DIGGING INTO THE PAST

25 Years of Archaeology in Denmark

DIGGING INTO THE PAST

25 Years of Archaeology in Denmark

Edited by Steen Hvass and Birger Storgaard

The Royal Society of Northern Antiquaries

Jutland Archaeological Society

DISTRIBUTED BY AARHUS UNIVERSITETSFORLAG

1993

DIGGING INTO THE PAST
25 Years of Archaeology in Denmark

© The authors 1993, The Archaeological Board
Editors: Steen Hvass and Birger Storgaard
Design: Christian Adamsen, Ulla Lund Hansen and Birger Storgaard
Editorial board: Bent Aaby, Christian Adamsen, Ulla Lund Hansen, Jørgen Jensen,
Kristian Kristiansen, Niels-Knud Liebgott, Poul Otto Nielsen, Erik Brinch Petersen

Translation: John Hines
(The following parts were translated by Joan F. Davidson:
Preface, 25 years of archaeology in Denmark, The Middle Ages and more recent times,
Castles and fortified sites, Crafts and skills)

Cover: Gold figure from Slipshavn Skov, Fyn. Photo: Lennart Larsen, National Museum.
Graphic design: ReproGården a/s, Them
Cover: Elsebet Morville, Moesgård
Composition and repro: ReproGården a/s, Them
Printed by: BB Grafik i/s, Allingåbro
Font: Times Ten
Paper: 100g Silverblade
Binding: Nordisk Bogproduktion

Published by:

The Royal Society of Northern Antiquaries, Prinsens Palais
Frederiksholms Kanal 12, DK 1220 Copenhagen

Jutland Archaeological Society, Moesgård, DK 8270 Højbjerg

Distribution:
Aarhus Universitetsforlag, DK 8000 Århus C

ISBN 87-7288-568-8

Publication funded by:
THE AUGUSTINUS FOUNDATION
KNUD HØJGAARDS FOUNDATION
THE DANISH MINISTRY OF CULTURE

Preface

In September 1993 the 19th Nordic Archaeological Congress will take place in Denmark. Twenty years have gone by since the archaeologists of the Nordic countries last met on Danish soil to deliberate matters of common interest, and this meeting presents us with a welcome opportunity to take stock of what has happened in Danish archaeology in the time-span of the last generation.

This we have done in the present book, which is being published in both Danish and English — the latter because of the significant interest shown in Danish prehistory by our professional colleagues in large parts of the world. This interest is to a large extent conditioned by the history of the discipline itself. Denmark was indeed one of the pioneering countries in prehistoric archaeology in Europe. But even today we have much to offer the world's archaeologists. Without wishing to sound self-congratulatory, we can nevertheless risk saying that Denmark is among the countries which have the most comprehensive knowledge about their ancient monuments. Our strength is not just an inheritance from the distinguished academics who in their day founded and developed the subject, but also derives substantially from the fact that archaeology here enjoys a totally unusual degree of sympathy within the population. It is not too much to say that prehistoric archaeology, over the last hundred years or more, has been something of a national science in Denmark. Throughout the whole country there are amateur archaeologists and interested others who follow vigilantly what comes out of the Danish soil and who make sure that the archaeologists in the museums are informed of new finds and observations. It has also been an advantage for archaeology that from far back in time there has been an obligation to hand over rare finds of prehistoric objects, in return for compensation. But the main point is that the Danish people, who in other respects are not given to following the dictates of central authority, have accepted the demands of archaeology with respect and understanding.

During the last generation, when society in so many ways has developed explosively, our activities have been strengthened by the passing of comprehensive antiquarian laws which chiefly ensure the right to undertake archaeological investigations in places where finds of ancient monuments are made. What is even more important for the subject, however, is that there are now many more of us to carry out the work. Growth has been particularly dynamic in the local historical museums, which in most cases were previously looked after by amateurs, often as a spare-time activity, but which now are run by professional archaeologists. This has brought into being a fine-meshed network for identifying and studying new archaeological finds.

It is striking that the rapid growth in local museums continued right into and through the 1980s, although otherwise, in Denmark as in the rest of Europe, these were crisis years for the Humanities. It is clear that there must have been a strong demand for these local activities. But archaeology in the universities, which had been developing strongly, has meanwhile been weakened by diminishing resources, and now the crisis has also reached archaeological rescue-excavations; today we only have means to undertake these important excavations on such an inadequate scale that the threshold of irresponsibility has been crossed. And where it is at all possible to set major research projects in motion, this is chiefly because of the major private foundations in Denmark which have always been among the close friends of archaeology and have proved indispensable partners in cooperation.

Today Danish archaeology feels under pressure in many ways from lack of resources, and we are worried about all the tasks which cannot be carried out. But amidst this worry we should not overlook the fact that strong work-pressures are also a sign of health, and that they are due not least to the very significant extent by which we have raised our own level of ambition. This book bears witness to this, reporting on 25 years in which Danish archaeology has blossomed and borne fruit as never before.

The publication of this book is the responsibility of the Archaeological Board, which has as its chief task the coordination of archaeological activity in Denmark - not by compulsion but by means of extensive cooperation among colleagues. To the book's editor and 76 authors I should like to convey the warm gratitude of the Board - as well as to the Augustinus Foundation, Knud Højgaard's Foundation and the Ministry of Culture, without whose ready support the book could never have appeared.

Olaf Olsen

Contents

The Iron Age
and the Viking Period

The Middle Ages
and more recent times

The archaeological institutions

25 years of archaeology in Denmark

By Jørgen Jensen

European history provides us with several instances where the approach of the end of a century has been accompanied by decisive changes in hitherto well-established patterns in the surrounding world: ideological systems are demolished, scientific concepts disintegrate, definitions dissolve. This is happening now, in our own era, with the current disruptions in East and West; it happened at the end of the last century with the breakthrough of modernism in the arts, and it happened in the 18th century in the wake of the French Revolution. In times of such change new demands are made of historical consciousness. Comprehensiveness of vision, in the interests of counterbalancing confusion, becomes a very pressing requirement. This can also be observed in the account of Denmark's past during prehistoric and medieval times which has been compiled, from the contributions of 76 scholars, in this book.

The choice of a 25-year period for this account is a reasonable one. The end of the 1960s, chosen as the starting-point of the time-span under consideration, was not only the beginning of a period of social upheaval. It was also a time when a new generation appeared on the academic scene and when the universities expanded as never before. In the Danish welfare state, 1969 was the year when legislation took account of the onset of a new era of almost overwhelming growth. The Nature Protection Act, which came into force that year, was not only an attempt to control the development of the landscape in a society undergoing rapid expansion. The Act also included a paragraph providing for the protection of all archaeological finds made during soil-displacement. And there was more and more soil-displacement: motorways were built, towns grew, extraction of sand, gravel and other raw materials took place on a scale larger than ever before, and new agricultural methods came into use. All this meant that thousands of previously invisible traces of the people of the past were exposed and in danger of being destroyed.

In cases where ancient monuments were found which were not visible on the surface or could only barely be perceived in the landscape, the Act only provided for their protection if they were of exceptional value. On the other hand it contained a special clause which required that ancient monuments found during digging should immediately be reported to the State Antiquary, who had the power to stop the work and to carry out excavations on the site before the remains were lost.

This was a totally new situation, and one which placed on the Danish museums and archaeologists an overwhelming responsibility. Colossal quantities of finds were brought to the attention of the archaeologists, and new cultural-historical evidence was harvested on a scale previously unknown. Again and again routine construction-work had to be interrupted because new discoveries made it necessary to excavate. Today Danish archaeologists carry out between 400 and 500 rescue excavations a year.

But the archaeologists were not totally unprepared for this new situation. As early as 1958 legislation had opened up possibilities for decentralisation of the Danish museum structure. In the European context this was a quite unique decision, but one which is characteristic of Danish cultural policy. Until then the National Museum had been the only institution in Denmark responsible for carrying out excavation activities on any significant scale. With the Act of 1958, however, it became possible to expand the museums outside Copenhagen and to employ professionally-trained staff. This meant that when the large volume of new tasks flooded in during the 1960s it was, to an increasing extent, archaeologists and museum-staff with sound qualifications behind them, who were also in close contact with local authorities and local communities, who undertook the work. Today there are 48 museums throughout the country which have university-educated archaeologists on their staff.

The academic tradition - in retrospect

It was possible to develop the museum structure in this way solely because of the fact that the universities had also undergone expansion in the 1960s. Two university institutes, a relatively recent one in Århus and a slightly older one in Copenhagen, were responsible for the academic education of archaeologists. Teaching was carried out in the context of a strong, unbroken, tradition stretching back via a series of outstanding personalities to the founder of the discipline, and of the National Museum, Christian Jürgensen Thomsen (1788-1865) (J. Jensen 1992). From as early as the beginning of the 1830s, on the basis of the rich collections in the Museum of Northern Antiquities, he developed the form of an empirical science which became the tutelary system around which large sections of European archaeology grew up, incorporating not only his classification of the prehistoric finds into a Stone Age, a Bronze Age and an Iron Age, but also the collaboration which he had initiated with the new Natural Sciences. Thomsen was one of the first to formulate a coherent synthesis describing the development of cultures in European prehistory. He created a comparative cultural research and a taxonomy of prehistory which had sufficient capacity to encompass all of the knowledge then available relating to civilizations of the past. The developments taking place in Copenhagen in those years have rightly been seen as an intellectual breakthrough of worldwide significance.

Thomsen's pioneering contribution, which was founded on ideologies characteristic of the "Golden Age" of the 19th century, along with an incipient evolutionism, was further developed by his successor, J.J.A. Worsaae (1821-1885). In those years Danish archaeology was at the forefront of European archaeology, with a wealth of international contacts. On Worsaae's initiative, in 1873, the systematic nationwide collection of information on finds and ancient monuments began; this now forms the basis of the Danish National Record of Sites and Monuments (DKC) in the National Museum (P.O. Nielsen 1981b), and provides a unique resource for archaeological research. In no other part of the world have archaeological structures and finding-places been recorded as systematically and accurately as in this register.

The middle of the 19th century, however, was also a period when national archaeology emerged - in many countries - and was increasingly forced into the service of nation-states. This was the background for what is known as the modern breakthrough of Danish archaeology in the years after 1870, a development which can be credited almost entirely to one person, Sophus Müller (1846-1934), a pupil of Worsaae (J. Jensen 1988). Müller in his research played an active part on the radically changing European academic stage in those years. He was deeply conservative in political terms, paradoxically enough, and for him the "revolutionary" new trends signified taking up arms against the idealistic historical notions of the preceding generation. These historical notions had arisen out of national liberalism, but had collapsed with the defeat of 1864. The new realistic positivism, and the theoretically value-free scientific attitude which Müller stood for, were symptoms of new academic ideals coming into ascendancy. But evolutionary theories and positivism also reflected the emergence of new social classes as conveyors of culture and as political forces within society.

In the first decades after the turn of the century, Müller was still the leading personality in Danish archaeology. Undoubtedly he was not uninfluenced by contemporary German archaeology, which was focusing exclusively on ethnic interpretations of the source material. But his fundamental academic stance continued to be a firm positivism, linked to inductive methods. This meant that, like other contemporary historical researchers, he thought that historical explanations should emerge more-or-less spontaneously during the study and comparison of facts, i.e., where archaeology is concerned, of the finds. He attributed little significance to formulation of theory in historical synthesis.

The same fundamental stance was held by Johannes Brøndsted (1890-1965), who was to become the leading figure of the next generation in Danish archaeology. Brøndsted carried out an organisational reform of the discipline in the period after 1930, but in terms of theory and method there were few changes. At this time German archaeology in particular was developing in the pseudo-scientific direction which was to become dominant after the Nazis came to power in 1933. Brøndsted's answer to this challenge was to develop a special popularized form of archaeology which is propounded in his major work "Danmarks Oldtid" (Danish Prehistory) of 1938-40. In this book he was able to demonstrate the wealth and variety of source material which was available to Danish archaeology. This publication came to be immensely important for relations with the general public. In terms of theory and methodology, however, it still rested on the same positivism which Sophus Müller had developed a generation before.

Post-war archaeology
In the years following the Second World War Danish archaeology continued with the methodological basis which had been developed before the war years. Attempts to write cultural history on the basis of archaeological finds were largely relegated to popular literature. Fundamental research, in contrast, confined itself to what was absolutely indisputable; the positivist tradition was still well and truly alive. This might seem somewhat unimaginative, but

the caution at work here arose partly from negative experiences during the war, in particular with the exploitation of archaeology in Nazi ideology.

A positive result of the demands for academic rigour was, however, that cooperation with the natural sciences was instigated. There were high expectations of pollen analysis in particular. In that area Denmark had been in the forefront since the First World War, and in 1944 the Bog Laboratory was set up in the National Museum. According to J. Troels Smith, its director, its primary task was to date the cultural periods of prehistory and to describe human influence on nature.

A few years later the range of scientific dating methods was extended to include the Carbon 14 method. In 1951 the first laboratory outside the USA was set up in Copenhagen, under the direction of Henrik Tauber. In 1956 the Natural Science Laboratories became an independent department of the National Museum. In the years which followed, a long-term contribution to environmental history was made by this department, although this did not immediately lead to integrated cooperation with traditional archaeology. In the academic world of the Humanities, in this case that of archaeologists, there was still too great an attachment to individual research. There was quite simply no willingness yet to embark on major interdisciplinary research projects, and there was probably a suspicion that such projects could threaten the integrity of the disciplines involved.

A decisive step forwards in traditional archaeology was taken, however, when C.J. Becker, who had succeeded Johannes Brøndsted as professor in Copenhagen, in 1961 began major excavations, to last several years, of the Iron Age villages at Grøntoft in western Jutland. In the same year Olfert Voss began the excavation of the Iron Age settlement at Drengsted in south-western Jutland. These two large projects were in their own way a continuation of the investigations in Nørre Fjand carried out in the 1930s by the ethno-geographer Gudmund Hatt (1884-1960). His excavations had been the first in Denmark to include the areas between Iron Age houses in order to gain an overall impression of the settlement. In Grøntoft and Drengsted the excavations were carried out, as a complete innovation, using machine power; digging machines were used to remove the plough-layer and uncover the ground-plans of the houses beneath. By this method such large areas could be exposed that one could study the settlement as a coherent whole and in some cases follow the existence of a village and its movements through centuries.

The importance of this progress in research into prehistoric communities can hardly be exaggerated. In 1969 the Danish National Council for Research in the Humanities (SHF) agreed to set up an "Archaeological Settlement Committee" and through that body it financed a 5-year research programme which was without parallel until that time in Danish archaeology. The excavations, certainly, began as one-man projects, but the scale of the enterprise rapidly made it clear that larger, integrated, cooperative activities would be necessary. By the end of the 1960s the preconditions were thus present for the genuine renewal of Danish archaeology which gave the results presented in this book.

New archaeology

It has already been mentioned, as one of the preconditions for the renewal of Danish archaeology at the end of the 1960s, that a new generation emerged then from the universities. This was a generation which was open to the very important theoretical and methodological influences which reached Denmark at that time from American and British archaeology. There was talk of a "New Archaeology", but in fact it was greeted with deep scepticism by the archaeological establishment in this country. This was because the new ideas turned particularly against the methodological constrictions which had been characteristic of the discipline, especially in the post-war years. Taking inspiration from the social sciences, English-speaking archaeologists, and later Danish ones also, sought to impart to the study of prehistoric societies an ecological and social-anthropological perspective. The interplay between different aspects of life in prehistoric times became the centre of archaeologists' interests. Prehistoric societies came to be seen as systems which functioned in accordance with various patterns, e.g. of an economic or social nature. This arose from the premise that prehistoric societies were once *living* societies, and that it was only the study of the processes within those societies which could lead to understanding of the course of development in prehistory. The 1970s and the beginning of the 1980s thus became a phase of lively experimentation in Danish archaeological research, when attempts were made to use new forms of detailed analysis, e.g. using statistical methods (Randsborg 1974) and using new forms of synthesis (J. Jensen 1978, 1982; Randsborg 1980, 1991; Kristiansen 1984, 1986). At the same time there was also a growth of interest in the representativeness of archaeological finds, their significance and symbolic content. The increased use of models, a method borrowed form neighbouring disciplines, also gave rise to discussion of the whole issue of value-free methodology.

Whereas the positivist research up to this time had almost exclusively used inductive methods, the new archaeology had recourse to deductive methods. The idea was that, by taking as starting-point models of a social-anthropological nature, for example, new and fruitful questions could be posed of the source material. The models were used as a sort of explanatory sketch which either would be filled in with relevant data as the research went on, or - possibly - would have to be abandoned. This led to a positive interplay between theory and data - a feature which is characteristic of modern research in the Humanities. The method has proved of value, for instance, for the understanding of economic processes in prehistoric societies.

At the theoretical-methodological level, in Denmark the end of the 1980s witnessed a certain loss of impetus. The influence of English-speaking archaeology has declined. This is particularly because elements of British archaeology have developed in directions which are remote from Danish archaeology. In British universities, for example, in the last decade there has been a trend away from the strong influence of the Natural Sciences, and economic and ecological aspects have been considered much less interesting than the force of the symbolic content of the archaeological source-material. One thus treats the material culture virtually as a language consisting of symbols, as a kind of non-verbal discourse (Shanks & Tilley 1987). In many instances this has led to the recognition of relationships in the material culture which had not previously been noticed. But because of its strong empirical tradition and the depth of its involvement in settlement studies, which in fact shed light on ecology and economy, Danish archaeology has not felt particularly attracted to the new tendencies in Britain, but has to a greater extent found a community of interest with north-west German and Dutch archaeology, which are both working with issues very similar to the Danish ones.

Administrative archaeology

Methodological discussion is one thing; everyday experience of archaeology is quite another. The harsh reality is that 90% of archaeological excavations are not a matter of free selection by researchers, but are rescue excavations, often undertaken at short notice when ancient monuments are faced with destruction. The administration of this major antiquarian work is today the responsibility of the State Antiquary and the Archaeological Board, a cooperative body which was set up in 1984. The board, comprising representatives of the central and regional museums together with the Agency for Forestry and Nature and the universities, establishes priorities for archaeological rescue excavations. By far the majority of the excavations are carried out by the regional museums.

The whole mass of information which is available to archaeologists from these excavations is fed into the central data-base in the National Museum, the Danish National Record of Sites and Monuments, which is a facility for use in conjunction with the topographical records which have been kept by the country's central museum for more than a century. At the end of the 1970s young professional archaeologists trained in information-technology began to put modern data-processing to use in this work, and in 1984 the National Record was officially set up. Right from the start it could build on information about finds from more than 100,000 sites. Now, barely a decade after the establishment of the database, there are about 2000 find-places which are registered each year. All of this quantity of information is now being made accessible by computer for administrative, research and educational purposes.

Archaeological investigations are taking place, meanwhile, not only on land but also underwater. Large parts of Denmark actually consist of water. The National Record has therefore also initiated cooperation with the Maritime Institute of the National Museum, the Agency for Forestry and Nature and the regional museums about a maritime register, to contain information on ancient monuments and wrecks on the sea-bed. This is connected with the impressive growth which, over the last 25 years, has made Denmark one of the leading countries in maritime archaeology. And it is important that maritime archaeology does not only cover the study of ships but also deals with sea transport as an integrated part of prehistoric societies. Many important results have been achieved in this field, particularly with regard to the history of the Viking Age and early Middle Ages.

The period since the beginning of the 1970s has also seen a significant growth in activities within medieval archaeology. In 1971 the subject acquired official status with the establishment of the chair at Århus University, and medieval archaeologists now play their appropriate role in antiquarian work in many parts of the country.

In connection with antiquarian work, it should be mentioned, in conclusion, that over the whole country there are large numbers of amateur archaeologists and divers whose cooperation is valuable to the museums during excavations and survey-work, and who contribute by spreading knowledge about archaeological work. Many of the amateurs use metal-detectors, and in contrast to Sweden, for instance, where there is a total ban on the use of detectors to search for ancient artefacts, the Danish museums are relying on maintaining a relationship of trust with the amateurs who use detectors for field surveying. This positive cooperation has meant that the quantities of *danefæ* (treasure trove) reaching the museums in the last decade have multiplied many times, and our knowledge about settlements has become much more sophisticated.

New structures and environments for research
Seen from outside the Danish antiquarian system appears impressive and effective. But there is always a danger of loss of perspective in such a large administrative apparatus. There should therefore be a continuous, academically-rooted, examination of priorities for allocation of the limited resources available. With a museum structure decentralized to the extent that the Danish one is, this is a task which can only be carried out if, alongside the administrative apparatus, there exist a number of active research bases where researchers can keep up to date with topical archaeological issues, formulate new tasks, maintain the discipline's international contacts, and ensure, through academic publications, that there is a suitable foundation for assigning priorities within archaeology. Only through large-scale, and preferably also complete investigations of specially selected sites can one reach understanding of the otherwise kaleidoscopic picture provided by the many small rescue excavations, since normally investigation of only a limited area is possible in such cases.

In the effort to keep this large variety of knowledge coherent it is of invaluable help that, since 1979, a small group of Nordic archaeologists has altruistically managed to publish, annually, an English-language bibliography of all archaeological publications: Nordic Archaeological Abstracts. Similarly, since 1984, the Archaeological Board has published an annual review of all the archaeological excavations in Denmark. Taking this in conjunction with the National Record of Sites and Monuments, Danish archaeology has an information system which is unique in the international context.

But information also has to be processed and analyzed in academic research in order to produce feedback which will influence further antiquarian work. Here it is sometimes difficult to strike the right balance between the academic tasks on the one hand and the antiquarian, museological or educational tasks on the other. In recent years, in fact, because of financial cuts, a number of drastic changes have been witnessed in the priorities established for university and museum activities. One of the consequences is that the resources available for work related to rescue excavations are inadequate in many cases. We cannot ignore the fact that irreplaceable cultural treasures are continuing to be lost because the funds available often only permit the most strictly necessary investigations before the archaeological remains are destroyed by building or construction work. The present economic situation is in many ways a threat to the unique archaeological potential that we have in Denmark, and also to the maintenance of an international standard of research.

The increased political demand for a greater emphasis on museums' public-oriented activities also manifests itself in a tendency towards permanent staff posts being emptied of academic content, while basic research is left to temporarily-employed staff, often young project-assistants. Since basic research actually requires lasting and stable surroundings, this has to be viewed as a regrettable tendency, threatening the valuable continuity in the Danish archaeological tradition, and as something to be resisted, e.g. through more rotation of posts within both the universities and the museums.

But against all the odds, research projects have sprung up in large numbers in recent years. It is also encouraging that the newly established Danish National Research Foundation has identified archaeology as one of the strongest fields of research in Denmark. In research activities there has in fact been a clearly visible tendency for the one-man-projects of earlier times to be replaced by cooperative projects which have often grown into lively research environments. Some of these, for example, have placed great weight on international cooperation and have built up contacts e.g. with Eastern European countries which in the aftermath of many years of Communist rule now have to develop completely new research strategies. Another novelty is projects involving foreign archaeologists excavating in Denmark. And other projects again aim at the publication of major works, e.g. in collaboration between Danish and German archaeologists. Finally, there are some which include in their purpose a significant extent of involvement of amateur archaeologists.

There is one field in particular which has given rise to a variety of collaborative projects: settlement investigations. This applies to Stone Age and Bronze Age research, but above all to work on the Iron Age. It is doubtless in that area that Danish archaeology has made its most important contribution to research in the last 25 years. One could mention, for example, the large-scale investigations of the Atlantic period settlement in the Vedbæk area, north of Copenhagen, and around Norsminde, south of Århus. There are also the investigations of the late Stone Age settlements on Bornholm and the islands south of Funen, the collaboration on the publication of the Bronze Age settlements in the Viborg district, the Limfjord project on natural and cultural development from the Ice Age to the present, the investigations around Ribe covering all the prehistoric periods, the village investigations on Funen and in the Køge area, and the Gudme-Lundeborg project, which is being carried out in one of the richest settlement areas of the Iron Age. One can also add the "Medieval Town" project, the main aim of which was to determine the age and early topographical development of our medieval towns, and last but not least the major excavation-projects which have given us sites of truly international significance and which will occupy a central position in research for many years to come: Hodde, Vorbasse, Nørre Snede, etc.

In addition to the many regional projects there are a number of others which have crossed geographical or chronological boundaries: investigations of traces of use on flint tools, of prehistoric textiles, of iron extraction and of the physical-anthropological conditions in prehistory.

It is Iron Age research in particular that has benefitted from the many projects. Special mention should be made in this context of an initiative financed by the Danish National Council for Research in the Humanities (SHF), on "From Tribe to State in Denmark", which by means of a coordinated effort has resulted in distinct progress being made in Iron Age research, and has resulted in the production of a series of substantial publications. Finally it should be mentioned that the newly-introduced Ph.D. degree has opened up possibilities for bringing a number of long-running research projects to a fruitful conclusion.

Within the related natural science disciplines there has also been remarkable development. Since the 1970s dendrochronology has achieved results which along with C 14 datings have radically changed the presuppositions underlying many traditional archaeological issues. Today a process of comprehensive coordination of investigations in settlement-ecology and environmental history is also underway. It is now possible, specifically through pollen analysis, to draw up a picture of differentiated exploitation of the landscape; this is a necessary precondition for understanding the results that archaeological settlement research has reached.

This is the sum of the major efforts which the following pages describe in detail. If one compares this with the state of Danish archaeology 25 years ago, the results are immensely impressive. The contours of development of prehistoric society can be outlined today with much greater clarity. And just as important: research has progressed to formulate totally new issues, which is, and must inevitably be, a distinguishing feature of a thriving academic environment. It is difficult to say whether what has happened in archaeology in the last generation is indicative of a paradigmatic shift, or whether it continues in the tradition now nearly 200 years old. In any event the archaeology of the post-war period, with its scarcity of theory and somewhat arid style, has now turned in a direction which reveals what immense potential exists in archaeological source-material for those who seek to write history on that basis.

General perspectives
"He for whom actual academic enquiry lies close to his heart will seldom of his own volition produce a large-scale interpretation' wrote the main figure in

Danish archaeology at the turn of the century, Sophus Müller. Here he pinpointed a dilemma which characterized research based solely on the academic criterion of positivist empiricism right up to the 1960s. For methodological reasons, detailed archaeological analysis was considered academically more sound than the formulation of syntheses. Exactly the same point of view can be found in historical research, e.g. when the historian Kristian Erslev, around the turn of the century, pointed out that "no historian who deals with a subject of even moderate breadth can accompany his presentation with exhaustive evidence", and that the writing of history, in contrast to detailed academic analysis, must therefore in significant respects lack the character of science.

In archaeology it was not until the shift in methodology in the last 25 years that opinions changed on this matter and it became evident that there is no scientific distinction between the study of detail and synthesis. It has been recognised that it is methodological operations which provide the criterion of whether one is engaged in science or in fiction, and it is precisely these methodological operations which new archaeology has concerned itself with, in its debate on methods, when it sought, on the basis of analyses of the archaeological sources, to give a description of the once-living society.

It is in direct extension of this that during the last 25 years attempts have also been made to return to the superseded but never completely abandoned holistic theories (e.g. J. Jensen 1978, 1982; Randsborg 1980, 1991; Hedeager 1990, 1991). The works that are the outcome of these attempts have contributed to the formulation of new academic issues. But it is also evident that without synthesizing presentations the discipline would not have been able to produce the general surveys (e.g. Hedeager 1988; J. Jensen 1988; Sawyer 1988; Liebgott 1989) which are a precondition for maintaining the interest of the general public and of grant-giving bodies in archaeological research.

Syntheses, however, also have another role to play. Developments within archaeology, especially within administrative archaeology, have led to increasing regionalization, i.e. deeper concentration on local finds. This is characteristic, for instance, of the whole of settlement archaeology. A corresponding development can be seen in other European countries. For interchange and communication between the many regional archaeologists, it is of great importance that syntheses are published. They contribute to the internationalization of research, which is sought after by administrative bodies such as the research councils, and in the last analysis they also help to place archaeological research in a larger cultural context. As should be apparent from this book, in the last 25 years Danish archaeology has demonstrated the immense potential the archaeological sources offer in an international context.

MAN AND THE ENVIRONMENT

Man and the environment

BY BENT AABY

There is a long tradition of co-operation between archaeology and the natural sciences, and insights into the Late Glacial environment, early agriculture and changes of sea-level are amongst the areas where Danish research has always been of international standing. Such co-operation has grown in recent years, and through farsighted research projects in settlement archaeology and environmental history our knowledge of prehistoric cultural and natural landscapes has developed markedly (S.Th. Andersen *et al.* 1983, 1991).

Chronological questions have been central to this research. Through systematic dating of bone material we now have an overview of the history of the arrival of animal species in Denmark (Aaris-Sørensen 1988), and the spreading of trees up through Europe and Denmark (Huntley & Birks 1983). The widespread use of C 14 dating has proved to be the means of solving a number of culture-historical problems: for instance whether certain cultures were contemporary or sequential. At the same time, the calibration of C 14 dates to calender years has revolutionized our view of pre-

historic cultural developments in many ways. New scientific dating methods such as dendrochronology and thermoluminescence have come into use in the last 25 years, to supplement and extend the scope for establishing a reliable chronology, which is one of the foundation stones of archaeology.

Extensive excavations in recent years have produced numerous human bones, which together with earlier collections provides a basis for studies of disease, nutrition etc., while C 13 analyses have shown the composition of the diet at different times. These and other palaeoenvironmental topics are discussed in the following chapters, while the history of the cultural landscape is described here as an essential preliminary to a deeper understanding of prehistoric Man, his behaviour, and his interaction with the natural environment.

The cultural landscapes of western Jutland

Western Denmark has distinctively sandy soils, and up to just a century ago heathland was a characteristic feature of this unforested landscape. The history of the heathland was studied earlier (Jonassen 1950), and with Bent Odgaard's careful research into lakes and soil profiles the interrelationship between Man and nature was revealed, and changes in the cultural landscape were dated.

Solsø, west of Herning, was studied first (Odgaard 1985, 1988), and it transpired that heather expanded on sandy till around 2800 B.C., the earliest heathland-formation recorded in this country. Later results from Skånsø, which lies on the fluvioglacial sand north-east of Holstebro, show a development of vegetation that is similar to that of Solsø in many respects although there are also important differences (Odgaard 1991a). At both sites, heathland-formation took place in the Subboreal, but at Skånsø heather first expanded 1,000 years after it did at Solsø, and did so much more slowly. Thus when the landscape at Skånsø changed character in the Bronze Age, the forest was superseded by grass-dominated pasture vegetation, whereas heathland directly replaced the forest at Solsø. Differences in the nutrient content of the soil may partly explain this contrast, but the use of fire and grazing was also important to the spreading of the heathland, as is also known from present heathland tracts. Provisional studies on Kragsø on the Karup sandur plain show that the destruction of the forest and the formation of heathland was relatively late, as at Skånsø

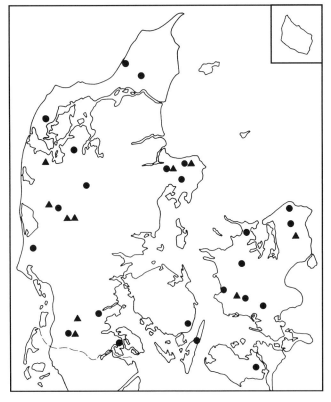

Map of sites from which regional (●) or local (▲) pollen diagrams have been derived.

(Odgaard 1991b). Heathland is thus a culturally determined vegetation type and its expansion and maintenance are governed by the nutrient status of the soil and human impact.

Pollen diagrams from lakes in western Jutland also reveal continuous and extensive exploitation of natural resources since the Neolithic (Odgaard 1991b). This development resulted in a still more open landscape structure and finally an almost tree-less region.

At certain sites, tree cover has, however, been preserved to the present as small oak shrubs, and palaeo-ecological studies in these coppiced woods reveal what they originally looked like (Odgaard 1985). If we take account of the variance in pollen production and dispersal in forests, it appears that at Hønning in southern Jutland there was a mixed deciduous forest stand with lime and beech as prominent tree species and less common oak where today oak dominates. Forest clearance, heathland-formation and grazing affected the area for a time, and the forest as such disappeared completely changing into heathland. This human interference with nature favoured oak more than other species, and after the maintenance of the heathland vegetation ceased it was the oak that triumphed in the emerging woods. The present coppiced oakwoods are thus the result of earlier cultural activity, and the forest composition seen today is not necessarily primeval or ancient.

Eastern Denmark

The nutrient status of the soil is of great importance to the range of vegetation, but just as in western Jutland it is primarily prehistoric Man who, through felling, grazing and arable farming, has affected the development of the cultural landscape in eastern Denmark. The few investigations that we formerly had concerning the development of the cultural landscape indicated a very uniform course of development, which Johs. Iversen described in 1967 and which also was supported by later studies (S.Th. Andersen 1978). But more pollen analyses in other eastern Danish areas have since produced a more elaborate picture, which enables us to present a much more varied and detailed model of the development of the cultural landscape than we could before. New features come from the Holmegård area of southern Sjælland, where it can be shown that beechwood was widespread in the Late Bronze

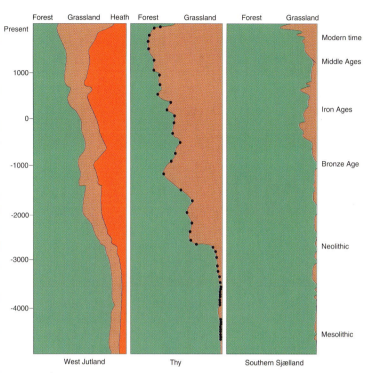

Pollen diagrams from western Jutland (Solsø, Odgaard 1988), Thy (Hassing Huse Mose, S.Th. Andersen 1991a) and southern Sjælland (Holmegårds Mose, Aaby 1986). The diagrams show the ratios of pollen from forest, agricultural land (including arable) and heathland.

Age (Aaby 1986). Then came the investigations at Hassing Huse bog in Thy which testify to landscape development in a densely populated cultural landscape (S.Th. Andersen 1991a). Here, a massive expansion of grassland at the expense of forest vegetation at the beginning of the Single Grave Period was demonstrated. The open landscape of Thy was used for grazing and cultivation and shows significant and continuous cultural influence that has increased right down to the present.

A closer analysis of earlier pollen diagrams from West Himmerland (S.Th. Andersen 1991b) and the western coast of Sjælland (Aaby 1992) shows that these areas have seen similar continuous exploitation to that in Thy. The development of the landscape here differs from the other areas of eastern Denmark studied, where cultural influence has been discontinuous, with irruptions interchanging with periods of forest regeneration on abandoned farmland. In the Holmegård area, cultural influence was thus relatively strong at the beginning of the Neo-

17

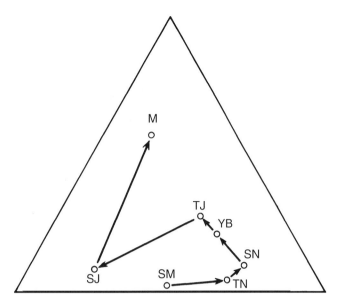

Scattergram showing the development of the landscape from the Late Mesolithic to the present around Abkær Mose, west of Haderslev (Aaby 1988, 1990). Pollen spectra dominated by high forest (lime, elm, oak, beech) bottom left, with secondary woods (birch, hazel) bottom right, and open grassland at the apex. It can be seen that the farming culture of the Early Neolithic (TN) caused significant change in the species composition of the forest while only minor open areas were created, though these expanded in the middle of the Single-grave Period and the Late Neolithic (SN) at the same time as secondary shrubby woods became commoner at the expense of high forest. The relationship between high forest and shrubby woods now stabilized, while open land became more common in the Late Bronze Age (YB). This development continued in the beginning of the Iron Age (TJ), but after ca. 500 A.D. (SJ) high forest returned. The landscape was well-forested until the mid-1100's, after which it became largely treeless (M). The diagram exemplifies discontinuous development in the landscape.

lithic, in the Iron Age down to ca. 500-600 A.D. and again from the Early Middle Ages. Another example of discontinuous landscape development comes from the Abkær area, west of Haderslev. Cultural irruptions are not synchronous in all places but vary in duration and intensity according to local and regional factors. There is, however, a clear tendency for farmland areas to become marginal around 500-600 A.D. when the beechwood expands. This change in the landscape was formerly explained by plague, emigration, soil-exhaustion, ecological crises and so on. The results from Thy and the coast of western Sjælland show that these explanations do not hold here, and probably do not in other areas either. What might the explanation be?

Modern cultural landscapes may give us a clue. It is interesting that all those places where, as yet, continuous exploitation of the landscape has been evidenced lie in treeless areas while in areas with discontinuous exploitation a lot of old deciduous forest is preserved today. It might therefore appear that modern cultural landscapes contain features that can tell whether prehistoric cultural influence has been continuous or not (S.Th. Andersen 1991b). We still need a number of palaeoenvironmental studies from treeless areas, but a picture is beginning to emerge of Late Iron-age development with intensive cultural influence in some areas (centres?) that now are treeless and reduced density of settlement in other areas (marginal?) that now have old woodlands. The western part of the Limfjord area was such a centre, as was the west coast of Sjælland, and the treeless areas of for instance Odsherred and the area between Copenhagen, Roskilde and Køge may have had a similar function. Was it changes in the power structure, trading connexions or other factors that governed this difference in landscape exploitation? This question has to be answered by co-operation between Science and the Humanities, for which there are strong precedents in archaeological research.

Agricultural ecology

A determinative factor in the development of agriculture has been a continual striving to increase the nutrient content in the ecosystem to support greater food production. In recent years there has been great interest in clarifying the ecological function of different agricultural methods (Olsson 1988), and on this basis four greatly simplified models have been constructed (Emanuelsson 1988).

In hunter-gatherer society (model 1) it was only small quantities of natural nutrients that were brought to the settlement site. The impact of Man on the environment was probably the same as that of large omnivorous animals and it is thought that 0.5 to 2 persons could be supported by 1 square km.

The introduction of swidden cultivation and pastoral agriculture (model 2) had much greater environmental impact. Cereal was grown in burnt areas, and the ash improved the fertility of the soil for a time, after which new areas were cleared and cultivated. The woods and clearings were grazed. Such extensive agriculture could support about 20 persons per square km.

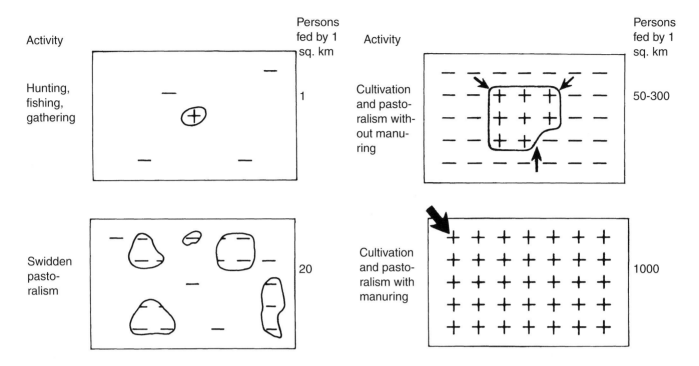

The general structure of the four food-supply strategies. Areas from which nutrition is taken are shown (-) and those to which it is added (+).

Permanent field-systems are known from the Iron Age, perhaps the Late Bronze Age too. This cultivation strategy (model 3) requires the fields either to lie fallow for longer or shorter periods for natural nutrients to build up or to be adequately manured if they are cropped every year, as was the case at the beginning of the Middle Ages, for instance on Mors. This form of agriculture, summarized by model 3, has in fact been in use right down to the present century, although the form of the field-systems changed around 100-200 A.D., when the square Early Iron-age fields disappear, and around 1200 A.D. when ridge-and-furrow fields appear. Depending on how advanced the cultivation technique was, this system could support 50-200 persons with 1 square km., a number which rose to about 300 after the introduction of fen irrigation at the end of the 18th century .

The last and present system (model 4) is based on the use of artificial fertilizers, rendering meadows, pastures and other outfield areas redundant as necessary producers of nutrients because these materials no longer set the limits of food-production.

Archaeology and the natural sciences

Recent years' studies of the fill of barrows have revealed previously unknown possibilities for discovering a lot of details of the vegetation of the cultural landscape at well-dated time intervals (S.Th. Andersen 1993). Pollen in fossil ploughsoil and grain and weed seeds in postholes are evidence of manuring, yields and so on. Together with many analyses of human and animal bone, scientific and archaeological research is elaborating a picture of the prehistoric cultural landscape.

On many occasions, botanical analyses have surprised us by revealing previously unknown features of landscape development. These clearly show that development was much more diverse than we had thought. Several regional studies of the landscape and a better understanding of the factors that have governed its development are one of the many urgent challenges that should be met in the coming years.

Land and sea

BY CHARLIE CHRISTENSEN

Distinctly low-lying, Denmark has changed considerably in size and shape as a result of often marked shifts in sea-level. Since the 19th century, Scandinavia has been treated as a perfect example of the general mechanics of the formation and melting of an ice cap and the consequent raising and sinking of land and sea levels. This view has not been seriously disputed. Quarternary geological research of the last 25 years has consequently been partly a matter of fine tuning, but we can report distinctly new results in the following fields: 1, the configuration of land, sea and ice in the Weichselian; 2, the plotting of a great rise in sea-level of the Early Atlantic Period; 3, the plotting of changes in the Littorina Sea and their relation to archaeological cultures; 4, marine geology and archaeology.

The Weichselian Period

In the Weichselian, Denmark was covered by ice for only a short period, 20,000-13,000 years ago, when the ice advanced to the main stationary line of western Jutland. For the rest of the approximately 100,000-year-long Ice Age the land stood as tundra, populated by, for instance, mammoth and possibly Man. These are the results of recent years' work on the dating of glacial strata and mammoth bone (Aaris-Sørensen *et al.* 1990). The use of ther-

moluminiscence dating of water-deposited sand and silt has been of great importance. These investigations have made it possible to produce a series of maps of the land-sea configuration at various points of time (Strand Petersen 1985; Houmark-Nielsen 1989).

From the Late Glacial to the Boreal Period

This period, in which Denmark had a much greater land area than now, is generally called the Continental Period.

It is not known whether the Late-Glacial reindeer-hunting cultures exploited coastal resources but there are indications that the following Maglemose Culture did (Clutton-Brock & Noe-Nygaard 1990).

Fishing and sand-dredging often produce finds from now sunken landscapes. These are usually trunks and stumps from drowned forests, as for instance the newly-found Pre-Boreal pine stumps from the bottom of the Storebælt (A. Fischer 1991b). Archaeological finds from the sea-bed have so far been limited to Maglemose tools from North Sea fishing banks.

The great Atlantic rise in sea-level

Around 6500 B.C., in the Early Atlantic Period, Denmark obtained very much its present outline.

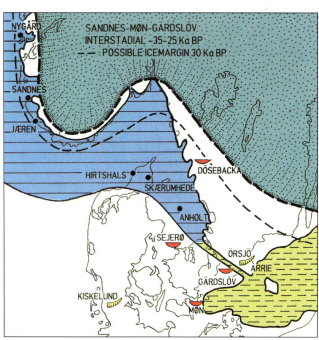

Example of a palaeogeographic map of the last Ice Age: the configuration of land, sea, lake and ice cap between 35,000 and 25,000 years ago.

Denmark 9,000 years ago (green) and 6,000 years ago (dark grey).

The sea-level, which when glaciation was at its peak was 90 m. lower than now, gradually rose through the Late Glacial, Pre-Boreal and Boreal Periods to around 30 m. below the present level. The subsequent rise to about the present level, beginning around 7000 B.C., took place in just 600 years, meaning a rise of 5 m. per 100 years, a truly extraordinary situation. The cause is thought to be the collapse and rapid melting of the large American ice-caps. In Denmark the rise has been detected in the Limfjord area (Strand Petersen 1981) and the Storebælt (H. Krogh 1973, 1979a).

This was an event that can very reasonably be thought to be the origin of the Biblical Flood story, and it must have been appreciated as a dramatic change in the landscape by the Danish Stone-age population too. This violent rise in sea-level linked the freshwater Baltic (Ancylus Lake) and the ocean through Storebælt, Lillebælt and the Sound, and in a short time Denmark became an area of islands and fjords. Access to marine resources was easy, and there was plenty there. From 6500 to 4000 B.C. we therefore find many settlements concentrated along the coasts.

The Atlantic and Sub-Boreal Period

After the great rise in sea-level came a series of minor changes in sea-level of between 50 cm. and 2 m., the so-called Littorina fluctuations. These were identified around 1940 and dated by pollen analysis (J. Iversen 1937; Troels-Smith 1942). An Early, a High and a Late Atlantic and a Sub-Boreal transgression could be distinguished, divided by regressions.

Only 30 to 40 years later were new investigations of the Littorina fluctuations undertaken, especially through the Vedbæk project in 1975. Through thorough studies of numerous profiles in association with settlements around the Vedbæk fjord, and with the extensive use of C 14 datings, the sea-level changes were identified and dated (C. Christensen 1982a-b) and compared with cultural phases in the Øresund region (Vang Petersen 1984). In Trundholm bog, north-western Sjælland, changes in sea-level were identified in purely geological studies (Maagaard Jacobsen 1982, 1983). In north and central Jutland, new results came both from archaeological excavations of coastal settlement sites (S.H. Andersen 1970, 1976) and from geological studies (Strand Petersen 1976). From the south-western

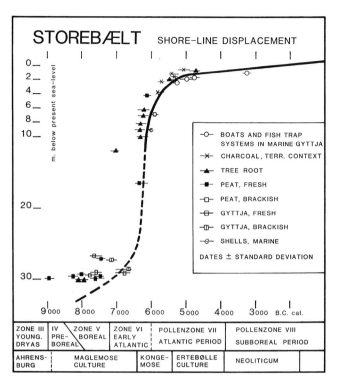

Curve showing the rise in sea level in the Storebælt area in the Early Atlantic Period. Various symbols show C 14 datings of, inter alia, *peat and mud from low-lying freshwater basins and trunks and stumps of submerged trees.*

coast of Jutland we have only scattered data (H. Krogh 1979b).

This leaves us with a rather more varied picture. Danish and southern Swedish studies show 3 to 5 Atlantic and 1 or 2 Sub-Boreal transgressions. There is, then, no agreement on the numbers. There are also problems with comparing different sites. This is usually due to the short duration of the fluctuations in relation to the coarsity of C 14 dating.

After the latest adjustments, the shoreline displacement curve for Vedbæk is thought to have been reliably fixed. It appears that the changes are of the order of about 1 m. and the peaks fall at intervals of about 500 years. Such fluctuations in sea-level are climatically determined and we apparently are faced with a periodicity that is double the length of what can be seen in Denmark's raised bogs (Aaby 1976).

The later uplift and downwarping of the shores of the Littorina Sea is more simply modelled as a rocking movement around the well-known line that runs across Denmark from northern Falster to Nissum Fjord (Mertz 1924; Strand Petersen 1985). Northeast of this the land rose, while the Stone-age coastal settlements south-west of this line now lie below sea-

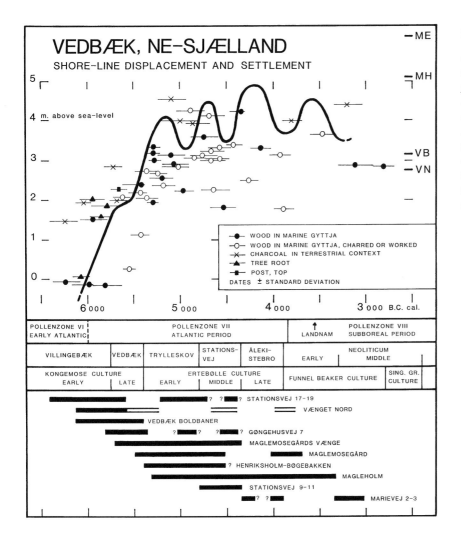

Shore-line displacement curve for the Vedbæk fjord. C 14 datings are marked according to date and height above present sea-level (see key on figure). The height of four settled islands is given on the right. Below the curve, the upper row shows pollen zones and the point of time of the Landnam-phase in Vedbæk. The middle row shows cultural phases in the Øresund area (Vang Petersen 1984) and the lowest row Danish cultural phasing. The duration of settlement at 10 excavated sites is shown at the very bottom.

level. It is from the latter area that marine archaeological excavations have produced settlements with incredible levels of preservation (Skaarup 1983; S.H. Andersen 1987).

The regional pattern of land uplift described here seems accurate, but local exceptions have been discovered in recent years. Clear evidence has been produced of local land uplift above salt domes in the ground. Læsø too, lying in the Fenno-Scandinavian border zone where faults occur in the ground, seems to have been subject to 'neotectonic' movements in the most recent millennia (J.M. Hansen 1980). Differences in the rate of uplift between Øresund and the Storebælt area have been suggested (Maagaard Jacobsen 1983), and confirmed to a degree by new studies around the Storebælt (author, unpublished).

The Atlantic marine environment
As stated, Kongemose- and Ertebølle-culture settlement sites are found overwhelmingly by the coasts.

Regional differences in tool inventories seem to show that the population was sedentary in different parts of the land (Vang Petersen 1984). $\delta^{13}C$ analyses of dog bones from one inland settlement indicate that in the late Ertebølle Culture there may have been a sedentary population by the extensive inland wetlands (Noe-Nygaard 1988a).

Earlier attempts to assess the size of the population on the basis of nutritional resources underestimated the importance of marine resources. Modern excavations where settlement layers are sieved prove fish bones to be very common. The importance of sea food is also clearly shown by $\delta^{13}C$ analyses of human bones (Tauber 1981, 1989b). Measurements of the size of fish bones from the settlements indicates that different forms of stationary fish-trap systems were used in the fjords (Bødker Enghoff 1983), and recently some such have in fact been found, for instance in the latest excavations by the Storebælt. The wide range of coastal activities is also shown by the large

22

number of new boat finds. 15 years ago, mesolithic boats were unknown. We now have about 20, all from the coasts (C. Christensen 1990).

Agriculture was introduced to Denmark around 4000 B.C. and the inland areas were settled. The lack of resources has been proposed as one possible reason for the shift in subsistence strategy. Are there demonstrable changes in the environment, then, that could have caused a reduction in the important marine resources around this date? We can point out here that several southern Scandinavian studies have revealed a marked fall in sea-level that must have cut off many of the important fjords. At the same date we can see a marked shift in Jutlandic kitchen middens from a predominance of oyster to cockle. One suggested explanation of this is a decrease in the tidal range and thus in salinity (Strand Petersen 1992). A consequent change in the level of water replacement in the often long and narrow fjords and straits would certainly diminish the scope for fishery.

The Sub-Atlantic Period

In the last 3,000 years, the coasts have been approximately stable, but in places processes of coastal regularization have caused considerable changes. Most marked is the accumulation of Skagen Pit by the repeated formation of beach ridges (Strand Petersen 1991). Also the southern Jutlandic salt marsh area were mostly formed during this period because of the continuing downwarping of the land in the south-west of Denmark.

The exploitation of marine resources in the Bronze Age is poorly documented. Iron-age fishery is evidenced at certain settlement sites and the exploitation of shellfish and snails is documented in kitchen middens (Løkkegaard Poulsen 1978). Settlement in the Bronze and Iron Ages seems to have very little connexion with the coast. Throughout the Iron Age, however, we see a clear increase in the number of marine finds in the form of pieces of ships, barriers and so on (Crumlin-Pedersen 1991c). Only in the Viking Period, when trade reaches a substantial level and coastal towns appear, does it seem reasonable to speak of a 'maritime cultural landscape'.

Future research

The Ice-age landscape of Denmark is still only partially described. New results can therefore be expect-

Fish weir, Halsskov. During excavations in advance of the construction of the Storebælt tunnel, parts of 7 logboats were found in marine deposits (including the oldest in Denmark, 5480 B.C.), a complete wicker trap and several fish-trap systems. The fully preserved section of a fish weir shown here is Early-neolithic.

ed, it is to be hoped touching on the possible presence of Man in ice-free times as well.

In the classic field of study, the Littorina Sea fluctuations, the publication of recent studies in eastern Denmark, including the Storebælt, is in hand. We still lack a final overview of sea-level changes and cultural phases in Jutland. From that, a final assessment of the occurrence of post-Glacial tectonic movements can be undertaken.

The salt marsh area of south-western Jutland has been only partially investigated. The coastline has shifted much more in this flat area as the sea-level has fluctuated. More effort should clearly be put into settlement-historical research here from the Late Stone Age to the present.

The investment in marine archaeological investigations in recent years can be expected to produce new and unfamiliar find groups. The coastal settlements of the Maglemose Culture, Stone-age fish-trap systems and Late Stone-age and Bronze-age seagoing boats could be amongst these. To these can be added wrecks of various periods that in good circumstances provide us with snapshots of prehistory.

Research into periodical changes in sea-level have gained new topicality. The large artificial increase in the level of atmospheric carbon dioxide (the greenhouse effect) is though to be causing a rise in sea-level of the same order as the Littorina transgressions. Like Stone-age Man, we may have to move our settlements a bit further inland.

Flora

BY BENT AABY

25 years ago, Johs. Iversen published his description of 'Nature in Denmark since the last Ice Age'. In this, he gave a vivid account of research, showing where attention had been focussed in studies of prehistoric flora. Subjects such as the environment in the Late Glacial Period, forest ecology and the phase of neolithic settlement are fully described, while other topics are dealt with quite summarily, simply because evidence was lacking. There were, as a result, relatively few pollen diagrams that could clarify the general development of vegetation and those at hand lacked a definite chronology.

An attempt was subsequently made to rectify this lack through palaeobotanical research in several of our extended raised bogs, where deep peat layers were analysed and dated. Lakes can be informative too, and in recent years they have played an important role in research into the history of flora (Odgaard 1988, 1991a; S.Th. Andersen *et al.* 1991). Alongside this work, our knowledge of pollen production and dispersal, especially in forests, has increased significantly (S.Th. Andersen 1970; Tauber 1977), and local vegetational and geological developments have been revealed through studies of the podzol soils and small bog hollows (Aaby 1983; S.Th. Andersen *et al.* 1983; S.Th. Andersen 1984, 1991c). A fundamental topic in this work and a spur to new understandings has been the interrelationship between prehistoric Man and his natural environment.

The large number of macrofossil analyses from archaeological sites and natural deposits has also contributed a lot of new evidence on Denmark's prehistoric flora (H.A. Jensen 1985, 1991).

From pollen to biotype
Iversen's monograph of 1967 shows pollen analysis to be a skilled tool for palaeobotanical studies, but it has its limits too. It is not possible, for instance, to convert pollen assemblages into species composition in various biotypes. Research in this area was underway and results had been produced earlier, but only with S.Th. Andersen's thorough research into the relative pollen production of forest trees and their pollen dispersal in forests could experimentally based corrections be made for tree pollen so as to reflect the areal range of tree cover within about 30 m. of a sampling site (S.Th. Andersen 1970, 1980).

The large and small scales
Empirical tests show that pollen found in large lakes or treeless bogs nearly all comes from the vegetation within 5 or 10 km. of the sample site (C.R. Janssen 1973; Aaby 1985). These means that the so-called regional pollen diagrams from such sites give an average view of the range of vegetation in a large area. The advantage of this is that main tendencies are revealed while underlying processes and other detailed points are normally hidden. In addition we need local diagrams that can be obtained from studies of acid soils, natural waterholes or bogs which are so small that the tree canopy covers the sample site and pollen rain comes mainly from the surrounding 30 m. area. Local diagrams are absolutely necessary for understanding the distribution of plants against the quality of the soil and human activities, while regional diagrams give a good overview of the distribution and density of, for instance, human influence. Both types of diagram are thus necessary to the construction of a detailed picture of prehistoric vegetation and its development.

The spread of trees
The systematic application of C 14 dating to pollen analyses of long-term series together with a series of datings of charcoal and various other finds has made it possible to construct a chronology for the arrival of trees in Denmark after the last Ice Age.

Finds of large plant remains are the definite sign of the presence of a species, but they rarely form the earliest evidence of its occurrence.

Tree-species	Corretion Factor
Birch	0,25
Oak	0,25
Alder	0,25
Pine	0,25
Hazel	0,25
Hornbeam	0,33
Elm	0,50
Beech	1,00
Ash	2,00
Lime	2,00

Correction factors for the most important tree-species in Denmark.

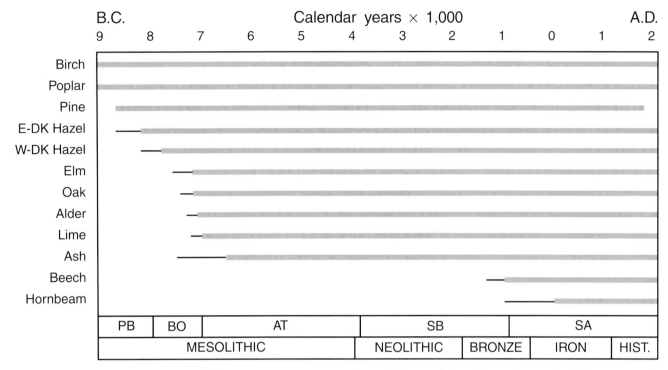

B.C.				Calendar years × 1,000						A.D.	
9	8	7	6	5	4	3	2	1	0	1	2

Birch
Poplar
Pine
E-DK Hazel
W-DK Hazel
Elm
Oak
Alder
Lime
Ash
Beech
Hornbeam

PB	BO	AT		SB		SA	
	MESOLITHIC			NEOLITHIC	BRONZE	IRON	HIST.

The immigration and disappearance of the most important species of tree in Denmark, based on pollen analysis. In assessing the date of arrival, note is taken of the specific pollen production of each species and forest pollen distribution. The University of Washington's calibration programme 1986 with the generalized 20-year atmospheric curve from Radiocarbon 1986 is used for calibration, and B. Becker et al. (1991) for C 14 dates earlier than 8200 BP.

At the end of the Ice Age, juniper was already growing in Denmark. Birch spread out along with juniper, and aspen appears at this time too. Their swift response to the rise in temperature indicates that they probably survived in the Younger Dryas in favourable sites in Denmark or a little to the south.

The Ice Age ended around 9000 B.C., but despite the favourable climate no new tree species arrived for 300-400 years. They were growing too far away, but the warmth set their northern expansion underway. Pine was the first arrival, around 8600 B.C. Hazel arrived in the east shortly after, but did not extend to Jutland until about 500 years later. Elm immigrated around 7500 B.C., quickly followed by oak, alder and lime. It is much more difficult to determine by pollen analysis when ash appeared here as ash remains rare far into the Atlantic Period and has a relatively low level of pollen production. Charcoal finds however show that it was certainly growing on Sjælland around 6500 B.C.

More than 5,000 years now pass before new tree species add to the flora, as beech begins to spread out around 1400 B.C. in southern Jutland, Djursland and Sjælland (Aaby 1986). Hornbeam is the last invading species, found mainly in the south of Denmark.

Post-Glacial expansion of trees thus saw three chronologically separated waves, dating to the Preboreal, Boreal and Subboreal.

The primeval forest
For the first 5,000 years after the last glaciation, Denmark was covered by primeval forest where the soil, the climate and the competition of trees and their history of movement governed the composition of the forest. Regional pollen diagrams show that birch dominated at first, followed by birch and pine and then hazel and pine before lime took over as the most common species in the country. Only with the many local diagrams of recent years, the knowledge of pollen distribution and the calculation of correction factors (see above) has it been possible to produce a detailed picture of the forest in different contexts.

On high and fertile soil, lime was quite dominant in the Atlantic, while hazel and oak did better on poorer soil. They were especially found in light, open areas that could be created by storm

25

damage or where individuals or groups of trees died. On dry and poor soil, as was then found in parts of western Jutland, the primeval forest was rather open, with grasses and flowering heather on the forest floor. Birch and lime were most common but hazel was a substantial presence too. Oak played a minor role here and there (Odgaard 1988) but in other places, on sandy soil, it must have been a presence.

Alder was the commonest species on wet and rich soil. It thrived where it was wettest while elm, ash, oak and hazel grew most on damp soil. On poorer soil alder and birch were the dominant species but lime and oak were also present. Alder did not only grow on the rich and wet land we particularly associate it with today but was also important on poorer and less wet soils.

The culturally influenced forest

The forest was an essential natural resource in pre-history that provided leaf hay and fodder for the farmer's grazing animals besides timber and fuel. Here one could indeed reap without sowing.

Coppicing reduced the trees regularly to their stumps, and the quickly growing shoots provided materials for fencing and many other tasks. Natural growth was exploited, and nearly all species of tree could be used although hazel was particularly common in the coppices of the time (S.Th. Andersen, below).

The trees provided winter fodder. Some was obtained in connexion with coppicing, but leaf fodder was also collected from tall trees whose side branches were lopped (branch pollarding). Some local diagrams show signs of this form of collection of leaf hay from as early as the Neolithic (S.Th. Andersen 1985), but in the Iron Age and Middle Ages too pollen analysis reveal this system (Aaby 1983), which church wall paintings also testify to. We now have archaeological evidence of leaf foddering in the Neolithic from Switzerland too (P. Rasmussen 1990, 1991).

Grazing in the forests was extensive, so that regeneration became difficult if the herds were too large. This is one of the main reasons for the forest declining in periods of heavy cultural intervention while the tree cover expands when the pressure of grazing reduces. The multiple functions of the forest meant that it formed an integral part of agriculture at the time, and it was only 200 years ago that a clear functional division of the landscape into forest and agricultural areas took place.

Open pasture and heathland

Under intensive grazing the forest disappears, and shrubs and bushes start to dominate. On more or less fertile soil a highly diverse pasture vegetation forms, with ribwort as one of the most important wind-pollenated herb species. This therefore is a good diagnostic species for pasture in pollen analysis (Behre 1981).

If the soil is poor, however, the grassed areas turn to heathland with a general cover of heather. This both produces and spreads a lot of pollen, and is therefore valuable for tracing heathland vegetation in pollen diagrams from lakes and soil sections. Heathland and pasture can then reflect the same form of land use, and the fertility of the soil decides which biotype will develop. In eastern Denmark, consequently, open pasture is the common biotype on grassed areas while heathland belongs mostly to the sandy soils of western Jutland.

The great advantage of heathland over open pasture is that the heather can be grazed in the winter. The collection of fodder for winter use was a very labour intensive task in early times, and it was the quantity and quality of the fodder that governed the size of the herds. Although the heathland was an infertile biotope, certain types of agricultural activity did better here than on richer parts of the land.

Arable land

Research of recent years into the prehistoric flora of arable land has refined the picture that, for example, Hans Helbæk (1954) drew on the basis of his many analyses of macrofossils gathered in connexion with archaeological excavations. At the same time, new facets have been added, as shown by H.A. Jensen's survey article (1991). Pollen analysis has contributed to the evidence.

To begin with, only rye pollen could be certainly identified while other cereals' pollen was normally just labelled "cerealia". Statistical and morphological analyses of recent pollen from cereals and other grasses have now provided a much better basis for identifying the species of fossil pollen (S.Th. Andersen 1979). It has proved, in consequence, that barley-types include not only the cultivated species but also wild grasses such as manna grass. This species often grows in small waterholes, and only with care-

HUMIDITY / TROPHICAL CONDITION	DRY	DAMP	WET
EUTROPHIC	Lime-Hazel-(Oak)	Alder-Elm-Ash-Oak Hazel (Lime)	Alder-Oak-Birch Willow
OLIGOTROPHIC	Birch-Lime-Hazel-(Oak) Heather-herbs	Birch-Alder-Oak herbs	Oak-Birch-Pine mosses

Conspectus of the distribution of the most frequent species of tree against soil-types in the Atlantic Period, based on local pollen diagrams.

ful measurements can it be determined whether barley or other grass species are present in the barley-type.

In contrast to other vegetation-types of the cultural landscape, arable land is difficult to detect by pollen analysis as the cereals - apart from rye - give off little pollen on flowering. The same applies to flax, while pollen from, for instance, cameline cannot be distinguished from wild plants of the cruciferous family. There are therefore many cultivated plants whose importance cannot be seen in pollen spectra (Aaby 1990). This is true for regional pollen diagrams, and new studies from small hollows lying hard by identified Iron-age fields show that the situation is the same with local diagrams, as even under these favourable circumstances both cereal pollen and pollen from annual weeds is very rare (S.Th. Andersen et al. 1983; S.Th. Andersen 1985). Instead, the cultural phase is primarily reflected in pollen from perennial weeds such as wild grasses, ribwort and mugwort, and sheep sorrel also seems to be associated with cultivated land in many pollen diagrams (Aaby 1990). Sheep sorrel grows on sandy open pastures but also does well in fields with winter crops that are cultivated in a rotation system. It occurs regularly in the Bronze Age and Iron Age, but first becomes general in the Early Middle Ages when rye too increases and cornflowers regularly appear. In early times cornflowers grew almost exclusively in winter-sown fields (V. Mikkelsen 1986). Its very rare occurrence before the Middle Ages may indicate that there were no suitable habitats on cultivated land. There are thus several points to indicate that winter-sown fields first appear at the beginning of this millennium, and that

rye was normally cultivated in these fields from then on.

The rich pollen production of rye means that it can easily be found in pollen assemblages, and its first appearance is dated in various parts of the country to 200-100 B.C., the end of the pre-Roman Iron Age (Odgaard & Aaby 1988), while the earliest macrofossils come from the 1st century A.D. (Helbæk 1977). Rye could have appeared as a weed to begin with, but macrofossil finds indicate that it was cultivated around 300-400 A.D. (Robinson & Siemen 1988). Macrofossil analyses have refined the picture that Helbæk (1954, 1977) could draw of cereal cultivation in other areas too. Thus the finding of naked barley from Mortens Sand has added to the debate over harvesting methods of the Single Grave Culture (Robinson & Kempfner 1988). The find shows that selective harvesting was employed, by which the heads were individually gathered while the stems and weeds may have been harvested later. In this way grain loss was minimized and the inclusion of weeds in the cereal harvest avoided.

It should finally be noted that urban excavations in Svendborg (G. Jørgensen 1986; H.A. Jensen 1979), Ribe (H.A. Jensen 1986, 1991), Viborg (Robinson et al. 1992), Copenhagen and so on in recent years have provided much macrofossil material and added to new insights into the normal diet and hygiene of the Middle Ages through investigations of organic culture layers such as latrine pits.

Palaeoethnobotany has grown stronger in the last decade, and by involving new methods of dating and scientific analysis the composition of the diet, cultivation strategies and the history of cultivated plants will be central topics in research in coming years.

27

The Fauna

BY KIM AARIS-SØRENSEN

Quarternary zoological research has concentrated in recent decades on providing a more complex and regionally more detailed picture of the wild fauna of the Full, Late and Post-Glacial Periods. This can best be done in step with new finds and ever more accurate datings of both new and old finds. Changes in the composition of the fauna are primarily climatically governed and form one of the most important factors behind the cultural developments that archaeology describes.

The Full Glacial Period

In step with the variations in temperature of the Weichselian, the Scandinavian ice cap expanded and retreated. As Denmark lies on the south-western edge of the maximal extent of the Weichselian ice, it is of great importance to date these variations accurately. Problems include how often and how long the land, or parts of it, were parts of a substantial, ice-free tundra or steppe area, habitable to animals and Man.

Through stratigraphical studies that can be aligned with, for instance, a number of C 14 datings of mammoth remains and TL datings of the deposits themselves (Houmark-Nielsen 1989; Aaris-Sørensen *et al.* 1990), a picture has now emerged of a very long cold stage, but mainly a cold stage *without* an ice sheet covering the Danish region. From the start of

the Weichselian, 115-110,000 years ago, right down to the start of the Middle Weichselian, the land was free of ice. After this the south-east was affected by the so-called Old Baltic ice advance, the duration and extent of which is not entirely clear yet but which seems, chronologically, to fall within the period *ca.* 70-60,000 BP. Then the land was ice-free again, until the main advance built up and reached the well-known main stationary line between 20,000 and 18,000 years ago. The deglaciation had already begun around 16,000, and by 13,000 the land was free of ice again.

In the long ice-free Middle Weichselian the ice front was about 300 km. north of Denmark, and southern Scandinavia formed part of the North European steppe tundra in respect of flora and fauna. Most mammoth finds date to this period. Mammoth *(Mammuthus primigenius)* is the representative animal of the period in all of Eurasia and northern America, but finds of the other animals that characterize this ice-age community, particularly migratory flocks of grazing ungulates, have been made in Denmark too. Thus along with the many Danish finds of mammoth we can note bones of giant deer *(Megaloceros giganteus)*, reindeer *(Rangifer tarandus)*, saiga antelope *(Saiga tatarica)*, musk ox *(Ovibos moschatus)*, steppe bison *(Bison priscus)* and woolly rhinoceros *(Coelodonta antiquitatis)*.

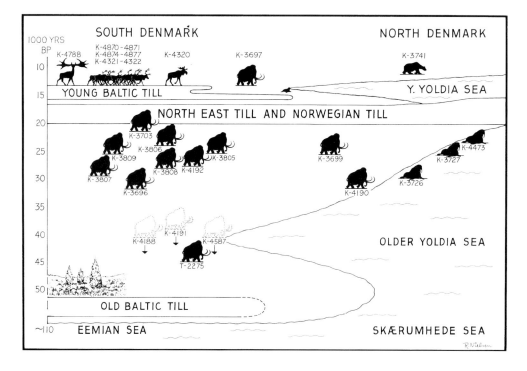

Land and sea distribution and till formation (= stationary line) in the Weichselian seen in a N-S section through central Denmark. The age of analysed mammalian remains is shown by animals placed on the resulting date. The stipled mammal outlines and arrows pointing back in time show that the datings cannot be given an upper limit. The juniper landscape around 50,000 BP derives from Kolstrup & Havemann (1984:128).

Earlier generations' views of the Weichselian gave neither time nor space for all these finds to belong to the period itself. It was thus thought that saiga antelope belonged to the Eemian interglacial and that the bones were simply moved by the Weichselian ice (Degerbøl 1932:176). Now, however, they fit well into the ice-free Middle Weichselian, when human settlement was also a *possibility,* before the main ice advance came and turned the whole situation on its head.

The Late Glacial Period
When the ice retreated from the area, the ecosystem had undergone a total rejuvenation. The speed and order in which different plant and animal species recolonized the land was governed by the change in temperature and the dispersal abilities of each species. Thus a clear delay in the response of many plant species to the improvement in the climate can be seen, reflecting their speed of dispersal. The fauna had to wait for this delay to be overcome for suitable habitats to grow. The first invasions immediately after the retreat of the ice naturally enough represent a spreading of the North European steppe tundra fauna, with, for instance, recolonization by mammoth before 13,000 and by giant deer *ca.* 11,700 BP. Mammoth seems to die out in southern Scandinavia around 13,000 and there are no dated mammoth finds in central or northern Europe later than 12,000 BP. The giant deer flourished briefly, dying out in northern Europe around 10,700 BP. Reindeer coped right down to the early Preboreal, but moved north as soon as the melting ice and the land rise in Scandinavia allowed.

In contrast to the analyses of the Full-Glacial fauna, our knowledge of Late-Glacial fauna is almost entirely based on large skeletal finds *in situ.* There is a great deal of Late-Glacial material, more complete and easier to date, and it gives an impression of a very varied fauna comprising both alpine and arctic/subarctic tundra elements and steppe and temperate mixed woodland elements with species such as desman *(Desmana moschata),* arctic hare *(Lepus timidus),* suslik *(Spermophilus sp.),* beaver *(Castor fiber),* field vole *(Microtus agrestis),* wolf *(Canis lupus),* brown bear *(Ursus arctos),* wolverine *(Gulo gulo),* giant deer *(Megaloceros giganteus),* elk *(Alces alces)* and reindeer *(Rangifer tarandus).* Marine arctic-subarctic elements are known from deposits in Vendsyssel in particular, and include polar bear (-

In 1983, the Zoological Museum excavated a whole aurochs skeleton at Prejlerup in Odsherred. 15 microliths and a 4 cm.-long piece of a pinewood arrowshaft were found amongst the aurochs' bones. One rib has been C 14-dated to ca. 7470 B.C. (K-4130).

Ursus maritimus), ringed seal *(Phoca hispida),* bowhead whale *(Balaena mysticetus)* and white whale *(Delphinapterus leucas).* This 'disharmonious' fauna represents an environment quite without modern parallels, and can hardly have been radically different from that which held sway in the ice-free periods of the Early and Middle Weichselian. It should be noted that the traditional view of the Late Glacial as a period characterized not just by reindeer but by the wild horse *(Equus ferus)* and European bison *(Bison bonasus)* too is not attested: the latter two species first appear at the transition to the Post-Glacial Period.

Post-Glacial
Wild horse, European bison and aurochs *(Bos primigenius)* lead Post-Glacial colonization. Since Preboreal faunal history has still to be written on the basis of individual bog finds, we have only additional evidence for the presence of red deer *(Cervus elaphus)* and wild boar *(Sus scrofa),* both of which arrive in the middle of the period. With supplementary evidence from settlement sites in England and northern Germany we can, however, confidently suggest that the main Post-Glacial immigration took place around the middle of the Preboreal.

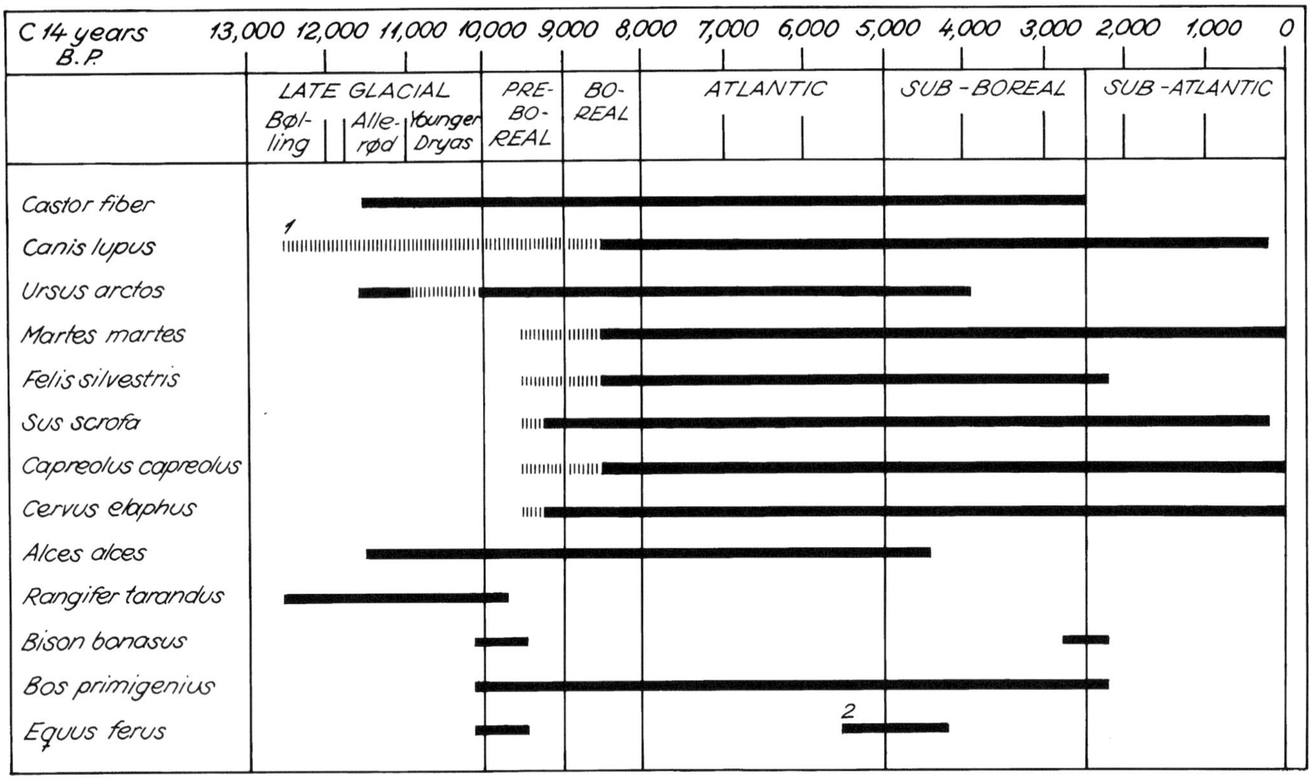

C 14 years B.P.	13,000 12,000 11,000 10,000 9,000 8,000 7,000 6,000 5,000 4,000 3,000 2,000 1,000 0
	LATE GLACIAL: Bøl-ling / Alle-rød / Younger Dryas — PRE-BO-REAL — BO-REAL — ATLANTIC — SUB-BOREAL — SUB-ATLANTIC

Castor fiber

Canis lupus — *1*

Ursus arctos

Martes martes

Felis silvestris

Sus scrofa

Capreolus capreolus

Cervus elaphus

Alces alces

Rangifer tarandus

Bison bonasus

Bos primigenius

Equus ferus — *2*

Late- and Post-Glacial history of a number of terrestrial mammals. The unbroken line is based on dated bone remains, while the broken line shows the probable distribution of the species - a qualified guess based, inter alia, on the present geographical distribution of the species and their ecological needs. 1) The only Late-Glacial find of wolf cannot be more closely dated within the period on the basis of pollen analysis; a C 14 dating is awaited. 2) For the author's views on the wild/domesticated horse debate, see Aaris-Sørensen 1988:145.

Where previously we worked with a more "extended" and differentiated immigration, everything now points to the rapid, early and unified immigration of Post-Glacial mammals. The later absence of certain species on various islands was thus not due to so late an immigration that channels, sounds and so on had emerged as dispersal barriers but should be explained primarily as the *result* of island-formation in connexion with the major rise in sea-level in the Early Atlantic Period. This led to the splitting up and isolation of animal herds so that vulnerable island populations were created. In the worst cases this led to local extinction (Aaris-Sørensen 1980, 1988). This zoogeographical model, which also permits chance recolonization by individuals and, now and then, the re-establishment of populations on the islands, best explains the fluctuations that can be seen. As previously suggested (Aaris-Sørensen 1985:459), palaeozoology (and archaeology) understandably ought to be cautious in interpreting negative evidence, just as the representativity of unique finds should be carefully evaluated.

After agriculture and pastoralism were introduced we see a gradual reduction of the wild fauna, in Jutland too. Here it is not the isolation of populations but rather a strong cultural influence which is the primary reason for the local extinction of certain species in certain areas. Cultural impact also affected the vulnerable island fauna. At the same time, the clearing of the landscape and the development of an open cultural steppe cleared the way for the immigration of new species that were originally found on rocky and mountainous terrain and open steppe such as the house mouse *(Mus musculus)*, black rat *(Rattus rattus)*, brown rat *(Rattus norvegicus)*, harvest mouse *(Micromys minutus)*, common vole *(Microtus arvalis)*, striped fieldmouse *(Apodemus agrarius)*, stone marten *(Martes foina)*, and birds such as the rock dove *(Columba livia)*, black grouse *(Lyrurus tetrix)* and partridge *(Perdix perdix)*. A poor substitute for what was lost, perhaps, but still another indication of the dynamics of fauna whatever changes are brought about by natural or cultural processes.

Domestic animals

BY TOVE HATTING

On the whole, the early history of domesticated animals in Denmark in respect of earliest appearances and the general situation through prehistory and the Middle Ages was alredy well documented 25 years ago. This means that it has been finds that have enabled us to judge, for instance, economic exploitation, variation in size and aspects of breed that have proved of greatest importance since then.

What was regarded as the central problem in the study of early domesticated animals 25 years ago was the sparsity of modern skeletal evidence for primitive breeds available. For this reason, the co-operative work that the Zoological Museum put in hand in association with the creation of the Historical-Archaeological Experimental Centre at Lejre was of great importance.

In the case of sheep in particular, it has been possible to build up a series of well-documented skeletons, i.e. of individuals of known sex, age, weight and height with data on their lives such as the number of offspring or particular illnesses. At the same time, it was possible to carry out a series of castrations so that variations in secondary sexual characteristics such as horn growth and pelvic form could be studied. The whole project was based primarily on the desire to obtain a well-documented body of comparative data for the assessment of bone finds.

Unlike an earlier time, when excavations of Early Stone-age settlements produced very comprehensive bone finds, the last 25 years have been distinguished by major excavations in medieval layers of market towns. Since these layers are midden deposits the majority of the animal bones come, predictably, from common domestic animals.

Comparisons between the urban bone finds and those from forts show how extensively the burgers' diet differed from that of the nobles, the latter having exclusive rights to game. In connexion with the analysis of these great quantities of bone, a debate began over how far the number of bone fragments of individual species reflects the real proportion of beasts in the living community at the settlement. The problem is a central one, but awkward, as so many different factors affect the bones from the time the beast is slaughtered to deposition. The method of excavation itself can significantly affect how much bone gets on to the zoologist's table.

Where, earlier, percentages of bone-types were rather uncritically used as evidence of settlement economy, it is now clear that distortions created by the level of butchery and the durability of the bone by virtue of size and structure mean that the smaller and slenderer species are underrepresented. A comparison between different sites where the structural form, the soil type and the method of excavation are different will produce quite unreliable results if one bases one's interpretations on the number and proportion of fragments.

Dogs

Our earliest domesticated animal is the dog, already present on mesolithic settlements. These were large hunting dogs, but a smaller type is found in the Late Stone Age, the spitz, an exceptional herding dog. It

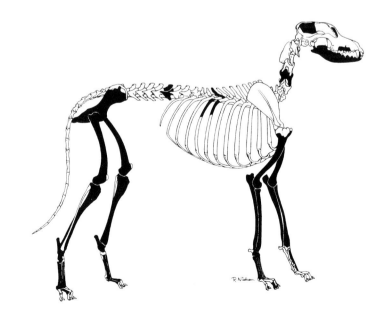

Amongst the many weapons that were excavated from Ejsbøl Mose near Haderslev in 1960 were some much decayed dog bones. Closer study showed that these came from one animal, with small fragments present from the whole body. Only parts of the crown of the skull were there, the upper jaw and a fragment of the lower with a full row of teeth. These very strong teeth and the long leg bones show that this was a large dog, and since its association with the weapon offering is definite one can suppose that it was part of a warrior's accoutrements.

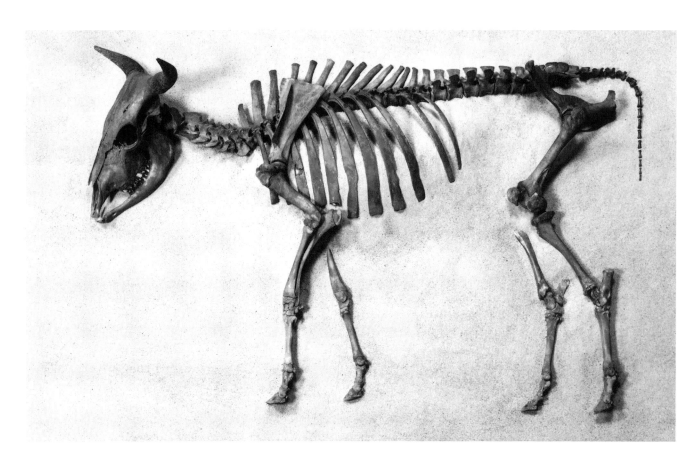

From a trial section across the main basin of Store Åmose in the early 1960's the skeleton of a large ox was excavated, C 14-dated to ca. 3300-3100 B.C. (K-2779). This was a young beast with immature teeth and open cranial sutures. The leg bones were not fully grown as evidenced by the bones (epiphyses) not having grown together. The animal is thought to have been about 2 years old. It had long, slender horns and relatively slender leg bones but was too heavy to be a cow. On the basis of comparison with a roughly contemporary find of an ox about 18 months old from Snoldelev, which had shorter and stronger horns and shorter leg bones, it can be suggested that this animal is a bullock and the Snoldelev one a bull. Studies of the effects of castration on cattle do not yet tell us whether it was practised in the Stone Age, but this find suggests that was the case.

is mostly from the Iron Age, however, that finds of dog have been made in the last 25 years. These finds confirm that Man then kept a wide range of different breeds, from the large fighting dogs of the warrior through the greyhound-like hunters to the small pets of which we have an example in a Viking grave at Lejre.

Cattle

An important contribution to our knowledge of what early cattle were like comes with a number of C 14 datings of skeletons from bogs on Sjælland. In Store Åmose, for instance, several cows and calves have been found, and one complete young bull's skeleton was found in a trial trench across the basin at Husede. The earliest find of cattle yet known

however was made in Snævret Hegn, north of Esrum, where unfortunately only parts of the skeleton and a highly fragmentary skull remained.

Horse

Datings do not however always give satisfactory answers; they can lead to ever more questions arising. At various sites from the Ertebølle Culture and the Late Stone Age, occasional bones and teeth of horse are found in circumstances that are too uncertain to determine whether we have a clear connexion with other cultural remains in the layers. Definite finds of wild horse in Denmark are from the Pre-Boreal Period, and the first certain finds of domesticated horse here come from Bronze-age layers. The finds of horse we now have from the

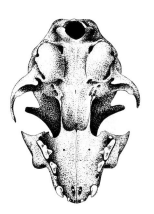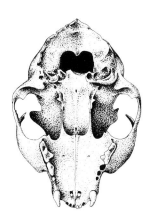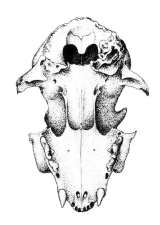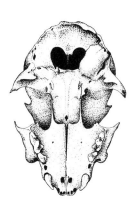

In the excavation of a medieval settlement in the centre of Odense in 1971, a pit full of small bones and dated to the end of the 11th century A.D. was found below a cellar floor. These turned out to be the remains of more than 60 young cats that had been flayed and dumped in the pit with lumps of slake lime. There were also a couple of foxes and,

At Raklev Høje near Kalundborg in 1942, the skeleton of a young sheep was found. Only one horn core remained, but this provides the earliest known evidence of castration in the Late Stone Age. It is larger than a ewe's horn but the surface is smooth, without the ram's deep grooves, and a break on the inner surface shows that the cavity inside the core reaches nearly to the point. These are precisely the characteristics found on specimens in the Experimental Centre at Lejre castrated at the age of about 6 months. We cannot however tell whether this was the result of deliberate action by the Stone-age farmer or of an accidental injury to the animal.

Late Stone Age pose the question, domesticated or wild? The bones do not answer the question, partly because we only have a few teeth and leg-bone fragments and partly because the processes of domestication do not leave diagnostic traces on the horse skeleton. Although the domesticated horse is common in eastern European finds of this period, we cannot exlude the possibility of the few individuals on Danish sites being stray wild horses.

But with the improving scope for C 14 dating of microscopic samples by the accelerator method and through further experimental work with recent animal breeds, plus, naturally, new, well-preserved and well-excavated finds, we can hope that the next 25 years will shed yet more light on the beasts in the prehistoric farmer's stalls.

The people

BY PIA BENNIKE

Since the 19th century, archaeological finds of human remains have customarily been passed on to the Institute of Anatomy at Copenhagen University. The Anthropological Laboratory, a subdivision of this institute, is located at the Panum Institute, and it is here that the large and unparalleled collections from Danish prehistory and the Middle Ages are kept and studied by anthropologists specializing in physical anthropology, physicians and dentists from both within the country and abroad.

Physical anthropology is a subject based upon both archaeologically excavated skeletal finds and studies of biological variance in modern populations. Close collaboration with archaeologists is therefore essential for placing anthropological results in their proper culture-historical context.

Physical anthropology around 1965

About 25 years ago, research in anthropology was upgraded and coincided with a growing public interest in anthropological studies. Besides the existing skeletal exhibits at the monasteries of Øm in Jutland and Æbelholt in northern Sjælland, a third permanent exhibition - on leprosy in the Middle Ages - was opened in 1964 at the Museum of Medical History in Copenhagen. P.V. Glob's world-famous book on the well-preserved bodies from Danish bogs also helped to awaken interest in prehistoric people (Glob 1965).

Two general studies were published in the 1950's. One dealt with eskimo skeletons from Greenland, written by Dr. J. Balslev Jørgensen (1954). The second dealt with skeletal finds from the Stone Age in Denmark, and was published by Dr. Kurt Bröste, Dr. J. Balslev Jørgensen and the archaeologists Johs. Brøndsted and C.J. Becker (Bröste *et al.* 1956). Both publications were the product of a laborious process of recording and measuring a very extensive number of bones. This form of publication, with catalogues and columns of figures, may not win the praise it deserves in archaeological circles, but it does at least provide a quite crucial basis for subsequent analytical anthropological studies.

There was also a study of medieval diseases based on several hundred skeletons excavated at Æbelholt monastery (Møller-Christensen 1958). Close to the ruins of the monastery Vilhelm Møller-Christensen managed to establish a small museum with an exhibition of selected specimens from the site, a museum that still attracts many visitors. It was through these studies of leprosy in the Middle Ages and the description of bone deformation caused by the disease that Møller-Christensen achieved international recognition (Møller-Christensen 1953, 1961).

Anthropological studies since 1965

Archaeology developed rapidly after 1965, and skeletons correspondingly streamed out of the ground all over Denmark. There were neither the resources nor the capacity to cope with this heavy load, and the anthropological examination of many skeletal finds from major excavations was delayed far too long. In addition, attention was focussed on material from other regions (Greenland, Thailand, Nubia) which for various reasons rated higher priority. Jørgen Balslev Jørgensen participated in an ambitious international research programme concerned with human-biological studies of the Arctic populations, while Ole Vagn Nielsen's studies were primarily focussed on the Nubian skeletal collection (Vagn Nielsen 1970). Further, and quite uniquely, previous studies on leprous deformation in Danish medieval skeletal material were combined with a clinical study of leprosy in India (J.G. Andersen 1969). Phillipe Grandjean (1973) undertook a renewed analysis of the lead content in these bones and compared it to the values found in the contemporary population. The number of odontological studies of the Danish material almost exceeded the number of anthropological bone studies in the first 10-15 years of this period (Alexandersen 1967; Danielsen 1970; Lunt 1978; Helm & Prydsö 1979a-b; Brøndum 1981). Skeletal studies were mainly limited to a series of minor publications on a particular topic and a single or small group of skeletons from one site (Vagn Nielsen & Alexandersen 1965; Lund Hansen *et al.* 1973; Balslev Jørgensen 1973; Albrethsen *et al.* 1976; Gilberg 1976; Schou Jørgensen *et al.* 1978).

Research in recent years

Fortunately, our knowledge of the prehistoric population of Denmark is now much greater than it was 25 years ago. In the 1980's a number of larger and smaller anthropological studies were carried out, and the number of skeletal finds has increased substantially, partly as a result of new excavations and partly through datings of hitherto undatable material at the C 14 Laboratory in Copenhagen.

The Mesolithic

Our knowledge of the earliest humans in Denmark, from the Mesolithic and Early Neolithic periods, has increased considerably as the result of excavations carried out in the recent decades. Just 25 years ago, knowledge of Man in these periods was sporadic, based on just a few skeletons. In the above-mentioned book of 1956, 'Prehistoric Man in Denmark', there were only 4 skeletal finds from each of these periods whereas now we have between 50 and 100 mesolithic skeletons and around 50 Early-neolithic ones. The increase in the number of mesolithic finds is mainly due to the excavation of 23 graves at Vedbæk in northern Sjælland around 1974-76. Subsequently more skeletons from the same period were found both in this area and in other parts of Denmark (Kannegaard Nielsen & Brinch Petersen, below). Similar finds have been recorded in southern Sweden providing us with significant comparative material (Alexandersen 1988; Persson & Persson 1988). A proper, comprehensive analysis of the large number of new mesolithic finds from Denmark is thus awaited with great expectation.

From the studies that have already been carried out, a picture of the first people in Denmark is slowly emerging. It is now known that a number of general changes took place in and after the Mesolithic, with the bones and skulls generally becoming less sturdy and the teeth smaller.

The Neolithic

A general account of the many new and newly-dated skeletal finds from the following period, the Early Neolithic, is also awaited, but several of the finds have already been published individually (Bennike *et al.* 1986; Bennike & Ebbesen 1987).

New C 14 datings of these finds have shown, *inter alia*, that skeletons found in bogs and showing evidence of violence, cannot, as formerly believed, be attributed to the end of the Bronze Age and the Early Iron Age but can be dated back to the Early Neolithic. Several of the Early-neolithic skeletons have proved to be those of very young people, but whether they were placed in the bogs sacrificially or as a punishment is considered uncertain.

An anthropological examination of over 2,000 bones and bone fragments excavated from a passage grave on Langeland (Hulbjerg) has formed the basis for our knowledge of people living in the Mid-

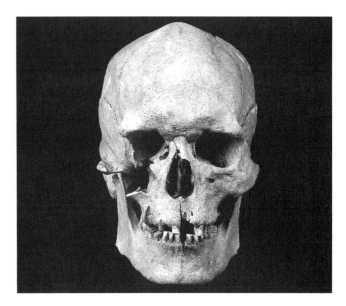

The male skeleton from Fannerup on Djursland is one of many new mesolithic finds in Denmark. It belonged to a small, stocky, muscular man aged 40-45. The skull has a ridged crown and narrow temples. Low, wide eye sockets, a long, narrow nasal cavity, a protruding nose bone together with broad cheek bones and a face of medium length characterized the man's appearance. This marked shape of the skull was partly due to functional factors such as strong chewing capacity and thus strong muscles, as are commonly found on mesolithic skeletons.

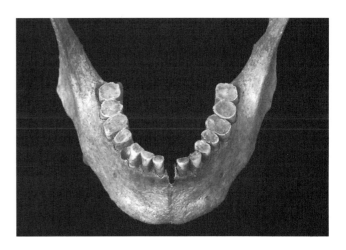

The odontology of prehistoric skeletons provides much important information on age, developmental disorders and lifestyle. A set of teeth such as the Fannerup man's is fairly typical of mesolithic Man. The teeth were generally very worn. In particular the crowns of the front teeth may be quite worn away and the surface of the roots evenly rounded. This is found slightly more frequently in women than in men. On the other hand some men have greater attrition in one corner of the mouth where fractured teeth may also be found as a result of the teeth having been used as a tool. Toothpicks were frequently used and tooth-decay did not affect mesolithic.

35

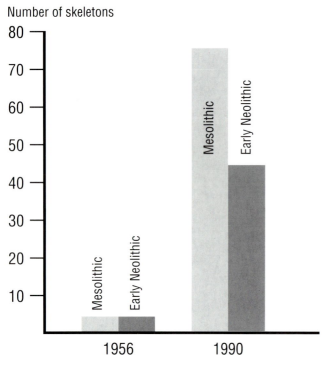

Number of skeletons

Skeletal finds from the Mesolithic and Early Neolithic, 1956 and 1990. The increase in finds from these two earliest periods from which skeletal material is known is quite significant. Such finds are of special anthropological interst as the change that takes place between the periods in respect to both subsistence and diet should be reflected in both bones and teeth.

dle and Late Neolithic (Bennike 1985b). The skeletal remains were retrieved under unusually favourable archaeological conditions under the direction of Hakon Berg in 1960. Individual bones were marked and their position in the chambers of the passage grave were recorded. The anthropological study of the bones became an integrated part of an interdisciplinary project involving zoologists, geologists and archaeologists. The goal was to illuminate a variety of aspects in a limited geographical area rich in finds, the islands south of Fyn (Skaarup 1985). The anthropological objective was to determine the age and sex ratios in the skeletal remains of a total of 53 individuals. Analysis of the mutual positions of the bones showed that defleshed skeletons must have been pushed to the side when a new body was buried. This produced the very jumbled deposit of bones. It was unfortunately impossible to determine whether those buried in the passage grave comprised a select group, or for how long the grave was used for burials.

The Iron Age

Thirty years had to pass before 'Prehistoric Man in Denmark' could be followed up with volume III,

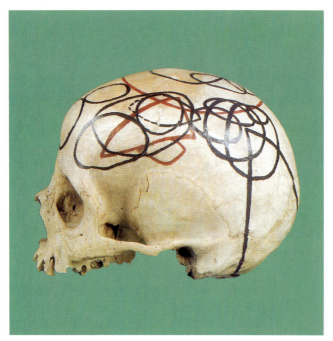
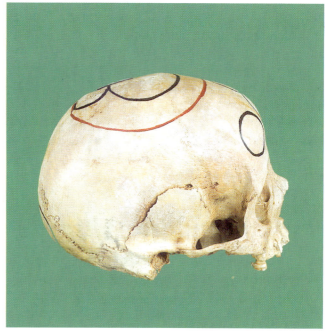

A study of the large number of prehistoric skulls from Denmark revealed 18 examples with traces of treatment - so-called trepannation. All of these are drawn on to the skull here. The red colour shows trepannations with no signs of healing around the edge, the black examples with signs of partial healing - in other words, of survival. It is interesting that the great majority of examples are located on the left side of the skull. This is where most lesions from blows from an opponent's right hand are inflicted. This location indicates that trepannation may have been a way of treating already existing lesions.

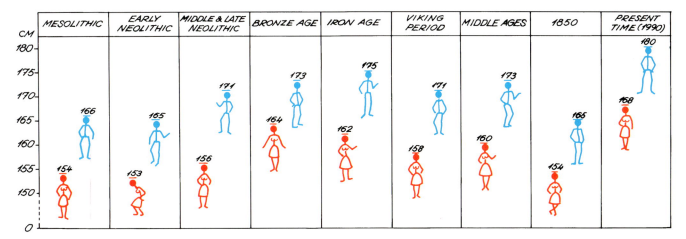

| | MESOLITHIC | EARLY NEOLITHIC | MIDDLE & LATE NEOLITHIC | BRONZE AGE | IRON AGE | VIKING PERIOD | MIDDLE AGES | 1850 | PRESENT TIME (1990) |

Through systematic studies of prehistoric and medieval skeletal finds it is possible to make calculations of average height through several millennia. The curves for men and women respectively show that there has not been a steady increase since the Mesolithic but variations in both directions throughout time. The average height in recent centuries, when living conditions were poor, seems to have been the lowest. Note also the fall in average height in the Viking Period.

'Iron Age Man in Denmark', with an anthropological description and catalogue of all the uncremated skeletal finds from the Iron Age. This work was carried out by the anthropologist Berit J. Sellevold and the archaeologist Ulla Lund Hansen in co-operation with Jørgen Balslev Jørgensen (Sellevold *et al.* 1984). It received a warm welcome, and is now the basis for comparative anthropological studies between the periods of Danish prehistory and for new studies of skeletal material from the Iron Age and Viking Period. Archaeological and anthropological collaboration has made it possible to focus on archaeological aspects such as artefact-types, grave length or status factors in relation to sex, age, height and diseases that leave their mark on the bones. It is, however, no secret that it has been difficult to interpret the range of differences and similarities between cranial measurements and other skeletal data. This is rendered difficult, for instance, by the great variation present even within small local groups of the same cultural period. This situation may itself be the reason that the substance of the anthropological studies has slowly changed from the purely descriptive to a more analytical form. Special attention is now paid to the circumstances in which prehistoric Man lived, his illnesses and demographic composition. On the other hand, less attention is being paid to prehistoric Man's appearance, distribution and origins, which the numerous earlier studies of cranial measurements were intended to determine.

The Middle Ages

Major excavations of medieval churchyards have taken place in the last 25 years at, for instance, Grenå, Svendborg, Randers, Næstved, Odense, Ålborg, Holbæk and Tikøb. From most sites, the number of skeletal finds is so large and representative of the past population that it will be possible, in studies of this material, to use the information that cranial measurements can provide in statistical ways. With his background in biology, and using a number of statistical analyses, Jesper Boldsen has tried to illuminate the medieval population structure on the basis of skeletal finds (Boldsen 1984, 1988). The medieval skeletons from Svendborg have also formed the basis for a comprehensive but more traditional anthropological and odontological study carried out by the anatomist Izabella Tkocz and dentist Niels Brøndum (Tkocz & Brøndum 1985). However, many of the other large medieval collections are still to be studied.

Sickness and health

Even after retiring as professor of medical history in 1973, Møller-Christensen continued to publish (Møller-Christensen 1967, 1978). His many publications contained new knowledge concerning sickness and health in the Middle Ages. Similar studies of prehistoric skeletons, however, were sporadic. As a result, an investigation was launched in 1980, focussing on diseases in antiquity based on a survey of around 2,000 Danish prehistoric skeletal finds. This involved

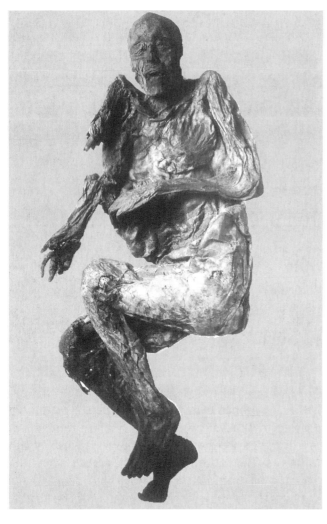

an extensive recording of all forms of change in bones and teeth. The result was 'Palaeopathology of Danish Skeletons' (Bennike 1985a). This included *inter alia* an assessment of traces of trepannation on a total of 18 skulls. The conclusion could be drawn that these skulls were not only geographically widespread but also chronologically, from the Early Neolithic to the Middle Ages.

A quite unique find was a neolithic skull from the Hulbjerg passage grave with a carious tooth that had been treated by drilling (Bennike 1984).

Current anthropological research

In the publications of the last 25 years one can detect a tendency for anthropological studies to be based increasingly on interdisciplinary collaboration. This not only includes archaeology but a wide range of other fields too. These fields of research have much the same aim: to reveal as many aspects as possible of our forefathers and their lives. Dentists and specialists in various medical fields are of course frequent participants in such interdisciplinary studies. Odontological studies of the Danish skeletal finds however play a special role in anthropology. This is to a large degree thanks to the dentist Verner Alexandersen, who has contributed much new knowledge on prehistoric teeth in Denmark (Alexandersen 1989). Specialists in a wider range of more technical fields are also becoming increasingly involved.

A current research project on the incidence of osteoporosis in the populations of various cultural periods in relation to the present sees the participation of, for instance, chemists, engineers, physicians

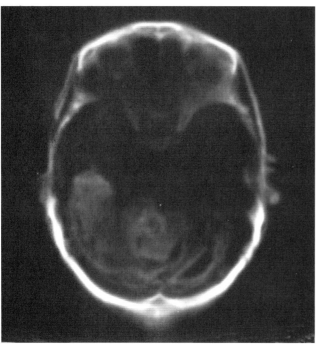

It is a long time since well-preserved bog corpses have turned up in the Danish peat. On the other hand, an exciting find of a very well-preserved pre-Roman Iron-age body was made in a museum storehouse. The woman's body, which was clothed, was found in Huldremose on Djursland in 1879. It was then sent to Copenhagen, where the well-preserved clothes were exhibited in the National Museum. The body ended up in a wooden box where it was left until recently. The body was completely untreated, and it has proved possible to CT-scan (computed tomography) the whole body. CT-scanning allows the internal study of the body through cross-section pictures. All the dried-up and shrunken inner organs seem to be preserved, and on the cross-section of the skull both the brain and the eyeballs can be seen. A sample from the stomach region showed the presence of rye, spurrey, other vegetable remains and possibly meat (Brothwell et al. 1990).

In 1964, a permanent exhibition on leprosy was opened at the Museum of Medical History in Copenhagen. This was based on a study of about 700 skeletons from a leper hospital known as St. Jørgensgård at Aaderup near Næstved, southern Sjælland. There were 30 such hospitals in Denmark alone in the later Middle Ages. The sick were committed there for life. The exhibition includes both medieval leprosy and the disease which still exists in underdeveloped countries, where 10-15 million people are afflicted.

and dentists from a number of different institutions (Bennike & Bohr 1990).

Comprehensive surveys such as 'Iron Age Man in Denmark' and 'Palaeopathology of Danish Skeletons' that include catalogues and records with information on the whole or large parts of the Danish skeletal material render the finds well-documented and readily accessible. Such surveys may serve as a basis for future studies of a more analytical character or for the testing of many new methods. They are certainly of great value for researchers in other countries who are interested in an extensive survey of the Danish skeletal material. In the future, however, continued research on the skeletal collection will be faced with great difficulties, unless it receives a radical upgrading, as it did 25 years ago. If the skeletal collection is to retain its value it should not be parcelled out to random projects. A research programme should be planned to assure continuity: older students could be supervised and younger ones taught.

As a whole, the Danish skeletal collection, the Greenlandic, the Faroese and the Nubian, the famous collection of leper skeletons and a pathological skeletal collection from the last century with more than 1,000 bone samples (Bennike 1991), form a unique collection. Together these should form the basis for a bone-research centre for interdisciplinary and international co-operation.

Physical anthropology has expanded enormously outside Denmark in the last 20 years, with the creation of new university departments, research centres and special museum departments dealing exclusively with archaeological bone finds.

This is clearly reflected in the European Anthropology Association, an organization that held its first conference in 1975. It now has 1,000 members and continues to grow. Although there are only a few Danish members, Denmark has been chosen to host the 9th conference in 1994, in an effort to increase knowledge of the subject in our part of Europe. This event should be used as a springboard for the development of the field in Denmark. It should serve the purpose of emphasizing that the Danish skeletal material definitely ought to occupy a central position internationally, and be the centre of a range of anthropological research activities.

Dating methods

By Henrik Tauber

The last 25 years have seen dramatic developments in the field of absolute dating. Ever more refined calibration curves have made it possible to convert datings in C 14 years to absolute ages in calendar (solar) years. Concurrently, two new dating methods, dendrochrology and thermoluminescence dating, have been developed into practical tools for archaeological use. Finally, ice-core datings from Greenland (Hammer *et al.* 1986), and an absolute dendrochronology from Central Europe, have contributed to the dating of the Late-Glacial periods and, thus, the last phases of the Palaeolithic.

This development means that most archaeological finds can now be dated on an absolute scale, and that earlier relative chronologies based on conclusions and estimates drawn from stratigraphy, typology and pollen-analyses etc. can be supplemented with a coherent absolute chronology that covers all the main archaeological periods of the last 13,000 years or so, when Denmark was free of the ice.

Each of these absolute dating methods dates slightly different events (the formation of carbon compounds in living organisms, the felling year of timber, the heating of mineral grains). The methods therefore cannot be expected to give exactly the same age for a specific archaeological event. These differences have a certain effect in the chronological delineation of archaeological periods too.

Carbon 14 dating

The C 14 method is based on the measurement of radioactive carbon (C 14) in plant and animal remains. If one knows the original C 14 content of living animal or plant tissue, and measures the amount remaining in surviving fragments of these tissue types (wood, charcoal, nutshells, turf, bone, seashells), one can use the known rate of decay of C 14 atoms to calculate how long has passed since the plant and animal remains were part of living organisms.

In the last 25 years, the C 14 method has been developed in several ways. A refined measuring technique has led to the statistical uncertainty of datings being reduced, in favourable circumstances, to 40-50 years or less (conventional C 14 dating). At the same time, a completely new measuring technique for mass-spectometric analysis of the total number of C 14 atoms in a sample (Accelerator Mass Spectometry: AMS) has been developed. With the AMS technique it is possible to date very small

samples - as little as a thousandth of the amount that is needed for conventional dating.

Contributing to a higher accuracy has also been a more extensive chemical pre-treatment of samples to ensure that all non-original carbon compounds that may be absorbed by a sample lying for a long time in the soil are removed before dating.

The most important step in the development of absolute datings has however been study of the time-dependent variations in the C 14 content of plant and animal tissue. By measuring the C 14 contents in growth rings in long dendrochronological series both from America and from Europe one can directly determine what the original C 14 content of plant and other carbonaceous materials was. Measurements of C 14 content have been made over to coherent dendrochronological series back to 9,700 years BP (Radiocarbon 1986; B. Becker *et al.* 1991). A reliable calibration of C 14 datings can therefore be applied over that range. Recently, attempts have been made to extend the European dendro-series back to 11,300 years BP (B. Becker *et al.* 1991), but the extension is still somewhat uncertain. Measurements indicate that in the Late Glacial Period, absolute ages are about 1,000 years older than those given in C 14 years. New ice-core measurements indicate that the correction might be 1,500 years (Hammer, pers. comm.).

These studies have shown that the original C 14 content has been subject to significant fluctuations, with levels up to 10% higher in the Post and Late Glacial Periods. At the same time, minor, short-term fluctuations, lasting a couple of centuries, were superimposed on the major fluctuations. In periods with rapid fluctuations in C 14 contents one cannot give precise C 14 datings in calendar years but only probable time intervals. This is most marked in periods of the pre-Roman Iron Age and Late Bronze Age, the Late Stone Age and the transition to the Mesolithic.

Besides periodic fluctuations there is also individual variance between different types of material caused by the fractionation of C 12, C 13 and C 14 during the absorption of carbon dioxide and the synthesis of carbon compounds in living organisms. The magnitude of these individual variations in samples can be calculated from measurements of the content of stable C 13 isotopes in the samples, and do not cause extra uncertainty in the C 14 determinations if a correction for isotope fractionation is made. The

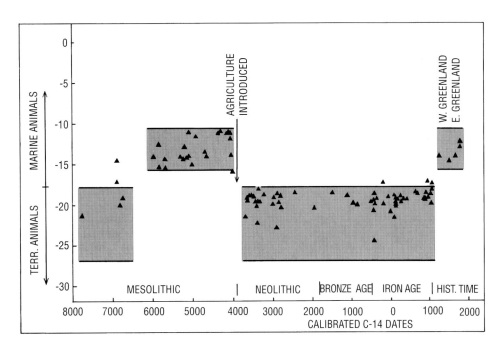

The δ¹³C contents of prehistoric skeletons from Denmark and of eskimo skeletons from Greenland ca. 1200-1750 A.D. Each triangle shows the analysis of one skeleton expressed in δ¹³C values. Normal δ¹³C values for land and sea animals are shown for comparison. From ca. 6000-4000 B.C., the δ¹³C contents of analysed skeletons from Denmark are as high as in the skeletons from Greenland, where food from the sea was dominant. In this period, fishing and hunting of marine animals was predominant. After the introduction of agriculture food came mostly from land animals and plants.

greatest differences occur between material from terrestrial and marine food chains. These differences can be used directly in dietary studies (Tauber 1981, 1986b, 1989b).

Most finds are C 14 dated nowadays. It is therefore impracticable to discuss individual results here. Instead, the chronology table shows the C 14 chronology that has emerged from the last 25 years' work. With the Iron Age periods, however, fine adjustments have been made on the basis of historical parallels etc.

Characteristic of the C 14 chronology is that - in contrast to what was earlier thought - clear overlaps between the main archaeological periods do not occur. Instead we have a simple, almost unilinear development. This applies as much to the transition from the Ertebølle Culture to the Early Neolithic (Tauber 1988, 1989a) as the transition from the Middle Neolithic to the (Jutlandic) Single Grave Culture (Malmros & Tauber 1977; Tauber 1986a). Also the Pitted Ware Culture, which is not mentioned in the table, essentially seems to fall after the Middle Neolithic, period V (Tauber 1986a). The above-mentioned short-term fluctuations in C 14 levels may however hide short chronological overlaps.

The C 14 chronology has brought great changes to earlier proposed dates of the archaeological periods. The date of the transition to the Neolithic, i.e. for the introduction of agriculture, has moved 1,400 years earlier. These changes, and corresponding shifts in cultural development in neighbouring areas, have been of great significance for the understanding of possible cultural relations between northern Europe and contemporary cultures in the Aegean and the Near East. One of the great advantages of the C 14 method is precisely that it can be applied to finds worldwide, and can thus contribute objective evidence on where cultural developments began and by what routes they were diffused.

New C 14 datings have also shown that Denmark was ice-free for a period of more than 20,000 years prior to ca. 22,000 years BP, when the last glaciation began. In this long period the land was covered with a sort of steppe vegetation with mammoth and other large animals (Aaris-Sørensen *et al.* 1990). It would be strange if people, at least seasonally, did not follow these large animals and leave traces in the form of tools and weapons. If this is the case, there is a whole cultural complex here that in future years it will be an important task to try to investigate.

Dendrochronology

Dating by means of timber growth-ring measurements presupposes the accumulation of long and continuous master curves and a great deal of comparative study before unknown growth-ring series can be confidently aligned with a master curve. Although this method has been known since the 1920's, it only became a practicable dating method after computer technology became generally available.

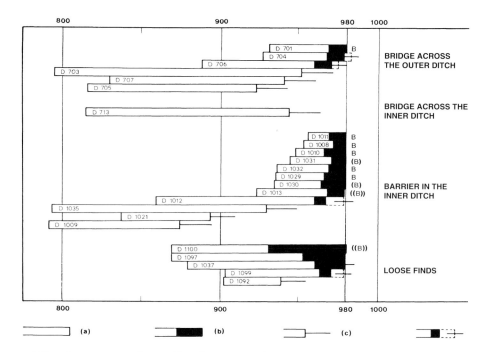

Diagram showing the dating of wood from Trelleborg: (a) heartwood, (b) heartwood and sapwood, (c) samples lacking sapwood, (d) samples with heartwood and some of the sapwood. B marks the bark ring.

Thanks to extensive collecting, a continuous master curve for oak now running back to 109 B.C. - the longest in Scandinavia - has been constructed in the National Museum, Copenhagen, together with a number of shorter, local master curves. The dendrochronological laboratory at the Wormianum, Århus, has also constructed a long Jutlandic master curve. Master curves for oak from southern Sweden, Schleswig-Holstein and Poland, worked out in the Universities of Lund and Hamburg, are also used in Danish dating.

Dendrochronological dating in Denmark is carried out on oakwood with reasonably long series of growth rings, normally 100-150. If the outermost ring (the bark ring) is preserved, felling can be dated to within 6 months or a year. Thus dendrochronology is potentially by far the most accurate dating method that archaeology has at its disposal. If the outermost growth ring is absent but some of the sapwood remains in the oak, felling can usually be dated to within 5-30 years, while series of heartwood alone provide a *terminus post quem*.

The precision of this method is decisive in the interpretation of finds from historical and late prehistoric periods. The dendrochronological dating of Trelleborg to 980/81 A.D. excludes the ring fort having been primarily built as a camp associated with the early 11th-century invasions of England. Instead, the dating links Trelleborg to the period of conflict between Harold Bluetooth and Sweyn Forkbeard over the Danish throne (Bonde & Christensen 1984).

Because of differences in regional master curves it is also possible to get information on the origins of wood samples. An example is Skuldelev ship no.2 from Roskilde Fjord. 13 samples from the ship are dated to *ca.* 1070 A.D. but this was only possible by using a master curve constructed on the basis of material excavated in Dublin. It is therefore overwhelmingly probable that the ship was built by vikings in Ireland (Bonde & Crumlin-Pedersen 1990). Gradually, as more regional master curves are established, the possibility of such determinations of provenience increases. This may contribute to a determination of the extent of timber trade etc. over much of northern Europe at different periods.

Amongst other important results can be noted the dating of the northern barrow at Jelling to 958 A.D. while the southern is 10-20 years later (K. Christensen & Krogh 1987). The earliest sections of Danevirke are dated to 737 A.D. (H.H. Andersen *et al.* 1976) while samples from the Nydam boat are dated to 310-320 A.D. (Bonde 1991; Bonde *et al.* 1991). Finally the Mammen grave chamber is dated by the Wormianum to 970/71 A.D. (Iversen & Vellev 1986).

A number of our Bronze-age coffins have now been absolutely-dated thanks to the synchronization of growth-ring series with the central German master curves established at the University of Cologne. The final growth ring in the Egtved girl's coffin is thus dated to 1370 B.C. (K. Christensen & Jensen 1991). As the growth-ring series in several of the great oak coffins can be put together into one long series, a large number of the Bronze-age coffins can thus be dated.

Work continues on developing and extending the Danish growth-ring series backwards. The ultimate goal is a complete Danish dendrochronology running far back into the Stone Age.

Thermoluminescence dating

Mineral grains, especially quartz and felspar, can store energy that comes either from internal radioactivity or environmental radiation. When the mineral grains are heated to 300-500°C the stored energy is given off in the form of a light signal (thermoluminescence). If all the stored energy has been released at a particular moment, the radiation that accumulates after this moment will be a measure of the time that has passed since the zero setting. If one knows the amount of radiation which is stored each year, the accumulated level can be converted directly into absolute years (Aitken 1990).

The release of stored energy (the zero setting) takes place, for instance, when pottery or brick is fired and when potboilers are heated etc., but can also take place with accidental processes such as housefires.

The TL method allows materials to be dated that cannot be dated by other methods and which normally are direcly associated with human activity. The TL method, like the C 14 method, is universal and, unlike the C 14 method, does not require calibration.

The datings are carried out in the Nordic Laboratory for Luminescence Dating, Risø, and with current techniques can be carried out with an uncertainty level of 5-6% (Mejdahl et al. 1980). A number of brick ovens, settlements and strongholds etc. have been TL-dated. Examples include the dating of a heap of burnt stones at Lejre, where two layers were distinguished, one dated to *ca.* 600 A.D. and one around 1000 A.D., as also indicated by C 14 datings, and the dating of a brick oven at Kalø with congruent archaeomagnetic and TL dating (Mejdahl 1990; Abrahamsen 1991).

Of especial importance for archaeological chronology is the possibility of direct dating of pottery with typological features. For material earlier than the Bronze Age, however, the uncertainty becomes so large that it sets a limit to practical applicability. This limitation may perhaps be overcome by a new technique based on optically stimulated lumines-

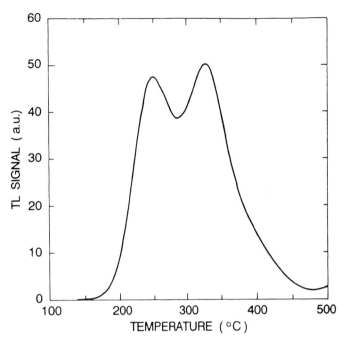

The dependency of the TL signal on temperature for a typical potassium feldspar, expressed in arbitrary units (a.u). The higher the TL signal emitted the older the sample.

cence (Bøtter-Jensen *et al.* 1991; Mejdahl 1991). This technique has not yet been fully developed but preliminary studies indicate that the level of uncertainty may be more than halved, while the sample size necessary may be reduced to a few grammes where up to now samples of 100-200 g. have been needed.

The TL method is also of great importance in the Late Glacial Period, where the calibration of the C 14 method is very uncertain and organic material is often poorly preserved. The method has thus been applied to the dating of a settlement of the Hamburg Culture at Jels in southern Jutland (Huxtable & Mejdahl 1992).

One of the TL method's basic advantages is that it can reach further back in time than the C 14 method. With quartz one can date back to *ca.* 70,000 years BP while dating with felspar can be extended back to about 500,000 years. This has been decisive in the dating of many Late-Glacial and Glacial deposits and might also have archaeological significance if we succeed in finding traces of mammoth hunters who pursued these huge mammals in the ice-free period prior to ca. 22,000 BP, or definite traces of hunters from earlier interglacial periods.

THE LATE PALAEOLITHIC AND THE MESOLITHIC

The Late Palaeolithic and the Mesolithic

BY ERIK BRINCH PETERSEN

How far our understanding of the Stone-age Hunter-Gatherers - the Late Palaeolithic and the Mesolithic - has changed in the last 25 years can perhaps best be shown by a comparison of the overviews that have been published during this period. While the first (Brinch Petersen 1973) attempted to provide a summary based on old excavations, of which a large number were effectively unpublished, more recent studies have been able to profit from modern excavations and their results (S.H. Andersen 1981a; Price 1985; L. Larsson 1990b). But even these, in fact, are already out of date in several respects, as the following essays show.

After the large settlement excavations of the 1940's and 50's in the Sjælland bogs such as Glarmosen, with Bromme (Mathiassen 1947), Holmegaard (C.J. Becker 1945), Sværdborg-Lundby (Bille Henriksen 1976, 1980) and in particular the Åmose (Troels-Smith 1953; S. Jørgensen 1956; K. Andersen 1951, 1961, 1983; K. Andersen et al. 1982), there was a decline in excavation. As the intensive peat-cutting gradually ceased, the sites were no longer so seriously threatened, and with this the motivation for large, systematic excavations disappeared. Only the Neolithic problem was still topical in the Åmose investigations (Troels-Smith 1982). It is typical, therefore, that the National Museum's excavations of the 1960's were led by the amateur archaeologist and sculptor Holger Kapel, who directed important excavations in Draved Mose in Southern Jutland (Sobotta 1991) and around the former Villingebæk fjord in northern Sjælland (Kapel 1969; Vang Petersen 1982). About 25 years ago a new generation of scholars arrived, leading not only to a change in the selection of areas and objects of study but also in the methods applied, which in turn could produce new and different results.

One of the difficulties facing the summary of 1973 was the problem of the large amount of unpublished data going right back to the beginning of the century. While the four fundamental publications in this area (A.P. Madsen et al. 1900; Sarauw 1903; Westerby 1927; Mathiassen 1947) appeared soon after the fieldwork, just as many equally important excavations had to wait their turn, or were only known through minor, provisional reports. The low rate of publication is regrettably still a problem. Fortunately, it has gradually been possible to get several of the earlier excavations published, above all the Maglemose huts from Ulkestrup (K. Andersen et al. 1982),

one of Denmark's most important finds. Other sites have been re-examined (Brinch Petersen 1967, 1972; Skaarup 1973; Bille Henriksen 1976, 1980; A. Fischer & Nielsen 1987), while others are still awaiting proper study and publication. It is not, however, necessarily the case that these old sites are still so interesting, as it can be difficult to apply new questions to earlier finds; an excavation really has to be well recorded for this to be possible. It has therefore to be fully understood that settlement excavations too can become out of date.

Post-war excavations in the Åmose of western Sjælland were first and foremost chronological-stratigraphic ones, as was quite reasonable in the circumstances, the work being carried out by bog geologists and pollen analysts. However it gradually became clear that pollen analysis was unable to support either the regional or the super-regional fine chronology that was looked for; C 14 dating in fact took on this job (Tauber, above). In consequence, it was predictable that first publications of the next generation dealt with typological and chronological questions (S.H. Andersen & Malmros 1966; Brinch Petersen 1967). This can also be seen as a development parallel to the typological and chronological debates in France (Sonneville-Bordes 1960; Tixier 1963) and Germany (Taute 1968, 1975) from where a great deal of inspiration in Stone Age archaeology has always derived. The interest in chronological studies has, naturally, continued right down to the present (S.H. Andersen 1979b; Vang Petersen 1984; B. Madsen 1992).

In the last 25 years there has been a significant growth in the culture-historical evidence from the Early Stone Age. Not necessarily because there are now more excavations per year than before, but at least equally because a new and in many respects quite unexpected body of material has been obtained. This primarily affects the Late Palaeolithic, from which all the classic cultures such as the Hamburg (J. Holm & Rieck 1992), Federmesser (Fugl Petersen 1974, A. Fischer 1990b; J. Holm 1993) and Ahrensburg (Vang Petersen & L. Johansen 1993) are now represented alongside the long-known Bromme Culture (A. Fischer 1991). Now, therefore, unlike before, the case can be made for unbroken settlement from the end of the last Ice Age, perhaps even from a time in the Bølling Period about 14,000 years B.P., down to the present.

46

B.P.	13	12	11	10	9	8	7	6	5
B.C.	11	10	9	8	7	6	5	4	3
B.C. (calibr.)	(12)	(11)	(10)	9.100	8.000	7.000	5.800	4.900	3.800
POLLEN ZONES	BØLLING	DR:2	ALLERØD	DR:3	PB:1	PREBOREAL	BO	EARLY ATLANTIC	HIGH ATLANTIC	SUBB
LAND/SEA								TR T R	T	RT
FAUNA	REINDEER				BISON HORSE	AUROX ELK	RED DEER – ROE DEER – WILD BOAR		DOM.
PERIOD	LATE PALAEOLITIC				MESOLITHIC				NEO
CULTURE/ PHASES	HAMBURG		AHRENSBURG		MAGLEMOSE	KONGEMOSE	ERTEBØLLE	TRB	
		BROMME			0 1 2 3 4 5	0 1 2 3	1 2 3	EN 1	
	FEDERMESSER								

Proposed chronology. By "Land/Sea" the trans- and regressions of the Littorina Sea are shown.

There are, certainly, persistent problems in studying the earliest phase of the Maglemose Culture, where there is still a find lacuna. This is first and foremost a gap in research, as the characteristic artefact-types from here are either part of the large body of stray finds or are known from a number of as yet unexcavated settlements. Systematic excavations in southern Sjælland (Johansson 1990), the Åmose (A. Fischer 1985c) and Draved Mose (Sobotta 1991), however, have helped to reduce this gap.

Recent excavations in Skåne (L. Larsson 1984) have shown that the transition from the Maglemose to the Kongemose was a gradual one and the same is being shown by uncontaminated settlement finds in Denmark. Finds like those from Skåne have long been known from several of the large, mixed settlement finds in the Åmose, like Øgaarde (Mathiassen 1943). Now, the underwater excavation at Blak in Roskilde Fjord (AUD 1991:121; S.A. Sørensen in prep.) shows that we must also reckon with an early phase of the Kongemose Culture with trapezes that can be regarded as a transitional point between the two cultures. How the transition from one culture to another in the Mesolithic is to be understood, however, is still something of guess both in Denmark and elsewhere.

The majority of Mesolithic excavations in these years have been concentrated around the coastal settlements. The larger excavations such as Norsminde, Ertebølle and Bjørnsholm in Jutland, and Vedbæk in north-eastern Sjælland, have concerned themselves precisely with these fossil fjords with many settlements with or without kitchen middens. It is no surprise, therefore, that it has proved possible to retrieve a body of material that can fill out the poorly evidenced periods that were formerly known as the 'earliest and earlier Coastal Culture'. These phases can now be assigned without difficulty to the Kongemose Culture.

The underwater excavations of the drowned landscape with its Stone-age settlements have provided new opportunities to discover settlements from periods and phases that had formerly escaped recognition on dry land (Skaarup 1983; A. Fischer et al. 1987; Grøn & Skaarup 1993). Furthermore, the exceptionally good preservative conditions at these sites have been able to provide completely new find-types such as the painted paddles and the woven textiles from Tybrind Vig, not to forget the well-preserved dug-out canoes (S.H. Andersen 1987).

Finally, a new, and quite different, set of finds is the many graves that have steadily been excavated at several sites, to which the most important parallels have appeared concurrently in Skåne (L. Larsson 1988). Graves like this, with well-preserved skeletons, have really helped to emphasize how Stone-age sites are not only sources for fine typological and chronological studies but rather are the settlements of a living community which contain the information that has to be used in a description and explanation of the adaptation of the Stone-age Hunter-Gatherers to the varying natural environments.

Interdisciplinary studies concentrating on a particular locality have been typical of this field since

47

its scientific inception in 1848. In the last 25 years too, intensive investigations of this kind have been carried out, first and foremost at Norsminde, south of Århus (S.H. Andersen 1976, 1991) and at Ertebølle and Bjørnsholm in the Limfjord (S.H. Andersen & Johansen 1987; S.H. Andersen 1993) and in the Vedbæk area, north of Copenhagen (Brinch Petersen et al. 1976, 1977, 1979, 1982). On the one hand, it has transpired that the more intensively an area is researched, the better the investigations will be. But conversely, this concentration of resources into relatively few areas has unfortunately meant that large areas of the country have still to be regarded as unstudied (Brinch Petersen 1992). This is quite important, as the mesolithic settlements are now, naturally, vulnerable to the same level of threat whether they are in the north of Sjælland or in Southern Jutland. Just now, the hardest pressed may be so classic a Danish find category as the kitchen middens which, however, are not distributed over the whole country (S.H. Andersen 1988, 1992).

In the course of the last 25 years there has been a shift from chronological-stratigraphic excavations with deep sections in long trenches to attempts to reveal the surfaces of whole settlements (Price & Brinch Petersen 1987; Brinch Petersen 1989). This tendency is naturally in line with Danish developments in the excavation of settlements of later periods. The inspiration for such excavations, and the subsequent analyses, however, derives from the large excavations of Magdalenian settlements in the Paris basin (Leroi-Gourhan 1984) and by the Rhine (Bosinski 1981). A further spur to conducting excavations as large open area excavations was, as noted above, the discovery of a large number of graves at the settlement of Henriksholmen-Bøgebakken in Vedbæk (Albrethsen & Brinch Petersen 1975).

But it is not only graves that are found through excavations of this type. Now we also find another previously undiscovered category of material, the many and varied structures of the settlements. This comprises not only the building, hut and tent structures that, undoubtedly, there are still problems with (Blankholm 1985, 1991; Grøn 1987a; S.A. Sørensen 1988), but also the large range of structural features which earlier excavations were not aware of.

At the same time as the excavated area of the settlements became larger, there was an intensification in the recovery of the very smallest objects. On those sites where systematic wet sieving has been carried out, there has been a significant increase in the quantity of small flint artefacts such as burin-spalls and arrowhead fragments. More important, however, is that the volume of microfaunal remains too, especially fish vertebrae, which could be very sparsely represented from earlier excavations (Rosenlund 1976), has now really exploded in quantity. Whether this means that the later Mesolithic ought now to be rechristened the 'Fishing Stone Age', as has been suggested (Tauber 1989b), may, however, be another matter.

The new excavation strategy has made it not only possible but in fact necessary to carry out different analyses from before. Previously, settlement finds were virtually only subjected to typological analysis and a description of the lithic tools. It was, of course, assumed that these studies would reveal the chronological and functional situation by means of comparison with other settlements.

The attempt to uncover and record a settlement horizontally aims primarily at retrieving a holistic picture of the prehistoric context, with the absolutely central problem being to understand, explain and define a 'settlement'. Ethno-archaeological studies, which have been so important a source of inspiration, have further shown that one must reckon with several different types of settlement in a Hunter-Gatherer society (Binford 1980). How such differences can be read in the archaeological material is still, however, a disputed matter (Gamble & Boismier 1991; Kroll & Price 1991). The individual settlement must, of course, be viewed first in light of the methods of excavation and then back through the thousands of years of possible destruction that separate the excavation from the prehistoric settlement.

The whole pattern of distribution of artefacts on the settlement is not the only matter of archaeological interest; so too is their relationship to the various features that can be observed. On the few sites where, as yet, lithic refitting has been carried out, it can also be seen how the image of a settlement can suddenly change from a static to a dynamic one. The same analyses are also good at illustrating the different stages of flint production, which in turn help to show activities on the settlement as well as sharpening insight into local raw-material consumption (B. Madsen 1992).

On the basis of experimental studies, it has also been possible to identify certain typical forms of damage from use, especially on flint arrowheads (A. Fischer *et al.* 1984). The microscopic examination of traces of wear that has been applied to a selection of finds from major settlements is also important (Juel Jensen & Brinch Petersen 1985). Only now is it possible to identify the function of the various flint tools, and to show that a very large proportion of the lithics found on settlements is in fact waste material (Juel Jensen 1988).

While the analysis of settlement flint has been refined, there has been a corresponding advance in the study of the faunal evidence, the second important category of finds. To begin with, the basic faunal range in the different periods has been sharpened up (Aaris-Sørensen, above). Then the taphonomic problems were studied (Aaris-Sørensen 1983; Grønnow 1987; Noe-Nygaard 1988b; Trolle-Lassen 1992), and finally now the very large quantity of fish remains has been subjected to careful study (Bødker Enghoff 1983, 1987, 1991, 1993).

The chronology has been refined too; it is now better founded than before. This depends primarily on the greater number of C 14 datings, combined with the recovery of new material. The Mesolithic chronology can best be regarded as a single line of development or change, with one culture superseding another and with gradual transitional phases. The chronological evidence for the Late Palaeolithic, by contrast, shows some overlap between the four classic cultures, which again raises questions about our understanding of them.

The problem of even earlier settlement has been raised above (Aaris-Sørensen; Tauber). A few hand-axes have also been found that on typological grounds could be very ancient (Grote & Maagaard Jakobsen 1982; C.J. Becker 1985; J. Holm & Rieck 1992). As always with stray finds, there are a number of problems affecting both the find circumstances and a definite dating. The latter also seems to be the case with the find and the excavated material from Vejstrup Skov in Southern Jutland (S.H. Andersen 1981a).

One of the reasons for the problems with dating in the Late Palaeolithic is that chronology cannot be viewed in isolation but must also be seen in the context of spatial distribution. In the Late Glacial Period, the Havelte finds (J. Holm & Rieck 1992) form the northernmost Hamburgian group in the same way as we can see the Bromme as the northern variant of the Ahrensburgian. The southernmost part of Denmark and Schleswig-Holstein can be regarded as a border area where the various cultures move forward and back. The same could, in reality, hold for the Maglemosian in the Pre- and Early Boreal Periods.

With the Kongemose and Ertebølle Cultures, a division between eastern and western Denmark appears, with a boundary line through the Storebælt between Fyn and Sjælland. In the Ertebølle, it has also been possible on typological-stylistic grounds to distinguish a series of local groups inside a limited area such as eastern Sjælland (Vang Petersen 1984).

Both the Late-palaeolithic and the Maglemose Cultures have always been regarded as inland cultures, and it is only with the Kongemose that the marine aspect begins to appear, subsequently to dominate in the Ertebølle. It is, however, far from certain that this dichotomy is so easy to explain. It may actually be the case that it is only with the Ertebølle that it is possible to see both aspects, and it can then be debated how this dichotomy is to be understood. Is it a matter of two populations, or is it the same population group that seasonally exploited both inland and coastal resources (Noe-Nygaard 1988a)? Here δ^{13}C analyses of skeletal material are of great importance (Tauber, above).

Many people see the Mesolithic developments in Denmark as an expression of changes from a Hunter-Gatherer society comprising mobile, egalitarian groups organized in small social units to larger and more complex communities settled in increasingly restricted areas (Price & Brown 1985). A diachronic model like this seems especially aimed at the description and explanation of the transition from hunting/fishing populations to farming (Rowley-Conwy 1984c; Zvelebil & Rowley-Conwy 1986; Price & Gebauer 1992).

This however presupposes that it is possible, in just these mesolithic finds, to measure phenomena such as population growth, stability of settlement (Kelly 1992), year-round settlement, group identity and changes in the social pattern.

Moreover, even though this material has now increased in many new and promising areas, it is still difficult to determine the function and seasonality of the individual settlements so thus as to be able to reconstruct settlement patterns in the various localities. A further problem with the rich Danish finds is that the data from different areas of study do not always agree amongst themselves.

Lithic refitting

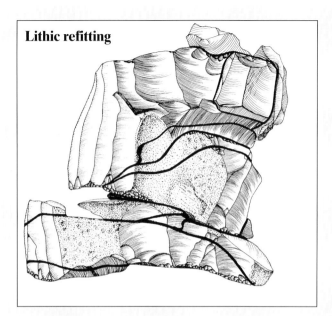
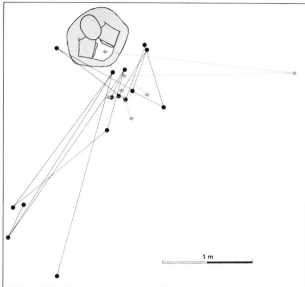

From blade-core to axe-blank. The reconstruction shows a flintknapper's attempt to use up the piece completely. The location on the settlement surface of the axe-blank and the refitted blades and flakes are marked in black. A fully equivalent series is marked in grey. The knapper's position is also shown.

Vænget Nord is a Kongemose settlement on an island in what was then the Vedbæk fjord, northern Sjælland. About 10% of the 50,000-piece flint assemblage has been refitted. The settlement site is typical, having several successive phases that could not be separated stratigraphically or typologically. Lithic refitting has identified four settlement phases in all, and movement around the island can thus be traced. It has been possible to identify three knapping sites where blades were produced, three for axes and three refuse areas with production debris. A further knapping place was found where the knapper first produced flakes on two cores and then attempted, unsuccessfully, to shape both cores into axes (see illustration). Serial production of both scrapers and burins has also been revealed. It has even been possible to differentiate between the detritus of production and use.

Finally, different tool-types showed different ranges of movement on the site. The scrapers were all limited to a small area while burins together with the burin-spalls and axes and their rejuvenation flakes often showed a considerable distance between the places of use and of resharpening.

Lithic refitting can thus be described as putting back together what the flintknapper has split. It is time-consuming work, but it provides a lot of information about Stone-age settlements. It is now possible to distinguish work areas, knapping sites and secondary deposits, and to clarify their relation to one another. It is possible to see where and how a tool was made, resharpened and re-used, at the same time as retrieving a lot of technological information. Most importantly, the basic problem of contemporaneity can be examined in detail as flakes that form part of a production series must also provide a picture of a brief moment, especially if one can exclude re-use. Settlements with several phases can thus be separated and the individual settlement starts to provide a dynamic rather than a static picture.

Not all sites, however, are suited to this technique. The culture layer has to be intact, without later disturbance, and the settlement has to be completely and carefully excavated. Since the method is expensive, it ought primarily to be applied where it can provide new information.

Lithic refitting is thus a method that allows us to get close to Stone-age Man: to look over the flintknapper's shoulder; to follow his work; to see what decisions are made in various circumstances; and to reconstruct the course of events.

Lykke Johansen

The Late Palaeolithic

By Anders Fischer

In the Late Palaeolithic Period, Man returned to northern Europe, from where he had been driven out by the ice cap and cold thousands of years before. The melting of the ice and the rising of the sea and the land meant that the geography of the area was under constant, dramatic change. There were marked changes in the climate at the same time and thus also in the flora and fauna on which Man was totally dependent.

The Late Glacial in Denmark and its neighbouring areas is therefore one of the most suitable fields for the study of how Man adapts to changes in his environment. It is, if possible, an even more appropriate field for the study of Man in a pioneering role.

Man spread out over the lowlands of northern Europe when the climate began to ameliorate and the huge glaciers melted away. This pioneer situation required deep changes in material culture and social organization.

This is immediately apparent if one compares the early and middle phases of the Magdalenian Culture and the Bromme Culture. The first represents the north-westernmost range of Man at the last peak of the Ice Age. The second belongs to the subsequent, milder period, in which settlement was fully established throughout southern Scandinavia. The former is evidently more complex than the latter in every respect. This appears, for example, in flintknapping techniques, the number of flint tool-types, artistic developments, the exchange of exotic materials from distant areas and perhaps too the number of inhabitants on the larger settlements.

The question then is whether the pioneers in northern Europe experienced these as negative changes. It may, by contrast, have been a liberating time in which it was possible to escape from innumerable practical and organizational norms and ties

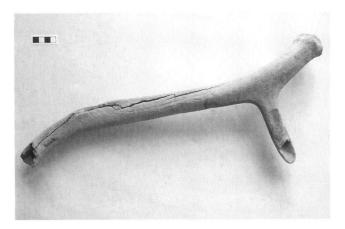

that had been essential for survival in the harshest times of the Ice Age. The situation in the Late Palaeolithic of northern Europe may thus have been, in its way, an 'Earthly Paradise', with a surplus of food, large amounts of easily accessible raw materials, few social ties and very few neighbours to cause problems.

The Late Palaeolithic is the only period of Danish prehistory for which stray and surface finds are still of decisive importance to archaeological research. This means that amateur archaeologists have made (and continue to make) an essential contribution to research into this period.Another peculiarity of work on the Danish Late Palaeolithic in the last 25 years is the small number of established researchers in the field. Initiative has passed overwhelmingly over to the youngest and least resourced practioners of archaeology.

This situation is largely due to the lack of impressive artefacts and, not least, the total absence of real culture layers and clear structures. With this, the institutions responsible for antiquarian work have rarely felt themselves required to consider this area of research when the limited resources for excavation are shared out.

This, however, has not curtailed the recording of new Late-palaeolithic finds or of sites threatened by destruction. The majority of finds from this period have been made in the last 25 years. This is partly due to the fact that there are now more amateurs and professionals who are able to identify Late-glacial settlement material, and also to the introduction of deep ploughing, which has brought a lot of Late-palaeolithic flint objects up to the surface from the sandy deposits in which they have been embedded since the Stone Age. These two factors have led to a huge increase in finds from the mid-1960's (A. Fischer 1985a) that has continued in one wave after another down to the present.

The small group of researchers working on the Late Palaeolithic has been characterized in the last 20 years or so by its great interest in the development of new excavation techniques and analytical methods. New developments have been concentrat-

The accelator method now makes it possible to date bone and antler artefacts without damaging them. Here, a reindeer antler axe from Arreskov, Fyn. It has an age of 10,600 ± 100 C 14 years (OxA-3173). It is thus one of the few finds that can certainly be attributed to the final, climatically harsh centuries of the Late Glacial. Scale in cm.

ed especially on attempts to wrest information from the settlements and their superficially uninformative flint objects. This has resulted in various forms of experimental archaeology concerned with settlement organization (A. Fischer *et al.* 1979), flintknapping technology (B. Madsen 1992) and traces of use on flint objects (A. Fischer *et al.* 1984; A. Fischer 1985b). This has also led to comprehensive refitting of settlement inventories (A. Fischer 1990a-c; J. Holm & Rieck 1992).

The new methods of excavation and analysis of settlements have increased the investment of archaeological resources in the site under study dramatically. Now, for instance, all excavated soil is sieved. This is not just done in order to 'take all the goodies home'. Most important is that one thus secures the uniformity and comparability in the horizontal and vertical distribution of the finds that is essential for any analysis of the structure of the settlement by quantitative methods (A. Fischer & Mortensen 1978). Unfortunately, this advanced method means that the excavation of a collection of flint, which could in principle take one person a single day to produce, often requires field and post-excavation work corresponding to a whole year's work for an archaeologist.

The new methods have, however, produced critical new results, with the horizontal distribution of artefacts proving to reflect the original organization of the settlement (e.g. S.H. Andersen 1973, 1988; A. Fischer & Nielsen 1987). In very favourable circumstances, indeed, it has been possible to get so close to the life of the inhabitants that it is possible to follow the behaviour and relationships between individual members (A. Fischer 1990a-c).

Paradoxically, in many ways we now have a clearer vision of human behaviour in the Late Palaeolithic than in the Mesolithic despite the generally much greater and better preserved evidence from the later period. A decisive factor here is that the Late-palaeolithic settlements were used for relatively short periods by relatively few persons, which usually leaves clearer evidence of individual persons and activities.

The finds of the Late Palaeolithic in Denmark represent a very limited fragment of the original material culture. The great bulk is flint, in the form both of characteristic single objects and of settlement assemblages. From some of the settlements we also have animal remains, charcoal and lumps of red ochre. There is additionally a small range of individual finds of tools and waste of bone and antler that on the basis of their context and/or parallels in dated finds abroad can be assigned with reasonable certainty to this period. A project attempting to date such items by the accelerator method has recently begun.

The finds of the Late Palaeolithic in NW Europe are normally divided into four archaeological groups: Hamburg, Federmesser, Bromme and Ahrensburg. At one time the Bromme Culture was the only one that was securely identified in Denmark. In the last 25 years the other three have been added to the list (C.J. Becker 1969c, 1970, 1971; Fugl Petersen 1974, 1993; S.H. Andersen 1977; A. Fischer 1978, 1982b, 1990b, 1991a; J. Holm & Rieck 1983, 1987, 1992). At the same time, pollen and C 14 datings and studies of flint technology have supported that this division reflects real chronological and cultural differences (Hartz 1987; A. Fischer 1990b, 1991a; B. Madsen 1992).

Knowledge of the geographical and chronological range of the four groups is as yet very limited. As a

Bromme flint point from three sides. From the hunting station at Ommelshoved on Ærø. The tip (at the top) is damaged. Experiments have shown that the breaks and microscopic marks were produced by use as a point on a spear or an arrow.

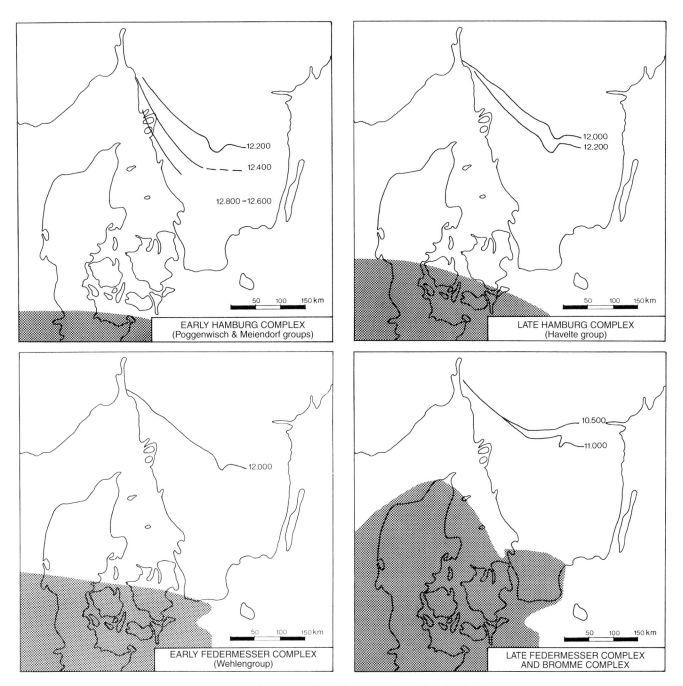

The retreat of the inland ice and the movement of Man into Scandinavia at the end of the Ice Age.

result, any attempt to assess their inter-relationship must remain preliminary. From a local, southern Scandinavian perspective, it is probable that they are basically sequential, representing stadia in one connected sequence of cultural development. In a larger European perspective it appears that human expansion northwards can best be described as a sort of budding.

The Hamburg Culture represents the first pioneer population in northern Germany. Culturally, its roots lie in the middle phases of the Magdalenian Culture in Central Europe and France. It probably reflects a special form of adaptation that emerged in connexion with the expansion of Man up over the lowlands of NW Europe when the Late-glacial climatic amelioration began. These two cultures existed side-by-side through the mild Bølling Period and into the still warm but drier Early Dryas (A. Fischer & Tauber

1986; Breest & Veil 1991; Stapert 1992), after which both apparently developed into the Federmesser Culture. It has not yet been established whether the earlier phases of the Hamburg Culture are represented in Denmark (J. Holm 1993). In what appears to be its final phase (the Havelte phase), however, it is fully established in southern Denmark. Settlements of the early Federmesser Culture (the Wehlen phase) are also as yet known only from the south.

Settlements of the Bromme Culture, by contrast, are found all over Denmark and in Skåne. This culture appears to have its origins in the early Federmesser Culture and again seems to represent a budding off, at the gradually expanding norhtern frontier of the human range. The Bromme and Federmesser may represent adaptation to two different natural environments (Bokelmann 1978) as at this time (the mild and humid Allerød Period) there was birch forest in Denmark but pine in Schleswig-Holstein and further south.

The Ahrensburg Culture, which apparently builds upon the traditions of the Bromme Culture, appeared in the final - climatically, the harshest - centuries of the Late Ice Age known as the Late Dryas. This culture is distributed over the whole of the NW European lowland probably reflecting a southerly expansion of northern adaptations alongside the climatically-determined southward movement of natural types.

A number of settlements and a quantity of tools of bone and antler, however, show that the Ahrensburg population remained in Denmark and Skåne,

An example of wasteful raw-material consumption in flaking technique at the Trollesgave settlement. A flint core (bottom left) with refitted blades, added in the order in which they were struck off. During the production process, the flintknapper tied to detach eight proper blades. Only the two best were taken from the worksite, and have not been found. They comprised about 1.5% of the original weight of the block. Many of the other flakes and blades were well suited for use as knives or for making burins or scrapers, but they were left unused at the knapping site. Scale in cm.

and may indeed have expanded further north. Late versions of the culture thus represent the earliest settlement traces in western Sweden and southern Norway from the period right on the transition from the Ice Age to the present temperate period (Taute 1968; A. Fischer 1978; Bang-Andersen 1990).

Up until quite recently it was believed the Man came to the Nordic countries on the heels of the reindeer that followed the retreating ice northwards (C.J. Becker 1969c; Rust 1972). The more detailed knowledge of the range of the ice and the location of settlement during the Late Glacial from more recent years changes this picture radically. It now appears more likely that for most of this period there was a

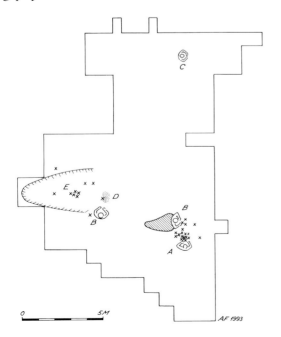

The structure of the Trollesgave settlement with flint worksites marked. The abandoned debitage at the knapping sites reflects three persons (A, B and C) with significantly different behaviour and skills. Also shown on the map is the distribution of pieces of flint from one core that was worked by an untrained child (A) - apparently under the instruction of the most experienced flintknapper at the site (B). The best of the child's efforts were taken to the hearth (D) and into the dwelling (E).

Excavation of the Trollesgave settlement in 1974, with a combination of horizontal and vertical inspection.

largely unsettled belt, several hundred kilometres wide, south of the ice. Man therefore clearly did not immediately follow the reindeer herds northwards into the newly deglaciated but still relatively inhospitable morain tracts.

A still unknown element in the history of human settlement in Denmark is the situation on the coast of the time, nearly all of which is now submerged. Further north, along the coast of Sweden and Norway, there has, by contrast, been such a substantial land rebound since the Ice Age that the coastlines from the end of the Late Glacial and the beginning of the present temperate period are mostly above present sea-level. Here it proves that the earliest settlement was very largely coastal (Lindblom 1984). Thus Man reached as far as North Cape virtually as soon as the west coast of Norway was free of ice. This can only be interpreted as evidence that, in the centuries immediately following the end of the Ice Age, Man mastered the intensive exploitation of coastal food resources and possessed seaworthy vessels (Bjerck 1990).

It falls to future underwater archaeology to establish whether similar circumstances were operative in the previous millennia, when the sea-level was some 100 m. lower than now. In this connexion it is worth noting that material from inland settlement in

France contains a number of indications of intensive exploitation of coastal resources far back in the Palaeolithic (Cleyet-Merle 1990; Clottes *et al.* 1992).

Recent years' excavations of Late-palaeolithic settlements are distinguished, *inter alia,* by intensive work on lithic refitting and the experimental reproduction of flint assemblages. This has provided a good basis for the assessment of the behaviour and technical capacity of the people of that time (A. Fischer 1990a-c; B. Madsen 1992). The flint from the Hamburg Culture settlement at Jels is thus characterized by technical care. This is reflected in a complicated process for the production of blades and a high level of exploitation of the raw material.

The flint material of the Bromme Culture is quite different. The way of producing blades was simple and very little effort was made to be economic with the raw material. The simple methods were not, however, the result of lack of skill. This is shown by the reconstructed knapping sequences from the Trollesgave settlement. It is rather a knapping tradition that was adapted to the abundance of flint in the new morain areas of southern Scandinavia.

In popular literature, the Late Palaeolithic is often called the Reindeer-hunters' Period. This term emerged under the influence of the extremely rich bone finds of that single species from the Stellmoor tunnel valley north-east of Hamburg (Rust 1937, 1943, 1958; Tromnau 1975). Both Hamburg and Ahrensburg Culture settlement in this area seems to reflect intensive reindeer hunting in certain seasons of the year (Sturdy 1975; Grønnow 1987).

We have virtually no idea what the people of these two cultures lived on for the rest of the year. Inland hunting and fishing are the most obvious probabilities. As the comments above on the coastal situation at the time imply, a notion of purely inland occupation may in time prove to be seriously mistaken. Indeed, if we are to judge by the evidence of modern hunting populations in the far north, reindeer hunting is not an especially dependable subsistence basis. Over short periods of time there can be very substantial changes in the size of reindeer herds. It is therefore by far the most prudent course to restrict reindeer hunting to a seasonal activity of variable scope, combined with the exploitation of other food sources, not least the sea (Burch 1972; Grønnow *et al.* 1983 and this volume).

Our knowledge of the Federmesser and Bromme Cultures' subsistence basis is even more limited.

From Denmark we have faunal remains only from the sites of Bromme, Trollesgave and Langå (Mathiassen 1947, A. Fischer & Mortensen 1977; B. Madsen 1983; Aaris-Sørensen 1988). Elk dominates here, and is the only species that occurs at all three sites. From Bromme there is also bone from reindeer, beaver, wolverine, swan, pike and possibly roe deer. Finally from Trollesgave there are two possible red deer bones.

The Late-palaeolithic sites vary markedly in extent, assemblage composition, and topographical location.This variance presumably reflects differences in the number of inhabitants, in season and in function. The majority of the sites can be assigned to one of the following four groups:

Egtved: a couple of handfulls of flint waste, representing a few minutes' knapping (A. Fischer 1990b). *Ommelshoved* and *Knudshoved Odde:* hunting stands on outstanding highlands where the finds are dominated by missile points while traces of domestic activity in the form of debitage, scrapers or burins are few (J. Rasmussen 1972; J. Holm 1973; A. Fischer 1976, 1991a). *Jels, Slotseng, Rundebakke, Løvenholm, Hollandskær, Ramsgård* and *Sølbjerg:* settlements dominated by hunting. They are located relatively high in the landscape and have numerous missile points but also a quantity of domestic tools of which some at least where produced on the site (B. Madsen 1983; Nilsson 1989; J. Holm & Rieck 1992; J. Holm 1993; Fugl Petersen 1993; Vang Petersen & Johansen 1993). *Bro, Bromme, Trollesgave, Fensmark Skydebane, Stoksbjerg Vest, Stoksbjerg Bro:* settlements with a broad economic basis, including fishing. These are located near the banks of lakes of the period and their inventories are dominated by the residue of domestic activity (S.H. Andersen 1973; A. Fischer & Nielsen 1987; A. Fischer 1976, 1990c).

Excavations up to now have been concentrated on the latter two groups. Here it has transpired that the Federmesser and Bromme Culture settlements are characterized by a main concentration of flint *débitage* and tools about 50 m.sq., often with traces of a fireplace in the middle. Corresponding sites of the Hamburg Culture are nearly twice the size but lack clear traces of hearths.

On the most informative of the settlements, Trollesgave, there are signs of a dwelling and traces of both adults' and children's activities. From its area, structure and artefact inventory, this site is inferred to represent one nuclear family's (summer) settlement for some weeks. Something similar may be the case with the other settlements of the Federmesser and Bromme Cultures. In the case of the Hamburg Culture we may possibly reckon with somewhat larger social units.

All the sites investigated so far represent inland settlement. This is also true of a number of stray finds of flint tools and a concentration of settlement flint from the sea-bed (A. Fischer & Sørensen 1983; A. Fischer 1993 and in prep.).

From the 2,500 years or so of the Danish Late Palaeolithic there are a couple of dozen more or less completely excavated sites. This is obviously too little for a reliable synthesis of the form and extent of human presence in the different areas of the land during the period. The basic requirement of investigation of the Late Palaeolithic must therefore simply be more finds, and especially more excavated settlements.

Some specific proposals can be added to these general points. We need many more finds dated by pollen or radiometric analysis, and many more chronologically homogeneous artefact assemblages, to improve our knowledge of chronology and culture. Organic cultural remains must be sought for the illumination of economy and technology. The studies of culture and individual behaviour based on flint technology and lithic refitting should be developed. Several comprehensive settlement studies should be carried out in order to clarify social organization and the general way of life.

In order to reach these reasonably realistic goals it is necessary for the institutions that are responsible for antiquarian work in the field to change their priorities. First and foremost, more resources have to be obtained for excavations of Late-palaeolithic settlements. On top of this, research groups should be established both competent in the special methods of excavation and analysis and with time to complete their work in the form of scholarly publications.

One further goal can be added: knowledge of the situation along the coasts of the period. Was there any coastal settlement? If there were, what was its range and character? An investigation of these questions will be methodologically far more demanding than the land-based tasks listed above. On the other hand, Danish underwater archaeologists have laid the foundations of practical and theoretical experience which should render them especially able to tackle this job.

Reindeer hunters on Greenland

The driving of a herd of reindeer, depicted ca. 1860 by the Greenlandic artist and hunter Jens Kreutzmann.

An important model for the study of Late-palaeolithic reindeer hunters comes from Arctic Greenland. The high grassy plains of inland western Greenland are the home of a wild reindeer population that has always attracted hunters. The Greenlanders had summer camps here, to provide themselves with a supply of dried reindeer meat and tallow.

The old settlement sites with tent-houses, middens and stone-built meat caches are still there, while many cairns, hides and other traces of the hunt are found in the field.

Many tales and legends of Greenland, old drawings, and maps with place-names tell of these hunting grounds. The first Danish missionaries and traders described massive hunting drives, and from the beginning of this century proper ethnographic studies were made.

Reindeer is a particularly unreliable quarry. Not only does the individual animal's state vary greatly throughout the year while the herds follow seasonal migrations but the herds also undergo dramatic fluctuations from good years to bad. These certainly climatically governed fluctuations occur at least once a century. At the settlement of Aasivissuit ('The great summer camp') layers with thousands of reindeer caught by massive hunting drives interchange with layers with only a few bones; later, stalking with rifles and smaller drives to shooting hides became the norm. Such marked naturally and culturally governed changes in behaviour can also be observed in the Late-palaeolithic reindeer hunters' settlements near Hamburg in northern Germany (Grønnow 1987).

In the hunting areas, many different settlement-types are used concurrently in a complex settlement pattern. These begin with assembly camps, out by the fjords, followed by transit camps on the traditional routes to the base camps, often by a river or lake rich in sea trout and centrally placed in the topographical bottlenecks that the reindeer must pass. Each family group had its fixed summer partners and its fixed base camp, from which smaller groups of hunters and women moved on to use overnight camps on their way in to especially good hunting fields where they established a special camp. Here the quarry was brought, from which the women there produced dried meat, marrow and other foodstuffs (Grønnow *et al.* 1983).

Of course one cannot transfer such systems directly into the situation in northern Europe 10-15,000 years ago. But as a source for new interpretations of the old settlements and as a guide to prospection for Late-palaeolithic settlements the Greenlandic sources are unparalleled.

Bjarne Grønnow

57

Mesolithic inland settlement

By Anders Fischer

Mesolithic settlements from inland bogs are one of the fields in which Danish archaeology gained an international reputation at an early stage. This honourable position was due not only to the evident skill of the researchers but even more to the unique preservative conditions for organic cultural remains in a number of bogs in eastern Denmark.

Mullerup, Holmegård and Sværdborg bogs are internationally classic sites that were excavated and published in exemplary form in the first quarter of the present century. New bog finds of the same quality, now, in addition, with well-preserved hut floors with criss-crossing pieces of bark, turned up in the next quarter century, especially under the intensive peat-cutting during the war. The fairy-tale continued, with a targeted campaign of excavation in the Åmose of western Sjælland down to the beginning of the 1970's. In spite of often only elementary publication, several of these later finds are amongst the most often discussed sites of the European Mesolithic.

Amongst the more important advances in the quarter century under consideration here are the interdisciplinary publications of a number of the earlier excavated finds from the Maglemose Culture (Brinch Petersen et al. 1972; Bille Henriksen 1976, 1980; Møhl 1980; I. Sørensen 1980; K. Andersen et al. 1982; Sobotta 1991). Valuable clearing-up works also include the analysis and presentation of the great body of material collected from the surface during the great years of peat-cutting in the Åmose (K. Andersen 1983).

A large number of settlement finds, however, including some of the most important internationally, still lie unprocessed in the storerooms of the National Museum. They form some of the largest unclaimed bonds of Danish archaeology. At the same time, their still unsolved fate reveals a basic problem in Danish archaeology during recent decades: an enormous number of excavations were set off but far too few of the really large and significant ones were carried right through to a complete, scholarly publication. This is primarily due to research having been a highly individual enterprise. There has been a fatal lack of institutions with the necessary competence for guiding prioritization, with sufficient power to obtain the resources needed and with the will to enter into constructive and mutually committed collaboration.

During the last quarter century only a few mesolithic inland settlements have been excavated. Most of these have been fairly poorly preserved. Thus, for instance, the lakeshore site of Flaadet (Skaarup et al. 1979) and the bog site of Barmose I (Johansson 1990), both of the Maglemose Culture. Nonetheless, several of these excavations have contributed significantly to the development of insight into the chronological, economic and social aspects of the North-European Mesolithic. In the future prioritization of excavation resources, therefore, it must be borne in mind that investment in mesolithic inland settlements evidently pays relatively well in terms of academic progress.

The changes in Danish agriculture in the last 25 years have meant that very large areas of the archaeologically famous bogs have been destroyed by draining and ploughing.

In the archaeologically richest parts of Åmose it can be observed, for istance, that peat cutting lowered the ground surface by 0.5 to 1 m. while the draining and cultivation of the following years has meant a further 0.75 to 1 m. fall. Every year from 1968 to the middle of the 1980's the ploughs have cut 3-4 cm. deeper into the bog layers with their internationally unique cultural treasure.

Bloated with bog finds from the peat-cutting period, the institutions responsible for antiquarian work paid no heed to the insidious destruction of innumerable Stone-age settlements in the bogs by agriculture. On the other hand, a large number of amateur archaeologists have for years enjoyed quite fantastic finds in the bogs of Sjælland. Everyone who wanted to could quite easily go out and find mesolithic bone and antler tools of a form and condition that would have put them amongst the jewels of the national museums of any other country. This has meant, for instance, that about a quarter of all European finds of the elegant barbed bone or antler points probably now reside in private collections on Sjælland.

The seriousness of the situation was recognized in the 1980's. In the hope of preserving at least a little bit of the very best bog areas in good condition for future research, the Forest and Nature Agency set in train a programme of protecting the culturally and palaeoenvironmentally most important parts of the Åmose (A. Fischer 1985c, 1991c).

The many small, well-defined and chronologically homogeneous settlement finds from inland bogs have been of decisive importance in the clarification of mesolithic chronology that the last 25 years has seen.

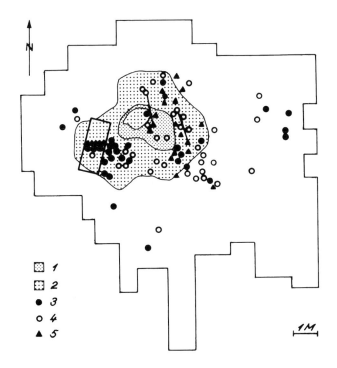

Typical ground plan of an inland settlement of the Maglemose Culture, Barmose I. 1: hearth of sand on a bark floor. 2: area with more than 100 pieces of flint per sq.m.; 3: flint axe. 4: microlith; 5: microburin;

The mixed cultures of the Danish interior, such as the 'Gudenå Culture', have now been definitively put down (S.H. Andersen & Sterum 1971). With the support of pollen analyses and not least of C 14 datings there is a straightforward sequence from the Maglemose through the Kongemose to the Ertebølle Culture (Tauber 1971; Brinch Petersen 1973).

New excavations have added a number of previously unrecognized phases to the earlier part of the series. A number of finds with combinations of microliths and flake axes (the 'Barmose Group') can thus be regarded as early stages of the Maglemose Culture (Johansson 1971, 1990; A. Fischer 1978, 1991a). Even earlier is the Bonderup phase, which belongs culturally to the Ahrensburg Culture and which lies chronologically on the transition from the Ice Age to the present temperate period (A. Fischer 1982b; Fredskild 1982).

The intensity of inland settlement varied during the Mesolithic (e.g. Mathiassen 1937; Troels-Smith 1967; S.H. Andersen 1978). At the same time, it appears that different regions followed generally the same pattern. There are very few finds from the first 500 years. The many phases of the Maglemose Culture, in contrast, are richly represented. The Konge-

mose Culture is rather less frequent in the finds but is known at least in its earlier and middle phases through excavated or surface-found material from all regions. The early Ertebølle Culture with asymmetrical transverse arrowheads is very sparsely represented. From the following phases, with symmetrical transverse arrowheads, there are once more numerous finds around the inland waters.

There are presumably both natural and demographic reasons for these fluctuations. The scarcity of finds from the beginning of the period may be due to there having been an especially low water level in the lakes then. Waterside settlements would therefore lie so low that in many cases they would be hidden underneath later deposits of gyttja and peat.

The high frequency of Maglemose finds and the subsequent gradual decline of the Kongemose and early Ertebølle Periods may well, however, reflect real changes in the geographical distribution of settlement. Many of the inland lake basins in fact became overgrown in this period (see, for instance, S.Th. Andersen *et al.* 1983). Thus the scope for living off fishing in these areas may have fallen so much that people preferred to live on the coast.

The question then is how the renewed flourishing of inland settlement in the final centuries of the Mesolithic is to be understood. It may be a question of growing population and thus more pressure to exploit marginal areas. The return of settlement in the bogs might therefore be an expression of a situation of shortage which might have been decisive for the introduction of agriculture shortly after (S.H. Andersen 1973a; A. Fischer 1974; Paludan-Müller 1978).

An amateur archaeologist's dream: a handful of bone points that had been lost during fishing in the Åmose, 9 to 10,000 years earlier.

59

It is largely the bog settlements that are the basis of the fame of the Danish Mesolithic. These finds make it possible to study the relationship between the hunting, fishing and gathering populations and the environment in more detail and over a longer period than anywhere else in Europe. The fine, interdisciplinary monographs of the last 25 years on Maglemose Culture settlements thus provide a quite unique insight into the way of life of the time.

All the bog sites of the Maglemose and Ertebølle Cultures, with their rich faunal evidence, seem to have been continuously occupied from spring to autumn. This agrees well with the notion that these sites would be too wet to occupy in winter. The large quantity of bone from these sites gives a well-focussed picture of the versatility and skill of the hunters. This picture derives more vitality and details of hunting techniques from the skeletons of large wild animals found in the bogs where they drowned with pieces of hunting weapons in their bodies (Noe-Nygaard 1974; Aaris-Sørensen (ed.) 1984; A. Fischer 1985b, 1989c).

The many shells of cracked hazelnuts from the bog sites are classic evidence that the Maglemose and Ertebølle people did not live solely off hunting. With the species that were available that would hardly have been possible. Man cannot live on a diet in which the protein content is more than about half of all the protein, fat and carbohydrate (Speth 1991). The population of the mesolithic inland settlements can only have obtained a balanced diet like this by extensive gathering of plant food in which starch-rich roots were probably dominant. Finding traces of these food sources lies somewhere in the future.

Otherwise the many finds of fishing equipment (barbed bone points and fishhooks) from inland summer settlements show that the Maglemose population certainly did not take all its protein from wild game. Fishing may indeed have been a more important food source than hunting. This was indicated by a small re-excavation at the long-known Maglemose site of Lundby I in 1979 where wet sieving produced a very large quantity of fish vertebrae. This notion was further strengthened in the 1980's by excavations in the Åmose (A. Fischer 1985c) where fishbone and scales often occur in such enormous quantities that they even form a major component of the late Ertebølle culture layers.

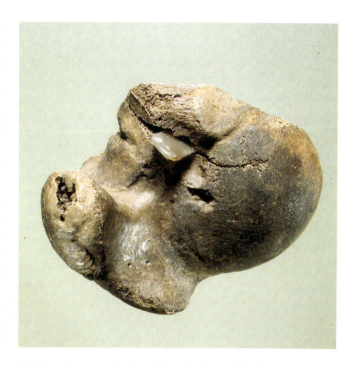

Red deer bones with rhombic point lodged in them. Found on the Kongemose settlement. The point of impact on an articular surface of the left foreleg shows that the animal had turned to face the hunter and that it was hit just when it had flexed the leg backwards at full gallop.

In very recent years, a number of Maglemose sites differing in topography, finds and extent have been identified as possible examples of inland winter settlements (Grøn 1987b, 1990; Sobotta 1991). Most important in this respect is the long-known site of Holmegård V. In a summary account of the site, C.J. Becker (1953a) had already noted that it could be a winter settlement. It lies mostly on dry land above the bog. Although bone is well preserved, it produced no barbed points.

New finds came from the site in 1970-71, strengthening the case for a winter settlement. This was a result of the 60- x 80-m. large and 50-cm. thick culture layer being destroyed for a factory building (A. Fischer 1975). In the larger body of material there is still no sign of fishing in the form of barbed points or fishbones. On the other hand a bone from a young beaver clearly belongs to the winter months (rep. K. Rosenlund, Zoological Museum). There are, however, indications of settlement in the warmer parts of the year, such as cracked hazelnut shells. This is only, however, on that part of the site that was out in the bog where there very well may have been a normal summer settlement.

Heaps of discarded artefacts in lacustrine deposits beyond the Ringkloster settlement.

The special character of Holmegård V in relation to the well-known bog sites is further underlined by the finding here of the clearest examples of ceremonial activity (A. Fischer 1975) and the two most plausible examples of graves from the Danish Maglemose Culture. These are two quite well presered human skeletons (rep. P. Bennike, Panum Institute) that were found during construction work at the periphery of the culture layer.

As far as the subsistence and seasonal basis of Kongemose Period inland settlement goes, we have still only provisional data from the Kongemose settlement itself to work from (Noe-Nygaard 1988b, 1989; Clutton-Brock & Noe-Nygaard 1990). It appears that this settlement, on a low island in the Åmose, was subject to many, short-term occupations at varying times of the year, including the winter months. The predominant object of these short visits was to hunt the larger, meatier animals of the forest. Fishing and fowling were of lesser importance.

The lakeshore site of Ringkloster in East Jutland, from the middle and late Ertebølle Culture, has an economic basis and seasonality reminiscent of the Kongemose settlement. There is evidence of specialized hunting of meat animals supplemented by trapping fur animals (S.H. Andersen 1975). Seasonal indicators suggest that the site was frequented at all seasons.

In contrast to this, Ertebølle bog settlement in the Åmose basin is reminiscent of Maglemose settlement in the same area in its broad subsistence basis

and its seasonality. The Præstelyng settlement in particular seems to have been continuously occupied from April to September (Noe-Nygaard 1988b). An innovation in relation to the Maglemose Period is traces of intensive gathering of large freshwater mussels.

In his survey of Stone-age settlement in the Åmose, K. Andersen (1983) has shown that sites of about the same age are more or less the same size and that the size of sites gradually increases through the Mesolithic. His conclusion from this is that the number of inhabitants per site must have gradually increased in the course of the period.

Younger scholars have subsequently put a lot of effort into clarifying how many inhabitants the individual sites actually housed and how the different parts of the sites were used (Grøn 1983, 1987a, 1987b, 1989, 1990; Blankholm 1985, 1991; Stapert 1992). These studies have concentrated on Maglemose Culture sites. The more or less intact hut floors with their associated artefact distributions from this culture form an invaluable starting point for studies of the structure and social organization of the settlements.

Besides the above-mentioned bog and lakeshore sites, mesolithic inland settlement includes a number of relatively small flint scatters on higher land (C.J. Becker 1952; Mathiassen 1959; Liversage 1981; Boas 1987). The question then is whether these three groups together represent the whole territory and seasonal circuit of the relevant populations.

From a number of inland settlements of the Maglemose, Kongemose and Ertebølle Periods,

Mesolithic "chewing gum". Two pieces of pitch or harpix with impressions of the teeth of a 7- or 8-year-old child and a juvenile over the age of 10. From the Barmose I settlement.

61

remains of sea animals are known that unquestionably must have been brought from the coast (Møhl 1971; Noe-Nygaard 1971; S.H. Andersen 1975). In consequence, for a long time it has been debated whether inland settlement is just part of a larger settlement pattern that included the coast too. The alternative would imply evidence for exchange between different population groups, living inland and on the coast respectively.

The last 25 years have clarified this situation to a degree. It has transpired that larger supplies of food from the sea leave lasting and measurable traces in, *inter alia*, the $\delta^{13}C$ levels in bone (Tauber 1981; Noe-Nygaard 1988a). By this it can be established that the two human skeletons from Holmegård V and two dogs from the approximately contemporary settlement of Ulkestrup Lyng have no clear signs of marine nourishment. By contrast a human bone from the Mullerup site clearly shows a certain intake of marine food (rep. H. Tauber & N. Noe-Nygaard). These facts have to be related to the distance of the find spots from the nearest coast at the time: in all cases the deep channel of the Storebælt (H. Krog 1973; A. Fischer 1991b). As the crow flies, the distances are about 55, 35 and 15 km. respectively. For water travel via the river systems they were probably a good three times longer.

It has correspondingly been established that two dogs from the Kongemose settlement had so large an intake of food from the sea that these beasts - and thus, presumably, their masters - must have lived a good part of their lives on the coast (Noe-Nygaard 1988a; Clutton-Brock & Noe-Nygaard 1990). This was about 25 km. off as the crow flies. Contrastively, $\delta^{13}C$ measurements of dog bones from the Præstelyng site indicate that the late Ertebølle Culture inhabitants here lived more or less permanently inland (Noe-Nygaard 1988a). The situation here agrees with C. Paludan-Müller's theoretical considerations (1978). He anticipated that it was inland groups that first went over to agricultural manipulation of nature and thus became less dependent on coastal resources.

If one omits the transition to the Neolithic, it thus appears as if mesolithic inland settlement in Denmark has two different settlement patterns. In the most 'continental' areas, people lived inland the year round and may have held their major social gatherings at special winter settlements. In contrast to this, inland settlement in a zone many miles wide along

Danubian shaft-hole axe. Length 15 cm. Found on a Late Ertebølle settlement in the Åmose. Imported from farming areas south of the Baltic.

the coast of the time was part of a settlement pattern whose economic and social centre lay by the sea (A. Fischer & Sørensen 1983; A. Fischer 1993).

In connexion with recent years' work in the Åmose of western Sjælland (A. Fischer 1985c), spot sampling has been carried out of a number of small, horizontally and chronologically well-defined bog settlements with flint, pottery and well-preserved food remains from the centuries around the transition from hunting to farming. On the basis of such finds from the bog it will be possible to construct a detailed sequence of snapshots which, with a combination of C 14 and pollen analyses, will be datable with hitherto unseen accuracy. Thus we will get a reasonable degree of certainty in the dating of the various tool-types, pottery-forms, species of domesticated animals, seed crops and interventions in the forest vegetation that appeared in the critical centuries of the change from the Mesolithic to the Neolithic.

With such a check on the chronological sequence, it will perhaps be possible to achieve more definitive agreement over the basic causes of this fundamental change in subsistence and lifestyle. Until then one must be satisfied with observing that in the Åmose there was apparently a gradual transition from the Ertebølle to the Funnel Beaker Culture. The transition lasted a good hundred years, corresponding to

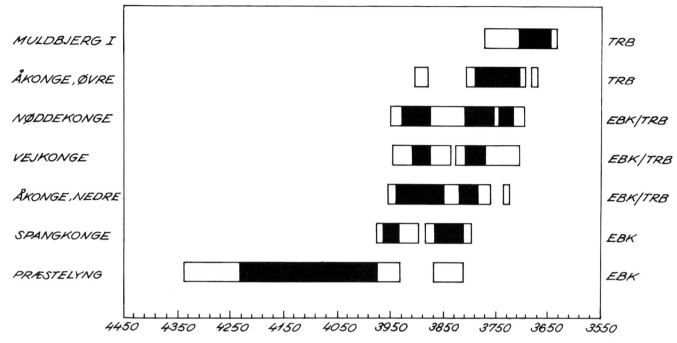

Chronological sorting of a number of short-term settlements in the Åmose from the period around the introduction of agriculture. Pointed-bottomed pottery is the sole type down to and including the Spangkonge site, and is certainly still found in the period of the Nøddekonge settlement. The earliest assemblages with funnel beakers and bones of domestic cattle are in the lower culture layers of the Åkonge settlement. In and after the upper layers there, ox bone is a common find and funnel beakers are the dominant form of pottery. Polished flint axes (including fragments) were first recognized at Muldbjerg I (Troels-Smith 1953, 1982). The datings, calibration and statistical presentation were carried out by the Radiocarbon Laboratory in Copenhagen.

the period between the Spangkonge site and the upper culture layer of the Åkonge site respectively (see figure).

Through the whole sequence of development from *ca.* 4100 (Præstelyng) to *ca.* 3675 B.C. (Muldbjerg I), the commonly occurring flint tools and general flint technology are clearly of the Ertebølle tradition. There can therefore be little doubt that the early Funnel Beaker Culture in the Åmose is culturally of local origin. It must then have been the local hunters here who learned the new subsistence strategies.

How they got access to the necessary know-how, the first breeding animals and the first crop seed, is indicated by the Danubian shaft-hole axes of which at least 5 examples are known from the Åmose (A. Fischer 1982a, 1983). These are axes of a distinctively striped rock that does not occur naturally in northern Europe. One has to go all the way to Central Europe, or even to the Balkans (Schwarz-Markensen & Schneider 1983), to find the sources of this stone, and thus the origins of the axe-type. Chronologically, these axes belong to the Ertebølle Period

(L. Pedersen 1989). At this time, agriculture had long been established in the areas the axes came from. Their presence in significant numbers over most of Denmark thus testifies to the existence of a well-developed trading connexion between farming communities south of the Baltic and hunting communities in the north. The earliest agriculture may thus have been introduced to Denmark via long-distance trading connexions.

With this established, it must finally be noted that in other places in western Sjælland further, presumably very early neolithic settlements have been found that may have a different origin. This includes, for instance, the material beneath the Early-neolithic long barrow at Lindebjerg (Liversage 1981; T. Madsen & Petersen 1984). On these sites, the shape of the tools, in combination with the somewhat hesitant manufacture and eceptionally economical use of flint, stands in clear contrast to the local Ertebølle tradition. These settlement finds should perhaps rather be associated with a population that migrated in from areas south of the flint-rich morain areas around the Baltic.

63

Mesolithic art

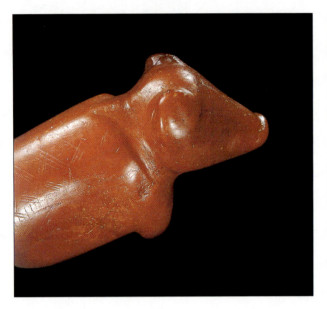

Amber figure, Resen, near Skive

Amber bear, Fanø

Decorated staff of antler, Åmosen, western Sjælland

Mesolithic coastal settlement

BY SØREN H. ANDERSEN

The study of coastal settlements has long traditions in Denmark, running back to the first half of the 19th century when the study of the most famous type of coastal settlements, kitchen middens *(køkkenmøddinger),* began as an example of inter-disciplinary collaboration between archaeology and natural science that has continued to the present. In 1850, the true character of these sites as settlements was established at Meilgaard. Later, excavations continued at the eponymous Ertebølle (A.P. Madsen *et al.* 1900), shortly after which, in 1906, the first coastal settlement that was not a kitchen midden was published (Brabrand: T. Thomsen & Jessen 1906). Bloksbjerg was published in turn (Westerby 1927) and Dyrholmen (Mathiassen *et al.* 1942). After a break, the systematic excavation of coastal settlements began again in the 1960's with new, large, interdisciplinary projects at, for instance, Ertebølle and Bjørnsholm in the Limfjord area (S.H. Andersen 1979b, 1992, 1993; S.H. Andersen & Johansen 1987, 1992), in East Jutland around Norsminde fjord (S.H. Andersen 1976, 1991) and in Vedbæk (Brinch Petersen 1977, 1979a, 1982, 1985). There are also major new excavations of the kitchen middens at Meilgård (unpublished), Ertebølle (S.H. Andersen & Johansen 1987), Norsminde (S.H. Andersen 1991) and most recently at Bjørnsholm (S.H. Andersen 1993).

In the last 25 years, the financial resources and a number of the largest excavations and new excavation methods, such as horizontal stripping and *décapage* of whole settlement areas, an increasing degree of stratigraphic detail, dry and wet sieving and refined methods of analysis have been significantly concentrated on research into Late-mesolithic coastal settlement. Another, equally new aspect is the development of systematic underwater surveying (Skaarup, below).

If some of the more important trends of research in recent years are to be picked out, they are a shift

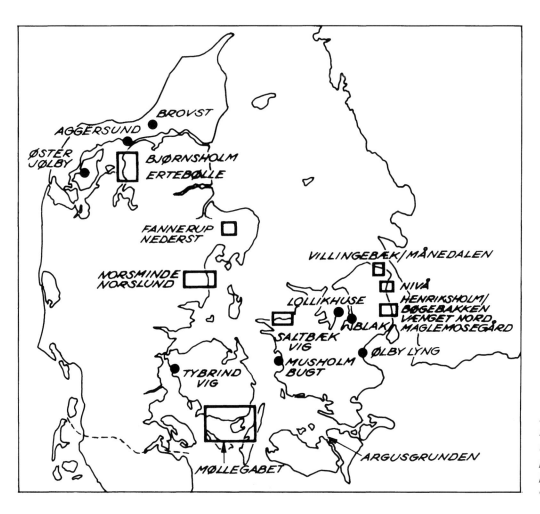

Areas of research into mesolithic coastal culture. Frames: regional projects; ●: *important published settlement excavations.*

65

from the excavation of segments of settlements to the excavation of whole sites, an increased level of detail, and, finally, an attempt to assess the individual settlement in a regional context.

The natural context of coastal settlement in the Mesolithic was a combination of the climatic and geological circumstances that characterized Scandinavia after the Ice Age - especially the iso- and eustatic movements, the combined effect of which was the erosion and submersion of substantial land areas. On top of this, the soil-type types were mostly clay, gravel and sand. The greatest impact of the rising of the world's sea after the Ice Age is really to be seen in the immense rise of the Early Atlantic Period, when sea-level rose about 30 m. over about 3,000 years (Ch. Christensen, above).

Since the topography of the land is also undulating, the total effect of these factors was an indented coastline with a variegated environment characterized by the frequent interface of land and sea. This meant a long coastline in relation to the land area, and since the marine environment was both warmer, saltier and more nutritious than now, with a larger tidal range, the marine biotope - in the second half of the Mesolithic at least - was much richer than it is today (J. Iversen 1967).

The geological circumstances also explain how the earliest coastlines (from the Late- and early Post-glacial Periods) now all lie in deep water; the later isostatic rising of the northern and north-eastern areas has meant, however, that the coastal settlements here are closer to dry land and that in theory at least even very old coastal sites could be found on land.

Renewed studies of the changes in sea-level and thus the position of the coast in the course of the Atlantic Period in various areas, especially on Sjælland, have produced much more secure and more detailed knowledge of the exact coastline than before (Ch. Christensen 1982a-b and above).

If we are to attempt to summarize the coastal settlements' character, we could say for one that they are more densely clustered and are always more extensive than other mesolithic settlements and contemporary inland settlements, and also that they are often characterized by a continuity of occupation that is reflected in stratigraphically thick series of culture layers. These layers often cover a very long period, not infrequently from the later Kongemose Culture to the beginning of the Funnel Beaker Culture, from *ca.* 5700-3500 B.C.

Section through the kitchen midden at Ertebølle.

This stability of settlement is rooted in the rich marine biotope.

Another characteristic of the southern Scandinavian coastal settlements is their consistently extremely find-rich waste layers with organic material, whether the artefacts are sealed in the shell layers of the kitchen middens or in wet, marine deposits (refuse layers). This means that the coastal settlements generally have great research potential for detailed studies of subsistence and technology in organic raw materials. On top of this come the sporadic, more surprising, insights into ideological aspects of Stone-age communities, such as in finds of decorated wooden paddles (S.H. Andersen 1985) or possible underwater graves (Skaarup & Grøn 1991). In respect of these aspects, it is the submerged settlements in particular that stand out with their remarkably good state of preservation (Skaarup, below). It is also to be noted that the number of decorated objects of amber, antler and bone from coastal settlements has grown markedly in the last 25 years (S.H. Andersen 1981b).

The earliest coastal settlements so far belong to the transition from the Maglemose to the Kongemose Culture, around 6600 B.C., but there are only a few, scattered examples. Such sites have been found in North Jutland (Nørholm Enge: S.H. Andersen 1990), the Storebælt (Musholm Bugt: A. Fischer 1989a-b), on Sjælland (Blak in Roskilde fjord: AUD 1991:121) and in Øresund (L. Larsson 1983).

From the Kongemose Culture, 6600-5400 B.C., rather more coastal settlements are known, especially from Sjælland though there are examples from Jutland: Brovst (S.H. Andersen 1970) and Ø. Jølby (S.H. Andersen & Malmros 1966), both in North Jutland. Overall, the amount of publication on this phase of the Mesolithic has been very small in the last 25 years, with only the submerged Argusgrunden published (A. Fischer et al. 1987).

The largest number of coastal settlements are of the Ertebølle Period, 5400-4000 B.C., totalling several hundred which have provided the basis for several major interdisciplinary projects. A significant number of the Late-mesolithic coastal settlements were still in use in the Early Neolithic and thus show site continuity between the periods: e.g. Norsminde (S.H. Andersen 1991).

Excavations of coastal settlements with several culture layers, especially kitchen middens, have in recent years made important new contributions to the assessment of the transition from the Mesolithic to the Neolithic, as at Norsminde (S.H. Andersen 1991) and Bjørnsholm (S.H. Andersen 1993). These settlements show that the change in material culture from hunter/ fisherman to farmer in Jutland was very rapid and abrupt, taking only about 100 C-14 years from *ca.* 3950 B.C. The change in subsistence, in contrast, seems to have been much more gradual (S.H. Andersen & Johansen 1992). In the kitchen middens, the transition from the Mesolithic to the Neolithic is marked by a clear shift from deposits dominated by oyster to layers dominated by cockle, at the same time as the artefacts change from the Ertebølle Culture to the Funnel Beaker Culture of the Volling type (S.H. Andersen 1991, 1993).

A characteristic feature of recent years' work in Denmark has been an increasing inclination not to concentrate exclusively on a single settlement site but also to assess it in a larger regional perspective as part of a whole settlement system. Such studies have begun in North Jutland by the former Bjørnsholm fjord (S.H. Andersen 1993), by Norsminde fjord (S.H. Andersen 1976, 1991), in the archipelago south of Fyn (Skaarup 1983) and by Saltbæk Vig (Paludan-Müller 1978; Price & Gebauer 1992), in Nivå

(Møller Hansen & Stummann Hansen 1992) and in Vedbæk (Brinch Petersen et al. 1976) on Sjælland. Although these studies are still in their infancy, certain results seem to be emerging. It appears that there were different settlement-types within the regions and some form of hierarchical system seems to be operating, for instance in East Jutland, where the largest settlements both lie centrally in defined resoure areas and are relatively regularly distributed in the coastal areas of the region (S.H. Andersen 1981a). At the same time, these studies show that regional settlement patterns adapted to local circumstances must be reckoned with much more than was previously supposed.

Regionally, the most recent years' work has clearly shown that there was contact between coastal and inland groups: this is true of Jutland (S.H. Andersen 1979a) and on Sjælland (Noe-Nygaard 1988b) but a detailed description of the form of such contacts is not yet possible.

On several occasions, regional aspects of the material and ideological evidence from the coastal culture have been described. These studies show that there are clear differences in material culture between an eastern Ertebølle group in Sjælland-Skåne (Vang Petersen 1984) and a western Jutland-Fyn one (S.H. Andersen 1973a). These two Ertebølle regions, which seem to be divided by the Storebælt, are also apparently reflected in the preference for certain patterns and compositions in art (S.H. Andersen 1981b).

A special (and famous) group of Danish coastal settlements are the kitchen middens, where new excavations began from 1970 after many years' break. It has now been established that the earliest Danish kitchen middens such as Brovst go back to the late Kongemose Culture, *ca.* 5700-5600 B.C. (S.H. Andersen 1970).

Although the kitchen middens are so well known, it has to be stressed that this type of coastal settlement is only found in the north and north-east of the country, and even in these areas there are always more coastal settlements in any given resource area without shell layers (ordinary coastal settlements) than kitchen middens. Quite a substantial amount of recent years' work has therefore also been done on these sites, such as Norslund (S.H. Andersen & Malmros 1966), Ølby Lyng (Brinch Petersen 1971), Vænget Nord (Brinch Petersen 1989) and Maglemosegård (Brinch Petersen 1979a).

Large new excavations of kitchen middens have been undertaken at Ertebølle (S.H. Andersen & Johansen 1987), Bjørnsholm (S.H. Andersen 1993) and Norsminde (S.H. Andersen 1991). This has provided an updating of the results from early excavations, while a finer and more secure dating of the sequences has been established with the help of systematic C-14 samples. This supports a better understanding of the course and rate of accumulation. The kitchen middens and the other coastal settlements seem also to have been structured: divided into areas characterized by particular activities (S.H. Andersen & Johansen 1987). Structural types such as various types of hearth, 'fire pits', pits, postholes and sometimes graves have been identified. Another, important detail is that there are apparently no large, comprehensive settlement or burial areas in the vicinity of the very largest Danish kitchen middens such as Ertebølle (S.H. Andersen & Johansen 1987). It is evident that the kitchen middens were the basis of all day-to-day activities but it is still an open question as to what sort of settlements these sites represent.

Amongst new sites, coastal settlements on shore banks exposed by the sea must be noted (Brinch Petersen 1982, 1990) and the sunken settlements described below. It must be stressed, however, that the submerged coastal settlements do not differ from the well-known settlements on land in any way other than their present location, and with that the often exceptionally good conditions for the preservation of organic remains.

Excavations and analyses of minor settlements have concurrently provided new evidence of a certain degree of economic specialization, such as sea-fowling and -hunting at Ølby Lyng (Brinch Petersen 1971) and swan-hunting at Aggersund (S.H. Andersen 1979b). The Limfjord area has a local character in respect of fishing which concentrated on eel both at Ertebølle and at Bjørnsholm (S.H. Andersen & Johansen 1987; Bødker Enghoff 1987, 1993 and below; S.H. Andersen 1992, 1993).

In studies of the economy new excavation methods (wet and dry sieving), new methods of analysis (δ^{13}C, Tauber, above), studies of charred foodremains from pointed-bottomed Ertebølle pottery with remains of fish soup (S.H. Andersen & Malmros 1985), and the finding of fishing sites and fish traps have further emphasized the great importance of this form of subsistence to the coastal population

of the Atlantic Period. It is important to stress, however, that we still know no coastal settlements where subsistence depended exclusively on the sea.

Total excavation of coastal settlements is another of the steps forward taken in research into the Mesolithic in Demark in the last 25 years. These excavations (at Vedbæk: Brinch Petersen 1977, 1979a, 1982, 1989) have significantly increased our knowledge of the structures and functional division of the settlements (Juel Jensen & Brinch Petersen 1985) and of a wide range of settlement structures such as various forms of hearth, pits, stone structures, driven stakes, flintknapping areas, concentrations of cracked stones, fixed fish traps, etc. The aim of these major settlement excavations is first and foremost to get as comprehensive picture as possible of the settlements of the period in order thus to understand what the Stone-age settlements really are, and to define their range of variation. An important new element in the work on settlement finds is the refitting of excavated lithics in order thus to illuminate behaviour and functional division on the settlements (Brinch Petersen 1989).

The modern stripping of large settlement areas has led to the identification of possible hut structures (Juel Jensen & Brinch Petersen 1985), some with slightly sunken floors, as at Lollikhuse on Sjælland (AUD 1991:121 ff.), though these occurrences are still somewhat uncertain and as yet have more the character of ghost structures than anything else.

The most important of the new discoveries on settlement sites is the appearance of graves both in groups and singly, giving a much more rounded picture of the mesolithic settlements than before (Kannegaard Nielsen & Brinch Petersen, below). But a number of major questions still remain, such as why there are no graves on any Ertebølle settlements where large areas have been uncovered, such as Ertebølle (S.H. Andersen & Johansen 1987) and Bjørnsholm (S.H. Andersen 1993), and where the graves of the later Ertebølle Culture may be.

In brief, the development within research into the coastal settlements can be described as a movement from artefacts and typology through studies of settlements on to settlement systems. Along with this, important excavations of individual settlements have been carried out.

Coastal fishing

The large quantity of fish remains that is retrieved in modern excavations now makes quantitative studies of the relative frequency of species, their size, and growth-rings in the bones possible. These studies in turn help to determine what fishing was carried out from a particular settlement and thus enable us to compare different sites.

The innovative technique of wet sieving of excavated soil has meant that there are now many more species on what has gradually become a comprehensive list, 42 species in all. The small species in particular, that were overlooked before, have proved to be richly represented. This is especially so with the three-spined stickleback, which apparently was important at several settlements! Also new are a group of species with a southern distribution (sea lettuce, bass and smooth hound) that are now rare in Denmark and which therefore help to confirm the warmer climate of the Atlantic Period. Finally, the quantity of fishbone indicates how important fishing was!

Although the earliest coastal settlements yet known in Denmark come from the Kongemose Period, the many new excavations of Ertebølle Culture settlements mean that fishing is best illustrated in that period. There seem to have been regional differences at this time.

Various species of fish were caught for the settlements, all of which could have been caught near the shore. Several of them live their whole lives there; others approach the shore in one season of the year or in their early years. The lists of species reflect uncritically gathered samples of the local inshore fish in the summer months. Most fishing depended on stationary traps furnished with lines and/or arms placed near the shore.

Differences in fishery appear to have followed differences in the local stocks. The classic Ertebølle site is special in that the dominance of roach (67%) indicates that the principal fishing for eel took place in freshwater despite the coastal location of the site. Otherwise, however, it fits with the general picture.

Inge Bødker Enghoff

Fish found at coastal settlements in Denmark.

Porbeagle *(Lamna nasus)*
Smooth hound *(Mustelus sp.)*
Spiny dogfish *(Squalus acanthias)*
Thornback *(Raja clavata)*
Sting ray *(Dasyatis pastinaca)*
Herring *(Clupea harengus)*
Allis shad *(Alosa sp.)*
Sea trout *(Salmo trutta)*
Whitefish *(Coregonus sp.)*
Pike *(Esox lucius)*
Tench *(Tinca tinca)*
Roach *(Rutilus rutilus)*
Rudd *(Scardinius erythrophthalmus)*
Bream *(Abramis braama)*
Eel *(Anguilla anguilla)*
Garfish *(Belone belone)*
Pipefish *(Syngnathidae sp.)*
Cod *(Gadus morhua)*
Haddock *(Melanogrammus aeglefinus)*
Whiting *(Merlangius merlangus)*
Pollack *(Pollachius pollachius)*
Coalfish *(Pollachius virens)*
Bass *(Dicentrarchus labrax)*
Perch *(Perca fluviatilis)*
Pike-perch *(Lucioperca lucioperca)*

Horse mackerel *(Trachurus trachurus)*
Sea lettuce *(Spondyliosoma cantharus)*
Sand eel *(Hyperoplus Ammodytes sp.)*
Greater weever *(Trachinus draco)*
Common dragonet *(Callionymus lyra)*
Thin-lipped grey mullet *(Liza ramada)*
Mackerel *(Scomber scombrus)*
Swordfish *(Xiphias gladius)*
Eelpout *(Zoarces viviparus)*
Black goby *(Gobius niger)*
Grey gurnard *(Eutrigla gurnardus)*
Short-spined sea scorpion *(Myoxocephalus scorpius)*
Three-spined stickleback *(Gastosteus aculeatus)*
Fifteen-spined stickleback *(Spinachia spinachia)*
Turbot *(Psetta maxima)*
Halibut *(Hippoglossus hippoglossus)*
Plaice *(Pleuronectes platessa)*
Flounder *(Platichthys flesus)*

The dominant species of fish at Ertebølle (Bødker Enghoff 1987), Bjørnsholm (Bødker Enghoff 1993), Norsminde (Bødker Enghoff 1991), Tybrind Vig (Trolle-Lassen 1984) and Vedbæk (Bødker Enghoff 1983 and unpubl.). The map shows the contemporary relationship between land and sea in the Atlantic Period.

Submerged settlements

By Jørgen Skaarup

From the end of the last Ice Age down to around the birth of Christ, the coastline of Denmark has undergone enormous changes (Strand Petersen 1985; C. Christensen, above). The huge amount of water that was still frozen in the polar ice caps at the beginning of the Late Palaeolithic had caused substantial falls in sea-level, so that in northern Europe particularly, large new hunting grounds were created for Stone-age hunters. Much of this area was drowned with the gradual melting of the ice which also, in north-eastern Denmark and the whole Scandinavian peninsula, set off a land-rise that is still going on.

As a result of this complicated interplay between eu- and isostatic forces, there are now many Stone-age settlements below the seas of southern and south-western Denmark. The earliest of these sites, from the Late Glacial and Boreal Period, may lie as much as 30-40 m. below sea-level and are still practically unknown (L. Larsson 1983). On the other hand, the last 20 years has seen various drowned settlements of the Atlantic Period identified, some examples, indeed, from the early part of this period. The deepest-lying and earliest of these is just 10 m. below the Storebælt (A. Fischer 1989b). Sunken settlements of the Sub-Boreal Period (the Neolithic) are also known. All of these are in shallow water (Skaarup 1983:155 f.).

The sunken Stone-age settlements have nearly all proved to have stood on former coastlines. They have, as a result, often been able to provide valuable and well-dated points for the successive shifts between land and sea through the Atlantic and Sub-Boreal Periods. Furthermore many of them contain rich, sometimes unique, finds which have supplemented, in important areas, the existing picture of the Atlantic-period hunting/fishing culture groups that had relied, essentially, on finds from northern and eastern Denmark.

Ever since diving established itself as a hobby after the Second World War, it had technically been possible to investigate the sunken Stone-age settlements. But the lack of archaeologists who were trained divers (Crumlin-Pedersen 1990) meant that this work was taken up only at the beginning of the 1970's.

In 1972, Langelands Museum was the first to test the water by undertaking a systematic reconnaissance of sunken settlements in the sea south of Fyn - one of the largest drowned morainic landscapes of Europe - in collaboration with a number of local diving clubs. On this basis, 1976 saw the beginning of a promising excavation of an Ertebølle settlement in the Møllegab outside Ærøskøbing.

A few years later, the Forhistorisk Museum Moesgård followed suit, beginning in similar circumstances to investigate a very rich settlement of the Ertebølle Culture in Tybrind Vig, western Fyn. The exciting results of these excavations led the Forest and Nature Agency to undertake underwater archaeological survey projects in the 1980's, supplemented by minor excavations in the Småland Sea, Roskilde fjord, the Storebælt and Århus Bay. The Maritime History Laboratory of the National Museum has also on occasion supported underwater Stone Age investigations, such as the excavation of a 7,000-year-old dug-out canoe by Fyns Hoved in 1988 (Rieck & Crumlin-Pedersen 1988). The latest to join in this little circle of institutions working in underwater archaeology is the Færgegård Museum, Frederikssund, which is uncovering a couple of Kongemose-culture settlements by the island of Blak in the Roskilde fjord (S.A. Sørensen, in prep.).

The investigations of sunken Stone-age settlements have as a rule been directed like comparable projects on land, with excavation and planning in a metre-square grid, drawing of sections, sampling, photography etc. Shovels, wheelbarrows and sieves, however, are replaced by injection pumps that suck the excavated fill into a fine mesh which ensures that fishbones, arrowheads and other small objects are retrieved. Levelling equipment is likewise replaced

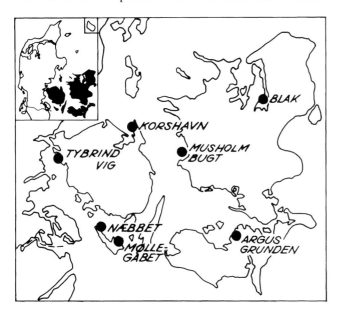

Important sunken Stone-age settlements found in Denmark.

by the depth-meter. Last but not least, care for the safety of the divers is something that obviously needs to be given more attention than with a traditional land excavation.

The survey projects have nearly all been carried out as a series of small trial investigations where divers have inspected sites that appear to be likely settlement places, from the study of charts for instance. This traditional, and quite successful, method has recently been supplemented in the sea south of Fyn by investigations using a sediment echo-sounder, which has made it possible to map the original topography - and with that, the ideal Stone-age settlement places - even in areas that are covered with thick peat deposits (Grøn 1990:85, 1991:27 ff.).

Møllegab is the name of a narrow but deep waterway leading into Ærøskøbing from the north. On its eastern side is a small island, Dejrø, from where a now sunken promontory runs west right out to the channel. At the end of this promontory, two settlements were excavated in 1976-80 and 1987-93, Møllegab I and II.

Møllegab I was sited on a coastline that is now 2.3 m. below sea-level. This settlement can be assigned to the late Ertebølle Culture and, despite erosion of the culture layers over thousands of years, still comprises a 60-m. long and upto 75-cm. thick culture layer. This layer is very rich in finds with many well-preserved hearths. No traces of buildings have been found. They may have stood on the higher, very eroded part of the headland behind the midden (Skaarup 1980b:3 ff., 1983:144 ff.).

Beyond the coastline of the time, a layer of gyttja more than 1.5 m. thick was formed which provided outstanding conditions for preserving the large quantities of flint, bone, antler, wood and clay waste that the population of the settlement threw into the water. Driven posts in the area may come from fishing weirs.

The copious faunal and floral remains show, as expected, that the economy of the site was based exclusively on fishing, hunting and gathering. The large number of flint, bone and antler tools and the pottery-types likewise produce no great surprises. One novelty, however, is a large flat piece of gneiss which seems, from a firmly attached mixture of soot and fat, to have been used as a palette.

As at most other sunken settlements, the wooden objects are the biggest asset of Møllegab I. The gyttja layers are thick with ash, chips and broken wood-

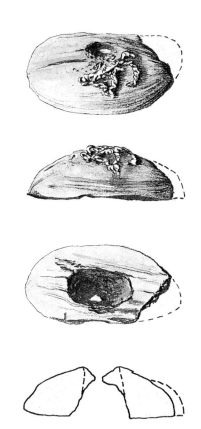

Wooden float with line of lightly-spun vegetable fibre. 1:2. Møllegab I settlement.

en tools which provide important evidence for the apparently advanced timber technology of the Ertebølle Culture. Shafts, pointed stakes, debarked logs and side-wings of leisters occur in large numbers, supplemented by fragments of bows and arrows, pieces with traces of engraving and club-like items. The wood shavings appear to come largely from the making of dug-outs that were used for transport and fishing. An interesting new discovery in the later field is a wooden float with a biconical perforation in which remains of a fishing line formed of spun vegetable fibre were found.

The occupants of the site are represented by a small collection of human bone, some of which apparently comes from disturbed burials. Other pieces, however, were split, and one burnt, and can therefore be taken as evidence of cannibalism.

Møllegab II lies only 20-30 m. from Møllegab I but at a significantly deeper level, apparently associated with a coastline about 4.5 m. below current sea-level. The tool inventory and C 14 dating have shown that the settlement is a good 1,000 years older than Møllegab I, and that it has to be attributed to the early Ertebølle Culture (Grøn & Skaarup 1993).

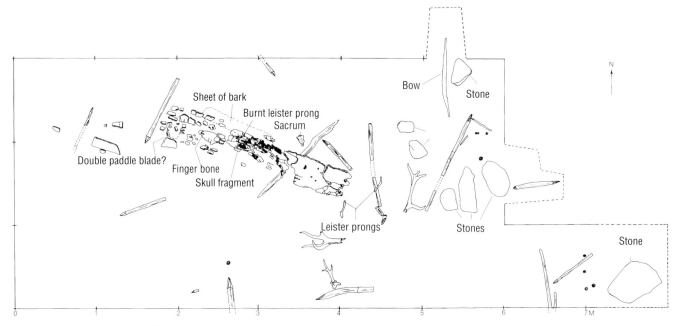

Boat burial from Møllegab II.

The settlement was established on an extended plateau in the lee of the headland, the outermost part of which was damaged by a straightening of the channel in the 1920's. The original extent of the settlement therefore cannot now be determined. The settlement layer appears as a grey sand layer without collected molluscs but characterized by decayed organic material and great quantities of worked, unpatinated lithics. At the west of the settlement area what is thought to be the remains of a dwelling was identified in 1992, with a floor formed of a layer of branches covered by bark flakes. This has a rectangular ground plan measuring 6 m. x 4 and containing at least one hearth. The bark layer is covered with a rubbish layer very rich in finds with large quantities of lithic *débitage*, nutshells, fishbones etc. This exciting discovery will be investigated in more detail in 1993.

In the water beyond the settlement a quantity of waste had accumulated: animal and fishbones, lithics, vegetable remains, discarded tools of bone, antler and wood, etc. Of the wooden objects, two bows and an axe handle attract attention. Stakes from former fishing weirs were found in several places.

The bank zone outside the building contained yet another great surprise, in the form of a boat grave (Skaarup & Grøn 1991). At the top of the gyttja the stern of a severely crushed dug-out that had functioned as the coffin for the corpse of a young man was uncovered. The body and the boat-section were wrapped in bark, placed, together with a set of paddles, in shallow water, and held in place by stakes. Some large red-deer antlers at the stern of the boat

may have served as a pillow for the corpse. This remarkable burial-form is as yet quite unparalleled in the Mesolithic. The closest parallel is a find nearly 1,500 years later from Åmose, Sjælland.

This boat burial seems not to have been the only grave at Møllegab II. In the course of excavating the channel in the 1920's the finding of 'two complete (ape) skeletons' was reported. This seems to be confirmed by scattered finds of human bone in the excavated area, where a small cemetery may have been situated on the dry land.

The excavation of the settlement in Tybrind Vig, western Fyn, took place from 1978 to 1987 and gradually developed into one of the most comprehensive underwater excavations in Danish territory yet (S.H. Andersen 1985). The findplace now lies about 2-3 m. deep, about 250 m. offshore, at the bottom of a west-facing bay of the Lillebælt. In the Mesolithic, this bay formed a protected lagoon, with access to the Lillebælt immediately south of the settlement.

The majority of the settlement area has been eroded away but the gyttja layer close to the shore south of the settlement, up to 2 m. thick in a bank zone 10 m. wide and about 50 m. long, has, conversely, proved to contain large amounts of abandoned tools and waste from the settlement with traces of several activities. This rich material comprising lithics, bone, antler and wood tools and, from the upper layer, pottery, together with a number of C 14 datings, has shown that the settlement in Tybrind Vig is to be attributed to the Ertebølle Culture and covers both its early and later phases: in other words a period of about 1,500 years at the end of the Mesolithic.

A fortunate find from a partly preserved segment of the settlement area provided an intact grave from a very early phase of settlement. A narrow grave contained the skeleton of a 15-17 year-old woman lying supine. The bones of a child, 1-3 months old, lay on her breast. There were no grave goods. The remains of a further 2 or 3 individuals - including a man with some healed lesions in the skull - were found scattered in the underwater area. These probably come from washed-out graves.

Like all other Ertebølle settlements, the economy of the Tybrind Vig site was based on hunting, fishing and gathering, as shown by the large quantity of food remains in the gyttja outside the settlement. The bank zone, however, did not only function as a dump. This is shown by a large number of fishing-weir stakes *in situ* in the mud and a concentration of angled leister wings that seem to indicate an especially favoured area for such fishing. Some bone fish-hooks, one with a piece of line preserved, further emphasize the importance of fishing (cf. Bødker

Scuba diver planning a section of the mud layers of the Tyrbrind Vig settlement. The section is recorded at 1:1 on a plexiglass plate hung on the surface.

Enghoff, above).

The occupants needed dug-out canoes for off-shore fishing and for transport. Two of these, both of lime, and one preserved to its full length of 9.5 m., were found in the mud outside the Tybrind Vig settlement, where traces of a landing place seem also to have been identified. The dug-outs were propelled with slender, spatulate paddles of which at least 13 have been found, three of which are uniquely decorated with complicated geometric patterns incised into the blades in low relief and with traces of coloured inlays.

The wooden objects are, as usual at sunken sites, the group of artefacts that attracts the greatest interest because of its rarity. The Tybrind Vig settlement has proved to be exceptionally rich in worked wood. As well as the items already noted, many bows, arrows, pointed stakes, handles, fish traps and perhaps the thwart of a boat have been found. Quite unexpectedly, towards the end of excavation the site

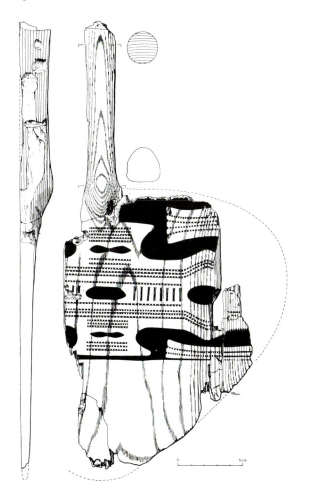

Decorated paddle from the Tybrind Vig settlement. 1:3.

produced textile finds in the form of small fragments of textiles made in a technique called 'needle-binding' with thread made from spun vegetable fibres. These textile remains are as yet the oldest found in Europe.

The sunken settlement traces south of the small island of Blak in the Roskilde fjord were discovered in 1983 and have seen annual investigations since 1989 (S.A. Sørensen, in prep.). As early as 1990, it could be shown, with the help of corings, that there were two chronologically distinct settlements in the area of investigation. In the Mesolithic this was a headland that flanked a river mouth to the east and reached into a deep channel in the fjord to the south.

The first settlement found, Blak I, appeared in the form of a washed-out and partly rebedded sandy settlement layer measuring *ca.* 50 m. x 10. The top of this layer is about 1.5-2 m. deep and is full of lithics: asymmetrical arrowheads, core axes, blade tools, borers etc. Amongst other tools, several axes made of greenstone, various fishing-weir or -trap stakes and a large piece of a bow can be noted. The wooden objects come from the bank zone of the settlement where many animal and fishbones were also found. The finds show that Blak I represents a coastal settlement of the early Kongemose Culture.

The Blak II settlement lies about 30 m. south of Blak I at a depth of 4 m. The finds are contained in a deeply charcoal-coloured culture layer about 10 cm. thick that has been found in a strip about 25 m. long along what was then the coastline of the headland. Beyond this were found heavy gyttja layers with rubbish deposits. No traces of solid structures have yet been found in the settlement layer but a marked concentration of burnt lithics and charcoal seems to indicate a hearth. The quantity of finds is at present very small, but the assemblage and find contexts indicate that the finds are not mixed. Arrowheads dominate the flint idustry, with about 30 trapezes and a few triangular microliths. A few core axes have also been found, and axe rejuvenation flakes, burins and various blade tools. The bone and antler finds comprise some awls, a flaking tool, a possible bone dagger and a fragment of a decorated slotted bone dagger. The faunal remains testify to the hunting of wild deer, boar, beaver and pond tortoise and coastal fishing of flatfish, eel and garfish. A human lower jaw indicates the presence of graves.

The trapezes are important in the dating of Blak II, as, together with a number of C 14 datings of the culture layer, they place the settlement in the otherwise practically unknown transitional phase between the Maglemose and Kongemose Cultures. The Blak II settlement will undoubtedly be a key site for the future understanding and description of the character of this phase.

The excavations in the Møllegab, Tybrind Vig and at Blak represent the largest but certainly not the only excavations of sunken settlements in Danish waters in the last 25 years. Minor investigations that have also produced exciting results have been carried out by the Protection Agency (now the Forest and Nature Agency) at Argusgrund in the Småland Sea and in Musholm Bay in the Storebælt, by the National Museum at Korshavn, Fyns Hoved, and by Langelands Museum at Skjoldnæs on Ærø.

The settlement at Argusgrund (A. Fischer *et al.* 1987) was found during gravel dredging in 1956 and provisionally investigated in 1984-85. Within an area of about 50 m. x 100 at a depth of 5-6 m. a culture layer with hearths and a rich refuse layer has been identified. A comprehensive flint inventory with core axes and rhombic points and a few antler and bone tools places the settlement in the Kongemose Culture, as is confirmed by C 14 datings. Some scattered skeletal material has been identified as the remains of two adults and two children. Presumably these bones come from washed-out graves.

In Musholm Bay, traces of a settlement contemporary with the earliest settlement at Blak were found at a depth of 9 m. in 1987 (A. Fischer 1989b). In this case too, the settlement seems to have been sited on a small promontory by a river mouth. The scanty finds comprise trapezes, axes and knives and food remains in the form of split bones, fishbones and hazelnut shells.

At a depth of 2 m. between Korshavn and Mejlø lies a very large and rich settlement of the early Ertebølle Culture. Great numbers of flint tools and a large number of deer-antler axes, flaking tools and awls have been collected over the years through diving at the site. In 1987-88, a well-preserved, 4.2-m. long dug-out of lime was located and excavated at the edge of the settlement area. Dated to 5200 B.C., this is one of the earliest boats found in Denmark (AUD 1988:214; Rieck & Crumlin-Pedersen 1988).

At Næbbet on the north side of Skjoldnæs, Ærø, in shallow water in a small bay that formed a coastal lake in the Stone Age, remains of a late Ertebølle settlement have been found (Skaarup 1981, 1983).

Once again, human bones from the disturbed settlement layers probably indicate the presence of graves inside the settlement area. The coastal lake was used as the rubbish dump for the settlement, as shown by the great quantities of disposed animal and fish-bones, wooden objects, and lithic *débitage,* bone and antler in the mud. The most important find from the site is the nearly intact lower part of a leister with a hazel shaft and thorn wings. The shaft and wings were firmly lashed together with cord made from twisted vegetable fibre. This piece is the first preserved example of the European Stone Age.

This short survey of the most important of recent years' investigations of submerged Stone-age settlements in Danish waters clearly shows, it is hoped, the significance of this special branch of underwater archaeology. Thanks to the reconnaissance projects and the underwater settlement excavations already carried out we have reached a much broader knowledge of the previously nearly unknown mesolithic coastal settlements in southern Denmark and, with this, very new prospects for identifying contacts between mesolithic groups in and outside modern Denmark. In a couple of cases it has also been possible to find and uncover settlements of a phase of the Mesolithic that was practically invisible in Denmark, the transition from the Maglemose to the Kongemose Culture.

The frequently outstanding preservative conditions for organic material in the gyttja layers of the bank zone have provided new evidence of a wide range of activities in the shallow water outside the settlements. This particularly concerns activities associated with fishing and water transport (dug-outs, landing places) but also a special use of the area as a burial ground. At the same time, the very high level of woodwork in the southern Danish Ertebølle Culture has been thoroughly documented by several finds, amongst which there is reason to emphasize the internationally unique wooden objects from the Tybrind Vig settlement. The conditions in the mud layers have also meant that many of the sunken settlements have been able to make very important contributions, both qualitatively and quantitatively, in the form of faunal and floral remains that illustrate the economy of mesolithic culture.

Surprisingly enough, the submerged settlements have frequently been able to confirm the close physical association of settlement and cemetery that has

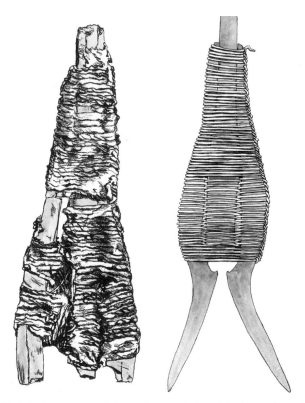

Slightly fragmentary leister with nearly intact lashing of vegetable-fibre cord. 1:3. From Næbbet, Ærø.

appeared in some recent excavations of mesolithic sites on land (Kannegaard Nielsen & Brinch Petersen, below).

The sunken settlements also seem to be able to play an important role in the future in charting the extensive shifts between land and sea throughout the Stone Age. This is because the majority of the settlements prove to have been placed on the coastline, the level and date of which can thus be determined.

Research into the hundreds if not thousands of sunken Stone-age settlement sites on the sea-bed over large areas of Denmark is still a new phenomenon, but one with international implications, as it is already clear what great research potential these sunken settlements hold. Fortunately this is recognized in Danish law. Since 1984, all ancient monuments on the sea-bed have been protected against disturbance.

Protection, however, can only be given if the monument is known. An important future task for Danish archaeology will therefore be to train archaeologists who will be able to cope with underwater archaeological recording and excavation and who will thus be able to maintain and develop Denmark's hard-won expertise in this field.

Burials, people and dogs

BY ESBEN KANNEGAARD NIELSEN AND ERIK BRINCH PETERSEN

Between the 1960's and the autumn of 1992 about 50 mesolithic graves have been excavated. It is difficult to give a precise figure. At several sites skeletons and skeletal material have been found lying on settlement surfaces or embedded in the shell layers of kitchen middens. Are these graves? There are other possible cases of disturbed graves and perhaps washed-out graves at the sunken settlements; other cases suffer a straightforward lack of evidence on the context of the skeletal finds. On top of this it can often be difficult to date a grave with absolute certainty to the Mesolithic. There is finally a question of whether a pit which may or may not contain finds or ochre but certainly has no skeletal material can be called a grave. The find total has also been increased by the re-examination of uncertain earlier finds, especially with C 14 dating.

While graves from earlier excavations such as at Ertebølle and Bloksbjerg could be doubtful, especially because they were so devoid of artefacts, the new graves show a remarkable range of variation in both form and contents. There are both inhumations and cremations, and boat graves under water and on dry land. There are single, double and multiple graves of as many as 8 persons. There are unfurnished graves or very sparsely furnished ones, but there are also graves with rich personal equipment such as reflects not only age and sex but also a degree of social differentiation. All age groups are now represented, even the newborn and children, who in fact have always been very difficult to find. There are empty or exhumed graves, and finally there are dog graves. Altogether, a new, unexpected but especially interesting body of material has emerged to enrich our understanding of the Mesolithic.

Graves have been found from Djursland in Jutland across Fyn and Ærø to the east coast of Sjælland. This distribution, however, only reflects those areas in which excavation has taken place in recent years (Brinch Petersen 1992). The graves are found, for instance, in the course of excavations of coastal settlements, and only a newly-dated Maglemose grave from Holmegaard V is from inland.

Chronologically, the newly-found graves are spread (with the exception of the Holmegaard V grave) from later Kongemose to the end of the Ertebølle Period. Three categories emerge in this

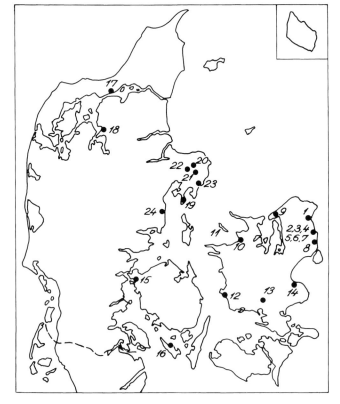

Distribution of graves.

List of graves. 1: Nivågaard (excavated by Hørsholm Museum). 2: Vænget Nord (Price & Brinch Petersen 1987). 3: Vedbæk Boldbaner (Mathiassen 1946; Kunwald 1954; Vang Petersen 1977). 4: Henriksholm-Bøgebakken (Albrethsen et al. 1976; Albrethsen & Brinch Petersen 1977). 5: Gøngehusvej no.7 (Brinch Petersen 1990; Brinch Petersen et al. 1993). 6: Maglemosegaard (Brinch Petersen 1979a; Alexandersen 1979). 7: Stationsvej 19 (excavated by the National Museum). 8: Bloksbjerg (Westerby 1927). 9: Melby (Lund Hansen et al. 1973). 10: Dragsholm (Brinch Petersen 1974). 11: Sejerø (excavated by the National Museum). 12: Korsør Nor (Norling-Christensen & Brøste 1945). 13: Holmegaard V (excavated by the National Museum). 14: Strøby Egede (Brinch Petersen 1988). 15: Tybrind Vig (S.H. Andersen 1985). 16: Møllegabet II (Skaarup & Grøn 1993). 17: Brovst (Newell et al. 1979). 18: Ertebølle (A.P Madsen et al. 1900). 19: Vænge Sø (S.H. Andersen et al. 1986). 20: Holmegård (S.H. Andersen et al. 1986). 21: Fannerup (Hougaard Rasmussen 1990; Bennike & Alexandersen 1990). 22: Nederst (AUD 1990:145 f.). 23: Koed (Hougaard Rasmussen 1990). 24: Norsminde (S.H. Andersen 1991).

group, with the first series comprising cremations that are now known from France too (Ducrocq *et al.* 1991), Holland (Arts & Hoogland 1987) and Poland. The second series, of inhumations, comes from the period of the late Kongemose and very early Ertebølle Cultures and comprises both the largest number and the richest of the new discoveries. The last series comprises the late Ertebølle graves that have been found in kitchen middens especially and which with one exception, Dragsholm, all seem to be unfurnished and without red ochre.

After the discovery of the large number of graves at Bøgebakken in Vedbæk it has been usual to describe a site with several graves as a cemetery. This, however, is difficult to justify, as the graves do not occur in separate areas, rather on the settlement itself. Many graves lie in the central parts of the settlements, the children's graves, perhaps, simply associated with hut construction, such as can be most clearly seen on the site of Gøngehusvej no.7 in Vedbæk. On the Ertebølle settlement at Nederst on Djursland the graves were sited in the area between the shell heaps, while the Fannerup grave, also on Djursland, was dug through the original shell layers.

The number of graves on one settlement must also be looked at in the context of the size of the settlement. The larger the settlement, the more graves would be possible. The provisional C 14 datings from Bøgebakken in Vedbæk also show that there is quite a chronological range amongst the graves found there. It further transpires from the excavations in Vedbæk that graves can be found on each and every settlement, graves having been excavated at six different sites here. Since several of these are also contemporary, we can conclude that people were buried where they lived and died. At Gøngehusvej no.7, graves have also been found in two clearly different layers about 500 years apart. Other settlements show that only one grave was constructed there, so that it is clear that graves must always be looked at in the context of the settlement, its size and its chronological range. It is thus these factors that are primarily determinative of the number of graves and their location. But it is, of course, most important that the excavation should be of appropriate character for the detection of structures, including graves, to be possible: *i.e.* large open area excavation.

Even where there are several graves on a single site, they seem to respect one another. Some graves were marked on the surface with stones. Large stones in graves, such as at Bloksbjerg and Vedbæk Boldbaner, have in the past been interpreted as expressions of a practical or symbolic entrapment of the deceased in the grave. It is, however, more likely that the stones served as above-ground markers for the graves which fell down on to the body when the grave sank. There may be a single large stone or several. In one case, Strøby Egede, Stevns, a limited stone frame was found outside one end of the grave. A special group is that of the small children's graves from Gøngehusvej no.7. Here a stone circle was found at the top, protecting an open grave pit, at the bottom of which the child's body was laid on a wooden tray or something similar.

The boat-grave rite, which is well-known from late prehistory, can now be found back in the Mesolithic, though here, of course, in the form of burials in or under dug-outs. At Møllegabet II outside Ærøskøbing in the archipelago south of Fyn a dug-out together with a skeleton were found in the refuse area beyond the settlement during an underwater excavation at the depth of 5 m. There were also similar burials on dry land, as the soil discolorations around a couple of the graves at Bøgebakken can really best be interpreted as the remains of a dug-out that was placed here above the deceased. The same observations have also been made at Skateholm in Skåne (L. Larsson 1988).

Gøngehusvej no.7, Vedbæk. Cremation burial under excavation.

The skeletons are nearly always found lying supine and extended at the bottom of the grave pit, with the arms by the sides and the feet right together. We can therefore suppose that the bodies were laid to rest wrapped in skins or something similar. In one grave at Gøngehusvej no.7 remains of a roe-deer hide were found around the skeleton, the pseudo-hooves of its lateral toes hooves being preserved. A newborn baby in grave 8 at Bøgebakken had been buried on a swan's wing, while three other bodies on this site had been laid upon a set of antlers, all from slaughtered red deer.

It is most common for only one body to lie in the grave; this holds for both children and adults. Two children in one grave have been found only once, at Gøngehusvej no.7, with one set of grave goods at either end of the grave indicating that two children must have lain here. It is more predictable that a younger woman should be found with a newborn baby. This occurs four times, each of which can be regarded as a joint burial of mother and child neither of whom survived birth problems.

The newborn also occur in the two mass burials known, the cremation of five individuals from Gøngehusvej no.7 and the Strøby Egede grave of

eight persons, three of them newly born. A one-year-old child was found with two adults in grave 19 from Bøgebakken and a three-year-old accompanied a woman of about 40 in the most recent grave from Gøngehusvej no.7. Slightly older children occur too in the two mass burials. Apart from the three graves just mentioned, adults are found together only in the double grave from Dragsholm and in a severely disturbed grave from Nederst. In two cases, both from Bøgebakken, a man's grave was added on to an earlier grave of a young woman and newborn baby. This could be taken as an expression of family unity both in life and death (Albrethsen *et al.* 1976).

At the settlement of Gøngehusvej no.7, a well-preserved dog's skeleton was found beside a grave pit. There was unfortunately neither grave goods nor red ochre with the dog, as there is with several examples from Skateholm in Skåne (L. Larsson 1990a). On the other hand there is equally no sign of the skinning of the dog, so that this dog can plausibly be interpreted as a companion to the person buried - even in death. That, as in Skateholm, dogs were buried in Denmark, is shown by the large number of dogs that have now been found in the kitchen midden at Nederst. However no grave pits, grave goods or red ochre have been found here either.

The great majority of the new graves appear as ochre graves, and there is often more ochre with infants and children than with adults. With the adults, a lot of ochre is usually found around the head and the pelvis, and the richer the grave, the more ochre is found. It is really surprising that such strongly coloured ochre graves were not discovered earlier. In the deep double grave from Gøngehusvej no.7 two layers of ochre were also recorded at the top of the grave pit.

The red ochre can vary considerably in colour and intensity from grave to grave, depending, perhaps, on the temperature at which it was produced and the Iron Oxide thus formed. From minerological and chemical studies of various samples it can, however, be seen that the red ochre was always locally produced.

Under excavation it can be difficult to define the red ochre exactly in relation to the skeleton. For the same reason, the interpretation of the occurrence of ochre in the graves is a much debated problem. Does it derive from skin clothing and hides that were originally treated with this colouring to tan them and conserve them, or is it a funerary ritual? In

Gøngehusvej no.7, Vedbæk. Dog's grave?

favour of the former is the fact that the red ochre can have a well-defined distribution within the grave and on the skeleton so that the pulverized ochre cannot have been powdered over the body. In favour of the latter is the occurrence of large quantities of ochre and flint flakes with ochre gloss in some graves.

In the great majority of cases we have to suppose that the dead were buried in their clothing. This is shown first and foremost by the location of the tools and jewellery around the skeletons. It is also interesting that all age groups are now represented, from babies two months premature and children of all ages through adults to the elderly of about 50 years old. Thus variation in equipment in which sex and age especially play their role appears.

From the grave goods, we can divide the people

Nederst grave 6. Child's grave with flint knife and tooth pendants.

Nederst grave 2. Man's grave with axes, flint knives, arrowheads and tooth pendants.

into three categories - unfurnished; with some grave goods; with rich grave goods - even though the state of nature they lived in makes it difficult to measure wealth. The absence of personal equipment may not always be a sign of poverty; other factors may be in play too. It is possible that the eldest no longer carried distinguishing equipment, or perhaps they could not be buried with it. The oldest woman from Bøgebakken, for instance, was found with no personal equipment at all but was still laid on a set of antlers like only two others at Bøgebakken.

In another case from Bøgebakken, grave 9, an adult man was buried with only a single red deer tooth bead while the woman in grave 8 - the grave that his grave was an extension of and with whom, therefore, he may have been connected - had jewel-

79

lery with tooth pendants from at least 37 red deer (Brinch Petersen 1979b). In contrast to this, however, stands the oldest man buried at Nederst (grave 2), who had not only a greenstone axe, a flake axe and a deer antler axe but also two large knives, six transverse arrowheads and a fine set of tooth pendants.

Persons of all age groups are found without grave goods but if several were buried together there are always some grave goods with the adults at least, though often with the children too. With this no view whatsoever is expressed on whether the other persons, adult or infant, were obliged to accompany the first into the grave. Apart from the cases where a newborn baby lies with a young woman, it is practically impossible to give any cause of death for the deceased. The exception is (of course) the slain occupant of grave 19 at Bøgebakken. Although it is especially adults that are distinguished by rich grave goods, there are two interesting 3- or 6-year-olds, apparently boys, who fall into the rich category and who thus may reveal a heritage system in society.

Ertebølle 1896. Man's grave, now C 14-dated to 4200-4100 B.C. (K 4933).

One is the child's grave from Nederst (grave 6) and the other the new double grave from Gøngehusvej no.7 in Vedbæk.

The richest men's graves are the following four: Fannerup and Nederst grave 2, both on Djursland, and Bøgebakken grave 6 and Strøby Egede by the east coast of Sjælland. Each of these contains an antler axe, a couple of which are in fact decorated. There are also several flint knives, often very long, and other flint, bone and tooth objects varying from grave to grave.

Children, men and women could all wear flint knives. Some newborn children, however, seem most likely to have been buried with heirlooms: large knives and axes. From the age of 3, children can carry flint knives like adults. These flint knives are either long, pointed blades or broad truncated ones. A study of use-wear has shown that these are used tools such as food or skinning knives and knives for paring wood (Juel Jensen 1982).

The incisors, canines and upper canines *(Grandeln)* of red deer - the most common large game of the time - are the commonest element in jewellery at the time. Teeth of wild boar, dog, Man, aurochs, elk, bear and maybe wolf too were used for tooth beads. There are also whole sets of red-deer, roe-deer and dog teeth used, as well as jaws of red deer, pine marten and polecat. Perforated snail shells of the species *Neritina fluviatilis balthica* have been found in one grave, and on one occasion a bone-like white stone with a natural hole for suspension was used as a special bead.

Quite different natural objects have also been found with those buried, such as hooves and the lower ends of fore- and hindlegs, and the astragalus, all of roe deer. A wing of a bird the size of a jackdaw was used, while ducks' feet and the beaks of grebe also occur. Small pieces of unworked amber have been found in a couple of graves, and on one occasion a piece of iron pyrites. Such items can very reasonably be regarded as amuletic.

The richest women's graves are Nederst grave 5, the double grave from Dragsholm, and Bøgebakken grave 8. In these we can see, amongst other things, that the women used tooth beads in arm-bands and around the neck and breast, and for the richest individuals also in a girdle of 60-90 beads, ranged according to size and gathered into clusters. A couple of these belts also contained several hundred perforated snail shells (Brinch Petersen 1979b). In these belts, which have only been found on Sjælland so far in Denmark but which are also found in Skåne (L. Larsson 1988), there is always one exotic tooth (Vang Petersen 1990). Bear, aurochs and elk had long disappeared from Sjælland by the Ertebølle Period but still lived in Jutland, Skåne and the Baltic area (cf. Aaris-Sørensen, above). This then may reveal a connexion between Sjælland and these areas.

A few men and one child wore a fore-girdle comprising tooth beads from wild boar, aurochs and red deer. With small children, tooth beads may be found on the head as if they were sewn on to a hat or bonnet.

While the deer-antler axe was a male accessory, the woman's grave from Nederst (grave 5) and that from Bäckaskog in Skåne (Rydbeck 1945; Gejval 1970) now show that the slotted bone point has to be regarded as a female item. The young woman from Dragsholm who, as well as tooth beads, had an ornamentally perforated bone skinning knife, also shows that it will probably be possible in the future not only to relate the various items of jewellery but also bone and antler tools and their decoration to sex, age, status and group (Newell *et al.* 1990; Brinch Petersen 1991). Even with the flint tools, it appears to be possible to differentiate male from female types and between men's and women's knives.

Generally, the mesolithic population can be characterized as healthy and robust, with few traces of chronic diseases except for arthritis, which increases with age. The average height was about 168 cm. for men and around 155 cm. for women. Compared with modern Danes, the mesolithic folk were smaller and more robustly built (Bennike & Alexandersen 1990). The average lifespan was about 35 years, but there are individuals who reached an age of 50 to 60.

In the skeletal material there are no signs of malnutrition, and isotopic analyses show that the diet was predominantly marine (cf. Tauber, above). The teeth, correspondingly, show absolutely no sign of decay (cf. Alexandersen, below). Traces of direct violence occur in a couple of cases, with the slain occupant of grave 19 at Bøgebakken to be noted in first place. This was a case of a frontal arrow shot so precisely targeted that it looks very like an execution. Several skeletons show signs of blows to the head without these lesions having been fatal (Bennike 1985a). Such traces of killing and violence should perhaps be interpreted as reflecting considerable population density (Meiklejohn & Zwelebil 1991).

Teeth - health, disease and use

The most striking feature of the mesolithic population's dentistry is their worn teeth. In children as young as 5 or 6, worn milk teeth are seen, and children later began to use their teeth for biting, gripping and softening hide.

Something similar to the flattening of a leather strap can be seen in the smoothed inner sides of the upper front teeth; this is found with various adults of both sexes. Later in life the front teeth were worn down to flat chewing surfaces, and with the oldest individuals only the rounded roots are left.

With adult males we see larger and smaller breaks in teeth at the front and the corner of the mouth. This is certainly due to the teeth being used to hold working material; the front teeth are commonly more worn on one side rather than the other, reflecting a favoured side for biting. Women more often show uniform wear of all the front teeth, canines and the foremost side teeth, corresponding to wear from working with hides.

Age-governed wear on the front teeth is substantial for both sexes but appears earlier with women. The side teeth, however, wore slowly, so the Stone-age hunters had few teeth with clear cavities revealing the pulpa nerve and few lost their front teeth. However a great deal of scratching and chipping of the surface of the teeth is evident.

Verner Alexandersen

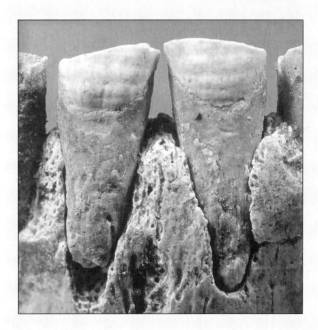

Newborn infants thrived on their mothers' milk, but at the age of 3 to 6, when the teeth are especially sensitive to external factors, disruption of enamel formation (enamel hypoplasia) often occurs in the teeth, revealing a less healthy situation. In general, however, the diet was good and wholesome.

THE NEOLITHIC

The Neolithic

BY POUL OTTO NIELSEN

Before the beginning of the Neolithic in Denmark, knowledge of cultivation and pastoralism spread slowly from the Near East, Asia Minor and south-eastern Europe to the rest of the European continent apart from the northernmost areas. From *ca.* 5400 B.C. an early agricultural culture appeared in Central Europe, the *Bandkeramik* Culture, whose population lived in village-like communities and dwelt in large, timber-built longhouses. The successors to this farming population moved further north between 5000 and 4000 B.C. and settled along the rivers that flow into the North Sea and the Baltic: the Rhine, Elbe and Oder. They were in contact with the hunting and fishing population of the Ertebølle Culture in southern Scandinavia who amongst other things learnt to produce pottery as a result of these contacts. One of the topics that has concerned archaeologists in the last dozen years indeed is possible influence on our local, late Ertebølle Culture at the end of the Mesolithic, before the farming culture could really establish itself here in the North. The importation of the so-called Danubian shaft-hole axes from Central Europe has been interpreted as evidence of gift-exchange - primitive trading connexions - which in time provided both the technology and the knowledge that was needed to practise agriculture (A. Fischer 1983; Jennbert 1984).

Was the introduction of agriculture the result of cultural influence or colonization? It has always been hard to answer this question categorically. We lack, for instance, sufficient finds of human remains from the periods before and after the introduction of agriculture. In the long perspective, there are clear differences in physique between the hunting and farming populations. But is this due to differences in ancestry or in circumstances? Earlier research assumed that the Ertebølle Culture continued to exist far into the Neolithic (C.J. Becker 1955a). This question can now be answered definitively. To begin with, a large number of C 14 datings show insignificant overlap between the Ertebølle and Funnel Beaker Cultures (Tauber 1988). Secondly, recent years' excavations of kitchen middens have shown quite a sharp differentiation between layers of the late Ertebølle Culture and the early Funnel Beaker Culture, C 14-dated to around 3900 B.C. (S.H. Andersen 1991, 1993).

Was this change in subsistence and culture the result of internal pressures, environmental changes, or both of these? One possible factor is population growth matching the growing coastal food resources in the Atlantic Period, forcing some of the population to move inland where agriculture was an alternative to the Ertebølle Culture's traditional, coastal subsistence strategy (Paludan-Müller 1978). A second possible factor might be changes in the natural environment. The end of the Ertebølle Culture coincides with the beginning of a new climatic period, the Sub-Boreal, which began with a fall in temperature and a fall in sea-level. This may have changed the conditions in which the coastal population lived in such a way that they were compelled to seek other subsistence strategies (Rowley-Conwy 1985b:194). The intensive gathering of oysters, for instance, ceased (S.H. Andersen 1991:38), and this may be a symptom of more extensive changes in the coastal environment.

All the same, the old hunting and fishing sites of the Ertebølle Culture continued to be used by the early farming population, who supplemented agriculture by hunting and fishing for a long time (Skaarup 1973). This is one of the features that is interpreted as evidence of continuity from the Ertebølle to the Funnel Beaker Culture. Despite the appearance of new tool-types and pottery-forms, we can also - for instance in the mastery of flintwork - see more signs of linkage between the two cultures than of a break.

C 14 datings have added several centuries to the duration of the Neolithic and have also significantly affected the dating of the individual cultures in relation to one another. But new chronological lines have also been produced by more traditional methods. Within the Funnel Beaker Culture the pottery chronology that was worked out in the 1950's (C.J. Becker 1947, 1955a) has been developed, producing new phases and groupings. Different labels and identificational criteria are now in use for some of the periods: see the diagram opposite.

The Early Neolithic (EN) was divided into three phases, EN A, B and C, on the basis of pottery finds 45 years ago (C.J. Becker 1947). We now have a more intricate image of the developments, and talk more about "groups", some of which are geographically specific and some chronological. The original phase A, now called the "A group" or the "Oxie Group", was distributed in the eastern, coastal areas of Jutland, on the Danish islands and in Skåne (P.O. Nielsen 1985a). The remains of the A Group appear, *inter alia,* in the earliest Neolithic layers of Jutlandic

C 14 YEARS B.C.	3000	2500	2000	1500
CULTURES	ERTEBØLLE · FUNNEL BEAKER CULTURE		SINGLE GRAVE CULTURE · PITTED WARE	BELL BEAKER

	EARLY NEOLITHIC			MIDDLE NEOLITHIC									LATE NEOLITHIC			BRONZE AGE	PERIODS
MESOLITHIC	A	B	C	A					B				A	B	C		
	I		II	Ia	Ib	II	III (-IV)	V	I	II	III		I		II		
	Svale-klint / Volling / Oxie		Fuchsberg/Virum	Troldebjerg	Klintebakke	Blandebjerg	Bundsø	St Valby	Bottom grave period	Ground grave period	Upper grave period		FLINT DAGGER TYPES I II III IV V				

CALENDAR YEARS B.C.	4000	3500	3000	2500	2000	1700

Diagram of Danish Neolithic chronology based on about 400 C 14 datings. Calibration to calendar years following Pearson et al. *1986 and Pearson & Stuiver 1986.*

kitchen middens (S.H. Andersen 1993). Amongst newly found settlement sites are several small ones and one large one, Sigersted on Sjælland (P.O. Nielsen 1985a). A man's grave that was found near Dragsholm in 1974 is still the only known burial of the A Group (Brinch Petersen 1974). In Jutland, the majority of the finds from the earlier EN are assigned to the Volling Group (Ebbesen & Mahler 1980; T. Madsen & Petersen 1984), including the finds from the earliest long barrows with timber structures (see below). Various labels are given to finds related to the Volling Group on the Danish islands: the B Group (P.O. Nielsen 1993), the Havnelev Group and the Svaleklint Group (Ebbesen & Mahler 1980; E. Koch 1990).

The last phase of the Early Neolithic, EN C or EN II, can now be described much more clearly than hitherto thanks to new finds, including the large causewayed camps of the Sarup type (see below). A characteristic pottery style, the Fuchsberg style, appears in western Denmark in this period (N.H. Andersen & Madsen 1978). Its eastern counterpart is the Virum style (C.J. Becker 1947:151ff.; Ebbesen & Mahler 1980). The decorated pottery of the megalith period first developed in this period. The earliest megalith graves, the dolmens, were raised in EN C.

Two new structural types have added important details to the picture of the EN culture: the long barrows with timber structures and the causewayed camps. The former have long been known in, for instance, the British Isles, northern Germany and Poland, but they were first recognized and studied in Denmark in the last 25 years (T. Madsen, below). The long barrows testify to the emergence of an elite given monumental burial already in very early farming society.

The causewayed camps have roughly the same European distribution as the long barrows, and again are a feature that has long been known abroad. As N.H. Andersen's contribution to this volume shows, these are surprisingly large structural works where special rituals took place. The use of Sarup sites ran from EN C to around the middle of MN A.

Today, the Early Neolithic strikes us as an era characterized by dynamic expansion. The land lay open to agricultural pioneers who shared their lifestyle with other groups living at the same time in other parts of Europe. There were common traits in methods of cultivation, in the organization of society and in religion. External connexions included exchange of goods, very probably for "political" rather than economic purposes. The earliest imported copper artefacts arrived in this period (Randsborg 1979; Menke 1989). Metal objects had no great practical importance, and did not inspire any local metal production. They should be set alongside the other luxury or prestigious items that were circulating in the Early Neolithic. Amongst these belong the thousands of locally made amber beads and super-large flint axes that are known in hoards and as loose finds (P.O. Nielsen 1979a). The surplus was "wasted" in ceremonial sacrifices and sunk in bogs and lakes, a fate shared by some animals and people (Ebbesen, below). In the course of the Early Neolithic a society developed that was strongly governed in the social and religious fields and was apparently characterized by surplus production. At the same time there was an agricultural expansion, producing a more open landscape by the end of the period (S.Th. Andersen, below).

The early part of the Middle Neolithic, MN A, is dominated by the material from large settlements and the passage graves, most of which seem to have been raised in Period Ib. New grave-types have appeared from Periods II-V: simple burials on the islands (Lund Hansen 1974; Liversage 1981) and stone-packing graves in Jutland (E. Jørgensen, below). The number of cult houses from the passage-grave period, known in Jutland since the mid-1950's, has increased as a result of continued investigations (C.J. Becker, below). The finds from the passage graves are treated in new syntheses that are especially concerned with the development and geographical variation of pottery styles (Ebbesen 1975, 1978a, 1979a; Gebauer 1979). The construction of the passage graves has been illuminated by recent years' investigations associated with the restoration of protected monuments (S. Hansen 1993), while the find material has been added to particularly through the excavation of ploughed-out sites (Skaarup, below). The last phase of the Funnel Beaker Culture, Period V, has been subjected to thorough new studies (Davidsen 1978). Period IV is now weakly represented in the picture, with no finds in the last 25 years. A late local development of the Funnel Beaker Culture on Bornholm was identified in the 1980's through the excavation of house-remains from this period (P.O. Nielsen, below).

One of the most hotly debated questions has been the relationship between the Funnel Beaker and Single Grave Cultures, previously regarded as contemporaneous. We can now say that each belongs largely to its own phase of the Neolithic, only overlapped for a short period (Tauber 1986a), and that development in the transitional phase varied from area to area in Denmark. A number of works published between 1977 and 1980 have contributed to this new picture of cultural development, with new datings, new stratigraphic studies and new analyses of the finds (e.g. Lomborg 1977b; Malmros & Tauber 1977; Davidsen 1977, 1982a; P.O. Nielsen 1979b; Malmros 1980; Ebbesen 1982a).

The beginning of the Single Grave Culture around 2800 B.C., at the transition from MN A to MN B, is now regarded as the beginning of a new expansion in subsistence and settlement. New palae-ovegetational studies show that the Single Grave settlement in Jutland was accompanied by forest clearance and evidence of extensive agriculture with the main emphasis on animal husbandry (S.Th. Andersen, below). The grave finds, which are quite predominant as a source for our knowledge of the Single Grave Culture, indicate that a period with changed social relations and clearer individual marking than before began at the same time. In subsistence terms, the break in development here can also be believed to coincide with changed natural circumstances. It is perhaps in light of this that we should assess the intrusion of Pitted Ware settlements along the coasts in the early Single Grave Period. New Pitted Ware settlements on Djursland (L.W. Rasmussen, below) provide an insight into a very diverse subsistence pattern, based not least on rich natural resources.

In the broad perspective, a new era began with the Single Grave Culture. To emphasize this, some use a new term: the "Younger Neolithic", synonymous with the "Single Grave Period" (Ebbesen 1978a:116f.). Like the early Funnel Beaker Culture, this new culture rose on common European foundations. Did the Single Grave Culture come to Denmark as a result of migration? Discussion of this question has started again (Kristiansen 1991b).

New datings show that the Late Neolithic must have lasted a considerable time, around 600 years. The period is divided either into three phases, LN A, B and C (Lomborg 1973a), or two, LN I and II (Vandkilde 1989a). Connexions with north-western Europe in particular, including the British Isles, now brought metal objects to Denmark in the form of simple copper axes and, for the first time, gold. At

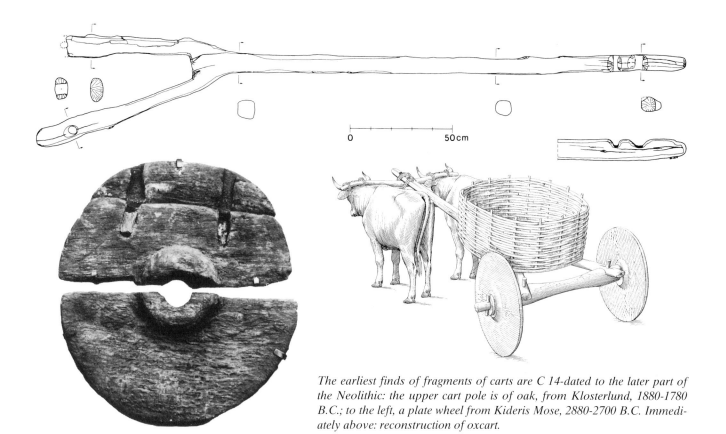

The earliest finds of fragments of carts are C 14-dated to the later part of the Neolithic: the upper cart pole is of oak, from Klosterlund, 1880-1780 B.C.; to the left, a plate wheel from Kideris Mose, 2880-2700 B.C. Immediately above: reconstruction of oxcart.

the end of the period, in LN C/LN II, metal objects began to be produced in Denmark, and the quantity of these grew at the expense of flint tools and weapons. We still need comprehensive studies of the many Late-neolithic finds, to which new grave finds have added (Hansen & Rostholm, below). The settlements of the period have produced new evidence, particularly on building construction; an unknown area 25 years ago (P.O. Nielsen, below).

The basic features of the development through the Neolithic have become clearer thanks to absolute datings. The relative chronology has also been improved through specialized studies of specific artefact-types such as flint axes (C.J. Becker 1974; P.O. Nielsen 1979a,b; Ebbesen 1983a), stone axes (Ebbesen 1985c), battle axes and clubs (Ebbesen 1975, 1978a, 1988) and flint daggers (Lomborg 1973a). It has also been possible to date finds by the C 14 method that could not be dated by purely archaeological methods. The earliest cartwheels, for instance, have been dated to *ca.* 2800 B.C., in agreement with datings of the earliest pieces of wagons, in Holland for instance, to the beginning of the Single Grave Period (Rostholm 1978). The construction of brushwood tracks, formed of layers of twigs that are held in place by vertical stakes, can now be traced

back to the Early and Middle Neolithic on Sjælland (Elverhøj Veje: V. Hansen & Nielsen 1979; Tibirke Vej: Malmros 1986). The use of dug-outs in the Neolithic is well-illuminated by the re-assessment and dating of earlier finds. In contrast to most mesolithic boats, the neolithic examples are found in inland lakes and bogs (C. Christensen 1990). New finds of fishing weirs at the coast, some of considerable size, are dated to the Early and Middle Neolithic (L. Pedersen 1992).

Important contributions to the understanding of cultivation methods, resource-use and technology in the Neolithic have emerged from experimental archaeology in recent years. A series of experiments in flint technology in particular have made valuable contributions to analyses of prehistoric working methods (B. Madsen, below).

The conditions of human life and social relations changed comprehensively with the introduction of agriculture. Was this for the better? The view has modified under the influence of ethnographic studies both of the life of gatherers and hunters (Sahlins 1972) and of working conditions in present farming communities (Boserup 1965). Were our first farmers tied by their culture more than the hunters were to Nature?

Early agriculture

By Svend Th. Andersen

The most reliable evidence of the introduction of agriculture to Denmark is remains of crops and farm animals found at settlement sites. New research has significantly increased our knowledge of these aspects of early agriculture.

We have now found einkorn, emmer, wheat and naked and hulled barley from the Early-neolithic Funnel Beaker Culture, with emmer dominant (Hjelmquist 1975; G. Jørgensen 1977; Rowley-Conwy 1979). We can also note new cereal finds of the Middle-neolithic Funnel Beaker Culture. Emmer and einkorn were the commonest types, and barley first became important in the final phase (G. Jørgensen & Fredskild 1978; Rowley-Conwy 1979; G. Jørgensen 1982; Rostholm 1987).

Grain impressions and charred grain show that barley was the leading cereal of the Single Grave Period (Rostholm 1986a; Robinson & Kempfner 1988), and barley continued to dominate in the Late Neolithic, when spelt wheat also appears (G. Jørgensen 1982).

Remains of domesticated animals such as cattle, pig and sheep or goat are known from several Early-neolithic settlements. Pigs were gradually superseded by cattle and to a degree by sheep or goat in the Middle-neolithic Funnel Beaker Culture (T. Madsen 1982). Farm-animal remains of the Single Grave Period are as yet lacking. Finds from eastern Danish settlements (Rowley-Conwy 1985a; J. Richter in Hedeager & Kristiansen 1988) show cattle to be dominant, and pig and sheep to be rare.

Settlement finds thus show a change in early cereal cultivation, with wheats yielding to barley in the Middle and Late Neolithic and domestic pig giving way to cattle in the Middle Neolithic.

Field traces

Marks found under grave mounds show that the ard was in use from the final phase of the Early Neolithic (Thrane 1991a). The ardmarks are usually ascribed to cultivation preceding the construction of the barrow, and signs of ritual ploughing are rare (Kristiansen 1990; Thrane 1991a). Usually only one set of criss-crossing ploughmarks is found, more rarely several sets. This could be evidence of extensive agriculture with short periods of cultivation (Hedeager & Kristiansen 1988: 47; Thrane 1991a:118).

Forest clearance in Eastern Denmark and North Jutland

To learn more about the use of natural resources in early agriculture we must turn to pollen analyses of layers from lakes and bogs.

Pollen analyses from lakes and bogs larger than 100-200 m. produce a representative regional picture of the landscape within a 10-km. radius. Pollen diagrams showing the impact of early agriculture have been known and discussed for many years. A problem has been the lack of precise datings. Consequently, the production of C 14-dated pollen diagrams has been an essential task in the last 20 years (S.Th. Andersen et al. 1983).

A starting point for discussion has been a fall in the pollen curve for elm dated to between 4000 and 3800 B.C. and contemporary with the earliest settlement finds of grain and domesticated animals, while traces of earlier agriculture (Kolstrup 1988) are vague and unreliable. The decline of elm has been attributed to exploitation of leaf-fodder for farm animals (Troels-Smith 1953) but no new evidence to throw light on this has appeared (P. Rasmussen 1990).

Shortly after the decline of elm, there are regular changes in pollen curves in eastern Denmark known as 'the landnam': a peak of birch, then one of hazel, and the occurrence of cereal pollen, ribwort and other weeds originally attributed to the burning of the forest, cereal cultivation, grazing and forest regeneration in several stages (Iversen 1941). It later became clear that hazel woods must have been

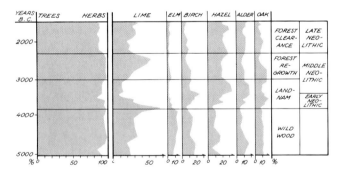

Early agriculture in the area around Fuglsø Mose on Djursland. In the Early Neolithic, elm was cleared, but lime peaked and birch, hazel, alder and oak increased. Herbaceous pollen scores are low. In the Middle Neolithic, lime is cleared, and hazel and alder replace birch. Herbaceous pollen scores increase. Late in the Middle Neolithic, the lime forest reappeared, and herbaceous pollen scores are very low. In the Late Neolithic, lime is cleared and herbaceous pollen scores

maintained for considerable periods and were not simply a transitional phase in reforestation (Iversen 1967: 419). Newly dated pollen diagrams (Aaby 1985, 1986, 1988) confirm this. The peak of birch begins shortly after the decline of elm and coincides with the Early-neolithic Funnel Beaker Culture (3900-3300 B.C.) while the peak of hazel is contemporary with the Middle-neolithic Funnel Beaker Culture (3300-2800 B.C.).

Characteristic of Early-neolithic agriculture in eastern Denmark, then, is the decline of elm, a flourishing of birch, and a lesser increase in hazel, alder and oak, while lime remains unchanged or peaks, and herbaceous plants are weakly represented. The decline of elm can be explained by the clearance of elm from damp sites in favour of oak (and hazel) for pannage and grass for grazing (T. Madsen 1982). The peak of birch might reflect repeated burning (Aaby 1986), but the very low herbaceous pollen values do not indicate the creation of large grazing areas.

The great Middle-neolithic peak of hazel in eastern Denmark shows that lime forest was then extensively being cleared in favour of hazel coppices. Grazing areas increased at the same time, while cereal cultivation still makes little impact on regional pollen diagrams.

The decline of hazel and re-establishment of lime forest coincides with the end of the Middle-neolithic Funnel Beaker Culture. These features recur in several eastern Danish pollen diagrams, showing that some districts were abandoned and agricultural areas given up. On Djursland, besides forest clearance in the Single Grave Period (Troels-Smith 1942), new clearances of the Late Neolithic have been found (Aaby 1985, 1988).

On the boulder clay areas of Thy, the decline of elm, and the peaks of birch and hazel in the Early- and Middle-neolithic Funnel Beaker Cultures, recur (S.Th. Andersen et al. 1991). At the beginning of the Single Grave Culture (2800 B.C.) there was sudden and drastic forest clearance. Hazel declined severely and wild grasses, ribwort and other herbaceous plants became common. At this point the coppice-based agriculture of the Funnel Beaker Culture was abruptly superseded by that of the Single Grave Culture which was based primarily on large open grazing lands and a small amount of cereal cultivation. The rapidity of the clearance indicates the arrival of a new population, the Single Grave people (Kristiansen 1991b), a supposition which is strengthened

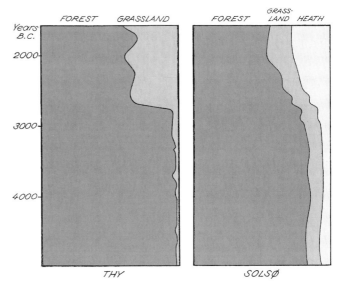

Single Grave Culture forest clearances in Thy and western Jutland (Solsø) ca. 2800 B.C. In Thy there was great expansion of grazing areas; at Solsø it was heather heath in particular that increased as a result of the expansion of agriculture.

by the sudden change in land use. In the Haderslev area, at the eastern edge of the heath tracts, there was a similar but less violent change, with less extensive forest clearance (Aaby 1988).

Early agriculture of the heaths of western Jutland

A new element appears in the heathlands of western Jutland, the heather heath. The emergence and age of this have long been discussed. Pollen studies of western Jutlandic lakes have provided relevant new evidence (Odgaard 1985, 1988, 1990, 1991a-b).

The primeval forest here originally contained the same species as in eastern Denmark, but was significantly more open with more birch, heather and grass. Some traces of forest clearance are seen as early as the Early Neolithic, with an increase in heather, grass and ribwort and weak traces of cereal cultivation, but these were small-scale up through the Middle-neolithic Funnel Beaker Culture. There is certainly no sign of the 'landnam' phases characteristic of eastern Denmark. With the introduction of the Single Grave Culture (2800 B.C.) there was extensive forest destruction and expansion of heath- and grassland, especially near Solsø (Odgaard 1991b). This cultural impact continued in the Late Neolithic.

As B. Odgaard has shown, the open forests here offered good conditions for grazing farm animals, with grass the most important fodder in summer and heather in winter. Forest clearance of the Single

89

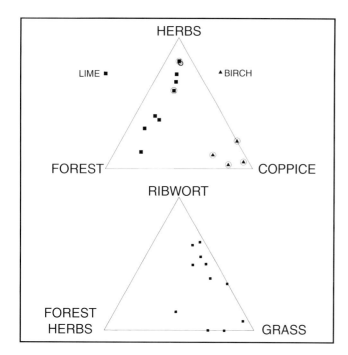

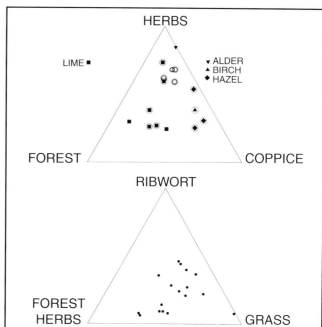

These two scattergrams show the cultural landscape (above) and land-use (below) in the Early Neolithic on the basis of pollen analyses from soil in grave mounds. The circles show soils from which tree-cover has been burnt off. The cultural landscape comprised forest, secondary coppice woodland and open land dominated by herbaceous plants. There were lime forests in the neighbourhood of the barrows which were raised in clearings in the lime forests created without burning. In other cases, birch wood was burnt off shortly before the barrows were built. Ribwort was very common in the open areas that were used for intensive grazing of domesticated animals.

In the Middle Neolithic, there were still patches of lime forest near the barrows, and these were cleared by burning. Secondary coppice woodland, especially hazel but sometimes of alder or birch, or mixed coppice of hazel and lime, was also burnt off to produce open areas dominated by herbaceous plants. Forest herbs were common in the coppices, and ribwort was less frequent than in the Early Neolithic, indicating lesser pressure from grazing.

Grave Culture indicates increasing population pressure. Cereal cultivation is evidenced, but animal husbandry was probably the most important agricultural activity.

Land-use in early agriculture

Regional pollen analyses give an averaged view of the changes that early agriculture caused in the forest and landscape in an area within a certain range of the bog or the lake. The forests were mosaics of different tree communities at this time, but these cannot be distinguished; spatially and chronologically discrete agricultural activities are generalized too. Better resolution for such detail comes with pollen diagrams from small forest bogs (S.Th. Andersen 1984, 1985, 1991c).

The sharpest spatial and chronological picture is obtained from pollen analyses of contemporary ground surfaces. Pollen analyses from a sealed layer of brown earth give a picture of the local vegetation,

which is narrowly delimited in space and time. In more acid soils such as mor humus or podzol the pollen grains are preserved longer, and can show sequential changes in the local vegetation. Brown earth layers and podzol sections are preserved under barrows, which themselves are built out of material dug from the immediately surrounding ground. Pollen analyses from the ground beneath the barrows and from the barrows' fill therefore give a well-focussed picture of the conditions at the site where the barrow was constructed and in its surroundings when it was raised. Archaeological excavations and C 14 datings provide precise datings of the barrows. Since, as a rule, these were raised in open terrain, we can use pollen analyses to obtain a new and unexpected view of human land-use.

A hitherto unobserved point is that pollen grains that are heated change their appearance, with the pollen wall swelling up as much as threefold (S.Th. Andersen 1988). When trees are felled and burnt, the pollen grains that were in the uppermost soil layer are deformed by the heat from the fire. Deformed pollen grains thus unambiguously testify to burning on the site, and are often found in the soil together with unaffected pollen from the subsequent vegetation. It was earlier thought that swidden cultivation was practised in early agriculture (Iversen 1941), but it has also been argued that there is no sign of this in regional pollen diagrams (Rowley-Conwy 1981). Pollen analyses from the soils provide a new opportunity to examine this problem (S.Th. Andersen 1990).

Pollen analyses are now known from soil layers and the fill of 6 Early-neolithic burial mounds (S.Th. Andersen 1992 and forthcoming). Two forest-types are represented, lime and birch. Lime dominated the original primeval forests on dry ground (S.Th. Andersen 1984). In these lime forests, clearings were formed by felling, and these areas were used for intensive cattle grazing. Open grazing areas were thus already used at the beginning of agriculture in Denmark, though the regional pollen diagrams show that the lime forest was not reduced and that the grazing areas were small. Pure birch forest on dry land must have emerged after the original lime forest was cleared. Birch spreads profusely in cleared forest areas and reproduces itself easily after burning by self-seeding. Traces of cereal cultivation following the burning off of areas of birch have been found, indicating that these birch woods were the basis for swidden cultivation as has been the case in Finland in modern times. The peak of birch in the Early Neolithic in the regional pollen diagrams can therefore now be explained as the result of extensive swidden cultivation.

Pollen analyses from the ground under Middle-neolithic grave structures, two dolmens and five passage graves, show substantial changes in land-use. We still find traces of lime forest, but above all communities rich in hazel. This vegetation represents secondary coppice woodland with bracken and mugwort, most of which was cleared by fire. Traces of cereal cultivation are found, but most cleared coppice woodland was subsequently used to graze cattle. Middle-neolithic Funnel Beaker-culture agriculture was thus shifting coppice agriculture, in which secondary coppice woodland was used for short-term cereal cultivation and subsequently for grazing. This coppice woodland probably regenerated by sprouting from the stumps. Land-use was extensive, hence the high peak of hazel in the regional pollen diagrams.

In soil sections from beneath Single Grave barrows in western Jutland, pollen from earlier brown earth phases is buried in the sand by burrowing animals and the sand was covered by mor humus (-Odgaard 1985, 1988, 1990). The original forests of lime, hazel, birch and alder were used for grazing during the Funnel Beaker Culture, and shortly before the raising of the barrows the heather heath was extended and renewed by burning. It was earlier supposed that these heaths spread over abandoned fields, but no traces of cereal cultivation are found in the soil sections, and ardmarks are rare in western Jutland (Rostholm 1987; Thrane 1991a). The new results show that heather heath rather emerged from the burning of forests and was used for grazing as early as the Single Grave Period.

Future perspectives

The natural sciences have made substantial contributions to the understanding of early agriculture, and Danish research in this field has been fundamental in international discussion. There has, however, also been a certain lull, and a growing level of criticism has made its mark (see Rowley-Conwy 1981, 1982; T. Madsen 1982). New initiatives can contribute to changing this situation.

It is especially important for palaeobotanical participation in archaeological settlement-site studies to be intensified, so that the opportunity to get a fuller picture of the subsistence basis of early agriculture is exploited.

The new, regional pollen diagrams have provided knowledge which enables new participation in the debate at the international level. But the east of Denmark is very sparsely covered, with one dated pollen diagram from Sjælland and two from eastern Jutland. Even the regional pollen diagrams are affected by local cultural developments that varied from district to district. At a national level, our knowledge of land-use in early agriculture is therefore seriously incomplete. This applies not least to the Single Grave Culture and the Late-neolithic expansion in eastern Denmark. Both the national and the international need for new studies is clear.

A new initiative, pollen analyses of soil horizons from burial mounds, is a promising prospect. Denmark is rich in barrows from nearly all periods of prehistory and almost all of these are suitable for pollen analysis. The potential here is, therefore, virtually limitless.

Settlement

BY POUL OTTO NIELSEN

The rich finds of the Neolithic in Denmark have not only spawned much research and publication on individual finds and complexes in the last 25 years but have also encouraged a series of studies of the settlement and its development. Contributing to this has been the renewed interest in settlement archaeology that emerged in the mid-1970's (Thrane 1974, 1976). Work in this research area was done both in narrowly focussed and large regional areas, sometimes covering all of prehistory, sometimes concentrating on the Neolithic or specific problems in this period: see the map on this page.

New topographic and geological maps, especially the Ministry of Agriculture's soil map of 1979, formed the basis for mapping, while older topographical maps helped to add to the number of ancient monuments and to provide a better starting point for reconstructing the landscape (Knudsen 1982). The problem of the representativity of the archaeological sources was taken up at the same time both in connexion with the new settlement excavations and in relation to research history (cf. Kristiansen (ed.) 1985).

The largest comprehensive publication of finds from museums, private collections and excavations is the survey of the Neolithic on the islands south of

Fyn, which are amongst the best studied areas of Denmark for this period (Skaarup 1985). In other areas, it has been possible to increase weaker sources significantly by new registration (S. Jensen 1984; Skamby Madsen 1984; F.O. Nielsen 1988). The potential and problems of fieldwork are clearly revealed by the experience of the south-western Fyn settlement project (Thrane 1989:21-4). Examples of analyses of settlement come from south-western Fyn and eastern Jutland, where different settlement-types have been identified and the relationship between their position and the topography has been worked out in order to produce a settlement model (N.H. Andersen 1981; T. Madsen 1982).

Studies of the internal structure of neolithic settlements are unfortunately still very few. Again we have to refer to eastern Jutland, where analyses of activity areas have been made on the strength of structures and find-distributions at two Funnel Beaker Culture settlements, at Mosegården and Hanstedgård, in one case alongside functional analyses of the flint tools (T. Madsen & Juel Jensen 1982; Eriksen & Madsen 1984).

The development of settlement

In the Early Neolithic, at the beginning especially, we find relatively small sites that are situated by preference on light soil or in areas with varying soil-types. This agrees with the picture that pollen analyses provide of a population employing swidden cultivation and moving round in small groups. The settlement at Mosegården in eastern Jutland, for instance, occupied an area of only 500-600 sq.m. (T. Madsen & Juel Jensen 1982:65). The settlement at Mosegården was preserved because it was subsequently covered by a long barrow. This applies to several other Early-neolithic settlements too, and suggests that grave mounds were deliberately raised on the levelled remains of a settlement. In some cases, the later long barrows

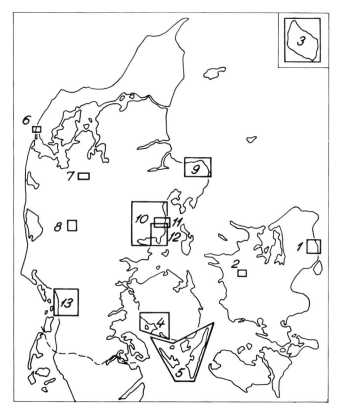

The more important local and regional studies that have contributed to our knowledge of settlement in the Neolithic: 1. Søllerød and Lyngby-Tårbæk districts (Knudsen 1982); 2. Store Åmose (K. Andersen 1983; A. Fischer 1985c); 3. Bornholm (F.O. Nielsen 1988); 4. south-western Fyn (Thrane 1989); 5. the islands south of Fyn (Skaarup 1985); 6. Lodbjerg (Liversage 1988); 7. Vroue Hede - Sjørup Plantage (E. Jørgensen 1977a); 8. Skarrild (Rostholm 1977); 9. northern Djursland (Vedsted 1986); 10. East Jutland (T. Madsen 1982); 11. Norsminde Fjord (S.H. Andersen 1976); 12. Hads herred (Skamby Madsen 1984); 13. the Ribe area (S. Jensen 1984).

were mistakenly identified as remains of longhouses, as at Barkær on Djursland (Glob 1975; Liversage 1992) and probably too at Stengade (Skaarup 1975). No certain traces of longhouses of the size found in the lands south of the Baltic from the 5th millennium B.C. have been found in Denmark. But this is a general characteristic of the Funnel Beaker Culture across the north European lowlands. The buildings were small, and their construction is difficult to establish. Structures found on Sjælland, Bornholm and in Skåne are interpreted as small buildings with a few central posts. Some of these have preserved wall posts that define an oval ground plan.

Kitchen middens with rubbish layers of the Early Neolithic have been excavated in Norsminde Fjord (S.H. Andersen 1991) and near Bjørnsholm, where the existence of both settlements and graves behind the midden indicates that the coastal zone was used for more permanent settlement in some places (S.H. Andersen 1993). Inland too, new hunting sites have been found. In the find-rich Store Åmose, western Sjælland, new registration through protection work led to the discovery and excavation of several small sites where gathering, fishing and hunting went on continuously from the Late Mesolithic to the Early Neolithic (A. Fischer 1985a). At the end of the Early Neolithic, TN C (TN II), when there is plenty of evidence for dense settlement over much of the country, a new type of site appears: the large, fortified structures or Sarup sites that clearly played some role in the organization of settlement. On the map of settlement in eastern Jutland we see a clear connexion between fortified sites and the occurrence of both settlements and megalithic graves. The same is evident in the area around Sarup on south-western Fyn (N.H. Andersen, below) and by Lønt, south of Haderslev Fjord (E. Jørgensen 1988).

At the transition to the Middle Neolithic the settlements increase in size and settlement becomes more concentrated and longer-lived. Investigations on Langeland show that the settlement area increases: Troldebjerg is at least 30,000 sq.m., Klintebakken at least 37,000 sq.m. and three sites from MN AV cover areas between 70,000 and 2-300,000 sq.m., amongst them the new MN AV settlement at Spodsbjerg (Skaarup 1985:363, 367). Several of the large, Middle-neolithic settlements of the Funnel Beaker Culture have proved to be placed over Sarup-type sites from which perhaps they derive. This is true for Blandebjerg, Trelleborg and Bundsø at least;

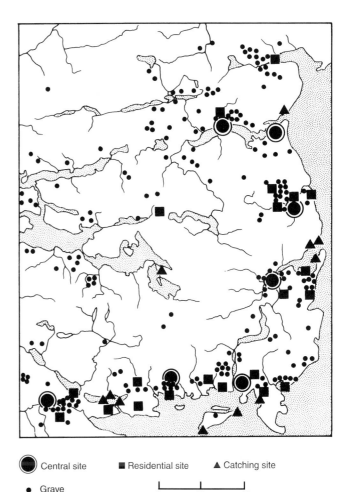

Central site   ■ Residential site   ▲ Catching site

● Grave   0   5   10

Map of Funnel Beaker-culture settlements and graves in East Jutland.

Troldebjerg is a case under discussion. Several settlements of this period have locations reminiscent of the positions of fortified sites, surrounded by watercourses and low areas. These may be determined by the need for grazing areas for cattle, which took on great economic importance in the course of MN A (Rowley-Conwy 1984: 92; Nyegaard 1985:454).

The D-shaped buildings and longhouses at Troldebjerg that were earlier used to show the building-type of the beginning of the Middle Neolithic are now the subject of debate. There is, for instance, disagreement over whether these are building structures or parts of features pertaining to fortified structures of the Sarup type (Eriksen & Madsen 1984:7781; Skaarup 1985:351). The excavation at Hanstegård in eastern Jutland, however, indicates that buildings of D-shaped or semicircular ground plan did exist at the beginning of the Middle Neolithic (MN AIa) (Eriksen & Madsen 1984). The cul-

93

Photograph of a circular structure of the late Funnel Beaker Culture at Grødbygård, Bornholm.

Photograph of Late-neolithic building under excavation at Hemmed Plantage, Djursland. The postholes are marked with white discs.

tural watershed around 2800 B.C., at the beginning of MN B, also meant a change in the settlement pattern, most markedly in Jutland where the Single

Grave Culture made its entrance. At the same time we find settlements of the Pitted Ware Culture in North Jutland and the Kattegat area (L.W. Rasmussen, below). On the Danish islands there seems not to be any sharp break in settlement development (Skaarup 1985:379ff.). On Bornholm, two settlement sites, Limensgård and Grødbygård, each of 6-8,000 sq.m., have produced remains of 18- to 20-m. long, rectangular longhouses with central posts. These belong to long-term settlements that run from MN AV some way into MN B (Kempfner-Jørgensen & Watt 1985; F.O. Nielsen & Nielsen 1985, 1986a,b, 1990). Besides longhouses, circular buildings or post circles of as yet uncertain function were found at Grødbygård.

The cultural changes were more abrupt in Jutland, where the settled area increased and where also less fertile soils were ploughed or grazed. In the area around Herning it has transpired that Single Grave settlement often appears in the same areas that were settled at the end of the Funnel Beaker Culture (Rostholm 1977, 1986b), while at Vroue and Karup Hede we have very different settlement patterns (E.

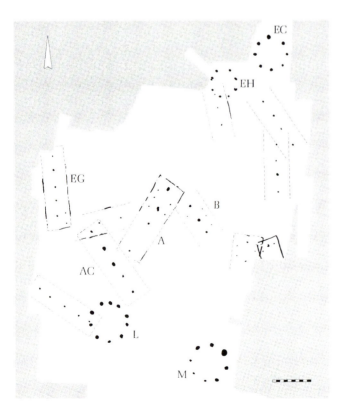

Plan of the settlement at Grødbygård on Bornholm with rectangular longhouses and circular structures of the late Funnel Beaker Culture.

Jørgensen 1977a). In the Viborg-Salling area a number of small settlements on very sandy soil, located near watercourses or fjords, have been excavated (Simonsen 1986, 1987). Small patches of culture layer with building traces in the form of groups of postholes have been found at Vorbasse (S. Hvass 1978, 1986a) and underneath a barrow at Lustrup a structure has been excavated that is interpreted as a round building (Rostholm 1986b). The only rectangular longhouse from the Single Grave Culture (the Upper Grave Period) so far was excavated at Hemmed Church on Djursland (Boas 1993).

The best insight yet into the economy of the Single Grave Culture comes from a seasonal settlement on Kalvø in Norsminde Fjord for hunting, fishing and the collection of molluscs, but where beef was eaten too. Summer grazing was possible here (S.H. Andersen 1976, 1983a; Rowley-Conwy 1985a). At a second coastal site, at Lodborg in Thy, amber was collected and worked (Liversage 1988). Grain finds, for instance from Lodborg, and grain impressions in pottery, show that barley was the main crop of the Single Grave Period (Rostholm 1986a; Robinson & Kempfner 1988). Despite the frequent poverty in finds and sparsity of Single Grave settlements, we can conclude, from the whole picture the finds give, that the land was comprehensively exploited and the population numerous. In this respect, the picture is the same as in the following Late Neolithic.

At the beginning of the Late Neolithic we again find settlements with clearly preserved building traces. The first was found at Myrhøj in Vesthimmerland, with buildings with central roof-bearing posts and sunken floors (J.Aa. Jensen 1973). More buildings of similar type have since been found in northern Jutland (Simonsen 1983). In recent years, settlements with large, regular, post-built longhouses have been excavated, completely changing the picture of Late-neolithic settlement. Buildings from the latter part of the period reach up to 30-45 m. in length. The largest group of such longhouses has been excavated at Limensgård on Bornholm (F.O. Nielsen & Nielsen 1986b). The development of longhouses with central posts can be followed from the transition of MN A to MN B through the Late Neolithic and further to the beginning of the Early Bronze Age. At the transition from Bronze Age Periods I to II this building-type is superseded by longhouses with paired roof-bearing posts, the nor-

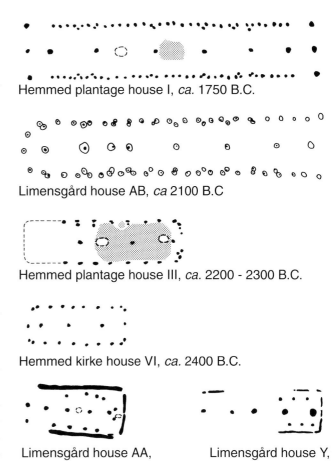

Hemmed plantage house I, *ca.* 1750 B.C.

Limensgård house AB, *ca* 2100 B.C

Hemmed plantage house III, *ca.* 2200 - 2300 B.C.

Hemmed kirke house VI, *ca.* 2400 B.C.

Limensgård house AA, *ca.* 2700 B.C.

Limensgård house Y, *ca.* 2700 B.C.

Mid- and Late-neolithic buildings with central posts. Examples from Limensgård, Bornholm, and Hemmed, Djursland.

mal type then right up to the beginning of historical times. The development of building-forms from the Late Neolithic to the Bronze Age is most clearly shown by the excavations at Hemmed on Djursland (Boas 1991, 1993). Several sites with Late-neolithic longhouses are now known both in Jutland and on Sjælland (Asingh 1988; Kjer Michaelsen 1989; AUD 1990:105-6).

Although there are still many unanswered questions, for instance on the development of building-types, settlement studies and excavations in the last 25 years have contributed a great deal to the knowledge of settlement in the Neolithic. It is, however, the experience of many excavators that settlements from this period are amongst the monuments most vulnerable to the effects of modern agriculture. Continued settlement excavations must therefore have a high priority in the future if this source is not to be lost.

Barrows with timber-built structures

BY TORSTEN MADSEN

The many impressive megalithic graves attracted a lot of early attention, and were made synonymous with the ealier part of the Late Stone Age in expressions such as "Dolmen Period" and "Passage Grave Period". In the first half of the present century, however, it was realized that early in the period there were also non-megalithic graves. These often appeared as simple hollows with or without simple stone-set bottoms. For this reason they were called (simple) earth graves (Friis Johansen 1917; K. Thorvildsen 1941). The finding of the grave at Konens Høj made it clear that whatever these graves lacked in the way of impressive stone structures they may have made up for in timber (Stürup 1966).

The frequently limited scope of early excavations meant that the earth graves could rarely be seen in a larger context. It occasionally appeared probable that there had been a mound over the graves, but as a rule they were regarded as graves under level ground. Increased excavation in the 1970's and not least the use of ground stripping machines changed this picture. It became clear that the earth graves were extensively associated with long barrows, and that the long barrows themselves could be complicated structures with timber features. Structures such as Barkær too (Glob 1949, 1975), originally

interpreted as buildings, could be re-interpreted as long barrows (T. Madsen 1979; Liversage 1992). This picture consolidated in the 1980's (Kjær Kristensen 1991). We can now be fairly certain that most if not all earth graves had timber structures in the form of coffins if nothing else, and we can therefore refer to them as timber-built graves.

The distribution of the timber-built graves of the Early-neolithic Funnel Beaker Culture in Denmark is distinctly westerly. A difference between East and West in Denmark is also apparent from the easterly distribution of early dolmen-types (Aner 1963) and the lack, so far, of association of the timber-built graves with the easterly Oxie Group. We have only one grave of this group, Dragsholm, with markedly mesolithic characteristics (Brinch Petersen 1974). The explanation may however be that research activity has been significantly higher in the West than in the East. A timber-built grave structure has, for instance, been excavated at Lindebjerg, western Sjælland (Liversage 1981) and new finds of timber structures on Sjælland may be a first indication of a coming change in the picture (Kaul 1988b). The discovery of a timber-built grave in the heart of a long dolmen is particularly interesting as it shows that long dolmens may include earlier phases with timber structures (Gebauer 1990).

Various types of timber-built graves of the Early-neolithic Funnel Beaker Culture are found. The Konens Høj type has deep foundation pits at either end of the base to hold the ends of a raised timber chamber (T. Madsen 1979:309). These ends were regarded as part of a tent-shaped superstructure with a ridge supported by the ends. The finding of a well-preserved chamber of this type at Haddenham, near Cambridge in England, however, shows that we are dealing with a large, coffin-like chamber with sides and a ceiling of horizontal planking that reached from end to end (Morgan 1990). So far, 16 graves of this type have been recorded in Denmark (Kjær Kristensen 1991:83).

The Troelstrup type had a rectangular chamber that was open at one end (T. Madsen 1979:309). The three closed sides were made of timber in foundation trenches supported by massive stone-packing or just by positioned stones. The ceiling was of wood,

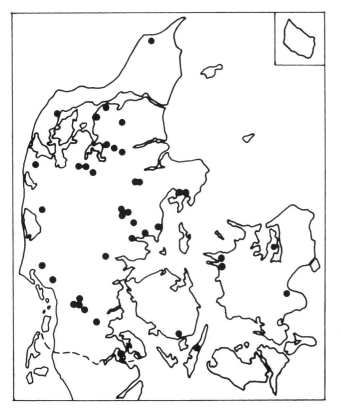

The distribution of known Late-neolithic timber-built graves in Denmark is distinctly westerly.

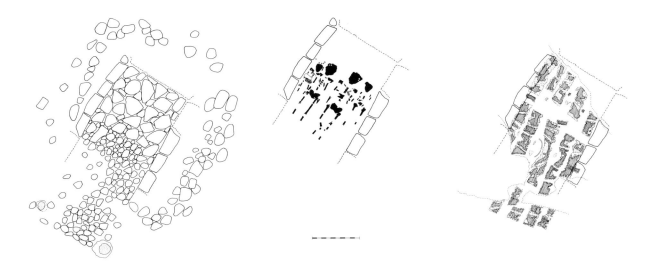

Three stages in the uncovering of the Skibhøj grave. To the left, a flagstone floor with a stone frame and two postholes at the open end to support the roof. In the middle, five very burnt skeletons of persons aged from new-born to 20-30 years. To the right, the split, charred planks from a burnt roof.

which one lucky find shows to have been split planks (E. Jørgensen 1977b). At present, 15 graves of this type are known (Kjær Kristensen 1991:84).

Examples of plank coffins are also known (e.g. Rønne 1979:6; Kjær Kristensen 1991:76f.), and we also find a number of graves with a covered stone frame surrounding the grave-bed. It is likely that the stone frame supported a timber cist of some form but no traces of wood are ever found. At least 22 graves of this type are known (Kjær Kristensen 1991:84).

A high proportion of the timber-built graves, but not all of them, were located in (long) barrows. How many may have lain under the level ground is unclear because the absence of a mound does not

necessarily mean that there was not one originally. The situation is also complicated by the fact that what we call "long barrows", on the basis, for instance, of palisaded enclosures, in many cases never had a mound (Faber 1976; Rieck 1982). In all, 36 "long barrows" with timber-built graves are currently known, of which 32 lie west of the Store Bælt (Kjær Kristensen 1991:86). The structures are frequently trapezoid and predominantly oriented east-west. In seven cases palisade enclosures of the mounds have been observed, but as a more general rule there seems to have been no upstanding delimitation of the barrows. Where real lines of boundary stones are found it is demonstrably probable that they are later additions linked to megalithic graves.

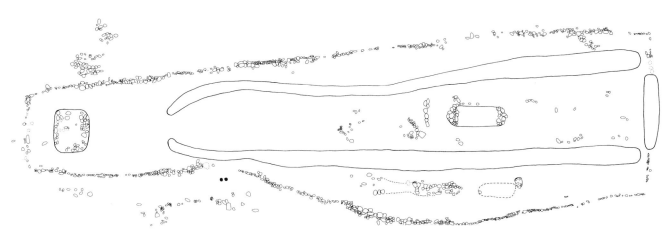

The Storgård IV long barrow with two phases. An earlier, trapezoid barrow with an end facade, flanking ditches and a single, central grave, and a later long barrow surrounded by a palisade and with a grave at the western end.

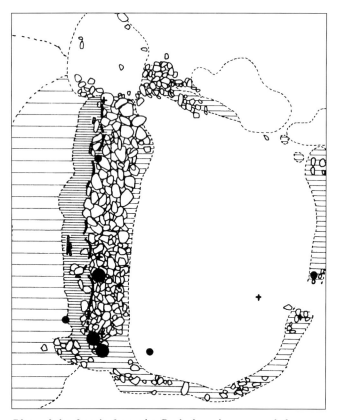

Plan of the facade from the Rude long barrow and the areas defined by wicker fences associated with it. The split logs, marked by their charred outlines, stood in the densely hatched, stone-free area. Three pots were found on the stone pavement, marked with filled circles on the plan.

In some cases flanking ditches have been found, but this appears not to be a common feature.

At no less than 17 of the mounds substantial facades have been uncovered at the broader, eastern end, and most of the mounds presumably had such features. The facades appear mostly as a deep foundation trench across the barrow, with traces of logs up to 1 m. thick placed side by side and stabilized on the outside by stone packing. In several cases the logs were split in half and placed with the flat side in towards the barrow (T. Madsen 1980:89; Kjær Kristensen 1991:75). In other cases whole logs were set up, sometimes singly in separate pits. At Rude long barrow there was an area in front of the facade enclosed by a wicker fence (T. Madsen 1980:89), and at Bygholm Nørremark long barrow too post-settings associated with the facade were found (Rønne 1979).

As a general rule, the timber-built graves were placed in the centre of the mounds with a common long axis. A single type, Troelstrup, conversely, is placed across the barrows with the open side out to the edge of the mound. A barrow often covers more than one grave, and the long barrows can appear as complex, composite structures. Extensions can be made in two ways: either by building over, with new barrows and graves placed on top of earlier ones, or by sequential extension, with new graves added to the end of existing structures. In the latter case, wicker fences are often found separating the different sections.

Because of the often chalk-poor soil by the long barrows, skeletons are rarely preserved in the graves. We have, however, a few lucky finds. In the Skibhøj grave, for instance, five persons were found (one adult and four children) buried side by side (E. Jørgensen 1977b) and in a plank coffin in Bygholm Nørremark long barrow four adults were found, buried in pairs foot to foot (Rønne 1979). It is striking that the two cases in which we have preserved skeletons also show multiple burials, though this is too weak a basis for generalizations. It does however emphasize that we cannot permit ourselves to assume that the timber-built graves were usually meant for the burials of one particular individual.

The graves are generally poorly furnished and, as a rule, lack pottery. We do however find pottery deposited by the facades. Anything between one and a dozen pots may have been placed here. (To judge by its description, the Volling "grave" (K. Thorvildsen 1940) was no grave but the facade of a barrow.) It appears, therefore, that the facades played an important role in connexion with the burials.

One of the more noteworthy features of the long barrows is the systematic destruction of both timber chambers and facades that can be observed in several cases. This destruction often took the form of the burning both of the grave chamber and the facade. It is clear that the funeral ceremonies, which may have been lengthy and perhaps have included several temporally separate stages, were not completed until

Three pots from the facade of a long barrow at Bjørnsnholm.

98

Bygholm Nørremark Plank cist supported by stones with four adults placed in pairs foot-to-foot.

the burial area was "closed" in some way. This "closure" found expression in a regular destruction of both chamber and facade before the final covering.

The timber-built graves in long barrows pertain, in the earliest cases, exclusively to the Volling and Svaleklint Groups, which represent closely related pottery traditions that are distinct from the pottery tradition we find in the third early group, the Oxie Group. There can be no doubt that the Volling Group at least and thus the timber-built graves start at the beginning of the Neolithic in western Denmark. The now plentiful C 14 datings support this, together with the location of Volling pottery in shell middens on top of Ertebølle layers and the fact that the Oxie Group in Jutland is restricted to certain coastal tracts (T. Madsen & Petersen 1984).

In a broader perspective, the pottery of the Volling and Svaleklint Groups shows close relationship with the pottery of the Svenstorp Group in Skåne and the central Swedish Vrå Culture. Looking southwards, we can point to the north-western German lowlands as a possible source for aspects of this ceramic tradition. Local groups in Lower Saxony (Schwabedissen 1979) and now in Holland too (J.A. Bakker, pers.comm.) that emerged on the margins of the late Rössen Groups show general similarity and certain genuinely shared characteristics with the Volling Group. There is, for instance, a special type of corded loop in two-ply cord for the decoration of pottery (Schwabedissen 1979:216) which is also occasionally found in the Volling Group.

The south-western contact area of the Volling and Svaleklint Groups is certainly not without interst

when we turn to the graves. It has been suggested (T. Madsen 1979:318f.) and later confirmed in various ways (Midgley 1985:199ff.; Kaul 1988b:73f.; Kjær Kristensen 1991:85), that the nearest parallels to the Danish long barrows are at present found in England. This applies first and foremost to the facades at the eastern ends of the mounds, the use of graves that are structurally identical to the Konens Høj type, and the burning of both graves and facades. It also applies to the use of trapezoid barrows, flanking ditches alongside the barrows, and the partitioning of the barrows with wicker fences.

The close English parallels do not have to mean that there was intense direct contact between Jutland and England - as a comparison of the material culture would also deny. The similarity, however, draws attention towards the south-west. The low-lying lands along the North Sea are especially interesting. Now, for the first time, cultures are being found here that are parallel to the early Funnel Beaker Culture in Denmark, and it is probable that we shall find much of the basis here for the earliest Neolithic in Denmark, which the parallels in southern England presumably also reflect.

Since the Second World War, Danish archaeologists have focussed their attention very much to the south-east when external impulses towards the Early Neolithic were to be sketched. The studies of recent years of, for instance, the timber-built graves in long barrows have opened our eyes to the fact that there is also a very relevant context to be found to the south-west. Researches of coming years will probably produce much that is new from this angle.

99

Causewayed camps of the Funnel Beaker Culture

By Niels H. Andersen

During the last century, a great deal of knowledge of fortified sites of the 5th and 4th millennia B.C. in western and central Europe has been gained. These sites are specific areas delimited by palisades and ditch-systems, i.e. major features of uniform character which form part of a large system. The function of these fortified sites is still a topic of discussion. They have been interpreted as defended sites, fortified settlements, astronomical observatories, market sites and more (Burgess et al. (eds) 1988; Kaufmann 1990). It was only in 1969 that it was discovered in Scandinavia that fortified structures also appear amongst the otherwise well-studied structural types of the Funnel Beaker Culture. By 1991, 23 sites had been found within Denmark (N.H. Andersen 1990b).

Only a few of the Danish structures have been extensively excavated, but the two sites at Sarup are well-investigated, all of one (Sarup II) having been uncovered and two-thirds of the other (N.H. Andersen 1988a-b, 1990a). Only minor segments of other sites have been dug, usually parts of the ditch-system.

The Danish structures of Sarup type, or Sarup sites, were all raised in the period from ca. 3500 to 3100 B.C., i.e. in the Fuchsberg/Virum, Troldebjerg and Klintebakke phases around the middle of the Funnel Beaker Period. These phases together form a period that is characterized by marked human impact on the environment in the clearance of land for cultivation and grazing (S.Th. Andersen, above). In the same period the building of megalithic graves began, and very high quality pottery ornamented in

a uniform manner that is found over all of southern Scandinavia was produced. It was in this watershed on the road to a pure agricultural economy that the Sarup sites were built and used.

The structures are characterized by ditch-systems and/or palisade ditches which enclose natural promontories or heights. The sites are placed where they were easy to find and reach in the Neolithic. The sites vary greatly in size, the smallest (Bjerggård) being only 1.6 ha. while the largest is thought to be more than 20. Very few sites are sufficiently investigated for their form to be known: forms vary from elongated structures (e.g. Sarup I), triangular ones (Hygind, Lønt, Sarup II, Trelleborg) and rounded ones (Store Brokhøj, Bjerggård, Toftum). With the elongated and triangular sites, natural slopes are used for the sides, while the rounded sites seem to have been fully enclosed by ditch-systems. One site (Vilsund) has no ditches, but the remainder have between one and four parallel rows; two, however, are most common. At the two fully excavated sites at Sarup, 43 and 32 ditches were recorded respectively. These were laid out in two parallel rows, linked by various fence courses. At Toftum the two rows seem not to have been dug at the same time (T. Madsen 1988:315). In form and size there is great variation amongst the ditches, which can range from small, square holes with sides up to 3 or 4 m. long (Sarup II, inner row) to ditches over 100 m. long (Sarup I, northern part). The ditches are 0.3 to 2.5 m. deep; their base is flat and level and up to 2 m. wide. Up to 10 cm. over the base of the ditch there is usually a natural fill: layers that have blown, washed

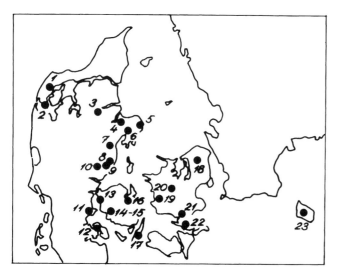

Sarup sites in Denmark. 1: Liselund, Sjørring (AUD 1989 no.190); 2: Vilsund (AUD 1988 no.165); 3: Lokes Hede (AUD 1987 no.299); 4: Store Brokhøj (B. Madsen & R. Fiedel 1988); 5: Grenå (N.A. Boas, pers. comm.); 6: Ballegård (AUD 1988 no.307); 7: Voldbæk (T. Madsen 1988:303ff.); 8: Toftum (T. Madsen 1978a, 1988:311ff.); 9: Bjerggård (T. Madsen 1988:309ff.); 10: Årupgård (T. Madsen 1988:309); 11: Lønt (E. Jørgensen 1988); 12: Bundsø (T. Madsen 1988:316); 13: Hygind (AUD 1986 no.149); 14-15: Sarup (N.H. Andersen 1988a-b, 1990a-b); 16: Åsum Enggård (AUD 1988 no.136); 17: Troldebjerg (J. Skaarup 1985:47ff.; T. Madsen 1988:318); 18: Skæving Boldbaner (AUD 1986 no.16); 19: Trelleborg (N.H. Andersen 1982); 20: Sigersted (P.O. Nielsen 1985a); 21: Bårse (AUD 1986 no.82); 22: Ellerødgård (H.H. Nielsen 1988); 23: Vasagård (F.O. Nielsen 1988:68ff.).

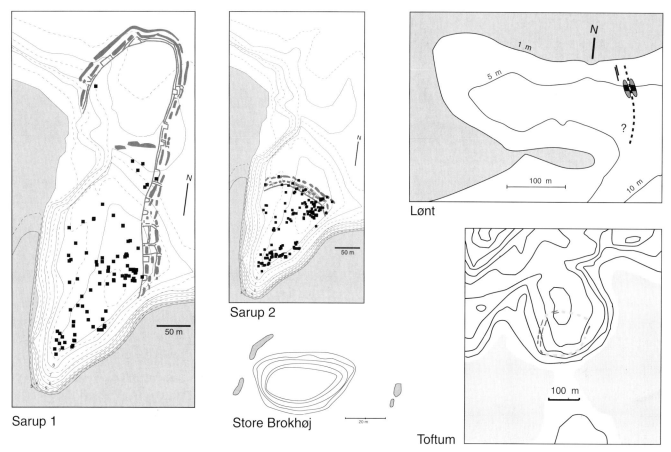

Plans of five Sarup sites.

or slipped down. Above this natural bottom layer the ditches have been deliberately refilled, i.e. the upcast has been put back into them. The form in which the replaced soil is deposited shows that the upcast lay on both sides of the ditch - in other words there was no regular rampart to one side. In the outer ditch-row at Toftum, however, the fill seems to have been naturally deposited (T. Madsen 1988:315). A lucky find of sherds from one pot in three ditches and four pits at Sarup II shows that these features were open at the same time (N.H. Andersen 1988a:47, 1990a:fig.21).

At several places at the bottom of these ditches traces of activities that can be regarded as ritual have been found, with whole pots lying at the bottom (Bjerggård, Bårse, Lønt, Sarup I and II, Liselund, Store Brokhøj, Toftum), heaps of tools (Bjerggård, Sarup I), heaps of animal bone, sometimes human skulls (Bjerggård, Hygind, Sarup I and II), parts of skulls (Hygind, Sarup I, Åsum), traces of fire, sometimes covered by soil while it burnt (Bjerggård, Toftum, Sarup I), and dark, greasy layers of decom-

posed organic material (Bjerggård, Toftum, Sarup). These presumably ritual layers were swiftly covered and the ditches completely refilled. Some time later - probably a few years - some of the ditches were redug, often right down to the original level. In these re-excavations are left traces of rituals of the same kind as before, and they are quickly re-covered by re-filling the ditch. Such redigging and refilling may take place several times in individual ditches, but we cannot see any uniform pattern.

At some sites culture layers rich in finds are deposited in the upper fill of the ditches. These may have been formed when the ditches were re-dug (Toftum, Troldebjerg, Liselund) or later (Bjerggård, Hygind, Sarup I and II). Some of these culture layers are deposited in refills (e.g. Toftum A 11 and A 9 (T. Madsen 1988:314f.)).

Palisade ditches, which always run parallel to the inner ditch-row, have been found on 5 sites (Hygind, Lønt, Sarup I and II, Troldebjerg). At Sarup I, the traces show that the palisade was an impressive timber construction made of oak logs 3-4 m. high and

101

A ditch at Sarup II (site 15) uncovered.

Section of ditch at Sarup II (site 15) with traces of recutting.

Votive pits in the inner area of Sarup II (site 15).

about 40 cm. thick. Up against the outer face of this fence traces of pottery offerings have been found that match the offerings by timber structures of long barrows and at megalithic graves. At the approximately 150 years later site of Sarup II the palisade was merely a fence of many small stakes hammered down into the ground. The palisade fence at Lønt was replaced several times (E. Jørgensen 1988).

Curiously, on the outer sides of the palisades of Sarup I and II a series of enclosures were constructed, between 6 m. x 7 and 7 m. x 20 at Sarup I. The importance of these enclosures is shown by the fact that the ditch-system of Sarup I was laid out to respect the position of the enclosures, and the inner row of ditches at Sarup II was constructed inside these enclosures. Matching forms of enclosure are found at the contemporary site at Büdelsdorf (Hingst 1971:Abb.1,6), and are seen at sites of the Lengyel and Michelsberg Cultures (Boelicke 1978; Kowalewska-Marszalek 1990; Bertemes 1991).

The large number of causeways between the ditches may have served as entrances to the enclosed area. At Sarup I an entrance structure comprising a double fence from the outer ditches running to a 1.6 m. wide opening in the palisade was found. In front of the opening a protective wall was found. This is a very small entrance to an area 9 ha. in size!

The areas that were enclosed by ditch-systems and sometimes palisades have usually seen only very limited excavation, revealing a few contemporary features. Large areas were excavated at Lokes Hede, Sarup I (6 ha.) and Sarup II (3 ha.). These area excavations show that the enclosed areas were only very partially used. At Sarup II, for instance, 149 pits of various functions were found: storage pits, post holes, rubbish pits and ritual features. In the latter category fall 28 pits which contained whole pots, axes, battle-axes, and in a few cases human bone.

The extensively-studied sites at Sarup show traces of very special activities. Most of these took place in the ditches. For the Stone-age farmers it must have been important to dig into existing ditch-systems, as no more effort would have been required to dig new ditches in the relatively light soil which most Danish sites lie upon (T. Madsen 1988:320). Possibly individual groups had the right to use particular ditches.

The Sarup sites played a role in the ritual life of the Stone-age farmers at a point when the population lived in small, scattered settlements in territories

Reconstruction of entrance area of Sarup I (site 14).

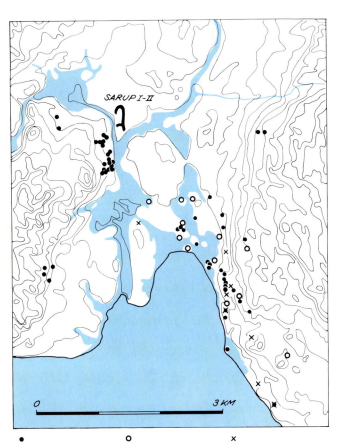

Location of megalithic graves and contemporary settlement sites within a few kilometres of Sarup. ●*: megalithic grave;* ○*: settlement site;* ×*: stray find.*

centred on megalithic graves (N.H. Andersen 1981: 77ff.). A scattered tribal community like this could be imagined to have had the Sarup sites as a primary centre. The construction of such sites must have relied upon the collaboration of many small units, and the activities on the site itself and later in the re-dug ditches maintained these links. The Sarup sites may have been raised and used in a period of great expansion in the early farming culture; an expansion that they may have tried to govern through rituals at, for instance, the megalithic graves and the Sarup sites. When the farming culture was no longer in serious turbulence, but found a natural home in large settlement units, the Sarup sites fell into disuse. The construction of megalithic graves ceased at the same time. These were henceforth used as collective graves, and pottery decoration lost its symbolic force.

Studies of the Danish Sarup sites have provided and will continue to provide important new insights. In the future, it is important to look at the function of the sites in the surrounding landscape, by which is meant their connexion with contemporary settlements and burials. Settlement studies based on the Sarup sites are underway in relation to the sites at Lønt, Sarup, Toftum and Vasagård.

103

Megalithic graves

BY JØRGEN SKAARUP

About 7,000 megalithic graves are now known in Denmark, many of them just as destroyed sites. Of these 7,000 recorded structures, dolmens formed about 90% while the rest were passage graves. Recent studies of the rate of destruction of megalithic graves seem however to confirm that the original number of such structures in Denmark could have been around 25,000 (Ebbesen 1985a). Of these only about 10% are now preserved and, just as importantly, less than a third are recorded.

The large number of megalithic graves destroyed early, which in many cases have disappeared without trace, must of course affect distribution maps. The main features of these, for instance that megalithic graves are a distinctly easterly/North Jutlandic phenomenon primarily associated with the fertile morrain clay areas, seem, however, to be secure. Sjælland and the southern islands together provide about half the recorded megalithic graves of Denmark.

This situation has not been reflected much in recent years' work on megalithic graves. Apart from a concentrated, problem-orientated and newly published project on the islands south of Fyn (Skaarup 1985) and - to a lesser extent - south-west-ern Fyn (N.H. Andersen 1981), there have only been a few, scattered excavations on the islands. Jutland has fared better, and here excavations of some preserved structures have produced crucial new evidence on the construction and use of the graves (Kjærum 1970; E. Jørgensen 1977a). New, well recorded and not least published excavations of individual examples or, even better, groups of megalithic graves, such as we know from southern Sweden and Mecklenburg (Strömberg 1968, 1971; Schuldt 1972; Blomqvist 1989) are, regrettably, still wanting.

The Danish megalithic graves have been increasingly used in recent years in the context of studies concerning the settlement history of the Funnel Beaker Culture (N.H. Andersen 1981; T. Madsen 1982; Skaarup 1985). The graves all seem to have been raised in the period ca. 3500-3200 B.C., and since many excavations have confirmed that they are often built close by or on top of contemporary settlements it seems fully justified to let the distributions of the megalithic graves and the still all too little known settlements of this period supplement one another to produce as detailed an image as possible of settlement at that time. The large amount of evidence of the continued use of the graves right through the Middle and Late Neolithic further seems to show that this relationship really did not change in the later Neolithic and indicates - in eastern Denmark at least - strong continuity in the settlement pattern throughout the Neolithic.

Of the more recent excavations mentioned above, the southern Fyn project has been much the largest. It was clearly inspired by exciting excavation results from neighbouring countries. As a general survey of 1985 (Skaarup 1985) shows, around 600 megalithic graves are known from an area of just 485 sq.km. on the islands south of Fyn. A third of these graves have been excavated, 50 of them - mostly just sites - in the last 25 years. The most recent, very extensive excavations, have produced no small amount of new evidence of the building of megalithic graves and their role for Neolithic society with regard to a number of aspects.

The same holds for the excavation of a considerable number of destroyed dolmens and passage

Distribution of dolmens and passage graves in Denmark. The darkest colour shows parishes with more than 20 megalith graves.

Excavated and restored passage grave "King Sweyn's Barrow" on Lolland.

graves around the northern part of Helnæs Bugt, south-western Fyn (N.H. Andersen 1981 and above).

From north-western Jutland too, in the areas around the Karup river, important new contributions to the understanding of the development of the Funnel Beaker Culture in this region and its relationship to the Single Grave Culture have emerged from excavations of several megalithic graves in the 1960's and 70's (E. Jørgensen 1977a and below). The use of megalithic graves here seems to be gradually supplemented and then superseded by burials in extensive systems of stone-packing graves in the later Middle Neolithic.

Because of the terms of the Preservation Act, the excavation of preserved megalithic graves is rare in Denmark. Since the very productive excavation of the passage grave "Jordhøj" by Mariager Fjord in the 1960's (Kjærum 1970) excavation has on the whole taken place in preserved dolmens and passage graves only in connexion with restoration. Some of these excavations have produced particularly exciting results. This is the case, for instance, with the excavation of the dolmen chamber "Klokkehøj" on

south-western Fyn, where the chamber proved to contain a well-preserved primary grave (Thorsen 1981.). Most recently, in connexion with the Forest and Nature Agency's restoration campaign which is being effected in collaboration with the National Museum, work on some of the large passage graves on Møn and Lolland has revealed various hitherto unknown constructional features such as phased mound construction, a regular, vaulted roof over the cap-stones of the chamber formed of flat stones laid in a mortar-like lime mass and dry walling "pointed" with lime mass between the slabs (Kaul 1989a).

The male skeleton in an extended supine position on the bed of the Klokkehøj grave is one of the very few Danish examples showing the funerary practice of the earliest dolmen builders. These early dolmen burials seem otherwise to be characterized by narrow, coffin-shaped chambers with side stones of even height closed with one large capstone. The chambers are placed in long cairns and have the same long axis as the barrows. As in Klokkehøj, the grave goods often consist of a collared or lugged flask and/or a funnel beaker (P.O. Nielsen 1984; Ebbesen 1990).

The earliest dolmen graves contain one or very

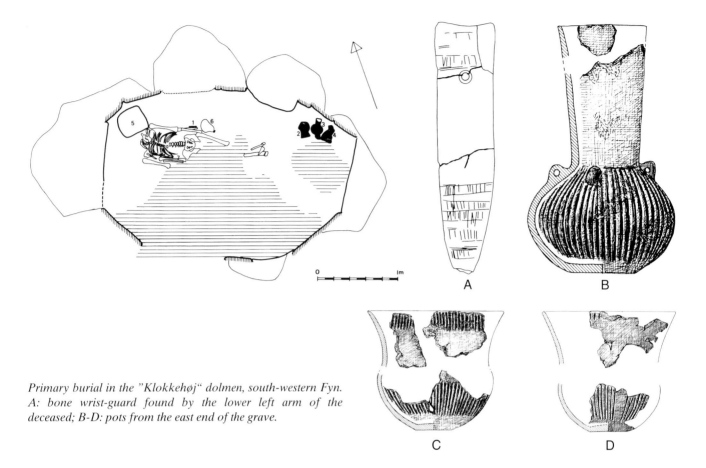

Primary burial in the "Klokkehøj" dolmen, south-western Fyn. A: bone wrist-guard found by the lower left arm of the deceased; B-D: pots from the east end of the grave.

few bodies. The grave structures therefore were not, as earlier thought, raised as collective graves. Men, women and children are all buried in the barrows, apparently showing that membership of an important family was as important as sex or age. The occurrence of several double burials of men and women indicates that monogamy was the common practice, but may also be evidence of women in the leading families sometimes being sacrificed to accompany their spouses in death.

Both dolmens and passage graves have frequently proved to overlie earlier features. The majority of these are remains of Funnel Beaker Culture settlements though other types are found as well. Under the site of a round cairn on southern Langeland, the disarticulated bones of three young people were found. Two were placed in roughly correct anatomical order in one, narrow grave pit while the third body was represented only by a skull placed in a small hollow. These unique burials are probably to be associated with a small ring-ditch structure that was also covered by the cairn.

On the neighbouring island of Strynø, a completely destroyed dolmen covered an earth grave with a

child's body, close to traces of a small, wooden cult building of U-shaped plan. In the centre of the building lay a thin-butted flint axe (Skaarup 1991).

Excavations of megalithic graves in the last 25 years have, on the whole, confirmed earlier notions of a development in which the early dolmens with narrow, body-length chambers were gradually superseded by structures with increasingly large chambers: extended dolmens, polygonal dolmens and large dolmens, built in rectangular or round, stone-lined barrows. The large dolmens form the structural link with the zenith of megalithicic construction, the passage graves, all of which belong to the final phase of construction around 3200 B.C.

Although the size of the chambers grows steadily throughout the period in which megalith graves were raised, it is very uncertain, with regard to the large dolmen chambers and passage graves, whether these ever functioned as real collective graves. It transpires that some passage graves were raised with a separate grave bed at one end of the chamber, and even with very large passage grave finds, with over 100 bodies, analyses of the grave goods show that the burials continued steadily throughout the later

Stone Age: over about 1,500 years in other words. This produces far too few burials per generation for the megalithic graves to have served the population of a complete settlement. The explanation, in respect of eastern Denmark at least, must probably be that throughout this long period, burial in a megalithic grave was reserved for a small social overclass.

Again in the case of the later dolmens and passage graves, the finds have not produced much evidence on the location of the bodies and grave goods. Thorough anthropological studies of the skeletal material of southern Fyn, and above all the unusually well preserved bones from the Hulbjerg passage grave on southern Langeland (Bennike 1985b), seems, however, to have established that the bodies were not - as often stated - disarticulated before deposition in the grave chambers and that the disturbed state of the bodies on excavation is attributable to a mixture of natural decomposition and interference in connexion with later burials. The deceased are evenly divided between both sexes, with no significant age clusters. Children are commonly represented.

The disturbance of earlier burials has also been a serious obstacle to efforts to establish the composition of individual grave furnishings in recent excavations. Pottery, presumably containing foodstuffs, appears as grave goods throughout the Neolithic. So too do flake tools, discoid scrapers and transverse arrowheads. Awls, bone chisels and animal-tooth or amber beads are also frequently found. Amber jewellery is often shaped as miniature versions of the exclusive status-giving stone battle-axes and clubheads. In the later Funnel Beaker Culture and the following Single Grave Period pottery is increasingly rivalled and replaced by flint axes and chisels.

The construction of the dolmens and passage graves, and the demonstration of local characteristics, has been the subject of several recent studies (Ebbesen 1975, 1978a; E. Jørgensen 1988; Kaul 1989a; S. Hansen 1993). As mentioned early on, new constructional details are continually appearing, increasing our respect for the architects of the megalithic graves. The mounds and chambers seem to be raised on the basis of a number of fixed and well-tried principles, which must have derived from a deep knowledge of the properties of the raw materials in respect of stability, strength, drainage, durability, etc. To this is to be added the architect's ability to organize and execute such major projects.

Dolmen sites with large dolmens under excavation at Nørreballe on Langeland.

Two passage grave excavations (Skaarup 1985: 251; Kaul 1989a:96) have produced observations that seem to confirm Frederik VII's hypothesis on how the large megalithic capstones were put in place (Frederik VII 1857). In both cases, organic or sand layers on a level with the upper edge of the side stones showed that the raising of the mound much have seen two stages. There must have been a long enough time between these for the fill of the first phase to have settled sufficiently for it to be possible to move the large capstone into place with the help of rollers.

Other excavations have revealed how long cairns and long barrows with several chambers were created by successive additions to an originally simple structure (Kjærum 1977; E. Jørgensen 1988), or how passage graves too could in some cases be raised over earlier grave structures with earth graves and timber cult houses (Rønne 1979; AUD 1986:84f.).

The sacrificial rituals of the Stone-age farmers associated with burials in megalithic graves have been extensively illuminated by a large number of studies. The Funnel Beaker peoples' ceremonies frequently included the placing of substantial quantities of sacrificial gifts on or by the kerb stones of the barrow, concentrated as a rule around the passage entrances. Something new is that these rituals have

The runs of dry walling between the supporting stones of the chambers can be very fine workmanship. Passage grave at Kragenæs, Ærø.

Ardmarks beneath the passage grave Jordehøj on Møn.

occasionally been traceable right back to the end of the Early Neolithic, when sacrifices at dolmens comprised thin-butted flint axes, funnel beakers and bowls etc. (P.O. Nielsen 1979a:103; Skaarup 1985:356; E. Jørgensen 1988:203). In one, thought-provoking case two sets of pottery, each comprising

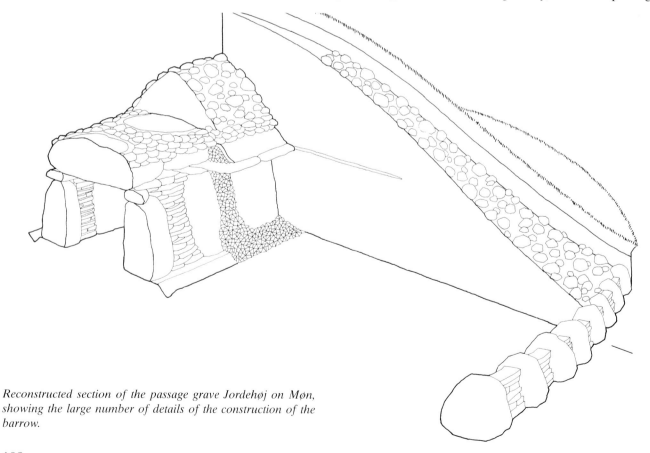

Reconstructed section of the passage grave Jordehøj on Møn, showing the large number of details of the construction of the barrow.

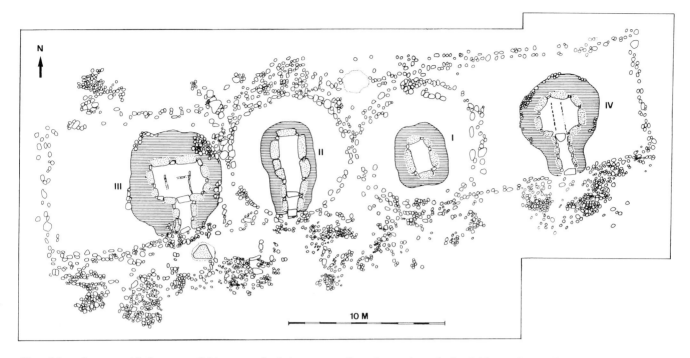

Site of long barrow with four megalithic graves built into one at Lønt in southern Jutland. The earliest is the small round dolmen with the closed chamber (I). On this the round dolmen with the open chamber was built (II). Finally the passage grave chambers (III-IV) were added on, each in its own rectangular plot.

a funnel beaker and a lugged jar, were placed in a pair of flat pits at distances of 8 and 9 m.(!) respectively from the kerb stones of a round cairn on southern Langeland.

In the Middle Neolithic, the offerings comprise pottery in particular: often special, finely decorated vessels that can be supposed to have contained food offerings to the dead. Vessel-forms such as pedestalled bowls and pottery spoons seem to have been specially made for this purpose. The number of pots can vary substantially, from just a few pieces to several hundred. Analyses of pottery finds seem, however, to show that even the very large groups can be attributed to a relatively few, large depositions in the first phase of the Middle Neolithic (Gebauer 1979:142).

Around 3100 B.C. there was a change in sacrificial ritual, when pottery was almost entirely replaced by flint axes and chisels, which can be deposited in great quantities by megalithic graves. The flint tools sometimes show deliberate damage to the edges or destruction by fire, presumably to discourage desecration of the sacrifice. The deposition of large flint tools such as axes and daggers outside graves, more rarely supplemented by pottery, continues right down to the end of the Neolithic, around 1700 B.C.

Besides giving us a very important insight into the ancestor cult of the Stone-age farmers and their technical capabilities, and the need to demonstrate territorial rights in small farming communities, the megalithic graves have also proved to contain striking new evidence of the contemporary landscape (S.Th. Andersen 1990 and above). Hidden in the fill of the barrows or protected by their mass are remains of ancient ground surfaces and undisturbed areas of Stone-age soil which offer outstanding opportunities for pollen analysis.

Ardmarks have been found under 20 Danish dolmens and passage graves so far (Thrane 1991a). The earliest traces of this method of cultivation can be dated to the second half of the Early Neolithic.

The thousands of ploughed-out megalithic sites in Denmark still contain, as the above has, I hope, shown, a lot of new information on Stone-age society. The same holds, of course - even more - for the circa 2,400 preserved and protected dolmens and passage graves that form a characteristic and valued feature of the Danish landscape. As for the destroyed sites, it is urgent to secure these data, because such sites are currently being ploughed to bits at a hitherto unseen rate under ever more efficient agriculture. Since the sites can hardly be protected, the only solution seems to be excavation.

Cult houses of the Funnel Beaker Culture

BY C. J. BECKER

The excavation of a stone-set, rectangular building at Tustrup on Djursland (Kjærum 1955) in the middle of a group of megalithic graves provided new and unexpected knowledge of the religious activities of the period. Only five years later, at Ferslev, south of Ålborg, a similar find was made (Marseen 1960). The last 25 years or so have brought at least 8 related structures to light, albeit with new details practically every time. For this reason, a short description of this material is offered here, nearly all of it as yet only provisionally published if at all.

The new finds, numbered 3 to 10, are marked on the map, together with Tustrup (no.1) and Ferslev (no.2): 3. Herrup 26, Sevel parish, Ringkøbing *amt* (C.J. Becker 1969b). 4.-5. Herrup 43 and 46, Sevel parish, Ringkøbing *amt* (unpublished). 6. Søndermølle III, Sevel parish, Ringkøbing *amt* (unpublished). 7. Trandum Skovby II, Sevel parish, Ringkøbing *amt* (unpublished). 8. Engedal, Daubjerg parish, Viborg *amt* (Faber 1977). 9. Foulum, Tjele parish, Viborg *amt* (Langballe 1985). 10. Tange Sø, Højbjerg parish, Viborg *amt* (JDA 1, 1982:170; unpublished; supplementary information from Mette Iversen, Viborg Stiftsmuseum). This building (not illustrated) has suffered some disturbance in recent times. It was of the same type as nos.7-8, with a porch to the east. The main chamber was about 3 m.sq. and the porch about 1 m. The foundation

Cult house from Herrup (nr. 3), seen from the NE.

trenches were covered by small stones; seven quite substantial posts could be seen in the partition wall. The building was probably burnt. At the floor level only a quantity of small potsherds was found, including bits of a funnel beaker with vertically striped sides.

The dense clustering in north-eastern Jutland is striking.

Architecture. Nearly all the structures have a rectangular chamber with an opening in one end. A division into main chamber and porch is found in five cases (nos.3, 7, 8, 9 and 10). No opening is visible in the ground plan in one case (no.5). In several cases the roof was carried on two large posts in the centre of each end, marked either by a stone pedestal (nos.1(?) and 7) or large postholes (nos.2, 3, 4, 6, 8 and 9); in two cases there were four large posts, one in each corner (nos.4 and 5), while three buildings had either two or more posts in or by the partition wall (nos.9 and 10). - In several cases, the inner wall was constructed of vertical planks, standing in a foundation trench. On the outside the walls were supported by fist-sized or larger stones. In some cases the outer face was finished off with heavy stones placed on edge (nos.1 and 2; perhaps no.9). But there has been no trace of such megalithic finishing with most new finds.

Size varies greatly, with internal dimensions from about 9 m. x 6 (no.3) to 1.7 m. x 1.5 (no.6).

Alignment varies similarly.

Burning. Clear traces of destruction by fire have

The reliably recorded cult houses noted here. The numbers correspond to those in the text.

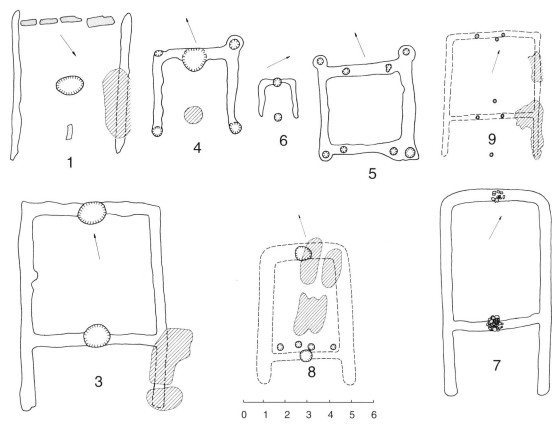

Ground plans of the inner chambers of the cult houses with roof-bearing posts, drawn after the publications noted in the text or original plans (some with reservations). Hatching shows secondary interventions or modern disturbance. Same scale.

been observed in four cases (nos.1, 2, 3 and 8), less certain traces with nos.9 and 10, while four examples certainly had no such traces (nos.4, 5, 6 and 7).

Finds. In five cases a considerable quantity of originally complete pots and spoons had been placed on the floor, often in clusters (nos.1, 2, 3, 7 and 8). In the small no.6, only one pedestalled bowl was found while the contents of nos.9 and 10 comprised only a few fragmentary `domestic potsherds'. Two examples lacked any finds (nos.4 and 5).

Neighbouring megalithic graves have been found by nos.1, 2, 7 and 8. Such graves may have been destroyed at the other sites long since.

Dating. Most pottery-dated examples are from MN Ib (the Klintebakke phase) (nos.1, 3 and 6-10); no.3 may have been constructed in Period Ia. Only no.2 is later (MN III), but it contains so many Period-Ib sherds that it is either a case of long-term use (Marseen 1960:51; Kjærum 1967a:194) or of two cult houses built on the same site (C.J. Becker 1969b:25).

Demolition later in the Neolithic is demonstrable at no.8 - the construction of a number of stone-packing graves of MN III (Faber 1977) - and no.9 - the

raising of a Single Grave barrow (Langballe 1985); the same holds for a poorly recorded structure that is not counted here (Lille Bundgård, Nørre Onsild parish, Randers amt; cf. Ebbesen 1975:270, 1979a:75).

The interpretation of the earliest examples found was primarily based on the Tustrup example: they could represent sacrificial rituals or other ceremonies connected with burial in the large megalithic graves (Kjærum 1955:23ff.). A second suggestion was as graves in their own right, mausolea for especially important persons (Kjærum 1967a:190). It was clear that they were no ordinary houses such as are known from other finds, and they never produce cultural deposits. - The absence of basic sets of the normal grave goods of the period (in more durable materials such as flint, other types of stone and amber) of itself weakens the idea of direct association with a death cult or funerary ceremonies. The great increase in the group of finds points in one direction, that of sacred structures: cult houses or, if you like, small temples (C.J. Becker 1969b:26ff.).

Jutlandic stone-packing graves

Danish archaeologists really became familiar with the Middle-neolithic stone-packing graves of the Funnel Beaker Culture in the 1950's. At that time, just 20 sites in north-western Jutland with a total of 50 graves were known (C.J. Becker 1960). The number of sites has nearly doubled since then, and the number of graves excavated is approaching 500, particularly as a result of deliberate research in the 1960's and 70's (C.J. Becker 1967; E. Jørgensen 1977a).

The stone-packing graves, which are always below the level ground, often comprise two parallel bath-shaped hollows in the ground filled up with stones, the so-called "graves". At one end of these is the so-called "mortuary house", normally a quadrangular stone setting that covers a similarly quadrangular hole in the ground that divides into two narrow oblong ditches near the bottom.

Besides typical stone-packing graves with two graves and a mortuary house, structures with mortuary houses and anything from one to eight graves are known.

The stone-packing graves were constructed in order in one or more parallel rows. At some sites the rows of pits seem to follow contemporary routeways. Only in relatively few cases do such features overlap.

The artefacts that are found in stone-packing graves are most often lying in the mortuary houses although they do - occasionally - appear in the graves too. The objects are predominantly of flint and comprise heavy axes, pointed-butted gouges, thin-bladed axes, chisels and blades. On rare occasions double-edged greenstone battle axes are found, and amber beads have appeared in a few examples. From a few stone-packing graves come flint arrowheads of triangular cross-section.

Potsherds have been found by several stone-pack-

Distribution of stone-packing graves.

ing graves. Usually the sherds represent a single vessel. In several cases, the sherds were found on or in between the capping stones of the mortuary house or at the top of the graves. This position indicates that the pot was placed by the stone-packing grave either after the mortuary house was covered by a layer of stones or after the graves were filled with stone.

At other stone-packing graves, the pot or pots were found down in the mortuary house; in other words at the same level as the other buried objects. This position shows that the vessels were placed in the mortuary house before it was sealed with a layer of stones.

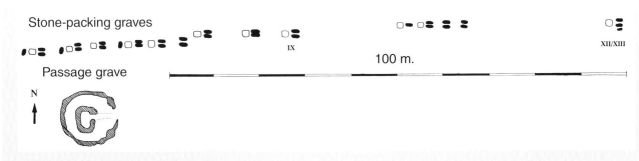

Vroue Hede II. The situation of the stone-packing graves in relation to another and to a passage grave.

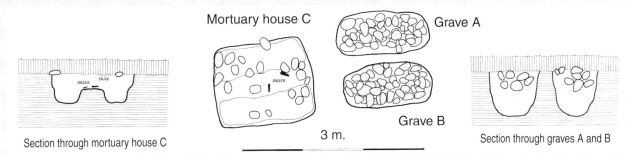

Mortuary house C   Grave A

Grave B

ØKSER   SKÅR   ØKSER

3 m.

Section through mortuary house C   Section through graves A and B

Vroue Hede II. Structure IX in plan and section. The finds have been plotted on to the section through the mortuary house, C.

The earliest stone-packing graves come from Period II/III of the Middle Neolithic (MN A) while the latest are from the end of MN A. The latest structures are probably contemporary with the earliest single graves and the beginning of MN B (Damm 1989). The great majority of stone-packing graves come from Periods IV-V of the Middle Neolithic.

The interpretation of the stone-packing graves is very problematic, for despite sophisticated methods of excavation still no traces of human bodies or skeletons have been detected in the features. It has been cautiously assumed that burial took place in the so-called graves while the ditches in the mortuary houses formed the foundations of a building where the deceased could rest, temporarily, before the interment itself (C.J. Becker 1963, 1967).

An alternative interpretation assumes that the "mortuary house" was itself the real grave while the two "graves" contained a sacrificed ox-team (P.O. Nielsen 1981a). This view is based on finds of ox teeth closely associated with certain graves (C.J. Becker 1960).

New finds show that domesticated oxen or parts of them were deliberately deposited in stone-packing graves (Stidsing 1989). The demonstration of high concentrations of phosphate in the graves and low levels in the mortuary houses (F. Christensen 1989) has neither proved nor disproved the above theories conclusively.

At several sites, the stone-packing graves are located near dolmens or passage graves of earlier construction.

Erik Jørgensen

Vroue Hede II. Finds from mortuary house C in structure XII. This structure overlay structure XIII.

Vroue Hede II. Finds from mortuary house C in structure XIII.

113

Pitted Ware settlements

By Lisbeth Wincentz Rasmussen

For decades, recurrent finds of cylindrical cores and tanged arrowheads clustering at coastal settlements have been known in Denmark. Such finds were described in 1951, and attributed to the Danish "Pitted Ware Culture" on the grounds that comparable types of arrowheads and flakes were particularly found on sites with pitted ware in southern Sweden (C.J. Becker 1951). The Danish sites were located in the North-East and East, around the Kattegat, on islands and by fjords. It was therefore believed that these sites were the remains of a culture based primarily on hunting and fishing, as in Sweden. The most informative finds came from two settlements in the Limfjord area, Smedegårde and Livø, which were excavated at the beginning of the 1960's. The finds from here comprised flint and stone tools and a little pottery, recovered from a ploughed-out culture layer (Marseen 1963).

From cross-finds, the earlier Pitted Ware Culture was dated alongside the Funnel Beaker Culture phases MN III-IV(V) and the later Pitted Ware Culture the earlier phases of the Jutlandic Single Grave Culture and the Swedish Battle Axe Culture and possibly MN V (C.J. Becker 1982a:25). Further, the Danish Pitted Ware Culture was seen as part of a common Scandinavian phenomenon.

The continuing lack of informative finds gradually led to a degree of agreement to treat the Danish Pitted Ware Culture as an independent group. The finds were viewed in various lights, as the hunting activities of a farming culture or as a sign of Swedish hunters' invasions of Danish coasts (Malmros 1980; S. Nielsen 1979a; Wyszomirska 1984:34, 42).

In the 1980's, however, two settlements were excavated that have provided new and secure information on the Pitted Ware Culture in Denmark. These are two outstanding coastal sites, Kainsbakke and Kirial Bro, lying about a kilometre apart on the same water system around 5 km. west of Grenå on Djursland. In the Stone Age, Kainsbakke lay on an

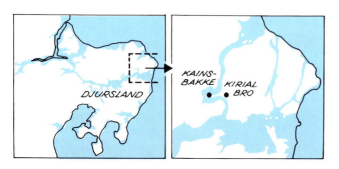

Kainsbakke. Uppermost shell layer in rubbish pit, above sherds of Pitted Ware pottery.

island, while the excavated part of Kirial Bro was situated right on the shorebank (L.W. Rasmussen & Boas 1982; L.W. Rasmussen 1984; L.W. Rasmussen & J. Richter 1991). Kainsbakke comprises an extended, now thin and ploughed-out culture layer that covers about half of the ½ km. large island. Thirteen settlement pits were excavated here, most of which contained oyster, snail and mussel shells. There was also a lot of well-preserved animal bone, which together with pottery and flint-, bone- and antler tools forms a comprehensive and varied assemblage. Kirial Bro is a multiperiod settlement with a culture layer with material from the Mesolithic and later. But at the edge, running over about 20 m. in a strip parallel with the then shoreline about 1-2 m. broad, a layer of shells was also found. The finds from this layer are pure Pitted Ware Culture.

According to the tools, Kainsbakke and Kirial Bro both belong to the earlier Pitted Ware Culture, with tanged arrowheads predominantly of type A, especially type A3. The other flint-types are also common to the two sites, though the grouping is different. At Kirial Bro there were many more arrow-heads and knives than scrapers, for instance, and they are better formed than those at Kainsbakke. This could indicate that hunting and butchering were more important at Kirial Bro. The pottery shows similar variation: vessels with small bases, high bodies and short necks, decorated at the mouth and shoulder and sometimes on the neck with various forms of pitting in horizontal rows. There is great similarity to pottery on the sites of western Sweden (Malmer 1969). Bone awls, stamps, cylindrical beads, a bone chisel and a fragment of a harpoon are the limited range of bone and antler objects.

The faunal remains from Kainsbakke show a mixed economy with both sea and land animals, domesticated animals, fish, fowl and shellfish represented. Red deer were particularly hunted, but as many as 19 other species of wild animal were found, ranging from shrew to bear and elk! The quantity of meat obtained from wild and domesticated animals, especially cattle, seems to have been about equal, with perhaps the wild contributing a little more. Kainsbakke could have been permanently occupied, but this cannot be confirmed.

The bone finds from Kirial Bro show the same species. Thus hunting formed an equally important part of the subsistence strategy which also included cattle raising, gathering and possibly cultivation. $\delta^{13}C$ analyses of human bone show that about half the diet consisted of land animals. Both tool-types and pottery match, in detail, what is found in the Pitted Ware Culture of south-western Sweden. There are also details in the finds, such as figure modelling, shell beads and miniature vessels that are also common in the "classic" Pitted Ware Culture, for instance on Gotland. These features link the Danish sites to the large area with Pitted Ware settlement in the rest of southern and central Scandinavia. But the finds from Kainsbakke and Kirial Bro represent a local tradition too. The clay disc, for instance, so characteristic a type of the Funnel Beaker Culture, is common, and all the thick-butted flint axes are of the Valby type (A-axes). Some small flint objects too are shared with the Funnel Beaker Culture. The special features are manifest on the pottery and its decoration, in the cylindrical core technique and tools that were especially suited to hunting and gathering. Finally it is also a special and unique phenomenon in the Neolithic to have so markedly mixed an economy in which hunting played such an important role.

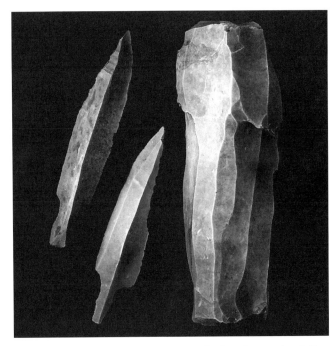

Kirial Bro. Tanged arrowheads and cylindrical cores (ca. 1:1)

A series of C 14 datings show that the two sites were settled in the period 2910-2550 B.C. (L.W. Rasmussen 1986; Tauber 1986a). This means that the phase of the earlier Pitted Ware Culture that we have represented here is contemporary with the earlier phases of the Jutlandic Single Grave Culture and generally later than the Funnel Beaker Culture. On the basis of, for instance, the special ceramic assemblage, it is not possible to see Kainsbakke and Kirial Bro as a special hunting group belonging to either the Funnel Beaker or the Single Grave Culture. These sites, and others around the Kattegat, must belong to an independent group, locally developed on the basis of the late Funnel Beaker Culture, but formed on the model of the hunting groups on the other side of the Kattegat. In terms of subsistence, ideology and material culture this can be seen as a countermove to the formation of the Single Grave Culture in Jutland.

Through continued excavations of Pitted Ware-culture sites in Denmark, it should be possible to place them more accurately chronologically and geographically and to gain a better knowledge of internal development. The new finds and results have created stimulating possibilities for research into the dynamic relationship between contemporary, culturally and economically different groups in the later Neolithic.

Single graves and Late Neolithic graves

BY MOGENS HANSEN AND HANS ROSTHOLM

A very large number ploughed-out neolithic grave mounds have been excavated in the last 25 years. It has become increasingly usual for the mounds and their immediate surroundings to be completely excavated. For the Single Grave Period (MN B) this has produced, amongst other things, ring-ditches and various timber structures. The burial customs thus appear much more varied than they did before.

Ardmarks have been found beneath the mounds in at least 30 cases (Thrane 1991a). Under some mounds there are settlement traces (*i.a.* Rostholm 1977; 1982a: 30ff., 62ff.; Simonsen 1981; Boas 1986; Asingh 1988). Votive deposits are also found by the mounds (A.H. Andersen 1986:127; Rostholm 1991:118ff.).

From 1966 to 1990, at least 592 sites with graves datable to the Single Grave Period and Late Neolithic on the basis of their contents, type or stratigraphy were excavated in Denmark. These sites include 454 mounds of the Single Grave Period/Late Neolithic, 54 megalithic graves and 36 sites without mounds. More than half the grave mounds of the Single Grave Period/Late Neolithic contained only one grave, while about 50 had more than two. A few mounds had around 15 graves. The mounds excavated were typically entirely ploughed out, or nearly so. It must be assumed, therefore, that the late Single Grave Period and the Late Neolithic are seriously underrepresented. This is confirmed by a critical analysis of the grave finds of south-western Jutland (M. Hansen 1985, 1986).

The great majority of the grave finds are from Jutland (*ca.* 88%). Most barrow excavations have been in Ribe *amt,* where amongst others Esbjerg Museum has excavated several large groups (Eriksen 1979; Lauenborg 1980). Many of the other finds are from the islands south of Fyn (Skaarup 1985).

Chronological problems

The chronological relationship between the Single Grave and the Funnel Beaker Cultures is clarified by the grave finds, which have produced both stratigraphic evidence and material for C 14 dating. At the end of the 1960's, a number of C 14 datings indicated that C.J. Becker's chronology was unreliable (C.J. Becker 1960:73ff.; Tauber 1971:128).

Stratigraphic observations from Skarrild and Lille Hamborg in Mid-Jutland in 1973 and later also showed that graves from the Bottom Grave Period were cut through settlement layers of the end of the

Funnel Beaker Culture (MNV) (Rostholm 1977). This could be confirmed by a number of earlier finds (Davidsen 1977). These finds confirmed that at most there could have been a short overlap between the Funnel Beaker and Single Grave Cultures, or that the two were sequential, as a large number of new C 14 datings indicate (Malmros & Tauber 1977). Furthermore, a critical re-assessment of the archaeological finds raised doubts about the old chronology (Sterum 1978; P.O. Nielsen 1979b).

The new chronology has provided an opportunity for renewed discussion of the origins of the Single Grave Culture and has necessitated a re-assessment of cultural development nationwide. A number of arguments against attributing the changes to immigration rather than a shift in religion or basic subsistence have been put forward (*i.a.* Ebbesen 1978a: 114ff., 1984: 131f., 1986c; J. Jensen 1979a:132ff.; Malmros 1980). This view had been aired before (Malmer 1962:810ff.). Others maintain the usual migration theory (*i.a.* Davidsen 1975:174, 1977:66ff.; E. Jørgensen 1977a:212; Kristiansen 1991b).

Regional differences

With the re-assessment of the Single Grave Period it has become clear that regional differences are great. In the early Single Grave Period there seem to have been three zones (Ebbesen 1986c:41f.): 1. Northeastern Jutland and the northern part of the islands with Pitted Ware Culture (see L.W. Rasmussen, above); 2. North and East Jutland and the islands where dolmens of the Funnel Beaker Culture and passage graves are frequently re-used and flint axes are the dominant grave goods; 3. the classic Single Grave Culture area in Mid- and West Jutland, dominated by low grave mounds, with battle-axes and amber beads as the most important grave goods.

For Single Grave-period grave finds, this means that the typical Single Grave barrow is a local Mid- and West Jutlandic form while the most common (and the only ubiquitous) grave-form of both the Single Grave Period and the Late Neolithic is secondary burial in megalithic graves (Lomborg 1973a:97ff.; Ebbesen 1984:127).

Graves without mounds

The category of graves "without mounds" includes both graves described as flat graves by their excavator and graves where no mound could be detected. Most cases are probably examples of mounds that

Single grave from Vedbæk near Esbjerg with traces of a plank coffin with a few supporting stones and skeletal traces. In front of the face lies a battle axe.

have disappeared (cf. Sterum 1976:80ff.; Olesen 1988:36ff.)

True flat graves from the Single Grave Period have been excavated at a few sites in Jutland (Thrane 1967a). In other cases it is less certain whether there had been a mound (e.g. Rostholm 1982b). At Fuglsbølle on Langeland there is a cemetery with flat graves of both the Single Grave Period and the Late Neolithic (Skaarup 1985:330ff.). In the Late Neolithic, flat graves appear on the islands especially (Lomborg 1973a:99ff.). There are recent excavations at Gundsølille near Roskilde (S.A. Sørensen 1982). In Jutland, graves without mounds have been excavated at Allestrup near Randers and Højris near Lemvig (Fiedel & Nielsen 1989:36f; Tauber 1990:232). An unusual Late-neolithic structure with a square stone paving about 15 m. across and a smaller circular stone mound has been excavated at Tønning Skov in Mid-Jutland (H.H. Andersen & Kjærum 1968).

Graves in dolmens and passage graves
It is common to find remains of graves of the Single Grave Period and Late Neolithic during the excavation of megalithic graves. But there is usually no further information about these secondary burials. In a couple of cases, large Single Grave Culture pots with so-called "short-wave moulding" below the rim have been found as votive vessels at megalithic graves (E. Jørgensen 1977a:185f.; Rostholm 1991:109ff.). This vessel-type is known from Single Grave Culture settlements (C.J. Becker 1955b).

Grave mounds (barrows)
In Mid- and West Jutland, a typical grave structure in a Single Grave barrow is a plank coffin that has collapsed and rotted away. There are often coffin traces in the form of darker fill or charcoal layers. Around the coffin may be stones, both from a heavy stone wall or frame and scattered supporting stones. In some graves coherent, often very thin, charcoal layers from the sides, lid or base of the coffin are found. An explanation of this is that the surface of the planks was singed so that the wood would hold together longer. There are examples of fires having burnt on the bed of the grave before the body was laid (C.H. Christiansen & Skelmose 1969; Eriksen 1979:17; Lauenborg 1980:12).

In the Late Neolithic the graves were constructed at the top of Single Grave barrows which were thus enlarged. The graves are often covered with a large pile of stones. In North Jutland, log coffins (i.e. hollowed-out oak trunks) seem to be very common. On the islands and in North and East Jutland Late-neo-

117

A half-excavated circle grave at Kideris near Herning. The pit measures 3.3 m. x 2.5 and 1.2 m. deep from the old surface. The grave was excavated in 1972 and contained a battle axe of type C. A plank coffin, now entirely disappeared, had stood in the large pit. A characteristic funnel-shaped feature can be seen in the section. The dark fill represents the earliest phase of the barrow which has sunk down into the grave, and the light sand, which surrounded the coffin, has fallen into the grave.

lithic barrows contain stone coffins, especially flagstone cists. New barrows are raised in the Late Neolithic too (e.g. Vorting 1977; Simonsen 1979). In some cases the piles of stone are like small cairns (Asingh 1988). The various grave-forms of the Single Grave Period and the Late Neolithic can appear side by side with the same furnishings. Thus burial practice seems to be independent of grave-form (cf. Ebbesen 1986c: 40).

Circle graves. The so-called circle graves comprise a circular or more often oval hollow with vertical sides up to 1.3 m. deep. The grave pit is usually 2.5 - 3 m. in diameter. In the centre of the pit stood a large plank coffin. A circle grave at Blåbjerg in Ribe *amt* had a pit of 4.0 m. x 3.6 (Albrethsen 1976:30).

Ring-ditches. In the course of the last 25 years, at least 70 ring-ditches associated with Single Grave-culture graves have been dug. Nearly all are from Mid- and West Jutland. Single Grave Culture ring-ditches are also known from Sarup on Fyn (N.H. Andersen 1979).

The outer diameter of the ring-ditches varies greatly, from about 1.4 to 19 m. The majority are between 3 and 5 m. in diameter. Most ring-ditches were formed as a separate ditch around the grave pit. Some of the smaller ring-ditches lie at the outer edge of the same hollow as the grave itself, with circle graves, for instance. Late-neolithic ring-ditch structures have been excavated at Runegård on

Bornholm (Wagnkilde 1986) and Løsning, Vejle (Ethelberg 1982). There is no doubt that ring-ditches were overlooked in earlier excavations which only dug the centre of the mounds.

Traces of posts or planks sometimes remain in the ring-ditches, which are often between 50 cm. and 1 m. deep, so that the posts or planks must have stood some height above the ground. By a ring-ditch at Skarrild near Herning lay the remains of a 2 m.-long, carbonized plank (Rostholm 1982a:50f.). A second structure at Skarrild had a ring-ditch measuring 3.7 m. with a secondary grave placed between the ditch and the central grave and a further grave added on to the outside of the ditch (Rostholm 1982b). In a mound at Bøel in Ribe *amt* two secondary burials were found inside a ring-ditch 7 m. in diameter.

The ring-ditches were undoubtedly foundation trenches for a fence or structure around the grave. No mound can have been raised over the small ring-ditches while the enclosure or structure was in use. There may be one or more openings where the ditch is broken or is not cut to full depth. There seems to be a close relationship between graves with ring-ditches, especially the smaller ones, and timber-built grave cists (see below).

Stone-built grave structures. Stone-built grave structures of various types occur, not all of them clearly defined. By flagstone cists is meant cists made of flat stones with or without an entrance. Both body-length and small flagstone cists are known.

Small flagstone cists were formerly called Oder cists. They are known primarily from North Jutland and have been found in large numbers in Himmerland and near Randers. There are often many small stone cists on a site, for instance at Malle, Løgstør (B. Jensen & Vellev 1971) and Skringstrup north of Viborg (Vellev 1971, 1972, 1973, 1975). It has been shown that this grave-type is not connected to the Oder area, and that contrary to earlier beliefs the graves do not appear in flat-grave cemeteries. The small stone cists are placed tangentially in the periphery of earlier barrows (Sterum 1976) and often lack grave goods.

"Grave cists" here means all grave chambers with access at one end or with a corridor. They were built of stone or timber or both. They occur in a pear-shaped form that is often referred to as the large North-Jutlandic stone cist. Amongst these, North-

South orientated examples are separately known as Bøstrup cists (Ebbesen 1985b).

The most remarkable of the stone-built grave cists is the Kobberup grave, where remains of a wooden coffin and organic material were preserved in the cist (Kjærum 1967b). Another find is from Blære near Års in Himmerland. Here, remains of the primary burial were found in a pit outside the entrance while the stone cist was filled with at least 14 secondary burials, of the whole of the Late Neolithic (Fabech 1988).

Body-length Late-neolithic flagstone cists occur over the whole country. In North Jutland they are usually aligned North-South, while a ”Sjælland type“ is oriented East-West with an entrance to the east. In recent times, barrows with flagstone cists have been excavated at Himmelev near Roskilde (Schiellerup 1992). On Bornholm, remains of a barrow with several large and small flagstone cists were excavated at Runegård (Wagnkilde 1986) and further examples have been excavated at several other sites (Watt 1978; Kempfner-Jørgensen 1983).

Undisturbed grave from Kobberup, near Skive in North Jutland. A wooden chamber was found in the stone cist, with remains of a wooden vessel and two bark beakers. The grave goods also comprised a battle axe, a flint axe, both without any trace of a handle, and amber beads. The grave is from the Ground Grave Period, and there had been no later burials in the stone cist. Outside the entrance to the chamber were remains of a timber passage.

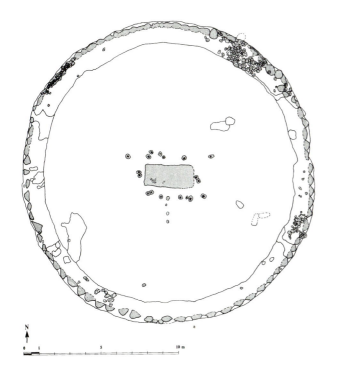

Single Grave barrow at Gantrup, north-west of Horsens. In the middle, a grave surrounded by small postholes from a mortuary house. The grave contained a plank coffin, 2.5 m. x 1.1, with a battle axe of type F2, a hollow-ground flint chisel, a thin-bladed flint axe and 7 small flakes. The ring-ditch around this is 19 m. in outer diameter and about 90 cm. deep. At the outside of the ditch were traces of close-standing, probably split posts.

Timber-built grave structures. Since 1970, about 20 wooden grave cists have been found. Their ground plan, including possible entrances, matches that of the stone grave cists described above. One of the first timber structures was found at Hald (Noe 1971). A group of four structures has been dug at Aars. That at Kjeldgården contained both a Jutlandic battle axe and a Swedish boat axe (M. Hansen 1980). The other three were at Vesthimmerland Airport. One grave there could be dated to the later Bottom Grave Period and another to the early Late Neolithic (SN A) (M. Hansen 1982). The timber-built grave cists, unlike the stone ones, could only have been used for a short period, at most a few decades. The grave goods can consequently be used to date the structures closely. It has also proved possible to divide both the stone- and the timber-built grave cists into types that are chronologically diagnostic and run from the later Bottom Grave Period to the early Late Neolithic (M. Hansen 1982).

At Dalbyneder, Randers, a grave chamber measuring 3.4 m. x 4 has been excavated, with a foundation trench with vertical planks, an entrance to the south and four burials of the Ground Grave Period (B. Madsen & Nielsen 1987).

Closed timber-built grave chambers (without entrances) are known from a small number of finds

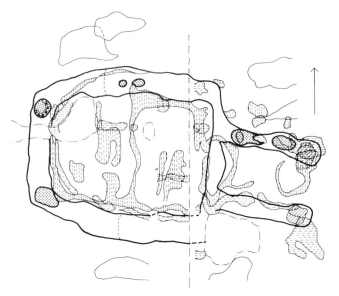

Timber-built grave cist from Vesthimmerland Airport with entrance from the east. The structure has foundation trenches with postholes and traces of decayed wood from the walls and ceiling. An amber ring was found in the chamber.

in East and Mid-Jutland. They are rectangular, and constructed of vertical planking. One structure is of the Late Neolithic; the others are from the Single Grave Period, the Bottom- and Upper Grave Periods. A small example was dug in 1987 at Gårslev (L. Hvass 1989; L. & S. Hvass 1990).

A timber structure with a ground plan strikingly similar to a passage grave has been found at Vroue in North Jutland (E. Jørgensen 1985a). Postholes around graves from Gantrup, Horsens, and Stendis, Holstebro, (Olesen 1988) are interpreted as traces of tent-like buildings surrounded by a large and a small ring-ditch respectively. A barrow at Hjordkær near Åbenrå contained a circle grave of the earlier Single Grave Period surrounded by 8 large postholes from a building of about 6 m. x 5 (E. Jørgensen 1991).

At Foulum, between Viborg and Randers, a grave structure with a small ring-ditch 2.6 m. in diameter has been dug. Around this was a post circle about 16 m. in diameter, while a row of posts 43 m. long ran out from the barrow (L. Jørgensen 1984).

Postholes and culture layers below a barrow at Lustrup near Herning are interpreted as remains of a settlement with a round building of the earliest Single Grave Culture and precede, stratigraphically, a grave with a battle axe of Glob's type B (Rostholm 1986b).

Late-neolithic timber grave structures are also known. A mound at Løsning, Vejle, contained remains of a plank coffin in a building placed in a hollow of 5 m. x 3 and 1 m. deep. There were probably at least two graves. This building was surrounded by a post circle around which there was a ring-ditch 16 - 17 m. in diameter with traces of posts (Ethelberg 1982).

A stone cairn at Diverhøj on Djursland covered the charred remains of what is thought to have been a tent-shaped building measuring about 5.5 m. x 5 and surrounded by small postholes (Asingh 1988).

In a mound at Hjordkær near Åbenrå a flat stone cairn shaped like a 5-spoked wheel was found (E. Jørgensen 1985b).

At Nautrup in Salling was a Late-neolithic grave surrounded by postholes in an oval pattern (Simonsen 1981), and 6 postholes were found beneath a flagstone cist at Krusegård on Bornholm (Watt 1978).

The contents of the graves

Skeletons rarely survive (E. Johansen 1977). Tooth-enamel or skeletal traces are, however, commonly found. There is normally one body in the grave though there are examples of double graves (C.H. Christiansen & Skelmose 1969; H.J. Madsen 1971; M.R. Madsen & Thomsen 1972; Noe 1973; Vellev 1973). The large grave cists may hold the remains of several bodies. The poor preservation of the bone means that it has been possible to undertake anthropological studies in only a few cases (E. Johansen 1977:67; Rostholm 1977:105; J.-H. Bech & Olsen 1985:38ff.).

Amber is known, especially in West Jutlandic graves (Mahler 1986). The earliest Single Grave male graves have large amber discs. Smaller amber beads are especially common in women's graves, sometimes in considerable numbers. In recent years at least 16 graves with over 100 beads have been found. A grave at Tarp, Ribe *amt,* had 375 amber beads in a single heap (M.R. Madsen & Thomsen 1972). A grave at Ottinggård in Ringkøbing *amt* had 428 beads (Rostholm 1982c) and one at Fly near Skive had over 500. To cap it all, a privately dug barrow at Vammen in Viborg *amt* allegedly contained about 1,000 amber beads. The beads are sometimes found in patterns that show they were part of complex jewellery (Lauenborg 1980).

Pottery is common only in graves in Mid-Jutland in the second half of the Single Grave Period. Pottery of the Single Grave Period and Late Neolithic

120

Grave structure from Hjordkær, Åbenrå. A cairn about 5 m. across was surrounded by a stone circle about 10 m. in diameter and linked to the cairn by 5 lines of stones like the spokes of a wheel. This was all surrounded by a post fence about 15 m. in diameter. In the cairn were found both a grave surrounded by an oval foundation trench with traces of timberwork from a building 3.5 m. long and a double grave with a flint dagger.

has been subjected to new chronological studies (Lomborg 1977b; M. Hansen 1986; L. Hvass 1986) and the few known Late-neolithic strainers are published (Ebbesen 1978b).

Several studies deal with the flint axes (Højlund 1975; P.O. Nielsen 1979b; Ebbesen 1983a). Flint axes and chisels occur in graves nationwide, but are most common on the islands. Battle axes are relatively rare on the islands, with only a few Bottom Grave-period finds known (Davidsen 1982a). The shaft-tongued battle axes and the so-called food knives of the Single Grave Culture have also been analysed (P.O.Nielsen 1976; Ebbesen 1984). The Late-neolithic finds have been examined with special attention to flint daggers (Lomborg 1973a).

The Kobberup grave noted above contained preserved items of bark and wood, though its battle axe had no wooden handle (Kjærum 1967b). Remains of such a handle were found in a battle axe in a large wooden chamber at Vroue, Viborg *amt* (E. Jørgensen 1985a). In some other graves, traces of containers of wood or some other organic material may have been found (e.g. Eriksen 1979:19).

Empty graves or graves with very little furnishing are often found. Three Single Grave mounds with 15 graves in all, 13 of which were empty, were dug at

Lund near Skive. At least 20% of the graves that can be dated to the Single Grave Period or Late Neolithic by stratigraphy or grave-type have no grave goods.

Conclusion

In the coming years, attention should be directed particularly at those areas where Single Grave Period and Late-neolithic graves are poorly represented: i.e. material from the islands in both periods (especially the early Single Grave Period) and the late Single Grave Period and Late Neolithic in Mid- and West Jutland. This calls for the excavation of large, well-preserved barrows.

We need to improve our knowledge of the often complicated grave-forms and to exploit the opportunities for studies of well-preserved structural traces beneath or beside barrows. There is also a need to obtain material for C 14 dating from the Upper Grave Period and Late Neolithic.

In light of the results that pollen analysis has produced, new excavations should see systematic soil-sampling from well-dated fossil layers even though we do not, at present, seem to have the capacity to analyse these samples. Both grave finds and samples have to be rescued before the grave mounds are totally ploughed away.

Sacrifices to the powers of nature

By Klaus Ebbesen

A very important set of finds from the Neolithic are religious in character. We can conclude from this that myths and cult practices were an integral feature of society.

The religion of the time was linked especially to graves and, not least, wetlands. It is in the ancient lakes, rivers and bogs that we find most traces of the Stone-age farmers' cult practices.

The last 25 years have produced only a few new finds. The incipient protection of the wetlands probably means that the coming years will produce even fewer. Most of the finds revealing Stone-age religion were recovered as a result of the intensification of agriculture around the beginning of this century and extensive peat-cutting during the Second World War (P.O. Nielsen 1985b). This large body of data has been subjected to intensive study in the last 25 years, producing both chronological and typological results and drawing a new picture of votive practice in the Neolithic (Rech 1979; P.O. Nielsen 1979a, b; Ebbesen 1979b, 1980, 1981,a,b,c,d,e, 1982b,c, 1983a, 1986a,b, 1989).

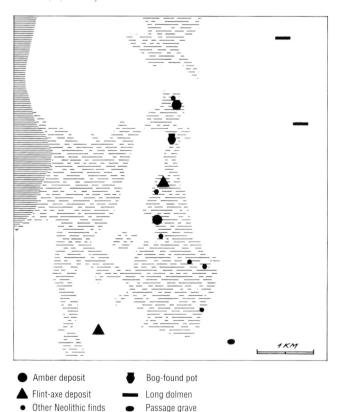

● Amber deposit   ▮ Bog-found pot
▲ Flint-axe deposit   ▬ Long dolmen
• Other Neolithic finds   ◖ Passage grave

The wetlands at Højslev in north-western Sjælland. The votive deposits were placed by the bank or out in the wetland; the megalithic graves were built higher up the slopes. The finds form a local topographical system.

Most striking are the results of the study of human remains. A number of skeletons have been found in Danish bogs, some with clear marks of violence. At Sigersdal, north-eastern Sjælland, remains of the skeletons of two persons were found, one about 16 years old, the other about 18, both, probably, women (Bennike & Ebbesen 1987). Around the neck of the elder were still the remains of a cord. The skeletons lay about 5 m. apart, and a large lugged vessel of EN C was found close by. The skeletons are C 14 dated to *ca.* 3500 B.C., the later part of the Early Neolithic. Some dramatic sequence of events must have been played out before these two people ended up in the bog (Ebbesen 1986a: 24ff.). These are probably the earliest human sacrifices in Europe.

A similar find is known from Bolkilde on Als, where two skeletons were found, both male, one about 16 years old, the other an invalid of about 40 (Bennike *et al.* 1986). Traces of a rope were found around the older man's neck. The skeletons are C 14 dated to 3370-3490 B.C., the same period as the Sigersdal sisters.

Human sacrifice is a newly discovered feature of Early-neolithic votive practice. It shows, along with the other votive deposits and the extensive megalithic architecture, that as early as the beginning of the Neolithic, Danish society was developing into a strongly governed community with social differentiation. As well as complete skeletons, sacrificial deposits include human bones, deposited together with the bones of various animals. They are the remains of huge cult feasts, where the chewed and sometimes split bones of humans and animals were sent down to the powers of water as part of the ceremonial. A find in Gammellung at Troldebjerg, Langeland, includes five young domesticated oxen, four pigs, one goat, one dog and three humans. At least two of the oxen and a 40-year-old woman were slain with a violent blow to the head. The bones were split so that no small delicacy would be wasted.

Votive deposits of the Neolithic include literally all sorts of objects. The humblest blade knife was not too simple. But there is a clear system to the deposits, reflecting the religion of the Stone Age farmer. The deposits are concentrated in fixed, especially sacred wetlands where sacrifice was made time and again. These sites are located some way from the settlement and are part of a local topographical system in which the settlement is placed on a river, lake or other water bank; somewhat higher up were the fields where graves were constructed for the dead, while votive hoards were deposited in the wetlands below. Here, hoards of flint axes were placed right by the bank while pots, for example, went in deeper water. In several places, wooden structures to stabilize the bank, probably for the ceremonies that accompanied the sacrifice, have been found.

Most sacrifices were hidden away, as it were. Often the objects were arranged in quite a definite manner on deposition. The blades of flint axes may lie like the spokes of a wheel; flint daggers may stand point downwards or sickles can be packed in. Very rarely, however, have the objects been burnt or otherwise ritually destroyed during the ceremony. Super-large objects, produced solely for sacrifice, are also rare. There are however examples of whole flint cores being broken up simply so that the blades could be sacrificed (Ebbesen 1981f). Most frequently the sacrifices comprise daily items or semi-finished versions of them.

Jewellery offered includes a few bone pins and slate pendants of the Late Neolithic, a few necklaces of boar's teeth (Müller 1896:366ff.) and, through the whole period, amber (Ebbesen 1983b). Amber deposits can vary from a single bead to over 13,000 deposited at once. The beads were often laid in a pot or wrapped up before deposition.

The great majority of the amber deposits come from the end of the Early and beginning of the Middle Neolithic. They also form a distinctively North

Early-neolithic lugged vessel from Sigersdal.

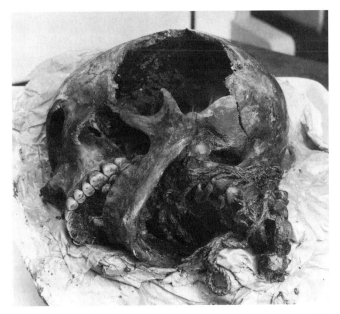

"The rope was still around the girl's neck when she was found."
Sigersdal, skeleton A, Stenløse, north-eastern Sjælland.

Jutlandic practice: common in just that area where amber naturally occurs plentifully. Outside North Jutland amber beads were relatively rare. The North Jutlanders kept the amber beads very much for themselves. Instead of setting up extensive amber trade, the beads were given to the dead in the grave or drowned in the water to the powers that resided there.

Some of the amber finds comprise just raw amber, others of a small number of beads. But there is no difference in composition between the small, medium and large amber hoards. On the contrary, it is typical for the finds to comprise raw amber, various forms of half-made beads, new beads, used and worn beads and fragments of old broken beads. It appears that it was the amber itself that was the gift.

The end of the Early and beginning of the Middle Neolithic also saw the peak of flint-axe deposition (P.O. Nielsen 1979b:61ff.). This is the age of the large, thin-butted axes, bride-prices in the opinion of some, deposited in wetlands to bring fertility to the young couple (Ebbesen 1986a:28ff.).

Axe deposits begin as early as the late Ertebølle Period and continue unbroken into the Bronze Age (Lomborg 1973a:20ff.; Ebbesen 1981d:41ff.). Usually just one axe, with a handle, is deposited. But the handle then rots so that only the blade is found.

Votive hoard from Sortekærs Mose, West Jutland. Nearly 1,800 amber beads lay in the vessel, which was buried in the ground.

Sacrificial hoard of axe blanks from Lisbjerg, Århus. The find comes from the Single Grave Period.

Neolithic flint axes found like this in Denmark are practically innumerable, and any attempt at counting them is pointless. On the other hand axes with handles are still extremely rare (Ebbesen 1979b). Frequently two or more unfinished axes or axe blades are deposited together in hoards, which may also include chisels and flint "scrap". These finds are important because they allow us to study the various stages in the process of axe-manufacture (B. Madsen, below). At the same time, they tell us something of the distributional system and the sacrificial rites. The finds are most common, and largest, in parts of Denmark where natural flint is most easily accessible. Pure blank deposits are found only here (Ebbesen 1980). To some degree, then, a surplus was sacrificed.

The largest flint-axe deposit has been found at Knud in Southern Jutland (Ebbesen 1981c, 1989). In a small pool here, at short intervals during MN V, three deposits totalling 99 axe blades and chisels were made. They were carefully placed in piles.

Recently too, no less than 70 axe and chisel hoards of the Battle Axe Period have also been identified (Ebbesen 1983a). In form of deposition, composition and distribution, these finds match the other neolithic axe hoards. Thus the practice of sacrificing axes shows a special degree of continuity.

In the earlier Neolithic, there was deposition of pointed-butted flint axes. These were followed by the many finds of thin-butted flint axes. These are directly superseded by the late, Middle-neolithic deposits of thick-butted flint axes, which continue into the Single Grave Period, in the middle of which they are superseded by hoards with flint adzes (gouges). From here there is direct continuity into the Late-neolithic hoards of both adzes and axes and the latest finds of broad-edged flint axes belonging to Bronze Age Periods I/II.

Axe-sacrifice is, as noted, supplemented during the Neolithic by other practices. In the Early Neolithic and early Middle Neolithic it is very common, for instance, for pots to be deposited in wetlands

(C.J. Becker 1947). Amongst the many and varied pottery-forms of the period it is by preference the medium-sized, slightly coarse funnel beakers that were used. It is probable, then, that what was of importance was the pot's contents. Analyses of preserved food scraps have not yet revealed whether these were wheat porridge or other food. Comparison with the pottery that was deposited at that time in front of the megalithic graves has show that there were two different cult traditions. The deposits by the Middle-neolithic megalithic graves were part of the funeral rites and linked with intense ancestor worship. Sacrifices in wetlands were by contrast most probably an element of the fertility cult so important to the Stone-age farmer.

At the beginning of the Late Neolithic, the dagger fashion reached Denmark. Quite extensive sacrificial deposition of flint daggers in wetlands begins at the same time (Lomborg 1973a). Again, the finds are concen-trated in the flint-rich areas, especially North Jutland. From the old Single Grave area in the Jutish peninsula, by contrast, hardly any Late-

neolithic flint-tool sacrifices are known. The situation is much the more peculiar in that at this date flint daggers were distributed far to the north, in Norway (Ebbesen 1980). In Mid- and West Jutland, however, there was extensive sacrificial deposition of simple shaft-hole axes.

Together with the flint daggers, other flat-trimmed tools of the period were sacrificed, including spoon-shaped scrapers, more rarely spearheads, but very frequently flint sickles. Many of the crescentic sickles had been used, and show definite wear. They are often deposited singly, or in small groups. These finds are interpreted as harvest offerings.

The large, Early-neolithic votive hoard of copper objects from Bygholm, Horsens (illust. Brøndsted 1957:188) is an example of the rare metal finds of the early Neolithic. It is first towards the end of the Late Neolithic that gold and bronze came here in considerable quantities and metal consequently became a regular element in votive hoards (Vandkilde 1990a). With this a new period, with new votive practices, was on its way.

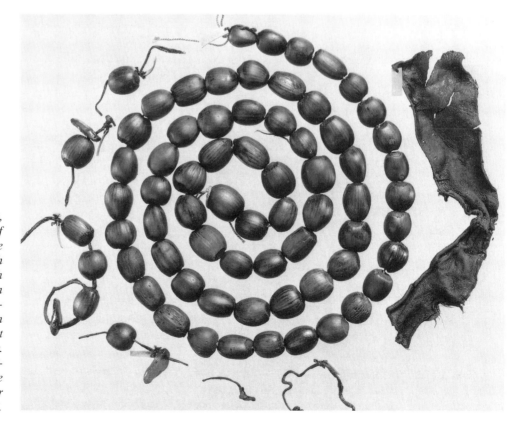

In Tværmose, Ejsing parish, about 3 m. below the surface of the bog, a piece of calf hide measuring 16 cm. x 3.5 with holes along the edge through which a leather throng had been drawn was found. Three perforated pieces of amber had been on the thong together with about 70 perforated hazelnut shells. The find is C 14-dated to 3090-2951 B.C. (Ua 329) and is the only known fragment of leather clothing from the Stone Age. 1:3.

Flint - extraction, manufacture and distribution

BY BO MADSEN

South-west Scandinavia is one of the chalk-rich areas of Europe. Formations deriving from the upper chalk are common in all deposits of the last Ice Age. The *in situ* layers below ground are between a half and nearly two km. thick. Eastern Sjælland, Lolland-Falster and North Jutland in particular formed one of the world's largest areas where raw flint could be obtained in prehistory. In the Late Mesolithic and the Early Neolithic the rising of the Littorina Sea meantthat the coast line became much longer, with the erosion and exposure of flint-bearing layers as a consequence. The most important deposits of the Cretaceous Period, the lower Maastricht stage, were exposed around Møn and the eastern Limfjord. In the later deposit - Danium - the flint was deposited in hard chalk and limestone. This, as the name implies, is richly represented in Denmark, especially in eastern Sjælland and several outcrops in East Jutland. There are two types of Danium flint: a grey,

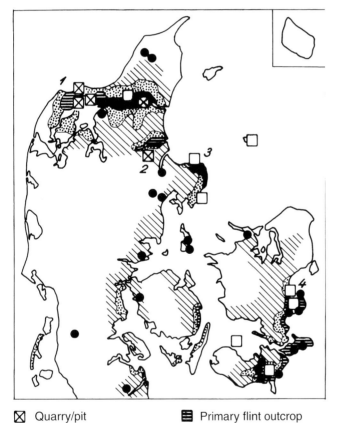

☒ Quarry/pit
☐ Worksite
● Hoard of blanks
▤ Primary flint outcrop
▨ Secondary flint outcrop
▨ Random flint outcrop

Occurrences of raw flint, flint quarries and the most important knapping sites and hoards of semi-manufactures. 1: Thisted; 2: Blegvad; 3: Fornæs; 4: Hastrup Vænge and Frøslev (axe worksites).

rough-grained type and a dull translucent type that is difficult to distinguish from the very varied but usually clear flint from the white chalk.

It is not possible to determine the origin of the different varieties of flint with certainty, unlike, for instance, in France, the Low Countries and Poland. The Danish occurrences are also too homogeneous. The archaeological value of provenancing is particularly limited by the muddled nature of morrain flint deposits. One of the few distinctive types for example, the East Scanian Senonian Kristianstad flint, is found in "indicator blocks" in the border morrain of southern Djursland. It is, nevertheless, informative to investigate the local and regional areas of supply in relation to settlement studies and analyses of spheres of trade and exchange (B. Madsen 1983:26). As, to some extent, in earlier studies (C.J. Becker 1953b, 1988), it is sensible to divide the country into a number of natural resource areas, and not least to remember that over large areas little usable flint was to be found in the neolithic landscape.

A type of flint that was of considerable importance for neolithic flint production is the so-called "Blue Falster" quality (B. Madsen 1984:52). In *in situ* chalk this is known only from minor surface sites on eastern Lolland and Falster. But in secondary, chalk-rich clay deposits this flint is found along the Storebælt coast of Sjælland, along the coasts of South and East Jutland and in the especially flint-rich East Jutlandic morrains. It is fine-grained, matt and porous. The blue cast is visible in a zone around the core. As fresh flint, its surface is rapidly affected by light. The raw material occurs in impressively large and homogeneous lumps up to a metre long. The large neolithic blades in the hoard from Høng (Ebbesen 1982c) and the famous Hindsgavl dagger were made of this flint.

In the European context, Denmark possesses a unique source of material in the form of composite finds (hoards) of finished flint tools whose size and quantity reflects exchange or the hoarding of a surplus. In eastern Denmark and North Jutland concentrations of significant artefacts and large thin-butted axes are found within the naturally flint-rich areas (Lomborg 1973a:37). The artefacts in the individual hoards are often produced from one type of flint and in a very consistent form (P.O. Nielsen 1984). In Indonesian New Guinea, where stone axes are still used and where the production of the largest axes is a highly specialized trade amongst the semi-agriculturists of the highlands, there is a close geographical relationship between quarries, worksites and the length and quantities of stone axes (Pétrequin 1988).

Flint quarries

Flint mines and pits are rarely found in Denmark. By Thisted on the white chalk of North Jutland three sites have been identified, two of the Early Neolithic and one of the Late, matching an equally old pit complex by Ålborg (C.J. Becker 1980a). After a break of 25 years, another flint quarry has been found, unexpectedly southerly in East Jutland, at Blegvad by the Kousted river north of Randers. In the early Battle Axe Period, at the edge of a small valley, flint was quarried from the white chalk. Larger knapping areas around the pits show that small axe blanks in particular were made here. Tool preforms indeed appear as a distinct group of hoards

(Ebbesen 1980) that include axe-forms and, now and then, material for large blade cores. To these can be added the large finds of rejected axe preforms in raised shore-banks, a group of finds that still has not been paid much attention. East Jutland and the islands have, altogher, 7-800 km. of coast running through relatively flint-rich deposits in which it will be possible to identify many knapping sites. There are also many finds of semi-manufactures and much evidence of worksites in the collections of local museums that are waiting for systematic study.

Axe worksites - experiments

Several excavated worksites for specialized axe production from the earlier Funnel Beaker Culture are now known around Stevns. Hastrup Vænge, close to Køge, was the first systematically analysed site. A methodological short-cut in interpretation

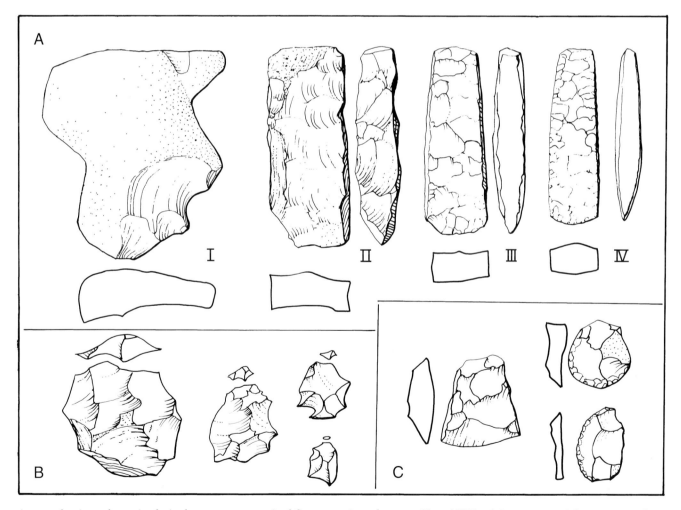

Axe production schematized. A: the process comprised five operations; between 60 and 80% of the raw material was removed. B: typical axe-core flake with faceted platform and jagged polygonal outline. C: tools, typical of earlier Funnel Beaker settlements, made from axe-core flakes: flake axes, flake scrapers and backed knives.

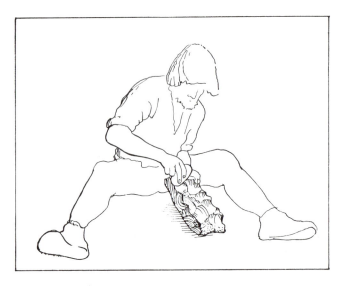

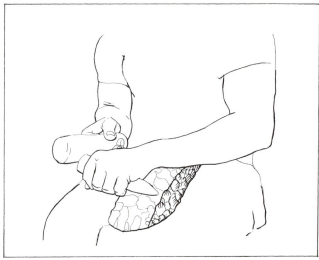

Blank manufacture with hammer-stone by a natural flint out-crop: 5 to 10 minutes' work.

Further knapping of the axe blank by indirect percussion with antler flakers - around 2 hours' work for a medium-sized axe.

was the reconstruction of the worksite through knapping experiments which revealed the distribution of flint debitage and the variance in size and form of the flakes (P.V. Hansen & Madsen 1983). The conclusions from this and many later studies are that the knapping of a four-sided axe, which requires great experience, saw the reduction of the piece in stages during which one had to pay heed to the size, form and quality of the material. The process required the maker to have a precise notion of the finished product. The production of a thin-butted axe required five operations: 1. the finding and selection of the raw material; 2. the shaping of a square blank with a hammer-stone; 3. further indirect shaping of the piece with medium flakers of antler; 4. finally the formation of the blade and edges with accurate, indirect flaking; 5. polishing. This process includes grinding, polishing and sharpening.

Stages 2, 3 and 4 are represented in the worksite finds in different forms of waste flakes detritus which essentially reflect decisions taken in series by the neolithic flint-knapper. The experiments showed that by analysing the by-products - several thousand flakes per axe - one can read the production process in the very consistent variation in the size and weight of the flakes. The worksite area at Hastrup Vænge - just one of many - produced 168 kg. of flint waste, a good 30,500 pieces in all, representing the production of about 25-30 thin-butted axes. Theoretically, these could have been knapped on the site by two craftsmen - to judge by the two sep-

Hoard with 16, polished all-over, thin-butted flint axes found in 1971 in a ploughed field at Hagelbjergård near Ringsted on Sjælland.

arate clusters - over 4 to 5 working days. And it should be noted that more than 250 kg. of flint were brought to the site.

Perspectives

The qualitative and quantitative, technical studies have been productive in respect both of methodological development and classification. The production of axes and large flint daggers was a stage-wise process and the most careful knapping took place at special worksites. Semi-manufactured pieces, however, were produced by the flint-rich coasts or, in a few cases, at mines.

The production of the large flint objects was apparently undertaken by specialists in the areas richest in flint. This specialization was the result of several processes. In the case of the Funnel Beaker Culture it was a matter of technological progress coinciding with the development of special social and economic structures, such as are amply illuminated by the large Sarup sites and monumental megaliths.

One of the experimental large axes in stage 4 and 5. Knapped in 3 hours and then polished for a good 30 man hours. This removed 420 g. of flint and the axe moved through 47 km. across the polishing stone. The total production time would be a good 32 hours, including the delicate sharpening of the bit of the cutting edge. It is thought-provoking that many Funnel Beaker-culture votive hoards contain 5 to 12 of these very large flint axes, perfectly formed and often resharpened, possibly the product of 2 or 3 months' specialist work.

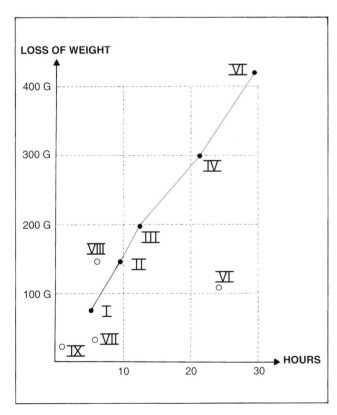

Experimental polishing of a replica thin-butted axe in 1983-84 by J. Pelegrin and B. Madsen (B. Madsen 1984). Medium-sized work axes could have been polished for 6 to 10 hours, depending on the quality of the knapping.

Experiments in flint techonology, as, for instance, the controlled testing of polishing methods in 1983-84, have now been followed up with studies of worksites by the Krzemionki mine complex in Poland, the Great Langdale axe worksites in England and analyses of Magdalenian sites in France (Böeda & Pelegrin 1985). In respect of the history of flint technology, a future job of international importance to be done is the study of worksites and flint production in the late Middle Neolithic and Late Neolithic especially, when daggers and long blades were exchanged alongside copper artefacts. Several large flint centres were established in northern, eastern and western Europe.

THE BRONZE AGE

The Bronze Age

By Jørgen Jensen

Research into the Bronze Age in Denmark in the last 25 years can in many ways be regarded as having undergone a revolution in relation to what went before. In the years up to about 1970, research was particularly directed towards study of the dependency of the Scandinavian Bronze Age on Continental contacts. Imported bronzes in particular were the subject of thorough studies intended to pinpoint their origins and date (Lomborg 1969; Randsborg 1974; Thrane 1975). But with the emergence of a new, socially-oriented and anthropological archaeology in the 1970's, attention shifted towards the local context. Attempts were made to clarify the multiplicity of ecological, demographic, economic and social factors that governed the development of Scandinavian Bronze-age society in the period *ca.* 1700-500 B.C. This change in the direction of research has produced a stream of publications,

especially articles (J. Jensen 1988a), of which, however, only a few are the product of larger, formally organized collaborative projects. There are a few exceptions: principally the Dano-German collaboration in a systematic and comprehensive publication of Early Bronze-age material from graves and hoards (Aner & Kersten 1973 etc.), a project which, with its high standards of documentation, stands quite alone in Europe. So far 11 volumes of this publication have appeared, covering the Danish islands, South Jutland, and the adjoining areas of Schleswig-Holstein. The rest of the Danish finds will be published in six further volumes (see general map).

Amongst other major initiatives that the last 25 years have seen, I would draw attention to a comprehensive topographical study of the area of southwestern Fyn supervised by Fyns Oldtid Hollufgård (Thrane 1989). There is also the large number of settlement-site excavations in western Jutland in the triangle between Ringkøbing, Herning and Holstebro carried out by the Archaeological Settlement Committee of the National Humanities Research Council (C.J. Becker 1982b), and a large, international project in Thy, which, down to 1995, will try to clarify settlement in one of the most important settlement areas of the Bronze Age. These projects, and a large number of rescue excavations financed by paragraph 26 of the Museum Act, underlie a massive increase in Bronze-age material. In this context, the need to look at the newly-harvested results in a larger context has arisen.

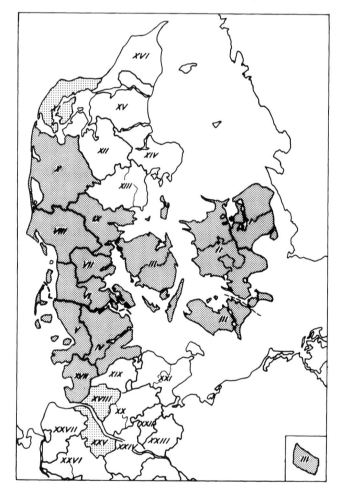

Chart of the publication of 'Die Funde der älteren Bronzezeit des nordischen Kreises' by Ekkehard Aner and Karl Kersten. Published volumes are shown by dark shading and volumes in preparation in a lighter tone.

New approaches

Two approaches have been dominant in recent Danish Bronze Age research. Under the first, scholars have concerned themselves with the subsistence system and settlement pattern of the agrarian society that developed in Denmark from the end of the Neolithic at the beginning of the 2nd millennium B.C. down to the beginning of the Iron Age around 500 B.C. The starting point for this is the numerous settlement excavations of the last 25 years, and the results have, in many respects, been radical. Where, right up to the 1960's, knowledge of the form of Bronze-age settlement was utterly lacking, excavations of a large number of settlements in the last generation have made it possible to follow the main lines of the development of the smallest productive unit of the agrarian society, the farmstead, from the large longhouses of the Late Neolithic down to the

132

earliest Iron-age farmsteads. It has at the same time become possible to derive an incipient understanding of how the individual productive units joined into a larger whole, and how the cultural landscape in which they were situated was exploited.

Under the second approach, scholars have tried to understand the role of metal in Bronze-age society and economy. Given that bronze has to be regarded as an exotic material in southern Scandinavia, there is no doubt that its importation and use in Bronze-age society can testify to important aspects of the social organization and the underlying socio-economic system of the period. Much research has therefore been aimed at clarifying just those processes that governed the development of the distinctive social form of the Bronze Age.

Development of the landscape and settlement

In settlement studies, it is of importance that natural-scientific research has provided us with a clearer and more detailed picture of the prehistoric landscape in which Bronze-age culture evolved. In general one can say that the earlier image of a single course of development has been changed, and that instead we are more conscious of the great differences that there were between separate parts of the country (Aaby, above).

As early as the Neolithic, intense exploitation of the forest was underway. Clearings were made for fields and buildings, the forest was grazed by cattle, leaf-hay was collected for winter fodder, firewood, and building timber, and so on. This intense land-use led to the decline of the forest, albeit in different measures in different places. On the thin soils of western Jutland, for instance, pollen analyses have shown that as early as the beginning of the Bronze Age the destruction of the forest was far advanced, and had led to regular heath-formation in some places, while other places saw grass-dominated pasture vegetation at this date. On the fertile soils of Thy, one can see a very forceful expansion of treeless areas as early as the Single Grave Period. In the Bronze Age, the cultural landscape here was densely settled and open, and used for grazing and cultivation. A similar development seems to have taken place in the equally densely settled (in the Bronze Age) area of Himmerland. Along the Storebælt on Sjælland, and probably in the other coastal areas of the island where settlement was dense, we can see continuous landscape exploitation that is very like that which

Early Bronze-age amber figure from a grave at Sejstrup near Ribe (Asingh 1990). It is possible to see the figure as a model building, although the architecture does not fully match the results of settlement excavations (see Feveile 1992). Ca. 2:1.

can be seen in Thy. Further inland on Sjælland, on the other hand, a picture emerges of many breaks in agriculture, followed by periods of reforestation on formerly agricultural land. The cultural breaks are generally not synchronous, but rather determined by local or regional circumstances.

It is on this basis amongst others, that the large number of settlements excavated have to be assessed. As shown below (Rasmussen & Adamsen), a complicated picture of the development of settlement through the 1,200 years or so of the Bronze Age emerges. We have not achieved a dependable typology and chronology of buildings. It is clear, however, that already in the Early Bronze Age an original, two-aisled building-form was superseded by a three-aisled construction, and that there was a definite development from very large, strong building-types to smaller and slighter forms. These slighter buildings, however, also seem to be present at an early date in the Bronze Age. The changes in building technique, including, for instance, the transition from log-walls to daub, may very well be explicable through the evident impoverishment of the forest at the same time. But it is also a fact that in many places local conditions confuse the general picture.

There is also still a great deal of uncertainty about the structure of settlement. The main question here has been what differentiates Bronze-age settlement from the pre-Roman Iron-age village such as appears, for example, at Grøntoft and Hodde.

Bronze-age settlement generally shows a quite different, more open character, with a relatively large distance between individual farmsteads. Perhaps this settlement can best be described as "clustered settlement". It is often, however, very difficult to determine how many buildings existed at any one time at a particular site. But generally, development through the Bronze Age seems to tend towards increasing numbers of house-holds in the individual clustered settlements. An important task for future research is to determine how, in the course of the 1st millennium B.C., Bronze-age settlement develops into the type of village we know from the early pre-Roman Iron Age. A second important task will be to establish a connexion between the cemeteries and settlement, in order to investigate whether the graves do not, in one way or another, reflect the organization of settlement.

Despite many uncertainties, a much more detailed picture than that of 25 years ago can be seen. Bronze-age settlement now appears as stable and organized in a quite different way than previously thought. And it seems to be a fact that the finds already known will be able to yield much more information and thus contribute to the creation of a more convincing general model than we have so far had. With this alone, we will be able to give the many rescue excavations the research-oriented perspective they need.

Social form
Down to the 1960's, the discussion of Bronze-age social form led to very general propositions. Bronze-age society was described either as a "society divided into classes" (Brøndsted) or a society without major social difference (Broholm). At the beginning of the 1970's, however, a number of studies moving in new directions were published (Randsborg 1974). Through a number of simple quantitative analyses of grave goods in Early Bronze-age burials, it was shown that there must have been great variation in wealth and social status in the Bronze-age population. Certain individuals could now distinguish themselves through the possession of metal objects. By weighing the furnishings of Early Bronze-age graves one could show that there was significant qualitative and quantitative differentiation of wealth. One could also show that most of the gold occurred in the relatively few graves with a lot of bronze, as well as those objects that could be interpreted as symbols of

political power: heavy bronze swords, palstaves, folding chairs, staves with bronze mounts and certain dress-ornaments. This observation was interpreted in terms of the highly-positioned individuals being representatives of the leading stratum of society and not of the population as a whole. Furthermore, the social pattern reflected in the Early Bronze-age graves correlates with the social anthropological concept "chiefdom".

Related analyses were also made of the finds from the Late Bronze Age (Thrane 1981, 1984; Freudenberg 1989). Here too it could be shown that the grave goods, despite their paucity, testify to clear differentiation in wealth. But what was really significant for the perception of the social pattern of the Late Bronze Age was the excavation of Lusehøj on Fyn (Thrane, below), which showed that even in Period V chieftains' barrows were raised over lavishly furnished graves.

Investigations of grave finds have produced a picture of a hierarchically organized Bronze-age society that at certain periods was characterized by the extravagant consumption of metal and other status-marking objects in graves and hoards. These could be personal ornaments and weapons or symbolic objects such as horse gear, drinking vessels, helmets, shields etc.

It has also been suggested that there was a system of ranks within the elite of this society: a sort of warrior aristocracy in which chieftains with ritual functions formed the apex, above a group of warriors without special ritual functions (Kristiansen 1984).

It was predictable that such a social pattern should be reflected in the organization of settlement. A lot of importance has thus been attached to identifying so-called centres of wealth in the Bronze Age. In the Late Bronze Age such centres can be identified in the areas of both south-western Fyn and south-western Jutland (J. Jensen 1983; Thrane 1984). Centres of wealth have been conceived of as meeting points in the network of exchange connexions that linked the separate settlement areas, from which, throughout the Bronze Age, the elite (the chiefly dynasties) controlled the exchange of prestige goods and probably of people too in a continual competition for social status.

From these studies, it may appear to be quite a leap across to the more technical analyses of craftwork that have been undertaken at the same time but which are of no less importance: experimental

Reconstruction of a Late Bronze-age longhouse. This building, which was raised in 1987 at Fyns Oldtid - Hollufgård, is based on the results of a gas pipeline excavation at Højby on Fyn in 1982.

archaeology, for instance, which has tried to penetrate the secrets of bronzecasting. A number of valuable studies have succeeded in determining the truth of many of the fixed notions concerning Bronze-age decorative techniques (Rønne 1991 and below) and in showing that it relied extensively on punched ornament. These studies provide us with an entirely new starting point for the study of Bronze-age metal craft and the distribution of bronze objects from individual workshop areas.

The European prospect

Although Bronze Age studies in the last 25 years have been undertaken with quite new approaches in many respects, the chronological analyses that are the backbone of all archaeological research have not

been neglected. Much new insight has been obtained through scientific dating methods in particular. One should emphasize especially the application of dendrochronology to the Bronze-age oak coffins (Randsborg, below). We now have a solid foundation for a broad perspective covering cultural development in the whole continent of Europe, where important events took place throughout the last two millennia B.C. and where one can detect certain pulses running across the various regions of Europe at the same time. What at first glance may have appeared to be very local studies have in many cases proved to yield results that open up the way for the writing of a truly European prehistory in which the connexion between the near and the far is becoming ever clearer.

Settlement

BY MARIANNE RASMUSSEN AND CHRISTIAN ADAMSEN

It may be impossible to explain how a category of finds can remain wholly unknown for a long time. Although other sets of Bronze-age remains had been familiar for a long time, settlements stayed hidden for more than 50 years after the first Iron-age buildings were discovered. The first Bronze-age buildings were found at Fragtrup in Himmerland in the mid-1950's, but only in the late 1960's did excavations achieve any real momentum: A series of settlements were excavated near Ristoft in western Jutland (1967-68), followed by, most importantly, Hovergårde, Spjald and Bjerg (1969-74). Here, the stripping of large areas by machine made it possible to investigate several longhouses in context. An initiative taken by the National Humanities Research Council, the Archaeological Settlement Site Committee, made these excavations possible. Once recognized, the number of buildings rose rapidly, and from the mid-1980's problem-oriented excavations have produced crucial new insights. There are various aspects of the settlements that have been subject to special attention:

First, naturally, the buildings themselves. At Fragtrup (1955-62), Egehøj (1969-73), Hemmed Church and Hemmed Plantation (1987-92) the level of preservation was exceptionally good. Well-preserved

building plots and an unusual quantity of artefacts in cultural layers supported detailed observation of the construction and fitting out of the buildings and their dating. Separated by protective blown-sand layers, the different settlement phases at the Hemmed sites show nearly unbroken building development through 1,500 years. While these finds have provided important details, other sites have directed interest into larger contexts.

Through the excavation of virtually complete settlements covering several hectares, the relationships between buildings and thus the size and organization of the settlements can be illuminated. This strategy was inspired by the major excavations of Iron-age settlements, and affected Spjald (1969-71), Bjerg (1971-74), Vadgård (1971-76) and Højgård (1984-90).

A long-nourished desire to study settlements along with the whole cultural landscape came fruition at Bjerre. Here, for the first time, one could identify a field system associated with a Bronze-age settlement. This investigation is the latest development in the growth of important results and it concurrently points the way towards new perspectives.

Danish settlement studies have made a crucial contribution to research into a settlement pattern that is common to north-western Europe. Comparison with Central Europe, where exchange of bronze was largely carried on, becomes harder however. So far, for instance, no fortified central places have been found in Danish territory, while more ordinary settlement in Central Europe is still very obscure.

The buildings

The earliest Bronze-age buildings are of the so-called two-aisled type (Egehøj). This means that the

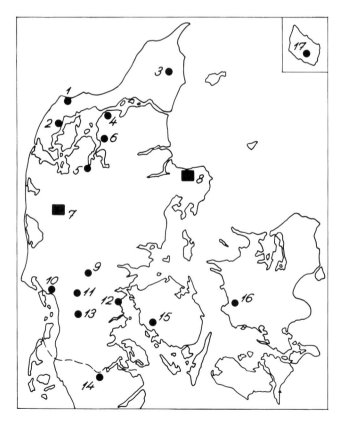

Bronze-age settlements. 1: Bjerre (Bech 1991); 2: Ås (M. Mikkelsen 1992); 3: Store Tyrrestrup (Nilsson 1991); 4: Vadgård (Lomborg 1973b, 1976; M. Rasmussen, in press, b); 5: Jegstrup (Davidsen 1982b); 6: Fragtrup (Draiby 1985); 7: The Nr. Omme area, with the settlements Ristoft, Hovergårde, Spjald, Bjerg, Grøntoft, Nygård, Kærholm and Omgård (C.J. Becker 1968, 1972b, 1980b, 1982b; J. Jensen 1971; L.C. Nielsen 1981b); 8: The Hemmed area, with the settlements at Egehøj, Hemmed church and Hemmed plantation (Boas 1983, 1991, 1993); 9: Vorbasse (S. Hvass 1983); 10: Grønnegård I (Siemen 1990); 11: Stavnsbjerg (Rindel 1992); 12: Trappendal (Boysen & Andersen 1983); 13: Højgård (Ethelberg 1987, 1993); 14: Handewitt (Bokelmann 1977); 15: Voldtofte-Kirkebjerget (Müller 1919; J. Jensen 1967; Thrane 1980a; J. Berglund 1982; Nyegaard 1993); 16: Hyllerup (J-Aa. Pedersen 1986); 17: Grødbygård (P.O. Nielsen 1989).

roof was borne on a single row of strong posts placed along the mid-line of the building. After more than 2,000 years' use, this structure was superseded by the three-aisled construction: i.e. with two rows of roof-bearing posts. What underlay this change is not clear, but the three-aisled form requires less strong timbers, and changing requirements in fitting out and the use of the buildings may also have been a factor.

A group of early buildings (Højgård, Bjerg etc.) are very solidly built, to impressive dimensions - the longest is the 50 m.-long Store Tyrrestrup building. That much slighter buildings are found at the same time (Trappendal, Bjerre) may reflect local timber shortages. The partly preserved sections of posts from Bjerre, accordingly, came from oak branches so badly misshapen that one would scarcely use their like in modern reconstructions. Wall structure itself varies greatly. Large intervals between strong wall posts indicate a log wall. Clay plaster with impressions of horizontal planks from such a construction was found at Hemmed Church. As yet it is mostly finds from eastern Denmark and the Late Bronze Age that show wattle-and-daub walls. Here one can see impressions of the woven withies that supported the daub in the surviving clay daub. In some cases traces of painting have been found on the clay surface (Skamlebæk, Voldtofte). Entrances to buildings change form through time. In the Early Bronze Age, entrances can be hard to identify. They are often no more than a larger gap between wall posts. As a rule, however, each long side has one entrance, and it is common for these to be placed at a diagonal to one another. In the Late Bronze Age, entrances are more clearly marked by extra drawn-in posts within the wall.

The early three-aisled buildings in particular have concentrations of cooking-stone pits at the western end (Ethelberg 1987) probably reflecting the repeated renewal of hearths. Some buildings, however, have hearths at both ends. Several of the early buildings also have one or two transverse partition walls (Trappendal, Hyllerup, Højgård, Handewitt etc.), showing that the building may have been divided up for several functions or groups of people. Some such buildings are found on settlements together with unpartitioned buildings and where there may also be great variation in building-length on the same site (Højgård). This may indicate that the inhabitants of a site did not all have the same needs or the same importance. The use of different areas in the build-

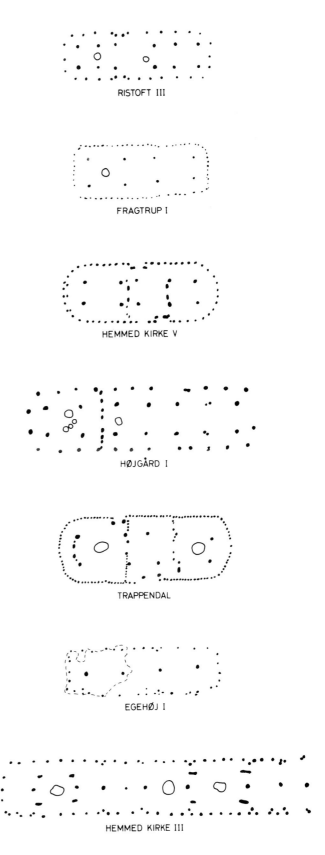

The development of Bronze-age buildings. 1:500.

137

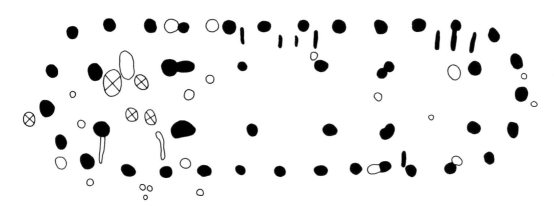

Spjald, western Jutland. The strongly built house XXX that has traces of possible stable partitioning in the eastern part. 1:200.

ing for different activities can, in favourable circumstances, be seen in the distribution of finds (Fragtrup, Egehøj).

The three-aisled structure ought perhaps to be looked at in the context of the creation of stalls, which were certainly found from the beginning of the Iron Age in the form of wooden box-partitions in two rows along the long sides at the eastern end of the building. So far, we cannot identify possible loose-housing stalls from the Bronze Age, while box stalls occur very rarely here, often questionably identified (Bjerre, Spjald). The issue of stalling is one of the most important factors in distinguishing the individual production units - the farms - in the settlement. A coherent unit of this kind can consist of more than a single building. Finds of special, often small and specially constructed buildings and other structures alongside regular, post-built longhouses, show that there was a need for outbuildings for particular economic purposes. Examples of such possible outbuildings are the circular structures at Bjerre, the turf buildings at Vadgård (M. Rasmussen 1993) and specially constructed minor buildings at Hemmed Church.

There are still major problems in the interpretation of the development of settlements. Datings of the individual structures and thus the question of contemporaneity pose especial problems. It is, however, clear that different building-forms are not necessarily to be assigned to different parts of the Bronze Age. Local resources, social organization and different subsistence strategies may affect the construction and fitting out of a building.

Excavation, preservation and finds
Knowledge of the whole appearance and size of a settlement is of course dependent on the extent of excavation. It is, sadly, usually only directly threat-

ened parts that are excavated, leaving the majority of the site unexplored.

With a few exceptions, it is only traces of the sunken features of the settlement such as posts from buildings or other structures like pits that are preserved. Everything above ground-level in the period of settlement (floor layers, rubbish layers, hearths, pavements etc.) have usually been ploughed away. A combination of the thickness of the soil layers, the size of the culture layers and the local topographical circumstances has, however, meant that on a slope near the village of Voldtofte, south-western Fyn, Kirkebjerget, thick and productive culture layers have been preserved. These were formed from rubbish and manure that gradually accumulated from a settlement of considerable size.

A special situation occurs with a good quarter of modern barrow excavations, where sealed settlement traces are found (Torslev, Diverhøj; E. Johansen 1985; Asingh 1988; M. Rasmussen, in press, a). Since these have been undisturbed since the barrow was raised, they form an especially good source with, for instance, examples of some our best preserved building plots from the Early Bronze Age. Both at Trappendal near Kolding and Hyllerup in south-western Sjælland, however, there was cultivation in between the lifetime of the buildings and the raising of the barrow. In the latter case, the building plot was extensively ploughed over. With good finds, it is possible to observe the sequence and duration of the events that took place on the site. Under the large barrow of Lusehøj on south-western Fyn a settlement area of the end of the Early Bronze Age was found (Thrane 1984). This was ploughed over twice, and then several minor grave mounds of the beginning of the Late Bronze Age were constructed. After this, the area was finally used for raising the

Diverhøj, Djursland (East Jutland). Ardmarks under an Early Bronze-age barrow (Period II). The barrow was built over a stone-built mound of the Early Late Neolithic, and the ardmarks date to the period in between. The series of furrows comes right to the edge of the Late-neolithic mound, the extent of which is shown by the curved layout of the parallel ardmarks. Below the neolithic mound a culture layer and three longhouses (all Late-neolithic), which had been ploughed over before the first mound was built, were found.

large barrow from the middle of the Late Bronze Age. The same relatively small area was thus used in different ways, apparently without break, by the local community for years.

Traces of fields are found under a good half of the recently excavated barrows in the form of the characteristic criss-cross furrows of the ard. But with a few lucky exceptions, these are difficult to date (Thrane 1991a). The same holds for another phenomenon, the finding of rows of pits filled with fire-crazed stones running several hundred metres but lacking other finds providing precise dating or evidence of function. These have now been found at several sites (e.g. Låddenhøj at Roskilde; T. Christensen 1986). By means of C 14 these structures can most often be dated to the Bronze Age, but they remain inexplicable.

Settlements are remains of the most central places in the life of Bronze-age Man. In all but a few exceptional cases, however, they are extremely poor in bronze finds. The finds primarily comprise potsherds and flint tools and detritus from the production of these. These are day-to-day objects, and precious bronze was only rarely left here. Although the quantity of artefacts basically depends on the conditions for preservation of the particular site, we do see differences governed by other factors. The quantity of finds is generally low in the middle of the Early Bronze Age, while a lot of pottery may appear in the Late Bronze Age, usually, however, from just a few large rubbish pits. It is also Late Bronze-age settlements that produce most finds deriving from bronze-casting. We can see regional differences in the quan-

tity of flint on settlements in the same period: the eastern Danish sites have considerably more flint than, for instance, those of western Jutland.

Flint is a fundamental material for tools throughout the Bronze Age, but only rarely can it be used for dating. The situation is different with pottery, where knowledge of the development of particular forms can be used as a means of dating (J. Jensen 1966, 1967; Draiby 1985; M. Rasmussen, in press, b). The same settlement may, however, have several phases,

Vadgård near Løgstør. Pottery was found on the fundament to a turf wall and can thus be used to date the small building.

139

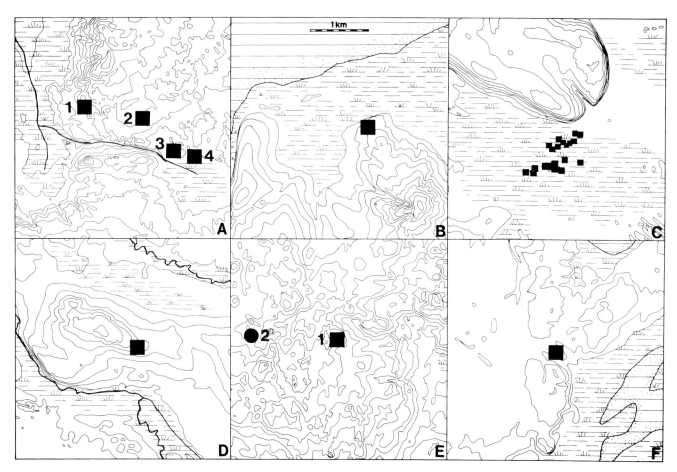

The topographical position of Bronze-age settlements in the landscape. A: The Hemmed area (1: Hemmed Kær, 2: Egehøj, 3: Hem-med Church, 4: Hemmed Plantation; B: Vadgård; C: Bjerre; D: Højgård; E: (1) Voldtofte, (2) Lusehøj; F: Jegstrup. Equ. 5 m.

so that if, for instance, a particular building does not itself produce datable finds, one cannot simply link it to other datable structures in the vicinity.

Finds of tools like sickles, arrows, sinkers and the like tell us what the people did to get their daily food. Important finds in this respect are larger and smaller stores of grain (Vadgård, Lindebjerg, Egehøj and Voldtofte; G. Jørgensen 1979; Rowley-Conwy 1979, 1984a-b; Jæger & Laursen 1983), which show that barley was the most important cereal-type but that the various types of wheat played a major part too. As in the Iron Age, most bone finds come from eastern Denmark, nearly all, in fact, from the Late Bronze Age. Early Bronze-age bone finds can still be counted on the fingers of one hand, and comprise pretty small collections. The Bronze-age bone finds have recently been analysed by Georg Nyegaard, with important results. A high proportion of ox bones, for instance, and the fact that many of their tarsal bones are worn in a particular way, may reflect

the importance of the ox as a draught animal and, thus, extensive arable agriculture at Kirkebjerget (Nyegaard 1993).

The structure of settlement

Excavations of settlements in the last 25 years, with some solidly built Bronze-age structures, have changed our view of the basis of society fundamentally. While descriptions of the early 1960's still spoke of a labile system, the impression now is of quite different, stable and organized settlement.

It is still, however, less than entirely clear how settlement as a whole is to be understood. Some settlements contain various buildings (Spjald), some very few (Vorbasse/Lille Bavn). Some have clustered buildings, of which several overlap (Højgård), while others show a more scattered pattern (Omgård). It is difficult to see how many buildings really stood at any one time. Although a term such as »village« is used in general studies, no references

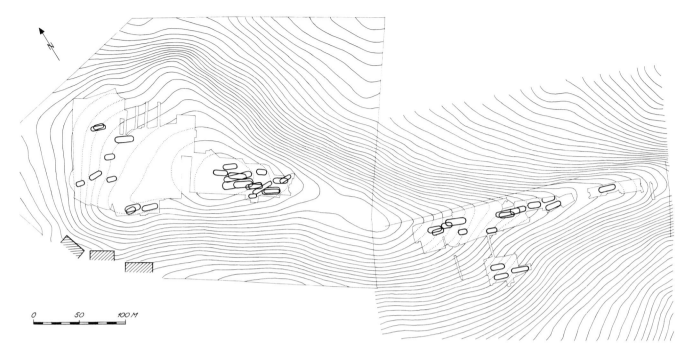

The settlement Bjerg A and B (western Jutland) with Bronze-age buildings and contour lines (equ. 0,5 m).

can be made to evidence for this, amongst other things because the fences that are so helpful in delimiting Iron-age farmsteads and in the analysis of their chronological interrelationship are virtually unknown on the Bronze-age sites. In many cases, however, the relative placement of the buildings indicates common organization. As a rule, several people, or what could be assessed as a single farmstead, must have lived together in a limited area. It is a matter of seeing several intermediary stages between the model of a single farmstead and the traditional notion of a village. Several examples of sites with widely scattered buildings (Grøntoft-Pøl, Omgård) are not all to be regarded as reflections of single-farmstead settlement. They probably shall seen as the key to understanding the denser settlements (Spjald, Bjerg) which can then be interpreted as the accumulation of many phases of a scattered settlement.

There was probably a change through time from a few contemporary buildings in Early Bronze-age settlements to more in the Late Bronze Age. How far the degree of settlement continuity and the extent of circulation in the resource area changed is a still unsolved problem.

Settlement structure may also differ from region to region. On south-western Fyn a settlement hierarchy with a hinterland of minor (and dependent?) settlements around a central place (Voldtofte-Kirkebjerget) has been identified (Thrane 1980b).

It is not only the broad settlement patterns that differ. So too do the individual sites, extensively. Associated with the large building at Store Tyrrestrup was the only bronze hoard so far known from a settlement, comprising *inter alia* large bronze axes. Contemporary with this site were settlements with much smaller longhouses (about 15 m. long) and no bronze finds at all (e.g. Vadgård). The majority of Bronze-age settlement sites fall between these extreme examples of different lifestyles and opportunities.

The Bronze Age is a central period for the study of the conditions of settlement and the basis of prehistoric society in a longer-term perspective. Fundamental changes took place in this period that were to be of importance much later on - in building construction as in the general settlement pattern. An understanding of why such important changes took place at just this time must take account, amongst other things, of the concurrent development of the cultural landscape and the basic subsistence strategies.

Many details still need to be mapped, analysed and interpreted. There is still a long way to go, but the topic discussed here can indeed be put forward as one of those in which the greatest progress has been made in the last 25 years.

141

Settlements on the raised sea-bed at Bjerre, northern Thy

Trial trench through an area of Bronze-age fields. In the foreground a small hollow under the yellow layer of blown sand. A field begins by the ranging rod and ends in a small bank beyond the tractor. The Hanstholm headland can be seen in the background.

Excavations of Bronze-age settlements and fields on the raised Littorina sea-bed carried out by Thy and Vester Hanherred Museum, Thisted, in 1990, have provided crucial new information on Bronze-age landscape use and subsistence strategy in north-western Jutland. Thanks to exceptionally good preservative conditions at Bjerre Enge, south of the Hanstholm headland, traces of a complete Bronze-age cultural landscape have been preserved. The construction of settlements in this area began early in the Early Bronze Age and continued into the Late Bronze Age.

These good conditions were not only the product of the high water table (the area now stands between 5.0 and 6.5 m. above sea level) but also of later sand-blows, which deposited a protective sand layer over all of the Bronze-age settlements and fields. The wetness of the area has meant that pollen grains in soil layers are well-preserved, and also that, in the deeper deposits in particular, the preservative conditions for faunal remains are good. The Bjerre finds form the largest collection of bone yet known from the Early Bronze Age. Organic material such as wood sometimes survives too. A few of the excavated buildings have, in consequence, produced the first examples of preserved building timbers of the Danish Bronze Age.

On the basis of the provisional results of S.Th. Andersen's pollen analyses, the Bronze-age landscape at Bjerre can be described as an open, dune landscape characterized by wetland vegetation. Small, flat dunes covered in grass and sedge were interspersed with minor hollows and larger wetlands with sedge and pondweed. Even now this interchange between wet and dry places stands out in aerial photographs of the area. Bjerre Sø, which dried out in the 1800's, was certainly in existence in the Bronze Age and thus bounded the area to the west.

Fluctuations in the ground-water level also affected the extent of the areas that could be exploited throughout the Bronze Age. It was apparently driest in the earlier part of the period.

Settlement 2 at Bjerre. This settlement belongs to the middle of three phases that can so far be identified at Bjerre and is to be dated to the Early Bronze Age (Period II). Several small, circular enclosures and three three-aisled longhouses apparently superseded one another. The western end of one of the buildings may have been used as a stall. Regular stalling has also been demonstrated in a longhouse of the Late Bronze Age at Bjerre. 1:400.

Pollen analyses have show that there were extensive grazing areas on the high land in Thy in the Early Bronze Age (S.Th. Andersen 1992). That such wetland as at Bjerre was also exploited is surprising, and demonstrates the great variance within Bronze-age land-use.

As far as one can tell from what has been found, subsistence at Bjerre was based almost entirely on pastoral and arable farming. Georg Nyegaard's studies of the animal bones show that cattle herding was of great importance, while in respect of arable, there were fields for longer or shorter periods in practically every part of the area where it was not too wet.

The excavations at Bjerre were set in train by plans to construct a large motor-racing track, and were undertaken under the aegis of paragraph 26 of the Museum Act. Because of shortage of money only a small selection of the many finds in the area were excavated. Only two of the settlements, for example, saw relatively comprehensive excavation while others were recorded only through strip trenches or small trial excavations (Bech 1991:41ff.).

The settlements are nearly all relatively small and contain traces of just one, or very few, buildings. In several cases various circular ditches or post-settings have been found as well. As on settlements in Holland, both ditches and post-settings could have surrounded special storage places (for corn, hay or manure?). Alternatively, some of the large circular post-settings could also have been used as animal pens.

Jens-Henrik Bech

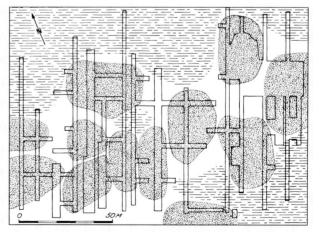

Part of a field system of the Late Bronze Age with quite small, irregular fields. Hollows of varying size occur between these. 1:2,000.

Roads

Plank road in Speghøje mose. In the middle of the Early Bronze Age, this originally 300 m.-long road ran straight through a birch bog across the narrowest point of the Pårup bogland.

Nearly a century ago, Bronze-age barrows were the basis point for Sophus Müller's sensible observations on Bronze-age routeways. Heavier-handed interpretations of later years by contrast proved to last less well: the barrows reflect the location of settlement, which was determined by the terrain. With just a few fixed points, in the form of special structures, the prehistoric road network can hardly be located any more precisely than as broad communication corridors, delimited by natural barriers in the landscape (S.W. Andersen 1983; Schou Jørgensen 1988a).

Some finds of wheels and parts of wagons from the Late Neolithic and the Bronze Age show that a constructional tradition ran unbroken from the earliest Danish wagons: a group of disc wheels from two-wheeled ox-carts that is known from the beginning of the Single Grave Period, probably a feature of and derived from the new tool-inventory of this period (Rostholm 1978; Schovsbo 1987). Light wagons with spoked wheels deriving from the Central European Urnfield Culture appear in the Late Bronze Age in finds from Egemose (Jacob-Friesen 1970) and Lusehøj (Thrane 1984) on Fyn, but these were most likely for ceremonial use, not for transport as such.

A paved road is essential for wagon transport on soft terrain, and its construction - a path expanded to a roadway - is a direct consequence of this. In the main,

the Danish finds conform to other European structures. Simplest, and most common, are simple brushwood and log roads. The earliest known structure built of shaped planks in Denmark is the Speghøje road of the Early Bronze Age (Schou Jørgensen 1982), but such roads were apparently being constructed from the very beginning of roadmaking.

Stone-paved roads are a purely Scandinavian phenomenon in prehistory, and the earliest are known from Denmark. Many explanations of their emergence have been suggested, several of them based on climatic change. With precise calibration of C 14 dated limiting horizons, however, it seems that the uncertainty around climatic variation is too large for this to be used as an explanation of changes in roadmaking. As yet incomplete investigations of both a road-complex in the Nørreå valley at Kvorning and the long familiar Krogsbølle road seem to show, however, that the earliest stone-paved roads may belong to the Late Bronze Age. The appearance of this type at that time could be a consequence of the incipient change in the landscape to more open forest (Aaby 1985; J. Jensen 1988b:282). Access to timber was thus restricted, while access to and the transport of stone was easier in the pastures of the open country.

Mogens Schou Jørgensen

144

The earliest metalwork

By Helle Vandkilde

Metal technology was first introduced to Denmark in the course of the Late Neolithic and the first period of the Bronze Age (*ca.* 2350-1500 B.C.). In the last 25 years, research in this area has mainly been directed towards the classification and dating of objects. This has laid the foundation for future research directed at a social understanding of the adoption of metal.

E. Lomborg in particular has worked on this period, and in 1969 and 1973 he published a division of the Late Neolithic into three parts, based on flint daggers, and a division of Bronze Age Period I into two on the basis of the formal and stylistic development of selected metal objects (Lomborg 1969, 1973a). In the years that followed research stood still, but in 1989-90 the present author proposed the main lines of a new chronology for the Late Neolithic and Bronze Age Period I. This chronology is constructed mainly on the basis of metal objects and thus supplements the flint dagger chronology. It is also built upon a comprehensive recording and re-assessment of all metal finds and on the seriation of associated finds. The numerous flanged axes are well represented in associated finds and thus naturally stand at the centre of this study, which has made it possible to date the majority of the large number of single finds of metal objects (Vandkilde 1989a-b, 1990a).

The large and quite neglected body of metal analyses (Junghams *et al.* 1968, 1974) can be profitably brought in as a supplement to archaeological analyses of chronology, cultural interaction, regionality, technology and economy to illuminate the period. C. Cullberg's thesis showed this as early as 1968, as did later research (Liversage 1989a; Liversage & Liversage 1989; Vandkilde 1992a-b). The archaeological possibilities of metal analysis are still far from exhausted.

On the basis of this re-assessment of typology and chronology, the earliest metalwork can be divided into four periods: the earlier and later Late Neolithic (LN I and II) and Early Bronze Age Periods IA and IB (Vandkilde 1989a-b, 1990a). The new chronological system, the basic, comprehensive assessment of the finds and the inclusion of the metal analyses have improved the basis for archaeological interpretation, and underlies the subsequent discussion of the social effects of innovation in metal technology.

The archaeological material is evidence of significant technological and social changes through the 800-900 years we are concerned with (Vandkilde 1993). The adoption of metal runs through three stages which break the simple Stone Age-Bronze Age sequence. This development moves in pace with the clear increase in availability of metal at the transition to LN II and to Period IB.

LN I: the beginning

As early as the Early Neolithic, in the 4th millennium B.C., the first copper objects reached Denmark from Central Europe. To begin with, however, these foreign metal objects did not inspire any local production. It is towards the end of the 3rd millennium, at the beginning of the Late Neolithic, that local metalwork may first be detected in outline. It comprises simple gold sheet ornaments in particular, perhaps flat copper axes too. A few items of Central European copper ornaments can also be seen, and a single copper dagger of west European origin. Compared with Early-neolithic copper, the copper of LN I contains more impurities and quite often a trace of tin. The chemical composition of the metal indicates that most of it came from Central Europe, while forms are strongly marked by the west European Bell Beaker Culture.

The number of metal objects in this period is very limited, and flint is the most common material for weapons and tools. Metal objects certainly marked social status rather than anything else. Sharpening and damage to copper axes sometimes show that

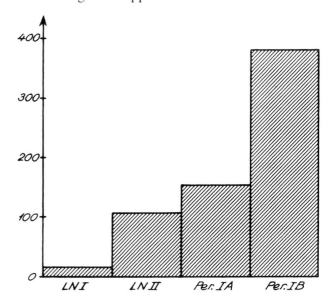

Denmark's metal supplies, ca. 2350-1500 B.C. (number of objects per 100 years). Significant changes take place at the transitions to LN II and to Period IB.

145

Metal analyses

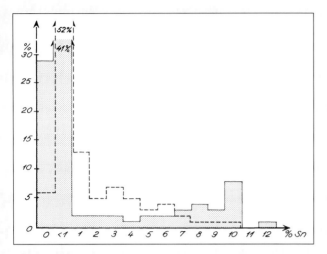

Percent tin content in (full line) a large sample of 849 objects from a broadly east Alpine area at the transition to the Bronze Age, and (stippled) of 116 Late-neolithic objects from Denmark.

One of the new developments in Bronze Age studies is the study of the metal itself - archaeometallurgy or paleometallurgy as it is called. One part of archaeometallurgy is quantitative chemical analysis of the metal of which ancient tools and ornaments are made, showing which elements are present and in what proportions.

The elements can be present as alloying metals which have been deliberately added to give the metal different working properties than copper alone would have. Copper plus tin makes bronze, copper plus zink makes brass, and there can be leaded bronzes and brasses. As well as these deliberate additives that make up a few percent of the total composition before they significantly change its working properties, there are natural impurities and trace elements that derive from the ore. Such elements are arsenic, antimony, silver, nickel, bismuth, cobalt, etc. If they amount to more than about 0,03% of the metal we may call them impurities, if less they are described as trace elements. The early smiths were hardly aware of their presence, at least not by name, but modern science can study them and obtain new information about early metal technology and supply. This may be illustrated with two examples, one reflecting on technology, the other on supply.

The small diagram shows the frequency of different percentages of tin in two samples from around 2200-1750 BC. The full line shows metal from around the eastern Alps, the stippled line from Denmark. A majority of the objects in both areas are still of unalloyed copper (the dividing line between 'copper' and 'bronze' can be set at one percent), but a substantial minority (30-42%) are of bronze. The difference between the two graphs is that in the sample from central Europe the tin is carefully used and most of it went into making an alloy with over 5% tin which was as much as possible kept separate from the unalloyed copper. In the sample from Denmark on the other hand no such careful separation can be seen and it is the intermediate values that predominate. It seems that the inhabitants had not yet learned to distinguish properly between copper and bronze and were letting their tin be diluted until it was little use. The comparison shows a difference in technical knowledge between central Europe and Denmark, with the higher skill being as expected in central Europe.

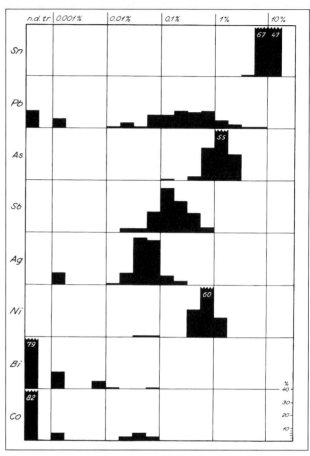

Impurity pattern of all shafthole axes of Fårdrup type from period I of the Bronze Age in Denmark. The percents of the impurities are shown on a logarithmic scale according to the method of H.T. Waterbolk.

The larger graph shows the amounts on a logarithmic scale of the most important trace/impurity elements in a sample of 67 bronze axes from about 1750-1500 B.C. in Denmark. The impurities are present in the pattern As > Sb > Ag < Ni, with Bi and Co at low values. Lead is unreliable and may be ignored. Most of the impurities are spread over a fairly narrow range and the largest number of analyses lie around the middle of the range.

Exactly the same pattern of the impurities is found simultaneously in the area around the eastern Alps. The impurities occur in the same order and have almost the same average values and range. The resemblance is so close that is shows that the same source of bronze must have been used in both regions. In Austria nearly 100% of the analysed objects had this impurity pattern, but in Denmark only about 80%, so there are other metal supplies as well that still need to be identified, though the largest part of the Danish metal must have come from the eastern Alps.

This gives an idea what can be learned from the study of metal analyses (Liversage in press). These two examples are only a foretaste of how the study of the composition of ancient bronze can be used to cast new light on the history of technology and trade in prehistoric times.

David Liversage

146

they were put to use; metallographic studies, however, reveal that the axes were only slightly cold-hammered on the edge, which was therefore very soft and not very effective. A metal axe could hardly stand comparison with a flint one for chopping wood.

Gold and copper are particularly found deposited singly in fields and bogs, maintaining an old tradition. Such field and bog deposits are normally regarded as linked with communal rituals (e.g. Kristiansen 1987:21f.). That the metal objects predominantly appear in hoards and are virtually absent from graves is a sign that it was the kinship group that controlled metal objects not the individual.

In LN I, North Jutland stands out as an important area, with large-scale production and distribution of lanceolate flint daggers (Lomborg 1973a:figs.12-20; Wincentz Rasmussen 1990:33ff.). These flint daggers imitate the west European Bell Beaker-culture copper daggers and may have had a similar ideological and social symbolic meaning. Influence from the Bell Beaker Culture is especially clear in the material culture of North Jutland, where society seems to be characterized by limited social differentiation and a strong emphasis on male prestige, just as in the Bell Beaker Culture (Case 1977:81f.; Harrison 1980:10f.; Shennan 1982:155f.).

It is no coincidence that the early metal objects cluster in North Jutland. The first local experiments with metal were closely linked to local adoption of the ideological and social concepts of the Bell Beaker Culture. Metal objects were certainly rare, but their significance was clearly great, given how eagerly the copper dagger was copied in flint.

LN II-Period IA: Bronze Age without chieftains?
At the beginning of LN II (*ca.* 2000 B.C.) the quantity of metal increases markedly and remains fairly constant for the next 400 years. Local metalwork has now established itself and locally produced metal objects are much more common than imported ones; in particular, flanged axes, but also halberds and small spearheads. Uniformity here contrasts with the variety of imported goods, which included metal-hilted daggers, halberds, large spearheads, several types of rings, especially from the Central European Únětice Culture, and large, decorated axe blades from the British Isles. Imported objects were probably regarded as exciting and precious exotica, and also provided raw material for local production.

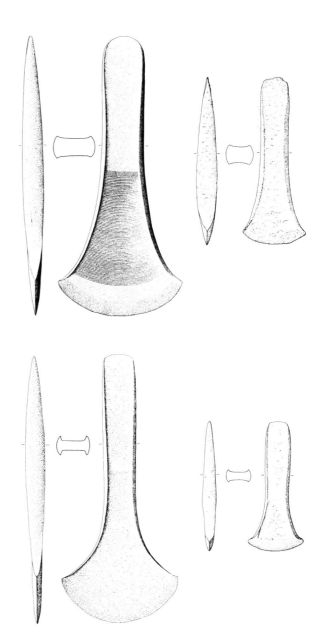

Much sharpened axes with asymmetrical cutting edges of primarily utilitarian function (right) and unsharpened, undamaged axes of primarily prestigious function (left). LN II axes at the top, Period IA axes below. 1:3.

In this period, the copper contains a large quantity of impurities and a fluctuating amount of tin that only occasionally could properly be called bronze. Tin bronze is, however, dominant from Period IA. Both copper-types and tin levels closely match the situations in Central Europe, and raw metal unquestionably came mainly from there. Imported objects and foreign influence in local material culture point towards the metal sources in Erzgebirge and the

Gold sheet ornaments and copper flat axes of LN.

Harz in central Germany, with a possible Alpine inclusion towards the end of the period.

Flint daggers and flint axes grow less common amongst the finds, and metal objects are about to take over the role of flint in both practical and symbolic action. The metal axes are now provided with flanges along the edges in order to sit more firmly in the shaft. Many of these flanged axes were clearly used as tools for felling trees and other woodwork; quite a large proportion of the axes have damaged cutting-edges or have had the blade shortened by sharpening. Microscopies show that the edge was often heavily cold-hammered to a great hardness. The ritual find contexts of the flanged axes, their occasionally outré form and fine decoration, and their occurrence in certain rock-carved scenes, further show that they still marked social status and position and that they played a part in ritual actions.

Amongst the flanged axes are found quite simple pieces that one would *a priori* assume to have been utilitarian tools alone; similarly there are some splendid axes that could only realistically be status symbols. But on the whole there is a typological and functional continuum, in which the majority of axes seem to have had both practical and symbolic use. This faint specialization in metalwork distinguishing practical from prestigious objects may reflect a social order moving towards a breakdown of an egalitarian framework.

Through the use of material symbols and through symbolic and ritual activities, the structures of society are confirmed and reproduced, so that changes in ritual practice can be interpreted as signs of social change. In this period, metal objects were still virtually exclusively ritually deposited, in fields and bogs, and the right to dispose of metal objects probably still resided with kinship groups as a communal matter. While in LN I metal objects were deposited singly, more rarely in pairs, there is now great variance in the number and form of deposited artefacts. This can be interpreted as expressing new differences in wealth and position between the kinship groups. Kinship groups manifested their social status and position in relation to the outside world by the ritual deposition of one or more, more or less exclusive metal objects at sacred sites. Still most common are deposits of one, locally produced metal axe. Far rarer are hoards of several objects of the same type, most often local flanged axes or spearheads, while hoards with a lot of local and imported ornaments, weapons and tools are very few (Vandkilde 1993:figs.6-7). Particularly representative of the last group are the hoards from Gallemose (J. Jensen 1979b:fig. p.75), Skeldal and Pile (Oldeberg 1974:no.832), but Torsted, Åbjerg, Virring (C.J. Becker 1965:Abb.4 & 8; Jacob-Friesen 1967:Taf.12) and Vigerslev (Vandkilde 1992a) are also in this category. This pyramidical pattern surely reflects essential differences in wealth and social position between the different kinship groups, and it was probably only at the top of the hierarchy that there were contacts with metal-controlling elites south of the Baltic.

Graves of the period are thoroughly indistinctive by comparison. Metal is buried only rarely and sparingly, but the metal objects in graves have parallels in the large, multitype hoards, so that a connexion can be detected. Behind large hoards such as Gallemose and Skeldal, the outlines of a social elite of powerful kinship groups can thus be made out, an elite that allowed individuals to be distinguished only to a very limited degree. A suitable term for the social structure of the period might be a group-oriented hierarchy.

Along with these technological and social changes, the distribution of metal objects is transposed, and with it the economic and social focus moves from the flint-rich north of Jutland to central and eastern Denmark, concentrated in areas without good flint (Vandkilde 1989a:figs.14 & 17; 1990b: figs.4-8).

The changes sketched here for Denmark were taking place at the same time as the formation of a complex centre in the Únětice Culture in central Germany, by the rivers Unstrutt and Saale, near rich

The late Late-neolithic hoard from Skeldal near Silkeborg with locally made flanged axes, chisel, beehive-shaped jewellery box and dress rings including so-called gold Noppenringe *from the Central European Únětice Culture. The trapezoid axe is of high-tin bronze; the other objects are of copper or low-tin bronze. The tin level and metal composition are typical of LN II and the contemporary Early Bronze Age phase in Central Europe.*

metal sources of copper, tin and gold. It is reasonable, therefore, to see these events as connected. The central German centre is clearly located at a level of social development which allows the organization of huge-scale metal extraction and the distribution of the products both near and far. Demand in the northern periphery was presumably large, and it is certainly not unlikely that the greatest advantage was taken at the centre, which was able to control the trade in metal. Obtaining metal of course demanded some form of exchange or payment. We do not know what was provided in exchange, but providing it presumably necessitated the achievement of an increased productive surplus. The use of a large number of flanged axes for felling trees and cultivation was perhaps a practical prerequisite for the immediate production of such a surplus. An elite of powerful kinship groups in the marginal

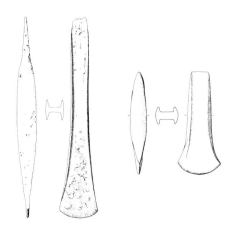

Flanged axes of Period IB of the Bronze Age. Sharpened utility axe with asymmetrical cutting edge (right) and long, slender cult axe (left). 1:3.

zones - including Denmark - was essential in a situation where a surplus had to be assembled, converted into something to be exchanged for the metal, and redistributed. The changed social structure in Denmark may thus have been a result of contact with the Únětice centre itself, or perhaps with subordinate centres in Mecklenburg and Pommerania.

Period IB: Breakthrough of the classic Bronze Age

From around 1600 B.C., in Period IB, the archaeological finds again testify to major technological and social changes. The production of metal objects increases very markedly, and local products now show great variation in form and style. The flanged axes undergo functional specialization, so that the group divides into a very large set of small, often badly damaged work axes and a small set of long, slender cult axes, which may be decorated. This final separation of tools from prestige objects may reflect a social system that is no longer egalitarian.

Unlike before, the bronze has a very uniform chemical composition, and this standard metal is found widely in Europe at this time. A material-cultural orientation towards the Central European *Hügelgräberkultur* and related cultures to the southeast in Hungary and Transsylvania might indicate that the raw metal for local production is now coming from here.

Most metal objects are still ritually deposited in field or bog, and two hoards from Valsømagle (Aner

& Kersten 1973ff.:nos.1097-98) are exceptional representatives of this category. Metal objects are now quite frequently deposited in graves; clearly, individuals can now distinguish themselves socially by the possession of metal objects. The graves also reveal a social pattern that is familiar in a later part of the Early Bronze Age and which agrees with the concept of 'chiefdoms' (Randsborg 1974:45ff.; T.B. Larsson 1986:113ff.). Within the social elite that the Period-IB graves seem to represent we find striking differences in the quantity and quality of grave goods, indicating substantial social inequality (Vandkilde 1993:fig.9). Period IB thus lies socially and technologically close to the second period of the Bronze Age.

The Únětice centre by the Saale river disappears from the archaeological map between 1700 and 1600 B.C., and new socioeconomic centres appear to the south. The disappearance of the centre may have meant a break in political alliances and thus the associated lines of metal supply. It is reasonable to see the development from a group-oriented to an individualized rank system as closely connected with these events in Central Europe.

Future research

Settlement excavations and pollen analyses already seem to have revealed new aspects of the structural break between LN I and LN II. Towards the end of the Late Neolithic, houses, indeed, become markedly larger, reaching 45-50 m. in length, but apparently only in the heartland of early Scandinavian metal culture, central and eastern Denmark and Skåne (P.O. Nielsen 1991:62; Björhem & Säfvestad 1989:108). On top of this, pollen diagrams indicate extensive open-land expansion in all of southern Sweden around 2000 B.C. (Digerfeldt & Welinder 1988:fig.9, 134) - in fact at the transition to LN II. This landnam could be evidence of forest clearance with metal axes and thus indirectly testify to increased agricultural production in order to obtain metal. Similarly extensive expansion cannot immediately be seen in the pollen diagrams from eastern and central Denmark (e.g. S.Th. Andersen et al. 1983), but these diagrams are predominantly from small, local areas which have been thinly populated through most of prehistory down to the present. More representative, by contrast, is the series of South, West and North Jutlandic pollen diagrams which fall outside the heartland of the metal culture in LN II. Here, as expected, we see no, or only faint, signs of an assault on the forest around 2000 B.C. A systematic comparison of archaeological data and pollen analyses, however, would require new, representative pollen diagrams from central and eastern Denmark.

The social system sketched above, the group-oriented hierarchy, which, chronologically, covers LN II and Period IA, is sociopolitically and technologically located in between relatively egalitarian Neolithic societies and stratified Bronze-age societies. This type of community that can be detected in outline poses new questions to the archaeological material and demands a more detailed description of its contents, origins, maintenance and further transformation. Contemporary Europe - especially studies of the organization of trade in metal - forms an important source to shed light on this. With what we already know, there appear to be systematic similarities and differences in social development at the European level, and the European connexions seem to change direction and character through time. The trade apparently is organized within a changing framework that can perhaps best be described as one of regularly recurring shifts between core periphery and peer polity interaction.

The end of the 3rd millennium B.C. (LN I) thus seems to be characterized by parity between and within the individual cultural zones of Europe. At the beginning of the 2nd millennium (LN II - Period IA) complex socioeconomic centres and less developed peripheries appear which, from 1600 B.C., with the emergence of the *Hügelgräberkultur* (Period IB), are in turn superseded by regional parity, albeit between many smaller, hierarchically structured communities. A decisive step in the direction of a real historical reconstruction of the transitional period between the Stone and the Bronze Age would be to plunge firmly into European archaeology and to study the metal artefacts themselves here: i.e. their geographical and chronological distribution, their quantity, form, style and function, their archaeological and topographical context, and their chemical composition and relationship to the rest of material culture. Since the exchange of copper, bronze and gold with the North stems primarily from the region between the Baltic and the central German/Bohemian mountain range, this area would be a natural starting point for archaeological investigation.

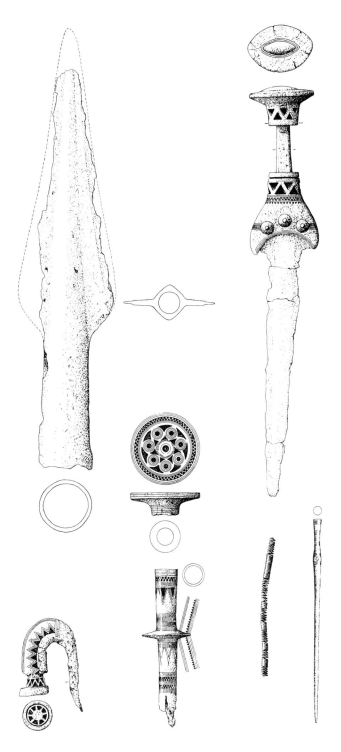

Period IB grave goods of gold and bronze from Buddinge in Copenhagen amt. *To judge by the quantity and type of the objects, the deceased must have held a leading social position. The dress pin with spiral gold wire may come from the middle Danubian area. The Buddinge gold has a quite different composition from the large amount of ring gold of Early Bronze Age Periods II and III which evidently comes from the Central European* Hügelgräberkultur. *1:2.*

151

Metal deposits

By Jørgen Jensen

Throughout the Bronze Age, it was practice to deposit gold and bronze valuables in waste or inaccessible wild places. The many wetlands, bogs, meadows, lakes and watercourses of the landscape were preferred depositional sites, and it is finds from these in particular that have filled out our image of the distinctive culture of the Bronze Age. From wetlands come such prominent finds as the chariot of the sun from Trundholm, the large cult axes, the lurs, the imported bronze shields, drinking vessels of gold and bronze and numerous deposits of both male and female objects - weapons, jewellery and tools; various items with both practical and religious functions.

Many interpretations of this group of finds in religious terms have been proposed, especially the so-called hoards, which usually comprise precious jewellery or weapons or tools. But the fact that this find group includes a large number of objects found singly which in principal have to be taken along with the multiobject hoards has often been overlooked (J. Jensen 1973). The term 'deposits' is used for all of these find-types, particularly because the circumstances of deposition of the items are only rarely known. Usually the find spot is a peat bog or some other wet area. But there are cases of deposition at grave barrows, by large natural boulders, and so on.

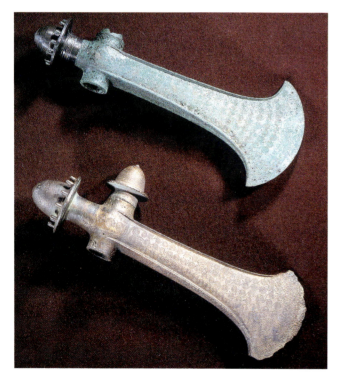

Cult axes from Egebæk in Hjørring amt.

The category of metal deposits is taken here in its widest possible sense, including all bronze and gold objects of the Bronze Age deposited with no reliably identifiable connexion with a burial or the daily life activities of a settlement. Thus this category includes (1) individually deposited bronze objects (weapons, jewellery, tools, sacral objects etc.), (2) so-called single-type hoards (i.e. several examples of a particular artefact-type, such as neckrings, found together), and (3) multitype hoards (i.e. several different artefact-types found together).

Although the metal depositions in all probability were part of or concluded ritual ceremonies, a religious interpretation is not aimed at here. On the contrary, the numerous finds will be looked at in the light of the economic and social development of Bronze-age society; i.e. as an expression of fluctuation in the supply of metal from abroad and of changes in the social order. It is this line of analysis that has been pre-eminent in archaeological research of the last 25 years.

The representativity of the deposits

The general representativity of the multitype hoards of the Late Bronze Age was examined in a valuable study by Kristiansen (1976). On the basis of a series of statistical observations the conclusion could be drawn that from the beginning of the 1800's there has been a close correlation between modern economic activities and the discovery of hoards. The type of land management, the extent of peat cutting, construction works such as, for instance, railways, all are amongst the factors that have affected the frequency of finds of Bronze-age hoards.

However the study also showed how in the present century Bronze-age layers have gradually been dug away from the majority of Danish bogs. In the years of and immediately after the Second World War peat cutting generally affected those layers of the bogs that were formed before the Bronze Age. In spite of increased peat cutting, the number of finds has consequently fallen in this century. This is a tendency that can be expected to continue. But the predictions of the study in respect of the number of future finds have proved to be too low. It was predicted that the years 1975-85 would produce 2-3 new finds. Subsequently the norm would be 1-2 finds per decade. In fact, an average of one find per year has proved to be the norm since 1975: a great deal more than expected. This

Spiral ornament

Detail of the belt plate from Langstrup Mose. The small pits in the surface were formed during casting. By the arrow one can see that the maker has tried to hide the flaws by hammering the metal.

"The fine ornament of the Bronze Age was punched into a smooth, cast metal surface". For centuries, up until quite recently, this has been the undisputed belief of Scandinavian archaeology. Lately, however, a few voices have started to question this dogma.

Spiral ornament is an important point from which to approach the study of the techniques behind Bronze-age ornament. Evidence is, however, difficult to obtain because of the problems of preservation and later treatment of the metal.

The most splendid belt plate that we have comes from Langstrup Mose, northern Sjælland. If you look very closely at these you can see details that show that the spirals could only have been produced by casting. The most important of these are casting flaws in the decoration. Small air pockets were formed in the metal during casting, and these appear as small pits in the finished product. Such flaws appear, naturally enough, both in spiral ornament and in other forms of decoration. On one occasion the caster attempted to rectify the situation. He hammered the metal out in a small area, but soon stopped, as the surface was changing character in a way that was more conspicuous than the small pits. The spirals

from the different ribbons are a little different, but within each ribbon the spirals are virtually identical. Even identical microtraces that can barely be seen with the naked eye can be found to recur on several spirals. This indicates that the spirals must have been formed with a stamp. The belt plates were cast by the lost wax method: they were first formed in wax; a clay mould was then built up around the wax model; the wax was melted out; and in the cavity left by the wax model bronze could be cast. The spiral stamp, which may have been rolled-up metal wire, was pressed down into the wax model, and thus the ornament would have been formed in the casting.

The idea of spiral stamps may have originated locally in Scandinavia, but the model of rolled-up metal wire stamps could have been imported. Such spiral ornament is found in Greece, albeit in gold not bronze. A small box from Mycenae has four thin gold plates with complicated spiral ornament. The thin gold plates were clearly pressed down over rolled-up spiral metal wire and so that the spirals were impressed upon the gold. Basically this is exactly the same idea as that underlying Scandinavian spiral ornament.

Preben Rønne

153

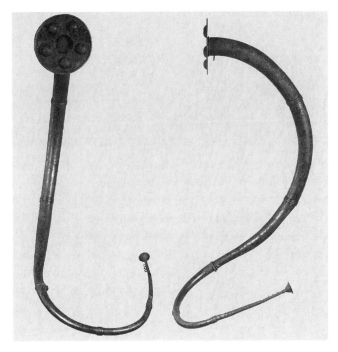

One of the two lurs from Ulvkær in Vendsyssel amt.

does not, however, affect the main conclusion of the study: that the distribution maps of multitype Bronze-age hoards really show the settled areas in which the Bronze-age population was in the habit of depositing bronze or gold hoards.

Although this study considered only multitype hoards of Periods IV and V of the Late Bronze Age, there is no doubt that its conclusions hold for all Bronze-age deposits to the extent defined above. With this find group too we thus have a source of data that is representative in quite another way than the preserved grave mounds of the Bronze Age, the national distribution of which shows a significant bias deriving from regional variance in intensity of agriculture (Baudou 1983), or settlements, whose appearance is closely dependent on the development of the museum service and archaeology (Thrane 1985).

New finds

As noted, the clear drop in the frequency of finding Bronze-age deposits since the start of this century does not mean that no new finds are made. The last 25 years have produced about 25 multitype hoards, particularly as a result of ploughing or construction work in former meadowlands. There is also a considerable number of single deposits of, for instance,

flanged axes and socketed axes of the Late Neolithic and Early Bronze Age. Amongst the most important finds must be mentioned the two sets of large cult axes from Viby on Sjælland and Understed in Vendsyssel respectively (J. Jensen 1978), each with around 15 kg. of bronze, showing that large quantities of metal were invested in ritual deposits around the middle of the Early Bronze Age. From about the same time comes the rich hoard of two sets of female jewellery from Vognserup Enge, western Sjælland (Rieck 1972). An important Period-II hoard was found in the excavation of a building at Store Tyrrestrup in Hjørring *amt* (Nilsson 1991). Finally, from somewhat earlier in the Bronze Age come the rich hoards from Skeldal near Silkeborg (Vandkilde 1990a) and Røjlemose near Strib on Fyn respectively (Thrane 1973).

There are important finds of the Late Bronze Age too. Particularly to be noted are a pair of lurs from Ulvkær in Hjørring *amt* (Lysdahl *et al.* 1992) and a cult axe from an unknown site in northern Sjælland. For multitype hoards, the finding of an imported bronze bucket with cruciform handle-mounts together with two hanging bowls, three spectacle brooches and two spiral armrings from Vaseholm in Ålborg *amt* requires special mention, together with a number of yet unpublished Period-IV to -V hoards of female jewellery from Mariendal in Gamtofte parish and Vestergade in Bogense parish, both in Odense *amt*, and Lysemosegård in Nr. Brody parish and Kildekrog in Øster Hæsinge parish, both in Svendborg *amt*. From the final phase of the Bronze Age, Period VI, there are groups of neckrings found at Brunsvang on Lolland and of large, hollow-cast ankle rings from the highway construction near Roskilde (J. Jensen 1982).

The earliest deposits

An analysis of the total number of deposits from field and bog will be able to reveal a number of fundamental features in the development of Scandinavian Bronze-age culture. Through its history of more than a thousand years, bronze and gold objects seems to have been treated as sought-after exotica which, beyond their more or less practical functions, marked social status too. Metal deposits either in fields or bogs or as grave goods can be supposed to have had an important social function in that the metal objects, to all appearances, were attributed with symbolic significance which *inter alia* could

Cult axe from unknown site in northern Sjælland. Length 22.5 cm.

mark male or female prestige. In this way they expressed an ideology that was common to the geographically large regions in which the common rituals were practised. Changes in these rituals and in the mode of deposition can therefore be regarded as reflections of changes in society itself. At the same time, the foreign objects that appear in the deposits are able to illuminate how the centres for the exchange of metal objects were continually shifting.

Even the metal objects that appear before the beginning of the Bronze Age proper in the Late Neolithic can illustrate this. Helle Vandkile has shown, above, in an account of the earliest metalwork in Scandi-navia, that development took place in waves: the quantities of metal deposited varies markedly from period to period. It was further noted that the marking of individual status, as is seen in burials, appears in varying degrees from period to period.

At the beginning of the Late Neolithic, in LN I, the quantities of metal were still quite small. But in the second part of the period, LN II and Bronze Age Period IA, there is a large increase in the number of deposits. Nearly all objects pertain to the male sphere. These are first and foremost locally produced or imported flanged axes, with a lesser number of massive bronze axes and small spearheads. Most common are single-object deposits; multitype

hoards are very rare. In this period, there is very little deposition of metal objects in graves. The foreign metal objects come particularly from Erzebirge and the Harz. One must also reckon with some Alpine element in the imported bronze.

A first peak of deposition

In Bronze Age Periods IB and II, the great increase in the number of deposits continues. The number of finds now reaches a first peak with practically a doubling of quantity. In the country as a whole, for instance, there is an increase from just over 200 deposits of LN II/Period IA to *ca.* 400 in Periods IB/II. Distribution is skewed in both periods, with two-thirds of the finds on the islands. By the far the majority of the metal objects of Periods IB/II are singly-deposited socketed axes which are known from more than 200 sites in Denmark. Swords and spears are now deposited too, so that it is still objects pertaining to the male sphere that dominate. There is also a very large number of sacral objects such as, for instance, large cult axes, the heaviest examples of which weigh more than 7 kg. As a rule, sacral objects are deposited alone; i.e. unaccompanied by weapons, tools or jewellery.

Metal objects are now invested in graves too in large numbers, both in male and femal graves, although quantitatively the male graves dominate

155

Gold armrings from Neble near Boeslunde, western Sjælland.

(Randsborg 1974). The foreign metal objects of this period found were principally manufactured within the Central European *Hügelgräberkultur* and related areas to the south-east.

In the following period, Period III, there was a very sharp fall in the quantity of bronze deposited. From all of Denmark we know of only about 40 Period-III deposits, about a tenth of the number known from the preceding period. Only a few of these are multitype hoards, and these have much humbler contents than in Period II. The remainder of the deposits comprise celts, swords, daggers, sickles, armrings etc. deposited singly. The whole impression is one of a shortage of metal.

Period III, which runs at least through the 13th and 12th centuries B.C., is a period which is characterized by significant archaeological discontinuity in the rest of Europe too. It is contemporary with the transiton from the palace culture to the Iron Age in Greece, and from the Middle to the Late Bronze Age in Central Europe. It is also contemporary with substantial natural changes such as the huge volcanic eruption in the North Atlantic, Hekla 3 (Baillie 1989). But how all these factors are to be related to one another is as yet unknown. In Danish archaeological finds it is also in Period III that cremation graves appears. Nevertheless, many of the rituals that were associated with earlier inhumation burials were maintained for a good time. The new burial rite first broke right through at the beginning of Period IV. But there was still a degree of continuity, as burials were often carried out as secondary burials in grave mounds that had been raised in the Early Bronze Age.

Late Bronze-age deposits

At the transition to Period IV, the number of bronze deposits rises sharply again. Single-item deposits comprise male equipment in particular, mostly deposited in wetlands: swords, for instance, are known from 65 sites, spears from 20. The majority of the finds, however, are celts deposited singly, which are known from several hundred sites of which at least half were certainly wetlands. With the celts, however, it is often difficult to determine whether they belong to Period IV or V. Multiobject deposits also increase in number. About 120 finds are known from Denmark as a whole, about 50 in Jutland and 70 from the islands, more than half being from wetlands. Women's jewellery is now a substantial element in multitype hoards, especially belt fittings but also neck and armrings. Sacral objects such as lurs, gold bowls, imported bronze vessels etc. also appear in great numbers in finds from wetlands, but usually unaccompanied by other artefact-types.

The large number of deposits contrasts sharply with the grave finds. Cremation has now fully established itself, and the quantities of metal that are invested in the graves are quite small. Although the material is sparse, the grave finds still show that Late Bronze-age society must have known clear social differentiation (Thrane 1981; Freudenberg 1989). The majority of foreign objects originated in the southeastern Urnfield areas, in western Hungary, Bohemia, Moravia, Slovakia and Austria. They reached the western Baltic lands via the regions along the Oder and the Elbe.

The tendencies that could be seen in the previous period continue in Period V. The number of single-object deposits is still very high: swords are known from 45 sites, of which 30 are areas of water; spears are known from 47 sites, of which 20 are areas of water. Finally a very large number of deposited celts are known, so that male equipment continues to dominate in the single deposits, although female jewellery such as, for instance, belt fittings and neck-rings is now very common.

In relation to Period IV, the multiobject hoards increase sharply in Period V. From Denmark as a whole, more than 130 finds are known, of which a little over 40 are from Jutland while the islands contribute about 90. Period-V hoarding apparently took two forms. To begin with, one can start to see a shift in the practice towards the east. In Period V, the number of deposits on the Danish islands increases in relation to Period IV. The same phenomenon can be observed in Sweden, where Period V produces 72 multiobject hoards against 32 of Period IV. Secondly, female jewellery is now a substantial element in multiobject hoards, where amongst other things sacral objects such as small statuettes also appear. However sacral objects such as lurs, bronze vessels, display shields etc. are most commonly found alone in finds from wetlands; i.e. unaccompanied by other artefact-types.

The large number of deposits continues to contrast sharply with the graves, where generally only small quantities of metal are invested and where the individual marking of status is very limited. There are, however, important exceptions, above all the great barrow 'Lusehøj' (Thrane, below), which is situated in the middle of a centre of wealth in south-western Fyn. Similar centres of wealth elsewhere in Denmark can be supposed to have had matching chieftains' graves (J. Jensen 1981).

Amongst foreign objects, forms originating in the western area of the Urnfield Culture in Switzerland, south-western Germany and eastern France are particularly dominant (Thrane 1975). They reached the Baltic area via a sharply delimited 'channel' along the Rhine and across Thuringia, and here formed the basis for extensive local production.

The end of the custom of hoarding

In the final phase of the Bronze Age, Period VI, the quantity of metal deposited remains quite high but the number of multitype hoards falls sharply against single-type and single-object deposits, of work axes, neckrings, armrings and dress pins in particular (J. Jensen 1973). The shift in the concentration of metal deposits to the east that could be seen in Period V continues in Period VI. Generally, the custom of depositing metal objects is now far more widespread in the eastern parts of southern Scandinavia, including the Danish islands, than in Jutland and Schleswig-Holstein. Related situations can be seen south of the Baltic at this time, where deposits of bronze are also much more common in the eastern parts of the North German/Polish lowland area in the final phase of the Bronze Age than in the west.

New types of neckrings also appear in Period VI in large numbers. It is difficult to tell, however, whether these were male or female accessories. Sacral objects, by contrast, are very scarce. Relatively small quantities of metal are invested in graves. Some items come from the Central European Hall-

Hollow-cast ankle rings found during highway construction near Roskilde, Sjælland.

statt Culture, from the eastern area in fact. But the majority of imported objects come from the wide lowland zone along the Baltic coast of Germany and Poland, where a lot of metal is deposited to the east while the western parts had almost completely abandoned the old hoarding customs.

Fluctuations in hoarding: crises or steady adaptation?

The picture of Bronze-age depositions of metal in field and bog is thus a very complicated one. Quantitatively, two peaks emerge, in Period II and Period (IV)-V. These are separated by a period, III, in which deposits of metal objects diminish sharply, and funerary rituals undergo considerable change in respect both of the labour and the precious metal invested. It is probable that these changes reflect fluctuations in the amount of metal that came to Denmark from abroad, primarily from Central Europe. And the phenomenon is not limited to Denmark; it is also known over much of northern and western Europe. A sharp fall in the quantity of metal that was in circulation can be seen in England, for instance, at a date corresponding to Scandinavian Bronze Age Period III (Burgess 1985).

Looking at local circumstances, there are considerable qualitative differences between the two peaks. In Period II, very substantial, prestigious barrow building dominates, at the same time as both male and female status is marked in graves by grave goods of gold and bronze. Metal depositions, especially in wetlands are extensive in this period.

In Period V, prestigious barrow building has been reduced to a few examples, and the marking of personal status in graves is correspondingly greatly reduced and highly stereotyped in both men's and women's graves. Great quantities of metal, by con-

157

trast, are invested in ritual depositions. This involves both personal equipment such as weaponry, jewellery and tools, and cult items such as lurs, sacral drinking vessels and so on, the number of which grows in comparison with the Early Bronze Age. In the category of multiobject deposits, female accessories fill a much more prominent place than in the first peak of this sequence in Period II.

General interpretations of this complex sequence of development have been attempted on several occasions. It seems reasonable to suppose (Vandkilde, above) that the sequence from the Late Neolithic to the peak in Bronze Age Period II marks a development from a group-oriented hierarchy towards a society with dominant families that increasingly marked the status of individuals (Randsborg 1974). It was the elite of this society that marked themselves so conspicuously at the zenith of the Early Bronze Age, in Period II.

Rather less certainty resides in interpretations of the serious decline in the quantity of metal deposited in the following period, and the subsequent sharp rise in the number of depositions in Period V. Some suggestions focus on the increased representation of female jewellery in the hoards in the course of the Bronze Age and see the changes as the result of changed ideological and religious notions (Levy 1982). It has been proposed, for instance, that while the marking of male status was overwhelmingly predominant in the early deposits, female status took its place in the later ones. This simply isn't correct. If we look at the deposits as a whole, i.e. both multitype hoards and single deposits, the quantity of female jewellery does rise through the Bronze Age. But male objects continue to form the largest numerical group. It is probable, however, that the higher quantity of female jewellery in hoards does reflect the growing importance of women in the political alliances of the Bronze-age elite (Kristiansen 1986:306).

More interesting are the interpretations that attempt to look at the metal deposits in relation to the development of settlement (Kristiansen 1986). At the basis of these lies a perception of an ecological crisis, growing through the Bronze Age. At the end of the 2nd and through the 1st millennium B.C. a reduction in the productive capacity of agriculture is thus supposed to lead to the collapse of "the hierarchical communities of the Bronze Age and consequent social reorganization" which can be observed in the village society of the pre-Roman Iron Age (Kristiansen 1986:307). The theory is interesting because it attemps to involve as many factors as possible in a comprehensive perspective. But it probably is too dramatic. Amongst other things, the peak of depositions in the periods (IV)-V is seen as the result of shortage of metal and an expression of a "growing opposition between the politico-economic superstructure with its need to mark status and the ecological and economic substructure with its failing capacity to achieve the necessary productivity" (Kristiansen 1986:306). The increased range of deposits in Periods IV and V would thus be a reflection of the leading families' attempts to overcome the crisis by maintaining old social and religious norms.

It is difficult to see, however, how the deposits of the Late Bronze Age could be the result of a situation of shortage. On the contrary, imported goods pour into Denmark in this period at a volume never seen before. There is, however, clearly a case of shortage in Period III of the Early Bronze Age. But this was at a date at which the postulated agricultural crisis had not yet begun. The shortage of metal in Period III rather shows the vulnerability of Bronze-age society to the continual shifting of the centres of exchange.

All the same, there is no doubt that through the Bronze Age we can see a gradual transformation of the settlement pattern and the subsistence basis (Rasmussen & Adamsen, above). This certainly indicates change but not any acute crisis. What we can observe is rather the gradual adaptation of society to the cultural and natural circumstances that changed through the centuries. For this development to be made clearer many factors need to be brought into a comprehensive view: climatic changes, changes in agricultural productivity, in the level of population, in social patterns and in connexions with the rest of Europe, such, for instance, as are reflected in metal supply. A fully persuasive comprehensive explanation cannot yet be offered, as our knowledge of the substructure of Bronze-age society, i.e. the development of settlement and subsistence, is as yet too limited. But an exciting task for future research will be to join together these diverse factors and indeed to see the deposits of metal objects, for instance, in the light of the changes that society as a whole underwent in the 2nd and 1st millennia B.C.

The cult house at Sandagergård

In 1985, Gilleleje Museum, at Ferslev, northern Sjælland, excavated a unique feature that sheds light on Bronze-age cult (Kaul 1987). A double stone frame, measuring 18.5 x 7.5 m. externally, was uncovered. This well-formed stone setting represents a building, for on the whole finds were only made inside it (potsherds; crucible and mould fragments) while the area outside, apart from the southern end, was virtually void of finds. At the south, where the entrance is thought to have been, lay four rocks incised with a hand mark below four lines. These were enclosed by three menhirs, of which one was fully preserved, having clearly been deliberately thrown down and buried in the Bronze Age itself; a second was broken up in more recent times and the third could only be traced through its socket. Three cremation burials were found in the building. The rock carvings, the stratified potsherds and the urns all date to Period IV of the Bronze Age.

The square, stone-set building, the cremations, the rock carvings and the menhirs show that this was no ordinary building, but rather a cult house. Stones with the hand mark are always associated with graves if anything. These stones, the significance of which is underlined by the menhirs, must therefore be associated with death: perhaps marking a deadly taboo against entering the cult house.

The following year, a settlement of the same period was found on a hillside about 100 m. east of the cult house. No settlement traces were found in the immediate vicinity. Excavation revealed only scattered postholes and pits. It was apparent that erosion had removed most traces; dark blown soil lay in hollows all around. The layers sealing the cult house themselves showed how considerable sandblows took place from

The cult house seen from the south. Outside the southern end of the building can be seen the area in which the rock carvings and the menhirs were found.

the time of its construction in Bronze Age Period IV and the transition between Periods II and III of the pre-Roman Iron Age, when some cremation graves were dug down from a somewhat higher level.

Other comparable square, stone-set buildings are known. There are some near barrow groups in Sweden. An excavation at Tofta Högar in Skåne has clearly shown such a building with timber roofbearing posts and walls. Several squares of this kind are known from Denmark; at Godensgård a rock carving with a foot mark was associated with such a struc-ture. A new find below Diverhøj in eastern Jutland, of a stone-set, rounded quadrangular building, the wooden parts of which were burned before the barrow was raised, shows that the tradition of stone-set cult houses goes back to the Late Neolithic (Asingh 1988).

When our cult house was excavated, 15 rocks with the familiar hand below four lines were known from Sjælland, Fyn and Østfold. Another has since been found built into Grevinge church, from where one was already known (Kaul 1988c), and in 1992 a further example was found at Udby Vig. Bohuslän has now joined the distribution map, with two hand-mark stones from Askum and Mosse Myr, while two more examples have been discovered, from Hoderöd and Utmark, albeit only in the form of drawings (Nancke-Krogh 1989). With these finds, we now know of 25 stones of this type.

The four incised stones with hand-marks that were found outside the southern end of the cult house.

Flemming Kaul

159

The graves

BY HENRIK THRANE

The balance between the classic find-type of the Bronze Age, the graves, and the settlement sites that have been so intensely sought after in recent years has clearly shifted in favour of settlements, both in the field and in the offices where money for excavations is shared out.

The publication of Early Bronze-age graves has made slow but steady progress since 1958, when Karl Kersten's project was accepted by the then state antiquary. With nearly 4,600 finds to date in the 11 published volumes from Schleswig and Denmark (see J. Jensen, above) the material might appear horrifyingly large. But thanks to its thoroughness, and the quality of presentation, Aner and Kersten's work stands on its own against its Swedish counterpart and in a European perspective. I am certain that interest in using this large body of finds for internal Danish studies will rise as soon as the work is complete. A solution for this work is therefore one of the primary needs of Danish archaeology.

There is no corresponding corpus of the Late Bronze-age material. Here we still have to make do with H.C. Broholm's work of the 1940's with all of its gaps and E. Baudou's major work of 1960, works concentrated on artefact-types. This unfortunately has led to Bronze Age research being split across the middle. Publications of the last 25 years show this as clearly as one could wish. The only opportunity there has been for treating the whole Bronze Age as one dwindled into an isolated, technical line of enquiry. By this I mean the analyses of Danish gold finds (Hartmann 1982), the significance of which was also limited by the impossibility of including the Swedish finds.

Most recent Early Bronze-age tumulus excavations are or will be published in Aner & Kersten's series. But many will not be included. These comprice important excavations of classic Jutlandic barrows as Krudhøj (Thorsen 1977). Nor should re-excavations of important barrows be forgotten. Egt-

ved (Alexandersen *et al.* 1983), Borum Eshøj, Tobøl (Thrane 1963) of the Early Bronze Age, and Lusehøj of the Late, are good examples of what new techniques can retrieve from the ruins of barrows.

The tendency only to excavate tumuli that stand in the way of public construction works is growing. Ploughed-out barrows rarely attract funding unless there are especially good arguments on their side although it is just these barrows that can advance research.

Ploughed-out barrows are undeniably one of the most crucial sources. With the techniques available to modern archaeology and the questions raised in most recent research a lot of relevant answers may be obtained from good ploughed-out barrows. I have in mind not just the graves but other structures too, both in the barrows and below them, either ploughed-out in prehistory or protected against the erosion that similar features have suffered in the open Danish landscape by the mass of the mounds. We would not, for instance, know much about Early Bronze-age buildings or pre-Iron-age agriculture without the house sites and ardmarks below barrows.

There is a strange tendency for more careful barrow excavations to produce fewer finds. I am thinking of grave goods. It is striking how few spectacular grave goods have been found in the large number of barrow excavations of the last generation. In all, 297 excavated barrows/graves/cemeteries have been recorded in the years 1976-90. But relatively few of them have been published as anything more than an entry in AUD (see however J. Jensen 1987).

Interesting aspects of the barrow excavations include the observation of earth-covered cairns in several parts of Denmark, not only on Sjælland, where they seem to have a long history. Recognition of this may blur the erstwhile clear distinction between earth-barrow and cairn landscapes. In the Scandinavian context, the appearance of cooking-stone cairns may be even more interesting. Apart from one example dated to the Germanic Iron Age, datable cooking-stone cairns belong to the Late Bronze Age and are just as intimately connected to contemporary settlements as in Sweden. They are found not only in Odsherred on Sjælland but also from the classic settlement site on Kirkebjerget in Voldtofte.

While cooking-stone cairns pose their own problems, small barrows of the same date belong to the

Lusehøj, Fyn. The 'minibarrow' sealed by the large mound.

normal barrow complex. There can be no doubt that tiny grave mounds, about 50 cm. high and 5 m. in diameter, must have been common from the beginning of the Late Bronze Age, at least on Fyn and probably over the whole country. Lusehøj and Lerbjerg (Håstrup) have provided the best examples of small barrows. These were only preserved because they were soon covered by large tumuli and thus protected from agricultural destruction in the course of the following millennia. The relationship between the small barrows and the earlier grave mounds used at the same time for secondary burials may raise new interesting questions.

As in many other contexts, we lack comprehensive studies of groups of grave mounds. With the enormous number of ploughed-out barrows it ought to be easy enough to find discrete groups. But instead we continue to excavate one particularly threatened barrow here and another there, which will never let us find the contexts that are necessary for the grave mounds to occupy their proper place in the study of the landscape and settlement in a broad synchronic perspective (a prerequisite for the study of diachronic development).

A step has however been taken at Brydegård, south-western Fyn, where 4 barrows, two stone circles and 8 flat graves proved to belong to the middle of the Late Bronze Age (C. Madsen & Thrane 1992). The barrows were all raised and used in this period alone. One of the barrows contained a secondary burial with richly-decorated male equipment - without weapons, although the furnishing of the other graves followed the norms of the period: at most one bronze object. Just one ruined and one protected mound remain uninvestigated in this closely connected barrow-group.

Two excavations have shown that the former certainty that no new large tumuli were raised in the Late Bronze Age is no longer tenable. The re-investigation of Lusehøj demonstrated that a barrow 36 m. in diameter was raised in Period V. The excavation of the remains of Lerbjerg, Håstrup, showed the existence of a barrow 38 m. in diameter. This was raised in Period VI! It was raised over several smaller barrows and stone circles with urns in stone cists (Albrectsen 1951, grave 1; C. Madsen & Thrane 1992), which immediately preceded the raising of the large mound. The analogy with the history of Lusehøj is obvious, and it is difficult to see the Håstrup barrow as anything other than a later

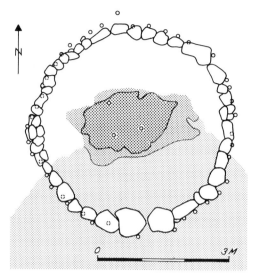

Håstrup, Fyn. Cremation pyre layer with stakeholes below funerary urn of Period VI.

attempt to demonstrate the same phenomenon as at Lusehøj.

Favourable condiations at Lusehøj made it possible to identify slender wicker hurdles that must have had a function in the raising of the barrow. Temporary structures of this kind can only be detected in special circumstances. A matching temporary phenomenon is the stakeholes from a structure associated with cremation that that was first seen below Lusehøj. These have now been found in 4 Period-VI barrows on Fyn. It would be remarkable if we have thus found all the existing examples.

The stakes had been driven into the ground and pulled up early enough for remains of the pyre to fill the holes. Exactly what stood above the ground we cannot say, of course, but we can guess it was some form of scaffold on which the deceased was placed.

Of the same character is the enclosure around a cremation-pit below Lusehøj with associated straw matting. The stake settings and the associated pyre show how much more complicated Late Bronze-age funerary practice was than we once believed. Unfortunately, older excavations are not easily compared with modern ones, so a reasonably comprehensive picture of the archaeologically identifiable features of such practice is a long way off. The latest contributions show how modern archaeology can reveal quite unexpected aspects of prehistoric behaviour.

But perhaps the most distinctive tendency of Danish Bronze Age research is following well-trodden paths. The interest in richly furnished grave finds has always overshadowed the humbler graves. In 1974,

161

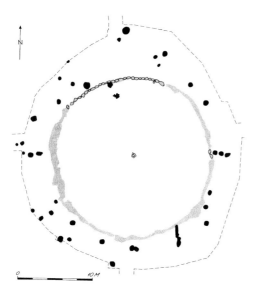

Hannemose, Fyn. Single-period grave mound of Period VI surrounded by Early Iron-age cremation graves.

carrying on from the gold analyses mentioned above, Klaus Randsborg analysed the grave finds of the Early Bronze Age in terms of the expression of material wealth. His quantitative analyses show a clear tendency to clustering, which was interpreted as reflecting social differentiation, with relatively few individuals being much more richly equipped than the majority, but also with groups of graves containing substantial gold and bronze furnishings.

Earlier research rejected out of hand the possibility of finding social difference in Late Bronze-age burials. The reduction of grave goods as a result of the transition to cremation makes direct comparison with the Early Bronze Age impossible. Nonetheless, analyses of Late Bronze-age grave goods also show clear clusters (Thrane 1981). A fundamental difference is that gold is now overwhelmingly deposited not in graves but in hoards. But there still are graves with massive gold objects or with gold foil on bronze pieces, just as in the Early Bronze Age. A number of artefact-types disappear from grave inventories: weapons (on the whole) and large items of jewellery.

Once again it is the Lusehøj excavation that has dotted the i. Despite the destructive effect of the pyre, which itself was abnormal for the Scandinavian Late Bronze Age, the unique cremation pit beneath the large barrow contained enough to show an exceptionally varied and comprehensive assemblage of gold and bronze. When the grave find of 1861 is added, Lusehøj stands unchallenged as the richest site of the Late Bronze Age in Scandinavia and quite apart from all other regions. Thanks to the

excavations, Lusehøj is the best known feature of the Late Bronze Age in SW Fyn, but it is not the only find showing the special status of the region. Further, though poorly recorded, grave finds with gold and bronzes (including types that are not put in graves elsewhere in Scandinavia) show that wealth was concentrated north of Helnæs Bay, especially in Period V.

The same chronological weighting is found on the major settlement on Kirkebjerg near Voldtofte that has been investigated several times between 1908 and 1986 (Berglund 1982). This settlement is distinguished from other Danish examples by its thick culture layers, rich in finds, which were deposited in hollows in the very uneven terrain of that time. More recent erosion has removed nearly all traces of buildings, but fromone cleared plot we have quite a lot of pieces of fine, polished, red- and black-painted wall plaster. The Kirkebjerg settlement is also distinguished from the others by a broad ditch that must have formed an eastern boundary and which was filled up in Period VI. How the boundary was marked to the west is not yet clear.

Apart from the traces of flimsy structures already mentioned, it is the identification of centres of wealth that emerges alongside the settlement studies as the most important discovery of the last 25 years in Bronze Age research. Although the information could be found in old material, as Klaus Randsborg's and Jørgen Jensen's studies and work in south-western Fyn have shown, it was the Lusehøj excavation that first put the old grave finds into a comprehensive context. We now see that wealth is not constantly expressed in the finds. Centres shift from period to period - from century to century. It is rare for a region to maintain wealth for more than a few generations. Such changeability probably reflects the character of social structures. Despite the importance we should properly attach to the families as the bearers of power and wealth, heritable power cannot have been as important as it became at the end of prehistory.

No doubt, as in the case of Migration-period Gudme, other cases of expressions of wealth similar to these in eastern Denmark will turn up around Scandinavia. It will be an important task for future Bronze Age research to investigate variance in such expressions: to determine where and how wealth moved from region to region and in what ways wealth could be displayed.

Lusehøj on Fyn

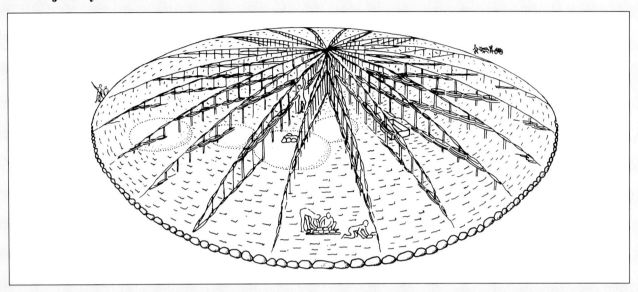

'X-ray photograph' of Lusehøj. The large barrow under construction. The two rich graves are marked and the earlier, smaller barrows picked out.

Lusehøj is situated 1.7 km due west of Voldtofte, with its classic Bronze-age settlement site on Kirkebjerg (J. Jensen 1967; J. Berglund 1982). The barrow was dug in the 1860's, as part of the efforts to provide new finds for King Frederik VII after the fire in Frederiksborg Castle of 1859. It was these efforts that made the Voldtofte area the richest area in Denmark of the Late Bronze Age, Period V in particular. The great majority of the finds have no information beyond that they come from barrows in Voldtofte Mark.

Even the grave found in Lusehøj was not properly described. We know, however, that the burnt bones lay wrapped in fine woven cloth of nettle fibre in an imported bronze bucket with its own lid. The lid was embedded in a thick layer of resin (or birch pitch) in which several pieces of amber and small bits of bronze were stuck. At the bottom of the vessel, with the bones, were an oath-ring and two toggles, all of gold. There were also two similar buttons, and two razors, of bronze and some amber. Outside the vessel, on the floor of the grave, lay a bronze axe and, right beside the vessel, three small bronze beakers. The lidded vessel and the beakers were wrapped in woven woollen cloth, beyond which an ox hide had been packed. All of this was placed in a cist of split stones, about a metre wide.

This grave find has remained the richest of Late Bronze Age Scandinavia, characterized by rare and exotic artefacts that are only matched far to the south.

In order to obtain more data on the find and its location, the ploughed-out barrow was re-investigated in 1973-75 (Thrane 1984). The barrow was originally about 36 m in diameter and 6 m high. It was made of grass turves layed in concentric rings distinguished by their varying contents of subsoil materials. It has been calculated that grass turf was stripped from an area of 7.3 ha to build the barrow.

Several wicker fences ran radially from the centre of the mound and are interpreted as gauges used while the barrow was being constructed. It was raised on top of a burial site with at least four small barrows and two flat graves of Period IV. These graves overlie a ploughed-out settlement from the end of the Early Bronze Age.

The large barrow was raised over the grave from 1860 and over a cremation pit with a stake structure. Cremation pit and stakeholes alike were filled with charcoal from the pyre with burnt remains of artefacts of bronze and gold. There are remains of at least 15 different bronze objects, an iron ring and at least three different sorts of gold foil. Amongst the Scandinavian items, a sword, a bossed belt and a chain with jingling pendants are remarkable because such objects are not normally found in graves. Several objects must have been imported, including a number of ornamental nails and other pieces that are interpreted as belonging to horse harness and a wagon body.

Each of the graves far outstrips even the richest graves of Scandinavia, with the sole exception of the Seddin grave in Mecklenburg.

The combination of exotic and rare artefact-types must reflect the social status of the deceased men in a way that emphatically contrasts with the otherwise highly uniform grave goods provided in the Late Bronze Age.

Lusehøj is situated on the morrain hills high above the plateau of south-western Fyn, with a prospect over the plain down towards the neighbouring bay of Helnæs, with further large barrows. Thus Lusehøj is part of a concentration of barrows, both richly furnished and of unusual size. No comparable archaeological expression of wealth and power is known anywhere else in Scandinavia. The closest parallels are at Albersdorf in the Dithmarsch and Seddin in Mecklenburg, both of which are contemporary with the Lusehøj group.

Henrik Thrane

Oak coffins and Bronze Age chronology

BY KLAVS RANDSBORG

The oldest method of obtaining absolute chronological dates is relative dating on the basis of imported and exported artefact-types. In this way, a pattern of interlinked regional sequences crossing Europe and the Near East was ultimately aligned with the historical chronology of Egypt. This so-called historical method is still, however, beset with many difficulties. The C 14 method, introduced in the 1950's, provides an independent means of establishing archaeological chronologies, but this technique is not without its own difficulties, and offers only probable dates. There is, incidentally, no discrepancy between the Egyptian historical dates and C 14 datings from the area (see Hassan & Robinson 1987). Dendrochronology, a dating-method developed in the 1920's, was not seriously used in Scandinavian archaeology until the last decade or two, but it has already yielded impressive results of great historical and international significance.

Some of the revised dendro-dates for the famous Danish oak-coffin graves of the Early Bronze Age have recently been published (Christensen & Jensen 1991; Randsborg 1992). A number of comments can be added to the archaeological datings and the other evidence concerning the oak coffins and their contents (Boye 1896; Th. Thomsen 1929). After the last identified year, the approximate felling date is given. This work was done by Kjeld Christensen.

1. Borum Eshøj, grave A (1373 B.C.; *ca.* 1353 B.C.): primary (central) grave in mound. No well-dated artefacts. (For secondary graves, see grave B.)

2. Borum Eshøj, grave B (1365 B.C.; *ca.* 1345 B.C.): secondary grave in the same mound as grave A. Period II/Reinecke C(2) (dagger).

3. Guldhøj, grave B (1401 B.C.; *ca.* 1381 B.C.): secondary grave (child) in mound. No well-dated artefacts. (Primary (?) grave, grave A (not yet dendro-dated), Period II.) See also grave C.

4. Guldhøj, grave C (1401 B.C.; *ca.* 1381 B.C.): secondary grave near grave B (contemporary?). Probably Period-II (wooden double button). (Primary (?) grave, see grave B.)

5. Lille Dragshøj (1390 B.C.; *ca.* 1370 B.C.): grave in mound. Possibly early Period-II (dagger).

6. Trindhøj, grave A (1376 B.C.; *ca.* 1356 B.C.): primary (?) grave in mound. Period II/Reinecke C(2) (sword, resembling the octagonal-hilted central European specimens; razor).

7. Trindhøj, grave B (1359 B.C.; *ca.* 1333 B.C.): secondary (?) grave in the same mound as graves A and C, lying parallel with and very close to grave C.

Grave B must therefore be contemporary with grave C. Rich equipment, probably dating quite late in Period II (sword, brooch, double button; also tweezers, tutulus, etc.).

8. Trindhøj, grave C (1356 B.C.; *ca.* 1330 B.C.): secondary (?) grave (child) in the same mound as graves A and B; contemporary with grave B (cf. above). Probably Period-II (bracelet).

9. Storehøj at Barde (1380 B.C.; 1373 B.C.): grave in mound. Period II, perhaps of an early phase (golden bracelet (?), tweezers; also belt-hook).

10. Mølhøj (1422 B.C.; *ca.* 1396 B.C.): grave in mound. No artefacts.

11. Egtved (1370 B.C.; 1370 B.C.): grave in mound. Period II (belt-plate, bracelets).

These dates indicate that the above graves all belong to a relatively short phase, Nordic Period II. This is corroborated by the artefacts. The graves were constructed within a relatively short period of time during the 14th century B.C. No graves of the 15th (nor of the 13th) centuries have come to light in this sample. The dendro-dates also seem to confirm observations about the relative dating of the some of the graves, both within the particular mound and with regard to the artefact-types. Finally, the graves without, or with only a few, metal artefacts are mostly early, suggesting that conspicuous investment in grave goods made from exotic raw materials (primarily metals) in Period II, as well as, of course, in (early) Period III, may have been restricted to a very short period of time. All the graves are from Jutland and are located on the poorer soils suited to a pastoralist subsistence economy.

Among the remaining dendro-dates, the analyis of which is not yet complete, there are several of great archaeological interest. It must be emphasized that the following dates are provisional ones:

12. Muldbjerg, Hover parish, Ringkøbing amt (Boye 1896:30f.), of classic Period II and with rich male garments, jewellery (two bronze brooches, two bronze tutuli and a wooden double button) and (in a wooden scabbard) an imported flange-hilted sword of central European phase Reinecke C(2). Preliminarily dated to sometime after 1396 B.C. plus *ca.* 20 years, i.e. sometime after 1376 B.C.

13. Nybøl, Hjortkær parish, Åbenrå amt (Boye 1896: 107f.; Aner & Kersten VI, Ke 3022). Preliminarily dated to *ca.* 1275 B.C. Contents: a bone comb and a wrapped Period-III bronze razor.

14. Nøragerhøj, Emmerlev parish, Tønder amt

(Boye 1896:119f.; Aner & Kersten VI, Ke 2909). Preliminarily dated to *ca.* 1296 B.C. Contents: a Period-III sword with a full metal handle, a gold spiral bracelet and a cattle horn.

The transition between Period II and Period III in western Jutland can thus be pinpointed to the decades between *ca.* 1330 and 1300 B.C., a remarkably precise date which furthermore agrees with findings based on other methods (Randsborg 1992).

What makes the oak-coffin dendro-dates particularly interesting for European research is that they are so well dated archaeologically, that they contain foreign artefact-types, and that they are the only dendro-dates from the Continent between about 1500 and a little before 1000 B.C. where in both cases we have a series of Alpine datings from lake-dwellings (as well as other dendro-dates). The Danish findings are thus of great importance for the Bronze Age chronology of the 14th and 13th centuries B.C. in Europe (the late Middle Bronze Age in Central Europe) and beyond. Furthermore, the oak-coffin dendro-dates have proved the historical chronology to be correct. For a time, there were serious discrepancies between the (too-highly) calibrated C 14 datings and the historical chronology.

For the first phase of the Early Bronze Age in central Europe, the new dendro-dates of the 20th and 19th centuries B.C. for the rich Leubingen and Helmsdorf graves (late phase A 1) in eastern Germany respectively are of particular importance for dating the beginning of the Nordic Bronze Age since these graves are contemporary with the end of the Late Neolithic in southern Scandinavia (B. Becker *et al.* 1989; Randsborg 1992).

The end of the Late Bronze Age (the Urnfield Culture) in central Europe, phase Hallstatt (Ha) B 3, is contemporaray with Nordic Period V. Ha B 3 dendro-dates from, for instance, Switzerland now consistently put the end of this phase in the 9th century B.C., some 100-150 years before the historical chronology traditionally has it. However Ha D, the second phase of the Early Iron Age in central Europe and contemporary with both the very end of the Nordic Bronze Age (late Period VI) and the beginning of the Iron Age in Denmark, is firmly dated to the 6th century B.C. on the basis of both dendro-dates and a number of well-dated Greek imports.

In the table are summarized a number of absolute chronological observations from Scandinavia, central Europe and the Aegean, all of which seem to be very difficult to alter, at least with our present knowledge. (Thera refers to the volcanic eruption of the island now C 14-dated to the (late) 17th century B.C., contemporary with the famous later Mycenean shaft graves of the Late Helladic Bronze Age I.

Accepting the dates below, after almost 50 years of intense chronological debate we are close to the unification of historical, C 14 and dendro-dates; the only major outstanding problem seems to be the 8th century B.C. The social and cultural development of the Bronze Age can now be formulated anew, and European cultural connexions can be studied from a firmer starting point. Thus, for instance, the development of the Early Bronze Age in central Europe is contemporary with the establishment of the palace cultures in the Aegean, and the oak-coffin and other richly furnished Scandinavian graves with the period of intensive exchange between late Bronze-age Greece and Europe. The important transition between the Early and Late Bronze Age in central and northern Europe is contemporary with the transition between the palace culture and the Iron Age in the Aegean, and the end of the central and northern European Bronze Age, with its settlement landscapes of hill-forts and other centres, is parallel not only to similar developments in Italy but also to the emerging Greek city state or *polis*, the cradle of Western civilization. Chronology is indeed the eyes of historiy, and it sees far beyond regional traditions.

Centuries B.C.	Scandinavia	Central Europe	Greece
21st		A1 (starts earlier)	
20th		Leubinge (late A1)	
19th		Helmsdorf (late A1)	
18th			
17th		A2	Thera; LH I
16th			
15th			
14th	Per. II		
13th	Per. III	D	LH III B
12th			
11th		Ha A2 (HaB1)	Proto-Geometric
10th			
9th	Per. V	Ha B3, Bronze Age ends	
8th			
7th			Orientalizing
6th	Iron Age begins	Ha D	Archaic
5th		La Tène A	Early Classical

THE IRON AGE AND
THE VIKING PERIOD

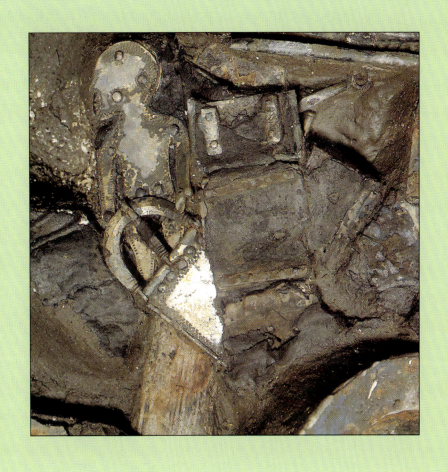

The Iron Age and the Viking Period

By Ulla Lund Hansen

The study of the Iron Age has developed in a very striking way in the last 25 years. Not all of its phases, however, have been subject to the same level of research, as different periods and topics have been in and out of favour in recent years.

In the 1960's, interest was particularly focussed upon the problems of the pre-Roman Iron Age. Less attention was paid to influences from the Celtic and Roman worlds than to the establishment of a chronology based primarily upon pottery (C.J. Becker 1961). This chronological research was to prove of the greatest importance in the study of the buildings and settlements that were uncovered in the great excavation projects of the following years (C.J. Becker 1966a-b, 1969a). These groundbreaking excavations were followed up with new settlement excavations over the whole country (S. Hvass, below). The Jutlandic material is at present the best known, but Fyn, Sjælland and Bornholm are not far behind.

There are only certain aspects of the steadily growing quantity of grave finds of the pre-Roman Iron Age that have interested archaeology in recent years: graves with weaponry, carts and imported vessels (J.L. Nielsen 1975; Schovsbo 1987). The excavation of the cemetery of Hedegård from period III of the pre-Roman Iron Age, with its unparalleled quantity of Celtic weaponry, early Roman bronze vessels, gold jewellery and previously unknown artefacts, created entirely new insights (O. Madsen 1992).

In the same way, the intense development of research into iron that appears to have begun will provide significant re-assessments of iron supply in the early Iron Age in coming years. An essential issue that must be tackled is how much iron was produced in Denmark rather than further south at the very beginning, and how extensive the trade in iron was between different parts of Scandinavia and the Continent (Voss, below).

After several years' neglect, the 1970's saw renewed interest in the Roman Iron Age, especially in its later phase. Inspired both by important new finds and a more general archaeological desire for entirely new social perspectives, new questions were asked of the rich and varied finds. Social development began to be looked at in a longer-term perspective with strikingly new consequences (Liversage 1980; Hedeager & Kristiansen 1982; Lund Hansen 1987, 1988a, 1991; S. Hvass 1988; Lønstrup 1988; Ilkjær 1991; S. Jensen 1991a; Hedeager 1992). Important research work on this period continues apace.

Archaeological periodization has been the subject of extensive re-evaluation in recent years, particularly in respect of the later Iron Age. This new situation is the product of the astonishing growth in new finds combined with increasingly problem-orientated research into the Earlier and Later Germanic Iron Age and around the beginning of the Viking Period. Happily, the last few years have seen considerable interest in the Viking Period amongst a group of young and talented scholars. We still lack, however, a modern and functional phasing of the period, so that, as a rule, it is only possible to offer datings to either the earlier or the later Viking Period. This is too coarse a phasing to answer the detailed questions that are now being asked of the archaeological evidence.

Interest in the Early Germanic Iron Age has held steady, although in recent years it has grown as a result of excavations at Sejlflod (J.N. Nielsen 1982; Ringtved 1991), Hjemsted (Ethelberg 1986, 1990), Gudme (Thrane 1987a, 1991b; Vang Petersen 1987), Lundeborg (P.O. Thomsen 1991b) and Sorte Muld (Watt 1991). The quantity of hoard finds has grown markedly (Fonnesbech-Sandberg 1991a-b; Hedeager 1991), and a number of find-categories have been subjected to new analyses (Andrén 1991; Axboe 1991). There has been a continuous re-assessment of the end of the Early Germanic Iron Age, partly on the basis of the finds of the period and partly in connection with analyses of the beginning of the Later Germanic Iron Age (Høilund Nielsen 1987; Lund Hansen 1992).

The conclusion is that the Early Germanic Iron Age was of shorter duration than previously thought. The end-date of the period is derived from analyses of the datability of the Scandinavian material compared with European relative and absolute chronologies (Lund Hansen 1992). A super-regional subdivision of the period is at present only possible on the basis of art style. The earliest and latest styles of the Early Germanic Iron Age, the Sösdala Style and Style I respectively, have been specially analysed (Lund Hansen 1970; Haseloff 1981). Above all, the study of the cemetery at Sejlflod can be expected to provide definite new points (Ringtved 1991).

In the later 1960's, after many years of inactivity, there began a new wave of research into the Later Germanic Iron Age. The foundation was laid in the 1950's with the publication of the Kyndby cemetery (Ørsnes-Christensen 1956), but at this point the clas-

In the last 25 years, considerable efforts have been put into chronological research, ranging from simple typologies to complicated matrices (Ørsnes 1966; Lund Hansen 1977, 1987, 1988b; Liversage 1980; Høilund Nielsen 1987; L. Jørgensen 1989, 1990; Ilkjær 1990). Substantial corrections have been made to absolute datings. This has been especially important in providing a uniform chronology on a national basis, and in enabling the assessment of phenomena in a European perspective. The latter has always been a primary concern of Danish archaeology and has led to the recognition of extremely interesting connections between the Continent and southern Scandinavia.

The pre-Roman Iron Age is divided into phases I, II, IIIa and IIIb (C.J. Becker 1961). The Roman Iron Age is the most finely subdivided of the periods of the Iron Age, with individual phases of just a few generations. The Early Roman Iron Age is divided into phases B1a, B1b and B2, the Late Roman Iron Age into phases B2/C1a, C1a, C1b, C2 and C3 (Liversage 1980; Lund Hansen 1987).

The transition to the Early Germanic Iron Age fell shortly before 400 A.D. This period is subdivided on the basis of styles; other generally valid criteria have not yet been worked out. The earliest style is the Sösdala Style (Lund Hansen 1970), partly overlapping with the Nydam Style (Voss 1955), which is followed by the Sjörup Style and Style I (Haseloff 1981). The Early Germanic Iron Age ends before the middle of the 6th century, probably around 520/530 A.D. (Lund Hansen 1992).

For the Late Germanic Iron Age we have both an artefact chronology and a chronology based on the animal styles B, C, D, E and F (Ørsnes 1966). It is not now so easy to date on the basis of the animal styles, as these seem to overlap substantially (Høilund Nielsen 1991). The relative sequence of the styles, however, is the same. The transition to the Early Viking Period has been the subject of great debate in recent years. Primarily on the basis of dendrochronologically-dated layers at Ribe, which are unquestionably to be attributed to the Viking Period on the basis of stratified finds such as Berdal brooches (S. Jensen 1991b), the transition has been re-assigned to the first half of the 9th century. The end of the Viking Period, by contrast, remains as it was: still identified with the historically-based transition to the Middle Ages in the middle of the 11th century.

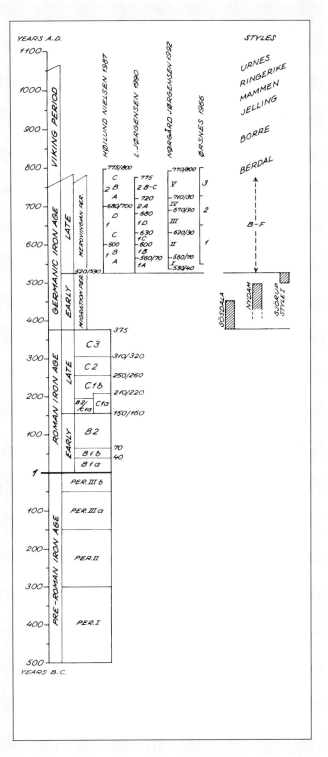

In 1979 and 1983, in connection with the construction of a road north of the village of Bakkendrup in Holbæk amt, a cemetery with 22 inhumation graves of the Late Germanic Iron Age and Early Viking Period was excavated.

One of the graves contained the well-preserved skeleton of a woman aged 20-35 at death. Her grave goods included this circular gilt bronze plate brooch. Plate brooches of this type, with imitations of 'Carolingian' coin portraits, had not previously been found in Scandinavia, being rather associated with the Middle Rhine and West Frisian regions in particular, where they are dated to the '9th century' (Hatz 1966). The Christ-like figure on the back of the brooch is unparalleled. The grave also contained a small iron handle and a necklace with 6 colourless glass beads (*ca.* 5 mm in diameter) and 50-60 opaque, whitish glass beads (*ca.* 1.2 mm in diameter). The grave is dated to the Late Germanic Iron Age/Early Viking Period.

Svend Erik Albrethsen

sification of the artefacts and their animal ornament became the focus of attention (Ørsnes 1966). The latter study came to be of great methodological importance for young archaeologists of the day: matrices had arrived in Danish archaeology.

Since then, the Later Germanic Iron Age has been a challenge. New aspects of the period are continually brought into the discussion (L. Jørgensen 1990, 1991b; Ulriksen 1990; Fenger 1991; Høilund Nielsen 1991; Nørgård Jørgensen 1991; Näsman 1991a-b), and the finds have increased considerably in recent years (Vang Petersen 1991 and below). From being a section of Danish prehistory in which the majority of the finds were concentrated on Bornholm this has developed into a far more comprehensively illuminated period, which very recently has been subject to quite drastic chronological revaluations in both relative and absolute terms (Høilund Nielsen 1987; Lund Hansen 1988b.)

Archaeological research into the Viking Period has been concentrated on several major sets of problems. Nearly all new insights into this period are the result of excavations, and immense progress has been made. From being a period that only a minority of archaeologists took seriously, the Viking Period has,

happily, become a challenge to the new generation of archaeologists, who have pitched into clear and as yet unsolved problems: above all the chronology. This concerns both the absolute-chronological boundary with the Late Germanic Iron Age and the subdivision of the period in order to solve a number of more general problems concerning Viking-period society.

The problems that the Viking Period poses are analysed below, but with regard to the pressing need for a chronological re-assessment of the grave finds of the period it should also be noted that the zoomorphic styles of the Viking Period urgently need new interest, and indeed have attracted it. In contrast to the Early and Late Germanic Iron Age, these styles are ill-defined and poorly distinguished from one another. They are therefore of limited use, while an interpretation of the very obvious use of several styles at one time should have consequences similar to those in the Late Germanic Iron Age.

In contrast to the grave finds, which only in exceptional cases, such as the Mammen grave (M. Iversen *et al.* (eds) 1991; L.C. Nielsen 1991), are accessible in any other than antiquated studies, civil and military settlement has enjoyed intensive study (T.E. Christiansen 1971, 1989; O. Olsen & Schmidt 1977; Roesdahl 1977, 1986; S. Hvass 1988; L.C. Nielsen 1990), as have urbanization, land and sea transport, and shipping (Rieck & Crumlin-Pedersen 1988; Crumlin-Pedersen 1991c).

Significant excavations, especially at Jelling and Mammen, have reawakened the debate over the conversion from paganism to Christianity (Krogh & Olsen, below), as has the growing volume of finds from the whole country which, if they are given close study, as, for example, on Bornholm, provide valuable evidence on this process (Watt 1988). General syntheses and interpretations of the Viking Period have been put forward (Randsborg 1980; Roesdahl 1980), which in themselves emphasize the clear need for new publications of many categories of finds.

With the enactment of the Nature Conservation Act of June 18th, 1969, which *inter alia* introduced a rule that in principle all ancient monuments found in the course of digging should be archaeologically investigated before they are removed (§ 49 of the Act; now Museum Act § 26), the number of rescue excavations in Denmark rose steadily to a level of about 400 excavations a year. A newly found monument is to be investigated as soon as possible, at most within a year of being recognized, and since efforts have been made to reduce the period between the discovery of the monument and the commencement of excavation as much as possible, the application of the law has meant that rescue excavation work in Denmark since the law came into force has been continuous. Only in the severest winter weather have rescue excavations - with some exceptions - been suspended.

The excavation at Bjergby on Mors was one of these exceptions (Albrethsen 1973, 1974). The discovery of a small cemetery with three inhumation graves (one man and two women) was reported to Rigsantikvaren between Christmas and New Year 1972. For various unfortunate reasons the excavation had to be carried out at the very start of the new year, in quite extreme conditions, with up to 8° of frost and light snow.

In the end, though, the extreme constraints on the Bjergby excavation proved to be a benefit. The excavators considered it necessary to lift the quite complex furnishings of the graves in blocks at a very much earlier stage in the excavation than would otherwise have been the case as the artefacts could not tolerate the sudden move from the relatively warm earth into the ice-cold air. At the end of 10 days' work in the field, the results of the excavation comprised plans and section drawings and four large plaster blocks with unknown contents. Only after X-ray photography in the Conservation Laboratory in Copenhagen and several months' intensive co-operation between conservator and excavator was it possible to see the graves' extraordinary contents. The largest of the blocks, shown here as an X-ray photograph and during excavation, was one of those with a remarkable collection of artefacts: the largest rosette brooch found in Denmark, a bronze pin with a trefoil head, a circular bronze pendant, a silver chain with 6 long links and two pins, 313 beads of amber and coloured glass (including 12 mosaic beads and 59 gold foil beads), and 7 small silver pendants.

The furnishings of the man's grave comprised an 84-cm long iron sword in a leather-covered wooden scabbard, bandolier disc, a gold finger ring, a silver brooch, a number of fragments of leather with gilding and a decorated handled pot.

The second woman's grave was furnished with a thin, twisted silver neckring with a keyhole-shaped catch, a silver brooch, an iron necklace, an iron ring brooch, two sheet-bronze pin cases, a small silver pendant, an iron knife with a bronze button in a leather sheath protected by sheet-bronze edging and decorated with 26 bronze rivets, one gold and two silver finger rings, and a cylindrical iron spindle whorl.

These three graves are dated within the first half of the Late Roman Iron Age (*ca.* 200-300 A.D.).

Svend Erik Albrethsen

Pre-Roman and Early Roman Iron Age

BY LOTTE HEDEAGER

Every period sees phases in which research leaps forward and phases of virtual standstill. So it has been with the Early Iron Age too.

At the beginning of the 1960's, the study of the "pre-Roman" Iron Age superseded the study of the "Celtic" Iron Age: *local* interest had supplanted a preoccupation with European connexions. Interest now turned from exotic luxury items such as the Brå and Gundestrup cauldrons to the humble grave finds, local pottery-types and brooch-forms, in order, if possible, to shed some light on the obscure local chronology of the period. More than anyone else C.J. Becker represented this field of research, and it was he, as professor in Copenhagen in the 1960's, who shaped the context for research into the Early Iron Age.

Settlement sites and settlement

In the typological-chronological jigsaw puzzle of the pre-Roman Iron Age, Becker made use of domestic pottery, and thus involved settlement features (C.J. Becker 1961). A first step was taken towards more detailed study of this enormous field, Iron-age settlement, which was made possible by a new excavation technique that Becker introduced to Scandinavia from Czechoslovakia.

Early Iron-age buildings had already been familiar to more than a generation. Gudmund Hatt above all had previously seen the need to study whole village communities,.as he tried to do at Nr. Fjand (Hatt 1957) although the practical problems of large area excavations by shovel hindered his designs.

It was the tractor with a drag that made the hitherto impossible possible, and in a campaign lasting more than a decade large areas were excavated at Grøntofte, Spjald, Bjerg and other sites north-east of Ringkøbing. Not just houses but villages were excavated here; detail had to bow to the general perspective, and the results were impressive. At Grøntofte, settlement could be followed from the late Bronze Age right through the pre-Roman Iron Age. Settlement in the late Bronze Age was dispersed, but from period I of the pre-Roman Iron Age the first village farmsteads with stalls appear. In period II, the village is surrounded with a common fence (C.J. Becker 1966a-b, 1969a, 1972a). At Grøntofte alone, nearly 300 buildings were revealed in an area of 16 ha., and 'the shifting village' appeared as an unchallenged concept.

Becker's excavations really opened the door to a new field of research, settlement archaeology, and with the foundation of The Archaeological Settlement Committee under The Danish Research Council for the Humanities the means were available to set this area of research on its feet. As a result, a number of villages of the Early Iron Age were excavated during the 1970's; the test case was Steen Hvass's excavation of the village at Hodde (S. Hvass 1985a). This village can be studied in minute detail through three phases from founding, *ca.* 150 B.C., to abandonment around the beginning of the Christian era, showing the establishment of a main farmstead and the laying-out of the village, fences around farmsteads and the village, changes in buildings, variations in stall-size, pottery-types associated with individual farmsteads and so on.

At Grøntofte and Hodde, Danish Iron Age research found two clear fixed points, and two village-types and settlement-patterns that were so different that they could easily be fitted into a simple developmental model: from small to large, from simple to complicated. Subsequent more or less complete excavations of Early Iron-age villages, however, show a more varied picture (S. Hvass 1988), while single farmsteads, that have particularly come to light in very recent years, are a new challenge to the current model of settlement.

At the end of the 1960's, considerable academic interest was focussed on settlement excavations. The great strides forward that new knowledge of Early Iron-age settlement undoubtedly represented were virtually halted by the mass of accumulated data. Interim reports were published but not monographs. An ideal level of documentation was not a practical proposition, and it was only with the publication of Hodde that this inbuilt problem was tackled in such a way that the results could be published in the form of a monograph (S. Hvass 1985a).

New excavations were no longer producing important new results but simply more material. Publications in the current framework of material publication and chronological studies were not possible, and money for large excavations gradually dried up as the demand for publication grew. Rescue excavations were the 1980's answer to the research excavations of the 70's. The parish records of the National Museum and the local museums' archives filled up with startling speed with settlement sites of the Early Iron Age, mostly from the later pre-Roman and Early Roman Iron Age, often on the same spot. Scholarly progress was no longer associated with the excavation of a single farmstead or a village but rather with the understanding of the whole settlement pattern in particular areas -shifting, density, basic resources and so on. The surveying of field systems, which Gudmund Hatt had organized in the 1930's and 40's (Hatt 1949) was developed on the islands by Viggo and Gudrun Nielsen (V. Nielsen 1984). Together with large area plans of ardmarks in Store Vildmose, these provide a detailed view of Early Iron-age cultivation (V. Nielsen 1987).

Settlement studies of the later 1970's on Fyn, in combination with a series of interdisciplinary settlement-historical symposia, put certain problems of settlement studies into focus in a still-relevant way (Thrane (ed.) 1976, 1977, 1979).

Settlement and the natural sciences

But archaeology will not achieve this on its own, and it is particularly important to involve other disciplines in settlement archaeology. This includes, above all, the natural sciences, which, however, have only very recently been seriously applied to settlement studies. Nobody now doubts that, for example, climatic studies, pollen and macrofossil analyses and bone studies are essential components of a fuller view of the conditions of a settlement: its economic basis, etc. The resources for such studies, however, fall far short of the great interest that there now appears to be in scientific research.

Grave and votive deposits

Besides the copious material from settlement sites, grave finds of the Early Iron Age are numerous. While, however, the number of newly-found settlements has grown explosively through the last 20 to 30 years (S. Hvass 1985b), the number of graves found has fallen in a similar way (Hedeager 1985), partly as a result of a definite devaluation of this category. New grave finds from both the pre-Roman and the Roman Iron Age supplement the existing picture rather than creating significantly new insights.

There are, naturally, exceptions, and the most striking of these is the large-scale excavation of the barrow cemetery at Årupgård, with its 1,500 or so graves of the early pre-Roman Iron Age (the site seems to start with a barrow with urns of the very end of the Bronze Age). The horizontal stratigraphy of the site will be a basis for the chronological clarification of an otherwise difficult part of the Iron Age, but publication is still awaited (interim report: E. Jørgensen 1975). To this can be added the full publication of the excavations at Nr. Sandegård (C.J. Becker 1990b).

The situation with burials of the Early Roman Iron Age is different. Through the 1970's and 80's were the subject of much greater attention, and were usually viewed as a part of the Roman Iron Age (1st-4th centuries) as a whole. An exception is Liversage's study (1980), in which domestic pottery is included to illuminate the chronology of grave finds.

A major chronological study resides in Ulla Lund Hansen's thesis (1987) on Roman imports to Scandinavia. Through chronological studies, the imports are closely dated by means of their local context in the graves. The chronological groupings provide a detailed insight into the distribution of the imports, into trade routes and the relationship with the Empire. A comprehensive catalogue gives an updated list of all the finds of imports in Scandinavia. A comparable but far less comprehensive or detailed work was published by Kunow (1983), who updated Hans Jürgen Eggers' European catalogue of the Early Roman Period (Eggers 1951).

Ulla Lund Hansen's monumental study closes - or at least ought to close, for a time - discussion of the chronology of grave finds of the Early Roman Period and the exchange relationship with the Roman Empire. Without critical new material, further investment of effort in this field would be a waste of resources. On the other hand, her book includes so much information and so much material that it is an excellent starting point for further research, for instance in connection with the thorough identifications of skeletal material (Sellevold *et al.* 1984).

Ulla Lund Hansen's thesis supports and refines the simple model of the use of Roman imports in the eastern Danish Roman-period culture which was proposed at the end of the 1970's (Hedeager 1978a-b). While the former is the consummation of the highly traditional chronological-typological method, the latter was the first attempt at applying an explanatory model rooted in anthropological theory to Danish Iron-age material.

The articles of 1978 were followed by others in the same theoretical framework although using different methods (e.g. Hedeager & Kristiansen 1982 followed up by Kaldal Mikkelsen 1990; Hedeager

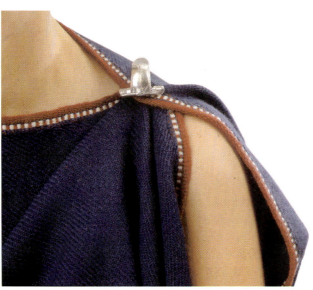

Reconstruction of female costume of the Early Roman Iron Age (1st century A.D.) by Anna Nørgaard. The reconstruction is based on remains of material found in a grave at Lønne Hede, Ribe amt, in 1969 (Munksgaard & Østergaard 1988).

1987). In my thesis on 'The Danish Iron Age - between tribe and state' (Hedeager 1990, 1992) the development of society is examined in a long-term perspective, in which all archaeological find groups from the whole Iron Age, 500 B.C. to 700 A.D., are included. This is the first synthesis of the Danish Iron Age since Brøndsted published his 'Danish Prehistory'. Just as 'Danish Prehistory' appeared in a popular version as vol. 1 of Politiken's History of

Denmark, 1977 (3rd.ed.), so the other has appeared in popular form as vol. 2 of Gyldendal and Politiken's History of Denmark (Hedeager 1988).

A number of theoretical works were the consequence of a new departure of the beginning of the 1970's, when positivistic archaeology was challenged by a new, socially-orientated anthropological archaeology that was cultivated in Britain and the U.S.A. But there were other departures too, such as a Marxist movement (Mahler *et al.* 1983), under which serious attempts were made to understand the transition from the Bronze Age to the Iron Age (Stummann Hansen 1980).

Apart from the examples mentioned, it is striking how few and far between have been attempts to work in a theoretically guided way with the Early Iron Age, and disturbing that these have been made by researchers who in a geographical sense at least are on the fringes of Danish Iron Age research. In the 1970's it was the German archaeologist Michael Gebühr who in several pieces explored the use of quantitative analyses and statistical methods on grave finds of the Early Roman Period (Gebühr 1974, 1976); in the 1980's it was the English archaeologist Mike Parker-Pearson who worked with a model of social development in Jutland from the Early Iron Age to the Germanic Period in Jutland (Parker Pearson 1984). The problem of transition from the late Bronze Age to the early Iron Age is the subject of Marie-Louise Stig Sørensen's research in Cambridge (Sørensen 1987) and of several studies by Kr. Kristiansen (most recently 1991a) and Jørgen Jensen (1973). However few the attempts have been to work in a modern theoretical framework, they nevertheless show how the rich and well-documented archaeological material of the Danish Iron Age can contribute to a dialogue with historical-anthropological research.

Technical archaeology/Laboratory archaeology

Through the 1970's and 80's, an important new niche has been carved out in the area of basic research through which new evidence is brought to light - not through new excavations, but through detailed technical analyses of material already known.

Most striking is the development of a new area of research in textiles, based on microscopic analyses of the often quite small fragments of material that metal grave goods have conserved as they decay. The Scandinavian material is analysed and catalogued in

Lise Bender Jørgensen's monograph (1986); the European finds are presented in her thesis from 1992. Considerable data and lot of information can be found in these catalogues that can also be profitably used in other areas of research. The manufacture of clothing can not least, for instance, shed light on the development of early industrial production in north-western Europe, as the author herself notes.

Technicians, craftsmen and archaeologists in a wide range of fields have now seriously set their eyes on the study of Iron-age craft and technology. Whether this is the question of building-construction (e.g. Lund 1982; Lund & Nielsen 1984; Draiby 1991), shipbuilding (Crumlin-Pedersen 1991b) or cartbuilding (Schovsbo 1987), iron-production (Voss 1991) or costume (Munksgaard 1974), goldsmithing and techniques of metalworking (Benner Larsen 1984; L. & N. Møller Andersen 1991), these studies bear consistent testimony to the far from primitive craft and technological standards of the Early Iron Age.

Detailed technical analyses are often directed towards the reconstruction of a costume, a building, a cart etc. One of the most remarkable reconstructions, achieved by the deliberate application of both technical and economic resources, has been the reconstruction and re-exhibiting of the Hjortspring boat. From the cellar of the National Museum, the remains of this, Scandinavia's oldest built boat, were retrieved, reconserved, reconstructed and re-exhibited. With the aid of talented technicians, this unique find was gradually recovered, not only for the public but also for the archaeological world, with C 14 dates now fixing the date of the boat to 350-300 B.C. (Kaul 1988a; J. Jensen *et al.* 1989).

C 14 dates have definitively halted discussions of date for more than the Hjortspring boat. The bog corpses, for instance from Borremose, Grauballe, Tollund and other Jutlandic bogs, are now dated. Most are from the end of the Late Bronze Age and the pre-Roman Iron Age. Some are late enough to belong to the Early Roman Period (Tauber 1980).

Conclusion
The great advances that settlement archaeology has seen in respect of the later part of the pre-Roman and the Early Roman Iron Age have not shed the same amount of light on the early pre-Roman Iron Age. It is understandable, therefore, that a new generation of scholars has focussed its attention on the period in which Iron-age society emerged.

Bog corpse from Tollund Mose, Mid-Jutland, found in 1950. After a series of comprehensive studies only the especially well-preserved head was conserved and exhibited at Silkeborg Museum. With the help of drawings, photographs and the dried, unconserved parts, by 1987 the body could be reconstructed in minute detail, so that the Tollund man could be exhibited in whole. The body is C 14 dated (K-2814) to ca. 200 B.C.

For the remainder of the Early Iron Age, the challenge of the 1990's is closely linked with the important results from the settlement archaeology of the 1970's and 80's. Farmsteads and villages should no longer be studied as isolated categories but should be included in a general analysis of settlement, the cultural landscape, the form of production and so on. The economic-ecological aspects of early Iron-age society need to be brought into focus through problem-orientated - and much expanded - co-operation with the natural scientists; the social context of settlement needs to be illuminated through the identification and excavation of associated graves and cemeteries. All in all, individual objects, whether they are settlements, grave finds or votive finds, should be analysed in both local and regional perspectives, in connexion with other categories of archaeological finds and with the active involvement of the natural sciences.

If a realization that the interpretation of this exceptional archaeological material does not simply grow spontaneously out of the data but through the methodology and hypotheses that are applied, research into the Early Danish Iron Age in the 1990's will be able to bring this period to the very zenith of the skies of international research.

Hedegård - a wealthy village on the Skjern river

The Roman bronze vessel after conservation. The vessel was made in Capue in southern Italy and is 42 cm. in diameter. The handles and the massive pedestal were added on.

An unusually rich village and associated cemetery of the late pre-Roman and Early Roman Iron Age is currently being excavated near the village of Hedegård in Ejstrup parish (O. Madsen 1992).

The village was enclosed by strong, palisade-like fences, covering an area of ca. 200 m. x 180: as yet the largest settlement from the period around the time of Christ. In several places the building plots are covered by nearly a metre of thick, artefact-rich culture layers. These layers contain masses of iron-smelting slag.

The cemetery, to the north of the village, contains both cremations and inhumations. The cemetery, like the village, is richer than most contemporary sites. There are more iron and precious metal artefacts than normal, and weapon graves are common, many with full weapon-sets. The graves also contain objects such as small tools and mounts which are rarely if ever found in graves of this period.

Three urned cremations are both unusual and unusually rich. In two of these the traditional urns were replaced by Roman bronze vessels, one of which - the pedestal type with a fixed handle shown here - had not previously been found in Scandinavia. Both graves also contained rich grave goods, such as gold finger fings, two very large iron knives and parts of further Roman bronze vessels.

In the third grave the urn, a large fluted vessel, was placed on top of the majority of the grave goods, which comprised more than 60 items. The majority of these came from a heavy, cast bronze belt, but also included parts of a Roman bronze strainer and three huge gold beads.

The special significance of the Hedegård complex for the study of the late pre-Roman and the beginning of the Roman Iron Age lies in the fact that both the settlement and the cemetery have been found and that both are exceptionally rich. This is thus a site with an unusually large amount of potential information.

Orla Madsen

Late Roman and Early Germanic Iron Age

BY ULLA LUND HANSEN

The Late Roman Iron Age runs from *ca.* 150/160 to shortly before 400 A.D. It is followed by the Early Germanic Iron Age, which ends a little earlier than previously thought, around 520/530 A.D. (Lund Hansen 1988b, 1992). The transition from the Early to the Late Roman Iron Age is a very clear one, characterized by changes in social structure, settlement, exchange of goods and the economy. The transition from the Late Roman Iron Age to the Early Germanic is less clear. Here both social structure and the range of artefacts generally show a steady development from the earlier period.

Re-assessments of the period have been provided by modern studies of many different find groups. They have led to new views on chronology, social structure, regionalism, contacts, external relationships such as exchange and other forms of communication, armament and war. A number of re-assessments are based on the many important graves and cemeteries that have been excavated in the last 25 years or so, of which I shall name just a few: Himlingøje (Lund Hansen 1978, 1979, 1981, 1991; Lund Hansen & H. Nielsen 1978), Skovgårde (Ethelberg 1989, 1991), Uggeløse (Thrane 1967b), Vindinge and Torstorp Vesterby (Fonnesbech-Sandberg 1990) on Sjælland; Møllegårdsmarken (Albrectsen 1968, 1971) and Løkkebjerg (Kjer Michaelsen 1990) on Fyn.

In Jutland, attention can be drawn to Bjergby on Mors (Albrethsen 1974), Hjemsted (Ethelberg 1986, 1990) and Sejlflod (J.N. Nielsen & Rasmussen 1986; Ringtved 1991). The latter are large cemeteries of the 4th and 5th centuries, previously a very rare phenomenon. Smaller but still important sites are Vorbasse (S. Hvass 1988), Sdr. Vissing (C. Fischer 1982), Stilling (N.H. Andersen 1980) and Nørreknold (AUD 1989:154 f.).

On Bornholm, we can note Slusegård (Klindt-Jensen 1978, S.H. Andersen *et al.* 1991), Rævekulebakke (AUD 1987:115 f.), Grødbygaard (Watt 1985), Nr. Sandegaard (L. Jørgensen 1988) and Levka (Seit Jespersen 1985).

Chronological study has been dominated by analyses of grave finds, but the votive weapon deposits have also been the subject of systematic study including typology and chronology (Ilkjær 1990). It is of importance that new Danish chronologies can often be correlated with Continental systems (Lund Hansen 1977, 1982, 1988b; Liversage 1980; Ethelberg 1986, 1990). It has been more difficult to create a common chronology for the later Late Roman Iron Age (C2 and C3) and the Early Germanic Iron Age than for the early Late Roman Iron Age, but the Sejlflod cemetery will certainly make a difference. A comprehensive publication of Jutlandic grave finds from both the Early and the Late Roman Iron Age is badly wanted: these form an invaluable set of data for a general assessment of a series of social phenomena.

Vindinge near Roskilde is amongst the most important of recently excavated eastern Danish cemeteries; with its Late-Roman and Early-Germanic graves it forms a chronological counterpart to Sejlflod, but with its own characteristic finds. On Fyn and Sjælland, however, no large cemeteries of the Early Germanic Iron Age have yet been found. The cemeteries of Bornholm have been intensely studied in respect of chronology, resulting in a quite finely-graded chronology which is readily correlated with the other recent Danish and European chronological systems. Analyses of the Bornholm graves has gone beyond the identification of social strata to possible family grave groups with primary and secondary spouse's graves (L. Jørgensen 1988, 1989). A different approach, analyses of regionalism in Jutlandic grave finds, has also produced a view on the material reflection of status (Ringtved 1988).

In the Early Roman Iron Age, weapon graves were the basis for theories concerning the warrior's role in society (Hedeager & Kristiansen 1982), but these theories cannot be applied to the following period on the strength of graves. Votive weapon hoards of the Late Roman and Early Germanic Iron Age, however, are reflections of organized armies (Ørsnes & Ilkjær, below).

Analyses of the political situation in the period are based on very varied evidence. In the Late Roman Period, the Sjælland graves show a principal centre in the east, around Himlingøje, Varpelev and Valløby, surrounded by a few subcentres. Similarly, weapon finds from graves and bogs cluster in a curve around the centre. Thus the centre on eastern Sjælland is protected by a retinue to the west; to the east, towards the sea, it must have been guarded in some other way. In the Early Germanic Iron Age both treasure and votive hoards reflect a changed situation. Fyn is now the dominant central place (Lund Hansen 1988a; Fonnesbech-Sandberg 1991a-b). The central places of Bornholm of the Late Roman and Early Germanic Iron Age comparably show traces of craft, trade and

Runes

The Skovgårde brooch comes from a woman's grave that is archaeologically dated to the first half of the 3rd century A.D. and the inscription is one of the earliest inscriptions in the older runes (the 24-rune futhark). These inscriptions - mainly on metal objects, jewellery, weapons and personal items - are widely distributed in the Germanic territory of the time but concentrated in Denmark. They often comprise just a few runes - individual words or short sentences - and are often now incomprehensible. There are runes on objects from the great weapon deposits at Torsbjerg, Vimose and Illerup and on brooches from women's graves. There are five such rosette brooches with runes in Denmark.

The peculiar layout of the Skovgårde inscription is noteworthy. It reads inwards from either edge towards the division mark: talgida : lamo, or, more probably, lamo : talgida, 'Lamo carved'. The similarity with the inscription on the rosette brooch from Nøvling near Ålborg, bidawarijaR talgidai, 'BidawarijaR carved', is striking.

The question of to what extent these inscriptions on metal were copied from exempla by illiterate carvers has been discussed, but the way in which the Skovgårde inscription was written and its contents indicate that Lamo - meaning 'the lame one' - understood runes. The name could be either male or female and it could be the owner of the brooch, as it was found in a woman's grave, or it could be the donor or the runemaster.

Runes formed a common Germanic writing system, derived from the alphabets of the Mediterranean lands, probably from the Latin. From a study of the earliest inscriptions it does not seem likely that it was developed as a magical or cult system, but of course, like any writing system, runes could be used for magical-religious

Rosette brooch from Skovgårde, Udby. Ca. 10 x 10 cm., made of silver with gold inlays. The runes, about 1 cm. high, are inscribed on the catch.

purposes. The runes on the Skovgårde brooch are used as phonetic symbols in an apparently thoroughly secular inscription in the writer's own language. This person belonged to a society which was strongly affected by Roman culture, with many members presumably familiar with Latin inscriptions such as manufacturer's or factory marks and coin legends. It is no coincidence that it is in this context that the earliest definite examples of runography are found. This need not mean that there was an extensive use of runes for utilitarian purposes in Iron-age society around 200 A.D., but it is probable that literacy - runic literacy - was associated with high status.

Marie Stoklund

cult activities (L. Jørgensen 1991a-b).

Contacts between the Danish regions in the Late Roman Period are illustrated by grave goods in particular. From eastern and southern Sjælland contacts were established at least with eastern Fyn, the area from the eastern part of central Jutland up to the Limfjord, and with Bornholm. Overseas exchange and communication too is reflected in graves and treasure and votive hoards. In contrast to the Early Roman Iron Age, Roman imports in Late Roman Iron-age graves show regular, organized contact with the Roman provinces. In the 3rd century this contact ran from the central place on Sjælland via a sea-route to the Rhine mouth, by-passing Continental land routes. From the middle of the 3rd century, eastern Fyn began

to take over this role, but Fyn has better direct southern overland links to the Roman provinces (Lund Hansen 1987). One can also see a connexion between Fyn and the Black Sea area (Werner 1988; Storgaard 1990). Late in the Late Roman Iron Age, probably in phase C3 (4th century), Jutland too achieved greater contact with the Roman Empire; this trade continued into the Early Germanic Iron Age and can be seen, *inter alia,* in imports at Dankirke and Sejlflod (Lund Hansen 1984; Jarl Hansen 1990; Fonnesbech-Sandberg 1991a-b; Ringtved 1991).

Numerous hoards have been discovered in the last 25 years in very varying circumstances; amongst the most significant is the Smørenge hoard from Bornholm, with nearly 500 denarii (latest coin, 195 A.D.)

Torstorp Vesterby

In 1989, Søllerød Museum's district archaeological section excavated a small, complete cemetery with eight interments at Torstorp Vesterby, south-east of Høje-Tåstrup near Copenhagen (Fonnesbech-Sandberg 1990). This is probably a family cemetery, with only one adult grave. Five of the graves were 90 to 120 cm. long and two 150 to 160 cm. long. These seven graves contained few grave goods. A woman aged 20 to 25 was buried in the largest grave, which was 2.5 m. long. Found with her were three necklaces of about 400 glass and amber beads together with a gilt silver-sheet brooch, a silver-inlaid bronze brooch, a stamp-decorated silver double button, several silver beads, small silver clasps and a Roman siliqua coin with a loop. The siliqua was struck under Constantius II in 340-351, and the grave goods are typical of the last phase of the Late Roman Iron Age, C3.

Eliza Fonnesbech-Sandberg

De luxe brooches from southern Sjælland

The area around Udby in southern Sjælland is famous for a number of rich grave finds, especially from the Late Roman Iron Age. A new cemetery was discovered and excavated in 1988 as a result of the building of the final stage of the southern motorway between Rødby and Copenhagen (Ethelberg 1989, 1991).

The cemetery, known as Skovgårde, comprised 18 inhumations aligned North-South and a horse grave. From the grave goods, all of these can be dated to phase C1b of the Late Roman Iron Age, possibly extending into the beginning of phase C2. Five of the graves can be described as princely graves of a common type, as is found, for instance, at Himlingøje. The Skovgårde cemetery stands out as a complete site, of which every grave has been identified and dug. The skeletal material is very well preserved and the majority of the graves are unusually richly furnished.

The cemetery provides important new evidence on both chronological and social questions, significant not just in the context of Sjælland and the immediate vicinity but for all of Free Germania.

The graves included a special disc brooch and certain types of Roman glass beaker (Eggers 1951:Type 203 and 205) which are usually dated C2 in southern and central Germany (Werner 1960, 1988) but which now appear in their earliest context in Free Germania in the C1b graves of Skovgårde.

The tutulus brooch from grave 400 shown here is quite unique in a Danish context. Tutulus brooches are usually regarded as of central or southern German origin (Steuer 1984:409), but a number of details show that this is not the case here. In fact there is a great deal to indicate that this de luxe brooch was manufactured in southern Scandinavia, probably on Sjælland.

Per Ethelberg

179

plus a solidus struck under Anthemius I, 467-72. The hoard confirms the suspicion that the denarius hoards of Bornholm could be deposited a long time after the coins were struck (Kromann & Watt 1984). On Fyn, too, many more Roman coins have been found, with examples of types and dies that were previously rare (Kromann 1987; Vang Petersen 1987). The number of hoards comprising various artefact-types such as brooches, bracteates etc. has increased on Fyn in particular, as has that of hacksilver hoards (Munksgaard 1987). The bracteate finds have been special subjects of study (Hauck 1985; Axboe 1991). The bracteates pose a chronological problem, but they were probably produced and used over quite a short period (Lund Hansen 1992). The hoards and their evidence have most recently been analysed at a more general level by Fonnesbech-Sandberg (1988, 1991a-b) and Hedeager (1991).

Something relatively new is the growth of technological analyses of archaeological finds from the Iron Age, e.g. thin-sectioning of pottery (Stilborg 1990) and iron analyses (Jouttijärvi & Lyngstrøm 1990). A large sample of Roman bronze vessels found in Denmark have been analysed; alloys and trace elements serve, amongst other things, to identify provenance, i.e. workshops, and mines for the copper ore (Lund Hansen & Bollingberg in print).

Today, the Late Roman Iron Age stands out as one of the most fully studied phases of prehistory. Most find groups appear to be well-published, but one could still list what more one would like; above all a survey of the rapidly growing number of Jutlandic grave finds of the Roman Iron Age along the lines of what has been done for Fyn (Albrectsen 1954, 1956, 1968, 1971, 1973) and for Sjælland in both the Early Roman Iron Age (Liversage 1980) and (forthcoming) the Late Roman Iron Age (Lund Hansen in print). There is a pressing need for an overview of the rapidly increasing finds from Bornholm. The Iron-age settlements of Sjælland are being published (Lund Hansen & S. Nielsen (eds) 1992), and the forthcoming cemetery and settlement-site publications will place many countrywide studies on a sounder footing.

Regional groupings in the Early Iron Age

Regional groupings are a striking feature of Early Iron-age find-distributions. There are clear differences between material from Sjælland and Fyn, and then in Jutland, while the Jutlandic peninsula itself has its own regional groups.

In the Late Roman and Early Germanic Iron Age regionality breaks through in many features such as burial and votive practices, building-types, personal equipment and domestic gear. The figure illustrates regionality in four Jutlandic grave finds of the 4th century: two from the north, two from the south, one of either sex. There are obvious differences in the quantity and type of grave goods, and the form of the pottery is regionally distinctive too.

These regional differences reflect social groups of one or more settlement units. The groups were mostly separated by water and marshlands, and at that time probably by forests too. It therefore seems reasonable to interpret the regional groups of the Iron Age as archaeological reflections of the tribe. The sources are insufficient to answer the question of how closely the regional group is related to the tribe.

The size of the regions, and the clarity with which they appear, vary in the course of the period, and this must mean that social identity could be redefined for instance in connexion with new leadership or, at a more general level, with new social and political alignments.

Jytte Ringtved

180

The Late Germanic and Viking Period

BY ULF NÄSMAN AND ELSE ROESDAHL

The Late Germanic Iron Age and Viking Period bridge prehistory and the Middle Ages, and the Viking Period has a special character for being studied by both prehistorians and medieval archaeologists together with their colleagues in the sciences, runology, numismatics, history and so on.

The Viking Period is both one of the best researched periods in Danish archaeology and the one that enjoys the greatest public interest. The last 25-30 years have seen new results from Danevirke, Jelling and the trelleborg forts, the excavation of a complete village at Vorbasse, major urban excavations, and much more.

Up to a few years ago, the Late Germanic Iron Age in Denmark was rather neglected, while interest in this period in Norway and, above all, Sweden, was much higher because of the relative richness of finds. Finland too is quite well off for material.

Bornholm, however, also has rich finds of this period, especially burials, and through the whole of the Late Iron Age this island has a special position both real and recognized. So too Gotland. Both islands are 'peripheral' in relation to Denmark and Sweden, and both developed special Baltic Sea cultures. These two islands were also annexed to Denmark and Sweden late: in the late Viking Period and early Middle Ages respectively.

In recent years, however, many new finds of the Late Germanic Iron Age have appeared in the rest of Denmark, especially from the 8th century. It is now primarily the 7th century that is obscure, although new results are on their way.

It would be wrong to omit important studies carried out in Skåne and Schleswig, which in the Viking Period were part of the Danish kingdom, from a review of Danish archaeology; they are included below on an equal footing with investigations in Denmark.

An impression of the results of Danish archaeology in the Late Germanic and Viking Periods in the last 25 years can be obtained by comparing Brøndsted (1960a) and A.E. Christensen (1969) with the latest synopses in Hedeager (1988) and Sawyer (1988). For the Viking Period one can also compare Brøndsted (1960b) with Roesdahl (1987a) noting also Roesdahl (1980) and Randsborg (1980). The latter is an exponent of the practices of the Anglo-American new theoretical school, which has also set a mark on the post-1968 period. A fine summary of the comprehensive German work on the North Sea area (Jankuhn *et al.* (eds) 1984; Kossack *et al.* (eds) 1984) shows the importance of the southern Scandinavian area in the German research traditon. A critical review of the literature on the Late Germanic and Viking Periods of 1976-1986 has been published by Näsman (1991b).

The basis of these good results is primarily new methods and techniques, together with strong public interest and increased international co-operation. Modern methods of excavating whole villages and the impact of metal-detectors and maritime archaeology are described elsewhere. Scientific reconstructions have given insights into ancient technology and raised new questions, at the same time as satisfying a latent popular need to understand the past better. One can mention, for instance, the full-size reconstruction of the Hedeby building at Moesgård, the hall at Fyrkat and several Viking ships (Schmidt 1985, 1992; Crumlin-Pedersen & Vinner (eds) 1986). Craft-techniques have been reconstructed too, e.g. for making oval brooches, glass beads and combs (Brinch Madsen 1984; S. Jensen 1991b:26 ff.; Gam 1992).

Dendrochronology has provided precise dates for the founding or development of several important structures, such as Ribe, Vorbasse, Danevirke, the Jelling mounds, the trelleborg forts, Ravning bridge and the Mammen grave. It is especially important that such structures are precisely dated in the Late Germanic and Viking Periods if they are to be located in the history of events and used in syntheses and general interpretations for which there are also written sources. This applies to crucial issues such as economic development, urbanization, state-formation and the introduction and establishment of Christianity. That the founding of Ribe goes back to *ca.* 704-710, and that the site was part of a large new long-distance trading network so early, has, for instance, caused great interest and changed views (Steuer 1987; Näsman 1990; Clark & Ambrosiani 1991; S. Jensen, below). But that the villages took on their Viking-period structure in the 8th century is also an important discovery. These results form a new basis for understanding the Viking raids: there was a surplus in Scandinavia, and the population was already familiar with the outside world. But while the chronology of the early Viking Period has had to be revised in important respects (much that was thought to be 9th-century is 8th-century), the chronology of the 10th and 11th

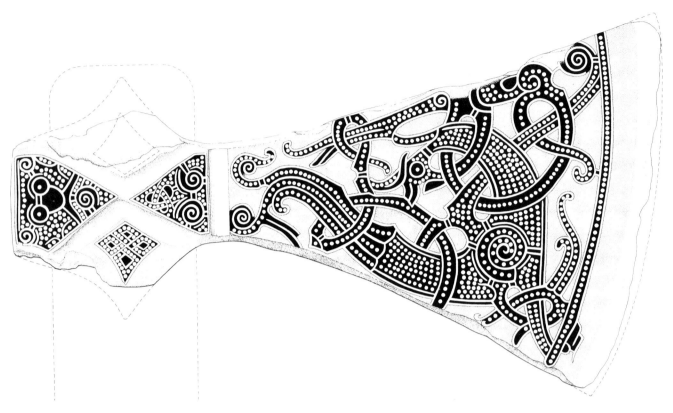

Reconstruction of an iron axe found in Bjerringhøj at Mammen. The decoration is inlaid silver and has given the Mammen Style its name. The grave and its other contents were published by J.J.A. Worsaae in 1869, the year after it was found. In 1986 the grave was re-excavated and preserved wood was dendrochronologically dated to 970/71. In 1991 both the Mammen grave and the Mammen hoard found in 1871 were published in a monograph with contributions from Danish and foreign specialists (M. Iversen et al. (eds) 1991). The precise dating gives a fixed point for the Mammen Style and a context for a new understanding of the this famous chieftain's grave from the transitional era between paganism and Christianity.

centuries has largely been confirmed by dendrochronology.

The question of when both the Late Germanic and Viking Periods begin and end has been discussed in recent years. The relative chronology of the Late Germanic Iron Age has been modified in crucial ways in relation to Ørsnes's phasing of 1966, and the absolute chronology has been sharpened (Høilund Nielsen 1987; L. Jørgensen 1990). The transition from the Early Germanic Iron age to the Late is now put at *ca.* 520/530 (Lund Hansen 1992). It is debated whether the transition from the Germanic Iron Age to the Viking Period should be put in the first half of the 8th century. But since there are good archaeological arguments for dating the changeover to *ca.* 760/790 (Høilund Nielsen 1987; C.J. Becker 1990a), we consider it sensible to keep to the traditional "*ca.* 800" when military expansion westwards also began. This agrees both with other disciplines and with international practice. There is no archaeological definition of the end of the

Viking Period, so the historically-determined date of *ca.* 1050 is also observed too.

Steadily growing international co-operation has made possible large exhibitions with objects from many countries, together with catalogues in which selected items can be seen in new and larger contexts and particular problems can be addressed. This has particularly affected the Vikings (Graham-Campbell 1980; Roesdahl *et al.* (eds) 1981; Roesdahl (ed) 1992).

Theoretical approaches of recent years have focussed on the development of complex societies into states (e.g for the Iron Age, Näsman 1988; Hedeager 1990; for the Viking Period, Randsborg 1980), and two publications of the research project 'From Tribe to State in Denmark' have appeared with cross-disciplinary contributions to the study of Danish ethnogenesis and state-formation (Mortensen & Rasmussen (eds) 1988, 1991; cf. also Fabech & Ringtved (eds) 1991).

Danish archaeology operates in a cultural landscape in which very few traces of earlier ages' use of the land have escaped damage from the efficient agriculture of more recent times. In the last 25 years, settlement archaeology has concentrated on the fundamental study of building typology and on village settlement patterns. This work has been rewarded with important results which are essential for studies of the agrarian landscape in the Germanic Iron Age and Viking Period to be carried further.

The time is ripe for analyses of the form of production in the Late Iron Age. This requires co-operation with geologists, palaeobotanists and place-name specialists, but it is above all the archaeologist's job to synthesize the varied data. Through new pollen analyses one can trace fairly clearly how the expansion of agrarian settlement that culminated in the early Middle Ages began in the Late Germanic Iron Age (e.g. S.Th. Andersen *et al.* 1988; Aaby 1990; B.E. Berglund (ed.) 1991). In Jutland the settlement pattern also changed at this time. The 'Viking-period village' was established around 700, and amongst other things a new farmstead-structure may be interpreted as reflecting a new agrarian system and the introduction of the mould-board plough, while rye and a shift to two-field rotation were probably introduced in the course of the period. Increased agricultural productivity is a prerequisite of state-formation.

Considerable effort has been put into clarifying the relationship between the settlement pattern and agriculture of the Viking Period and that of the Middle Ages. The dominant model has been one of discontinuity (e.g. Grøngaard Jeppesen 1981; Porsmose 1981). But is this right? The economy of the agrarian landscape seems to have been subject to much greater changes around 200 and 700 A.D. and again in the 14th century. The differences between the Viking Period and Middle Ages should not be exaggerated (cf. Callmer 1986). The theory of discontinuity may be largely the result of the difference between archaeological and historical sources and approaches. The study of the cultural landscape at the transition to the Middle Ages has to be seen in a long-term perspective.

Studies of the social landscape seek to answer questions concerning people's relationships with one another: what was their relationship with the nearest, with their neighbours or with foreigners? What was the significance of closeness or distance?

With the explosive growth of settlement-archaeological data and with a lot of grave finds these are realistic questions, and the testing of methods for analysis of the social landscape has begun, for instance on Bornholm (L. Jørgensen 1990:71 ff.; Watt 1991:101 ff.), around Ribe (S. Jensen 1991a) and in North Jutland (Ringtved 1991:65 ff.). Studies of the religious landscape of Denmark and southern Sweden should also be noted (Fabech 1991b:292 ff.). Studies of this type need extensive and varied data over broad geographical and chronological ranges plus researchers familiar with a wide range of disciplines. Thorough and explicit source-evaluation is also essential. A lot of work is waiting for a reliable methodology to be created, but such research will certainly be worthwhile.

Studies of the political landscape are particularly shaped by the central issue of the spatial organization of power (Näsman 1991d:325 ff.). For a long time the focus of the political landscape has been mid-Viking-period Jelling and the late Viking-period shift of power east to Roskilde and Lund. The dating of Danevirke, the Kanhave canal and the founding of Ribe to the early 8th century has shown that a centralized power existed long before the 10th century, and the age and development of the Danish kingdom is the subject of renewed debate (H.H. Andersen 1986; Sawyer 1988; O. Olsen 1989; Näsman 1991a). The Viking-period defence works also play a critical part in this. These cluster in the middle and second half of the 10th century, with town ramparts, a major extension of Danevirke, and the trelleborg forts.

Important sites have appeared, or changed their appearance, e.g. Stentinget and Bejsebakken in Jutland, Gudme on Fyn, Neble and Lejre on Sjælland, Uppåkra and Vä in Skåne and Sorte Muld on Bornholm (Callmer 1991; T. Christensen 1991; Vang Petersen 1991; Watt 1991). It is notable that these show continuity from the Early Germanic Iron Age or earlier, and that several sites continue into the Early Middle Ages. The Late Germanic Iron-age material is often especially rich, and the importance of this period for the growth of a centralized power structure in Denmark is ready for a radical reassessment. A closer study of these sites will undoubtedly also mean rewriting the history of the first phase of Danish urbanization. We can already see how the discoveries of the origins of Ribe and the trading site at Åhus have turned traditional

The excavations of the ring forts of Trelleborg, Fyrkat and Aggersborg turned the view of the Viking Period upside down. The full-size reconstructions of one of the halls at Trelleborg in the 1940's and Fyrkat in the 1980's have been of great importance for the presentation of the archaeological discoveries. The Fyrkat hall is illustrated (Schmidt 1985, 1992). Settlement excavations show that similar halls were main buildings on farmsteads over the whole country.

understandings upside down (cf. for instance the title of O. Olsen 1975).

Our knowledge of most 'central places' is still limited, but answers to questions on the ethnogenesis of the Danes and the origins of the Danish state must, *inter alia*, come from analyses of the central places' relationship with their region, with one another, and with communities outside Scandinavia. Several studies are already published (Callmer 1991; Fabech 1991b; L. Jørgensen 1990; Høilund Nielsen 1991; Thrane 1991c; Watt 1991).

Studies of rural settlement and early urbanization have also shed new light on long-distance trade. An established trade in luxuries continues to dominate into the Late Germanic Period, but around 700 the southern Scandinavian area joined the North Sea market in humbler goods. In the Viking Period this trading network was extended far into the Baltic area, and the new political freedom of the Baltic lands will undoubtedly lead to a review of the western Slavs' and the Balts' roles in northern European trade (cf. M. Andersen 1984).

Essential to wideranging connexions in the Late Germanic Iron Age and ever more in the Viking Period were a well-developed communications network and good means of transport. In 1960, really only a couple of ships were known in Denmark (the boat graves at Hedeby and Ladby) but there are now several examples of various types, especially from Skuldelev and Hedeby; a canal (the Kanhave canal on Samsø); a shipyard (Fribrødre river on Falster); and a harbour (Hedeby). We also know the capabilities of the ships (Crumlin-Pedersen, below). In the case of land transport, archaeological devel-

opments have been nearly as dramatic: the embankments and bridges of the period are now well-known features; C 14 dates and dendrochronology have rescued old familiar structures from chronological anonymity, and new ones have been found. Carts have also made a contribution, as yet just as fragments.

Several topics in the Late Germanic and Viking Periods have been the subject of large, comprehensive studies and discussion. Relatively few of these concern cultural-historical questions, especially artefact-based studies. The majority are either publications of particular excavations or structures with associated artefacts or extensive commentaries on one or more particular artefact-types. The Hedeby publications, mostly written by German scholars, are amongst the most important contributions in respect both of artefacts and of human exploitation of fauna and flora (e.g. Steuer 1974; Ulbricht 1978; Behre 1983; W. Janssen 1987). But major publications of the Ribe excavations are in hand (Bencard (ed) 1981, 1984; Bencard *et al.* (eds) 1990, 1991), and publication of later excavations in Ribe and Viborg are expected soon. The classic publication of a Danish town excavation with detailed presentation and discussion of all artefact-groups is Århus Søndervold (H. H. Andersen *et al.* 1971). This made it clear that many artefact-types pertaining to Viking-period daily life survived into the early Middle Ages, and that a major change in this range came first in the 12th century and around 1200 (cf. Roesdahl (ed) 1992). Besides Hedeby and Århus, Lund is the best investigated Danish town of the Viking Period (e.g. Mårtensson (ed) 1976).

184

The finds from town excavations are rich and varied but normally very fragmentary and often without any proper context. This is even more the case with finds from villages and farmsteads. Grave goods in pagan burials, however, allow one to study whole artefacts, or what remains of them, and to see them in the context that was created for them in the grave (e.g. Skaarup 1976; Roesdahl 1977; L. Jørgensen 1990). There is therefore a large and so far only intermittently exploited body of data for illuminating living conditions and many other culture-historical facets, especially in respect of Viking-period towns and the upper class. But the material is not fully representative. Real towns, with a permanent population, first developed in the course of the period and remained rare for a long time; only in the period *ca.* 900-975 did funerary practice demand rich grave goods (and only for the upper class, of course). Only on Bornholm do we find rich burials more generally throughout the later Iron Age.

Interest in special studies of particular artefact-types has been limited in Danish archaeology, with the exception of textiles and pottery. The newly found textile remains from Hedeby harbour and a shirt from Viborg have provided new evidence on common dress (Hägg 1985; Fentz 1989). The reconstruction of the Mammen costume from *ca.* 970 on the other hand reveals the elegant dress of the higher echelons of society (Munksgaard 1991), while a systematic study of all fragments of textile in archaeological finds has yielded information on, for instance, the different types of textile that were made locally or imported (Bender Jørgensen 1986, 1991, 1992). The involvement of textile studies with central archaeological problems produces totally new perspectives (e.g. Hägg 1991). Major surveys are available of Viking-period pottery (H.H. Andersen *et al.* 1971; H.J. Madsen 1991). In spite of all the modern methods, pottery is still the best basis for dating settlements, and it is therefore very satisfying that the difficult Late Germanic Iron-age pottery is also beginning to fall into place (Siemen (ed) 1989).

Late Germanic- and Viking-period art is also one of the traditional fields of archaeological study, but academic interest in it has fluctuated greatly in Denmark in recent decades. In 1965 and 1966 two monographs appeared, covering the Viking Period and the Late Germanic Iron Age in southern Scandinavia respectively (Wilson & Klindt-Jensen 1966;

Ørsnes 1966). Ørsnes's work, based heavily on Bornholm finds, stood out on a limb for many years, but eventually his path was followed. Høilund Nielsen has gone further on the basis of more finds from southern and eastern Scandinavia, and with new methods (1991); she also attempts to interpret the social background of this art: the manifestation and distribution of art is treated as dependent on regional power-structures and their development. The dating and classification of Viking-period art styles in Wilson and Klindt-Jensen's work has, conversely, been much discussed. Research on this subject in Denmark has paused for some time, but in Norway and Sweden the topic has been taken up by art historians. The basic classification of 1965 has proved to be practical, and is now refined (e.g. Fuglesang 1980, 1981, 1991, but cf. Karlsson 1983). The chronology of later styles has been confirmed by dendrochronological dating of critical finds from Jelling, Mammen and Hørning. For the early Viking Period, the results of dendrochronological dating of the Oseberg and Gokstad graves will be of fundamental importance.

Graves have always been one of archaeology's most important sources. Many new, and large, cemeteries have been excavated, and some are published: e.g. Stengade, Hesselbjerg, Fyrkat, Bækkegård and Glasergård (H.H. Andersen & Klindt-Jensen 1971; Skaarup 1976; Roesdahl 1977; L. Jørgensen 1990). Some very important finds have been re-studied and republished: Jelling, Ladby, Mammen, Søllested, Trelleborg and the boat-chamber grave at Hedeby (Müller-Wille 1976; K.J. Krogh 1983; H.H. Andersen 1987; Thrane 1987b; Bødtker Petersen & Woller 1989; M. Iversen *et al.* (eds) 1991). As noted above, the richest finds are of the 10th century, the last pagan phase, and interest has widely been focussed on the upper-class graves of this phase, interpreting them in both political-historical and religious terms. Perhaps the truth lies somewhere in between (Randsborg 1980; Roesdahl 1983, 1992; Müller-Wille 1991; Näsman 1991c). Within the social sphere, the male 'knightly' graves are matched by women's graves in wagon bodies, a burial-type first recognized in the 1960's.

Research into burials is much taken up with the questions of political power-structures and the Conversion. The deceased in the richest graves have been identified as kings and dynasties known from written sources (H.H. Andersen 1986); the only

Fragments of a basalt lava quernstone from Gl. Hviding, slate whetstone bars from the Ribe river and soapstone vessel fragments from Andersminde. Through settlement excavations and investigations of early trading sites and towns, archaeology has painted a new picture of the development of long-distance trade. Superficially uninteresting fragments of querns, whetstones and soapstone vessels have turned out to be important sources for the study of trade in daily goods in the Late Germanic and Viking Periods (S. Jensen 1990).

really convincing case, however, is Jelling. A lurking question is how and when the old cemeteries were abandoned for Christian ones. New excavations have shown that some time after the Conversion it was customary to delimit Christian graveyards with a ditch (Kieffer-Olsen & Engberg 1992). It is not known when churches became common. But it seems clear that after the Conversion, around 965, there was a period of at least a generation with transitional forms. Not until the mid-11th century do we find more uniform Christian observances (Roesdahl 1980:199 ff; Kieffer-Olsen 1990; M. Iversen *et al.* (eds) 1991). On the transition from paganism to Christianity see also Krogh & Olsen, below.

In the last two decades, attention has been focussed on settlement and other topics associated with the economy and social and political development, but much has been studied besides. Archaeology is a broad and free subject and so it should always be. There now seem to be tendencies towards a general new orientation, towards the more cultural-historical issues: a growing interest in archaeological interpretation in psychological and religious historical terms, and greater interest in living conditions, environment, technology and art. These require greater cross-disciplinary co-operation, for it is not enough to glean from other subjects' textbooks. It is equally necessary for the tradition of firm knowledge of the primary data to be maintained and strengthened. A deepening of the sources must underlie bold innovations if these are to be anything more than will-o'-the-wisps.

It is increasingly becoming clear again in Danish archaeology that cross-disciplinary co-operation is often a fruitful approach, and there is a growing recognition that local archaeological finds are profitably studied in a broad geographical context, both Scandinavian and European. The political opening-up of eastern Europe will provide new opportunities, and extensive contacts with this large area, which archaeologists of our generation have known little of, have rapidly been made. Archaeological finds have proliferated in the last 25 years, and happily many of them are sufficiently well-dated and published for other disciplines to make use of it. Historians are now re-assessing written sources in light of archaeological results, which now truly form part of nearly all other disciplines' syntheses of the Viking Period (e.g. Sawyer 1988; Meulengracht Sørensen & Steinsland 1990).

The birth of the Danes and the founding of the Danish kingdom took place in the long period from the Late Roman Period to the High Middle Ages. If only archaeologists, historians and others could come together and study the relevant processes as one! The interdisciplinary milieu is already there in Danish scholarship; it just needs to be made to bear fruit.

Settlement

By Steen Hvass

Most people have had a go at flying and have thus experienced the excitement of seeing the landscape spread out in a way that is rarely seen back on the ground. Aerial photography is an important aid to the search for early settlements that are not immediately visible from the surface. Differences in shade of vegetation have produced the most unexpected results in aerial archaeology. Crop marks depend on the quality of the soil, which requires only a little human intervention in the upper layers to influence the conditions for growth and thus the shades of vegetation for centuries afterwards.

In Denmark, archaeological air reconnaissance was carried out in a haphazard way before 1966. But from 1966 to 1970 the English archaeologist and aerial photographer K. St.Joseph carried out a comprehensive survey which resulted in the identification of more than 100 previously unknown settlement and cemetery sites in western and northern Jutland. In the years that followed, several of these new sites saw extensive excavations (C.J. Becker 1972b; Lund 1977; J.N. Nielsen *et al.* 1985). In 1982, the museums of south-western Jutland began annual aerial recon-

naissance to look for settlement traces (S. Jensen 1987).

In the coming years, aerial photography will be able to provide quite new opportunities for discovering hitherto unknown settlements and give detailed pictures of them without needing large area excavations.

The image of Iron-age settlement that was available around 1960 was poor and very coarse. Society was pictured as one that changed very little. The earlier period was practically unknown, and the settlements of the last seven or eight centuries of the Iron Age and Viking Period were known only superficially.

In the course of the 1960's the real breakthrough for Danish settlement archaeology came with the introduction of a new method of excavation. In 1961, two major excavations lasting several years began, at Grøntoft in western Jutland and Drengsted in the west of southern Jutland. At both sites the general culture layer had been removed by centuries of agriculture. For this reason machines were used for the first time here to strip the ploughsoil down to the

In the dry summer of 1992, aerial photography revealed new settlements in eastern Jutland. Two farmsteads from around the time of Christ stand out here in cropmarks near Jelling.

187

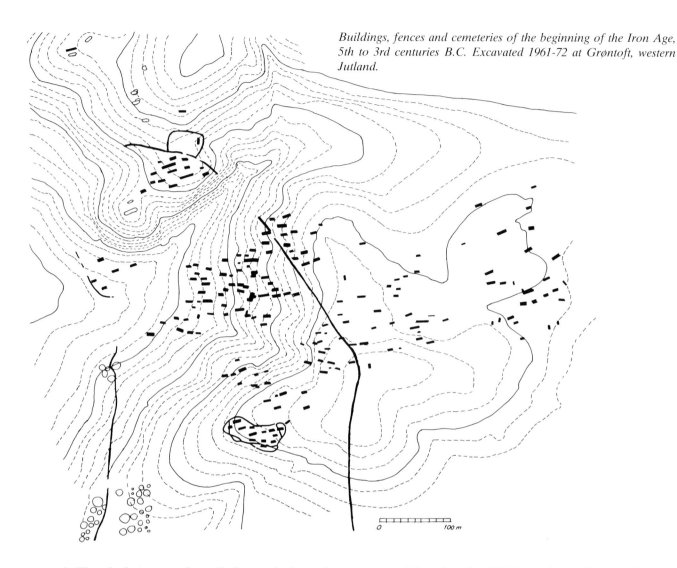

Buildings, fences and cemeteries of the beginning of the Iron Age, 5th to 3rd centuries B.C. Excavated 1961-72 at Grøntoft, western Jutland.

natural. The dark traces of postholes and, thus, the ground plans of the buildings, now stood out clearly against the lighter ground surface. Machines made it possible for very large areas to be excavated and for whole villages to be planned.

At Grøntoft, an area of 150,000 sq.m. was excavated, with about 250 buildings from the first three centuries of the Early Iron Age, the 5th to 3rd centuries B.C. The latest phase was a fenced-in village to the south. All the other buildings must represent one or more older villages which probably, in each new generation, moved around in a given area. Each slightly larger building with a dwelling area and stalls was the nucleus of a farmstead that is to be regarded as an independent economic and social unit.

The village here forms a shared settlement comprising a group of farmsteads which were linked together in some way. At Grøntoft two associated cemeteries have also been excavated, as have many

traces of the ploughed fields and two fences, 400 and 600 m. long respectively (C.J. Becker 1966a, 1969a, 1972a).

There has been a steady development of the excavation methods used at Grøntoft and Drengsted. Some major construction projects such as roadbuilding, housing development and extraction of natural resources have also provided the opportunity for more comprehensive excavations. These circumstances have been the basis for the establishment over the last 25 years of an astoundingly large body of data and insights of historical significance, that underlies a wholly new debate over social development through the Iron Age and Viking Period (C.J. Becker 1981; S. Hvass 1988; Mortensen & Rasmussen (eds) 1988, 1991; Hedeager 1990).

The house, farmstead and village together form the social and economic basis that more than anything else reflects 'real' life. Changes in this material thus reflect deep changes in the whole of society, looked at in a long-term perspective.

The most important building-type in the agrarian society of the time was the longhouse, the main building of the farmstead. It is now possible to follow an unbroken series of longhouses through 1,500 years, from the beginning of the Iron Age to the end of the Viking Period. Chronology is based on a very large number of buildings from central Jutland (Egebjerg Hansen *et al.* 1991). In the rest of the country the series of buildings is not yet complete, but in the last 10 years an increasing number of buildings that gradually prove to have completely preserved ground plans have been excavated on the islands too (Watt 1983; N.H. Andersen 1984; J.A. Jacobsen *et al.* 1985; Mahler 1985; T. Christensen 1991; Tornbjerg 1991). Many buildings however, especially from Sjælland, still present problems in respect of close dating.

From the beginning of the Iron Age down to about 1000 A.D. the basic architecture of the main building remained the same: a three-sectioned longhouse with a roof that was carried by two rows of heavy internal posts running the length of the house. These buildings have a constant width of about 5 m. with entraces in the middle of both long sides. The three-sectioned longhouse disappeared about 1000, with buildings then being constructed in just one section, with transverse beams from wall to wall. This one-sectioned building is really the source of the later timber-frame house. Through 1,500 years, buildings kept the same basic functions, with nearly the same internal division into a dwelling area, usually to the west, an entrance area in the middle and a stall, usually in the east. But if we go through the ground plans of the buildings in more detail, it transpires that for practically each century there is a distinctive architecture sufficient for many buildings to be dated purely on the basis of their ground plans.

This large body of data, mostly from Jutland, also shows regional differences, most clearly in the Early Roman Iron Age, with various forms of walls and entrances, determined by the availability of building materials, location etc. (S. Hvass 1982). Paving is also used in different ways, and on the high, exposed banks by the eastern Limfjord all of the farmstead's buildings are also sunk into the ground (Lund 1984).

Different uses of the same type of building may also reflect geographical differences in the agrarian economy. One type of building may, for example,

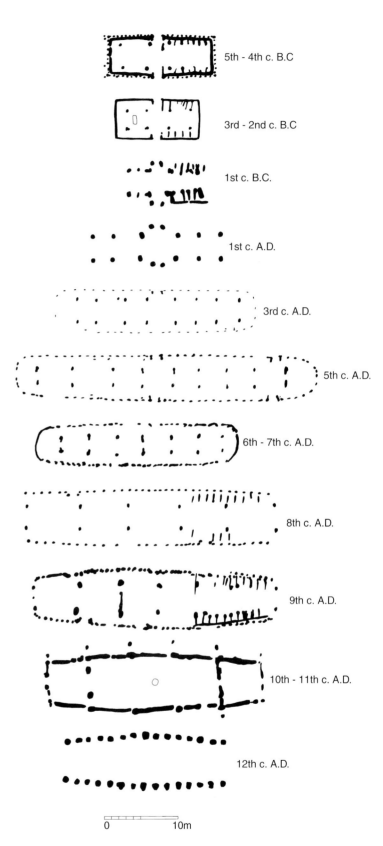

5th - 4th c. B.C

3rd - 2nd c. B.C

1st c. B.C.

1st c. A.D.

3rd c. A.D.

5th c. A.D.

6th - 7th c. A.D.

8th c. A.D.

9th c. A.D.

10th - 11th c. A.D.

12th c. A.D.

0   10m

The longhouse through the Iron Age and Viking Period.

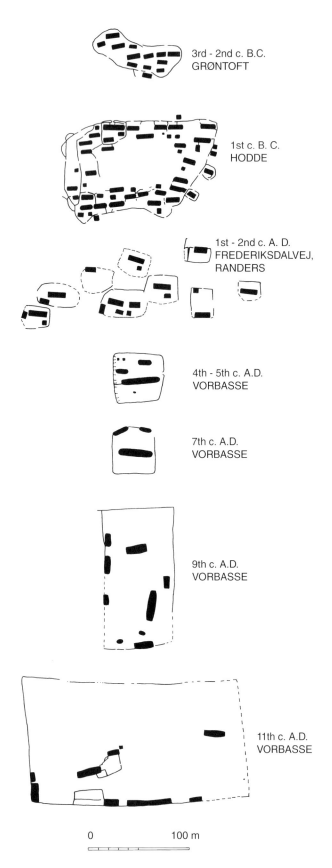

3rd - 2nd c. B.C.
GRØNTOFT

1st c. B. C.
HODDE

1st - 2nd c. A. D.
FREDERIKSDALVEJ,
RANDERS

4th - 5th c. A.D.
VORBASSE

7th c. A.D.
VORBASSE

9th c. A.D.
VORBASSE

11th c. A.D.
VORBASSE

0   100 m

The farmstead through the Iron Age and Viking Period.

function as an outhouse in eastern Jutland but form a main building with dwelling area and stall in Thy.

From the beginning of the Iron Age, the farmstead functioned as an independent social and economic unit based on the family holding. As the longhouse changes the whole farmstead's form changes too.

In the last village at Grøntoft, from the 3rd to 2nd centuries B.C., we find, for the first time, a common fence around the village. From all of the rest of the Iron Age and the Viking Period we now have excavated settlements, albeit only as yet from Jutland, where foundation trenches for a fence are found around the buildings of the farmsteads and the village. The fences show clearly which buildings form a particular farmstead and how many farmsteads there were at any one time in a village. The fences are the key to understanding the settlements. This sequence of fenced settlements is at present unique in Europe.

The main building of the farmstead, the longhouse, kept nearly the same size throughout the half millennium of the pre-Roman Iron Age, 8-14 m. long, occasionally 18-20 m., with place for up to 16 beasts in the stalls. The farmstead originally comprised one building, the longhouse. In the 1st century B.C. the farmstead starts to be expanded, often with one minor building, more rarely with two. These small buildings were used as outhouses, workplaces and such like; a small building in the large village at Hodde for example was used as a smithy.

The early settlements were a shared living place composed of a more or less scattered group of individual farmsteads. It is in the last village at Grøntoft that we first see a fenced village, with 13 contemporary farmsteads (C.J. Becker 1969a). From Hodde (1st century B.C.) comes the largest village of the period so far known, with 27 contemporary farmsteads and a total of 53 buildings that formed a village community regulated with rights and duties. For the first time at Hodde we can distinguish a regular chieftain's farmstead, larger in every way than the other farmsteads of the village. There is no equivalent chieftain's farmstead to be seen in other contemporary villages. The village at Hodde may have been some form of central place with a certain regional political importance (S. Hvass 1985a).

The chieftain's farmstead at Hodde is a large, separately fenced farmstead of a size that becomes the norm in the succeeding Early Roman Period, the 1st and 2nd centuries A.D. The longhouse grows to 15-20 m. long and the dwelling area is expanded with an

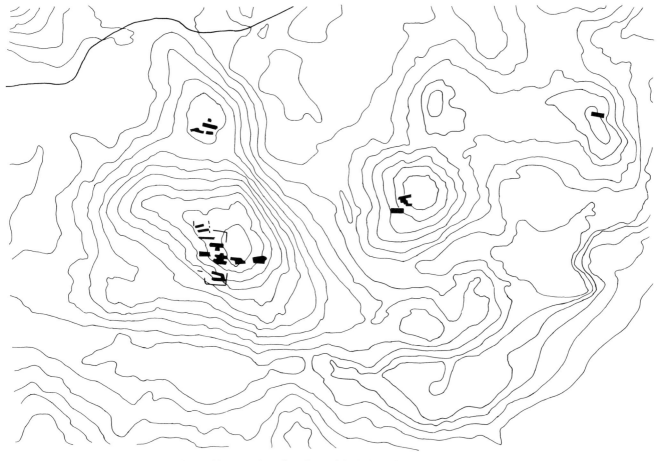

Several farmsteads and a village of the 3rd to 7th centuries A.D. Excavated 1983-88 at Køge on Sjælland.

extra bay or room placed beside the entrance. One or two minor outhouses become common. An excavation near Randers in 1990 has produced the first known village comprising a series of separately fenced farmsteads standing practically in a row.

The serious excavation of Iron-age buildings began after the discovery of the settlement mounds of Thy, several of which have seen major new excavations. In addition to Vestervig and Hurup, the large settlement mound at Heltborg in particular has shown a settlement comprising independent farmsteads gathered into a village (Kann Rasmussen 1968; Bech 1985; Vebæk 1988). In the last 25 years hundreds of these farmsteads have been excavated across the country, some clustered on villages such as Overbygård in North Jutland and Priorsløkke near Horsens, others as isolated farmsteds (Lund 1984; Kaul 1985, 1989b). Unfortunately relatively few farmsteads have preserved fences. From the Early Roman Period we know an isolated chieftain's farmstead at Jelling, where a fenced area of 50 m. x 40 holds a 20 m.-long main building and 4-8 minor

buildings (Kaldal Mikkelsen 1990).

The chieftain's farmstead at Jelling is the largest of the Early Roman Period, but this size becomes normal in the succeeding Late Roman Period, the late 2nd to 3rd centuries A.D. At the transition to the Late Roman Period the longhouse is extended again with a further dwelling bay, a new room. Later, in the 4th and 5th centuries A.D., the stall is expanded too, and the buildings can be divided into 4-6 rooms. Lengths vary from 20 to 50 m. Besides one or two minor buildings, a stack barn is now added for storing hay and, on one occasion, a sunken hut. Through 500 years, from the 3rd to 7th centuries, the size of the farmstead is virtually unchanged. Irrespective of the length of the main building, the settlement is practically the same; only the stalls and other rooms vary in length.

These farmsteads are known from a large number of excavations carried out during the last 25 years over all of Jutland and more recently on the islands. Just as before, they appear as individually fenced farmsteads, either isolated or grouped in villages.

191

'Croft' in an 11th-century village (showed in gray), above a nucleated settlement of the 3rd to 7th centuries A.D. Excavated 1974-87 at Vorbasse in South Jutland.

0   100m

The best preserved villages have been excavated in southern Jutland at the sites of Drengsted, Hjemsted, Vorbasse and Nørre Snede (S. Hvass 1979, 1988; Ethelberg 1988; Egebjerg Hansen 1988; Siemen (ed) 1989). In North Jutland larger settlements of the same date have been excavated, unfortunately without enclosing fences, at sites at Sejlflod and Stavad (Dehn 1982; J.N. Nielsen *et al.* 1985).

On Sjælland extensive excavations have recently been carried out in connexion with major construction worksboth at Høje Tåstrup north of Copenhagen and Køge. In spite of the difficulty of close dating, the provisional results give an impression of settlements of the 3rd to 7th centuries A.D. At Høje

Tåstrup these cover a large area, and excavations of 1989 here show separate, fenced farmsteads with well-preserved ground plans of longhouses, outhouses and barns. The settlements at Køge comprise both farmsteads densely clustered in a village and isolated farmsteads with their own defined resource area of fields and meadows (Tornbjerg 1985, 1989).

The settlements can be very large. At Vorbasse, excavations from 1974-87 covered an area of 260,000 sq.m., which is less than half the total settlement area from the 1st to 12th centuries A.D. Changes in the course of the Late Iron Age and Viking Period are very clear here (S. Hvass 1979, 1981, 1986b).

The 7th-century farmstead of about 2,000 sq.m. is

of the same size as in the 3rd to 6th centuries, but both building-construction and farmstead-structure now anticipate the Viking Period (Egebjerg Hansen *et al.* 1991). In the 8th century the changes are clear, and the fenced farmstead of the 9th century is quite different, with an enclosure 3½ times larger at about 7,000 sq.m. appearing as a regular, rectangular enclosure with the farmstead placed in the middle. At the end of the 10th century the farmstead changes again, with a rectangular enclosure 3½ times as large again, now of about 25,000 sq.m., around the farmstead buildings. In the 11th century the farmstead still comprises only a central main building and a couple of minor buildings. Inside the large enclosure a varying number of smaller buildings are raised, including, now, separate stalls. The 11th-century village must reflect planning at a level higher than that of the local village community.

At the end of the Viking Period, in the 11th century, the settlement of Vorbasse was a village in which all enclosures measured 120 m. across or some fraction of this. From around 1000 A.D. for the first time we see the fully developed 'croft'. In the agrarian laws of the Early Middle Ages, the croft determined each individual farmstead's share of the village's common resources. Archaeological and written sources now suddenly fall together to produce an integrated agricultural history (Hoff 1990).

25 years ago, only sections of a solitary Viking-period village were known in Denmark, but through the last 20 years a number of major excavations have been undertaken in rural settlements, and Viking-period villages are now familiar. Important new sites are Vilslev, Sædding, Omgård, Trabjerg and Vorbasse in Jutland, Lejre and Varpelev on Sjælland, and Runegård on Bornholm (Bender Jørgensen & Skov 1981; L.C. Nielsen 1981a; Stoumann 1981; Watt 1983; S. Jensen 1987; T. Christensen 1991; Tornbjerg 1991).

In the 1980's, the use of metal detectors gave a breakthrough in Late Iron Age settlement archaeology. Through the work of amateur archaeologists especially a wholly new type of settlement has been found, identified by the careful mapping of detector finds, usually from ploughed-out culture layers (cf. Høilund Nielsen & Vang Petersen, below).

At Vorbasse too, detector surveys have been carried out, with relatively few finds being made. Here we have the really local village level, and here excavations show that throughout the time from the 1st to

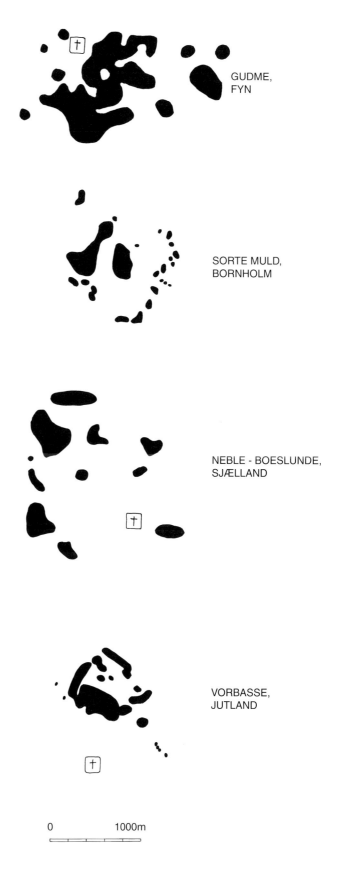

GUDME, FYN

SORTE MULD, BORNHOLM

NEBLE - BOESLUNDE, SJÆLLAND

VORBASSE, JUTLAND

0   1000m

The size of various Iron-age settlements.

193

7th centuries the settlement comprised both farm-steads grouped densely in a village structure and more scattered farmsteads, isolated or in small clusters, all located within the common settlement area. The different settlements move around the area at certain intervals. At any time, settlement can best be characterized villages and isolated farmsteads in symbiosis, both in a local village such as Vorbasse and in a super-regional centre of power such as Gudme.

The basis of settlements with buildings and farm-steads was agriculture. The investigation of pre-served ancient fields, especially on the heaths of Jutland, began at the end of the 1920's in a way that led the rest of Europe. A wide range of field systems have since been studied in the eastern Danish forests (V. Nielsen 1984). At the beginning of the 1970's the study of ancient fields began again with the use of air photographs. Nationwide surveys of 1954, 1968 and 1972 prove a quite new and unique source for the study of these fields (Harder Sørensen 1982).

At two sites, fields themselves have been extensively uncovered, showing preserved ardmarks. At Store Vildmose in Vendsyssel there is a total area of 200 ha. with ardmarks. Half a hectare (5,000 sq.m.) of these has been investigated (V. Nielsen 1987). At Grøntoft too areas with both ardmarks and boundary banks have been uncovered. It is of importance that it is possible here to demonstrate the relationship between the use of the fields and the associated settlement (C.J. Becker 1972a). One of the most difficult problems is the dating of these fields, but they are apparently found throughout the Early Iron Age (Hedeager & Kristiansen 1988).

In 1977, a unique find was made of about 100 kg. of carbonized grain and other plant remains representing a single year's harvest. This lay in an underground corn store of the village at Overbygård in Vendsyssel from about the time of Christ. Current analyses will have great significance for the study of cereal cultivation in the Early Iron Age (Lund 1980; Robinson & Boldsen 1991).

From the beginning of the Early Iron Age, the 5th century B.C., buildings have stalls; in other words the cattle were in stalls through the winter and it was possible to collect dung for the fields. analysis of the finds at Vorbasse shows it is possible to produce a holistic picture of the settlement and its associated fields from the decades around the birth of Christ through the 1st century A.D. The manured fields were around the farmsteads: the infield, separated by a fence from the meadow, the outfield. The manured infields of the 3rd- to 5th-century settlement can also be identified, but how the fields themselves stood in relation to the various settlements here cannot, unfortunately, be determined. This field-system may have existed from the very beginning of the Iron Age, as the 400- and 600-m. fences from the beginning of the Iron Age at Grøntoft may have been built for an infield.

We can now trace how villages move around inside the same resource area and are thus firmly associated with a particular site from the beginning of the Iron Age. This localization of settlements becomes ever more clear through the 1st millennium A.D. From the time of Christ and to the end of the Viking Period we can trace a very stable society in continual development and growth. Both excavated sites and those identified by detectors show long-term continuity in a very complex settlement structure. There is a gradual change in the structure of the farmstead in the 1st to 3rd centuries A.D. Bays are added to the dwelling end of the main building: changes that may reflect a steadily growing household. The farmstead itself becomes very much larger. Underlying this must have been strongly growing agricultural production, making it possible to release and sustain groups such as craftsmen, traders, warriors and servants, who function with the aid of dues and trade on the central sites, which appear precisely in the 3rd century and reflect a greater concentration of power and cult. In the 8th century royal power became a reality, with a strong governing hand in politics and trade that is also reflected in the regulation of the farmsteads that can be be seen at local settlements, again with strongly growing agricultural production. Late in the 10th century an even stronger royal power appears, again with radical changes in farmsteads, probably caused by the need to supply produce to the growing number of towns. This must be a reflection of agricultural policy governed from above.

A very large number of the historical villages that are now found spread over the Danish countryside have their roots far back in the Iron Age.

Air photographs and plans of ancient fields are a unique and as yet unused source for knowledge about the development of the cultural landscape through the Iron Age. The developments of the last 25 years have made it ever more clear what huge archaeological resources still lie preserved in Denmark.

Trading sites and central places

BY STIG JENSEN AND MAGRETHE WATT

Research into the archaeological evidence for Iron-age trade is an area that has seen immense progress in the last 25 years. One searches in vain for the term 'trading site' in Johannes Brøndsted's 30-year-old synthesis of the Iron Age. He treated Roman-period trade solely in terms of the distribution of imports, although he did entertain the hypothesis of the Danish islands functioning as 'intermediary posts for passing trade' (Brøndsted 1960a:177).

Finds of the Germanic Iron Age were still so few in 1960 that Brøndsted felt himself obliged to make the trade routes by-pass Denmark in this period. He did, however, point out the interest of the then newly excavated Lindholm Høje by the Limfjord in respect of trade as early as the Late Germanic Period.

The sensors of research are far more sensitive now because of the decentralization of Danish museum work. This, together with new excavation methods, not least the extensive use of metal detectors, has multiplied the number of finds that reflect craft and trade several times over (e.g. Vang Petersen 1991).

One is faced, in the scholarly literature, with a multiplicity of terms: e.g. trading sites, central places, market sites, storage places, emporia and centres of wealth and power - to list just the most frequently used examples of words whose meanings turn out to be largely the same.

On the basis of the very broad range of finds that has been made in recent years from a number of large settlement areas, it is necessary to state precisely what archaeological criteria must be fulfilled for material to be regarded as evidence of organized trade. The presence of small quantities of imported goods, coins, payment gold and weights is no longer of itself sufficient for identifying trade as the essential basis of a site.

We are, therefore, faced with certain problems of definition, and the question is whether one cannot often profitably replace the narrower term 'trading site' with the broader 'central place'. This implies sites which are distinguished from the general run of settlements in a larger geographical area on the strength of their 'strategic' location and their range of finds.

The economic basis of central places was undoubtedly complex, and the study of ship remains and road systems belongs here too. Votive finds and place names (as, for instance, around Gudme) show that the practice of religion too can be associated with larger central complexes where many people met.

It can be difficult now to see what factors determined whether one settlement site rather than another achieved dominance in a given area. In most cases it seems that a favourable location, strategically or in respect of communications, played a role. The most important central places all developed into economic centres with trade and specialized craftwork as their basic foundations as early as the Late Roman Iron Age. It is probable that the economic centres that appear in just this period reflect steadily more complicated political and social organization. The most successful leaders' ability to establish and develop trading contacts determined the relative status of these sites.

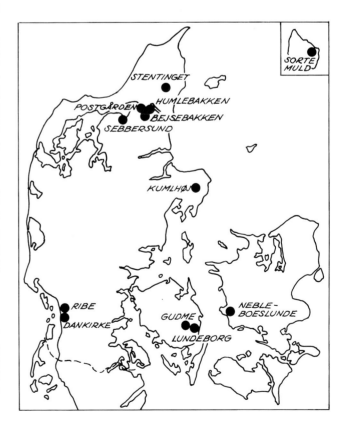

Iron-age trading sites and central places. The map is certainly not complete, as detector surveys are continually revealing 'new' sites that add to the general picture. It also appears that metal objects from sites that were hitherto regarded as central places may 'just' come from ploughed-out graves. This may, for instance, be the case with Kumlhøj and Bejsebakken.

195

	200	300	400	500	600	700	800	900	1000	1100	1200
Sorte Muld	————————————————————						—				
Neble-Boeslunde	———————————————————————————————									—	
Lundeborg	——————————————					—					
Gudme	– – ———————————————————————————————————										—
Stentinget	– – ———————————————————————————————————										—
Postgården				—————		– – ———		— —			
Humlebakken		– – ———————————————————————————									
Bejsebakken				——————————————————						—	
Kumlhøj			—————————	— —————				—			
Dankirke	——————————				– – —	—					
Ribe						———————————————————					

Most Iron-age central places are characterized by continuity of settlement for centuries, often far exceeding the richest period of the site. Ribe developed through the period from a trading site to a proper town.

Eastern Sjælland in the Roman Iron Age

For trade in the Early Iron Age, it is the Roman imports that are focussed upon, these illustrating the rise and fall of centres throughout the Roman Iron Age. This is the first period in which one can see connexions between larger geographical areas on the basis of find-distributions (Lund Hansen 1988a:79).

From the beginning of the Late Roman Iron Age, a concentration of especially richly furnished graves can be seen in the Stevns district of eastern Sjælland. The richest graves at Varpelev, Valløby and Himlingøje are interpreted as evidence of a southern Scandinavian nucleus of a wide-ranging and well-organized network of trading routes rooted in Continental Europe (Hedeager 1987c; Lund Hansen 1987:220 ff.). So far, however, the supreme settlement area has not been identified, nor have the landing sites that must have underlain the functioning of a central place. There are therefore no certain indications of real centralization, and it is possible that there were chieftain's seats here without the super-regional central functions that can be seen at Gudme (Näsman 1991a: 172).

Gudme and Lundeborg

Even while eastern Sjælland was at the peak of its success at the beginning of the Late Roman Iron Age, central places emerged in other parts of the country. These included the major central complex around Gudme on south-eastern Fyn. It is conceivable that even by the beginning of the Early Germanic Iron Age this had taken over pre-eminence in southern Scandinavia.

Proper archaeological excavations have been carried out at several sites in south-eastern Fyn, not only inside the central settlement complex around

A concentration of grave finds on eastern Sjælland with, inter alia, expensive Roman imports is evidence of well-organized trade in the Roman Period. Here a grave at Himlingøje with a rare glass drinking horn is being excavated.

196

Gudme but also by the coast at Lundeborg, where landing sites with evidence for trade and crafts have been found (P.O. Thomsen 1991a-b).

Although the Gudme area has been a centre of atten-tion for a long time by reason of its extraordinarily high quantity of gold finds, it was a surge of metal detector finds in the early 1980's that was the immediate cause of new investigations in the area (Thrane 1987a). On the strength of the distribution of detector finds, the settlements of Gudme are understood to cover about 5 sq.km. (Kromann *et al.* 1991:145). The buildings or farmsteads that have been found at various places in the area are not fundamentally different from those known in other parts of the country. All the same, the range of the finds - imported goods and objects that mark high social status - shows that this must be something more than a well-off farming community.

After the treasure deposits cease in the mid-6th century, it becomes less easy to measure the importance of the area as a central power in southern Scandinavia. The chronological range of the finds, however, shows that the settlement continued to be at least locally important for centuries after.

While Gudme is interpreted as the seat of an early royal power, Lundeborg is viewed as the area's landing, craft and trading site (Kromann *et al.* 1991:157). Excavations here since 1986 have made it possible to follow traces of craftwork over an area of 800 m. along the coast on both sides of the Tange river. Activity at the coastal site of Lundeborg peaked in

The finds from the Gudme area cover the period from the 3rd century to the 12th, but the densest concentration lies in the 4th-6th centuries. The finds include gold hoards with bracteates, armrings and scabbard mounts. The silver hoards include Late-Roman hacksilver, bars and local clasps. There are also numerous dress accessories such as brooches and buckles. From metal workshops there are fragments of gold, silver and bronze, weights and so on.

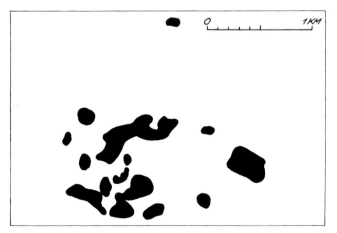

The settlements of the Gudme complex cover a virtually continuous area of more than 1 sq.km. The character of the large number of finds from both regular excavations and surveys in the area show that activities varied from place to place in the large settlement complex.

the Late Roman and Early Germanic Periods, when traces of craft and trade can be followed over the whole extent of the site. The level of activity then fell, but the site apparently did not lose its importance before about 700 A.D.

Sorte Muld

The area around Sorte Muld, near Svaneke on Bornholm, has been known as 'gold-rich' since the end of the Middle Ages. Through excavations at the end of the 19th century and after the Second World War at both Sorte Muld and nearby Dalshøj it could be established that there were settlements with thick culture layers and remains of building plots representing long-term settlement (Klindt-Jensen 1957).

A massive find of 'guldgubber', about 2,300 pieces in all, led to new excavations in 1986-87, this time in another part of the settlement area. These limited excavations (less than 2% of the settlement) have since been supplemented with repeated surface surveys with metal detectors. The results of this work, and provisional analysis of the many finds, have meant that the settlement site can be recognized as part of a large, central complex (Watt 1991).

The consistent use of water sieving in the most recent excavation has produced a lot of finds, including many sherds from various types of glass vessel, imported particularly from provincial Roman and Frankish areas. Weights, and many larger and smaller pieces of bullion supplement the hoards of solidi and denarii that are thought to have been deposited at the end of the 5th century and perhaps some way into the 6th. The relatively small number of later finds, such as sherds of a Tating-ware jug and fragments of Early Viking-period reticella glass, seem to belong to the period in which Sorte Muld gradually lost its importance as a central place.

Surveys on other settlement sites in the general complex have produced finds such as weights, worn denarii, scrap metal and casting remains, that show that all the larger settlement sites in the area housed specialized activities which must have included both trading and various crafts from iron extraction to brooch-casting. Excavation has not as yet uncovered any production sites themselves.

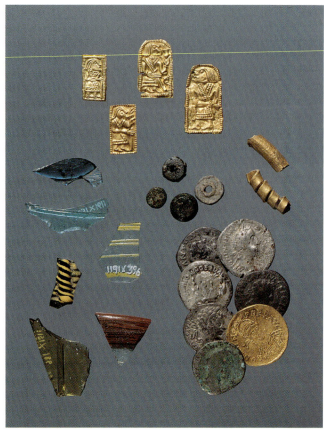

Finds from the centre of the settlement complex of Sorte Muld. The clothing of the 'guldgubber' shows contacts with the Frankish-Germanic princely world. Glass fragments may have been imported for secondary use. Coins, hackgold and weights testify to extensive trade.

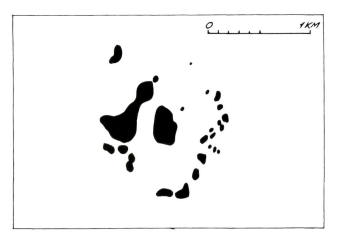

The settlement complex around Sorte Muld on Bornholm stands out in the landscape and comprises large and small settlements whose inter-relationships were apparently partly determined by the topography (after Watt 1991).

Dankirke - Ribe

When the rich Iron-age settlement at Dankirke, south-western Jutland, was discovered in the mid-1960's, it was without parallel in Denmark (E. Thorvildsen 1972; Jarl Hansen 1990, 1991).

Excavation revealed a settlement that could be traced from the pre-Roman to the Late Germanic Iron Age. In the Late Roman and Early Germanic Iron Age the settlement stands clearly above the general run of settlements in terms of both the quantity and the range of finds. These include, for instance, 38 denarii, a considerable number of sherds of glass beakers and many metal objects. A remarkable assemblage of glass is associated with a particular farmstead that burnt down at a late date in the Early Germanic Period and which was surrounded by a thoroughly normal Iron-age settlement (S. Jensen 1991a:77 f.). Apart from a single complete beaker, the glass is in fragments, but a number of types that come from Frankish regions can be identified.

Dankirke was probably the seat of a chiefly dynasty, and the range of finds indicates that some of the area's trade was organized from here.

Amongst the latest finds from Dankirke are 13 scattered coins, 3 of the Late Roman Iron Age, and 10 Frisian sceattas of the 8th century (Bendixen 1972a). Their distribution in the topsoil indicates that they cannot be attributed to a single deposit. It is probable, therefore, that they reflect an as yet undiscovered settlement at the site.

About AD 704 a market site was founded by the Ribe river, about 7 km. north-east of Dankirke (Bencard *et al.* (eds) 1991; S. Jensen 1991b). From the beginning this was a planned and well-organized trading community, probably created by an early royal power. The central power's large market site by the Ribe river must have knocked the supports from under Dankirke's trade with one blow, so that Dankirke should be regarded as representing the system that was superseded by the new market site rather than as a predecessor of Ribe.

It was no coincidence that the creation of a market site at Ribe accompanies a general shift in the pattern of trade (S. Jensen 1990:132; Näsman

A selection of the rich finds from Dankirke - Roman denarii, sherds of Frankish glass, brooches, a pin and small pieces of gold.

1990:105). In the first half of the 8th century the importing of daily goods such as basalt lava quern-stones and slate whetstones begins. Imports had previously consisted solely of luxury items. With this, the range of trade was widened, and excavations at Vorbasse in southern Jutland show that these wares spread immediately into the countryside.

Great variation

Research into the new central places is still in its infancy, and many points are still unclear. It can, however, be seen that the development of economic centres began as early as the late Roman Period and that they represent a stable new feature of centuries that followed.

Only a few central places have yet been investigated in anything more than small samples, and it is difficult to put them in an order of rank. There can, however, be no doubt that the Gudme-Lundeborg complex was one of the most important centres in the 3rd to 6th centuries. Sorte Muld, slightly smaller, had similar but more local importance.

Turning to Sjælland, the Neble-Boeslunde area demands attention. Concentrations of rich finds from the Late Iron Age have been observed here in an area stretching just 2 km. (Bendixen *et al.* 1990). These comprise a number of contemporary farm-steads, but whether these simply reflect local leading farmers or are part of a south-western Sjælland central complex with collection points at Skælskør Nor and Korsør Nor is not yet known. It is, however, noteworthy that the development of the Neble-

A small sample of the 150 or so Frisian sceattas so far found in Ribe. Such coins remained in circulation at Dankirke for years after Ribe was founded.

Roman coins

Thanks to the large number of major archaeological excavations and support from diligent detector users of recent years, the number of Roman coins found in Denmark has grown considerably in the last 25 years.

The new finds include about 1,700 coins, of which about 1,600 were found in archaeological contexts - in bogs, on settlement sites or in graves - while the rest must provisionally be regarded as casual losses.

Chronologically, the coins fall into four groups: a, denarii of the 1st to 3rd centuries; b, aurei and solidi of the 3rd and 4th centuries; c, solidi of the 5th century; d, siliquae of the 4th century.

The first three groups are well-known, but the siliquae are new. Bronze coins also appear, but only as single finds. In many ways, the coin-finds of the last 25 years confirm the picture that the earlier finds gave: Only in isolated cases did Roman denarii reach Denmark before 200 A.D. The majority of the coins were deposited in the 4th century or later, and there is a strong tendency to separate metals in the hoards.

But the finds have led to some new insights. From the excavations at Gudme and Lundeborg it transpires that Roman coins were used over a longer period, from the 3rd century onwards.

On Bornholm, where importation begins late but where the coins, conversely, are widely distributed, it has transpired that hoards were normally deposited in association with settlements. They are often buried right beneath the buildings, just as on Gotland.

The Smørenge (I) hoard, with a single solidus of the 5th century amongst 1st- to 3rd-century denarii, shows that denarii were still in use in the late solidus period. That these two coin-types are very rarely found together is attributable to the marked desire to separate the different metals, with an eye, for instance, to re-use. An investigation on Gotland, where denarius hoards are always found in earlier layers than solidi, shows it is unlikely that denarii and solidi were imported at the same time. It seems clear that a large proportion of the imported coins were intended to be melted down. The question of their monetary function has not been categorically answered, but there is more evidence: the Illerup finds indicate that many of the denarii from the Danish bogs were brought in by foreign soldiers and deposited without having circulated here. In major trading centres such as Gudme-Lundeborg and Dankirke, coins played an important role. But in other Iron-age villages their presence seems to have been extremely unusual.

On Bornholm, importation is very late and lasts for a relatively short time. It is difficult, as a result, to imagine any form of coin-economy even though coins are generally common. Their most frequent function may well have been as the solid kernel of a family's wealth.

Anne Kromann

Site	Latest coin	One hoard	Several hoards	Scattered hoard?	Loose finds	Denarii	Aurei	Siliquae	Solidi	Total	Bog	Settlement
Jutland												
Illerup	188		x			191				191	x	
Katrinelund	192			x	x	5				5		x
Dankirke	201			x	x	36				37		x
Fyn												x
Lundeborg 1	189				x	25				25		x
Lundeborg 2	355				x	42	1	2		47		x
Gudme 1a	355			x	x	35		6		41		x
Gudme 1b	355			x	x				11	11		x
Gudme 2	355			x	x	156		16	1	175		x
Gudme 3	367	x						287		287		x
Bornholm												x
Smørenge 2	192				x	x				26		x
Sorte Muld	193	x								105		x
Sylten 4	193	x								67		x
Smørenge 1	475	x				505			1	506		x

Major finds of Roman coins from archaeological excavations

Boeslunde area's separate but contemporary rich farmsteads matches the situation at Sorte Muld and Gudme very closely (L. Jørgensen 1993). The centre of wealth on south-western Sjælland may therefore have been of regional importance.

A different phenomenon is that of a series of small collection or landing sites that seem to have served just one or two local settlements. These circumstances appear most clearly in a comprehensive survey around Roskilde Fjord (Ulriksen 1990). Such local collection points must have existed in great numbers along most of our coasts.

Two new sites have recently been found in North Jutland, at Stentinget and Sebbersund. Both can probably be treated as central places of regional importance, in Vendsyssel and the eastern Limfjord area respectively.

Stentinget differs from most other central places in lying far inland. Provisional investigations show that the area of settlement covers about 1 sq.km., with both settlement traces and cemeteries from the Early Germanic Iron Age to the Middle Ages. From many hundreds of metal objects, a large number of weights are evidence of trade, and a miscast key and lumps of bronze and lead are evidence of metal-work.

Sebbersund, by contrast, is right on the shore of the Limfjord. Besides a large number of metal objects found by detector, sunken huts, smithing pits and so on have been dug. There is also an enclosed Christian cemetery of the 11th century (Birkedahl Christensen & Johansen 1992).

Long familiar are Lindholm Høje on the north side of the Limfjord and Bejsebakken on the south. While Lindholm Høje is perhaps to be regarded as a major settlement with associated cemetery, the volume of metal finds from Bejsebakken indicate that this site may have been of regional importance (Ørsnes 1976).

Given that a central place such as Stentinget could turn up quite unexpectedly in 1989, we must reckon with the possibility of further important sites appearing in the future, by chance or through well-aimed search. This also applies, of course, to the sites of slightly lower rank with many metal artefacts that distinguish them from the general run. Amongst the newly found sites that probably should be put in this category are Postgården and Humlebakken near Ålborg and Kumlhøj on Djursland (Vang Petersen 1991) plus various, newly discovered and very pro-

A selection of finds of the 5th-11th centuries from Stentinget: brooches, dress pins, belt buckles, weights, lead and bronze bars, unfinished keys and a large, silver gilt Carolingian belt mount. At Stentinget too, traces of trade and metalworking are seen.

ductive sites on Bornholm. It is important to note that several of these sites were discovered by chance, and that nationally the level of detector use and surveying varies enormously.

The picture of Iron-age central places that we now have and our view of the significance they must have had for the development of organized trade will undoubtedly change in the coming years. In recent years, the potential that resides in systematic field surveys to supplement traditional excavations has changed the body of data dramatically.

Early towns

BY STIG JENSEN

In the course of the Iron Age, craft and trade activities moved increasingly to central places and trading sites (cf. above). In the Viking Period these were gradually replaced by towns of more permanent character and more fixed structure. Underlying this totally new element in the settlement structure was increased exchange of goods, greater economic specialization and (not least) the growth of centralized power. Urbanization must also be seen in the context of the general flourishing of trade in northern Europe. The transition from trading sites to real towns is a fluid matter, with much depending on how one defines a town. Let us begin by looking at the situation at Ribe and follow the development from the late Iron Age to the Middle Ages there.

Ribe

There has been considerable archaeological work in Ribe in recent decades, and the town is now one of the best known Viking-period Danish communities. Excavations took place in the years 1970-76 (Bencard (ed) 1981, 1984; Bencard *et al.* (eds) 1990, 1991) and again from 1985 (L. Frandsen & Jensen 1988; Feveile *et al.* 1990; S. Jensen 1991a-b).

With the help of dendrochronology, we now know that Ribe was founded between 704 and 710 (Bencard & Bender Jørgensen 1990:137 f.; K. Christensen 1990). The market site stretched over 200 m. along the north bank of the river. It was about 65 m. deep and was cut by a street with plots 6-8m. wide on

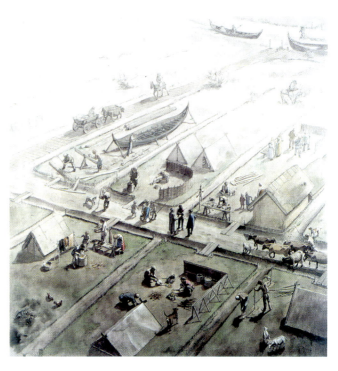

The eastern part of the market site at Ribe, ca. 725. The use of the plots varied greatly: some crafts required a whole plot while in other cases there was room for several different activities.

either side. One row of plots ran down to the river, the other away from it.

It is clear that the market site was well-organized and divided into plots when the first merchants and craftsmen were there around 705 A.D. Their workshops were the individual plots, which apparently

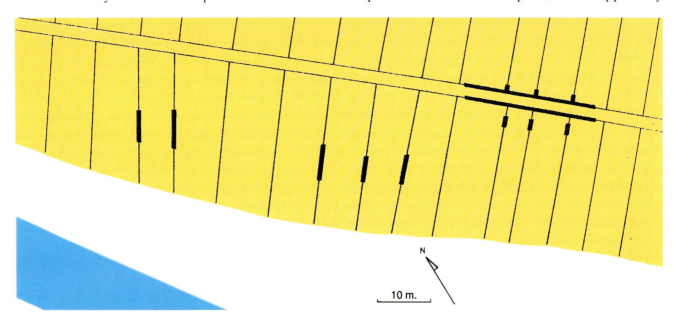

10 m.

N

The structure of the market site at Ribe, ca. 725. The places where the plots and the street are recorded by excavation are shown in thick lines. Unfortunately we have not found the western and eastern ends of the market site.

they hired for longer or shorter periods. Plots were often subdivided to accommodate several activities concurrently. The market site's most important function was of course to provide a context for trade. The more goods that were exchanged, the more successful the site. And Ribe did succeed. The incredible quantity of goods and craft detritus that is found in the culture layers is evidence of a high level of trade. The purpose of the market site - the control of a high proportion of trade - thus seems to have been met.

So who founded Ribe? Since it is now decided that the market site was the result of a well-organized and meticulously planned project, it is natural to raise the question of who stood behind it. It may have been a local chieftain, but we should really rather think of central - royal - power as characterizing the founder. Two major structures, Kanhave canal crossing Samsø in 726 and Danevirke of 737, indicate that there must have been a central power as early as this. Both structures have a strategic importance which makes best sense if the greater part of Denmark were already unified. It is a reasonable notion that Ribe was founded by the same royal power.

The founding of a market site at Ribe around 705 was undoubtedly of importance for the whole district, and must have brought with it considerable upheaval in the chieftain system which had previously organized trade - for instance the chieftain's seat at Dankirke about 7 km. to the south-west (cf. above). The latest finds from Dankirke are ten small coins, *sceattas,* of the beginning of the 8th century. Matching coins have been found at Ribe, and it can be accepted that these rare coins came to Dankirke in the decades after Ribe was founded. Thus the chieftain at Dankirke was still of some importance at this time. One can imagine, then, that the creation of the large market site by the royal power took place in some form of co-operation with the existing chieftain system, perhaps following the principle of 'divide and rule'.

The archaeological finds show that Ribe had widespread trading links. Whetstones, soapstone vessels and whale bone came from Norway. Presumably fur came from the north too. From the south-eastern quarter, gems such as cornelian, rock crystal and garnet from as far off as the Black Sea can be noted. Most goods, however, came from Francia, especially from the Rhineland. The largest category is that of glass beakers, but there is also a great volume of pottery.

A few of the many sherds of Frankish glass drinking vessels that were found on the Ribe market site. Most come from glass vessels with funnel-shaped rims.

The incredible volume of imported material found at Ribe cannot be explained by local demand alone and must mean that Ribe was an important gateway between western Europe and the rest of Scandinavia.

The majority of the finds at the market site, however, represent crafts. Traces of craftsmen's activities, mostly detritus, are found everywhere. With finds

A few of the more than 3,000 mould fragments found in Ribe.

203

from the workshop floors it is possible to follow work through from raw material to finished product. Amongst the most prominent crafts are metal-casting, beadmaking, amberwork, comb-making and shoe-making.

Life in Ribe changed a lot in over the years. When a market was held, the site bristled with people and activity, but in the winter months it stood virtually deserted. But it was not totally deserted. About 250 m. south-east of the market site remains of a settlement that was in use all the year round have been found. This comprises post-built buildings of various sizes, sunken huts, a street, a fence and a well.

The dead were buried immediately to the east of the market site. A row of 8th-century graves has been found here, which together with the permanent settlement fills out our picture of the trading site at Ribe.

In the first half of the 9th century, a ditch was dug around Ribe. Thousands of Viking-period finds have been made down in the ditch and in the area it encloses, but there are none beyond it. This, then, is a 'town ditch', marking the town's boundaries at this date.

Ribe, therefore, was not defended in the middle of the 9th century. At the same time as the ditch was dug, a large bank of turf was raised on the eastern edge of the town. This has not yet been studied in detail, but it is reasonable to imagine that it may have been the town's fortified retreat. In the second half of the 10th century, Ribe was given defences, with the symbolic town ditch being replaced by a flat-bottomed, 1 m.-deep and 8 m.-wide ditch and bank. The earth bank has now completely disappeared, but on the southern edge of the ditch a row of grass turf has been uncovered which was the foundation of the turf-built bank face.

In the course of the 11th and 12th centuries, Ribe outgrew the old, now filled ditch. In consequence, around 1000 A.D. a new, major defence work was built further east: a 12 m.-wide and 2 m.-deep, water-filled moat. This had a 8 m.-wide bank, covered on both sides with grass turf from the nearby marshlands. This impressive set of defences ran from the Ribe river north to the Tved river, and the town was thus surrounded by water, just as in Adam of Bremen's description of ca. 1070 "..Ribe, a town that is surrounded by a second river.." (Skovgaard-Petersen 1981:51).

If one has to sum up the development of Ribe through the Viking Period, it is the major changes that come first to mind. The difference between the seasonal market site of the 8th century and the strongly defended town of the 11th century is enormous, and undoubtedly reflects decisive changes in the functionof the site. It is, however, also worth focussing on some persistent features of this development. There is above all the level of organization that

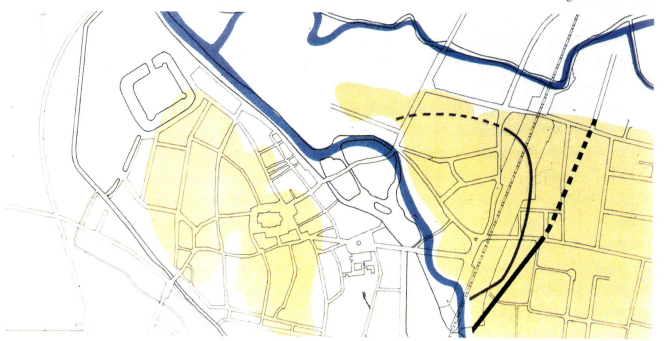

The 11th-century ditch and bank at Ribe was located a little further east than the earlier town boundary and linked the Ribe and Tved rivers. The town thus grew from about 10 to 16 hectares.

sets its mark on the site throughout the period: the planned market site of around 705, the town ditch of the 9th century, the defended town of the 10th century and the strong, expanded defended town of the 11th century. One can detect a governing hand throughout this period - presumably a royal one.

Other towns

The date at which Ribe developed from a trading site to a real town cannot yet be determined, and depends fundamentally on the criteria by which a town is identified. It is certain, however, that from its founding, Ribe was a centre for long-distance trade and not just local exchange.

The same is true of Hedeby, which was founded at the end of the Slien fjord at Haddeby Nor around 810 (Jankuhn 1986; Elsner 1989). Hedeby was a town of international character, with contact north to Norway, east to Sweden and the Slavic peoples to the south of the Baltic, and further to Asia through the great rivers. There were also western contacts, with Dorestad and England.

In recent years, excavations in Hedeby have concentrated on the harbour area where, besides great quantities of artefacts, well-preserved quays have been found (Schietzel 1984). It has been shown that the quays run into the water at intervals that match the plot-division on the land.

Birka in Sweden and Hedeby were Scandinavia's principal Viking-period towns. The role played by Kaupang in Norway and Ribe in this context is uncertain, but there is no doubt that all four towns were gateways for long-distance trade. This was hardly the case with the next generation of Viking-period towns: Aarhus, Viborg, Odense, Roskilde, Lund and Aalborg. These were evidently shaped by the regional context and the local market.

Aarhus, situated on the mouth of the Aarhus river, is first mentioned in 948 and described as the bishop's seat. Archaeological evidence of the Viking-period town comes primarily from a major excavation of 1963-64 (H.H. Andersen *et al.* 1971). This town lay in the centre of the modern city and was defended by a bank, enclosing an area of 4-5 ha. A wooden-paved street ran at the foot of the bank on its inner side.

A number of excavations have subsequently been carried out in the town, one of the most important of which was in Store Torv in 1982 (H.J. Madsen 1983). Comparing the results of this with various other

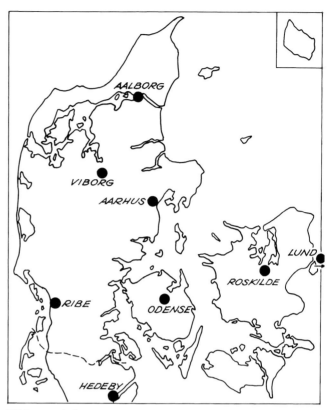

Viking-period towns.

observations produces a picture of a Viking-period town in which settlement was mostly clustered in the south and east - i.e. nearest the river - while large parts of the enclosed area seem to have been left more or less empty. In 1989, a trial trench through the town bank near the river showed, in contrast to earlier observations, that there apparently was a brief Viking-period settlement here before the bank was built sometime in the 10th century.

Viborg is in the centre of Jutland, where the Military Way meets a number of other routes. This, together with the fact that the site was apparently the seat of the Jutish moot, is presumably why a town appeared here in the late Viking Period. Very recently, archaeological excavation beside the Søndersø has revealed a new settlement, with a sequence of well-preserved settlement traces from around 1000 A.D. (Krongaard Kristensen & Vellev 1982; Krongaard Kristensen 1987). That such a development took place in a wet area may indicate that the best sites in the town were already occupied by this time. There have not been any major archaeological investigations of the earliest phases of the other Danish Viking-period towns in recent decades (- Clarke & Ambrosiani 1991).

Iron smelting

BY OLFERT VOSS

The growing use of iron that can be observed through the Iron Age and Middle Ages was probably dependent on more and more extensive domestic iron smelting. Excavations have shown that it is still possible to retrieve evidence of iron production. Several forms of smelting furnaces were used in Denmark down to *ca.* 1600, when local production ceased.

The earliest furnaces, from Maglegård on Bornholm and Hillerup on Fyn, of the 2nd and 1st centuries B.C. (Voss 1991), are so poorly preserved that their original appearance cannot now be established.

From the 1st century B.C. and 1st century A.D. there are now 11 finds of furnaces, with an opening at the base leading to a shallow work pit. Jutlandic furnaces of this type have a stone-lined opening. The furnaces from Fyn and Sjælland have a clay plate here, a so-called 'tuyere plate'. These furnaces could be re-used several times, and the slag, which was removed after each firing, must have been left in heaps on the ground, though none of these have survived.

These early furnaces are found over the whole country, unlike the slag-pit furnace which belongs to the period of the 1st to 7th centuries A.D.; it is only known from Jutland south of Himmerland and primarily in western and southern Jutland. The slag from this furnace, about 200 kg. per furnace, lies in the 50 to 80 cm.-deep slag pit. In some slag pits that were fully or partly broken up immediately after firing, fragments of the furnace shaft are found. This was of clay, with four air inlets 3.5 to 4 cm. in diameter, and was placed a few centimetres above the ground. Only one fully preserved shaft has been found, at Scharmbeck outside Hamburg (Wegewitz 1957). Excavations have shown that in Jutland up to 175 slag pits can be found grouped in irregular clusters of varying density. So far, we know of slag-pit furnaces from more than 60 sites, 10 of which have more than one cluster of pits. Each slag pit represents one smelt, and excavation will therefore make it possible to determine the total volume of iron production. There are no finds of furnaces involved in iron smelting dated between the 7th and the 12th and 13th centuries, when we have slag heaps with planoconvex slags and tap-slags which show that the slag was drained out of the furnace into a bowl-shaped hollow in the ground. A few slag heaps from these furnaces are preserved in old forest areas. It is probable

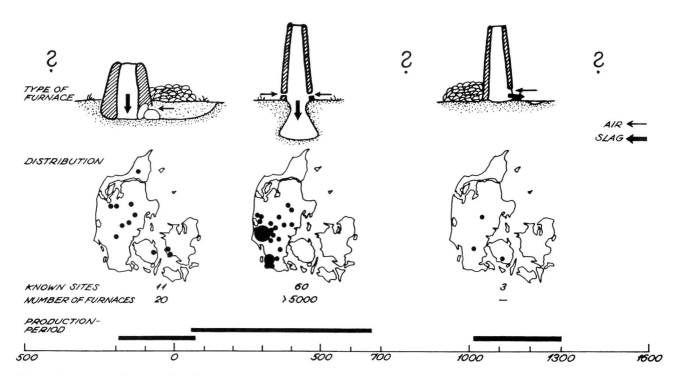

The various types of iron-smelting furnaces and their spatial and chronological distribution. The thickness of the topsoil makes it immediately apparent that apart from slag pits very little will have survived in cultivated areas.

206

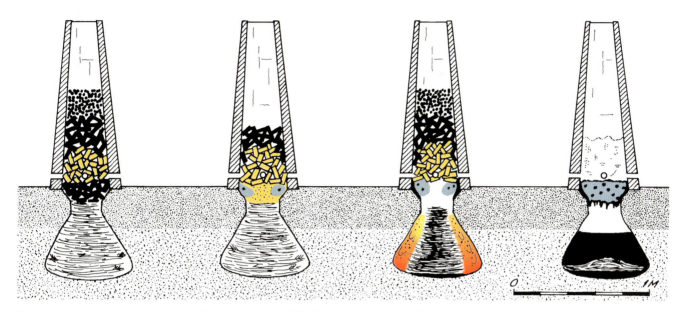

Reconstruction of the sequence by which a slag pit was filled during the iron-smelting process.

that this is the type of furnace that was in use in the Viking Period.

There are again no finds of slag or furnaces from the 14th and 15th centuries. Slag-rich iron clots may come from this period and may have been produced in a pit furnace (Buchwald 1992).

The process of iron smelting in a slag pit can partly be reconstructed from the results of excavation. After the club-shaped slag pit was dug, it was filled with straw - occasionally with heather - which was pushed, handful by handful, down into the pit through the 20 - 25 cm. wide opening (the connecting pipe). Thus the fill was densest in the centre, where the individual handfulls lie on top of one another in various directions, so that they could appear to be twisted together, as has been shown by earlier reconstructions (Voss 1986).

The straw filling had two purposes. The first was to prevent charcoal and ore from falling to the bottom of the pit. The second was to prevent the first slag from running straight into the pit where, because of the low temperature below ground level, it would solidify within the connecting pipe and thus block in the slag behind it. In the 'bowl', directly below the hottest part of the furnace, the slag could be kept above its melting point of 1150°. Gradually, as the pressure from the accumulating slag grew, the straw packing would be compressed and the slag would run, all at once, to the bottom of the pit, where it would form a perfectly flat plate of slag (the

base slag), of *ca.* 15 litres, which can weigh up to 60 kg. This heats the whole furnace up so much that slag can then flow right down into the pit without solidifying.

The location of iron-smelting sites was determined by the need to keep the distance as short as possible to both the bog ore and the forest from which the charcoal came. The clay from which the furnace was built also needed to be at hand, and the people who were to dig the ore, fell the trees and burn the charcoal should not have to go too far to work. When charcoal could no longer be obtained within a reasonable distance, production was moved to a new site.

Only in the area of Snorup, north of Varde, has an attempt been made to map all iron-smelting sites, and this has demonstrated that although iron smelting was frequently moved from site to site, old sites were returned to frequently. In the Snorup area, 20 iron-smelting sites within an area of 500 m. x 700, with between 28 and 171 slag pits each, show that new production was started more than 20 times in the period 100 - 700 A.D.

The 780 pits to the north-east are treated as five densely clustered sites. The explanation of the 20 or more breaks in production could be attributed to nothing but the lack of charcoal. Timber for the charcoal was certainly cut in a coppice which could be harvested every 20 years, and it was this that determined when iron could be produced at the site

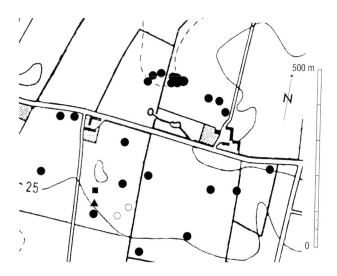

The iron-smelting area of Snorup, north of Varde, western Jutland.

again. The charcoal in the slag pits seems to have come mostly from oak. The best wood for charcoal is pieces 5 - 12 cm. thick and this is the thickness obtained in a 20-year-old oakwood (Duhamel du Monceau 1761:9). Oak grows quickest as a young tree, and coppicing thus produces the highest yield per area unit (B. Jakobsen 1973:367). 170 furnaces will consume nearly 43 tons of charcoal, which can

be produced from a coppice of a maximum of 20 ha. Coppices certainly existed since the introduction of agriculture, perhaps even before (Worsøe 1979:105). This was the source of palings for fencing and laths for roofs (Draiby 1991:122), wood for cart axles, bolts and spokes, shafts and so on, as well as charcoal. Before felling, the oak could be stripped of its bark for tannin smelting.

The coppice was also a valuable grazing area, allowing haymaking, and a place where domestic animals could feed in the winter (B. Jakobsen 1973).

If charcoal burning was not the most important activity for the village, the varied uses of the coppice may be an explanation for the different amounts of iron smelting on the sites within the Snorup area.

Of the more than 20 iron-smelting sites around Snorup, seven are surveyed and partly excavated, with more than 1,000 slag pits clustered in groups, often slightly oblong and at varying intervals. The number of slag pits in the different groups is 20, 80, 145, 150, 171 and 175.

In the south-eastern part of the area with the 780 slag pits a small oval pit, 75 cm. long, 30 cm. wide and 10 cm. deep, was found; in the middle of the pit, the ground around which was baked red, lay a

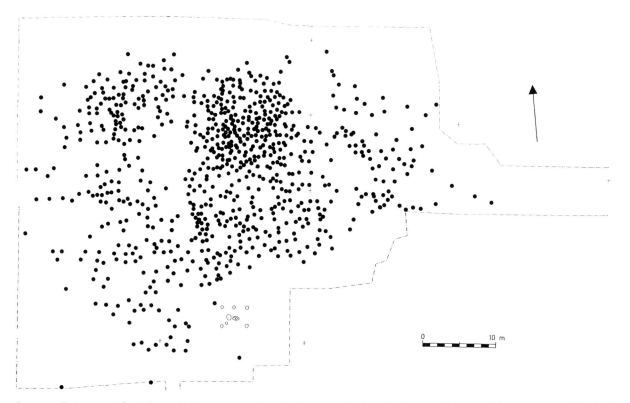

Snorup, Tistrup parish, Ribe amt. *Excavation plan showing several densely clustered iron-smelting sites. Individual slag pits are marked as circles. Earlier settlement traces on the site are not shown.*

planoconvex slag measuring 15 x 13 cm. Immediately west of this was a large pit, about 75 cm. in diameter. This pit, and a smaller one 35 cm. in diameter, contained significant quantities of hammerscale; this is identified as the remains of a smithy where the raw bloom was worked. Around the smithy were six postholes, two of which had planoconvex slag in the fill. The postholes might have come from a smithy's shed.

An isolated hoard of iron bars was found on the Snorup iron-smelting site. At the bottom of a pit measuring 30 x 30 cm. were six pieces of iron weighing 3.2 kg. in all. Above these were 100 so-called axe-bars, about 20 - 30 cm. long and weighing about 130 g., and a rusted mass containing about 100 small bars, 16 - 20 cm. long and weighing 25 - 30 g.; in all, nearly 20 kg. The hoard contained no datable artefacts.

Investigations of iron-smelting structures have been limited to the excavation of those furnaces which are being destroyed by agriculture. Only in Starup and Snorup north of Varde has this resulted in total excavation of several sites within the same area. The results of this show that it is necessary to undertake total excavation of all the sites which make up an iron-smelting area, and to analyse all the charcoal to determine whether this recurrent production was dependent on charcoal from one coppice, as proposed here. Because of the depth of the slag pits every single one can be identified, and thus it is possible to calculate the total iron production within a site in the period 100 - 700 A.D. An assessment of the economic and social importance of the iron-smelting areas in western and southern Jutland will only be possible when the geographical extent and density of iron smelting sites has been investigated.

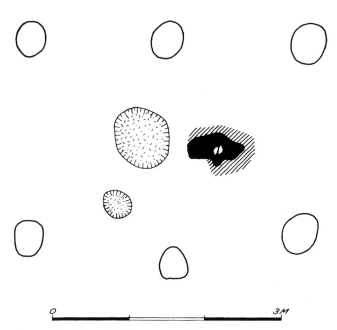

Snorup. Smithy with planoconvex slag.

After the use of the slag-pit furnaces had ceased, the use of iron continued to grow, and one must suppose that production continued, using other types of furnace that are simply so poorly preserved that we have not managed to find them. The possibility that the growing use of iron was based on imports cannot, however, be excluded.

Thanks to the number of excavated furnaces it has been possible to produce a reliable reconstruction of the slag-pit furnace; this has not yet been possible for other types.

It is supposed that local iron smelting goes back to the beginning of the Iron Age, but no certain traces of furnaces older than the 2nd century B.C. have yet been found.

Snorup. Iron bars from a hoard of nearly 20 kg. of iron.

Territorial defence

BY FLEMMING RIECK, STEEN W. ANDERSEN AND ELSE ROESDAHL

Aerial photograph of Trelleborg from the east. This circular Viking fort with extra-mural houses and cemetery is on western Sjælland on a headland between the Vårby and Tude rivers. The Storebælt can be seen in the background, and the hall reconstructed in 1942 in the foreground. Trelleborg was the first of the four Danish geometric ring forts to be excavated, in the 1930's. It led to a new perception of the Viking Period. The building of the fort is dendrochronologically dated to 980/81, when Harold Bluetooth was king of Denmark.

Barriers in fjords and inlets

For several years there has been a marked tendency to assess prehistoric social organization without the necessary attention to the 'maritime cultural landscape'. The development of wetland and underwater archaeology in recent decades has opened up an entirely new field for research. There is extraordinarily rich material on the seabed and in coastal zones that can lead to a wholly new understanding of both the regional and the national situation in the Iron Age and Viking Age.

Saxo's 'Chronicle of Denmark' mentions structures designed for defence against maritime attack several times: "Neither weapons nor towns were reckoned to secure safety but bays and creeks were blocked with long stakes and beams so that the pirates could not enter" (Horn 1911). Archaeological excavations have shown that such structures, raised against the Wends, did indeed exist in the periods

Saxo states. The late Viking-period/Early Medieval barriers at Skuldelev in Roskilde fjord, Vordingborg, Fotevik and so on are described below, but the structural type itself is known from much earlier.

The need to be able to protect the hinterland from attack from the sea grew as boat and ship technology advanced. As vessels became large enough to carry significant loads of men and weapons, the need for effective defence works grew. The most important Danish finds of Iron-age ships are the rowing boats sacrificed in Nydam Mose, of which the large oak boat was deposited around 350 A.D. This is just the period of the Iron Age from which the earliest well-documented barriers are found.

Let us turn our spyglass on the mouth of Haderslev fjord in the Lillebælt. For many years, two massive barriers have been known here, 'Margrethe's Bridge' and 'Æ Lei' ('The Gate'). Investigation of

Aerial photograph of barrier systems in Gudsø Vig, between Stegenav and Kidholm.

these two systems began in 1969 under the leadership of the National Museum's Institute of Maritime Archaeology, with Danish, Norwegian and Swedish archaeologists taking part (Crumlin-Pedersen 1975). Sometime later the site was revisited, and recently, in 1989-91, more extensive excavations have been carried out. The course of the barriers, their inner structure and dating have now been established in quite fine detail (Rieck 1991).

'Margrethe's Bridge', which lies nearer the mouth of the fjord, runs roughly north-south, and the presence of the structure has been observed on both sides of the modern sailing channel. No proper excavation has been made south of the channel. It can be noted that the southern end of the barrier is a small headland which was called Stagodde (or, locally, Stekshage). Place-names with elements such as "stik", "stek", "stage" or "pæl" (= "spit", "stake") are associated with many of the known barriers in Denmark (Wåhlin-Andersen 1964).

The system north of the channel is clearly divided into two separate structures. One comprises one or two rows of thick, vertical hammered oak and beech piles and a quantity of thinner driven or hammered stakes. Dendrochronological datings provisionally place this structure in the Middle Ages, so it will not be described in more detail here. The second structure, however, is dendrochronologically dated to the end of the Roman Iron Age. This appears as a 24 m.-broad zone of thousands of vertical, hammered stakes some of which brace heavy horizontal oak planks. These planks, called 'pontoons', lay athwart the sailing route and were held fast in the structure by vertical stakes placed through rectangular holes in them. Dendrochronological samples show that the structure was built in the second half of the 4th century and was probably in use to 400/410 A.D. It may, then, have specifically been boats of the Nydam type that were to be prevented from sailing into the substantial hinterland the Haderslev fjord is asssociated with.

'The Gate' was about 1 km. further west, inside the fjord. It has been possible to trace this roughly 10 m.-broad construction right across the fjord to a length of about 500 m. The alignment of this structure is southwest/north-east. Again, quantities of vertical hammered stakes are found (alder, hazel, ash, oak, maple) plus horizontal oak planks with rectangular holes. Many undressed alder logs were also included in the structure. A small heap of stones on the eastern side

of the barrier might perhaps be interpreted as ballast from a ship which was placed here. The dating of several oak planks gives 403 A.D. as an exact date of construction, but there may well be several phases of construction (AUD 1988:233 f.).

It is worth noting, that remains of a major warbooty deposit from the same period as the two barriers have been excavated on the land above Haderslev fjord, at Ejsbøl (Ørsnes 1984) - further evidence of troubled times.

Turning to the Viking Age, we find few Danish structures investigated. On the northern side of the Kolding fjord is the natural harbour of Gudsø Vig. This creek, which could certainly have served as an assembly point for Viking-period fleets, is bounded to the south-east by the headland 'Stegenav', the Kidholm islands and Hovens Point. As early as 1973, the strait between Hovens Point and Kidholm was surveyed, and a row of poles was seen here. One preserved pole is radiocarbon-dated to the Viking Period.

In 1985, the strait between Stegenav and Kidholm was investigated in connexion with seabed construction work, and several courses of stakes were found. More than 900 stakes were planned and at least three separate construction phases can be distinguished. Two zones with multiple stake-courses - mostly beech and hazel - are radiocarbon-dated to the 8th and 9th centuries (AUD 1988:225 f.), while a third, slighter course of oak and apple stakes is dated to the late pre-Roman Iron Age.

While there may be doubt about the defensive function of the pre-Roman structure, the Viking-period ones are so massive that they must be interpreted as properblockades. Again, a pile of ballast has been found at the end of the stake-courses. Together, the barriers between Hovens Point and the Kidholms and the Kidholms and Stegenav efficiently protected the inlet against ingress from the Kolding fjord. Looking at the topography, it may have been possible to get out of the Gudsø Vig to the north through the now blocked and overgrown Rands fjord, which runs south from Vejle fjord. The only obstacle to sea travel between Gudsø Vig and Vejle is a narrow morrain bank. The bank is called "Skibdræt", "Ship-drag": perhaps where ships were hauled across. "A clever fox has many exits," it is said. Is this how we ought to view the good natural harbours of Gudsø Vig, and Stavns fjord with the Kanhave canal?

FR

212

Defensive works of the Early Iron Age

Prehistoric forts and enclosures form a group of monuments which have been known from the infancy of archaeology. The members of this group vary greatly in respect of construction and size, including true fortresses, semicircular banks and extended barriers. They often have their own folk legends and interpretations, but only to a limited degree have they been dealt with in serious archaeological literature.

In recent years, however, interest in these structures has increased markedly. This is primarily due to C 14 dating and dendrochronology, which now give us much more chance of dating the structures and thus placing them in relation to other classes of monument. Without natural-scientific dating methods, the defensive works would remain a virtually intractable group of monuments, being generally poor in finds and lacking in datable construction features.

Research into this group of monuments is still so sporadic that it is too early to identify general characteristics, but the last 25 years have seen several individual studies, each of which has produced important new results.

Borremose (North Jutland *amt*): defended village of the pre-Roman Iron Age. A reassessment of the excavations that J. Brøndsted and P.V. Glob carried out in the 1940's, together with new, supplementary investigations, has shown, contrary to what was previously thought, that the fort is contemporary with the settlement that it encloses (Martens 1990).

Priorsløkke (Vejle *amt*): defended village of the Early Roman Iron Age. This fully excavated village lay on a small headland that projects into the Hansted valley north-west of Horsens. The headland is cut by a ditch with a palisade of heavy oak stakes (Kaul 1985, 1989b).

Trælbanken (Southern Jutland *amt*): ring bank of the Early Roman Iron Age, lying on the edge of a marshy area about 10 km. north of the Danish-German border. A minor excavation on the bank and associated ditch was carried out by Ole Harck, Kiel University, in 1978. From comparisons with, *inter alia*, similar ring banks on the North Frisian islands, Harck interprets Trælbanken as a ritual site with no real defensive function (Harck 1990:209 ff.).

Olgerdiget (Southern Jutland *amt*): defensive work of the Roman Iron Age, situated south-west of Åbenrå. The structure comprises up to three parallel palisades of closely spaced oak posts. To the southeast of this is a ditch, and there are traces of a low bank in some places. Altogether this feature can be traced over a length of some 12 km., of which, however, only 7.5 km. are really defended; the remainder comprises intervening tracts of bog. The excavator, Hans Neumann, believed that Olgerdiget faced the north, and that it was raised by the Angles against the Jutes. Olgerdiget was radiocarbon-dated to the 2nd to 6th centuries A.D. in the course of Neumann's studies (Neumann 1982). Some of the posts have since been dendrochronologically dated (provisionally) to 219 and 278.

The Bank (Southern Jutland *amt*): a long bank of the Late Roman Iron Age, running east-west between Åbenrå and Haderslev. This structure, which comprises a ditch and bank with a palisade on the northern side, has so far been followed over a distance of about 4 km. Both east and west of The Bank are natural obstacles in the form of eroded valleys, watercourses and bogs, so that the structure barred a narrow pass which had to be used to travel in or out of Jutland throughout prehistory. Olgerdiget (above) and Danevirke are similarly situated. The Bank is dendrochronologically dated to around 278 A.D. (provisional) (S.W. Andersen 1990).

Trældiget (Ribe/Vejle *amt*): long bank of the Iron Age, situated west of Kolding. Trældiget runs north-south, and according to old drawings it covered at least 12 km. An excavation undertaken in 1981 shows that the structure comprised a low bank and associated ditch with a palisade to the east. The excavator dates the structure to the Iron Age (S. Hvass 1987).

SWA

213

Viking-period banks and forts

The defensive works of the Viking Period have always been amongst Denmark's most popular ancient monuments. In the last 25 years, archaeology has both brought new examples to light and found new ways of understanding them (Roesdahl 1988).

Danevirke has been the object of archaeological research and publication for over a century. It is repeatedly named in written sources from the Viking Period and Early Middle Ages as a functioning structure. Dano-German co-operation over major excavations in 1969-75 produced new observations of some of the many banks and phases, certain of which have been precisely dated by dendrochronology. Some main phases of the bank-complex were delineated: three major defence lines that had superseded one another - the earliest constructed in 737 A.D., the second in 808 and the last, which was subsequently greatly expanded, in 968. This means that the earliest phase was built as early as the Late Germanic Iron Age, and that the latest is from the time of Harold Bluetooth (H.H. Andersen *et al.* 1976; H.H. Andersen 1977, 1984). Current excavations, however, are raising questions about this scheme. The situation is not yet clear, but basically it appears that the origins of the Danevirke may yet go back even further than 737.

In the course of the 8th and 9th centuries, the earliest towns developed in Denmark (cf. S. Jensen, above), but the earliest town banks are from the middle of the 10th century. None, however, are yet dated by dendrochronology. The semicircular bank of Hedeby has always been known, and recent excavations in the harbour basin have corroborated the view that this was protected by a semicircular palisade (Jankuhn 1984: 199; Schietzel 1984:187). Excavations of 1963-64 first showed that Århus's semicircular bank was constructed in the Viking Period, probably at the same time as the settlement (H.H. Andersen *et al.* 1971). That Ribe too had a Viking-period bank was not revealed before 1990 (S. Jensen 1991b).

The four geometric ring forts are still in view, and minor excavations have been carried out at each of them in the last 25 years. Fyrkat was published in 1977, and at the same time Trelleborg, Aggersborg and Nonnebakken were reviewed (O. Olsen & Schmidt 1977; Roesdahl 1977). The interpretation of the forts, however, was still not clarified, amongst oth-

er things because of disagreements over dating, which still had to depend on the artefacts found. Through the 1970's scepticism over the traditional interpretation of the forts as camps for the Vikings who conquered England for Sweyn Forkbeard and Canute grew (e.g. T.E. Christiansen 1971). The dendrochronological dating of the building of Trelleborg to 980/81 and of Fyrkat to about the same year meant that this theory had to be abandoned (Bonde & Christensen 1984; T.E. Christiansen 1984). The dominant view now is that the forts' primary role was a matter of internal politics: to secure Harold Bluetooth's power in difficult political circumstances, at the same time as being prestige monuments as so many other military buildings through the ages (e.g. Roesdahl 1987b). But there are other views too (e.g. H.H. Andersen 1988). There is, however, agreement that they were raised by the king. There are only provisional accounts of the largest ring fort, Aggersborg (Roesdahl 1986 and refs.) and scattered articles on Nonnebakken (most recently N.M. Jensen & Sørensen 1990). But all of the forts have been put into a perspective where they no longer stand quite alone in the world. There are related ring forts in the Netherlands - the best known is Souburg on Walcheren (O. Olsen & Schmidt 1977:92 ff. and refs.) - and a few years ago a circular ring fort was discovered at Trelleborg in Skåne (B. Jacobsson 1989). The Danish geometric ring forts are a unique phenomenon. They had a short life, without predecessors or successors. But they are one feature of aggressive military construction work that took place in the middle and later 10th century, and which ran alongside other major construction works such as the Jelling monuments and the bridge over Ravning Enge. Without doubt, many of these monuments are to be attributed to Harold Bluetooth, and they correlate well with the varying internal and external political circumstances of the period.

The structures considered here have proved to be of great interest. This has not been the case with the fortified refuges which must have existed in the Danish Viking Period. There must have been more than Gamleborg in Almindingen on Bornholm and Hochburg by Hedeby. There are various anonymous and undated banked structures around Denmark that are generally attributed to the Iron Age. At present, they attract little interest (cf. H. Andersen 1992). They may be guarding surprises.

ER

214

Votive deposits

By Mogens Ørsnes and Jørgen Ilkjær

In the last 25 years, the study of the great weapon deposits of the Iron Age has attracted especial attention, and it is this group of votive hoards that we shall consider in what follows. Very extensive excavations of such sites have been carried out since 1950 in the Illerup valley near Skanderborg (H. Andersen 1951, 1956; Ilkjær & Lønstrup 1983; Ilkjær 1990), at Ejsbøl bog near Haderslev (Ørsnes 1984, 1988) and Nydam bog at Sundeved (Vang Petersen 1988; Bonde et al. 1991). Alongside this, the chronological ordering of the finds and the diverse interpretative problems the finds pose have continually been worked over and re-assessed (Ørsnes 1969-70, 1988:9 ff.; Ilkjær 1976, 1990:13 ff.; Ilkjær & Lønstrup 1982; Fabech 1990, 1991a-b; Hedeager 1990:138 ff.).

The dating and interpretation of the weapon deposits have been debated throughout this century. The classic sites, Thorsbjerg, Nydam, Kragehul and Vimose, which Engelhardt excavated and published in the mid-19th century (Engelhardt 1863, 1865, 1867, 1869), were originally regarded as large, unitary weapon deposits, and Worsaae could therefore (1865), on the basis of accounts by, for instance, Caesar, Tacitus and Orosius (Hagberg 1967:65 ff.), identify the finds as sacrifices of war booty, each of which specially marked a victory over an invading enemy. It had, however, repeatedly to be recognized that they could not form the equipment of single armies or have been deposited all at one and the same time. While Brøndsted (1960a) as, earlier, Müller (1897) held to Worssae's view and simply observed that several successive war-booty offerings had taken place at the relevant sites, Jankuhn (1936) and many after him (Hagberg 1967; Geißlinger 1967; Raddatz 1970; Stjernquist 1974; Hines 1989; Müller-Wille 1989) saw the opportunity for a more radical re-interpretation whereby the weapon deposits, like other bog deposits, were regarded as accumulated small sacrifices in a local sacred bog. Both interpretative models identified the sacrificial site as evidence of a strong local votive tradition, but while the objects sacrificed in Brøndsted's view were foreign warriors' weapons, and the sacrifice reflected politico-military events, the same find material, according to the other model, served to illuminate the local population's weaponry and their socially governed religious practices. It was one of the primary tasks for the systematic excavations in Illerup and Ejsbøl and the bog-find studies that derived from these to try to tackle this problem.

The decisive method for establishing contemporaneity or lack of it between objects which are haphazardly spread over extended bog areas is the accurate description and recording of the placement of the individual items in relation to one another and to the sequence of natural layers in the bog. In this way, contemporaneity has been found where objects were deposited so tightly packed together that they have to be regarded as closed finds. This applies to a number of clusters of artefacts in Illerup bog which were found so far from the original lake bank that they must have been dropped into the lake on a single occasion, and it applies too to two compact clusters, each comprising more than 500 pieces, that were deposited near the bank of the then Ejsbøl lake. Contemporaneity between widely scattered items can also be identified in that the equipment sacrificed was often broken up before it was deposited or broadcast into the lake, and matching parts of a single item or of the same set thus can be found far apart in the area of excavation. The mapping of such matching fragments, which often also connect isolated finds with items that are part of closed groups, illustrates quite remarkably that on each individual site we are faced with a limited number of sacrificial deposits each of which comprised the equipment of a considerable number of warriors. Thus the latest excavation results accord with Brøndsted's interpretation of the finds as war-booty offerings, although it has to be recognized that we still lack adequate evidence that the weaponry sacrificed represents an invading foreign army.

In the case of Illerup and Ejsbøl, an assessment of the number and scope of the deposits is based both on the closed finds and the mapping of matching fragments, and on the distribution of various weapon-types in the area of excavation, as our knowledge of the chronology of weapon-types has also been substantially developed in recent decades (Slomann 1959a-b, 1977; Godlowski 1970; Ilkjær & Lønstrup 1974; Ilkjær 1976, 1990; Biborski 1978; Solberg 1981; Menghin 1983; Madyda-Legutko 1986). In Illerup, then, four, successive deposits have been identified (in periods C1b and D1) and at Ejsbøl two or three deposits (in periods C2-C3 and D1) as a number of items that are dated to period C3 and are not represented in the clusters of objects could be seen as an independent deposit which belongs, chronologically, in between Ejsbøl-North and Ejsbøl-South (Ilkjær 1990:304).

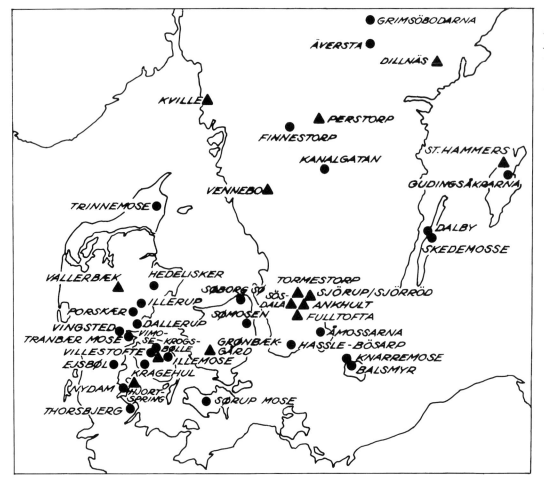

Find-places of supposed war-booty sacrifices marked by open circles. Other finds of weaponry or horse gear marked by triangles.

The finds from Illerup and Ejsbøl have provided quite comprehensive information about the composition and equipment of Iron-age armies. From site A at Illerup have come more than 775 javelin- and lanceheads and up to 350 shield bosses. A javelin, lance and shield form the basic equipment of the individual warrior in contemporary weapon graves which in accordance with means or need may be supplemented with a sword and bow and arrows, and since only a limited part of the probable sacrificial area has been excavated, the finds must represent a very substantial army. The many groups of objects deposited together that are characteristic of this votive hoard further provide specific insight into the individual warriors' equipment, so that, for example, it can be seen that each man wore two belts: an outer one, which was distinguished by a buckle with a backplate and a strap-end, to which a knife and strike-a-light were fastened, and an inner one, which carried more personal items, probably in a leather or textile purse: comb, toothpicks, hackmetal or coins. The latter can hardly have been in everyone's possession, and we can also see social stratification within the troop: there were, for instance, 5 silver and 40 bronze shield bosses while the rest were iron. Bridles for a dozen horses similarly show that some in the troop were higher than others - on horseback. A similar picture emerges of the group of warriors whose equipment was deposited about a century later in Ejsbøl-North. Here there are javelins, lances and shields for about 200 men, and 675 arrowheads that were found densely packed in clusters near the lake bank emphasize the importance of the bow and arrow. Social stratification is illustrated by 14 bronze buckles and 12 matching strap-ends that stand apart from the other belt fittings of iron, and 12-14 swords with silver-plated hilts and a matching number of heavy lanceheads encrusted with silver and brass. Finally, the find included expensive horse harness and saddle mounts for 9 horses, and spurs for 9 riders.

On the basis of these systematically excavated votive sites, one can now gain a certain understanding of the deposits at other sites. Comparisons

216

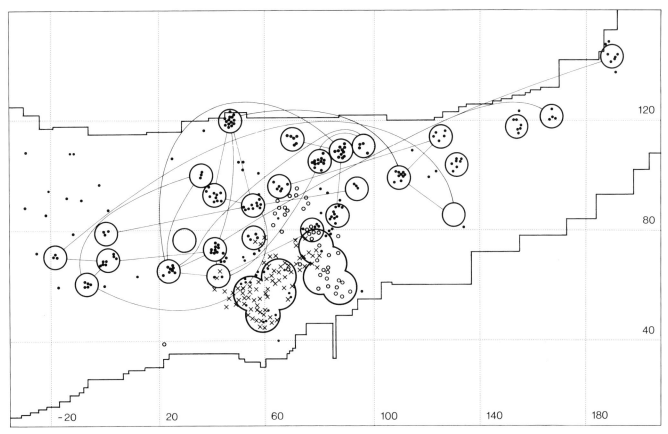

Illerup Sites A, B and C, shown by the distribution of three lancehead-types, each of which is characteristic of one of these sites (Ilkjær 1991:95 ff., 111 ff. & 53 ff.). ● : Site A, with lanceheads of the 'Vennolum type' of the beginning of period C1b, group 5; × : Site B, with lanceheads of the 'Skiaker type' from a later part of period C1b, group 6; ○ : Site C, with lanceheads of the 'Havor type' from period C3/D1, group 11. Circles mark the clusters of objects that all belong to Site A, and the lines between them indicate that the clusters concerned contain connected fragments of objects that had been broken up for deposition. It is quite clear that the widely scattered clusters of Site A must have been deposited at the same time, and their location far from the lake shore must mean that the objects were dropped into the lake from a boat or raft. A broken contour line marks the areas within Sites B and C where linked fragments occur in the same way, without connexions with artefacts in the Site A clusters. The material of both Sites B and C lies densely gathered in a zone near the shore, but more scattered further into the lake. The distribution indicates that the offerings were thrown out into the lake from the shore in both cases.

between the different votive finds, however, run into many problems. Some of the sacrifices (e.g. at Ejsbøl and Illerup site C) saw the material not only broken up, but also burnt, which completely destroyed organic material and often melted silver and bronze artefacts; in other places (e.g. Thorsbjerg and Trinnemose) the bog is so acid that it has destroyed iron objects and thus deprived us of essential comparative material; finally there are obvious problems in that some sites are only partly excavated, or known only through the random discovery of deposited weaponry. In order to distinguish 'war-booty offerings' from other categories of votive offerings and hoards that include weapons or horse harness, it is therefore necessary to define 'war-booty offerings' as containing several categories of weapon-types or

other classes of military gear in contemporary use, with the objectsshowing signs of ritual destruction, and having been thrown or dropped into inaccessible places in lakes or bogs. An assessment of the form and size of such deposits must, when other specific evidence for the find context is lacking, generally be based on an artefact chronology which is primarily derived from type-combinations in weapon graves. Each of these represents a single individual's current weapon-set, while weapon hoards represent a whole army-unit's equipment in which old and new weapons may well have been in use side by side. In the clusters of objects noted at Ejsbøl, where the majority of the material belongs to period C2, there are, for example, also objects that by the grave-find chronology are dated to periods C1b or C3. A cer-

217

tain caution must therefore be exercised with any purely chronologically based assessment of the date and extent of sacrificial deposits on any one site.

Apart from the finds from Hjortspring and, perhaps, Krogsbølle, which are dated to the pre-Roman Iron Age, the Vimose find is the earliest known comprehensive deposit of weaponry (period B2), although material from the Early Roman Iron Age has also been found at Thorsbjerg and in a number of minor, little known bog finds where the character of the deposit cannot be assessed in any detail. In the Late Roman Period (period C1b), the Vimose find shows a further massive deposit of weapons that chronologically seem to belong in between the two earliest, large deposits at Illerup (sites A and B). At the same time there were weapon deposits in, for instance, Trinnemose in North Jutland, Porskær in Skanderborg *amt*, Illemose on north-western Fyn and Søborg lake in north-eastern Sjælland. All of these sites share a location near the coast around the Kattegat and only a couple of minor finds from Lolland and Bornholm and a large deposit in Thorsbjerg mose differ in this respect; the Thorsbjerg find is also distinctive in its brooch-type inventory and Roman or Roman-inspired equipment which is foreign to the Scandinavian range of material that is characteristic of the other votive hoards (Ilkjær & Lønstrup 1982).

The distribution of votive hoards in the following period is quite different, and the range of objects that is dominant in Ejsbøl-North recurs in the material from Thorsbjerg and Nydam, Kragehul mose on south-western Fyn, Hassle-Bösarp in southern Skåne and Skedemosse on Öland. The deposit in Ejsbøl-North must, as noted, have taken place around the transition between periods C2 and C3. Before this, but still with period-C2 material, are other finds from Hassle-Bösarp and Skedemosse and votive hoards from Hedelisker in Randers *amt*, Vingsted lake in Vejle *amt*, Ballerup lake-bog on eastern Sjælland and Balsmyr on Bornholm, while a number of C3 forms in Nydam, including lanceheads, scabbard mounts and brooches, indicate a later addition to the sequence of deposits that is found at this site. The oak boat from Nydam, to which, according to Engelhardt, the Nydam brooches pertain, is now dated dendrochronologically to 310-320 A.D., agreeing well with the time-honoured but still debated archaeological dating of period C3 (Ethelberg 1990:29 ff.; Bonde 1991). Common to all of

these finds of periods C2-C3 is, Hedelisker excepted, a southern and eastern Scandinavian distribution and associations with the Baltic area. Renewed excavations at Nydam have decisively revised our understanding of the later deposits at this stie (periods D1-D2). While the Nydam II find, with its clustered, chip-carved scabbard mounds etc. was hitherto an isolated phenomenon that could be interpreted as a *pars pro toto* offering, just 100 m. east of here there has now been uncovered an extensive weapon deposit (Nydam III), with javelins and lances with interlace ornament on the shafts that at least belong to the same period (D1) as Nydam II (Vang Petersen 1988). About 100 m. further north a very compact and comprehensive, clustered deposit of weaponry (Nydam IV) that is perhaps a bit later has also been found (Bonde *et al.* 1991). The deposit at Ejsbøl-South is dated to period D1, with chip-carved scabbard mounts and buckles matching the 'Nydam Style' of Nydam II, and there were also contemporary deposits at Illerup (sites C-D), at the neighbouring sites of Porskær and Dallerup lake and at Kragehul on south-western Fyn where the interlace-ornamented spear shafts were for a long time a unique and debated phenomenon but which now can be compared with shafts from Nydam III and IV. Similarly late deposits are also known at Hassle-Bösarp in Skåne, Knarremose on Bornholm and Skedemosse on Öland, where the latest items (parts of sword hilts and lanceheads) belong to period D2. Thus the weapon deposits of the Germanic Iron Age are not so clearly associated with a limited geographical area as they once appeared to be, and the distribution map is further complicated by a series of Swedish finds of weaponry and horse harness which are often linked to the great weapon deposits but whose interpretation is very much open to discussion (Hagberg 1967:69 ff.). Finds from Sösdala and Fulltofta in Skåne and probably also Vennebo in Västergötland were deposited on dry land and may represent cemetery sacrifices as in Hunnic-influenced central Europe, while the finds from Sjörup and Tormestorp in Skåne are more likely to be hacksilver hoards, a well-known phenomenon in contemporary Danish finds (Fabech 1991b:284 f.). On the other hand, finds from Grimsöbodarna in Västmanland (periods D1-D2), Finnestorp in Västergötland (period D1), Gudingsåkrarna on Gotland (mainly from the Vendel and Viking Periods) and Dalby on Öland (period D1) can be put

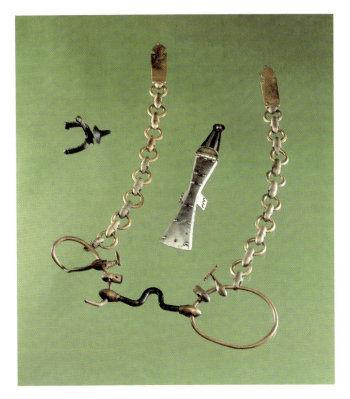 

Finds from Illerup Site A. To the left: horse harness and spur, of iron and silverplated bronze; to the right: shield bosses and mounts of gilt silver. Such richly decorated shields are often severely damaged, and parts of the same shield have been found up to 200 m. apart.

alongside the 'war-booty offerings' in that they all contain comprehensive and deliberately destroyed weaponry that was deposited in a lake or bog.

Regarded as war-booty offerings, the weapon hoards reflect military activies of quite considerable scope, as it has to be borne in mind that the war boo-ty probably only represents some of the equipment of the attacking army and that it is known that at all sites except for Illerup sites B and C and Ejsbøl-North considerable quantities of finds remain in the ground or were removed by others who had been digging there. Both the size of the army-units and the specialized and uniform weaponry presuppose social organization in which a central leadership had authority over considerable areas; the battles then more probably represent deliberate politico-military operations than haphazard raiding. Brøndsted (1960a) saw the concentration of the finds in eastern Jutland and Fyn as a war zone in which for centuries the Danes, penetrating from the east, sought to establish themselves in Jutland. The picture now is more complex. Through half a century (period C1b) one wave of attacks followed another in coastal tracts of the Kattegat, and in the next 100-150 years

(periods C2-C3) there was similar military activity in the lands around the Baltic from Öland to the east coast of Jutland. It is not possible to identify the homelands of the attackers because both attackers and defenders used a uniform, North Germanic weapon set, and we also know very little about how far this equipment may have been in use south of the Baltic where weapon graves are very rare. Certain locally produced items of person property and regionally specific raw materials will certainly prove more relevant to identifying origins. Certain distinc-tive comb-types that come from Illerup site A, Vimose and Nydam and also found in mainland Scandinavia, and arrows of pinewood, combs, chapes and firesteel handles of elk antler point in the same direction - or at least away from Denmark itself - while the pinewood boat that was excavated in 1863 at Nydam was not made of local timber. Bat-tles may nevertheless have been fought between neighbouring areas of whom one sought control over essential resources in the territory of the other - trading sites, routeways, raw materials and so on - and the late war-booty offerings in mainland Sweden most probably represent the same disputes.

Priorsløkke - a suggested interpretation

In 1980-83, the National Museum excavated a village of the Early Roman Iron Age on a promontory that juts out into the Hansted valley close to the innermost branch of Horsens Fjord, Nørrestrand (Vebæk 1980; Kaul 1985, 1989b). The settlement was excavated in full. It covers an area *ca.* 150 m. x 75 and had two main phases. We shall focus only on the second main phase here. 8 farmsteads can be distinguished, each comprising a main building 15-16 m. long, aligned NW-SE, with 6 pairs of roof-bearing posts as a rule and one or two outhouses of which one is usually aligned the other way and has 3 pairs of roof-bearing posts. The settlement seems to have been abandoned late in the Early Roman Iron Age.

The village at Priorsløkke has a special position amongst the villages of the period because it was partly enclosed by a rampart that blocked the only passage from the promontory to the mainland. This comprised a ditch 1.3 m. deep, 3 m. wide at the top and 1.5 m. across its flat bottom. A palisade backed the ditch. At the highest point of the promontory the ditch was interrupted by a gate structure. The rampart was found only in dry areas; as soon the surrounding wetlands were reached it became smaller, with the wetlands eventually taking over its function. The ditch was 121 m. long but the palisade ran on into the wetlands to a total length of 220 m.

In the wettest parts, palisade timber was preserved, mostly to the south-east where sections of posts up to a metre long were recovered. All of the identifiable timbers were re-used building pieces. Buildings were evidently demolished when the palisade was built. It is equally significant that study of the ditch and of several sections

Well-preserved section of the palisade: re-used oak building timbers, just removed. A fork formed as a support for the horizontal roof-beams. This piece is so well preserved that each axe cut is visible.

shows that the settlement itself must have been abandoned just when the rampart was constructed.

With copies of Iron-age tools, and on the basis of the excavation plans and drawings, a reconstruction of part of the Priorsløkke rampart was made at the Historical-Archaeological Experimental Centre at Lejre. The work was closely analysed so that information could be gained on the use of resources, time and manpower, and on the most appropriate methods. Since building timbers were used in the palisade a knowledge of the construction and size of Iron-age buildings could be used to infer its height.

Analysis shows that the Priorsløkke rampart could be built in about a week by a gang of some 40 men in four teams. Labour to demolish the buildings needs to be added to this. The amount of timber included in the palisade and its gate-structure was calculated. Since these were re-used building timbers, the amount of timber available for this project from the second phase of the village was also calculated (roof-bearing posts, roof-beams etc.). This produced the surprising discovery that the quantity of wood in the rampart matched the quantity available in the village's buildings closely. In other words the whole village was demolished in order to build the rampart!

If we do not simply reject this extraordinary coincidence as sheer chance, these calculations provide information of great culture-historical significance. We can immediately conclude that the demolition of the village and the raising of the rampart reflected needs that were far greater than the village's alone. We must further conclude that the village was part of a larger, tribal territory, and that a strong chieftain could peremptorily order it to be demolished and put to defensive use. Through this information about the fate of Priorsløkke we gain a view of the power that the local chieftains could exercise, at least in a crisis. The existence of large territories or defensive confederacies in the relevant period in the Iron Age is underlined by large structures such as the stake-built sea-barriers and ramparts and the bog-deposits of military gear, the distribution of which points to tribal areas or petty kingdoms extending for about 40 km. from north to south.

When we consider the location, there can be no doubt that there were sound strategic reasons for raising the rampart at this site. From here one coud control both the north-south traffic across the Hansted valley and access to that valley. If an enemy wished to penetrate the land behind the present Horsens-Skanderborg area an armed local force based at Priorsløkke could be a major hindrance. An army could come from inland, but an attack from the sea was also possible. The rampart seems to have been designed to withstand a mounted attack, and we know, from the great weapon deposits, that cavalry was used. The location of the rampart at the inner end of Horsens Fjord and the total destruction of a village shows that it was not scattered and haphazard coastal raids that were expected.

If we risk the conclusion that the demolition of Priorsløkke and its transformation into a strategically situated stronghold show a response to a truly hostile attack we could sketch a scenario for the last days of Priorsløkke.

"An enemy fleet is sighted from the east coast around Gylling, and news of the imminent danger is quickly sent to the local leader and his men. A swift decision is taken to demolish the village at Priorsløkke, this being the site an enemy army with ships and cavalry would have to take. As the building commences the first battle is fought a good 20 km. further east, where some of the enemy had landed and were taking horses. The battles may have taken place around the (undated) fortification called Ulvedige, near Gylling. Demolition work is well under way within a couple of days, with the ditch being dug while the palisade is raised. Fighting men are drafted in from surrounding villages to help with the work. While the buildings are being demolished, and the inhabitants' homes thus destroyed, women and children move to securer villages further inland. The enemy ships are now slowly coming up the fjord, supported by men mounted on stolen horses; but the ships are held up by one or two sea-barriers, one near Sundet in Horsens (undated). This delay provides the time needed to get the stronghold battle-ready. After one week, it is a small but strong enclosure surrounded by wetlands."

How the battle went, archaeological evidence cannot tell; the only military find from Priorsløkke is a iron spearhead socket found in the palisade ditch.

With a radical interpretation of the context of the end of the Priorsløkke village like this, the idea of associating the site with the battle that is reflected by the great weapon deposit at Illerup is unavoidable. The very strategic situation of Priorsløkke, together with the fact that it is the coastal site with the nearest access to the Illerup valley whether one assumes a route along the recorded medieval track or a route up through the Hansted valley, force one to assess the possibility. We must, however, point out that there are problems in chronological assocation with Illerup, although perhaps another bog deposit in the area, i.e. the Porsmose find, could be considered, as the minor weapon offering here seems to be a little earlier that the main deposit at Illerup. The dendrochronological datings of the re-used building timbers found in the palisade trench are for this and other reasons awaited with great interest.

Jens Henrik Jønsson & Flemming Kaul

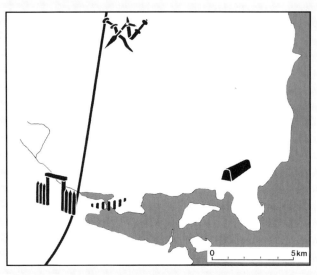

Map showing the situation of Priorsløkke and other sites and features referred to. Priorsløkke itself is marked as a palisaded stronghold, the Ulvedige ditch and bank furthest to the east, and a stake-barrier marked at the narrow passage at the end of Horsens Fjord, Sundet. The weapon deposit at Illerup, the medieval trackway and Hansted river are also shown. Priorsløkke lies at the narrowest part of the Hansted valley where several known routes of the Middle Ages and earlier cross. Since neither the barrier at Sundet nor Ulvediget have been archaeologically investigated and therefore cannot be dated, they are included in the scenario by hypothesis.

In 1988, 30 m. of the 2.3 m.-high palisade were reconstructed at the Historical-Archaeological Experimental Centre, Lejre. Along the inner side of the palisade the fill dug from the ditch forms a ramp from which the defenders of the stronghold could take up a position of advantage over the attackers.

221

From the excavations in Nydam bog in 1991. Some of the "Nydam IV" complex. The objects lay densely packed, surrounded by more than 25 swords driven down into the bog. As well as a large number of wooden objects, shields, shafts etc., a wooden scabbard with gilded mouthpiece can be seen and a sword-bead of rock crystal (upper right). Below these are lanceheads with angled or very rounded transitions to the socket, javelin heads with long, parallel barbs and shield bosses with angled collars and extended points. Altogether these are objects that testify to a votive deposit that was made at the end of the 5th or early 6th century (Period D2). A few earlier objects were found in the same area, which is only 20-25 m. from where, between 1859 and 1863, Engel-hardt excavated a vast range of military gear of the Late Roman Iron Age (Period C2-C3) and the Nydam boat that is dendro-dated to 310-320 A.D.

The war-booty offerings directly represent the attacking and defeated army, but they provide just as much information about the victorious society that was able to raise, train and equip armies of at least comparable size. As a social phenomenon, the votive deposits that followed the same rituals on the same time-honoured sites for generations served to affirm the military duties of the populations in ever larger tribal entities and their common dependency on a chieftain and the warrior elite that surrounded him. That these votive practices are generally abandoned in the course of the 5th century is no indication of more peaceful circumstances but rather that the elite in the relevant communities was now so well established that such esoteric ritual demonstrations were no longer needed (Fabech 1991b:287).

Research of the last 25 years has increased our knowledge of the great weapon deposits of the Iron Age and of the changing Iron-age societies that the finds reflect in many ways. This set of finds has attracted renewed attention as a large and comprehensive source for Iron Age history, and provides an opportunity for a concluding remark about certain basic work that future research on the votive hoards should not overlook in its eagerness to extort new interpretations from the finds.

It was the large, systematic excavations in Illerup, Ejsbøl and Nydam that made a re-assessment of this set of finds possible, and the continued analysis and publication of the finds from these sites will still be a key to any understanding of deposits on other sites. But it has to be recognized at the same time that we want just as badly publications of the extensive finds from Engelhardt's excavations in Vimose, Nydam and Kragehul that Engelhardt himself only described and illustrated selectively and quite sparingly, and that we want similar publications of a number of further finds that have only occasionally come into our museums: for instance the considerable quantities of finds from Vingsted lake in Vejle *amt* and Finnestorp in Västergötland. Klaus Raddatz's thorough cataloguing of the Thorsbjerg find (Raddatz 1987a,b), which includes such information as can be obtained from Engelhardt's diaries and find register, may serve as a model. A wider classification and assessment of the finds would also, obviously, be desirable, and analyses of materials and production techniques used will certainly also prove to be just as important as the artefacts themselves.

Most of the weapon finds that we are concerned with are still very fragmentarily documented, as the finds have emerged through chance digging work, often at intervals of many years. We know, however, that many of the sites may still contain intact layers of finds and it is therefore quite crucial to undertake soundings and detector surveys that could inform us about the state of preservation and the scope for finding material. On the basis of such knowledge certain sites could become the objects of supplementary excavations where the research situation seems to render this necessary, while others could be secured for future research by protection and precautionary measures. Future generations will no doubt find the excavations in Illerup, Ejsbøl and Nydam rather primitive.

Detector finds

BY KAREN HØILUND NIELSEN AND PETER VANG PETERSEN

"It's the work of the Devil's." This was Skalk's judgement upon the metal detector in 1983. These sharp words came after the finding that year of bronze axes and gold rings by using a detector along the edge of a forest track at Skeldal near Tjele Langsø.

Delight in a rare, 4,000-year-old metal hoard, which had been spared from destruction by forestry machines, could not dispel the fear of the growing popularity of detectors that gripped museum staff for most of the 1980's. Reports of the vandalism of treasure hunters came in from abroad; things were especially bad in England and on Gotland, and alarm bells rang. The 'English disease' of grave robbing and nocturnal looting of archaeological excavations has, happily, not happened here, and unlike in Sweden, which since 1991 has had a total ban on searching for archaeological finds with metal detectors, this new method of locating finds has in Denmark been allowed to develop into a significant factor in antiquarian study.

This positive development is due, amongst other things, to the Danish law of 'danefæ', which for centuries has stipulated that ancient finds of valuable materials or especial rarity must be handed over to the state (the National Museum). This law does not forbid citizens the pleasure of collecting objects (except at designated monuments and other specially protected sites), but certain types of find - all metal objects, for instance - are danefæ, and must go, for an appropriate reward, to the National Museum.

The use of detectors in archaeology was first experienced in the late 1950's. This originally military equipment has since been developed specifically for archaeological use, and metal detectors are now standard equipment on most excavations. They reveal artefacts still lying in the soil, and help the excavator select an appropriate method of further digging by machine, spade or trowel.

Detectors have played their most important part in the hands of amateur archaeologists who use them in field surveys. Many rare or quite unknown artefact-types have emerged, and the collections of several important jewellery-types have increased severalfold in just 15 years.

The growth in finds

The use of detectors has caused a veritable population explosion of metal finds. In relative terms, growth has been smallest in respect of the pre-Roman Iron Age, and increases through the Roman and Early Germanic Period. The greatest expansion has affected the Late Germanic Period, and since this period was previously the poorest in finds (except on Bornholm), the new finds have made a significant change to the situation visible in the mid-1960's (Ørsnes 1966).

Sites

Gradually, over the whole country but with marked clusters in south-western Sjælland, south-eastern Fyn, North Jutland and on Bornholm, many 'detector sites' have become known. Most sites appear to have been settlements, and detector finds from these sites come mostly from the period from beginning of the Late Iron Age down into the Middle Ages.

At Neble near Boeslunde, many metal objects of the Late Germanic Iron Age and Viking Period have been found, and everything suggests that there was a large and important settlement here (Bendixen et al. 1990). Slightly more humble in character are the finds from Sønderø/Veddelev north of Roskilde, where a small trial dig revealed, inter alia, a sunken hut. The site probably functioned as a landing place throughout the Late Iron Age far down into the Middle Ages (V. Jensen & Ulriksen 1989).

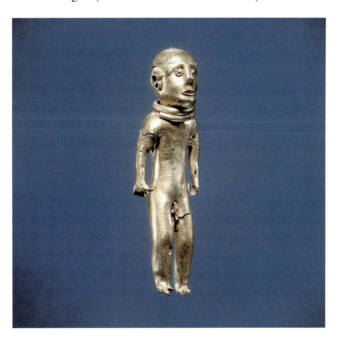

Germanic-period gold hoard at Slipshavn near Nyborg in 1981 was the starting signal for the detector-users' very profitable search for treasure in south-eastern Fyn.

Rich finds of, for instance, silver coins, weights and silver bars have come from Kalmargården in western Sjælland near where the Halleby river flows from Tissø. Besides the heaviest gold ring in Denmark, imported goods such as weights and enamelled mounts of Irish origin show that Kalmargården was a centre of power and trade of more than local importance.

On south-eastern Fyn, detector-users' interest has been focussed on two areas in particular, Gudme and Lundeborg (Kromann *et al.* 1991). The detector finds from Gudme are the richest in Denmark, and the excavations undertaken show that there was a rich settlement in this area including a large number of farmsteads of the Late Roman and Early Germanic Periods. The finds from Lundeborg, the Gudme settlement's collection place, which besides remains of a wide range of crafts has traces of small huts, are of the same period.

North Jutland too contains a number of detector sites of significant size. Most important north of the Limfjord are Lindholm Høje and Stentinget. On the southern side the main sites are Bejsebakken, Sofiendal, Postgården and Humlebakken south of

Using military bomb detection equipment, a new weapon deposit was found in Nydam bog (Nydam III) in 1984. Excavation was essential, during which iron weapons near the surface were recorded with a normal metal detector and marked with paper plates.

Ålborg. Amongst the most recently found sites is Sebbersund, halfway between Ålborg and Aggersund (Birkedahl Christensen & Johansen 1992).

Only Kumlhøj near Albøge on Djursland will be noted of Jutland's remaining detector sites. Finds of partially melted bronzework in the area around a large ploughed-out barrow suggested that there was a cemetery here. This suspicion was fully confirmed by subsequent excavations. A large number of sites on Bornholm too are being intensely surveyed in this way (Watt 1991).

Interpretation and dating of the sites

Detector finds nearly always emerge as stray finds, without secure associations with other artefacts or features. On many sites, metal objects appear only in

This silver hoard, with spiral clasps, bars, ring fragments and cut-up embossed Roman silverware, was found by detector-users Flemming Lyth and Johnny Kragekjær Hansen at Stenhøjgård, Gudme, in 1984. The silver, 1.282 kg. in all, was buried on the edge of a settlement of the Late Roman and Early Germanic Iron Age. Excavation on the site also produced melting crucibles and metal detritus from gold- and silverworking. The silver was probably brought to Gudme as scrap metal for remelting and re-use as jewellery or mounts.

Detectors have made it possible to find small objects such as, for instance, the bronze dies that Germanic-period goldsmiths used to press gold-foil ornaments. Chequered gold foil, used as a light-reflecting underlay to garnets, was produced on two positive dies from Gudme and Neble. We also have a few such dies for pressing square pendants from these sites. The negative die for gold D-bracteates is from Postgården near Ålborg, and half such a die for 'guldgubber' has been found at Neble, south-western Sjælland. The intact die from Møllegård on Bornholm was used to press some of the 2,000 guldgubber that have been found at Sorte Muld.

circumstances that indicate they come from ancient sites that are being destroyed. Some sites represent ploughed-out burials but on most sites we also find fire-crazed stones, charcoal, daub, sherds etc. indicating a normal settlement. Excavations at, for instance, Gudme show that the metal objects come predominantly from settlement layers, preserved in hollows, on slopes and as the fill of post holes or pits. It is rarely possible to say whether the jewellery, tools, weapons and mounts found were originally lost, stored or buried as hoards or sacrifices.

Chronologically, the distribution of the detector finds sees only a small number from the pre-Roman Iron Age and a steadily increasing number from the Early Roman Iron Age through to the Viking Period. The strength of continuity through the Late Germanic Iron Age and the Viking Period is especially striking. Most sites continue on into the Early Middle Ages. For the present, one must reckon that the distribution of detector finds gives a picture, as yet incomplete, of the better-off settlements of Denmark. Detector sites are an important new archaeological source, not only in terms of settlement history but in illuminating many other aspects of Iron-age society.

Craft

Data about crafts in the Late Iron Age are scattered, but in combination with other sources the detector finds add a lot to our knowledge. Regular worksites of the Late Roman and Early Germanic Iron Age

are found at Lundeborg, and we know of a number of sites from the beginning of the 8th century, for instance at Ribe. In the intervening period, however, finds are few, coming first and foremost from detector sites. Late Iron-age jewellery-making saw the use of pressed foils, with ornaments embossed in thin metal foils from positive or negative dies. These small stamps were previously unknown, but now we have, for example, a negative die for D-bracteates from Postgården; and since D-bracteates are concentrated most densely in Jutland it is very encouraging to be able to link their production with the area. Positive dies have been found at Gudme and Neble. One such from Neble, for making "guldgubber", deserves special notice. Such a die has also been found at Møllegård on Bornholm. This was used to make some of the guldgubber found at Sorte Muld, 20 km. away.

Trade

Roman silver (denarii) and gold coins (solidi) are found across Iron-age sites in the whole country. They are particularly numerous in south-eastern Fyn and on Bornholm. The Bornholm hoards show that fine 1st- and 2nd-century denarii circulated outside the Empire as precious metal far into the 5th and 6th centuries (Kromann & Watt 1984).

'Kufic' Arab silver coins are found singly at many Viking-period sites, and two small hoards have been found at Gjerrild on Djursland and Neble (Bendixen

Detector finds have turned the relationship between gold and silver finds upside down. Shining gold has always held popular attention, while oxidised silver is easily overlooked. At Gudme I, 7 gold coins (solidi) and 2 silver ones (denarii) were found in the period 1885-1978. When the detector-users got going in 1978 the finds of Roman coins were futher increased.

et al. 1990). Like the Roman coins, the Arab silver coins are characteristically of high-purity metal. Such coins were probably used by weight.

Weights and balances have been found on many sites, focusing the problem of the organization of trade. Weights found singly have little to tell us, but finds of several weights on one site indicate that the site played some role in the system of trade.

Small discoid lead and bronze weights appear in Denmark in the Early Germanic Iron Age. Weights are the category of objects that has grown most as a result of detector finds. They were lost on sites where trading was done or where traders frequented. Many weights and fragments of weights are found at centres of wealth such as Gudme, Neble and Stentinget, but extremely few such objects appear amongst the extensive Bejsebakken finds.

In considering the character of the sites, topographical location is naturally of great importance,

not least with coastal detector finds. On the shore of the Roskilde fjord, rich finds have been made at Sønderø and Jyllinge Helligkorskilde. Sebbersund on the Limfjord has a similar coastal location, and has also produced many finds of weights, balances and payment metal. Like Lundeborg, such coastal sites should be regarded as trading and collection points that traders visited.

Hoards

A detailed map of metal finds makes it possible to identify ploughed-up hoards, and in many cases surface finds have put archaeologists on the track of hoards that had not been entirely scattered by the plough. Up to 1991, 23 Iron-age hoards had been located by detectors in Denmark. These are often hoards of coins and small fragments of bars and jewellery. Many hoards had previously been found through ploughing, and further investigations of old find spots have in several cases enabled us to find more pieces of precious metal that had been overlooked when the hoard was discovered.

The recent excavations at Gudme, Neble and on Bornholm show that hoards on dry land were often buried at contemporary settlements, under house

Garnet jewellery of foreign origin found with detectors at Gudme: a silver Frankish bird brooch from Stenhøjgård, the backplate of a gold buckle from Gudmeløkken and a gilt bronze Rhineland brooch from Gudme II.

226

A small silver hoard: a scutiform bronze pendant and silver and glass beads on a linen string, deposited between two small silver dishes. A Viking woman hid her jewellery away, and for a thousand years it remained hidden and forgotten at Kalmergården near Tissø. Autumn ploughing in 1988 disturbed the hoard, and by good fortune the National Museum's detector survey discovered it before spring harrowing scattered the objects.

floors for instance. The motives for this are unknown. When valuables are deposited in bogs or watercourses, the motives were probably religious. Hoards buried in settlements may also be votive offerings, but here the hidden valuables were still so easily accessible that their deposition can be thought of a form of safe-deposit.

Aristocratic contacts

Imports and other material show that throughout the Iron Age there were social and trading connexions between the populations of southern Scandinavia and the rest of Europe. At Gudme, for example, several items of foreign origin have been found. These include a gilt silver bird brooch, a gold kidney-shaped buckle plate and a gilt bronze oval brooch, all decorated with cut garnets. The bird brooch and the oval brooch are Frankish, and date to the Early Merowingian Period (6th century). The buckle is interesing because very close parallels are known from European princely graves, for instance from the Frankish King Childeric I's grave at Tournai, now Belgium. Several of these graves have a Byzantine element combined with unmistakably Frankish items, and although the Danish buckle was made in Byzantium or somewhere close by it could certainly have come to Fyn via Francia.

The gold buckle and the bird brooch indicate contacts with Francia at a high level, perhaps even royal. It is quite natural to think so, as Fyn indeed seems to have been one of the central places in southern Scandinavia in the Early Germanic Iron Age and the beginning of the Late Germanic Iron Age. It would be natural for the central leadership to have had contacts with royal circles in other lands, including Francia. Gudme, however, is not unique in its foreign imports. At Stentinget in Vendsyssel, the richest site in North Jutland, a fragment of a 6th-century Langobard brooch has been found. Contacts with Langobard areas are also revealed by the Scandinavian gold bracteates that are found there.

Conclusion

The massive harvest of detector finds from certain sites lets one suppose that there was once intensive settlement there. Since in the pre-detector age we really didn't know any settlements from a period such as the Late Germanic Iron Age, the detector finds can be said to have brought this period out of obscurity. Finds from these new sites reveal previously unrealised aspects of the quality of top range art and craft of the period and its extensive trade.

With the detector finds, the comparable artefact material from the Late Iron Age has grown in an invaluable way, and it is now possible to undertake regional studies of the material remains of the period with real confidence. At the moment, the picture promotes Fyn as a central area through much of the Roman and Germanic Iron Age. Variation in the material is especially great here, running from simple brooches to exceptional hoards with regal gold objects. The Gudme settlement remains for centuries as a dynamic community with contacts at the highest level, for instance with Francia. The many hoards from Gudme include valuables and items of princely character, and several scholars have expressed the view that these finds reflect an early kingship centred upon south-eastern Fyn.

Land transport

BY MOGENS SCHOU JØRGENSEN

The physical remains of prehistoric land transport - wagons and roads - can rarely be closely dated by archaeological means. The scope for wider research was, consequently, decisively changed by the advent of C 14 dating. Before this, from the 1940's, careful and methodical excavations of roads and their surroundings had been undertaken (Kunwald 1964), but the usefulness of the results was limited by the absence of dates and, as a result of the lack of scientific interest, analyses. C 14 dating allowed material from old excavations to be analysed, and led to re-excavations and larger, problem-oriented digs. Roads gradually obtained higher priority in general excavation work, as there was a chance of concrete dating rather than just labelling something as a 'probable prehistoric track', which further increased the number of finds. C 14 dating was also the basis on which a number of finds of wheels and carts

The Viking-period bridge at Ravning Enge. The felling date of the timber, 979 ± 1, was a surprising dating of a structure that had been known for several years. At 700 m. long, with more than 1,000 supporting posts, a road area of at least 3,500 sq.m., great precision and close contemporaneity with the Trelleborg forts, this bridge was probably designed for the same general purpose as the forts. This is probably also the case for a series of smaller and simpler bridges of the same period. Here, white plates of the size of the posts mark identified sections of the bridge for part of its course, both a well-preserved section close by the Vejle river and a number of surviving posts of fish dams, the construction of which in the 1950's brought the bridge to light.

could be put in the right chronological slots. More than half of both the 37 definite finds of prehistoric carts and the 69 sites with in total a few hundred prehistoric roads depend upon C 14 dating. It is just as important that many 'probable' prehistoric tracks and finds have in fact turned out to date from the Middle Ages or later.

The earliest examples of the working carts of the Iron Age are represented by disc wheels and forked chassis in the Rappendam find (Kunwald 1970), a development of the simple vehicles of the Stone and Bronze Ages (Rostholm 1978). In the Roman Iron Age, a new four-wheeled wagon with spoked wheels appears. This is based on foreign models, but it is adapted to local tradition with a so-called wet technology that exploits the natural changes in timber from felling to finished state (Schovsbo 1987). Unlike day-to-day vehicles, the metal-trimmed wagons of the Early Iron Age, a group with the well-pre-

served Dejbjerg wagons at its centre, derived from the ceremonial carts of the Bronze Age, and have recently been added to by finds of wagon mounts from Dankirke (Jarl Hansen 1985) and Fredbjerg (S. Jensen 1981).

Iron-age roadbuilding sees continuation of earlier traditions, with technical differences being primarily determined by practicalities and varying according to the suitability of the ground surface. Roadbuilding is a solution to the problem of providing passage for wagons over soft ground. Individual structures do not reflect optimal answers rather than appropriate responses to practical problems.

Iron-age roadbuilding - in this context no heed is paid to the Roman road system - has been the object of studies in Europe since the early 1800's, concentrating on areas with a level of research encouraged by work in bogs: north-western Germany, Holland, southern England and Ireland. In recent decades there has been intensive excavation in all of thes areas, targeted on various problems determined by practical considerations: e.g. timber technology, the local and broader topography of the structures, chronological cluster-ing, the natural environment, transport and vehicles, exploitation of the landscape and settlement (B. & J. Coles 1989 and refs.). A special perspective with a long tradition comes from Swedish studies of Viking-period transport based on runestones and bridge inscriptions, while a series of bridle paths in Central Norway gives a picture of road-organization at the beginning of the Middle Ages (Smedstad 1988).

There are also various problems concerning Danish land transport that have been answered by

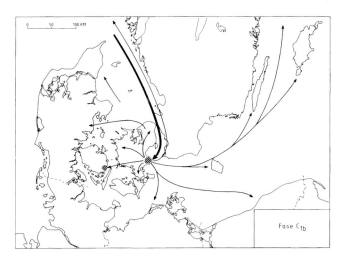

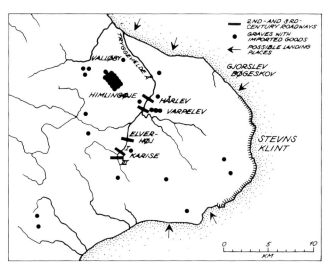

The main lines of road development from the Neolithic onwards can be traced across the Stevns and Tryggevælde valleys in eastern Sjælland. Here, existing causeways were changed from simple brush and branch crossings to stone-paved roads in the 2nd-3rd centuries at Varpelev, Karise (III) and Elverhøj, and stone roads were built at Hårlev and Karise (I). Roadbuilding can be seen in connexion with the centres of Roman imports, which appear at the same time in the area with centres at Himlingøje, Varpelev and Valløby. It is still unclear whether the roadbuilding was primarily due to the development of the settlement structure or the trading route that the imports reveal and which culminates in phase C1b (at the top of the map) - precisely the date of the roadbuilding, if all of them were built within a short period. The collection or trading sites presumably associated with these centres have not been located. Topographic circumstances provide several possibilities; certain indications point towards the mouth of the Tryggevælde river or Gjorslev Bøgeskov.

229

research. Dating of finds has revealed the main traits of Iron-age wagons (Schovsbo 1987) and roads (Schou Jørgensen 1988a). New finds, mostly retrieved in rescue excavations, have thrown particular light on eastern Sjælland in the Roman Iron Age (V. Hansen & Nielsen 1979) and on Viking-period bridge-building (Ramskou 1980, 1981; Schou Jørgensen 1988a), both of which are factors in many other areas of research. Natural-scientific perspectives have similarly opened up a new view of the landscape in which people travelled - both around the routes themselves (Schou Jørgensen 1988b; J.T. Møller 1988) and in the terrain where the roads ran as wheel-ruts (Dalsgaard 1985; J.T. Møller 1986).

Topographical circumstances are crucial to an understanding of prehistoric communication and seem to explain some of the peculiarities of Danish transport in relation to other European evidence. In extensive bog areas such as Holland/north-western Germany, with roads running for kilometres, parallel developments can be seen in road and wagon technology (Hayen 1989). This, however, is not the case with the Danish material, where transport on artificial causeways was a minor feature of the picture. Stone-paved roads are a Scandinavian and especially Danish phenomenon in prehistory. The substantial presence of these in the Early Iron Age may reflect a lack of timber and relatively easy access to stone and transportation of stone in the ever more open landscape where increased and more solid construction was demanded by radical changes in agriculture and settlements.

The necessity of transport for all sections of the community makes roadworks a multifaceted form of evidence. A basic requirement of all new finds is, therefore, the close determination of the dates of construction and use. The transition and extensions to causeways will be able to reflect local and regional developments, and attention should be paid to the denser chronological phases to produce greater and surer evidence. A general European problem is the precise courses and character of routes on dry land. In both the local and the general view, crossing points associated with navigable waterways and harbours are, therefore, important to an understanding of the obscure connexions between land and water transport, the system in which trading sites like Lundeborg and Ribe are important nuclei (Näsman 1990; Ulriksen 1990; S. Jensen 1991a; P.O. Thomsen 1991b). Also of importance in the study of land

Three elements of land transport: road, wheel and sledge. The cartwheel was broken and re-used in the foundation layer under the road that replaced a bridge across Risby valley around the year 1000 in southern Sjælland. On the sledge, the plank deck of which has been removed here, a boulder had been dragged out into a still boggy former watercourse to form the foundation for a plank-built path that constituted the road built in the softest area while the route over the rest of the valley was paved in stone.

transport are the extended banks that controlled communications routes - a problematic group of features here as elsewhere (Schou Jørgensen 1988a).

Since causeways were self-evidently built in wet areas, great quantities of organic material are often preserved. The circumstances of preservation are an important factor here (Schou Jørgensen 1990): drainage and changes in watercourses, even at a minor level, often mean rapid decay. Recent decades have produced much that is new concerning prehistoric transport, but we should ensure that new evidence will continue to be available from the data banks that the roads constitute, for instance on the topics of timber resources and technology, and the prehistoric landscape.

Boats and ships

By Flemming Rieck

Research into finds of boats and ships of the Danish Iron Age and Viking Period of the last 25 years are based to a very small degree on newly excavated material. The most important new observations have come from the re-analysis of 'old' finds, with decisive contributions from the natural sciences.

In the National Museum, the permanent prehistoric exhibition was enriched in November 1988 with the reconstructed Hjortspring boat. Behind this welcome re-appearance lay difficult re-conservation, reconstruction and analytical work, which despite the poor state of preservation of the boat timbers shed new light on this very important find (J. Jensen *et al.* 1989).

In the process of restoring the boat, a number of new observations were made, the most important of which will be noted here. Little, however, can be added concerning the basic constructional principles of the boat, which were described by the Norwegian naval architect Fr. Johannesen in G. Rosenberg's initial publication (Rosenberg 1937).

A more detailed picture of the vessel can nevertheless be given. Amongst other things, the conservators managed to find parts of the bottom plank of the boat that had not been recognized before. The bottom plank had a smoothly rounded cross-section and was a little thicker than the side planks.

During the work, parts of a rectangular cross beam that had supported the quarterdeck in the stern of the boat were also discovered. It is similarly suggested in the reconstruction that two pieces of wood with dog's-tooth ornament, which Johannesen could not place in the reconstruction first proposed, belong on the front and back edges of the quarterdeck respectively. The quarterdeck plates themselves are placed higher in the new version (Rieck & Crumlin-Pedersen 1988).

As we know, no metal was used in the shell of the Hjortspring boat. It was all sewn, lashed or pegged together. The joints were subsequently caulked with animal fat, not with resin as suggested in the original publication. New analyses also show that the boat may have been treated with linseed oil or something similar in order to protect the vulnerable limewood from dessication even in antiquity.

In the late summer of 1987, through a minor excavation in the sacrificial bog on Als, sufficient pieces of wood were found for C 14 dating to be carried out on fresh, unpolluted wood. The results show that the boat and the other finds must have been deposited in the period 350-300 B.C. There is, in other words, nearly half a millennium between the Hjortspring finds and the many bog finds of similar character of the Late Roman and Germanic Iron Ages.

In 1989, the National Museum began excavating in Nydam bog with the diverse aims of mapping the extent and character of the votive finds, of studying the Iron-age lake and the history of the surrounding cultural landscape, and of excavating supplementary boat timber. At the same time, new analyses of the boat timber excavated in 1863 were carried out.

At present, the large oak boat that is exhibited in Schloss Gottorf, Schleswig, has been dendrochronologically dated (Bonde 1991) to *ca.* 310-320 A.D. It has also been established that the boat must have been built in the area which the Danish standard curve for oak covers: Schleswig-Holstein, Denmark or Skåne.

At the same time as dendrochronological samples were taken from the oak boat, it was recognized that all strakes in the boat were made up of two lengths of wood (Bonde 1991). This disproves a persistent belief that the Nydam boat was constructed of unbroken planks more than 20 m. long (Engelhardt 1865; Rieck & Crumlin-Pedersen 1988). Analysis of this boat will continue in future years.

Investigations in the bog itself have so far led to the finding of several pieces of planking from the so-called 'broken oak boat' of which Engelhardt had found parts in 1863. In 1991, a plank more than 7 m. long from this boat was recovered (Rieck 1992). Closer analyses and a dating of the planking are currently awaiting the completion of conservation.

As yet, it has not proved possible to find any excavation drawings from Engelhardt's excavations of 1859, 1862 and 1863. As a result, a network of trial trenches are now being laid out in the area of the bog where it is thought that both the large oak boat and the pine boat that were found in 1863 (Engelhardt 1865) must have lain. When Engelhardt's sites have been defined, the plan is to re-excavate them, both to reveal the sequence of layers in the area and to find supplementary, 'fresh' boat timber by extending the areas a little; the stem of the pine boat, for instance, has never been found.

The boat timber that is excavated at Nydam is crucial to an understanding of the construction of the large rowing ships and their place in the sequence that leads to the clinker-built, sailing ships of Scandinavian tradition that are found in the Viking Period and the Middle Ages.

The very term 'the Scandinavian ship-building

The large oak boat in the Nydam hall, Schloß Gottorf, Schleswig.

tradition' has been discussed and illuminated through the analysis and publication of the boat graves from Slusegård on southern Bornholm (Crumlin-Pedersen 1991b). These produced evidence of the use of expanded log boats as coffins in the 2nd and 3rd centuries A.D.

Expanded log boats are more flexible and have more sweeping lines than simple dug outs. After the thin 'shell' is expanded, it is necessary to add ribs to the boat in order to maintain the shape and to counteract the pressure of the water on the shell. It is a short step from here to increasing the height of the sides with planks, a technique that is found on Finnish *espinger,* which follow this concept exactly (Nikkilä 1947). Thus the development of log boat to clinker boat begins.

There are a few new finds that advance the picture of Iron-age vessels. At Kongsgårde on Djursland a

Stone with incised ship found at Karlby Klint, Djursland, in 1987. An animal is incised on the back. The stone measures 22 mm. across.

large oak rib of the Nydam type from *ca.* 600 A.D. has been found; at Hjemsted Banke, southern Jutland, part of a boat plank of pine, provisionally dated to the 3rd or 4th century; and from the mouth of Mariager Fjord at Alsodde a 4.3 m. long oak oar has been retrieved, thought to be a steering oar used in the bows of a rowing ship as seen on several Gotlandic picture stones (Rieck & Crumlin-Pedersen 1988).

The boats from Skuldelev are discussed in detail below (Crumlin-Pedersen) and no new Viking-period ship finds have been made. Work is, however, under way again on the burial ship from Ladby on Fyn (K. Thorvildsen 1957). Since excavation in 1935, the impression of the ship has suffered from adverse climatic conditions, and in the future a more stable and controlled environment must be created for this important and informative find. An analytical study of the impression and the iron rivets stands high on the list of priorities of the Institute of Maritime Archaeology.

Although we have several important ship finds from Danish territory there are still gaps in the evidence. We do not know for certain when the transition from rowing ships to sailing vessels took place. Was it ships of the Nydam type that were provided with sails? A small sketch of ship inscribed on stone, found at Karlby Klint on Djursland, hints at this, but as a loose find the stone can only, unfortunately, be dated on the basis of ship typology. The form of the ship depicted, with raking stems, is more reminiscent of Nydam than of the steep-prowed Viking-period ships (Rieck 1992).

From Paganism to Christianity

By Knud J. Krogh and Olaf Olsen

The writer Martin A. Hansen once described the introduction of Christianity to Denmark as "an amazingly silent event". Any archaeologist who studies this event, which in the longer term was to affect, really to transform Danish society utterly, may be inclined to agree with Hansen. We find the new religion everywhere, but emerging from a long-term and apparently undramatic process. Of the point of conversion there are virtually no visible traces in Denmark other than the Jelling complex with its church squeezed in between two royal barrows and a large runestone with its monumental Christ and short runic inscription that declares the conversion of the Danes to be King Harold's work. It took place around 960 A.D.

The inconspicuousness of the change of religion is explicable, however. Norse paganism had, for all we can see, few monumental structures which the Church Triumphant would need to trouble to destroy or to convert to its own use. As far as we know, the old faith had no separate cult houses in the villages or at the main farmsteads. The notion of the 'temple' as a sort of pagan church was disproved by the many excavations of churches in the 1950's and 60's which showed no trace of Christian re-use of pagan ritual sites (O. Olsen 1966), a conclusion that has been corroborated by the evidence from Viking-period villages in the last 25 years. Not one of the many villages and farmsteads that have now been excavated has produced traces of buildings that bear evidence of use in pagan cults. The farmsteads do however generally have large dwelling houses, and there are impressive halls of the type that was first found in the excavation of the Viking-period fort at Trelleborg in the larger farmsteads. It is conceivable that, besides their daily functions, feasts of a ritual character were held here.

In the latest of the excavated Viking-period villages, Omgård in north-western Jutland, there are post-holes from an elongated building, 7 to 12 m. long with narrower outbuildings to the east. They are interpreted as churches by the excavator (L.C. Nielsen 1991), but the evidence is weak, and there are no associated burials. More interesting is the discovery that the Romanesque church at Lisbjerg near Århus lies within an enclosure that also surrounds a large Viking-period farmstead (J. Jeppesen & Madsen 1991). Together with the discovery of major farmsteads of the Early Middle Ages on sites that abut other churchyards, this strengthens the view that the first churches were mostly built by major landowners, the class that in pagan times can be supposed to have been responsible for communal religion in villages and settlements.

Excavations since the 1950's have shown that there are traces of one or more wooden churches that had stood on the same site below a large proportion of our Romanesque churches, or at least of Christian graves pre-dating the stone church. The only question is how early these wooden churches are. When excavation of wooden churches began, those involved cherished an optimistic belief that it would be possible to date at least some of the churches very closely (E. Møller & Olsen 1961), and it was expected that future years would see a large number of new finds of wooden churches so that the body of material on which to base datings would be large. In the latter respect, we were wrong. Excavations declined dramatically both in number and scope, paradoxically because the National Museum succeeded in restraining the violent assaults on church floors that were in fashion in church restoration in the 1950's. With most more recent church excavations, the archaeologist has therefore to content himself with noting that there are traces of earlier churches on the site. Total excavation is now exceptional, and finds that support close datings are rare.

An absolutely or very nearly absolutely accurate dating can be obtained when we have preserved timber from a wooden church that can be dated dendrochronologically. An important example is Nr. Hørning church, where with the help of computer-tomographic X-ray scanning it has been possible to date the so-called Hørning plank and thus to establish that the wooden church of which traces were found under the present Romanesque church in 1960 (K.J. Krogh & Voss 1961) was built ca. 1060-70.

Although we do not have anything like such close dates for other wooden churches, experts now generally believe that very few of the known wooden churches can be thought to have been built before the year 1000, and we have to ask ourselves whether we really have touched upon the very earliest series of churches under still standing churches. The question is sharpened by new evidence settlement excavations have provided us for the shifting of settlements. This did not end for good in the Viking Period, but clearly continued in many places to the 11th, 12th and perhaps even the 13th centuries. When whole villages moved, it should be supposed that the churches, as a rule, were moved too. These of course were wooden, and therefore easily reconstructed or replaced, and at the beginning of the Christian period people probably did not feel bound by the canonical proscriptions that later made it hard to abandon a church-site. We therefore cannot simply assume that the postholes from early wooden churches that are found so frequently below 12th- and 13th-century Romanesque stone churches belonged to the villages' earliest churches.

This uncertainty also means that it is not generally possible to use the results of church excavations to answer the question of when earlier burial sites were abandoned for burial in Christian churchyards. Here we have to rely on the evidence that pagan burials provide. They should at least provide a *terminus post quem* for the enforcement of Christianity and thus also for the establishment of churchyards. 10th-century graves are found in quite considerable numbers, but it is often difficult if not impossible to determine whether thay are pagan or Christian (Gräslund 1991), while they have usually to be dated within such broad limits that nothing can be made of them. But there are exceptions. In 1986, Viborg Stiftsmuseum undertook a re-excavation of the Mammen grave. The investigation, which has been published in an exemplary way (M. Iversen *et al.* (eds) 1991), produced wood that can be shown to have been felled in the winter of 970-1. But, typically, as far as the grave itself is concerned, we do not know how pagan the dead person was.

In recent years, the richly-furnished weapon and cavalry graves of the 10th century have attracted attention in archaeological discussion. They have been associated with the cult of Odinn (Roesdahl 1983) and thay have been used as a basis for bold theories concerning the development of power-structures in the period (Randsborg 1980; L.C. Nielsen 1991). The cavalry graves have however contributed little on the problem of the conversion. In this respect, as in the case of church studies, by far the most important results have come from a single site: from the investigations of the complex of pagan and Christian features at Jelling.

It was not least our knowledge of the Christian element of the Jelling monument that was improved by investigations of the ground below Jelling church that were carried out in 1976-79 in connexion with comprehensive conservation of the church building (K.J. Krogh 1983). Under the present church, which

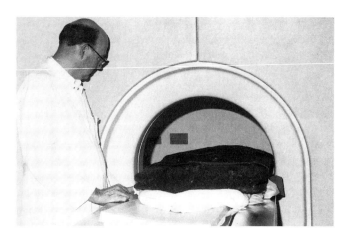

Picture showing the Hørning plank lying in the X-ray 1 scanner at Bispebjerg Hospital for computer-tomographic X-ray scanning in 1990. The growth rings on the scan were subsequently measured by Niels Bonde, the National Museum. The latest preserved growth ring was formed in 1036. Only the heartwood is preserved. Felling must have taken place after 1050, probably no later than the 1060's.

was built no later than *ca.* 1100, traces of no less than three wooden churches that had previously stood on the site were found. The largest of them all was the earliest. Not only the remarkably large dimensions, but also the fact that this first church at Jelling was apparently contemporary with the large runestone, makes it natural to believe that the large church was built by King Harold. The church must then have been built sometime in the 960's or 970's.

The supposed church of King Harold is not only exceptional in its size but also in that it was built as a mausoleum. While the church was being built, a grave was opened and the mortal remains of a man were translated to a large chamber grave that was constructed under the floor of the church. The question is, who was the dead man that Harold Bluetooth had incorporated into his church in this way? And where had he first been buried?

Since there is much to indicate that the chamber grave of the northern barrow was emptied at about the time that King Harold would have been building his church with its tomb, it is obviously appropriate to consider whether the man who was reburied in the church had come from the barrow. If so, it would be an example of a body translated from a pagan to a Christian grave. The King's father, King Gorm, who must have buried after pagan rites, must be a candidate.

We have a re-assessment of the evidence from the first investigation of the northern barrow of the 1820 which renders it probable that the intervention that

234

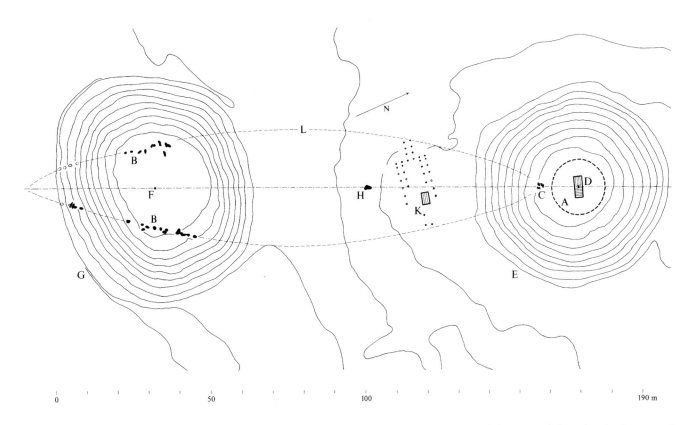

Plan of the Jelling monument. Contours at 1 m. intervals. A: Bronze-age barrow. B: Megalith or megalith socket in the ground beneath the barrow. C: large stone, perhaps a megalith, as B. D: Grave chamber, northern barrow, built into the Bronze-age barrow. E: Northern barrow. F: Central post in the barrow. G: Southern barrow. H: King Harold Bluetooth's runestone. I: Postulated church of Harold Bluetooth (postholes and grave chamber). L: Reconstruction of possible ship-setting.

could be seen to have taken place "in very ancient times" cannot be regarded as normal grave-robbing. Amongst other things it appears that those who entered the barrow subseqeuntly re-established the burial structure. Grave-robbers would hardly have done that. And it now appears that the intervention may have taken place while Harold Bluetooth was king, on the basis of a C 14 dating obtained from a candle that was apparently left behind by those who broke into the barrow.

On the subject of the precise geometrical form of the Jelling monument, the subject of speculation even in the 19th century, an excavation carried out in 1981 near the large runestone showed that the stone-has probably always stood where it now stands (K.J. Krogh 1983).

Another basic problem in Jelling studies, the question of the chronology of the complex, has also been clarified. In the 1970's and 80's, the National Museum worked on dendrochronological datings of pieces of wood from the two barrows, and it is now clear that the burial structure of the northern barrow was constructed around 958/9 A.D. (K. Christensen & Krogh 1987). The southern barrow could, theoret-ically, have been started on at the same time as the northern, though it seems more probable that it was started a little later. When a good half of this barrow was built, work stopped for a few years, eventually to be begun again and apparently first completed around 970. Why there was this interruption we do not know. One possibility is that it was because Christianity had been introduced, posing the problem of whether one should continue building a barrow. On the basis of the extent of lichen growth on the stone that belongs to the large block-stone structure that was partially uncovered below the southern barrow in Ejnar Dyggve's excavations of 1941-42 (Dyggve 1942), it is probable that this structure had stood on the site for a considerable period, presumably at least 20-30 years, before the stone blocks were covered by the newly built barrow. As we now know that the northern barrow may be a few years earlier than the first phase of the southern barrow, it can be established that the stone block structure pre-dated *both* barrows.

Ejnar Dyggve interpreted the rows of stone blocks as fragments of a large, triangular, sacred pagan enclosure. He called it a "vi" (shrine). This

235

hypothesis derived fundamentally from the supposed fact that the two rows of stone blocks did not just follow absolutely straight lines for a short stretch under the middle of the barrow but that they could be followed as straight lines for more than 40 metres. As Dyggve understood it, this made it impossible that the stones could be remains of a pointed-oval block-stone structure, a so-called ship-setting.

However an excavation carried out in the summer of 1992 in the southern barrow made it clear that the positions of the stone blocks and of voids where they had stood under the southern part of the southern barrow were incorrectly plotted in 1942. The correct course is not as long as thought. A new excavation and planning of the stones and stone-settings uncovered in 1942 at the south of the southern barrow and supplementary finds of traces of stone blocks in the same area shows that the two rows do not form perfectly straight lines but that both of them, as they run south, bow in towards the centre in such a way as to make the idea that they represent a large ship-setting now seem the most probable.

Only now do we have an accurate general plan of the excavations of 1941-42, giving us for the first time the precise locations of those elements that make up what we call the Jelling monument. The earliest feature is the hypothetical ship-setting. It appears that the large stone blocks that were noted under the northern barrow during King Frederik VII's investigations of 1861 are placed in such a way in relation to the axis of the block-stone structure that one has to consider that they might have come from the same structure as the stones below the southern barrow, and that in consequence the suggested ship-setting extended over the area shaded on the general plan. If so, this was a ship-setting of unusually large dimensions, about 170 m. long.

It would appear that this ship-setting was linked to a Bronze-age barrow, as the central axis of the block-stone structure is aligned towards the centre of the prehistoric barrow whose presence below the northern barrow was discovered in 1942 (Dyggve 1942). We cannot know what ideas underlay the linkage of these two monuments, but there can be no doubt that the prehistoric barrow was deliberately included as an element in the complex.

After the imposing block-stone monument had stood for a number of years, around 958-59 those changes and developments of the monument that - at least as far as the phases we know of are concerned -

were eventually to include the raising of the two great barrows, the northern barrow with a grave chamber and the southern barrow without one, and, at the point at which Christianity was introduced (i.e. probably sometime in the 960's or 70's), King Harold's raising of the large runestone on which he makes it known that it was he who introduced Christianity.

It is particularly noteworthy that the development of the Jelling monument continues to respect fully the axis that was the backbone of the monument in its earliest phase: the central axis of the block-stone structure. This is a fact that unquestionably implies that we are looking at a monument that was extended according to a single plan.

The precision in the geometrically governed plan of the structure is striking. The northern barrow was raised with the Bronze-age barrow as its starting point, and with its central point placed on the central axis described. In the same way, the southern barrow was sited with its centre, marked with a mighty central post, on the axis. King Harold's great rune-stone stands on the same line too, placed within a few centimetres of the mid-point between the centres of the two barrows. King Harold's runestone thus seems to be intimately associated with the two barrows, and there is therefore reason to suggest that the runestone and the barrows should be viewed as parts of one and the same monument. The inscription on the stone speaks of two dead people, King Gorm and Queen Thyra, and it is reasonable to believe that the barrows are in some way linked to these two. The southern barrow would then be Thyra's memorial and the northern barrow Gorm's, if it is the case that the man whose body was translated and incorporated in the first church at Jelling was moved there from the northern barrow.

The Jelling monument is unique in respect of its great size alone, and it is reasonable to suggest that this reflects the position of the Viking-period kings, Gorm and Harold, in their day. But what really distinguishes this monument is the way in which it spans jst that period in which the conversion took place. In this context it is noteworthy that the structure or monument raised in the pagan period was not ignored or destroyed when the new faith had arrived but on the contrary was preserved through developments and modifications which converted it into a Christian monument.

Could the example of the king have set the pattern in this respect too?

THE MIDDLE AGES AND
MORE RECENT TIMES

The Middel Ages and more recent times

By Niels-Knud Liebgott

During the 25-year period convered in this book, Medieval Archaeology achieved official status as a university subject. This happened in 1971, with the establishment of a Chair in Medieval Archaeology at Århus University. Archaeological investigations of medieval buildings, structures and finds had quite commonly been carried out, however, since the middle of the 19th century, both by museum archaeologists - the National Museum especially - and by capable amateurs. Drawings made by local archaeological enthusiasts in association with construction works have, for example, proved an important basis for modern archaeological work in a number of Danish towns. Without the interest of Engineer-General H.U. Ramsing and senior master H.N. Rosenkjær, for instance, our knowledge of Copenhagen's medieval topography would be significantly poorer than it is. The academic acceptance of the subject, reflected by the Chair at Århus, has also meant not only that it has been possible to establish and carry through substantial and coherent research programmes but also that the training of researchers has been markedly strengthened. Medieval archaeologists now naturally take their place amongst the archaeologists employed in museums all over the country.

Although medieval archaeology, despite being a relatively new subject, hardly needs to establish its legitimacy, there may still be reason to emphasize the special limits and possibilities inherent in the subject. In contrast to prehistoric archaeology, which is virtually exclusively focussed on remains left in the ground, medieval archaeology works in an area that has been dominated for generations by written sources, and therefore by historians. But medieval archaeology finds and interprets its own data through its own methods and techniques, and does not aim only to help illustrate situations that are otherwise reconstructed on the strength of the evidence in the written sources. Obviously, discoveries of new written sources for medieval history are now very rare. We have to assume that virtually all preserved documents and chronicles of the period are known and published. This does not, of course, mean that the possibilities of historical evidence have been exhausted. The sources can still be combined in new ways and read with greater insight and understanding. In medieval archaeology, however, it is the case that every time the spade is put in the ground, new evidence is found. And this evidence is frequently of aspects of medieval social life that are only sparsely,

if at all, reflected in written material from the period. The archeological structures and finds suffer, however, from the great limitation of not being able to speak for themselves. They are fragments from the past that have to be interpreted before they yield their evidence. When this can be done, medieval archaeology succeeds in making new and independent contributions, either to the illumination of already known situations and events or, better still, to the formulation of totally new theories.

The 1,700 or so village churches of the Middle Ages that still stand, more or less intact, evenly spread over Denmark, were, understandably, the "source group" that first attracted the interest of medieval archaeologists. As early as the beginning of the 19th century N.L. Høyen toured the Danish churches taking observations of their architectural history and historical decoration. This did not develop into real archaeology, but Høyen had taken the first steps in an area which for several generations was central to work in medieval cultural history. In 1933, the National Museum began to publish systematic descriptions and analyses of Danish ecclesiastical buildings and their furnishings in the comprehensive series entitled "Danmarks Kirker" (The Churches of Denmark). In this, each individual church is described in detail on the basis of all available sources. More than half the nation's churches are now described and published. Actual church archaeology, with excavations of church floors, began in earnest in the 1950's, and the results achieved from then on have been included in this work.

Church archaeology, however, does not only concern itself with what lies under the ground. The medieval archaeologist indeed enjoys the immense advantage over the prehistorian that he can often work on still standing buildings - not only churches but also secular buildings and sometimes fortified structures. Medieval archaeology thus also develops into building archaeology, including studies of the various traces of rebuilding and extension that lie in the walling of stone buildings. And since some of these buildings - especially the churches - still have medieval furnishings, the archaeologist's field of work extends far into the neighbouring disciplines of architectural and art history.

The work of the last generation in church archaeology has borne rich fruit. It is now possible to form a coherent picture of the development of Danish

The church at Gundsømagle in northern Sjælland was fully excavated in 1988. Large areas of the original mortar floor had survived, together with the bottom of two benches built along the length of the nave. In the course of the investigation of the walling, a fine western portal was discovered and a series of wall paintings of unusually good quality.

church building through the Middle Ages from the earliest Christian times around 1000 A.D. to the beginning of the 1500's (H. Johansen 1981). Such results are extraordinarily valuable in themselves. But some of the conclusions that the results lead to are so full of implications that they can serve here to show the special scope that medieval archaeology offers in relation to the historical areas of study with which it is most closely linked. The recognition of the high architectural quality of the earliest church buildings, the richness of their original decoration, and various features of original internal division, especially the now common evidence of special arrangements at the west end of the churches reserved for chieftains and church patrons, have rendered it necessary to revise theories as to who it was that supported the building of Denmark's earliest churches. Hal Koch's thesis that it was the parishioners themselves - i.e. the Danish farmers - who raised and paid for the churches is no longer tenable (H. Koch 1936). Thus church archaeology has made a decisive contribution to a new understanding of an early medieval society with an aristocratic structure as opposed to the democratic one Hal Koch described.

While the work with the churches has so far been carried out by the National Museum, where antiquarian responsibility also lies, a number of important areas of medieval archaeology have been looked after by the other museums in Denmark in the last twenty years. This applies particularly to urban archaeology. True enough, the earliest urban excavations of modern character in Denmark were carried out under the influence of the extensive excavations that went on around Europe in connexion with the rebuilding of blitzed towns - in Ribe, by the National Museum (Stiesdal 1968). But since then, urban archaeology has been the domain of the local museum of the town concerned.

The large Medieval Town research project, set in train by the Chair in Medieval Archaeology in 1977 and funded by the State Humanities Research Council, is the largest co-operative and most ambitious initiative in medieval archaeology in modern times (O. Olsen & Schiørring 1980). With the main aim of establishing the age and original topographical development of our medieval towns, 10 Danish market towns were selected for thorough analyses of existing written and archaeological accounts and small supplementary excavations. The project is nearly finished, in that the majority of the monographs planned are out. But the repercussions of the project are not diminishing. Interest in urban archaeology is growing in towns which were not included in the project, and the recovery of often substantial amounts of material has led to a deepening of research into the types of structures discovered and, not least, a virtually fundamental re-assessment of the artefact material found. The finds from the towns, with their advanced patterns of trade and

Coins from 8th to 17th centuries

In 25 years, well over a hundred thousand coins have been retrieved from the ground, providing a great deal of new numismatic evidence. First and foremost, the excavations in Ribe carried Danish coin history centuries back in time to the beginning of the 8th century (Bendixen 1981). We know now that in part of south-western Denmark at least there was a coin economy using small Frisian *sceattas* as currency. It has been suggested that these might also have been struck in Denmark. To corroborate local origin, we do not only need, as it has seemed, the local dominance of a single type (the Wodan/monster type) but also a large number of die-linked coins. The first set of finds did not provide this; it will be interesting to see if the most recent finds of around 80 coins will clarify the situation.

The use of metal-detectors both by professional museum staff and by amateurs, alone and alongside the archaeologists, has recently increased the known coin finds of the Viking Period significantly, not least on Bornholm (Steen Jensen 1988). Until around 1980, Viking-period Danish numismatics could be based on 19th-century hoard finds; the number of loose finds was limited and on average one Viking-period hoard was found per decade. This has changed. Re-excavations of old findspots such as Hågerup on Fyn, Store Valby on Sjælland and Iholm in Svendborg have produced significant new material, while new finds such as Neble near Boeslunde, Lillegærde on eastern Bornholm and Nr. Felding near Holstebro have appeared. The large number of loose finds that metal-detectors have turned up provides a much more varied picture of coin-circulation and coin-use than was previously visible.

The incredible number of loose finds from church floors (Bendixen 1972b; Steen Jensen 1977) or made by metal-detectors also allows us to argue for a much wider coin economy in the rest of the Middle Ages. This holds particularly for the period *ca.* 1280 to *ca.* 1330, when the debasement of coin seems to correspond to much increased coin production, so that the whole country, not just the towns, seems to have been part of a coin economy. Particularly informative are the yet unprocessed finds from Tårnborg, which include a couple of thousand late-medieval coins found in a fairly small area.

Some have thought and argued that the majority of major hoards were found in the 19th century, and these had been supported by statistical studies (Steen Jensen *et al.* 1992).

The last 25 years have taught us something quite new. Not only has Denmark's largest coin hoard of all, the Kirial hoard of 81,422 coins, deposited around 1365, been found, but also our largest hoard of gold coins (the nobles from Vejbystrand: 110 gold coins from a Prussian-built cog, lost in the early 1370's *en route* into the Baltic). To these can be added the largest 17th-century find, the Balle hoard (12,121 coins plus silver, *post*-1656), the two largest finds of Thalers, with 466 and 305 specimens respectively (the Staby find, *post*-1644; Torvet in Køge, *post*-1658), and the three very important finds of Frederik III and Christian V crowns (Brogade, Køge, *post*-1673; Bogøgård, Læsø, *post*-1672; and the coins from Ivar Huitfeldt's warship "Dannebroge" which blew up in Køge Bay in 1711).

Jørgen Steen Jensen

Sceatt of the Wodan/Monster type. Haloed head on obverse, dragon on reverse. 8th-century. Found in Ribe.

Norway. Olaf Tryggvason. This extremely rare coin, of which just one example has now been found in Denmark, was struck around 995 in imitation of a contemporary English coin. Found during the re-excavation of a site at Iholm in Svendborg Sund where a hoard dated to ca. 1000 was found in the mid-19th century.

Coin probably struck on the Rhine (Mainz?) at the beginning of the 11th century. Unidentified ruler on the obverse, while the reverse imitates an Arabic dirham. This poorly preserved coin is evidence of how Arabic and Central Asian dirhams were known all over Europe. Just one example of this rare coin has been found in Denmark, in the find from Lillegærde, Bornholm, deposited around the middle of the 11th century.

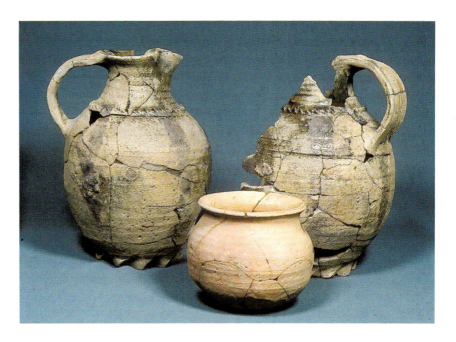

In recent decades, Medieval Archaeology has been much preoccupied with research on the range of artefacts of the period. As in Prehistoric Archaeology, our knowledge of medieval pottery is of fundamental importance. Here is a selection of mis-fired vessels from a pottery of the period ca. 1250-1350, excavated at Favrholm near Hillerød in northern Sjælland.

craft, have thus naturally encouraged studies of the conditions of medieval trade and of craft techniques.

The interest in medieval trade has amongst other things led to the excavation of a number of seasonal trading sites outside the towns from both the Middle Ages and more recent times (Liebgott 1979a; Berg *et al.* 1981). But of special importance in this connexion has naturally been the development of an entirely new area of archaeology, maritime archaeology. Following the recovery of the Viking ships from Skuldelev, a separate discipline has emerged - basically supervised by the Institute of Maritime Archaeology of the National Museum, which, during the last 25 years, has achieved international eminence in the field. This discipline concerns itself not only with the study of newly found wrecks and ship-types but with the broad economic and military historical context of these finds. Hence a long-term project, "Ship and Port".

Two major areas within medieval archaeology should receive more attention in coming years. These are agrarian archaeology and castles and fortifications. In agrarian archaeology it has proved possible in recent years - in some cases by means of relatively limited archaeological intervention - to establish quite firmly the main lines of the development of the village from prehistory to the present (Grøngaard Jeppesen 1981; Porsmose 1981). About 50 excavations of rural settlements are reported to Rigstantikvaren's Archaeological Secretariat annually, and despite the very limited scope of the excavations it is pleasing that such work is getting underway again after a period of stagnation since Axel Steensberg's pioneering work of the 1940's and 50's. We still, however, lack projects for major excavations of whole farm complexes and village structures, and until such projects are embarked upon we must note that we really known less about medieval and later villages than we know of those of the Iron Age and the Viking Period.

In medieval castle research, we must, regrettably, report a decline. All the ambitious registration projects that were undertaken at the start of the century and in the 1950's, covering the approximately 1,000 fortified structures in Denmark, have broken down. One can, however, rejoice that the large-scale excavations seen between the 1920's and the war have not continued. A large number of the principal monuments of Denmark - monasteries, and the royal castles of Kalø, Søborg, Gurre, Vordinborg and Kalundborg - were dug in this period, usually with methods more appropriate to large-scale building works. We ought to recognize that the time was not ripe for these great tasks; perhaps it still is not. Clearly, this category of structure could yield a range of evidence concerning medieval social relations, but we must first allow ourselves time to formulate the questions we wish to pose of the material before we throw ourselves into massive field projects. Until then, the Danish castles and fortifications stand secure and well-protected by legislation - against untimely archaeological assault as much as anything else.

Church and cloister

BY EBBE NYBORG

With eight bishoprics, nearly 140 monasteries and convents of friars, and more than 2,700 parish churches, medieval Denmark was the richest and the most European of the three Scandinavian kingdoms. Research into the standing churches and ruins has a good 200-year history. But only in the post-war years did church archaeology develop into any sort of independent discipline with its own methods and goals.

Unique to Denmark is the number of 12th- and 13th-century Romanesque churches that are preserved in more or less unchanged form. This derives from the position of the country: on the edge of Christian Europe, though not at the very limits. Further south, in the rich heartland of Europe, it was possible to renew the parish churches of the High Middle Ages comprehensively, several times over, while further north, in poorer parts of Scandinavia, the means were simply not everywhere available to raise stone churches in the Romanesque Period. In Denmark, however, by the middle of the 13th century practically every parish was able to have built a stone church, though that exhausted the resources. There have subsequently been additions and vaulting, especially in the decades preceding the Refor-

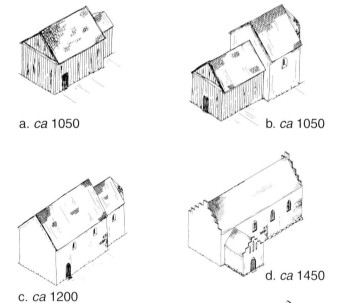

a. *ca* 1050

b. *ca* 1050

c. *ca* 1200

d. *ca* 1450

e. *ca* 1500

Typical history of a Danish village church. Most churches, however, especially in Jutland, have retained a complete Romanesque form (c), supplemented only by a late Gothic tower and porch.

mation. But otherwise it was enough for the parishes just to maintain the cherished temples from the nation's great days under the Valdemars.

The study of these numerous, virtually fossil, village churches has held an important place in Danish architectural and art history. And it is work on the small churches that has revolutionized Danish church archaeology and produced the most remarkable results.

The church floor became a field of archaeological work after excavations in Snoldelev (1953), Brørup (1953-54) and a number of other churches revealed unexpected results and opportunities. Above all, what had been sought was found in excess: evidence of earlier wooden churches in the form of floor layers, graves, and traces of posts and plank walls (E. Møller & Olsen 1961; Høgsbro Østergaard 1962). This led to entirely new perceptions of the missionary period (K.J. Krogh & Voss 1961; O. Olsen 1966) and new, early chapters could be added to the development of the parish church. In relation to the raising of stone churches, the floor excavations provided crucial new evidence, for instance of pauses in which a wooden church served together with the choir of the new, rising stone church. Such finds, together with the recognition of scaffolding holes etc. enriched the picture of the parish church as a building site and particularly sharpened the focus of research on the situation higher up in the walling and roof (K.J. Krogh 1960; E. Møller 1961).

The most distinctive results of the new Danish church-floor archaeology internationally, however, concerned the interiors of Romanesque stone churches. Successive floor raising was so extensive in many churches (up to *ca.* 80 cm.) that earlier layers were preserved with remains of altars, font podia, wall benches etc. This allowed the practically complete reconstruction of Romanesque furnishings, interesting not least in the raising of the west ends, with wider benches that are interpreted as a form of church patrons' seats (O. Olsen 1966). A careful screening of floor finds produced fragments of display items such as gilded altars and glass painting as well as quite unexpected amounts of coin which have proved crucial for dating as well as a godsend to the numismatist.

These developments have been the basis of Danish church archaeology in the last 25 years. A further important inheritance from the pioneering years that should be mentioned is extreme restraint in respect

242

of intervention in church floors (O. Olsen 1958). This protectionary approach has of course led to many fewer extensive church-floor excavations being undertaken.

All the same, the work of the last 25 years has been able to provide a stream of new discoveries and observations, some from church floors. This is not least due to the fact that church archaeologists have achieved an understanding that allows them to pose very precise questions and to find answers, often with limited means and quite minor interventions in the layers. Typically, one empties a couple of deep, later graves and from their sides alone ("extant sections") can make observations that clarify central archaeological issues and possibilities.

So far as the archaeologists themselves have been able to select their work, major excavations have only been carried out where there really was something to dig for. The testing of specified and ever broader hypotheses and theories has increasingly directed matters. The time has really gone in which excavations of churches and monasteries were only concerned with architecture and ground plans.

This does not mean that no important contributions have been made to architectural history in recent decades. The complex revelation of a basilica with a twin-tower front from around 1080 under St. Mikkel's town church in Slagelse can be noted (O.

Hammelev church was built ca. 1200 in a local, grey limestone. 15th-century Gothic changes and additions are in brick and are typically whitewashed.

Olsen 1972) and the recent clarification of the building history of Asmild (Vellev 1990) and Vrejlev minster churches. Characteristic of such studies now is the increased use of a combination of truly archaeological observations with close investigation of the standing walling (the so-called "vertical archaeology") of the buildings, such as in the remarkable, three-storey church at Lillehedinge (N.J. Poulsen 1977) and the Cistercian church Brahetrolle-borg (Hædersdal 1990). Numerous contributions come from the inventory, Danmarks Kirker, such as the publications of Ribe Cathedral and the large shrine at Holmstrup, with their excellent isometric reconstructions (Danmarks Kirker, Ribe amt: 145ff.; Holbæk amt: 1793ff.).

New and greater technical capacity is used, such as geological analysis of building and sculptural stone which has revealed importation from the Rhineland and England and shown in detail the location, exploitation and transport routes of local quarries (E. Thomsen 1983). Dendrochronology has contributed much more precise datings, as for the little stave church at Hørning which seems to have been raised in the 1060's. Attempts are being made in some areas to apply this new dating method systematically (Vellev 1983; P.K. Madsen *et al.* 1993).

Distribution of the parish churches of Medieval Denmark. In modern Denmark, only a few have been lost since the period of the Reformation (86% remain). In the areas east of the Øresund annexed by Sweden in 1658, however, the 19th century saw destructive renovation work.

243

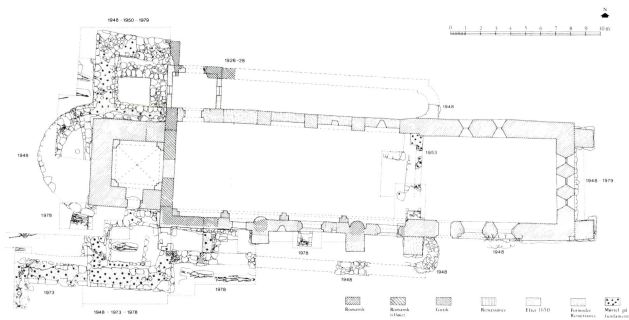

Plan of Asmild minster, Viborg, perhaps originally an episcopal church, with the foundations etc. planned from several excavations. The nucleus of the building is a late 11th-century basilica, the western section of which was replaced by an apse between two square towers in the mid-12th century. In the south tower can be seen a central woman's grave, probably a founder's. At the same time a nunnery was joined to the church. Extensive demolition after the middle of the 14th century probably reflects the problems the nuns faced after the plague of 1349 and the general decline.

It tends to date the buildings a bit later than previously thought.

Monastery excavations have been fairly numerous though mostly limited. As in neighbouring countries, there has been a distinct shift in interest from rich monasteries to small nunneries, and from the central, enclosed area of the complexes to the external facilities such as work buildings, mills, hospitals etc. (Sterum 1983). The largest excavation, however, was of the central area of an important Cistercian abbey, Øm or *Cara Insula*, famous for its unusually vivid chronicle. In the years 1975-78, a thoroughly strati-

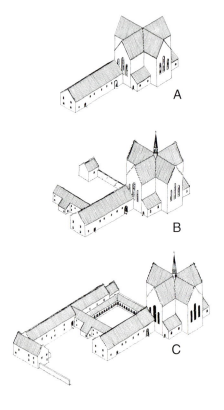

Excavations in the cloister at Øm. Work during the years 1975-78 produced nearly 23,000 precisely recorded finds of considerable importance for an understanding of life in the monastery in various periods. To the right, phases in the expansion of the monastery's central buildings, reconstructed on the basis of excavation. A: at the consecration of the church, 1257; B: around 1450; C: at the end of the Middle Ages.

graphic excavation strategy here revealed traces of an early timber cloister and identified and dated the phases of the stone-built structure. Just as the ambitious churches of the 13th century had to be finished in reduced form (without a proper nave), there were clearly problems with getting the stone abbey finished (O. Olsen 1979a). At Øm, as certainly at many other Danish monasteries, a fully extended complex with stone-built wings and perambulatories was first realized at the very end of the Middle Ages. A closer study of the wooden and wattlework buildings that were frequently still home to the monastic life in the 14th and 15th centuries is an interesting topic for future archaeologists.

Still, however, Danish church archaeology principally comprises work with the numerous old parish churches. New elements in their furnishings include timber rood lofts built as early as *ca.* 1200 and peculiar floor ramps linking the choir with the raised podium of the font at the west end of the nave which must have allowed the parish priest to make distinguished progress to the baptismal (E. Møller & Græbe 1972; Als Hansen & Aaman Sørensen 1975).

In Butterup church, in 1978-79, it proved possible not only to provide a detailed, comprehensive picture

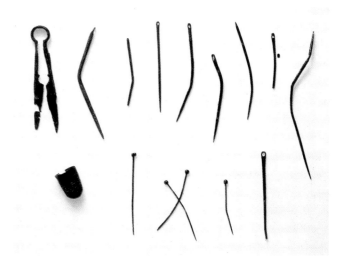

At Ring convent the sewing room was identified in the north wing in 1972. The bow scissors measure only 7.6 cm.!

of original furnishings of a clearly widespread pattern but also to identify quite thorough refurbish-ment shortly after 1300 - a sensation, with its walled stone benches in two complete rows. At the same time, the font seems to have been replaced with a Gothic one, and the Romanesque wall paintings, with saints in the

Butterup church, interior reconstructed on the basis of excavations 1978-79. Left: around 1175, seen from the podium at the western end of the nave; right: around 1325. Similar development could be seen in Gundsømagle church in 1988, where some of the phases could be dated dendrochronologically.

About one parish church in ten had a tower as early as the Romanesque Period. In Himmelev, Gothic brick additions partly hide the old limestone tower that is of the broad Skåne type. During excavations in 1972-73 remains of a finely constructed limestone sepulchre were found in the middle of the tower floor, probably that of a founder.

niches of the side-altars, were replaced in the same style. No new saint was painted in the northern niche, however, evidently because a new altar table in front of it was to carry a carved and painted saint's figure (Als Hansen & Aaman Sørensen 1979). Such images, holy roods and retables are otherwise preserved in great numbers, and contribute to a complete picture of the old ritual space (Nyborg 1977, 1988b). Another supplement (and corrective) is provided by the discovery of long planks with rows of incised bows that were found re-used in various contexts. These must be the arcaded front sides of long timber benches that could have replaced or superseded the stone-set ones (E. Skov 1979).

The western benches with slightly better seats have been found in various churches in recent years, always part of the original furnishings and removed in the 13th or 14th century. The dating of this phenomenon to the period in which the founders of the

churches could still dominate both church and priest strengthens the case that these were seats of honour. They can also, possibly, be regarded as a reduction of the towers with a raised gallery on the west wall of the nave that are known from a number of parish churches and which must imitate such western structures (westworks) in large churches. Here too, however, the use of the arrangement has been debated. There is, however, no doubt that outstanding church towers could serve as a local mark of power and status (Stiesdal 1983a; Nyborg 1985). This is emphasized by a number of interesting excavations of early towers which seem to have served as conspicuous mausolea for founding families (Stiesdal 1983b).

The growing recognition of the interplay between the church and contemporary social life and economic/ social structures has helped to bring surroundings into focus. This goes beyond a series of churchyard excavations that have carried on a very old tradition of major physical anthropological studies (summary by Kieffer-Olsen 1990 and Bennike 1990).

The parish churches have become important elements of settlement research, for instance as a guide to the manors of the period. A number of these have been recognized and excavated in direct connexion with churches, showing that the current place of worship was established as a form of manorial church (Stiesdal 1982). Most informative, indeed, are the recent discoveries at Lisbjerg. Here, a manor of the 11th century must have established a wooden church in the middle of its territory, the large stone-built successor of which soon pushed the farmstead out (Jeppesen & Madsen 1990). In other cases, the close relationship between a manor and a church can be followed down through time, as at Karlstrup,

Dragon's head from a house-shaped reliquary shrine (ca. 1200) found in 1980 in the apse floor of Eskilstrup church.

where manor and church partly shared fortification in the 14th century (Fraes Rasmussen 1982).

The relationship between churches and settlement is, of course, not just a question of association with manors. The explication of these complex connexions requires hypotheses concerning the social forces and impulses that made churchbuilding an increasingly public task in the 12th and 13th centuries. The written sources here are much sparser than in England, for instance, where the greatest progress has been made in integrating church archaeology with regional studies. Nevertheless, such studies have proved promising in Denmark too, thanks, *inter alia,* to the unique insight that the ubiquitously preserved and closely comparable Romanesque buildings provide (Nyborg 1986, 1993).

The same "statistical" quality of the small churches (recognized since the 1920's) has led in recent years to sociologically-inspired nationwide studies based on quantification. It has been possible to show a striking connexion between the occurrence of Gothic vaulting and the economic resources of the area (Wienberg 1986) as, for instance, represented by the modern soil map. This sociological influence has otherwise been more profound in Sweden, and typically it is a Swedish archaeologist who has most consistently tried to explain the Danish Middle Ages by ecclesiastical formulae (Andrén 1985; Nyborg 1990).

Church archaeology has moved a long way beyond what would have been assumed to be the natural limits of the subject 25 years ago. Professionalization has been followed by inexorable and rather contradictory demands for interdiscipliniarity (Nyborg 1987). This huge challenge must not weaken our fine tradition of empirical analysis and documentation. A respect for detail and for the complexity of past reality are the crucial requirements for anyone to progress from the narrow to the broad. An important path forward is co-operation - internationally, indeed. An essential step was taken on our initiative in 1981 with the first of a series of trans-Nordic symposia on church archaeology (published in Hikuin nos. 9, 12, 17 and 20). Such work will be even more international in future.

Romanesque holy rood in Asnæs church, ca. 1175-1200. The regal conqueror of death stands strong and stylized in front of the cross (the royal crown is now missing) which was originally much higher, and placed in the middle of the entrance to the choir, Christ's "triumphal arch". Original colours and gilding have been lost, but the wood has traces of Gothic and more recent repainting.

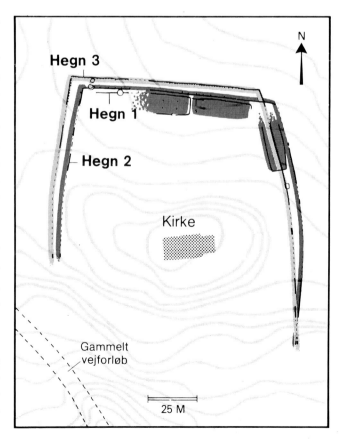

Lisbjerg church with traces of fences and longhouses uncovered in 1989 from a large manor of the 11th century (ca. 100 m. x 140). The Romanesque stone church's site in the centre of these features must have been determined by a predecessor, a wooden church associated with the central buildings of the manor.

247

The medieval town

By Ole Schiørring

In 1972, the present State Antiquary, Olaf Olsen, presented a paper on the current state of Danish urban archaeology at a symposium in Kiel (O. Olsen 1973: 72ff.). This included an outline of the information that was then available on the Danish medieval town; he also stressed the point that about 80% of the towns of Denmark were still undisturbed by archaeology and that the talk should perhaps have been postponed for 10 or 20 years as some major archaeological investigations were just beginning. He was right, for Danish urban archaeology has developed at an extraordinary rate since 1972, not least in its scope, so that now it is rather the case that larger or smaller excavations have taken place in up to 80% of the Danish towns that have a medieval history.

Interest in the archaeology of the medieval town, however, goes much further back. For many years the work had been left in the hands of capable amateurs. In towns such as Copenhagen, Viborg, Randers, Århus and Horsens these watched every trench and hole dug in the town centres. A great deal of topographical information was recorded for posterity in this way and can still be used. For most of these earliest urban archaeologists, the sole object of excavation was the monument *in situ*. The ground plan and topographical detail were central, while culture layers were not of great importance and artefacts were usually treated as an ornamental supplement to drawings and photographs.

Before the Second World War, research into the history of medieval towns was usually left to historians and art-historians both in Denmark and in Europe generally. Urban history was written virtually exclusively on the basis of documentary sources and surviving buildings. The archaeological dimension, however, became an important element after the War, and urban archaeology was properly established as a scholarly discipline just then. It was the extensive destruction caused by bombing in the towns of northern Europe that set investigations off. In the towns of what was then eastern Europe a series of major excavations were undertaken, and the results from the thick culture layers produced surprising new information on the medieval topography and development of the towns. In a number of western European countries similar opportunities were spotted. Comprehensive excavations were undertaken in several German towns, and in England there were rich opportunities on the large areas destroyed in Southampton and in parts of London. The experiences gained here led to a recognition of how rich a source of material the urban culture layers were and that these cultural remains should be protected by law so that they could be studied in advance of construction work. At the beginning of the 1970's, this understanding led to the publication of two important English works that were to be of great importance to Danish urban archaeology (Heighway *et al.* 1972; Biddle & Hudson 1973). These included plans of the archaeological potential of the town centres. An invaluable work tool had been created, and in the years that followed the work proceeded through a number of major excavations in English towns, amongst which the multi-year excavations in Winchester, York and Southampton should be picked out. The experience of these urban projects, in respect of the methods and techniques of excavation in particular, was profitably exploited in Denmark and the other Scandinavian countries during the 1970's.

25 years ago, Danish towns suffered many assaults. When the Store Nygade quarter in Aalborg was demolished to make way for a supermarket, capable amateur archaeologists were only able to investigate the wells found, even though invaluable archaeological material could have been excavated in the large areas.

Excavations in Store Torv, Århus, in 1982, uncovered the 15th-century town hall, sited immediately to the west of the cathedral. The square itself was laid out around 1300 on top of an earlier medieval settlement and forms part of the topographical changes that the old, ramparted Viking-period town underwent in the Middle Ages.

The first modern archaeological study of a town in Denmark was undertaken by the National Museum in 1955-56 in Grønnegade in Ribe (Stiesdal 1968). On a large building site it was possible to examine the metre-thick culture layers with a professioal method of excavation. The thousands of stratified artefacts provided not only a basis for dating but also considerable insight into Ribe's role as a medieval trading town. This pioneering excavation also showed how complicated it is to dig in our medieval towns as the metre-thick culture layers pose quite unique problems and the restricted areas dug often hinder an overview. An urban excavation can probably best be compared with a partial excavation of a series of settlements lying on top of one another. Successive buildings, demolition, levelling, the digging of pits and sometimes the removal of layers, over a long period of time, often make interpretation particularly difficult.

A positive development in urban archaeology was set off by the appointment of a growing number of trained inspectors in the local museums during the 1960's. This led to renewed and enhanced archaeological work in several Danish towns. In Ribe, Mogens Bencard continued the search for the Vikings, leading to a large number of excavations, large and small, within the area of the medieval town. The Vikings were not found to begin with, but on the other hand our knowledge of the develop-

ment of Ribe through the Middle Ages was extended in essential details, and the large number of excavations turned out not least to be of importance for research into medieval artefacts. In these years, Ribe became the place from which new inspiration and knowledge for urban archaeological work was sought. The first excavation in Viborg was in Riddergade in 1961-62. This was the prelude to a number of larger excavations in the town under the direction of Erik Levin Nielsen. These formed a series of systematic excavations that were based on a historical-archaeological hypothesis concerning Viborg's earliest history (Levin Nielsen 1966). For the first time in Denmark, a general view of the development of a medieval town was offered that could be either confirmed or rejected by carefully directed excavations.

In Århus, the 1960's saw continued development in research into the earliest history of the town. The main problem the town posed was the localization of the earliest, Viking-period settlement. The Museum of Prehistory, Moesgaard, carried out a major excavation in 1963-64 on the site that was later to be known as Århus Søndervold. On this relatively large site it proved possible to identify a settlement and the 10th-century town defences. Only sunken huts were found, and this is probably an outer area of the town where, for instance, craftsmen worked. The excavation also provided information and finds from the 13th- and 14th-century town. Light plank and

Building plots have been excavated in many towns, and these were usually buildings with roof-bearing posts. The restricted areas of excavation do not, as a rule, make it possible to uncover whole buildings. Here are two buildings separated by a pavement from Møllergade 6 in Svendborg. The buildings are dated by dendrochronology to 1308 and 1318 respectively.

wattlework buildings covered the site at this date and amongst other things housed some of the cattle that were an important element in the basic life of a Danish medieval town. Århus Søndervold is distinguished not only on the basis of the results that changed the perception of the earliest topographical development of the town fundamentally but also because the results and the large number of finds were published in an exemplary manner (H. Andersen *et al.* 1971). The investigations at Århus Søndervold were followed up systematically in subsequent years with new excavations at different places in the town, such as in the area by the first cathedral (H. Andersen & Madsen 1967), by Århus Cathedral School in 1969 (H. Andersen & Madsen 1985a:35ff.) and several small trenches in the 1970's west of the Viking-age town (H. Andersen & Madsen 1985b:97ff.). The excavations in Store Torv in 1982 produced new but as yet not fully tested ideas on the plan and function of the earliest Århus (-Schiørring 1983:221, 1984:12ff.).

Urban archaeological work expanded not only in these towns but also in Aalborg, Odense and Randers. In most cases it was minor areas that were excavated, and in comparison with the large excavations going on abroad at the same time the conditions were poorer and the possibilities fewer. This was not least the case in respect of the application of scientific methods that were used elsewhere. The reason why this potential was not fully exploited in Denmark was primarily the lack of resources. The investigations in medieval Svendborg were an exception.

In 1972, the ambitious project "The Archaeology of Svendborg" began under the direction of Henrik M. Jansen (Jansen 1988:198ff.). From the beginning of the project not only archaeologists were involved but also a large group of scientific specialists. Through pollen studies, grain analyses, wood identification, studies of both animal and human bone, the investigation of preserved insects and scientific dating it was possible to extend our knowledge of life in the medieval town, and with this the archaeological material was put into a much wider context.

In all, 23 archaeological excavations were carried out in Svendborg from 1972, covering a range of different settlements of both secular and ecclesiastical character (Reinholdt 1992:14f.). Amongst the most important of these has to be counted the excavation of Møllergade 6 (Jansen 1986), where remains of a sequence of buildings were found running from the late 12th century beyond the end of the Middle Ages. This excavation provided an insight into the various different building-types and constructions of the medieval town. The scientific studies, which were boosted by good conditions for preservation, provided information on the life and circumstances of medieval people, *inter alia* through lucky finds of latrine barrels (Jansen 1988:206f.). The project is not yet concluded, but five volumes have been published so far, dealing with selected themes and find-groups (Jansen 1988:219; Reinholdt 1992:18). Although the sciences are now used much more in Danish urban archaeology, the Svendborg project is still as yet the only one where they have been used so widely and consistently on a par with corresponding projects abroad. In future years, this is a field that should be exploited very much more.

Thus through the 1970's, urban archaeological work was making progress, and there was a need for certain main lines to be laid out for Danish urban archaeology. Because of the large sums that area excavation in the towns required, a different route had to be taken for new evidence to be retrieved from the medieval town centres. In 1977, the Danish

Research Council for the Humanities set the "Medieval Town Project" in train: an interdisciplinary project aimed at illuminating the age of the towns and their topographical development through the Middle Ages (O. Olsen 1982a:137ff.; Schiørring 1988:143ff.).

Eleven towns from modern Denmark were selected for the project: Roskilde, Køge, Næstved, Odense, Svendborg, Aalborg, Viborg, Århus, Horsens, Ribe, and the deserted borough of Søborg where the study was to be undertaken by the National Museum. The basic idea was that future excavations should be based on a synthesis of all accessible written sources, earlier excavations and loose finds, cartography and geological data. On the basis of an analysis of these sources, new investigations should be undertaken as carefully targeted, minor excavations that could solve specific topographical problems. In this way, larger and thus expensive area excavations could be avoided. The great work of registration required usually took place in collaboration with the local museums in the towns in question.

After the first phase of the project, about 45 small, carefully located excavations, distributed amongst the various towns and each with the goal of meeting some of the main aims of the project were carried out. A few larger excavations took place in collaboration with the local museums or the National Museum. The large number of results were then included in a publication for the individual town. At present, the results from seven of the towns have been published, namely Ribe (I. Nielsen 1985), Køge (M. Johansen 1986), Næstved (Aa. Andersen 1987), Viborg (Krongaard Kristensen 1987), Odense (Λ.S. Christensen 1988) and Svendborg (Reinholdt 1992), while Bodil Møller Knudsen has published the results from Aalborg as part of the history of Aalborg town (E. Johansen et al. 1992).

The guiding lines that the Medieval Town Project laid out assumed an exceptional degree of importance for research into Danish medieval towns. First and foremost, similar work began in a number of other towns, often on the basis of higher-degree dis-

sertations in Medieval Archaeology at Århus University. In consequence, systematic investigations began, for instance, in Nykøbing, Mors, Vejle, Kolding, Haderslev, Helsingør, Kalundborg, Randers and Ringkøbing. Several more followed later, and in a number of towns on Sjælland and in Copenhagen efficient excavation work is now established. Towns without museums are often covered by the National Museum, as with Slagelse and Nakskov. However another important factor in the increased amount of excavation has been that the culture layers in the town centres were protected by § 26 of the Museum Act so that it was possible to investigate urban sites in advance of construction work.

Urban archaeology in the last 10-15 years has provided fundamentally better knowledge and understanding of the development of the Danish medieval towns. In many towns, widely significant results have been obtained through a very large number of excavations (AUD 1984-1991) in larger monuments such as monasteries, hospitals and urban fortifications too. It would be too large a task to describe the many finds here. Up to now, the main efforts, however, have kept within the medieval bounds of the various towns and the results have rarely been compared with like results in other boroughs or with results from the surrounding countryside. The towns have been dealt with archaeologically like islands in the sea of medieval society, and, with a few exceptions (Andrén 1985), no attempt to discuss higher

The Medieval Town Project's small excavations produced many fine results. Here by the Søndersø in Viborg a well-preserved settlement from 1018 down towards the year 1300 was discovered. The local topography changed around 1300 with the damming of the lake, perhaps in connexion with the construction of the castle, Borgvold, for which a quarter of the town was abandoned.

Ecclesiastical institutions dominated the face of the medieval town. In a number of Danish towns, excavations in such institutions have been carried out, although current land occupation often places severe restrictions on their scope. Our knowledge of churches, monasteries and hospitals has increased fundamentally in the last 25 years in respect of their extent in the urban space, the dating of building phases and their appearance. This picture shows parts of the Franciscan friary church in Aalborg, excavated in a small town plot at the beginning of the 1980's.

questions concerning urbanization and general development, or causal explanations, has yet been made. The investigations have further usually been focussed on the topography and not on socio-economic conditions. Medieval artefact research is making substantial attempts to rectify this. The whole body of archaeological data gained from the work of the last 25 years provides the opportunity to extend our knowledge of these aspects.

The founding-date is of great importance for our understanding of the towns. On this question, the large number of excavations have not carried us much beyond the information in the earliest preserved documents. Only in a few towns, such as Ribe and Århus, have Viking-period remains of an urban character been found. The 10th-century settlements that have been found both in Næstved (Aa. Andersen 1987:11f.) and Horsens (Møller Knudsen & Schiørring 1992:9ff.) must for the present be regarded as villages preceding the urban settlement. It seems, then, to be in the 11th century that the earliest group of towns appears, as recognized in Aalborg, Viborg, Horsens, Odense and Roskilde, to name a few. With a view to possible town-shifting, new information could presumably be gained from investigations in the immediate vicinity of the towns.

On the development of the towns, archaeology has supplemented the information from the written sources in essential respects. The medieval towns of

In Roskilde, which was one of the largest medieval towns of Denmark, the last 10 years have seen a substantial series of excavations. It is the earliest development of the town in particular that has been focussed upon, both inside the 12th-century town fortifications and outside them. At the end of 1992 in Skt. Jørgensbjerg remains of an upper-class home with a house built of travertine, raised at the beginning of the 12th century and demolished around 1225, were excavated. It is as yet the oldest secular stone building in Roskilde.

Larger areas of excavation often produce surprising new insights, as here in The Square in Horsens, where remains of a regular fortification of the period around 1300 were found below the buildings of the square. This enclosed the area where the royal chapel of St. James the Greater was sited in the Middle Ages and where, perhaps, the king's own court was situated in the town. The structure was demolished just a few decades later.

Denmark change through the period, quite radically in some cases. In Ribe, for instance (S. Jensen *et al.* 1983: 156ff.), Roskilde (Liebgott 1989:242f.) and Aalborg (E. Johansen *et al.* 1992) it has been shown how settlements were cleared in order to make space for fortifications, ecclesiastical institutions and squares or for entirely new quarters to be established. Such a pattern appears clearly in Horsens, where the past few years have provided opportunities for excavations in large areas and in all of the medieval streets (Møller Knudsen & Schiørring 1992: 9ff.). The earliest phases found are a settlement and cemetery of the 10th century, an urban settlement of the 11th century and an expanded settlement of the 12th and 13th centuries. In the years around 1300 the town was completely restructured, with a completely new town area being added. At the same date, all of the streets and the town square were laid out and paved, and the town ditch was constructed, cutting off old town quarters. This radical change in the town plan was supplemented with new monasteries and hospitals and a town hall and ordinary houses, amongst which stone buildings were not so few as was previously assumed. These features of topographical development have proved to be general ones in the towns studied. It is probable, therefore, that the results from Horsens reflect a common development in Danish medieval towns, so that in the period 1250-1350 these became "European", presumably under the influence of

northern Germany. Køge, founded in the 1280's, is an illuminating example of the desires and needs medieval Man had in respect of a town's appearance.

Urban archaeology in Denmark is now in a transitional period. As a relatively new discipline, it has succeeded in finding its own basis with investigations in nearly all Danish boroughs. In the future, its work should be developed further, and above all resources need to be obtained for both excavation and publication so that the efforts invested can match the results from towns abroad. Resources need to be found for the excavation of larger areas so that large, unitary structures can be seen. This is often impossible with the small excavations that have characterized urban archaeology - with good results - for many years, irrespective of how well-placed they may be. The results from Horsens show that an understanding of a range of phenomena can only be obtained through larger area excavation.

The coming years should also see the increased processing of the results across the towns collectively with the aim of describing medieval town life and the factors that determined the founding and further development of the town. As it happens, this line is already being followed in artefact research, where comparative studies of the pottery (P.K. Madsen 1986:57ff.) for example have resulted in a greater understanding of differences both social and regional.

Ships and barriers

By Ole Crumlin-Pedersen

Ship and harbour

With the growth of towns in the Middle Ages, attempts were made to create an organized context for trade and craft inside the towns' limits. If the burgesses had their way, all the hinterland's trade would be forced through the town. But this was far from the case. The church and the nobility's trading activities were exempted from the towns' privileges. Stubborn traditions of light traffic with neighbouring coasts persisted around the coasts of Denmark which did not allow themselves to be knocked out by the merchant towns' attempts to gain a monopoly of trade. This struggle is reflected in the written sources in rules exempting skippers of small craft outside the towns, for instance in North Jutland and Lolland-Falster, from where local agricultural exportation was tolerated. In other places traffic continued without formalities from local landing places which in the burgesses' eyes were "illegal ports".

In Skuldevig, 12th- to 13th-century sanddrift has sealed a site where for several centuries previously people had gathered at the coast in booths or tents (Liebgott 1979). This was presumably in the fishing season, and clearly too with an eye to trade, as remains of two large merchant ships of the mid-12th century have been found in the bay by this beach market (Crumlin-Pedersen 1979a). The location, just inside the mouth of Isefjord, and the capacity of the ships, up to 60 tons for the best preserved example, indicates that this site could have played a central role in the export of agricultural produce from the hinterland of Isefjord and Roskilde fjord to, for example, Norway.

The finds along the shore of the Fribrødre river south of Stubbekøbing have a quite different character (Skamby Madsen 1987, 1989, 1991). Beside a now overgrown fjord-system sections of a shipyard from around and shortly before 1100 have been excavated. Ships were broken up here with a view to re-using planks and beams in new vessels. Finds and local place-names show a marked mixture of Danish and Slav elements, and the site is interpreted as evidence of a local Wendish colony under Danish control.

Otherwise it is, as yet, principally Roskilde fjord that has attracted interest in the study of the relationship between seafaring and settlement (Crumlin-Pedersen 1978:61ff.; Ulriksen 1990), though the Limfjord too and the coast of Fyn are now looked at in new light, and collaboration between land and marine archaeologists in such studies can be expected to contribute fundamentally new insights in the coming years (Crumlin-Pedersen (ed.) 1991).

The farmer's ship

The vessels used in light traffic are widely represented in finds of recent decades. Previously their size and form were practically unknown, as written sources said next to nothing of these mundane craft. Now the large boat Skuldelev 3 and the small ships from Ellingå and Gedesby provide a very detailed impression of such vessels in the earlier Middle Ages while the finds from Klim strand and Uggerby by Jammerbugten show the end of the long development of beach craft.

The natural harbour of Bøtøminde near Gedser is mentioned in several medieval sources as the starting point for local light traffic and ferries to the towns of northern Germany. In 1990, a small cargo lighter of the late 13th century was excavated here which, like other finds of light, local craft along the coasts, seems to represent a close local connexion between ship and port. The find place outside Gedesby is marked here on the Scientific Society's map of 1776.

No historic vessel is now more thoroughly known than Skuldelev 3, a small cargo ship 14 m. long (O. Olsen & Crumlin-Pedersen 1968:118ff.). This is due to the copy of the ship that was built in Roskilde from 1984-86 and which has since undergone extensive trials (Vinner 1986a-b; Crumlin-Pedersen 1987; B. & E. Andersen 1990). This mid-11th-century vessel can be sailed by a crew of 4-5. It holds 4½ tons of cargo and is regarded as the large boat of a farmstead. With it, the population of the farm could travel to moot and market, carrying the farm's own surplus to exchange for other goods, for instance at the market site at Skuldevig.

In an earlier natural harbour, now totally closed and overgrown, at Ellingå, north of Frederikshavn, a slightly larger cargo boat was excavated in 1968 and is now exhibited in Bangsbo Museum. The boat is 15 m. long and its capacity is reckoned at about 15 tons. It is dendrodated to *ca.* 1160 and apparently sank in its home harbour where luckily it settled in such a way as to preserve almost all of one side (C. Fischer 1969; Crumlin-Pedersen 1981). The boat was well-adapted to cargo transport in the Kattegat and Skagerak but there was no trace of its various cargoes.

There was, however, in the Gedeby ship (Crumlin-Pedersen 1989b; Bill 1991). Here a woven brush mat lay at the bottom of the ship, enclosed in deposits of fresh manure. This 13-m. long vessel of the late 13th century was thus one of the many small boats from Lolland-Falster that provided the Hanseatic towns on the south coast of the Baltic with live horses and meat animals.

Similar light vessels were also used to carry brick from the furnaces to building sites, as shown, for instance, by a couple of 17th-century wrecks outside Lundeborg (Skaarup 1980, 1984).

Light transport still played an important role in the Skagerak area in the 18th and 19th centuries. These small vessels carried Norwegian iron and timber to Jutland in exchange for provisions. During the war with England of 1807-14, Norway was severely afflicted by the English blockade and the widespread capture of these craft. In response, the traditional clinker- built vessels known from a wreck from Klim strand (Gøthche 1985, 1991) were supplemented with new, small carvel-built boats such as the Uggerby wreck (Gøthche 1986), probably built by craftsmen sent from Holmen in Copenhagen to help Norway through the crisis.

Large ships

The Skuldelev find with its five different ships contained a wide variety of types of the 11th century, including the 16.5-m. long sea-going ship Skuldelev 1, perhaps a *knarr* (O. Olsen & Crumlin-Pedersen 1968: 96ff.). It was built of pine planking and thus not of Danish origin; more probably western Norwe-

With the building of "Roar Ege", a close copy of Skuldelev 3, Danish ship archaeology gained the opportunity to test the potential of the Viking ships realistically in all weather conditions.

The Gedesby ship with its wickerwork "stall floor" amidships.

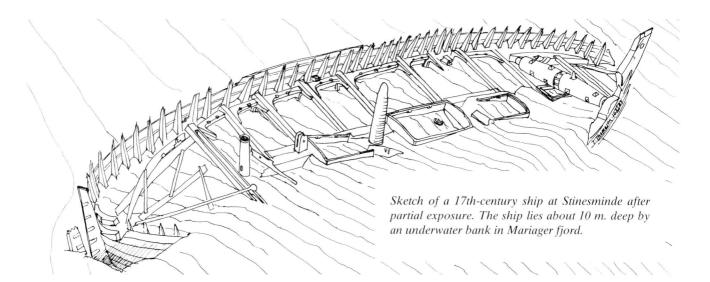

Sketch of a 17th-century ship at Stinesminde after partial exposure. The ship lies about 10 m. deep by an underwater bank in Mariager fjord.

gian. It is therefore very appropriate that a copy of this ship was built in Norway in close consultation with Danish scholars. The utility of the reconstruction in all conditions was clearly shown by a circumnavigation of the world in the years 1984-86 (Crumlin-Pedersen 1987; B. & E. Andersen 1990). The ship can be sailed by a crew of 5, and it could have carried a cargo of 20-25 tons, 4 or 5 times more than Skuldelev 3.

But there were very much larger cargo boats as early as the 11th century. This is shown by one of the three ships found in Hedeby harbour in 1979-80. Since the 1960's, there has been joint Danish and German work on the study of the ship finds from Hedeby (Crumlin-Pedersen 1969), and this has, amongst other things, led to the finding of a cargo ship of Skuldelev 1 type but considerably bigger, with a capacity of *ca.* 40 tons (Crumlin-Pedersen 1985b). To judge by the types of wood used, this ship may have been in its home port, but it is unclear who owned it or what it was carrying. Was it the king's, or a lord's ship, bringing natural tributes home, or was it a merchant's ship plying to Birka, Truso and Staraja Ladoga?

The increase in size of ships continued in the 12th century, as the Lynæs ship, with a capacity around 60 tons, shows (Crumlin-Pedersen 1979a, 1985b). This was probably linked to the growth of the towns, but hardly governed by this alone: the Lynæs ship and its sister were found outside a seasonal coastal site.

Large Scandinavian ships of the 13th and 14th centuries are known from Bergen in Norway rather than Danish finds. The finds clearly show that the shipbuilding tradition that created the Viking ships

did not stagnate but developed dynamically to meet the heavy transport requirements of the Middle Ages - in spite of an increasing shortage of suitable shipbuilding timber (Crumlin-Pedersen 1986, 1989a).

The following centuries were marked by quite different basic types of large ship: the cog, the *hulc* and carvel-built large ship-types of around 1500. Their appearance in our waterways is shown by Danish finds: in detail in respect of the cog but more haphazardly with the other types.

With the Dutch dominance of the sea in the 17th century, not least on the North Sea-Baltic route, Baltic shipbuilding came under strong Dutch influence. It can therefore be difficult to establish the origin of carvel-built ships closely in this period. This is the case with an unusually well-preserved cargo ship of the early 1600's that was excavated on the bottom of Mariager fjord by Stinesminde in 1990 (Gøthche & Rieck 1990; Gøthche 1992). The draft marks on the stem, measured by a foot of 29 cm., indicate that the ship was built for a merchant of Lübeck or Sweden, but its history is otherwise unknown, as with the majority of wrecks in Danish waters.

The cog

With German expansion into the Baltic and the estab-lishment of the Hanseatic league as an economic force in the 13th to 15th centuries the medieval *cog* came to play a decisive role as a vessel of trade and war. The written sources give us the name but little concrete information on the form and size of the cog. But wrecks found in recent years remedied this, after an unusually well-preserved wreck of

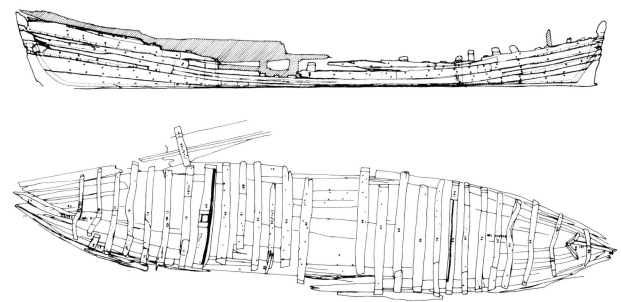

Drawing of the preserved parts of the Kollerup cog.

1380 was found in Bremen in 1962 and identified as a cog.

The peculiarities of the cog - the flat bottom with smooth planking, the straight fore and aft stems - have now been found in other wrecks, such as a medieval wreck that was studied by divers as early as 1943-44 in Kolding fjord (K.E. Hansen 1944; Crumlin-Pedersen 1979b, 1981). But new cog-finds have been made, for instance in Vejby, 1976, Kollerup, 1978, and Ll. Kregme, 1986.

These finds have shown that the coarse, simple construction of the cog differs radically from Scandinavian shipbuilding traditions even though in developing into a proper sea-going vessel the cog must have been influenced by Scandinavian shipwrights. This affected both the high, clinker-built sides and the long keelson with the mast slot.

Most important here is the Kollerup cog, excavated by Thisted Museum but later transfered to the National Museum (Crumlin-Pedersen 1979b; H. Jeppesen 1979; P.K. Andersen 1983). This ship, from around 1200, is a key find, the oldest medieval cog yet known in the whole north European area in which cogs were used. The hull is long, narrow and low compared to later cogs.

The Kollerup ship undoubtedly represents the first generation of sea-going cogs, built in the Low Coun-tries for sailing north of Skagen as "tramp ships". The closest parallels in construction come in much older finds from the Rhine area which confirm that the medieval cog was not, as some historians

have thought, a creation of the Hanse but derived from an earlier river or estuary vessel that developed greatly during the 13th century to reach, in the next century, the size of large Scandinavian ships and to supersede them (Crumlin-Pedersen 1985b, 1991d).

The Vejby cog, from the coast of northern Sjælland, was stranded around 1380 *en route* from western Europe. Its valuable Baltic cargo had been sold, and ballast had been taken on to supplement a light cargo of luxury items on the return voyage. In and around the wreck was found English metalwork and 109 English gold coins, while two coins from the Danzig-Elbing area found in the mast slot indicate that the cog was built there (Crumlin-Pedersen *et al.* 1976; Crumlin-Pedersen 1979b). The wreck was raised in 1977 with the intention of eventually being exhibited in Roskilde along with the Kollerup cog.

Finally, a cog of about 1400 was found in Roskilde fjord near Ll. Kregme. Here, in contrast to the Vejby cog, it is upper parts of the sides that have been excavated and planned so far. It is possible, however, that further excavations on the site will retrieve the rest of the vessel as there will be an opportunity for archaeological students to undertake fieldwork under water here in future years, some from the Archaeological Institute in Copenhagen, where a course in marine archaeology was introduced in 1991.

Warships

There are important 11th- and early 12th-century finds of warships of Scandinavian origin, but none as

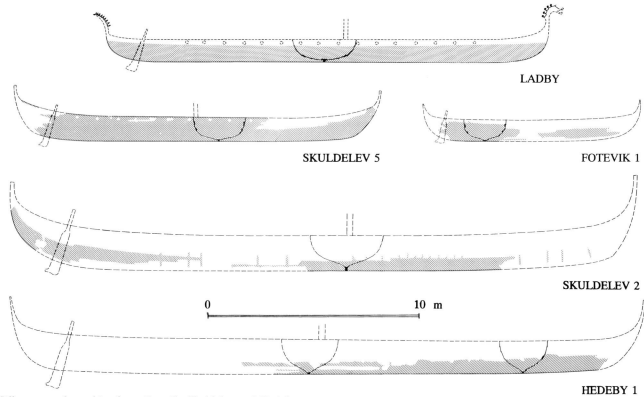

Silhouettes of warships from Fotevik, Skuldelev and Hedeby.

LADBY

SKULDELEV 5

FOTEVIK 1

0   10 m

SKULDELEV 2

HEDEBY 1

yet from the following centuries of the Middle Ages.

In a joint Danish-Swedish project in 1982, sections of a sea-barrier at the entrance to Fotevik in Skåne were excavated, with remains of five ships of very different size but of a single building tradition being found (Crumlin-Pedersen 1984). There is much to indicate that these were scrapped warships that had been used as stone-sledges on the ice during an extension of the barrier designed to hinder King Niels' invasion of 1134. Only the originally 10.3-m. long Fotevik 1 wreck, which carried about 14 oars and which must have been one of the smallest craft in the fleet, was fully excavated.

A more normal size is that of the 26-oar warship represented by Skuldelev 5 (O. Olsen & Crumlin-Pedersen 1968:132ff.; Crumlin-Pedersen 1988). This ship was partly built of re-used materials, and it was worn and patched to an as yet unparalleled degree before it ended up as part of the fill in the first phase of the Skuldelev barrier in the 11th century. Surviving Norwegian laws of the 12th century concerning the maintenance and refurbishment of warships indicate that it was hard to get the farmer-levy to build a new ship as long as the old one was at least in one piece. This probably explains the character of

Skuldelev 5 and thus implies that this ought to be an example of a ship built and maintained as a collective duty, not as a means of transport for a lord.

Quite different in character is the warship from Hedeby harbour found in 1953 and excavated in 1979 (Crumlin-Pedersen 1969, 1988:151f.; Schietzel & Crumlin-Pedersen 1980). The port side of the ship was burnt down to the waterline over its complete surviving length. The parts of the ship found clearly show that this was a high-class ship, with materials of special quality and outstanding construction. The wreck is interpreted as the remains of a royal long-ship that had been captured, and was used as a fire-ship during an attack on the harbour in the mid-11th century.

The Skuldelev 2 ship, about 30 m. long, was also a longship (O. Olsen & Crumlin-Pedersen 1968:111ff.; Crumlin-Pedersen 1988:151). It was built around 1060-70 and was used in the second phase of the Skuldelev barrier. Dendro-samples show that the ship was built in the Dublin area of Ireland but was later locally repaired in Denmark before being sunk (Bonde & Crumlin-Pedersen 1990). This ship shows how Denmark's western connexions continued after the end of the Viking Period.

Warships of later centuries, when the ships' ability to withstand a fusilade had become crucial, are found in Danish waters too. There is the wreck of the "Gideon", a Danish navy ship of 1584, excavated in 1990 off Helsingør (Probst 1993), while other Danish naval vessels have been more randomly investigated (B.Thomsen 1982; Christoffersen 1990). The English ship of the line "St. George" has provided material for a special exhibition at Thorsminde.

The Danevirke in the sea

Sea defence of the early Middle Ages was based on manned warships as mobile units, locally equipped and assembled in special levy harbours before they set out in larger fleets. Their home base must have been the boathouses in which the ships were kept when not in use. In Harrevig by the Limfjord the site of two such boathouses have been found (Ramskou 1961) though otherwise this is a type of structure that has yet to become more widely found in Danish archaeology (Crumlin-Pedersen 1991:184ff.).

The assembly places for the levied fleet were strategically situated natural harbours, and stake-systems to control ingress and egress have been found at several of these: for instance at Vordingborg's old harbour at Hvidanger between Oringe and the fort, where two stake-systems have been found, one undated and one dated to 1162 by one dendro-sample. The dated system was associated with a peculiar construction on the sea-bed, probably the foundation of a watch-tower to control transit (Crumlin-Pedersen 1979c, 1985a; Rieck 1985).

Fotevik, on the northern side of the Skanør peninsula in Skåne, probably served as protected assembly place of this kind. By the entrance here, a stake-barrier reinforced with stone has been observed. This structure was probably built in the 11th century and is in any case many years older than the second phase, in which the ships were used as stone-sledges before being sunk beside the barrier, probably in the winter 1133-34.

Sea-barriers are found in contexts other than assembly places. The Skuldelev barrier is an example of a structure protecting a rich hinterland or a town against sudden attack (O. Olsen & Crumlin-Pedersen 1968:91ff.; Crumlin-Pedersen 1978:29ff.). Here too there were two building phases, the latest perhaps on the orders of Erik Emune before the battle at Værebro river in 1133, the year before it was Fotevik's turn.

When mapping an underwater stake complex sealed in mud, one cannot plan the structure in the normal way. One has to move all the measuring points up to the surface and plan them there, as shown in this photograph of the mapping of the barrier at the military harbour at Vordingborg.

At Helnæs, southern Fyn, remains of barrier from around 1100 that was to control traffic to the Helnæs Bay with its hinterland, a good proportion of Fyn's good soil, have been found (Crumlin-Pedersen 1974; Rieck 1991). This had a refined design, with floats fixed between two stakes in a way that minimized the need for timber. This was, however, like all sorts of stake barriers, a type of structure vulnerable to winter ice, so that many similar barriers could have been constructed at other sites without leaving any direct traces in the terrain.

At the mouth of Haderslev fjord, at the place called "Margrethes Bro" (Margrethe's Bridge), there are clear remains of a pair of rows of stakes across the fjord, dated to *ca.* 1140, so solid that one is encouraged to believe that there really was a bridge here with the twin purpose of aiding land traffic and controlling sea traffic. The topographical circumstances see this structure directly overlying a comprehensive barrier of around 400 A.D. (Crumlin-Pedersen 1975; Rieck 1991).

With the future studies of the `Danevirke of the sea' it will be important to aim to clarify the connexion between underwater defensive works and matching structures on land, and with the details of local settlement and water transport. These factors together determined fundamental features of the cultural landscape that we now know in Denmark.

Castles and fortified sites

By Rikke Agnete Olsen

Twenty-five years ago the study of castles and fortifications from the Middle Ages was still a new research discipline in Denmark. In some ways it seems relatively new even now - partly because many of the fortified sites known in present-day Denmark - of which there are about 1000 in all - have not so far been the subject of detailed surveys or investigations.Many things have happened, nevertheless, in the intervening years. New structures have been identified, well-known ones have been investigated, and new Natural Science methods, particularly dendrochronology, have provided datings which in some cases have matched earlier theories and in others have stood them on their heads. The present state of research is detailed with full bibliographical references in *Dansk Middelalderarkæologi* (Liebgott 1989). Investigations of fortified sites carried out since the end of the 1970s have been recorded in the publications *Fortidsminder* and *Antikvariske Studier,* so in this article it is aspects of a more theoretical nature which will be the main focus of attention.

The few people who were involved in work on castles and fortified sites around 25 years ago were almost all associated with the National Museum and carried out this work in conjunction with their other duties in the museum.

By that time the major ruins, castles of kings and bishops, had been excavated long before, and because of the unsophisticated excavation methods of the early days, much information had been lost

On Næsholm castle mound one of the corners has been cut off and given particular protection with its own moat. On the mound there was a strong stone tower and a number of houses of different materials, brick and half timber. As a whole it is a good example of the individualistic and varied Danish castle mounds.

for good. Of course, new investigations have since then been carried out from time to time on these structures, e.g. because of restoration work or to provide the answer to specific, limited, problems. In some cases the context is also an effort to improve the presentation of the monument, as was the case with the ruins of Copenhagen Castle, under the present Christiansborg, where Johannes Hertz was responsible for the renovation and re-displaying of the structure in connection with the publication, in 1975, of a major work on Christiansborg Castle (Hvidt *et al* (eds) 1975). Hammershus on Bornholm has also been examined thoroughly in the course of recent years, in connection with restoration work and an exhibition about the castle, on the site itself, arranged by the The National Forest and Nature Agency. Over a period of years comprehensive excavations have been carried out at Kalundborg (Hertz 1990) and at other major ruins, and also at some of the smaller privately-owned sites, e.g. Sandgravvold near Århus (Krongaard Kristensen 1992).

By the middle of the present century, work on the major ruins and registration of the fortified sites in the whole country had reached a point where it could form a foundation for further studies. C.M. Schmidt's work on the major ruins had provided a general overview of castle-building and a detailed understanding of the architectural design of the castles and of the fortified elements. Around the turn of the century many fortified sites had been registered, in all their various forms, by P. Hauberg and Vilhelm la Cour (then a young scholar). Vilhelm Lorenzen had emphasized their importance as sources (Lorenzen 1949). Vilhelm la Cour resumed work on the fortified sites in the early 1940s and presented his ideas for the future study of them in *Historisk Tidskrift* (la Cour 1963). Together with Hans Stiesdal he was responsible for the publication of two volumes on the fortified sites in the districts of Hjørring and Thisted (la Cour & Stiesdal 1957, 63). The basis for this was a new registration of all structures, and in many cases surveys of them, together with a review of the written sources for each site. The goal was to produce a "corpus on fortified-sites", which like the series on Danish churches, *Danmarks Kirker,* would cover the entire country; comprehensive preparatory material exists, in the archives of the National Museum, for the districts of Frederiksborg and Århus. For the time being, however, there are no plans to continue this work; a general overview of the fortified sites in the country is to be found in *Trap Danmark,* 5th edition, which began to be published in 1958.

There have not been many new discoveries of fortified sites in recent years; some are listed in *Fortidsminder* (Borch Vesth 1985). On the other hand, there have been various investigations which have both contributed to archaeological knowledge and increased understanding of written sources. This was the case, for instance, at Eriksvolde on Lolland, which Vilhelm la Cour (1972) dated to the first half of the 12th century on the basis of the structure-type. Excavations have since shown that this remarkable double fortress was built on top of culture-layers from the 14th century, and it can be dated by dendrochronology to the beginning of the 1340s. It can only have had a short functional life, and although Eriksvolde is not mentioned directly in any written sources it must have been one of the Holstein-owned fortresses on Lolland which were destroyed by the *drost* (Royal Steward), according to the *Yngre Sjællandske Krønike,* actually in the early 1340s. The results of the excavation have most recently been described by Karen Løkkegaard Poulsen (1992).

The volume on Næsholm (la Cour 1961) is still the only complete publication of a total excavation of a fortified site with plentiful finds. There were, for instance, many coins which could date the site to within about 100 years, between the second half of the 13th century and the middle of the 14th century. For this reason Næsholm is still a focus of attention and the results of other investigations tend to be compared to this site and the finds from it. The most recent development is that timber from the bridge across the marsh to the castle islet has been dated by dendrochronology to 1278, but an up-dated analysis of the coin-material runs counter to that dating and upholds the earlier date of establishment indicated by la Cour's conclusions (Engberg 1992b; Steen Jensen 1992).

It was above all the typological considerations and the terminology used in the two volumes (la Cour and Stiesdal 1957, 1963) of the "corpus" on fortified sites which influenced subsequent research.

A clear terminology was necessary for systematic work with the castle sites, and it was important to find out whether a typological categorization could be used as the basis for dating. An attempt was made to borrow terminology used abroad, where medieval castles had existed and developed for periods of several hundred years before they came into use in Denmark. Castellologists there were using the designations "motte" for the fortified element and "bailey" for the residential and farm quarters of the castle. Structures with a fortified element resembling a classical motte, and a farm area similar to a bailey, do in fact exist in Denmark, but the Danish fortified sites are so varied and individualistic that it was decided to favour the designation *castrum-curia,* i.e. "castle and farm". These are the two elements which are characteristic of the medieval castle, no matter how it is positioned or equipped as regards mounds, ramparts, moats and walls.

This was a far-sighted choice, because with time it has become more and more evident that by far the majority of the Danish medieval castles, royal and private, belong to a relatively short period much later than the time when the motte and the bailey were typical elsewhere in the world as the fortified resi-

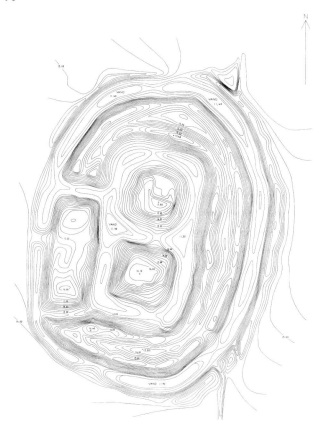

The remarkable double mound of Eriksvolde does not fit well with any typology. There is not enough space for living quarters on either of the mounds, and there was no farm attached. But sense can be made of the site if it is seen as a pure fortification for an emergency.

The little fortified island of Solvig also illustrates how the form of the fortification is conditioned more by need than by date.

dences of local potentates. The great degree of variety in the Danish castle-structures, and the fact that the background to the building of the individual structure is seldom known, make it difficult if not impossible to date them typologically. Apart from the large public structures there are few Danish fortified sites dated earlier than around 1300 (Stiesdal 1981). Among the privately-built structures which can be dated, Skådebakken, on Hjelm, was - and is still - the earliest. Coins were found there from the 1280s, when according to written sources Stig Andersen, the Marshal of the realm, and others who had been outlawed for the murder of the king at Finderup, took refuge on the island. Næsholm, as already mentioned, cannot readily be dated more precisely than to a period of functioning between the middle of the 13th century and about 100 years later, and nothing more is known about the site than that it was probably a royal possession. The lifetime of Næsholm, however, lies within the period which, around 1980, as a result of excavations and on the basis of evidence in the written sources, came to be thought of as the "century of the castle" - specifically the privately-owned castle - in Denmark.

This was the time after the death of Valdemar the Victorious in 1241, when war broke out between his sons, up to the reign of Valdemar Atterdag, from 1340 onwards, when royal power was gradually re-established, first by King Valdemar himself and then, conclusively, under his daughter Margrethe. This more or less covers the lifetime of Næsholm Castle, and just as it has only been possible to date a few private castles with certainty to the 13th century, it is unlikely that many new private castles were built after the middle of the 14th century. Probably none at all were built under Margrethe. The restoration of royal power received its ultimate confirmation with her decree of 1396 prohibiting the construction of private castles.

The written sources contribute substantially to the impression that throughout a period of nearly a century - the "century of the castle" - the conditions in the country were such that it was natural and possible for private individuals to fortify their homes and property. The evidence of this is summarized by Rikke Agnete Olsen in *Borge i Danmark* (Castles in Denmark) (1986), although there is no emphasis there on Margrethe's prohibition of private castle-building being an expression of restoration of royal power, i.e. the recovery of the monarchy's monopoly of castle-building for the defence of the realm.

Examination of written sources was in keeping with the suggestion by La Cour and Stiesdal that the castles should not purely be studied typologically with a view to dating. The goal should be to place them in their social and historical context. This was also behind Hans Stiesdal's recommendation (1981) to discontinue the use of the terms "motte" and "bailey" with reference to the Danish structures. Those terms in fact relate to fortifications from the infancy of the medieval castle in societies which were quite different from those found in Denmark in the high Middle Ages. Even though some of the Danish earthworks may resemble old French and German ones, their purpose was different and the historical preconditions were dissimilar. This can also be said of conditions in England in the years around and after the Norman Conquest of 1066.

There are a few motte-bailey structures in England which can be dated to the years before 1066, and during the campaign which followed up the victory at Hastings and secured the Conquest, hastily erected "mottes" were used as support-points for the army on the route through the country.

Eriksvolde is a Danish example of the use of earthworks in an acute war-crisis, and even in the 15th century Eric of Pomerania used small, hurriedly-erected mounds in his campaign to recapture the Duchy of Slesvig. The Valdemars had doubtless done the same in Wendland and in their battles against the North German princes in the 12th century.

During the reign of Eric of Pomerania there was still a need for private fortifications in Slesvig, but in the rest of Denmark private castles virtually came to an end during Margrethe's rule, following the active demolition she engaged in, with the help of the Church, and from which even her friends were not exempt. This is the historical reality which the written sources describe, and one has to be familiar with this to understand the archaeological evidence.

Much searching has been carried out, and is still continuing, for fortified sites from the period between the circular fortresses and communal defence systems of the Viking Age and the middle of the 12th century, or just after, when the major and minor royal castles were constructed. Vordingborg, Copenhagen and Kalundborg, along with Sprogø and Tårnborg near Korsør are a few of them. Helsingborg and Varberg, as well as Sønderborg and others should be added to the list; there are more which belong to the 12th century or perhaps earlier than has so far been thought likely. This may apply, for instance, to Søby on Ærø and Revshaleborg on Borgø in Maribo lake - all royal fortifications, not private ones.

There was certainly plenty of unrest in the kingdom after the murder of Knud Lavard in 1130, but it is questionable whether this gave rise to private castle-building. The few private fortifications which have been identified, such as the Bastrup Tower near Farum and Pedersborg near Sorø, belonged to members of the Hvide family, the most powerful in the country, responsible for putting Valdemar the Great on the throne. In both those cases the buildings, of stone, were of international quality, and at both sites the fortifications vanished at an early date. Most of the 12th century houses of local potentates were built for peaceful purposes, as was the stone house at Pedersborg, and more and more cases are being found where they are closely associated with the church. This highlights the fact that the "farmers" who built the churches were the big landowners, and their farms were modelled on the king's own farm and European patterns (Engberg 1992c). Houses built of stone or brick were reserved for only the very uppermost circles, within castles also. In Tranekær on Langeland the remains can still be found, in the masonry, of a 13th century brick house (Stiesdal 1974), but that was also originally a royal possession which later belonged to the Duke of Slesvig.

Wood was the normal building material of the castles which have been investigated, e.g. Egholm in Himmerland (Jantzen 1992). Wood and half-timber was usual even for the upper class throughout most of the Middle Ages, and by the middle of the 14th century the internal layout of one of the houses at Halkær/Hedegård in Himmerland was still virtually the same as in the long houses of the Viking Age. The houses on the late medieval manor-house sites were also more often than not timber-built or half-timbered.

Among the very few major investigations of castles and fortifications in the last 25 years, mention should be made of Søby Volde on Ærø, Tårnborg near Korsør and Søborg in North Sealand. At all three sites there were market-places or towns associated with the fortifications. Søborg developed for a period into a market-town, but in the two other places the settlement disappeared; Tårnborg may even have been as sizeable and important as Vordingborg, which is described as urbs in written sources.

Research into castles and fortifications, and maintenance of them, is now no longer centrally carried out by the National Museum's Medieval Department, but is divided up between several institutions. Local museums now have professionally-qualified staff who carry out excavations in their own area. Where previously it was historians, art historians or architects all from one institution who worked with medieval monuments, now it is often prehistorians from different museums.

This double decentralisation means that in future great care will need to be taken to ensure that all excavation plans and reports are still collected in one place. It must also be strongly emphasized that cooperation between different disciplines is extremely important. The questions one poses of the material are determined by the nature of one's own professional background, and this also applies to the guidance one obtains through the relevant literature. Without deep insight into the historical issues and their development, and the current state of research, there can only be registration, without any progress towards syntheses valid for the longer term.

Rural settlement

BY ERLAND PORSMOSE

Medieval and Renaissance-period rural settlement is still a poorly studied area given relatively low priority by medieval arcaheologists. In the last 25 years, however, it has been possible to outline how the change from the shifting village of the Iron Age to the stable village of the Middle Ages can be understood, mostly as a result of rescue excavations. Meanwhile, the structural development of the medieval and Renaissance-period village is still very weakly illuminated, and, shamefully, we have as yet no practically fully excavated medieval village.

There are many reasons for this. Axel Steensberg's pioneering excavations in the 1930's and 40's had pointed out the basic methodological problems facing village archaeology. As a rule, there are no postholes, making it hard to identify definite buildings. This particularly affects the outhouses, which are often impossible to recognize. Then, it follows from the stable nature of the village that the settlement layers from the 1,000-year history of the village are often thoroughly disturbed and difficult to separate. The result of this is that archaeological excavation is very time-consuming and thus expensive, which has presumably been extremely discouraging. The Scandinavian Deserted Village Project's mapping of the Late-medieval deserted village crisis therefore had to proceed with virtually no help (except via surveys) from archaeologists in its main period from 1970 to 1975 (Gissel 1976).

While Axel Steensberg's excavations were guided by an ethnological tradition of farmstead research, a special course in Medieval Archaeology was established 25 years ago at Århus University. However the head of this had to observe in 1976 that "Agriculture was the all-dominant occupation of medieval Denmark. One would think, then, that Medieval Archaeology would carefully nurture the study of evidence for medieval farmers, their farmsteads, tools and fields. With some shame we have to note that at present this is not the case" (O. Olsen 1977:10). Regrettably, the same could be said 15 years later (Engberg 1992a:115), even though the 1980's had seen important breakthroughs. In an attempt to counteract this unhappy tradition the "Village Group" was set up in 1987 between museums in Denmark and Skåne. As early as 1982, younger archaeologists and historians had established an annual symposium "Town and country in the Middle Ages". These two organizations now contribute to a more active environment

of research into medieval rural settlement in Scandinavia.

As well as the lack of a research tradition and the methodological difficulties, the slight research tradition of village archaeology lacks defined problems for research and faces the competition of historical geography. The geographical continuity of our villages before the 18th century has been dealt with primarily through retrospection from clearance maps and field books (V. Hansen 1964;; Hastrup 1964; Porsmose 1981; K.E. Frandsen 1983). This method has produced strong results, especially where it has been possible to underpin retrospection with contemporary material, documentary or archaeological. But it is in the very nature of retrospection to set up/discover a plausible course of development that could have produced the finished result known - there is an inevitable tendency to emphasize continuity because that is what the method assumes. Worse still, perhaps, is that retrospective studies have hidden our basic ignorance of village development in the Middle Ages and Renaissance Period. We are not in fact currently in a position to give any certain or reasonably detailed answers to the questions of when and how the geographical village structure of the 18th century arose (Porsmose 1992a).

Having said that, however, it must be noted that archaeological work of the last 25 years has decisively changed our views of the origin and development of the medieval village. Even in 1970, the description of settlement development from the Late Roman Period to the High Middle Ages (400-1200 A.D.) relied almost totally on place-name evidence. On this basis a chronology was constructed with three phases of development leading to the present villages. The earliest phase was characterized by village names ending in -heim, -inge, -lev, -løse and -sted, which were thought to go back to the transition from the Early to the Late Iron Age. A Viking-period phase was represented by names ending in -torp, -by and -toft, and there was finally a phase of expansion in the earlier Middle Ages with names ending in -rud, -rød and -tved. In the 1970's, through extensive Iron Age excavations in Jutland in particular, it became clear that a shifting village pattern did not belong only to the Early Iron Age but also the Late. At this time, a project on "The Origin and Development of the Village" was carried through on Fyn (Grøngaard Jeppesen 1981; Porsmose 1981), with one of its main aims being to date stages of the foundation of our modern villages through a series of problem-orientated excavations in 15 villages on Fyn. These excavations were later followed up by similar excavations in Jutland, on Sjælland (Hedeager 1982) and in Skåne (Skansjö 1983).

The common result is that the thousand-year wandering of the Iron-age village seems to have ceased in a period between the last decades of the 10th century and the beginning of the 12th. It appears that villages with an early church may have stopped moving relatively early while other villages could shift for the last time around 1100. Thus the church-village of Rønninge on eastern Fyn came to its present site in the late 900's while nearby Røjerup moved from the Viking-period site "Bytoften" ("village-site") around 1100 (Porsmose 1992b). This phenomenon implies that the earliest, 11th-century phase of the medieval village might often be excavated in a fairly undisturbed state as the settlement preceding a modern village, as in fact at Vorbasse and Røjerup Bytofte. In a similar way, part of the predecessor of the village of Veerst of the Early Middle Ages was excavated at Bulagergård (Adamsen 1982). The predecessors of modern villages can often be recognized in 17th- and 18th-century field names such as Gammeltoft or Gammelby (Old Farm, Old Town). A large number of these sites have gradually been identified on Fyn, Falster and Sjælland, and as a rule these names seem to pertain to Viking-period settlements. An extensive, systematically planned excavation of one of these "old" Viking-period settlements is currently underway at Varpelev Gammeltofter, Stevns (Tornbjerg 1991).

The emergence of the stable village belongs to a period of agricultural revolution when agriculture expanded and intensified greatly after the introduction of open-fields and the mouldboard plough. An increasing shortage of grazing resources made it necessary to regulate the group-cultivation that was reflected in the system of farms more closely; the crown derived taxation from just this system. On top of such heavy control and regulation of the exploitation of resources, church-building was a new and stabilizing factor. With Christianity, cemetery and settlement merged into the village and church, with the church eventually fortified as an apparently eternal stone building (Porsmose 1988: 220ff.).

The intensification of agriculture was accompanied by a decentralization of settlement. Out of the old villages ("adelby") "thorps" were set up, com-

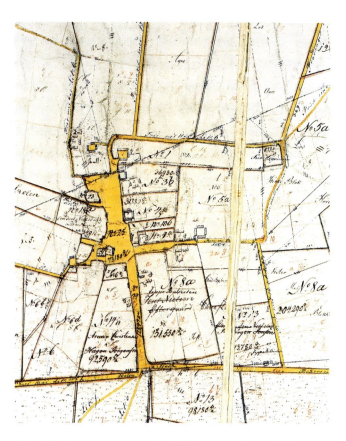

When Vorbasse was mapped in 1788 in connexion with clearance, the village comprised 6 large holdings, one of which had been divided into three farmsteads as well as the manse connected to the church. The holdings prove to be laid out in the same modular system as in the 11th-century village. At matriculation, in 1688, Vorbasse comprised 9 equally sized farmsteads (including the manse). These large crofts were then used for cultivation, haymaking and grazing.

prising one or a few farms. Many of these thorps were abandoned again in the Late Middle Ages. Some were deserted, while others merged with the old mother villages. The tendency was back towards centralization of settlement. Many "thorps" therefore had a functioning life of 100-200 years, and like the Iron-age settlements the abandoned thorps are often now under fields accessible to excavation. Field names and a few contemporary documents reveal the location of many such deserted thorps. Between 1951 and 1973 Axel Steenberg excavated one of these sites at Borup by Slagelse. Building plots were unfortunately very difficult to see, postholes being absent, but it proved possible to plan much of the associated common field, the parcels of which have since been covered by forest (Steensberg 1983).

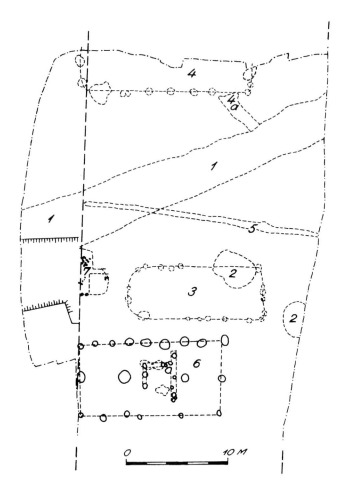

Rønninge manse. General plan. 1: Viking-period ditch; 2: Viking-period sunken hut; 3: building plot, Viking-period/ early Middle Ages; 4: building plot with associated ditch (4a), High or late Middle Ages; 5: minor ditch, 16th- or 17th-century; 6: post-built living room above predecessor, 16th- or 17th-century; 7: remains of the neighbouring manse's kiln, 19th-century. The boundary system of the clearance map, to which building 6 and ditch 5 belong, seems to have been established in the late Middle Ages. Beneath this system lies a different, earlier boundary system, marked by the ditches 1 and 4a with the associated building 4 (Porsmose 1989).

Better preserved building plots were found by excavation of the village of Jernkær near Ribe which seems to have been in use from *ca.* 1000 to 1350 A.D. This low-lying village may have been destroyed by a huge flood of 1362 (P.K. Madsen & Petersen 1983). In 1991, near Århus, a thorp called "Todderup" was excavated which proved to comprise a single farmstead, founded around 1230 and abandoned a century later. When parcelled off from the old mother village, a ditch was dug as a boundary marker. This 700/800-year-old boundary is still

part of the local map, just as the name "Todderup mark" has survived (Hoff & Jeppesen 1992). Ditches as boundary markers seem to have been common in the Middle Ages. Both in towns and villages, ditches often form farm or plot boundaries (Siemen 1991:74f.) while ownership boundaries can be marked in this way too.

The villages saw marked internal structural development in the course of the Middle Ages that gradually replaced the late Viking-period village of the 11th century with its farmyards characterized by evenly scattered buildings in large, enclosed crofts with the 18th-century structure of often four-winged farmsteads sited at the inner end of the croft hard by the village street. In some villages, as at Vorbasse, we must reckon with a basically unchanged pattern of crofts from the 11th century to the 17th. At Rønninge, in contrast, it can be shown that this structure changed decisively in the Late Middle Ages. Historians have shown that around 1300 many villages were shaped by a large-scale cultivation system with attending smallholdings that was superseded by a equally large fixed farm structure in the Late Middle Ages. The village continued - as at Rønninge - to house one main farm, which in the Late Middle Ages was often moved out or simply broken up. Such restructuring will often presumably imply the recasting of the pattern of crofts, but at present we simply do not know what a 12th- to 13th-century main farm, ordinary farm, partible farm or tied farm would look like archaeolo-gically, and it is therefore impossible to identify these fundamental Late-medieval structural changes. A contributory factor here is that the majority of the excavations that have been carried out have been excavations in more recent farm sites under which continuity is indeed often broken in the Late Middle Ages, which was probably the period in which the winged farmstead emerged. From 1000 to 1300, however, the complex of buildings has to be sought all over the croft behind the 17th- and 18th-century farm buildings (see e.g. Grøngaard Jeppesen 1982). Future investigations of the development of medieval farm structure must therefore, as far as possible, be at the level of the croft. In Ottestrup near Slagelse a regular row of four farmsteads of the earlier Middle Ages was excavated in 1982, immediately south and south-east of the Romanesque church. Here too settlement seems to have been re-organized in the Late Middle Ages (L. Holm & Nielsen 1983).

A two-winged, T-shaped farm of the Late Middle Ages from Pebringe (Steensberg 1986) was for decades the only example of a medieval composite winged farmstead. In recent years a similar T-shaped structure of this period has been excavated in Skåne (Kling 1992). Near Oksbøl an L-shaped farmstead dated to *ca.* 1200 was excavated in 1985 (U. Mejdahl 1987).

It seems that the 2-, 3- or 4-winged farmstead right beside the street triumphs in the villages in the Late Middle Ages and Renaissance Period. Excavations in Vorbasse town revealed such 3-winged farm buildings of the 16th and 17th centuries (Kieffer-Olsen 1987).

Building practice developed considerably in the course of the Middle Ages, although the relatively small number of excavated building plots in relation to the length of the period and the scope of development only yet allow us a notion of a few main lines of development in an inevitably very complex and regionally diverse pattern of development.

The roof-bearing posts of the three-aisled Iron-age headed structures were replaced by roof-bearing wall posts. Timber walling (vertical planking or later log-built structures) is replaced by clay-lined timber framing, and the sill beam on stone replaces the earth-fast posts of earlier times. Although archaeological building finds have grown strongly in the last 15 years, the material is still too slight for real differences to be seen between different regions, or between town and village (Fraes Rasmussen 1992).

Functional differences have to be taken into account as well as chronological and geographical variation in building practice. At the main farm of Hedegård in the second half of the 14th century there were both buildings with roof-bearing walls and stave-built planked walls on a sill beam and buildings with roof-bearing central posts and log-construction, or even roof-bearing central posts and wattle walls (Hyldgård 1987). Greater variation in building form and practice naturally accompanies the economic expansion and diversification of the Middle Ages.

Over the centuries, about 150 medieval churches have been abandoned as a result of the desertion crisis, parish mergers and the expansion of major farms. Often the medieval churchyard lies intact, with great potential for tracing population history in these centuries. In 1984 the site of such a church and its churchyard was excavated near Horsens. According to later field names the site was called Tirup. The church was apparently abandoned in the 14th century, and the great majority of the more than 600 graves that were excavated are of the 12th and 13th centuries (Boldsen *et al.* 1986). It is striking that the average height - 166 cm. for men and 155 for women - matches the situation in the same area in the mid-19th century exactly.

As well as agrarian settlements such as villages and farms, the economically differentiated medieval community included a series of settlement-types outside the market towns. Fortifications, forts and mills are discussed elsewhere. There has recently been an archaeological breakthrough, not least in the case of watermills. Mill sites are often very well preserved in their low, wet locations (C. Fischer 1990), and it can be anticipated that in a few years a chronological-typological framework will be established for the interpretation of this technological achievement of medieval society. Coastal "settlements" such as landing places, trading sites, fishing camps and harbours are still only slightly investigated. At present an interdisciplinary study of the coastal settlements of Fyn in the Iron Age and Middle Ages is being carried out under the aegis of the project "Atlas of the Coast of Fyn: 0-1500 A.D." (Crumlin-Pedersen 1991c).

Besides settlement archaeology, in the future a lot of effort needs to be put into interdisciplinary research into landscape and vegetational development in relation to the medieval agrarian economy. At the Cartographic Records Centre, Odense University, extensive registration of ridge-and-furrow field systems in the woodlands of Fyn is currently underway (under Per Grau Møller).

Altogether, an immense programme of research is required before archaeology can make serious inroads into the history of agrarian society of Denmark in the Middle Ages and Renaissance Period. But the potential is so clearly there for archaeology to change, radically, much of the assumed course of development.

Crafts and skills

By Niels-Knud Liebgott

During the transition from the Viking Period to the Middle Ages - as indeed in earlier times - there were people who acquired special expertise in making particularly sought-after products and who had these crafts as their main or only occupation. A few such crafts stand out: decorative artwork, weapon-making and silversmithing. Artisans undoubtedly worked in a very close "customer-producer" relationship, meaning that they produced their wares to the direct order of the future owner, being dependent on the valuable raw materials that the customer had at his diposal. This was how art was organized far into the Middle Ages.

Quite apart from this limited production of luxury goods and the virtually total self-sufficiency of the rural communities, there came into being a medieval "market economy", based on the growing division of labour in society and very closely linked to urban life and functions. Late-medieval craft - its organization, in particular - is fairly well-documented in written sources. The craft guild system can be traced back to the 13th century, from where it seems to develop parallel to the much earlier guilds concerned with trade. For the situation of craftsmen in the early Middle Ages, however, we only have archaeology to turn to.

Urban archaeology has been the major source of data on the large culture-historical area that is sometimes referred to as "daily life" and which includes such diverse matters as the physical structure of towns, the character and form of houses, and living conditions and standards - including all the material objects which the inhabitants of medieval market-towns gathered around themselves.

Because of their depth, the urban layers have proved very productive in respect of these sorts of finds, and it is possible to discern a close connexion between the development of urban archaeology and the study of medieval artefacts.

The chronological classification of the finds is, of course, crucial, and here the processing of the finds from Århus Søndervold has set a trend for Danish medieval archaeologists (H.H. Andersen *et al.* 1971). But find-processing also involves consideration of the use and relative function of the artefacts and questions of the techniques and circumstances of their production. Thorough analyses of the artefacts themselves, and finds of workshops and production sites, have recently contributed to a quite comprehensive new understanding of this field.

Characteristic of medieval craft is "professionalization". This is primarily to be seen in the "mass-production" of uniform craft goods, often of high technical quality and, in many cases, produced in workshops that required a lot of resources in the form of raw materials, power, fuel etc. This did not apply to crafts such as shoemaking. The needs of that craft were not massive, although the production of thin-soled and fashionable footware must have been large, to judge by the number of finds of semi-finished or abandoned shoes. In the early Middle Ages the shoemaker - like other leatherworkers - probably prepared the leather needed, and only later in the Middle Ages did tanning become a separate craft, as, for instance, is reflected in the street name "Skindergade" (Tanner Street) in several Danish towns.

Combmaking, a highly specialized craft, belongs amongst the earliest market-town crafts. There are early medieval workshop finds in the form of detritus and semi-manufactures from the towns of Ribe, Holbæk, Kalundborg, Næstved, Odense, Svendborg, Århus, Viborg, Kolding, Aalborg and probably many more. As well as ordinary combs, the comb-maker produced hairbrushes, cases, buttons and other small items of bone and antler. The raw material was generally taken from domesticated animals though a few finds have pieces of elk or reindeer antler, evidence of the deliberate and perhaps expensive collection of material. Although it hardly played a major role in the medieval economy, comb-making has come to play quite a major role in medieval archaeology. This is partly due to the fact that this craft seems, at present, to be the oldest specialized urban craft, and partly because the thorough study of comb finds has led to various comb-forms now being used as "leading types" (Ulbricht 1980).

It seems that there was also early specialization amongst metalworkers. We have not, it is true, excavated a single medieval smith's workshop in Denmark that could contribute evidence for this. There are also no complete finds of tool sets such as those of the Viking Period, although intermittent single finds of, for instance, medieval iron and stone anvils, tongs, hammers, files etc. have been made. However if we look at the richly varied medieval metal finds, from horseshoes through coarse building-mounts and ship anchors to fine chest-fittings and complicated locks, we can hardly imagine that such diverse items were produced by one and the same craftsman. At the very least, the separation of blacksmithing from bronzecasting had existed since the Viking Period.

The blacksmith's requirements for workshop facilities were less than the bronzecaster's, and this is the explanation of our much greater knowledge of bronzecasting and the techniques it involved than of smithing in the Middle Ages. The smelting of bronze requires very high temperatures, so that clay moulds, fire-flues and smelting furnaces were burnt to brick under heating and thus, like brick, became practically indestructible.

From the earliest phase of urban activity at Ribe both finished cast-bronze objects and innumerable mould fragments - crucibles for melting the metals and clay tuyeres in which the mouth of the bellows would have been fixed - have been found. But we know very little of the appearance of the hearths, or perhaps the furnaces, themselves (Brinch Madsen 1984). Both in Viborg and Næstved, bronze slags and hard-burnt, almost vitrified fragments of smelting-furnace caps have been found in 11th- and 12th-century layers but here too it has not been possible to describe details of the structures more closely (J.E. Petersen 1988). In 1991, bronzecasting workshops were found at Gudme on Fyn and Refshale near Maribo, apparently for bell-casting, but neither of these finds is fully excavated yet.

Best known as yet is a bronzecaster's workshop excavated in 1978-79 on the site of the former Dominican abbey at Odense (Vellev 1985). The preserved parts of this feature, which can be dated to the end of the 13th century, represent a bell-casting workshop. The smelting furnace, from which the molten metal ran in channels down into the mould, was placed on the ground surface and thus left no traces behind.

It is generally supposed that church bells were cast by peripatetic craftsmen in the immediate vicinity of the church where the bell was to hang. This may have been the case at Gudme, Refshale and Odense, where the Dominican abbey could have been a major customer. But excavation here produced moulds for many different sorts of bronze object: mostly pots, but also candlesticks and incense burners. The activities of the Odense bronzecaster must have continued for some time, and it is reasonable to imagine him as a lay brother at the abbey who added to the friary's income by means of his craft.

The brickmaking site of Bistrup by Roskilde. The latest of the brick kilns, from the 16th century, with the parallel stokehole, disturbed an earlier, 13th-century kiln (at the top of the picture) when built.

A distinctive feature of medieval craft is increasing "internationalization". The guild system mentioned above was a direct imitation of the situation in northern Europe. With the products themselves it is difficult, in the High Middle Ages at least, to identify distinctive Scandinavian or local artefact-types such as are characteristic of the earlier periods. The cast bronze candlesticks and three-legged pots made in Denmark are no different from such objects cast in, for instance, northern Germany or the Low Countries. Only when identifiable production marks are found on the objects can one hope to establish provenance (Vellev 1985).

One can suppose that many new crafts and skills were brought to Denmark by immigrant craftsmen, or that Danes learnt their trades abroad. In one important area, however, the movement seems to have been the other way; this is the case of brickmaking. Knowledge of how to make clay bricks had survived from the Roman Period in a small area in northern Italy but had been forgotten elsewhere in Europe until suddenly it flourished in Denmark, where suitable clay deposits are virtually ubiquitous. From the early Valdemar period in the mid-12th century, craftsmen from Lombardy must have been brought to Denmark to assist with the great building projects that were completed within a few decades -

The brickmaking site of Bistrup by Roskilde. The two connected tile kilns which, in the 14th century, produced relief-decorated floor tiles for a large number of churches in the area around Roskilde fjord.

from Valdemar's Wall in the Danevirke through the minster churches of Ringsted and Sorø to massive castles such as Søborg in northern Sjælland. Brickworks sprang up everywhere, and after 1200, as the technique gradually developed, both the art of brickmaking and the special brick architecture associated with it spread from Denmark to the Low Countries, northern Germany and the whole Baltic area.

Several hundred medieval and later brick kilns have been found in the present area of Denmark and many of them have been excavated (Als Hansen 1985). Two or three new examples are regularly found every year. As the various main types have gradually become known, it is now rarely necessary to undertake extensive excavations of these structures as a minor excavation can quickly determine the age and type of the kiln. Only in one case - Pamhule skov near Haderslev - has it been possible to excavate a complete medieval brickwork complex with associated drying stacks, puddling pits etc. (S. Nielsen 1979b). As a rule, only the kiln itself is excavated, with on occasion fairly simple structures raised in the vicinity of where the relevant building was to be constructed. Like the bellcaster, the brickmaker had to travel around following work. Larger, more permanent brickworks such as we know today were rare in the Middle Ages. Along the coast of

Fyn south of Nyborg brickmaking continued from the Middle Ages far into the succeeding centuries. But production here was not only aimed at nearby churches, castles and (eventually) noble homes. The coastal location made it possible and profitable to transport this relatively cheap building material over considerable distances. The same coastal position characterizes the brickworks at Bistrup a little north-west of Roskilde. Bricks were made here in the 13th century and again in the 16th century (Als Hansen & Aaman-Sørensen 1980). Products from here are known to have been taken to a number of sites in the area around Roskilde Fjord and further afield. But there was also the cathedral town here, with its many ecclesiastical buildings, which with their constant building activity ensured a ,steady demand for the brickmaker's products.

Bistrup brickworks is interesting, not only because of the size and complexity of the site but also because the great variety of its products. Its very large but traditionally constructed brick kilns produced not only ordinary bricks but also roof tiles and specially shaped building bricks for particular architectural requirements. The most surprising finds at Bistrup, however, were two kilns built together, one oval and one rectangular. These formed a special kiln for glazed floor tiles. Such kilns are well known in Britain, but the Bistrup kilns are as yet the only such find in Denmark. It seems as if glazed floor tiles were otherwise produced in ordinary kilns along with bricks, as can be seen at Farum Lillevang, Sorø and the monastery at Øm.

A number of attempts at reconstruction and firing have contributed to the interpretation of these kilns and an improved understanding of the technical problems that medieval brickmakers faced. At Bistrup, the narrow rectangular kiln was used for firing the floor tiles. The oval kiln was used for the glazing. The whole complex was covered with a walled dome and perhaps a clay cap. If the dome is reckoned to have been a metre or more high, about 2,000 tiles could be made in one firing, enough for about half of a tiled floor in a medium-sized village church.

Like the brickmaker, the combmaker, the smith, the bell-caster and the shoemaker, the turner, the cooper, the butcher, the baker, the tailor and the potter were numbered amongst the craftsmen. Domestic production of pottery continued throughout the Middle Ages, and from the end of the period far into more modern times the production of "Jute pots" was so voluminous that these distinctive pots, made particularly by women in various parts of Jutland, could be exported to neighbouring countries.

Grey- and black-fired wares produced without a potter's wheel and fired in charcoal stacks rather than kilns were manufactured throughout the Middle Ages. Up to the year 1200, pottery kept its prehistoric character in respect of both firing and forms. In eastern Denmark pottery of a type that Slavs had introduced to the Baltic area at the end of the Iron Age was still being made. But from the beginning of the 13th century, pottery changed character. Red-fired, glazed jugs and pots now become common finds. This pottery was professionally produced with a wheel and fired in proper kilns. For a very long time it was supposed that the red-fired and often richly decorated ware was imported from Holland, but the finding of a 14th-century kiln at Farum Lillevang in the 1950's showed that such wares were also made in Denmark.

As yet, no medieval pottery kilns have been found in other Scandinavian countries, and for more than 20 years Farum Lillevang was the only known example in Denmark. In the course of the 1970's and 80's, however, four more kilns have been found: first Faurholm near Hillerød (Liebgott 1976), then Hellum in Rold Skov (J. Kock 1984), Kragelund near Silkeborg (Reinholdt 1985) and Barmer near Sebbersund. The kilns were all in use in the period *ca.* 1200-1350. None of them had a long functioning life, and none of them produced anything like as much as the one at Farum Lillevang. It may seem surprising that none of the kilns currently known share quite the same construction. The reason for this is not chronological, as on the whole they are contemporary. And since the pottery they produced was not so very different, the explanation does not seem to be technical. It must therefore be most probable that each of these potters represents a tradition of the area in which he learnt his craft. The Low Countries is still the most likely candidate. There is, however, one common characteristic of these sites: they are all a long way from towns. We can conclude from this that easy access to fuel and raw materials must have governed the location of a medieval pottery. In the 16th and 17th centuries the picture changed completely. Every self-respecting market town then had one or more potteries within its limits.

View through one of the stokeholes in a late-medieval brick kiln excavated at Grønholt, northern Sjælland, in 1984.

The discovery and processing of the large number of brickworks and pottery kilns in recent years has, by means of analysis and experimentation, led to a significant improvement of our understanding of medieval craft techniques. We can hope, and urge, strongly, that the curiosity which has been fostered in this area will grow and extend to other fields, so that the usual questions concerning age and function will in the future be accompanied by questions concerning the production of the objects. For this, Medieval Archaeology has to form an alliance with colleagues who have the appropriate technical and scientific knowledge at their disposal, as well as the necessary analytical equipment.

THE ARCHAEOLOGICAL INSTITUTIONS

The archaeological museums

BY METTE IVERSEN AND POUL OTTO NIELSEN

The development of the museum service has been an important aspect of the development of Danish Archaeology in the last 25 years. Right down to 1970, only a few local museums were staffed with university-educated archaeologists. Many of the museums had nevertheless built up significant archaeological collections, and some had been involved in archaeological work since the 1920's or 30's. The employment of archaeologists in local museums began in the 1960's, and by 1990 48 museums had such staff.

In the course of the last 25 years, the museums have developed from being traditional, committee-run local collections to being institutions that often employ several staff members educated in archaeology or history. The archaeological exhibitions in the museums, often modelled on the National Museum's exhibition, were redesigned in the course of the 1970's. New, specialized museums have appeared amongst the local institutions, such as *Vedbæk-fundene,* a museum about the Early Stone Age graves and settlements near Vedbæk north of Copenhagen, and the Museum at Lindholm Høje, Nørresundby. Both of these museums represent new steps in museum presentation. The higher level of activity created the need for new buildings, larger storerooms and workshops. In the same period, 10 local conservation laboratories have been estab-

lished, 8 of which have the status of 'county' conservation labs. This area will see continuing expansion in the coming years.

As the local museum service has grown the National Museum has seen its staff and finances cut and has therefore had to reduce its involvement in excavations. It has, on the other hand, elected to maintain the units and functions that are of importance for archaeology at a national level and that enable it to provide services for the other museums: the central registration of finds and monuments, marine-archaeological work, natural-scientific dating and identification, conservation, numismatics and runology. Thus the Danish museum service has moved in the direction of decentralization and work-sharing.

Legislation

One of the reasons for the growth in local museums is the high level of public interest in archaeology. Another reason is the progressive legislation Denmark has seen concerning museums. The Local Museum Act of 1958 established a system of support whereby the state matched local financial support, sum for sum. In practice, however, subsidies did not keep pace with costs. In the later Museum Acts (1976, 1984) the subsidy to recognized museums was fixed at 40% of the total costs of the museum up to a certain ceiling. The current subsidy is below 40%.

The present Museum Act defines the branches of the museum service and the duties of the museums. The museum councils of each county supervise co-operation between museums at a regional level. Up to now these councils have been particularly important in the establishment of regional conservation labs. At the national level, archaeological work is regulated by The Archaeological Board, led by Rigs-antikvaren (the State Antiquary). Treasure trove ("danefæ") judgements are administered for Rigsantikvaren by the National Museum, which also runs The Central Register of Cultural History, which takes in find reports from the museums. The Danish Counsil of Museums has the job of regulating museum work nationally, of recommending new museums to obtain state subsidies and administering a budget that is distributed on application for specific projects at individual museums or for shared purposes.

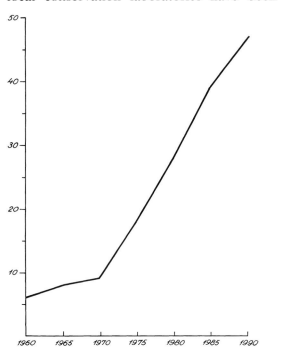

The number of local archaeological museums with staff with university qualifications, 1960 to 1990.

The museums and antiquarian work

It was in 1969 that a paragraph was included in

Denmark's Nature Protection Act to protect unlisted archaeological remains. Until 1973, the administration of this new, antiquarian side fell to Rigsantikvaren; from 1973-82 to the Environment Ministry; and from 1983 to Rigsantikvaren again. It was the museums, however, who carried out the majority of the rescue excavations that were financed either by Rigsantikvaren or by other public authorities. In 1983, the local museums entered into formalized collaboration with Rigsantikvaren over the supervision of archaeological duties: i.e. the scrutiny of local development plans, inspections and rescue excavations. The Museum Act of 1st July 1984 established The Archaeological Board, on which both the central and the local museums, together with the Protection Agency and the universities, had permanent representation, and where for the first time the museums could influence priorities within rescue excavation (Hertz 1985).

Rescue excavations, and the administrative work they involve, now occupy a great deal of the time and resources of the museums. Unlike before, when most excavations were caused by farmers ploughing up finds in their fields, it is cases involving building and construction that require attention both at the desk and in the field. Thus the museums take their share of responsibility for physical planning.

Research in the museums

The museums' excavations are just the first stage in a process of research which is pursued by the excavator himself through find processing and analyses down to publication. The local museums are behind nearly half the annual total of publications and this is not just a matter of contributions in museum periodicals but also articles in scholarly national and international journals and monographs.

Gradually, as the number and range of excavations has proliferated, and the associated administrative load has grown, it has become impossible - and indeed in some cases pointless - to process and publish every single excavation. Many of the new finds increase the source material quantitatively but do not provide radically new knowledge. An important task for the future will therefore be analyses based on comprehensive collections of data possibly supplemented by problem-oriented excavations. This requires new collaborative organizations. In the 1980's, several museums took on major research programmes in collaboration or in

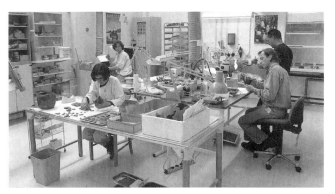

From Gram Conservation Laboratory.

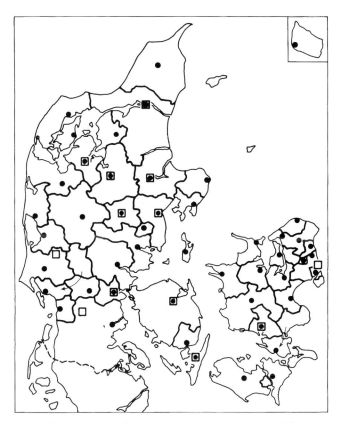

Map of archaeological museums ● and conservation laboratories □. The map also shows the division of Denmark into areas of archaeological responsibility.

interdisciplinary co-operation with other institutions.

For the archaeologists employed by museums, who have to perform several different tasks at once, it is a challenge to maintain the research perspective. In recent years it has only been possible to live up to such ideals by giving fixed-term work to unemployed archaeologists. A future goal must be to secure satisfactory work conditions for this large human and scholarly potential.

The excavations

BY SVEND E. ALBRETHSEN, JOHS. HERTZ OG SVEND NIELSEN

Ancient monuments *in situ*, the fixed remains of human activity upon and below the surface of the town and country landscape, and the loose cultural remains associated with these sites, form the true material of archaeology. They are a "vulnerable and irreplaceable resource" which, by international agreement, society is duty-bound to take care of (Hertz 1991).

In Denmark, general protection of ancient monuments was introduced in the Nature Protection Act of 1937; now, certain ancient monuments are permanently protected ("listed") under the current Nature Protection Act (see Kr. Kristiansen and T. Dehn, below) while all other ancient monuments, known and unknown, are covered by § 26 of the Museum Act. This coverage is temporary, meaning that Rigsantikvaren (the State Antiquary) can require earthwork that threatens to destroy an unlisted monument to be halted while the site is excavated, which should be completed within one year. In contrast to the rules in the neighbouring countries of Norway and Sweden, it is a principle of this Danish law that these rescue excavations shall always be publicly not privately funded. For this reason, the public authorities, including a rather vaguely defined circle of licensed groups, themselves pay for the excavations caused by the work that they undertake; Rigsantikvaren has to pay for excavations caused by private work.

A quite unique feature for ancient monument legislation is that archaeological excavations in Denmark are exclusively reserved for museums. The archaeological museums now form an elaborate network that is well-suited to take on the cases that require excavation under § 26, not least because the museums are closely involved with local planning.

The day-to-day administration of § 26 orders is undertaken by the museums together with the Archaeological Secretariat of the State Antiquary (RAS), which also functions as the secretariat for the Archaeological Board (DAN). According to § 30 of the Museum Act, it is DAN's job to define and provide basic guidelines for archaeological work and to prioritize § 26 excavations. This prioritization has, of its very nature, to take account of the archaeological importance and state of preservation of the individual site, and the nature of the threat it is under. As important tools in its work, DAN has two publications: the journal *Arkæologiske Udgravninger i Danmark (Archaeological Excavations in Denmark)*, first published in 1985, summarizes and comments

Funding

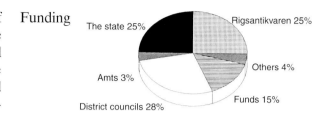

The proportional distribution of grants for archaeological excavations 1990-91. "Others" includes the licensed groups. In the years, when the major natural gas project was completed, it took far the largest share. "Funds" represents in particular a few projects that formed the majority of the museums' own chosen archaeological research. The total annual payments were about 16 million kroner, but this does not include the museums' own economic commitments, which are probably of about the same order.

Reasons

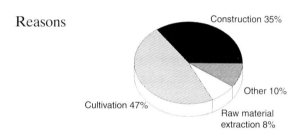

The reasons for § 26 excavations paid for by Rigsantikvaren ("P-cases") 1990-91, in percentages in proportion to the costs; a similar chart of § 26 excavations paid for by public bodies and licensed groups ("O-cases") would have been dominated by construction works (roads, pipelines etc.).

Features

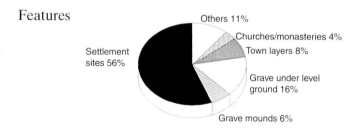

The proportional distribution of costs by objects, 1990-91, both P- and O-cases. The National Museum's excavations in churches in use are not included.

Dating

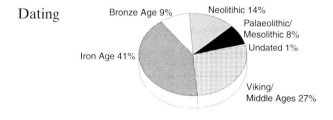

The proportional distribution of costs by archaeological periods, 1990-91, P- and O-cases.

276

upon a year's archaeological work, and offers overviews of *danefæ* (treasure trove), scientific analyses, etc.; *Arkæologisk felthåndbog (The archaeological field hand-book)* is continually updated.

In the period that this book is concerned with, legal provisions for rescue excavations have developed into the basis of virtually all field archaeology in Denmark. It is only right and proper that research efforts are directed first and foremost at those objects that are doomed to disappear, at least in so far as properly formulated questions can thus be answered; it is also, however, at present really only in this area that the money needed can be found. DAN has decided that a rescue excavation budget, irrespective of who has to pay, should include not only the costs of the excavation itself but also the production of a report, primary ("stabilizing") conservation of objects found, sampling in the field and basic analysis and urgent natural scientific datings; not, however, costs of post-excavation work including wider scientific analysis and publication.

The development of the archaeological capability of the local museums, an important prerequisite for the re-organization of 1983 (Hertz 1985), continued down through the 1980's and increased both the ability to follow up § 26 jobs and the pressure on Rigsantikvaren's funds, which did not grow in pace. There is therefore a pressing need for both Rigsantikvaren's resources for rescue excavation to be improved and the museums' own resources for further work on the material, including scientific analyses, selected research and, not least, publication. With a coming revision of the law, one must

In the years 1979-86, when most of the Danish natural gas network was established, the natural gas companies were the largest contributors to Danish archaeology. With large construction projects like this it has been usual for the developer to pay for the sites to be surveyed for ancient monuments in advance. The natural gas excavations are described in the publication Danmarks længste udgravning (Denmark's longest dig) (RAS 1986) and were also the subject of an exhibition.

argue for a clearer and broader definition of the circle of those required by law to fund rescue excavations. But the individual citizen should still be spared direct charges of this kind (of course we all pay something through tax) which could discredit archaeology. Popular support is Danish archaeology's greatest asset.

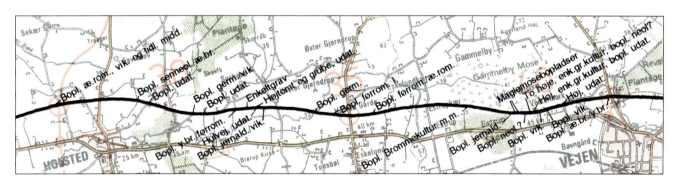

On the strength of the results of the natural gas and motorway excavations it can be seen that there are about 30 sites per square kilometre, while the parish description, with its current total of about 130,000 sites, indicates the presence of only 3. It is typical that the increase is accounted for overwhelmingly by settlements. On the 20-km. long and 60-m. wide track of the motorway between Vejen and Holsted there will be about 30 new parish description points when the Museum at Sønderskov has finished its work; only a couple of barrow sites were known beforehand. © Kort- og Matrikelstyrelsen (A 66-93).

Archaeology in the universities

BY ULLA LUND HANSEN AND JØRGEN LUND

The first Chair in Scandinavian Archaeology was established at the University of Copenhagen in 1855. However it disappeared again in 1866 not to be revived until 1930. Teaching in Scandinavian Archaeology and European Prehistory is now offered in both the University of Copenhagen and the University of Århus where it was introduced in 1949. In 1971, a further Chair, in Medieval Archaeology, was established in Århus. Prehistoric Archaeology covers the study of the development of cultures from the Palaeolithic down to (and including) the Viking Period, while Medieval Archaeology covers the period from *ca.* 950 to *ca.* 1550. Central to both subjects is the study of Scandinavian cultural history and its European background.

Archaeology at the University of Copenhagen.
Having for many years been housed in the National Museum, the Institute, together with the Institute of Classical Archaeology, moved to refurbished offices at Vandkunsten 5, close to the Museum (C.J. Becker 1979). The primary reason for this move was the urgent problem of space for the steadily growing number of students.

The Institute in Vandkunsten now provides offices for the staff, libraries, reading and study rooms for the students, and drawing offices, a computer room, store rooms, a laboratory with facilities for the treatment of finds, flint studies and experiments, and a laboratory furnished with microscopes and photographic equipment and equipment for the thin-sectioning of pottery, *etc.* The Institute also possesses a fine collection of samples of flint from many parts of the world and a teaching collection of artefacts and copies. In 1986, the Faculty of the University of Copenhagen decided to merge the Institute of Prehistoric Archaeology and the Institute of Classical Archaeology into one institute, though preserving the two subjects. In the summer of 1993 the Institute of Archaeology and the Institute of European Folk Studies were merged.

Staff
The staff now comprises four teacher/lecturers, of which two have the title of *docent.* In accordance with a research recruitment plan, a further teaching post in Arctic Archaeology was granted in 1987 (dropped again in 1991, but, provisionally, to be carried forward in two years' time) and in 1989 a lectureship in Marine Archaeology was granted. There is also a varying number of individuals studying for the *licentiate* degree attached to the Institute, externally funded stipendiaries and teaching assistants.

Since 1876, 16 academic doctorates have been awarded, and since 1990 four Ph.D.'s.

Schemes of study in Copenhagen.
The first Master's disputation *(mag.art.)* in Prehistoric Archaeology was convened in 1932, and in 1958 a supplementary subject *(bifag)* examination in Scandinavian Archaeology *(cand.art.)* was introduced.

The current scheme of study was introduced in 1990, and offers a three-year Bachelor programme followed by the *cand.phil.* examination after one year or the *cand.mag.* examination after two years; a disputation two years after the *cand.phil.* and/or a Ph.D. three years after the *cand.phil.* In the new schemes of study the academic content has been extended to include Medieval Archaeology, while dissertations could, in principle, be offered on material from anywhere in the world. Arctic Archaeology can be studied in a special two-year course after the Bachelor examination, and leads to a *cand.mag.* examination. An equivalent two-year advanced course in Marine Archaeology is also in preparation.

Archaeology at the University of Århus
Ever since the subject was introduced in 1949, there has been a symbiotic relationship between the Institute and Århus Museum, more recently the Museum of Prehistory. This close relationship is enriching and fruitful, not least for the students who have direct access to the museum environment. An additional advantage that should also be mentioned is the wide range of shared technical facilities such as a drawing office, a photographic laboratory, a reconstruction workshop and conservation, where the wear-mark laboratory of the Institute is also housed. The Institute also has a fine teaching collection. After changing address several times, at the end of the 1960's the Institute and the Museum finally settled at the Manor of Moesgaard, a little south of Århus. But the Institute has also changed its name in the meanwhile, reflecting its history very clearly. In 1962, teaching of Ethnography began, and from 1963 it was called the Institute of Prehistoric Archaeology and Ethnography. The final branch on the stock was Medieval Archaeology, which appeared in 1971, teaching having begun in 1969. In 1973 the Institute was given its current name, the Institute of Prehistoric Archaeology, Medieval Archaeology, Ethnography and Social

Anthropology, and thus comprises three independent departments.

Staff

On July 1st, 1992, the academic staff in Prehistoric Archaeology included one docent and five lecturers, and in Medieval Archaeology one docent and two lecturers. There are also eight technicians and secretaries. There are three *licentiate* students in Prehistory and one in Medieval Archaeology. There is also a number of externally funded research stipendiaries - on average, two to four. Over the years, Prehistoric Archaeology has been responsible for the awarding of a number of academic titles. Four doctors have been created, and a total of seven Ph.D.'s in the last four years.

Schemes of study in Århus

As early as 1972, both archaeological fields had schemes of study that allowed supplementary and major subject examinations and the disputation. The Ministry of Educations Order of 1985 changed the structure of studies in the Humanities radically, for instance with the abandonment of the supplementary subject. In 1990 a three-year Bachelor degree based on the English model was introduced, comprising a two-year basic course followed by a one-year Bachelor module. There have been changes at the other end too. The major subject *(hovedfag)* was formally discontinued, and replaced by an advanced course of two years' duration. A completed course of study at the third level leads to the title of *cand.phil.* The disputation, however, remains unchanged, and is reached after two years' further study. The last stage is the three-year, highly specialized, *licentiate* course, which is normally undertaken immediately after the *cand.phil.*

Internationalization

Archaeology has traditionally been of a strongly international character - a natural consequence of the fact that cultures and finds cannot be adequately understood in a limited local context. This important aspect of Archaeology has been further strengthened by the establishment of a large number of international research and teaching programmes in recent years. The archaeological institutes participate in a wide sweep of contacts, including, for instance, teacher and student exchanges, network arrangements, *etc.* It should finally be pointed out that the new political situation in eastern Europe has provided additional opportunities for increased con-

tact, and Archaeology is one of the Humanities that has taken full cognizance of this. It can be assumed that internationalization will continue apace over the next decade.

The new archaeological courses

The courses in Archaeology are aimed at making the students familiar with the scholarly problems and developing their ability to carry out independent studies. The course qualifies them to carry out specific jobs in research, in museums or in the public management of cultural history. Considering the high number of graduates, the possibility of finding employment has been better up to now than one would have expected. But permanent jobs are few, and most graduates have to manage with temporary posts or stipends for a number of years. The new schemes of study, however, create new possibilities. The course of study is individually shaped, and Archaeology can now be combined with other subjects in the Humanities or the natural sciences. Like archaeological research, teaching in the coming years will increasingly be based on greater interdisciplinary collaboration, and the possibility of employment outside of the traditional workplaces such as museums and universities thus grows. On top of this there is the possibility of specializing in, for instance, Arctic Archaeology or Marine Archaeology, while Experimental Archaeology, Laboratory Archaeology and Information Technology are playing an ever greater role as elements in the range of studies.

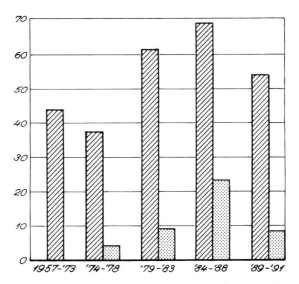

The output of candidates (cand.phil. *and* mag.art.*) in Prehistoric Archaeology (shaded) and in Medieval Archaeology at the Universities of Copenhagen and Århus.*

279

The amateurs

BY ELUF LYNGBAK

Many people evidently regard "collectors" and "amateur archaeologists" as one and the same thing. But there is a difference: the collecter is interested in the objects - the stone axes, the daggers, the flakes etc. - as objects in themselves; the amateur archaeologist is interested in the people and the culture behind the objects. Thus he values find contexts and surveys, and for this reason cultivates close co-operation with a museum and its professional archaeologists. Over the years, such co-operation has been established in many places, often very profitably.

Amateur archaeology has proud traditions in Denmark. A fundamental part of early archaeological research was based upon the efforts of people who cherished archaeology as an interest but who earned their living in other ways. From the 19th century we can note, at random, Vedel, a sheriff, and Sehested, a chamberlain, and from the present century there are people like Frode Kristensen, a teacher, Berthelsen, a dentist, and Erik Westerby, a chief of police.

Nowadays, the amateurs continue to contribute to new advances, despite the fact that the law has made it harder to have archaeology as a hobby. Being an amateur archaeologist is therefore a quite different thing now (bearing in mind the difference between collectors and amateur archaeologists noted above!). Both alone, and in local groups, efforts have been made to get involved with the museums and their specialists in surveying and sometimes excavation too. Some objects, of course, would never have been recorded or excavated if an interested layman had not given a warning at the right time and place.

It has been common for amateurs to get together in societies in recent years. There were less than a dozen of these in Denmark 25 years ago, but now there are about 30. This does a great deal to raise standards in respect of surveying and the handling of finds. A number of museums all over the country have learnt to make use of the potential workforce this provides. On the other hand the members of the amateur archaeologists' groups - and many freelance amateurs -have learnt to respect professional archaeology, in terms of recognizing one's limits, not least in respect of registration. A large number of rescue excavations in connexion with, for instance, motorway, natural gas pipeline and other construction projects, can be seen as the product of the crucial point in all of this: good collaboration between specialists and amateurs.

The amateur archaeologist has opportunities that the professionals cannot have. These consist primarily of the strength of numbers and institutional freedom. On top of this are the opportunities provided by important contacts that a local resident can have with his own neighbours, not least in his occupation. Finally, an amateur will often have a deeper historical and geographical knowledge of the immediate locality than a professional archaeologist could obtain.

From this, one can begin to distinguish the tasks for modern amateur archaeologists. In brief these are surveying, reporting and, on occasion, assisting.

In 1990, amateur archaeology took an important step with the inauguration of the *Union of Danish Amateur Archaeologists* (SDA). It is the aim of the union to further archaeological work in Denmark by defending the interests of amateur archaeologists, disseminating knowledge of archaeological work, working together with professional archaeologists and museums and raising the knowledge, standards and status of amateur archaeologists. Next comes the cultivation of more international contact and collaboration. In Scandinavia, we are already well under way, as since 1988 excavation camps for Nordic amateur archaeologists have been arranged (NAU camps). These have taken place in Denmark, Sweden, Noway and Finland. In 1991 an NAU camp took place in Tallinn, Estonia. It is intended that NAU-93 will be held in Denmark, near Vejle in fact.

The organized amateur archaeologists can thus, happily, see that there are plenty of tasks and challenges for them in the future.

Registration and records

By Henrik Jarl Hansen

We have a tradition of archaeological records going back for centuries in Denmark, the usefulness of which has been greatly enhanced in the last 10-15 years through computerization. Such registers are now an essential tool for the planning of rescue excavations and protection. Meanwhile their academic potential is also growing substantially.

A degree of interest in bygone ages can be seen as early as the beginning of the 17th century; the first collection of reports on ancient monuments was established by Ole Worm in the 1620's. More than two centuries elapsed, however, before this tiny initiative turned into anything more methodical. As a result of the increasing destruction of Danish monuments, a national survey of archaeological finds and monuments was begun 1873. The written result of this is known in archaeological circles as the Parish Record. The collection and classification of data from our cultural heritage is, therefore, no new phenomenon, but exactly 25 years ago a manual system of registration of archaeological objects and structures was presented in what was called a "central card-index". Although the idea really went back to 1950, it was novel that the processing of material with the help of punch-cards and computers was envisaged (Voss 1967). It was only at the end of the 1970's, however, that it was practicable to use computers in central archaeological registration. At that time, collaboration was established among the National Agency for the Protection of Nature Monuments and Sites, the National Council of Museums and the National Museum concerning computerized processing of the Parish Record maps and, later, of the associated, handwritten texts (P.O. Nielsen 1981b; Pauly 1982; Ebbesen 1985a). Underlying this effort was the district and regional councils' and the museum world's growing need to be able to use these archaeological maps in planning. In 1984, this work led to the creation of The Danish National Record of Sites and Monuments (DKC) in the National Museum.

Before electronic registration was set in motion, the Parish Record contained information on about 105,000 finds and monuments nationwide. The data included the marking of the individual find spots on maps and associated, handwritten descriptions. The transference of all the mapped data to computer was completed at the beginning of 1982. The field of the Central Register includes in principle all culture-historical finds and monuments from the earliest times to the present. In order to secure this broad basis, the Museum Act of 1984 requires state-funded culture-historical museums to contribute to the common register.

Watercolour showing the archaeologist Vilhelm Boye by the remains of a megalithic grave in Blovstrød parish on Sjælland. The monument, which was painted by E. Rondal during a tour in 1884, has now completely disappeared, but the antiquarian information about it is preserved in The National Record. All the data in this are accessible for administrative use and for research and display purposes from all sorts of different angles (C.U. Larsen 1986, 1989; Jarl Hansen 1990b, 1992, 1993; Christoffersen 1992).

A second important task for DKC is the registration of all newly-discovered archaeological finds. Since the unofficial opening of the register in 1982, about 14,000 new finds have been reported, distributed across the whole country, as well as much supplementary information about previously recorded sites: much more than was anticipated when the register was planned.

At present, The National Record contains data on slightly more than 130,000 finds.

Under the Forest and Nature Agency (SNS), alongside the work of DKC, the register of some 30,000 protected ancient monuments has been computerized, including administrative data, while new information from the revived inspection of monuments is continually added (Pauly 1992).

The Forest and Nature Agency administers not only the law protecting ancient monuments but also shipwrecks on the sea-bed. SNS and DKC have therefore, together with the Institute of Maritime Archaeology, begun to work on the creation of a marine register following the principles of the register of localized finds on land. In this way the marine finds will be given better protection at the same time as antiquarian knowledge is increased.

The rapid proliferation of computers that the 1980's saw was nothing less than a revolution that also, inevitably, set its mark on cultural history and archaeology: not just centrally, but also in the individual museums, which were able to begin to use computers for registration. In order to meet this need, a registration programme has been developed under the National Council of Museums called the Danish Museum Index (DMI): a programme that can be used by all museums, irrespective of the nature of their collections. In the DMI system registration can be tailored to the individual museum's need, but in such a way that ultimate uniformity is ensured, with a view, for instance, to later data-exchange.

Around the end of this millennium, the computerization of all the data in the National Museum's Parish Record will be complete. Then at last DKC will really be the full national register of located finds and monuments that was planned 15 years ago. As a result of the decentralized electronic registration of museum data anticipated, for example, through DMI, in future years DKC will receive and treat a wide range of other cultural history information from prehistoric and historic periods.

The descriptions in the central computerized register of finds and ancient monuments generally deal with whole groups and not individual artefacts. From what is in the DKC database, one can easily determine how many structures of a particular type are known from a certain period but not which objects are found. For that to be possible, a proper artefact register would be required, such as those now emerging from several Danish museums. The Prehistoric and Medieval Department of the National Museum, for instance, is now undertaking such a project. The future integration of local artefact registers with the DKC database would mean entirely new possibilities for archaeological research.

In a wider perspective, we can expect that many of the museums and heritage institutions in Denmark will be linked up in an electronic network, which will facilitate rapid updating and detailed searches of the networked databases. The Museum Act presupposes that the central cultural history perspective is taken care of by DKC, which will also be one of the places where recorded data can be processed through a number of advanced programmes. It will, for instance, soon be possible to present data using geographic information systems. With such systems the distribution of archaeological finds can be related to topography, soil-types and old coastlines - to mention just a few striking possibilities.

It is not unrealistic to imagine that development over the coming decades will reach the point where the central register will be able to provide data in the form of both text and images to a large number of different users via a national electronic network.

Within the same period we can also expect that international exchange of cultural heritage data will seriously get underway, eventually becoming quite commonplace for future archaeologists. Our modern boundaries had no meaning for prehistoric folk. We should not underestimate the difficulties that this will involve, but the prospects are so promising that they are worth seizing, especially in light of the furious development that has already taken place.

It is important to remind oneself, however, that without the careful antiquarian work of previous centuries, the future prospects would be different. The great challenge therefore is to continue and to intensify the quality-conscious collection and recording of cultural history data so that the future generations too can look back at this period as one of the fruitful ones for Danish archaeology.

Conservation and preservation

By Torben Dehn and Kristian Kristiansen

Apart from the automatic protection of ancient monuments under the new Nature Conservation Act of 1937 and the systematic protectionary surveys of the years that followed, there had never previously been so many and such important changes in the business of protecting archaeological remains as there were in the period from 1969 to 1993.

In the post-war period and from the 1960's onwards, the explosive development of society put increasing pressure on natural resources and the environment. In order to cope with this, a series of planning laws were adopted and a number of protective laws were sharpened up. In due course, in 1973, a Ministry for the Environment was established, with responsibility for such legislation. The protection of ancient monuments had been included in the Nature Conservation Act since 1937. As a result this moved, in 1975, from the Ministry of Culture and, thus, Rigsantivaren (the State Antiquary) and the National Museum to the National Agency for Nature, Monuments and Sites (later the Forest and Nature Agency) within the Ministry for the Environment - certainly the most discussed decision of this 25-year period.

In respect of legislation, there have been five central changes since the Act of 1937:

1. In 1961, a protected 100-m. zone became automatic, recognizing the fact that ancient monuments are also part of the landscape.

2. In 1963, a law for the protection of historical shipwrecks was introduced.

3. In 1969, it was determined that unlisted ancient monuments should be investigated before destruction and the funding of this investigation was secured; in addition a number of ancient monuments from historical times were included under the Act.

4. In 1983, historical shipwrecks were brought under the Nature Conservation Act and protection was extended to include a zone of 24 nautical miles and not just the Danish territorial waters. At the same time, the provison for investigations of unlisted monuments were transferred to the Museum Act.

5. In 1992, the Nature Conservation Act was renamed the Protection of Nature Act and in respect of ancient monuments saw an extension of the protection of monuments from historical times, such as stone and earth walls.

Two advisory boards has been established to give advise to the administration: the Ancient Monument Council in 1976 and the Archaeological Board in 1983 (Betænkning 467, 953; Naturfredningsloven 1973; Kristiansen 1985, 1992).

Conservation/Protection

So much for the legislative and administrative framework concerned with protection - how in fact has the (cultural) heritage been managed since the 1937 Act? It is a fact that at the end of the Conservation Survey in 1957 23,774 monuments had been registered for protection, while the score in 1992 is 28,674. Of these 23,774 monuments, for various reasons protection has been dropped in about 300 cases. The majority of the 5,200 new ancient monuments have been added in the period since 1969 and reflect, amongst other things, a stronger inclination to protect monuments from historical times. In 1957 virtually none were listed; in 1992 they number 1,542. Through the years, various thematic protectionary campaigns have been mounted, affecting, for instance, castle mounds, buried ruins, bridges, culverts, entrenchments, game park fencing and milestones. There has also been the inclusion of large, special groups of ancient monuments such as the saltpans on Læsø; currently work is in progress on the protection of defensive works from the 19th century.

Some of the newly added ancient monuments are, however, prehistoric, such as the burial mounds in forests. Under the Conservation Survey the ancient monuments in forests, especially those owned by the state, were regarded as protected and were not, as a result, always scheduled. In respect of the state-owned forests, we have followed a rolling plan of revision for 15 years, so that all known ancient monuments are now properly recorded and printed on the forestry districts' detailed maps of the forests.

A considerable proportion of the 5,200 newly added ancient monuments comprises structures that for one reason or another were not regarded as worthy of protection during the major survey of 1937-57. There is no doubt that the threshold of what one considers worthy has reduced since then. Now, for instance, small barrows and cairns less than ½ m. high are listed, in recognition of the fact that such humble structures can be of just as much scholarly importance as the larger barrows. Many structures that were formerly regarded as too badly damaged for protection have nevertheless been included eventually as excavations of such apparently badly damaged structures have shown us that they can still yield valuable information. In particular, since 1984

This picture shows a diver in the process of stereophotographing an early 18th-century wreck by Gåsehage near Ebeltoft. An excavation was carried out in 1990-91 as a collaborative project between Ebeltoft Museum, the Trade and Maritime Museum, the Museum of Prehistory, Moesgaard, and the Forest and Nature Agency. A team of 12-14 sports divers also took part.

the majority of the 1,628 burial mounds that from the survey of 1937-57 were given a status under which the owners had to give the National Museum three months' notice before they planned to clear them have been screened. This ordinance turned out to be very ill-conceived, and was removed by an amendment to the law in 1984.

Besides such protection of invidual monuments as is effected without compensation to the landowner, work has also gone on in this period on the conservation of a range of natural areas of cultural-historical importance. Since compensation is paid for this form of conservation, it is possible to halt agricultural work in areas with well-preserved ancient monuments - typically settlements. Cases like this require a lot of preparation; some have been completed, and a number are, after extra efforts in the past few years, on the brink of conclusion. Examples that can be noted are the conservation of the ring-fortress of Aggersborg, the votive bog in the Illerup river valley and, not least, Store Åmose with its Early Stone-age settlements. Conservation like this has also been built into the special planning projects concerned with the national ancient monument areas such as Jelling, Lejre, Dybbøl and Hammershus.

Alongside such area conservation, an account should be given of the protection of the landscape immediately around the listed monuments. Since 1961, it has not been permitted to change the terrain or to build within 100 m. of a listed ancient monu-

ment without the agreement of the local Conservation Board. This rule is based on the principle that one should preserve intact the relationship between the ancient monument and the landscape as far as possible, and it has meant that many monuments can now be appreciated without being surrounded by new buildings. With the new Protection of Nature Act, the administration of this protection zone has been transferred from the Conservation Boards to the County Councils. An important decision was made by the Main Conservation Board in 1983, that in respect of the protection of the surroundings of a monument from agricultural work, any destroyed parts of an otherwise protected ancient monument should be taken account of - for instance a filled and ploughed over moat around a castle mound.

The submerged heritage

While conservation of the heritage on land can build upon records of the National Museum going back over a hundred years, the protection of features on the sea-bed is another matter: only in 1984 did systematic survey and recording of ancient monuments under the sea begin - a step corresponding to that taken on land in 1873, when Worsaae received a grant to begin the systematic parish survey. The finds on the sea-bed fall into two principle categories, Stone-age settlements south of the fulcrum, which are sought out following topographic features in the now submerged Stone-age landscape, and shipwrecks which are sought out on the

Information board at the newly restored monastery ruin at Antvorskov. An aspect of the drive to inform has been a 3-year board project which has produced information boards to be set up by 500 selected national ancient monuments. This was a matter of cooperation with the County Councils, who take responsibility for controlling the vegetation and establishing access for the public.

basis of archival information and reports from fishermen, etc., just as one might go through a museum. For a number of years, the Forest and Nature Agency has undertaken systematic field registration in selected areas, with the help, inter alia, of seismic equipment. Up to now, 2,000 Stone-age settlements have been recorded out of an anticipated total of 10-20,000. 4,500 shipwrecks have been recorded, but only 200 have so far been identified as historical in legal terms. A total of 20-30,000 is anticipated. There is also a small number of navigation barriers, coastal forts, etc. On the basis of records up to now, we are beginning to pick out the sites of settlements and wrecks. In recent years, major investigations have been made underwater in connexion with bridge and harbour building.

Ancient monuments on the sea-bed are legally protected without having to be scheduled. The same applies to the great majority of types of ancient monument on land, although it has become customary here for the appropriate designation to be registered on the property (Mathiassen 1957; K. Thorvildsen 1978; C. Lund 1987; I. Nielsen (ed.) 1987).

Preservation

Protection and registration alone, however, do not preserve our ancient monuments. Human thoughtlessness continually causes ancient monuments to be destroyed, while natural causes slowly but surely take their toll too. To obviate the former, inspection and information is the strategy, while to hinder physical damage conservation and restoration is undertaken. While for earlier generations the policy was to save what could be saved from immediate annihilation, our aim is much more to work towards the long-term preservation of what has been saved. This applies first and foremost to the large group of medieval ruins (about 250) and passage graves (about 200) that were excavated, restored and opened to the public in the decades around the beginning of this century. This is being done, inter alia, on the basis of additional funds that were granted from 1986 for an originally 10-year, now a 14-year, "ruin campaign" and since 1991 for a megalith campaign (Ruinkampagnen 1991; S. Hansen 1993).

The future

The scheduling of ancient monuments is often done with a view to something surviving there for future archaeologists to work on. But when will it be the future? In one sense the future will come when all ancient monuments other than those that are listed have disappeared or been investigated. Years ago it was a common practice to excavate protected monuments on scholarly grounds, but in the last 25 years this approach has changed radically. We have recognized that remains from our heritage are a very limited resource that has to be treated with consideration and caution. Permission to excavate on scheduled sites is therefore strictly restricted by scholarly criteria. If it is to take place, the reason must be that the information anticipated cannot be gained anywhere else. Mere curiosity is not enough.

Maintenance work on passage grave "Røverkulen" in Southern Jutland. One of the supporting stones in the chamber has fallen and is to be raised. With work of this character, efforts are always made to disturb as little of the intact monument as possible; when that does happen, of course, a normal archaeological excavation is carried out. With more comprehensive conservation or restoration, the attempt is made, through a combined archaeological and restorational investigation, to re-create the original construction before using iron supports and cement.

The protection of the cultural heritage is not only a matter of listing and material conservation. Important protective work goes on at the many levels of planning. When, for instance, a decision is made to build a motorway, it is very important, to avoid major conflicts, that attention is paid to the ancient monuments and their setting right from the drafting of the first proposals for the course. With the construction of the natural gas network, for instance, not one protected ancient monument was lost. There is no doubt that the linkage of the protection of ancient monuments with planning and environmental conservation in the past 25 years, with the intensive exploitation of open land that they have seen, has saved many grave mounds from destruction, while landscapes of an important culture-historical character have been protected from building or other major structures.

With the enactment of the Protection of Nature Act in 1992, the possibility of protecting "new" historical monuments such as stone and earth walls has been created. The preservation of the material cultural heritage has thus extended, in these 25 years, to include not only the individual monuments but also the wider historical context in the landscape. In other words, we have further underlined the desire to keep basic structures in the landscape. This poses quite new demands of future preservative work.

A complete innovation is that under the new law one can also protect something that is not firmly sited, or tangible, like an ancient monument: namely stones and trees to which popular beliefs or historical traditions or accounts are attached. The situation in which one now attempts to conserve and protect impalpable things such as legends, beliefs and rituals really is a major new step that should give us food for thought (Vejledning 1993).

Annex

Part 1: The following types of ancient monuments are protected in accordance with § 12 of the Act if they are visible in the terrain:
1. burial mounds, cairns
2. stone cists, dolmens, passage graves
3. ship-settings
4. fortified or moated sites without visible building remins
5. fortifications
6. disused churchyards
7. ruins
8. runestones, monoliths
9. rock carvings
10. crosses, milestones, boundary stones around royal hunting areas, etc.

The ancient monuments covered by Part 1, with the exception of no. 10, crosses, milestones, boundary stones around royal hunting areas, etc., are surrounded by a protection zone as defined by § 18, subsection 1 of the Act.

Part 2: The following types of ancient monuments are only covered by protection in accordance with § 12 of the Act if the owner has received notification of their existence:
1. mills
2. dams and dikes
3. bridge and road constructions
4. stone banks and stone settings
5. earthworks and moated sites with buildings
6. holy wells
7. canals
8. structures near or in lakes, rivers and bogs
9. settlement sites.

Ancient monuments that are covered by Part 2 are surrounded by a protection zone in accordance with § 18, subsection 1 of the Act.

Part 3: The following types of ancient monuments are only protected in accordance with § 12 of the Act if the owner has received notification of their existence:
1. ancient monuments covered by Part 1 that are not visible in the terrain
2. stones and trees connected with popular beliefs, histori cal tradition or folklore
3. soldiers' graves
4. memorial monuments
5. boundary walls of stone or earth
6. traces of field cultivation
7. trapping pits
8. heaps of stones or branches near roads and bridges, accumulated as a result of local tradition.

Ancient monuments covered by Part 3 are not surrounded by protection zones in accordance with § 18, subsection 1 of the Act, cf. § 18, subsection 3.

The new Protection of Nature Act's list of types of ancient monument that can be protected.

List of figures

Literature

Abbreviations:

Aarb.: Aarbøger for Nordisk Oldkyndighed og Historie, København.
Acta: Acta Archaeologica, København.
Arbejdsmarken: Nationalmuseets Arbejdsmark, København.
Arkæol.Kunsthist.Skr.Dan.Vid.Selsk.: Det kgl. Danske Videnskabernes Selskab, Arkæologisk-kunsthistoriske Skrifter, København.
AUD: Arkæologiske udgravninger i Danmark, Rigsantikvarens Arkæologiske Sekretariat, København.
BAR: British Archaeological Reports, Oxford.
DGF Årsskr.: Dansk Geologisk Forenings Årsskrift, København.
DGU: Danmarks Geologiske Undersøgelse, København.
FRAM: FRAM, Fra Ringkøbing Amts Museer, Herning.
Hist.Filos.Skr.Dan.Vid.Selsk.: Det kgl. Danske Videnskabernes Selskab, Historisk-Filosofiske Skrifter, København.
JAS Skr.: Jysk Arkæologisk Selskabs Skrifter, Højbjerg.
JDA: Journal of Danish Archaeology, København.
MIV: MIV. Museerne i Viborg amt, Viborg.
MLUHM: Meddelanden från Lunds Universitets Historiska Museum, Lund.
NF: Nordiske Fortidsminder, København.
ROMU: ROMU. Årsskrift fra Roskilde Museum, Roskilde.
PPS: Proceedings of the Prehistoric Society, London
PZ: Praehistorische Zeitschrift, Berlin/New York.

Aaby, B. 1976. Cyclic climatic variations in climate over the past 5500 yr reflected i raised bogs. *Nature* 263.
- 1983. *Forest development, soil genesis and human activity illustrated by pollen and hypha analysis of two neighbouring podzols in Draved Forest, Denmark.* DGU II Rk. 114.
- 1985. Norddjurslands landskabsudvikling gennem 7000 år. Belyst ved pollenanalyse og bestemmelse af støvindhold i højmosetørv. *Fortidsminder 1985* (Antikvariske Studier 7).
- 1986. Trees as anthropogenetic indicators in regional pollen diagrams from eastern Denmark. In: Behre, K.-E. (ed.): *Anthropogenetic Indicators in Pollen Diagrams.* Rotterdam.
- 1988. The cultural landscape as reflected in percentage and influx pollen diagrams from two Danish ombrotrophic mires. In: H.H. Birks *et al.* (eds) 1988.
- 1990. Pollen og jordstøv fortæller om fortidens landbrug. *Arbejdsmarken* 1990.
- 1992. Sjællands kulturlandskaber i jernalderen. In: Lund Hansen & Nielsen (eds) 1992.
Aaris-Sørensen, K. 1980. Depauperation of the mammalian fauna of the island of Zealand during the Atlantic period. *Videnskabelige Meddelelser fra dansk naturhistorisk Forening* 142.
- 1983. An Example of Taphonomic Loss in a Mesolithic Faunal Assemblage. In: Clutton-Brock,J. & C. Grigson (eds): *Animals and Archaeology: 1. Hunters and their Prey.* BAR Int. Ser. 163.
- (ed.) 1984. *Uroksen fra Prejlerup. Et arkæozoologisk fund.* København.
- 1985. Den terrestriske pattedyrfauna i det sydfynske øhav gennem Atlantikum og Tidlig Subboreal. In: J. Skaarup 1985.
- 1988. *Danmarks forhistoriske Dyreverden. Fra Istid til Vikingetid.* København.
Aaris-Sørensen, K. & E. Brinch Petersen 1986. The Prejlerup Aurochs - an Archaeozoological Discovery from Boreal Denmark. In: Königsson, L.K. (ed.): *Nordic Late Quaternary Biology and Ecology.* Striae 24.
Aaris-Sørensen, K., K. Strand Petersen & H. Tauber 1990. *Danish Finds of Mammooth (Mammuthus primigenius (Blumenbach)). Stratigrafical position, dating and evidence of Late Pleistocene environment.* DGU Serie B, 14.
Abrahamsen, N. 1991. Arkæologiske magnetiske dateringer 1990. *AUD* 1990.
Adamsen, C. 1982. Bulagergård. En bebyggelse fra tidlig middelalder i Verst sogn. *Mark og Montre* 1982.
Adamsen, C. & K. Ebbesen (eds) 1986. *Stridsøksetid i Sydskandinavien. Beretning fra et symposium 28.-30.X.1985 i Vejle.* Arkæologiske Skrifter 1. København.
Aitken, M.J. 1990. *Science-based Dating in Archaeology.* New York.
Albrectsen, E. 1951. En gravhøj ved Håstrup. *Fynske Minder* 1951.
- 1954. *Fynske Jernaldergrave I. Førromersk jernalder.* København.
- 1956. *Fynske Jernaldergrave II. Ældre romersk jernalder.* København.
- 1968. *Fynske Jernaldergrave III. Yngre romersk jernalder.* Fynske Studier VII. Odense.
- 1971. *Fynske Jernaldergrave IV, 1-2. Gravpladsen på Møllegårdsmarken ved Broholm.* Fynske Studier IX. Odense.
- 1973. *Fynske Jernaldergrave V. Nye Fund.* Fynske Studier X. Odense.
Albrethsen, S.E. 1973. Og disse mennesker mener-. *Skalk* 1973:5.
- 1974. Bjergby - en jernaldergravplads på Mors. *Arbejdsmarken* 1974.
- 1976. Hvad klitten gemte - en enkeltgravshøj i Blåbjerg Plantage. *Mark og Montre* 1976.
- (ed.) 1977. *Antikvariske studier tilegnet Knud Thorvildsen på 70-årsdagen 18. december 1977.* København.
Albrethsen, S.E., V. Alexandersen, E. Brinch Petersen & J. Balslev Jørgensen 1976. De levede og døde... for 7000 år siden. *Arbejdsmarken* 1976.
Albrethsen, S.E. & E. Brinch Petersen 1975. Gravene på Bøgebakken, Vedbæk. *Søllerødbogen* 1975.
- 1977. Excavation of a Mesolithic Cemetery at Vedbæk, Denmark. *Acta* 47, 1976.
Alexandersen, V. 1967. The pathology of the jaws and the temporo-mandibular joint. In: Brothwell, D. & A.T. Sandison (eds): *Diseases in Antiquity.* Springfield.
- 1979. Beskrivelse af et barn - ud fra 23 tænder. In: Brinch Petersen *et al.* 1979.
- 1988. Description of the Human Dentitions from the Late Mesolithic Grave-Fields at Skateholm, Southern Sweden. In: L. Larsson (ed.) 1988.
- 1989. Tandforholdene i Enkeltgravstid/-stridsøksetid. In: L. Larsson (ed.) 1989.
Alexandersen, V., P. Bennike, L. Hvass & K.H. Stærmose Nielsen 1983. Egtvedpigen - nye undersøgelser. *Aarb.* 1981.
Als Hansen → Hansen, B. Als
Andersen, Aa. 1987. *Middelalderbyen Næstved.* Viby.
Andersen, Aa., T. Dahlerup, U. Lund Hansen, J. Steen Jensen & N.-K. Liebgott (eds) 1988. *Festskrift til Olaf Olsen på 60-års dagen den 7. juni 1988.* København.
Andersen, A.H. 1986. Enkeltgravstid på de danske øer. In: C. Adamsen & K. Ebbesen (eds) 1986.
Andersen, B. & E. 1990. *Råsejlet - Dragens vinge.* Roskilde.
Andersen, H. 1951. Det femte store mosefund. Våbenfundet i Illerup ådal. *Kuml* 1951.

- 1956. Afsked med ådalen. *Kuml* 1956.
- 1992. De glemte borge. *Skalk* 1992:1.
Andersen, H. & H.J. Madsen 1967. Nygade i Århus. Bidrag til teorien om det ældste Århus. *Kuml* 1966.
- 1985a. Byudgravning ved Århus Katedralskole. *Kuml* 1985.
- 1985b. Udgravninger i det gamle Vest-Århus. *Kuml* 1985.
Andersen, H.H. 1977. *Jyllands vold.* Højbjerg.
- 1984. Das Danewerk. In: H. Jankuhn *et al.* (eds) 1984.
- 1986. Hedenske danske kongegrave og deres historiske baggrund. *Kuml* 1985.
- 1987. Kongsgårdshøjen. *Skalk* 1987:4.
- 1988. Ringborgene og den militære begivenhedshistorie. *Kuml* 1986.
Andersen, H.H., P.J. Crabb og H.J. Madsen 1971. *Århus Søndervold. En byarkæologisk undersøgelse.* JAS Skr. IX.
Andersen, H.H. & P. Kjærum 1968. Senneolitiske gravanlæg i Tønning Skov. *Kuml* 1967.
Andersen, H.H. & O. Klindt-Jensen 1971. Hesselbjerg. En gravplads fra vikingetid. *Kuml* 1970.
Andersen, H.H., H.J. Madsen & O. Voss 1976. *Danevirke.* JAS Skr. XIII.
Andersen, I.F. 1982. Tre midtjyske enkeltgravshøje. *Kuml* 1981.
Andersen, J.G. 1969. *Studies in the Mediaeval Diagnosis of Leprosy in Denmark.* København.
Andersen, K. 1951. Hytter fra Maglemosetid. Danmarks ældste boliger. *Arbejdsmarken* 1951.
- 1961. Verupbopladsen. En Maglemoseboplads i Aamosen. *Aarb.* 1960.
- 1983. *Stenalderbebyggelsen i Den vestsjællandske Åmose.* København.
Andersen, K., S. Jørgensen & J. Richter 1982. *Maglemose hytterne ved Ulkestrup Lyng.* NF B, 7.
Andersen, L. & N. Møller 1991. Ældre jernalders mønstersvejsede sværd. In: B. Madsen (ed.) 1991.
Andersen, M. 1984. Westslawischer Import in Dänemark etwa 950 bis 1200. *Zeitschrift für Archäologie* 18.
Andersen, N.H. 1979. To grave fra tidlig enkeltgravskultur i Sarup. *Fynske Minder* 1978.
- 1980. Drik og du vil leve skønt. In: Glob, P.V. (ed.): *Danefæ. Til Hendes Majestæt Dronning Margrethe, 16. april 1980.* København.
- 1981. Sarup. Befæstede neolitiske anlæg og deres baggrund. *Kuml* 1980.
- 1982. A Neolithic Causewayed Camp at

Trelleborg near Slagelse, West Zealand. *JDA* 1.
- 1984. Jernalderbebyggelsen på Saruppladsen. *Hikuin* 10.
- 1985. Megalitgrave. *AUD* 1984.
- 1988a. *Sarup. Befæstede kultpladser fra bondestenalderen.* Højbjerg.
- 1988b. The Neolithic causewayed enclosures at Sarup, on South-West Funen, Denmark. In: C. Burgess *et al.* (eds) 1988.
- 1990a. Sarup. Two Neolithic Enclosures in South-West Funen. *JDA* 7, 1988.
- 1990b. Sarup. Zwei befestigte Anlagen der Trichterbecherkultur. *Jahresschrift für mitteldeutsche Vorgeschichte* 73.
Andersen, N.H. & T. Madsen 1978. Skåle og bægre med storvinkelbånd fra Yngre Stenalder. *Kuml* 1977.
Andersen, P.K. 1983. *Kollerupkoggen.* Thisted.
Andersen, S.H. 1970. Brovst. En kystboplads fra ældre stenalder. *Kuml* 1969.
- 1973a. Overgangen fra ældre til yngre stenalder i Sydskandinavien set fra en mesolitisk synsvinkel. In: Munch, G. Stamsø & P. Simonsen (eds): *Bonde - veideman, bofast ikke-bofast i nordisk forhistorie.* Tromsø Museums Skrifter IV.
- 1973b. Bro. En senglacial boplads på Fyn. *Kuml* 1972.
- 1975. Ringkloster. En jysk indlandsboplads med Ertebøllekultur. *Kuml* 1973.
- 1976. Et østjysk fjordsystems bebyggelse i stenalderen; Norsminde Fjord undersøgelsen. In: H. Thrane (ed.) 1976.
- 1977. En boplads fra ældre stenalder i Hjarup mose. *Nordslesvigske Museer* 4.
- 1978. Ertebøllekultur på Vestfyn. En oversigt. *Fynske Minder* 1977.
- 1979a. Pelsjægere. *Skalk* 1979:2.
- 1979b. Aggersund. En Ertebølleboplads ved Limfjorden. *Kuml* 1978.
- 1981a. *Jægerstenalderen.* Sesams Danmarkshistorie, Stenalderen 1. København.
- 1981b. Ertebøllekunst. Nye fund af mønstrede Ertebølleoldsager. *Kuml* 1980.
- 1983. Kalvø - A Coastal Site of the Single Grave Culture. *JDA* 2.
- 1985. Tybrind Vig. A Preliminary Report on a Submerged Ertebølle Settlement on the West Coast of Fyn. *JDA* 4.
- 1987. Tybrind Vig: A Submerged Ertebølle Settlement in Denmark. In: Coles, J.M. & J.L. Lawson (eds): *European Wetlands in Prehistory.* Oxford.

- 1988. A survey of the Late Palaeolithic of Denmark and southern Sweden. In: Otte, M. (ed.): *De la Loire à l'Oder. Les civilisations du Paléolithique final dans le nord-ouest européen.* BAR Int. Ser. 444.
- 1990. Limfjordens forhistorie - en oversigt. In: Ringtved, J. (ed.): *Limfjordsegnens kultur- og naturhistorie. Rapport fra seminar afholdt 4.-5. november 1989 i Nykøbing Mors.* Limfjordsprojektet, rapport 1. Århus.
- 1991. Norsminde. A "Køkkenmødding" with Late Mesolithic and Early Neolithic Occupation. *JDA* 8, 1989.
- 1992. Marin udnyttelse af Limfjorden i stenalderen. In: *Limfjordsfiskeri i fortid og nutid. Rapport fra seminar afholdt 1.-2. november på Krabbesholm ved Skive.* Limfjordsprojektet, rapport 4. Århus.
- 1993. Bjørnsholm. A Stratified Køkkenmødding on the Central Limfjord, North Jutland. *JDA* 10, 1991.
Andersen, S.H., T.S. Constandse-Westerman, R.R. Newell, R. Gillespie, J.A.J. Gowlett & R.E.M. Hedges 1986. New Radiocarbon Dates for Two Mesolithic Burials i Denmark. In: Gowlett, J.A.J. & R.E.M. Hedges (eds): *Archaeological Results from Accelerator Dating.* Oxford.
Andersen, S.H. & E. Johansen 1987. Ertebølle Revisited. *JDA* 5, 1986.
- 1992. An Early Neolithic Grave at Bjørnsholm, North Jutland. *JDA* 9, 1990.
Andersen, S.H., B. Lind & O. Crumlin-Pedersen 1991. *Slusegårdgravpladsen III. Gravformer og gravskikke. Bådgravene.* JAS Skr. XIV,3.
Andersen, S.H. & C. Malmros 1966. Norslund. En kystboplads fra ældre stenalder. *Kuml* 1965.
- 1985. Madskorpe på Ertebøllekar fra Tybrind Vig. *Aarb.* 1984.
Andersen, S.H. & N.T. Sterum 1971. Gudenåkulturen. *Holstebro Museum, Årsskrift* 1970-71.
Andersen, S.Th. 1970. *The Relative Pollen Productivity and Pollen Representation of North European Trees, and Correction Factors for Tree Pollen Spectra.* DGU II Rk. 96.
- 1978. Local and regional vegetational development in eastern Denmark in the Holocene. *DGU Årbog* 1976.
- 1979. Identification of wild grass and cereal pollen. *DGU Årbog* 1978.
- 1980. The relative pollen productivity of the common forest trees in the early

Holocene in Denmark. *DGU Årbog* 1979.
- 1984. *Forests at Løvenholm, Djursland, Denmark, at present and in the past.* Det Kgl. Danske Videnskabernes Selskab, Biologiske Skrifter 24:1. København.
- 1985. Natur- og kulturlandskaber i Næsbyholm Storskov siden istiden. *Fortidsminder 1985* (Antikvariske Studier 7).
- 1990. Pollen Spectra from the Double Passage-Grave Klekkendehøj, on Møn. Evidence of swidden cultivation in the Neolithic of Denmark. *JDA* 7, 1988.
- 1991a. Pollenanalyser fra Hassing Huse Mose, 1990. In: Andersen, S.Th., B. Odgaard & P. Rasmussen 1991.
- 1991b. Miljøhistorie. Kontinuitet og diskontinuitet i bebyggelseshistorien. *DGU Årsberetning* 1990.
- 1991c. Natural and Cultural Landscapes Since the Ice Age. Shown by Pollen Analyses two Small Hollows in a Forested Area in Denmark. *JDA* 8, 1989.
- 1992. Pollen Spectra from two Early Neolithic Lugged Jars in the Long Barrow at Bjørnsholm, Denmark. *JDA* 9, 1990.
- 1993. Early and Middle Neolithic agriculture in Denmark. Pollen spectra from soils in burial mounds of the Funnel Beaker Culture. *Journal of European Archaeology* 1.
Andersen, S.Th., B. Aaby, & B. Odgaard 1983. Environment and Man. Current Studies in Vegetational History at the Geological Survey of Denmark. *JDA* 2.
Andersen, S.Th., B. Aaby, B. Odgaard & E. Stenestad 1988. Bæredygtigt landbrug. *DGU Årsberetning* 1988.
Andersen, S.Th., B. Odgaard & P. Rasmussen 1991. *Pollenanalytiske undersøgelser 1988-89-90 i gravhøje, Hassing Huse Mose, Skånsø, Gudme Sø, Kragsø og Kobbelhøje Mose.* København.
Andersen, S.W. 1983. Hærvejen og bebyggelsen i Nordslesvig i den ældre bronzealder. *Nordslesvigske museer* 10.
- 1990. "Æ vold" ved Øster Løgum - et gammelt fortidsminde i ny belysning. *Sønderjysk Månedsskrift* 1990:1.
Andrén, A. 1985. *Den urbana scenen. Städer och samhälle i det medeltida Danmark.* Malmö.
- 1991. Guld og magt - en tolkning av de skandinaviska guldbrakteaternas funktion. In: C. Fabech & J. Ringtved (eds) 1991.

Aner, E. 1963. Die Stellung der Dolmen Schleswig-Holsteins in der nordischen Megalithkultur. *Offa* 20.
Aner, E. & K. Kersten 1973 ff. *Die Funde der älteren Bronzezeit in Dänemark, Schleswig-Holstein und Niedersachsen* I ff. København/Neumünster.
Arts, N. & M. Hoogland 1987. A Mesolithic settlement area with a human cremation grave at Oirschot V, municipality of Best, the Netherlands. *Helinium* XXVII,2.
Asingh, P. 1988. Diverhøj - A Complex Burial Mound and a Neolithic Settlement. *JDA* 6, 1987.
- 1990. Et hus af rav. *Skalk* 1990:3.
Augustsson, J.-E. 1992. Husbyggande i Halmstad under perioden 1300-1750. In: J.-E. Augustsson (ed.) 1992.
- (ed.) 1992. *Medeltida husbyggande.* Stockholm.
Axboe, M. 1991. Guld og guder i folkevandringstiden. Brakteaterne som kilde til politisk/religiøse forhold. In: C. Fabech & J. Ringtved (eds) 1991.
Baillie, M.G.L. 1989. Hekla 3: How big was it? *Endavour, New Series* 13 (2).
Balslev Jørgensen → Jørgensen, J. Balslev
Bang-Andersen, S. 1990. The Myrvatn Group, a Preborial Find-Complex i Southwest Norway. In: P.M. Vermeersch & P. Van Peer (eds) 1990.
Barton, N., A.J. Roberts & D.A. Roe (eds) 1991. *The Late Glacial in northwest Europe. Human adaptation and environmental change at the end of the Pleistocene.* Council for British Archaeology, Report 77. Oxford.
Baudou, E. 1983. Arkeologisk källkritik och modern odlingshistoria i Danmark. *Fortid og Nutid* XXX.
Bech, J.-H. 1985. The Iron Age Village Mound at Heltborg, Thy. *JDA* 4.
- 1991. Et bronzealderlandskab ved Bjerre i Nordthy. Om arkæologiske udgravninger forud for en planlagt motorbane. *MIV* 16.
Bech, J.-H. & A.-L. Haack Olsen 1985. Nye gravfund fra enkeltgravskulturen i Thy. *MIV* 13.
Becker, B., K.-D. Jäger, D. Kaufmann & T. Litt 1989. Dendrochronologische Datierungen van Eichenhölzern aus den frühbronzezeitlichen Hügelgräbern bei Helmsdorf und Leubingen (Aunjetitzer Kultur) und an bronzezeitlichen Flusseichen bei Merseburg. *Jahresschrift für mitteldeutsche Vorgeschichte* 72.
Becker, B., B. Kromer & P. Trimborn 1991. A stable-isotope tree-ring time-

scale of the Late Glacial/Holocene boundary. *Nature* 353.
Becker, C.J. 1945. En 8000-årig stenalderboplads i Holmegaards Mose. Foreløbig meddelelse. *Arbejdsmarken* 1945.
- 1947. Mosefundne Lerkar fra yngre Stenalder. *Aarb.* 1947.
- 1951. Den grubekeramiske kultur i Danmark. *Aarb.* 1950.
- 1952. Maglemosekultur på Bornholm. *Aarb.* 1951.
- 1953a. Die Maglemosekultur in Dänemark. In: Vogt, E. (ed.): *Congrès International des Sciences Prehistoriques et Protohistoriques. Actes de la IIIe Session Zurich.* Zurich.
- 1953b. Die nordschwedischen Flintdepots. Ein Beitrag zur Geschichte des neolithischen Fernhandels in Skandinavien. *Acta* XXIII, 1952.
- 1955a. Die mittel-neolithischen Kulturen in Südskandinavien. *Acta* XXV, 1954.
- 1955b. Coarse Beakers with "Shortwave-Moulding". *PPS* XXI.
- 1960. Stendyngegrave fra mellem-neolitisk tid. *Aarb.* 1959.
- 1961. *Førromersk jernalder i Syd- og Midtjylland.* Nationalmuseets Skrifter, Større beretninger VI. København.
- 1963. Kompliceret jordfæstelse. *Skalk* 1963:3.
- 1965. Neue Hortfunde aus Dänemark mit frühbronzezeitlichen Lanzenspitzen. *Acta* XXXV, 1964.
- 1966a. Ein früheisenzeitliches Dorf bei Grøntoft, Westjütland. Vorbericht über die Ausgrabungen 1961-63. *Acta* XXXVI, 1965.
- 1966b. To landsbyer fra tidlig jernalder i Vestjylland. *Arbejdsmarken* 1966.
- 1967. Gådefulde jyske stenaldergrave. *Arbejdsmarken* 1967.
- 1968. Bronzealderhuse i Vestjylland. *Arbejdsmarken* 1968.
- 1969a. Das zweite früheisenzeitliche Dorf bei Grøntoft, Westjütland. 2. Vorbericht: Die Ausgrabungen 1964-66. *Acta* XXXIX, 1968.
- 1969b. Grav eller tempel? En kultbygning fra yngre stenalder ved Herrup, Vestjylland. *Arbejdsmarken* 1969.
- 1969c. Ældste pil. *Skalk* 1969:4.
- 1970. Eine Kerbspitze der Hamburger Stufe aus Jütland. *Frühe Menschheit und Umwelt* Tl. I. Fundamenta Reihe A:2. Köln.
- 1971. Late Palaeolithic Finds from Denmark. *PPS* XXXVII.
- 1972a. Früheisenzeitliche Dörfer bei Grøntoft, Westjütland. 3. Vorbericht:

Die Ausgrabungen 1967-68. *Acta* XLII, 1971.

- 1972b. Hal og hus i yngre bronzealder. *Arbejdsmarken* 1972.

- 1974. Studien zu neolithischen Flintbeilen. *Acta* XLIV, 1973.

- 1977. Efterskrift. In: J. Brøndsted 1977.

- 1979. Nordisk arkæologi og europæisk forhistorie. In: Jensen, P.J. (ed.): *Københavns Universitet 1479-1979* XI. København.

- 1980a. Katalog der Feuerstein/Hornstein-Bergwerke, Dänemark. In: G. Weisgerber (ed.) 1980.

- 1980b. Bebyggelsesformer i Danmarks yngre bronzealder set i forhold til ældste jernalders landsbysamfund. In: H. Thrane (ed.) 1980.

- 1981. Viking-Age Settlements in Western and Central Jutland, Recent Excavations. Introductory Remarks. *Acta* 50, 1979.

- 1982a. Om grubekeramisk kultur i Danmark. - Korte bidrag til en lang diskussion (1950-80). *Aarb.* 1980.

- 1982b. Siedlungen der Bronzezeit und der vorrömischen Eisenzeit in Dänemark. *Offa* 39.

- 1985. Danske fund af istids-menneskets redskaber i Nationalmuseet. In: Nielsen, P.O. (ed.): *De ældste fund.* København.

- 1988. Sydskandinavisk flint i nordsvenske fund fra mellem- og senneolitisk tid. In: Edgren, T. (ed.): *XVII nordiska arkeologmötet i Åbo 1985*. ISKOS 7. Helsinki.

- 1990a. Anmeldelse af Gyldendal og Politikens Danmarkshistorie bind 1-3. *Historisk Tidsskrift* bind 90,1.

- 1990b. *Nørre Sandegård. Arkæologiske undersøgelser på Bornholm 1948-1952.* Hist.Filos.Skr.Dan.Vid.Selsk. 13.

- 1993. Flintminer og flintdistribution ved Limfjorden. In: Lund, J. & J. Ringtved (eds): *Kort- og råstofstudier omkring Limfjorden. Rapport fra seminarer afholdt 7.-8. november 1991 i Bovbjerg samt 23.-24. april 1992 i Aalborg.* Limfjordsprojektet, rapport 6. Århus.

Behre, K.-E. 1981. The interpretation of anthropogenic indicators in pollen diagrams. *Pollen et Spores* 23.

- 1983. *Ernährung und Umwelt der wikingerzeitlichen Siedlung Haithabu.* Die Ausgrabungen in Haithabu 8. Neumünster.

Bencard, M. (ed.) 1981. *Ribe Excavations 1970-76, vol. 1.* Esbjerg.

- (ed.) 1984. *Ribe Excavations 1970-76, vol. 2.* Esbjerg.

Bencard, M. & L. Bender Jørgensen 1990. Excavations and Stratigraphy. In: M. Bencard *et al.* (eds) 1990.

Bencard, M., L. Bender Jørgensen & H. Brinch Madsen (eds) 1990. *Ribe Excavations 1970-76, vol. 4.* Esbjerg.

Bencard, M., L. Bender Jørgensen & H. Brinch Madsen (eds) 1991. *Ribe Excavations 1970-76, vol. 3.* Esbjerg.

Bender Jørgensen → Jørgensen, L. Bender

Bendixen, K. 1972a. Mønterne fra Dankirke. *Arbejdsmarken* 1972.

- 1972b. Middelaldermønter i de sidste 10 års danske kirkefund. *Nordisk Numismatisk Årsskrift* 1972.

- 1981. Sceattas and Other Coin Finds. In: M. Bencard (ed.) 1981.

Bendixen, K., F. Kaul, A. Kromann, E. Munksgaard og H. Nielsen 1990. En vikingetidsskat fra Neble, Sjælland. *Arbejdsmarken* 1990.

Benner Larsen → Larsen, E. Benner

Bennike, P. 1984. Tandbehandling i oldtiden. *Medicinskhistorisk årbog* 1984.

- 1985a. *Palaeopathology of Danish Skeletons. A comparative study of demography, disease and injury.* København.

- 1985b. Stenalderbefolkningen på øerne syd for Fyn. In: J. Skaarup 1985.

- 1990. Middelalderens skeletfund. *Hikuin* 17.

- 1991. Datidens sygdomsspor. *En patologisk skeletsamling på Medicinsk Historisk Museum* 1.

Bennike, P. & V. Alexandersen 1990. Skelettet fra Fannerup. En antropologisk og odontologisk beskrivelse af jægerstenalderens mennesker. *Kuml* 1988-89.

Bennike, P. & H. Bohr 1990. Bone Mineral Content in the past and present. In: Christiansen, C. & K. Overgaard (eds): *Osteoporosis.* København.

Bennike, P. & K. Ebbesen 1985. Stenstrupmanden. *Fra Holbæk Amt* 1985.

Bennike, P. & K. Ebbesen 1987. The Bog Find From Sigersdal. Human sacrifice in the Early Neolithic. *JDA* 5, 1986.

Bennike, P., K. Ebbesen & L. Bender Jørgensen 1986. Two Early Neolithic Skeletons from Boelkilde bog, Denmark. *Antiquity* 60.

Berg, H., L. Bender Jørgensen & O. Mortensen 1981. *Sandhagen.* Rudkøbing.

Berglund, B.E. (ed.) 1991. *The cultural landscape during 6000 years in southern Sweden - the Ystad project.* Ecological Bulletin 41. Lund.

Berglund, J. 1982. Kirkebjerget - A Late Bronze Age Settlement at Voldtofte, South-West Funen. An Interim Report on the Excavations of 1976 and 1977. *JDA* 1.

Bertemes, F. 1991. Untersuchungen zur Funktion der Erdwerke der Michelsberger Kultur im Rahmen der kupferzeitlichen Zivilisation. In: Lichardus, J. (ed.): *Die Kupferzeit als historische Epoche.* Saarbrücker Beiträge zur Altertumskunde 55.

Betænkning 467. *Betænkning om naturfredning.* Betænkning nr. 467, 1967.

Betænkning 953. *Betænkning om samarbejdet mellem fredningsmyndighederne og museerne.* Betænkning nr. 953, 1982 (Møllmann-betænkningen).

Biborski, M. 1978. *Miecze z okresu wpłlywów rzymskich na obszarze kultury przeworskiej. (Épées provenantes du territoire de la civilisation de Przeworsk datées à la période des influences romaines).* Materiały Archeologiczne XVIII.

Biddle, M. & D. Hudson 1973. *The Future of London's Past: A Survey of the Archaeological Implications of Planning and Development in the Nation's Capital.* Worcester.

Bill, J. 1991. Gedesbyskibet - Middelalderlig skude- og færgefart fra Falster. *Arbejdsmarken* 1991.

Bille Henriksen → Henriksen, B. Bille

Binford, L.R. 1980. Willow smoke and dogs' tails: hunter-gatherer settlement systems and archaeological site formation. *American Antiquity* 45.

Birkedahl Christensen → Christensen, P. Birkedahl

Birks, H.H., H.J.B. Birks, P.E. Kaland & D. Moe (eds) 1988. *The Cultural Landscape - Past, Present and Future.* Cambridge.

Bjerck, H.B. 1990. Mesolithic site types and settlement patterns at Vega, Northern Norway. *Acta* 60, 1989.

Björhem, N. & U. Säfvestad 1983. Fosie IV - en långdragen historia. *Ale* 1.

- 1989. *Fosie IV. Byggnadstradition och bosättningsmönster under senneolitikum.* Malmöfynd 5.

Bjørn, C. (ed.) 1988. *Det danske landbrugs historie I. Oldtid og middelalder.* Odense.

Blankholm, H.P. 1985. Maglemosekulturens hyttegrundrids. En undersøgelse af bebyggelse og adfærdsmønstre i tidlig mesolitisk tid. *Aarb.* 1984.

- 1991. *Intrasite spatial analysis in theory and prectice.* Århus.

Blomqvist, L. 1989. *Megalitgravarna i Sverige.* Theses and Papers in Archaeology. New Series 1. Stockholm.

Boas, N.A. 1983. Egehøj. A Settlement from the Early Bronze Age in East Jutland. *JDA* 2.

- 1986. Tidlige senneolitiske bosættelser på Djursland. In: C. Adamsen & K. Ebbesen (eds) 1986.

- 1987. Rude Mark. A Maglemosian Settlement in East Jutland. *JDA* 5, 1986.

- 1991. Bronze Age Houses at Hemmed Church, East Jutland. *JDA* 8, 1989.

- 1993. Late Neolithic and Bronze Age Settlements at Hemmed Church and Hemmed Plantation, East Jutland. *JDA* 10, 1991.

Boëda, E. & J. Pelegrin 1985. Approche experimentale des Amas de Marsangy. *Archéologie Experimentale* 1. Beaune.

Boelicke, U. 1978. Das neolithische Erdwerk Urmitz. *Acta Praehistorica et Archaeologica* 7/8, 1976/7.

Bokelmann, K. 1977. Ein bronzezeitlicher Hausgrundriss bei Handewitt, Kreis Schleswig-Flensburg. *Offa* 34.

- 1978. Ein Federmesserplatz bei Schalkholz, Kreis Dithmarschen. *Offa* 35.

Boldsen, J.L. 1984. Palaeodemography of two Southern Scandinavian Medieval communities. *MLUHM* new series 5.

- 1988. Two methods for reconstructing the empirical mortality profile. *Human Evolution* 3.

Boldsen, J.L., J. Kieffer-Olsen & P. Pentz 1986. En nyfunden kirke ved Bygholm. *Vejle Amts Aarbøger* 1986.

Bonde, N. 1991. Dendrochronologische Altersbestimmung des Schiffes von Nydam. *Offa* 47, 1990.

Bonde, N., C. Christensen, F. Rieck & P. Vang Petersen 1991. Jernalderbåde og våbenofre. Nationalmuseets Nydamprojekt. *Arbejdsmarken* 1991.

Bonde, N. & K. Christensen 1984. Trelleborgs alder. Dendrokronologisk datering. *Aarb.* 1982.

Bonde, N. & O. Crumlin-Pedersen 1990. The Dating of Wreck 2, the Longship from Skuldelev, Denmark. *News WARP* 7.

Bonsall, C. (ed.) 1989. *The Mesolithic in Europe. Papers presented at the third international symposium, Edinburgh 1985.* Edinburgh.

Borch Vesth → Vesth, K. Borch

Boserup, E. 1965. *The Conditions of Agricultural Growth.* Chicago.

Bosinski, G. 1981. *Gönnersdorf. Eiszeitjäger am Mittelrhein.* Schriftenreihe der Bezirksregierung Koblenz 2.

Boye, V. 1896. *Fund af Egekister fra Bronzealderen i Danmark. Et monografisk Bidrag til Belysning af Bronzealderens Kultur.* Kjøbenhavn. (Reprint: Wormianum, Højbjerg 1986.)

Boysen, Aa. & S.W. Andersen 1983. Trappendal. Barrow and House from the Early Bronze Age. *JDA* 2.

Breest, K. & S. Veil 1991. The Late Upper Palaeolithic site of Schweskau, Ldkr. Lüchow-Dannenberg (Germany), and some comments on the relationship between the Magdalenian and Hamburgian. In: N. Barton *et al.* (eds) 1991.

Brinch Madsen _ Madsen, H. Brinch

Brinch Petersen _ Petersen, E. Brinch

Bröste, K, J. Balslev Jørgensen, C.J. Becker & J. Brøndsted 1956. *Prehistoric Man in Denmark. A Study in Physical Anthropology.* København.

Broholm, H.C. 1930. Broskov-Fundet. En Gravplads fra Folkevandringstiden. *Arbejdsmarken* 1930.

Brothwell, D., T. Holden, D. Liversage, B. Gottlieb, P. Bennike & J. Boesen 1990. Establishing a minimum damage procedure for the gut sampling of intact human bodies: the case of the Huldremose Woman. *Antiquity* 64.

Brøndsted, J. 1957. *Danmarks Oldtid 1. Stenalderen.* 2nd ed. København.

- 1958. *Danmarks Oldtid 2. Bronzealderen.* 2nd ed. København.

- 1960a. *Danmarks Oldtid 3. Jernalderen.* 2nd ed. København.

- 1960b. *Vikingerne.* København.

- 1977. *De ældste Tider. Indtil år 600.* Politikens Danmarkshistorie 1. 3rd ed. København.

Brøndum, N. 1981. The Jaws and Teeth of the Medieval Population in Svendborg. *Ossa* 8.

Buchwald, V.F. 1992. Jernfremstilling i Danmark i Middelalderen: lidt om bondeovne og kloder. *Aarb.* 1991.

Buck, D.-W.R. & B. Gramsch 1986. *Siedlung, Wirtschaft und Gesellschaft während der jüngeren Bronze- und Hallstattzeit in Mitteleuropa. Internationales Symposium Potsdam, 25. bis 29. April 1983. Bericht.* Veröffentlichungen des Museums für Ur- und Frühgeschichte Potsdam 20.

Burch, E. 1972. The caribou/wild reindeer as a human resource. *American Antiquity* 37:3.

Burgess, C. 1985. Population, climate, and upland settlement. In: Spratt, D. & C. Burgess (eds): *Upland settlement in Britain. The second millenium BC and after.* BAR British Series 143.

Burgess, C., P. Topping, C. Mordant & M. Maddison (eds) 1988. *Enclosures and Defences in the Neolithic of Western Europe.* BAR Int. Ser. 403.

Bødker Enghoff → Enghoff, I. Bødker

Bødtker Petersen → Petersen, S. Bødtker

Bøtter-Jensen, L., C. Ditlevsen & V. Mejdahl 1991. Combined OSL (infrared) and TL studies of feldspars. *Nuclear Tracks Radiat. Meas.* 18.

Callmer, J. 1986. To stay or to move. *MLUHM* new series 6, 1985-1986.

- 1991. Platser med anknytning till handel och hantverk i yngre järnålder. In: P. Mortensen & B.M. Rasmussen (eds) 1991.

Case, H. 1977. The Beaker Culture in Britain and Ireland. In: Mercer, R. (ed.): *Beakers in Britain and Europe: Four Studies.* BAR Suppl. Series 26.

Christensen, A.E. 1969. *Vikingetidens Danmark.* København.

Christensen, A.S. 1988. *Middelalderbyen Odense.* Viby.

Christensen, C. 1982a. Havniveauændringer 5500-2500 f.Kr. i Vedbækområdet, NØ-Sjælland. *DGF Årsskr.* 1981.

- 1982b. Stenalderfjorden og Vedbækbopladserne. *Arbejdsmarken* 1982.

- 1990. Stone Age Dug-out Boats in Denmark: Occurence, Age, Form and Reconstruction. In: D.E. Robinson (ed.) 1990.

Christensen, F. 1989. Fosfatundersøgelser ved Ø. Tørslev udgravningen. *Arkæologiske fund. Kulturhistorisk Museum, Randers. Virksomhed og resultater* 1987-88.

Christensen, K. 1990. Wood-anatomical and Dendrochronological Studies. In: M. Bencard *et al.* (eds) 1990.

Christensen, K. & J. Jensen 1991. Egtvedpigens alder. *Arbejdsmarken* 1991.

Christensen, K. & K.J. Krogh 1987. Jelling-højene dateret. *Arbejdsmarken* 1987.

Christensen, P. Birkedahl & E. Johansen 1992. En handelsplads fra yngre jernalder og vikingetid ved Sebbersund. *Aarb.* 1991.

Christensen, T. 1986. En lang historie. *ROMU* 1986.

- 1991. *Lejre - syn og sagn.* Roskilde.

Christiansen, C.H. & K. Skelmose 1969. Dobbeltgrav. *Skalk* 1969:5.

Christiansen, T.E. 1971. Træningslejr eller Tvangsborg. *Kuml* 1970.

- 1984. Trelleborgs Alder. Arkæologisk Datering. *Aarb.* 1982.

- 1989. Trelleborg og Pine Mølle. *Aarb.* 1989.

Christoffersen, J. 1990. Nyt om vraget af orlogsskibet Dannebroge. *Maritim Kontakt* 14.

- 1992. DKC, the National Record of Sites and Monuments. In: C.U. Larsen (ed.) 1992.

Clarke, H. & B. Ambrosiani 1991. *Towns in the Viking Age.* Leicester.

Cleyet-Merle, J.-J. 1990. *La Prehistoire de la Peche.* Paris.

Clottes, J., A. Beltrán, J. Courtin & H. Cosquer 1992. La Grotte Cosquer (Cap Morgiou, Marseille). *Bulletin de la Société Préhistorique Francaise* 98:4.

Clutton-Brock, J. & N. Noe-Nygaard 1990. New Osteolocical and C-Isotope Evidence on Mesolithic Dogs: Companions to Hunters and Fishers at Star Carr, Seamer Carr and Kongemose. *Journal of Archaeological Science* 17.

Coles, B. & J. 1989. *People of the Wetlands.* London.

Crumlin-Pedersen, O. 1969. *Das Haithabuschiff.* Berichte über die Ausgrabungen in Haithabu 3. Neumünster.

- 1974. Helnæs-spærringen. *Fynske Minder* 1973.

- 1975. "Æ Lei" og "Margrethes Bro". *Nordslesvigske Museer* 2.

- 1978. Søvejen til Roskilde. *Historisk årbog fra Roskilde amt* 1978.

- 1979a. Lynæsskibet og Roskilde søvej. *13 bidrag til Roskilde by og omegns historie.* Roskilde.

- 1979b. Danish Cog-finds. In: McGrail, S. (ed.): *The Archaeology of Medieval Ships and Harbours in Northern Europe.* BAR Int. Ser. 66.

- 1979c. Dronning Margrethes Stiger. *§ 48-udgravninger 1969-1979.* København.

- 1981. Skibe på havbunden. Vragfund i danske farvande fra perioden 600-1400. *Handels- og Søfartsmuseet, årbog* 1981.

- 1984. Fotevik. De marinarkæologiske undersøgelser 1981 og 1982. In: Bunte, C. (ed.): *Pugna Forensis - ?.* Lund.

- 1985a. Ship Finds and Ship Blockages AD 800-1200. In: K. Kristiansen (ed.) 1985.

- 1985b. Cargo Ships of Northern Europe AD 800-1300. *Conference on Waterfront Archaeology in North European Towns No. 2. Bergen 1983. Proceedings.* Bergen.

- 1986. Aspects of Wood Technology in Medieval Shipbuilding. In: O. Crumlin-Pedersen & M. Vinner (eds) 1986.

- 1987. Aspects of Viking-Age Shipbuild-

ing, *JDA* 5, 1986.

- 1988. Gensyn med Skuldelev 5 - et ledingsskib? In: Aa. Andersen *et al.* (eds) 1988.

- 1989a. Wood Technology and Forest Resources in the Light of Medieval Shipfinds. In: Villain-Gandossi, C. *et al.* (eds): *Medieval Ships and the Birth of Technological Societies.* Malta.

- 1989b. Skibet i Bøtøminde - en falstersk middelalderskude. *Lolland-Falsters Historiske Samfunds Årbog* 1989.

- 1990. Marinarkæologien i Danmark. *AUD* 1989.

- 1991a. Søfart og samfund i Danmarks vikingetid. In: P. Mortensen & B.M. Rasmussen (eds) 1991.

- 1991b. Bådgrave og gravbåde. In: Andersen, S.H., B. Lind & O. Crumlin-Pedersen 1991.

- 1991c. Maritime Aspects of the Archaeology of Roman and Migration-Period Denmark. In: O. Crumlin-Pedersen (ed.). 1991.

- 1991d: Ship Types and Sizes. In: O. Crumlin-Pedersen (ed.) 1991.

- (ed.) 1991. *Aspects of Maritime Scandinavia AD 200-1200. Proceedings of the Nordic Seminar on Maritime Aspects of Archaeology, Roskilde 13th-15th March, 1989.* Roskilde.

Crumlin-Pedersen, O., J. Steen Jensen, A. Kromann & N.-K. Liebgott 1976. Koggen med guldskatten. *Skalk* 1976:6.

Crumlin-Pedersen, O. & M. Vinner (eds) 1986. *Sailing into the Past.* Roskilde.

Cullberg, C. 1968. *On Artefact Analysis. A study in the systematics and classification of a Scandinavian Early Bronze Age material with metal analysis and chronology as contributing factors.* Acta Archaeologica Lundensia, ser. in 4, no. 7.

Dalsgaard, K. 1985. Matrikelkortet fra 1844 anvendt til rekonstruktion af det udrænede landskab. *Aarb.* 1984.

Damm, C. 1989. Stendyngegrave i enkeltgravstid. In: L. Larsson (ed.) 1989.

Danielsen, K. 1970. Odontodysplasia leprosa in Danish Mediaeval Skeletons. *Tandlægebladet* 74.

Danmarks Kirker 1 ff. København 1933 ff.

Davidsen, K. 1975. Tragtbægerkulturens slutfase. Nye C-14 dateringer. *Kuml* 1973-74.

- 1977. Relativ kronologi i mellemneolitisk tid. En diskussion af C.J. Beckers kronologisystem på baggrund af nye og gamle stratigrafiske fund. *Aarb.* 1975.

- 1978. *The Final TRB Culture in Den-*

mark. A Settlement Study. Arkæologiske Studier V. København.

- 1982a. Undergravstid på de danske øer. *Aarb.* 1980.

- 1982b. Bronze Age Houses at Jegstrup near Skive, Central Jutland. *JDA* 1.

Degerbøl, M. 1932. Et Fund af Steppe-Antilope (Saiga tatarica (Pall.)) i Danmark. *Meddelelser fra Dansk geologisk Forening* 8:2.

Dehn, T. 1982. Stavad. En jernalderboplads i Store Vildmose. *Fortidsminder og Bygningsbevaring* (Antikvariske Studier 5).

Digerfeldt, G. & S. Welinder 1988. The Prehistoric Cultural Landscape in South-West Sweden. *Acta* 58, 1987.

Draiby, B. 1985. Fragtrup - en boplads fra yngre bronzealder. *Aarb.* 1984.

- 1991. Studier i jernalderens husbygning. Rekonstruktion af et langhus fra ældre romersk jernalder. In: B. Madsen (ed.) 1991.

Ducrocq, T., A. Bridault & A.-V. Munaut 1991. Un gisement mésolithique exceptionnel dans le Nord de la France: Le Petit Marais de la Chaussée-Tirancourt (Somme). *Bulletin de la Societé Préhistorique Francaise* 88,9.

Duhamel du Monceau 1791. *Art du Charbonnier.* Paris.

Dyggve, E. 1942. La fouille par le Musée National danois du tertre royal sud à Jelling en 1941. *Acta* XIII.

Ebbesen, K. 1975. *Die jüngere Trichterbecherkultur auf den dänischen Inseln.* Arkæologiske Studier II. København.

- 1978a. *Tragtbægerkultur i Nordjylland.* NF B, 5.

- 1978b. Sikar og klokkebægerkultur. *Holstebro Museum, Årsskrift* 1978.

- 1979a. *Stordyssen i Vedsted. Studier over tragtbægerkulturen i Sønderjylland.* Arkæologiske Studier VI. København.

- 1979b. Flintøksen fra Føllenslev. *Museet for Holbæk og Omegn, Årsskrift* 1979.

- 1980. Die Silexbeil-Depots Südskandinaviens und ihre Verbreitung. In: G. Weisgerber (ed.) 1980.

- 1981a. Offerfundet fra Å Højrup. Bondestenalderens mejseldepoter. *Harja* 1981.

- 1981b. St. Aldrup-fundet. Et offerfund fra enkeltgravstid. *Historisk Årbog for Thy, Mors og Vester Han Herred* 1981.

- 1981c. Det store offerfund fra Knud. *Nordslesvigske Museer* 8.

- 1981d. Klæstrupfundet. Flintofre fra ældre bronzealder. *Vendsysselske Årbøger* 1981.

- 1981e. Offerfundet fra Suldrup i Himmerland. *Fra Himmerland og Kjær Herred* 1981.

- 1981f. Flintafslag som offer. *Kuml* 1980.
- 1982a. Enkeltgravskulturen - 100 år efter opdagelsen. *Aarb.* 1980.
- 1982b. Yngre stenalders depotfund som bebyggelseshistorisk kildemateriale. In: H. Thrane (ed.) 1982.
- 1982c. Flintflækker som offergave. *Fra Holbæk Amt* 1982.
- 1983a. Flint Celts from Single-Grave Burials and Hoards on the Jutlandic Peninsula. *Acta* 53, 1982.
- 1983b. Et offerfund fra Lomborg. *Hardsyssels Årbog* 1983.
- 1984. Yngreneolitiske tap-stridsøkser. Nyt lys på enkeltgravstiden. *Kuml* 1982-83.
- 1985a. *Fortidsminderegistrering i Danmark*. København.
- 1985b. Nordjyske gravkister med indgang. Bøstrup-kisterne. *Aarb.* 1983.
- 1985c. Tragtbægerkulturens grønstensøkser. *Kuml* 1984.
- 1986a. *Døden i mosen*. København.
- 1986b. Offerfundet fra Vejleby. *Fra Holbæk Amt* 1986.
- 1986c. Fred i enkeltgravstid. In: C. Adamsen & K. Ebbesen (eds) 1986.
- 1988. Tidligneolitiske tapkøller. *Aarb.* 1987.
- 1989. *Hoards of the Late Funnel Beaker Culture*. Inventaria Archaeologica. Denmark. 12.-14. set. DK 55 - DK 70.
- 1990. The Long Dolmen at Grøfte, South-West Zealand. *JDA* 7, 1988.

Ebbesen, K. & D. Mahler 1980. Virum. Et tidligneolitisk bopladsfund. *Aarb.* 1979.

Ebbesen, K. & E. Brinch Petersen 1974. Fuglebæksbanken. En jættestue på Stevns. *Aarb.* 1973.

Egebjerg Hansen → Hansen, T. Egebjerg

Egevang, R. (ed.) 1979. *Strejflys over Danmarks bygningskultur. Festskrift til Harald Langberg*. København.

Eggers, H.J. 1951. *Der römische Import im freien Germanien*. Atlas der Urgeschichte 1. Hamburg.

- 1955. Zur absoluten Chronologie der römischen Kaiserzeit im Freien Germanien. *Jahrbuch des Römisch-Germanischen Zentralmuseums Mainz* II.

Elsner, H. 1989. *Wikingermuseum Haithabu: Schaufenster einer frühen Stadt*. Neumünster.

Emanuelsson, U. 1988. A model of describing the development of the cultural landscape. In: H.H. Birks *et al.* (eds) 1988.

Engberg, N. 1992a. Middelalderlandsbyens huse - en oversigt over forskningen i Danmark, udviklingsteorier og udgravningsresultater. In: *Medeltida husbyggande. Symposium i Lund, november 1989*. Stockholm.

- 1992b. Næsholms datering - dendrokronologisk eller numismatisk? Brugerens dilemma. *Hikuin* 19.
- 1992c. Danske privatborge før 1250? Et bidrag til det omdiskuterede spørgsmål. *Hikuin* 19.

Engelhardt, C. 1863. *Thorsbjerg Mosefund, Søndersjyske Mosefund I*. København. (Reprint København 1969.)

- 1865. *Nydam Mosefund, Søndersjyske Mosefund II*. København. (Reprint København 1970.)
- 1867. *Kragehul Mosefund, Fynske Mosefund I*. København. (Reprint København 1970.)
- 1869. *Vimose Fundet, Fynske Mosefund II*. København. (Reprint København 1970.)

Enghoff, I. Bødker 1983. Size distribution of cod (*Gadus morhua* L.) and whiting (*Merlangius merlangus* (L.)) (Pisces, Gadidae) from a Mesolithic settlement at Vedbæk, North Zealand, Denmark. *Videnskabelige Meddelelser fra dansk naturhistorisk Forening* 144.

- 1987. Freshwater Fishing from a Sea-Coast Settlement - the Ertebølle locus classicus revisited. *JDA* 5, 1986.
- 1991. Fishing from the Stone Age Settlement Norsminde. *JDA* 8, 1989.
- 1993. Mesolithic Eel-Fishing at Bjørnsholm, Denmark. *JDA* 10, 1991.

Eriksen, P. 1979. Nygårdhøjfolket. En snes høje fra yngre stenalder. *Mark og Montre* 1979.

- 1985. Det neolitiske bopladskompleks ved Fannerup. *Kuml* 1984.

Eriksen, P. & T. Madsen 1984. Hanstedgård. A Settlement Site from the Funnel Beaker Culture. *JDA* 3, 1984.

Ethelberg, P. 1982. Gravens traditioner. *Skalk* 1982:6.

- 1986. *Hjemsted - en gravplads fra 4. og 5. årh. e.Kr.* Skrifter fra Museumsrådet for Sønderjyllands Amt 2. Haderslev.
- 1987. Early Bronze Age Houses at Højgård, Southern Jutland. *JDA* 5, 1986.
- 1988. Die eisenzeitliche Besiedlung von Hjemsted Banke, Skærbæk sogn, Sønderjyllands amt. *Offa* 45.
- 1989. Skrålbanken. *Skalk* 1989:3.
- 1990. *Hjemsted 2 - tre gravpladser fra 3. og 4. årh. e.Kr.* Skrifter fra Museumsrådet for Sønderjyllands Amt 3. Haderslev.
- 1991. Ein seeländisches Fürstengrab aus dem frühen 3. Jahrhundert. Skovgårde Grab 8. *Fundberichte aus Baden-Württemberg* 16.
- 1993. Two More House Groups with Three-aisled Long-houses from the Early Bronze Age at Højgård, South Jutland. *JDA* 10, 1991.

Fabech, C. 1988. Storstenskisten fra Blære. *Kuml* 1986.

- 1990. Sjørup - an Old Problem in a new Light. *MLUHM* new series 8.
- 1991a. Neue Perspektiven zu den Funden von Sösdala und Fulltofta. *Studien zur Sachsenforschung* 7.
- 1991b. Samfundsorganisation, religiøse ceremonier og regional variation. In: C. Fabech & J. Ringtved (eds) 1991.

Fabech, C. & J. Ringtved (eds) 1991. *Samfundsorganisation og Regional Variation. Norden i romersk jernalder og folkevandringstid. Beretning fra 1. nordiske jernaldersymposium på Sandbjerg Slot 11.-15. april 1989*. JAS Skr. XXVII.

Faber, O. 1976. Hus eller grav? *Mark og Montre* 1976.

- 1977. Endnu et kulthus. In: S.E. Albrethsen (ed.) 1977.

Fenger, O. 1991. Germansk retsorden med særligt henblik på det 7. århundrede. In: P. Mortensen & B.M. Rasmussen (eds) 1991.

Fentz, M. 1989. En hørskjorte fra 1000-årenes Viborg. *Kuml* 1987.

Feveile, C. 1992. Et sjældent ravhus. *By, marsk og geest* 4, 1991.

Feveile, C., S. Jensen og K. Ljungberg 1990. Ansgars Ribe endelig fundet - rapport over en udgravning ved Rosenallé i Ribe 1989. *By, marsk og geest* 1. Ribe.

Fiedel, R.B. & A.B. Nielsen 1989. Allestrup, gravplads, yngre stenalder. *Arkæologiske fund. Kulturhistorisk Museum, Randers. Virksomhed og resultater* 1987-88.

Fischer, A. 1974. Introduktionen af korn og kvæg i Sydskandinavien, en befolkningspres-model. *Kontaktstencil* 8. København.

- 1975. An ornamented flint-core from Holmegård V, Zealand, Denmark. Notes on Mesolithic ornamentation and flint-knapping. *Acta* 45, 1974.
- 1976. Senpalæolitisk bosætning i Danmark. *Kontaktstencil* 12. København.
- 1978. På sporet af overgangen mellem palæoliticum og mesoliticum i Sydskan-

294

dinavien. *Hikuin* 4.

- 1982a. Trade in Danubian shaft-hole axes and the introduction of Neolithic economy in Denmark. *JDA* 1.

- 1982b. Bonderup-bopladsen. Det manglende led mellem dansk palæolitikum og mesolitikum? *Fortidsminder og Bygningsbevaring* (Antikvariske Studier 5).

- 1983. Handel med skolæstøkser og landbrugets indførelse i Danmark. *Aarb.* 1981.

- 1985a. Late Palaeolithic Finds. In: K. Kristiansen (ed.) 1985.

- 1985b. *På jagt med stenalder-våben.* Forsøg med fortiden 3. Lejre.

- 1985c. Den vestsjællandske Åmose som kultur- og naturhistorisk reservat. *Fortidsminder 1985* (Antikvariske Studier 7). København.

- 1989a. Skovtur på havets bund. Stenalderboplads i druknet skov på bunden af Storebælt. *Havbundsundersøgelser. Aktiviteter 1988.* Skov- og Naturstyrelsen.

- 1989b. Musholm Bay. Excavation of a submarine settlement in a drowned forest 9 m below present sea level. *Mesolithic Miscellany* 2:2.

- 1989c. Hunting with flint-tipped arrows: Results and experiences from practical experiments. In: C. Bonsall (ed.) 1989.

- 1990a. On being a pupil of a flintknapper of 11,000 years ago. A preliminary analysis of settlement organisation and flint technology based on conjoined flint artifacts from the Trollesgave site. In: Cziesla, E., S. Eickhoff, N. Arts & D. Winter (eds): *The Big Puzzle. International Symposium on Refitting Stone Artefacts, Monrepos 1987.* Studies in Modern Archaeology 1. Bonn.

- 1990b. A Late Palaeolithic flint workshop at Egtved, east Jutland - a glimpse of the Federmesser culture in Denmark. *JDA* 7, 1988.

- 1990c. A Late Palaeolithic "school" of flint-knapping at Trollesgave, Denmark. Results from refitting. *Acta* 60, 1989.

- 1991a. Pioneers in deglaciated landscapes: The expansion and adaptation of Late Palaeolithic societies in Southern Scandinavia. In: N. Barton *et al.* (eds) 1991.

- 1991b. Træstubbe på havets bund - eller Syndfloden i Storebælt. *Varv* 1991:4.

- 1991c. Store Åmose - Danmarks hidtil største kulturhistorisk begrundede fredningssag. *Skov og Natur.* Skov- og Naturstyrelsen, Hørsholm.

- 1993. *Stenalderbopladser i Smålandsfarvandet. En teori afprøvet ved dykkerbesigtigelse.* Skov- og Naturstyrelsen, København.

- in prep.: *Stenalderbopladser mellem Jylland, Fyn og Sjælland.* Skov-og Naturstyrelsen, København.

Fischer, A., B. Grønnow, J.H. Jønsson, F.O. Nielsen & C. Petersen 1979. *Stenaldereksperimenter i Lejre. Bopladsernes indretning.* Working Papers 8, The National Museum of Denmark. København.

Fischer, A., P.V. Hansen & P. Rasmussen 1984. Macro and Micro Wear Traces on Lithic Projectile Points. Experimental Results and Prehistoric Examples. *JDA* 3.

Fischer, A. & B.M. Mortensen 1977. Trollesgave-bopladsen. Et eksempel på anvendelse af EDB inden for arkæologien. *Arbejdsmarken* 1977.

- 1978. Report on the use of computers for description and analysis of Palaeolithic and Mesolithic occupation areas. In: K. Kristiansen & C. Paludan-Müller (eds) 1978.

Fischer, A., U. Møhl, P. Bennike, H. Tauber, C. Malmros, J. Schou Hansen & P. Smed 1987. Argusgrunden - en undersøisk boplads fra jægerstenalderen. *Fortidsminder og kulturhistorie* (Antikvariske Studier 8).

Fischer, A. & F.O.S. Nielsen 1987. Senistidens bopladser ved Bromme - en nybearbejdning af Westerbys og Mathiassens fund. *Aarb.* 1986.

Fischer, A. & S.A. Sørensen 1983. Stenalder på den danske havbund. *Fortidsminder og Bygningsbevaring* (Antikvariske Studier 6).

Fischer, A. & H. Tauber 1986. New C-14 Datings of Late Palaeolithic Cultures of Northwestern Europe. *JDA* 5, 1985.

Fischer, C. 1969. Skibet skal sejle -. *Skalk* 1969:3.

- 1982. En romersk glasskål med jagtmotiv. Fra en yngre romersk jernaldergrav. *Kuml* 1981.

- 1990. Vandmøller i arkæologisk belysning. In: N.H. Jessen (ed.) 1990.

Fonnesbech-Sandberg, E. 1988. Vægtsystemer i ældre germansk jernalder. *Aarb.* 1987.

- 1990. De arkæologiske undersøgelser i Torstorp. *Høje-Tåstrup Kommunes Lokalhistoriske Arkiv. Årsskrift* 1990.

- 1991a, Guldets funktion i ældre germansk jernalder. In: C. Fabech & J. Ringtved (eds) 1991.

- 1991b. Centralmagt, centre og periferi i Danmarks folkevandringstid. In: Wik, B. (ed.): *Sentrum, periferi: sentra og sentrumsdannelser gjennom førhistorisk og historisk tid. Den 18. nordiske arkeologkongress, Trondheim 18.8-4.9.1989.* Gunneria 64,2.

Forsberg, L. & T.B. Larsson (eds) 1993. Ekonomi och näringsformer i nordisk bronsålder. *Rapport från det 6:e nordiska bronsålderssymposiet, Nämforsen 1990.* Studia Archaeologica Universitatis Umensis 3.

Fraes Rasmussen → Rasmussen, U. Fraes

Frandsen, K.-E. 1983. *Vang og tægt. Studier over dyrkningssystemer og agrarstrukturer i Danmarks landsbyer 1682-83.* Esbjerg.

Frandsen, L. og S. Jensen 1988. Pre-Viking and Early Viking Age Ribe. *JDA* 6, 1987.

Frederik d.VII 1857. *Om Bygningsmåden af Oldtidens Jættestuer.* København.

Fredskild, B. 1982. Nogle pollenanalyser fra prøveudgravningen på stenalderbopladsen Bonderup. *Fortidsminder og Bygningsbevaring* (Antikvariske Studier 5).

Freudenberg, M. 1989. *Studien zur vertikalen sozialen Strukturen. Eine Analyse der Grabfunde der jüngeren Bronzezeit in Dänemark.* BAR Int. Ser. 524.

Friis Johansen → Johansen, K. Friis

Fugl Petersen → Petersen, B. Fugl

Fuglesang, S. Horn 1980. *Some aspects of the Ringerike style. A phase of 11th century Scandinavian art.* Medieval Scandinavia Supplements 1. Odense.

- 1981. Vikingetidens kunst. In: Berg, K. (ed.): *Norges kunsthistorie 1. Fra Oseberg til Borgund.* Oslo.

- 1991. The axehead from Mammen and the Mammen style. In: M. Iversen *et al.* (eds) 1991.

Gam, T. 1992. Prehistoric Glass Technology - Experiments and Analyses. *JDA* 9, 1990.

Gamble, C.S. & W.A. Boismier 1991. *Ethnoarchaeological Approaches to Mobile Campsites.* International Monographs in Prehistory. Ann Arbor, Michigan.

Gebauer, A.B. 1979. Mellemneolitisk tragtbægerkultur i Sydvestjylland. *Kuml* 1978.

- 1990. The Long Dolmen at Asnæs Forskov, West Zealand. *JDA* 7, 1988.

Gebühr, M. 1974. Zur Definition älterkaiserzeitlicher Fürstengräber vom Lübsow-Typ. *PZ* 49.

- 1976. *Der Trachtschmuck der älteren römischen Kaiserzeit im Gebiet* zwischen unterer Elbe und Oder und auf dem westlichen dänischen Inseln. Göttinger Schriften zur Vor- und Frühgeschichte 18. Göttingen.

Geißlinger, H. 1967. *Horte als Geschichtsquelle*. Offa-Bücher 19. Neumünster.

Gejval, N.G. 1970. The Fisherman from Barum - mother of several children! Paleoanatomic finds in the skeleton from Bäckaskog. *Fornvännen* 65.

Gilberg, R. 1976. Stengade-vikingernes skeletter. In: J. Skaarup 1976.

Gissel, S. 1976. Om ødegårdsprojektets opgaver til arkæologien. In: H. Thrane (ed.) 1976.

Glob, P.V. 1945. Studier over den jyske Enkeltgravskultur. *Aarb.* 1944.

- 1949. Barkær. Danmarks ældste Landsby. *Arbejdsmarken* 1949.

- 1965. *Mosefolket. Jernalderens mennesker bevaret i 2000 år.* (3. udg.) København.

- 1975. De dødes lange huse. *Skalk* 1975:6.

Godlowski, K. 1970. *The Chronology of the Late Roman and Early Migration Periods in Central Europe.* Prace Archeologiczne 11. Kraków.

Gräslund, A.-S. 1991. Var Mammen-mannen kristen? In: M. Iversen *et al.* (eds) 1991.

Graham-Campbell, J. 1980. *Viking Artefacts. A select catalogue.* London.

Grandjean, P. 1973. *Bly i Danskere.* København.

Grote, K. & E. Maagaard Jakobsen 1982. Der Faustkeil von Karskov-Kliff auf Langeland. *Archäologisches Korrespondenzblatt* 12.

Grøn, O. 1983. Social Behavior and Settlement Structure. Preliminary Results of a Distribution Analysis on Sites of the Maglemose Culture. *JDA* 2.

- 1987a. Dwelling organization - a key to the understanding of social structure in Old Stone Age societies? An example from the Maglemose culture. *Archeologica Interregionalis. New in Stone Age Archaeology* 8. Warszawa.

- 1987b. Seasonal variation in Maglemosian group size and structure. A new model. *Current Anthropology* 28, 3.

- 1989. General spatial behaviour in small dwellings: A preliminary study in ethnoarchaeology and social psychology. In: C. Bonsall (ed.) 1989.

- 1990. Studies in Settlement Patterns and Submarine Bogs: Results and Strategy for Further Research. In: P.M. Vermeersch & P. Van Peer (eds) 1990.

- 1991. Skovtur. *Skalk* 1991:2.

Grøn, O. & J. Skaarup 1993. Møllegabet II. A submerged Mesolithic site and a boat burial from Ærø. *JDA* 10, 1991.

Grøngaard Jeppesen → Jeppesen, T. Grøngaard

Grønnow, B. 1987. Meiendorf and Stellmoor revisited. An analysis of Late Palaeolithic reindeer exploitation. *Acta* 56, 1985.

Grønnow, B., M. Meldgaard & J.B. Nielsen 1983. *Aasivissuit - the great summer camp. Archaeological, ethnographical and zoo-archaeological studies of a caribou-hunting site in West Greenland.* Meddelelser om Grønland, Man and Society 5.

Gundestrup, B. 1991. *Det kongelige danske Kunstkammer 1737 I-II.* København.

Gøthche, M. 1985. "Sandskuder" - Vessels for Trade between Norway and Denmark in the 18th and 19th Centuries. In: Cederlund, C.O. (ed.): *Postmedieval Boat and Ship Archaeology.* Stockholm.

- 1986. Uggerbyvraget. Et eksempel på Nationalmuseets skibsarkæologiske udrykningstjeneste. *Arbejdsmarken* 1986.

- 1991a. Three Danish 17th-19th Century Wrecks as Examples of Clinker Building Techniques versus Carvel Building Techniques in Local Shipwrightry. In: Reinders, R. & K. Paul (eds): *Carvel Construction Technique.* Oxbow Monograph 12. Oxford.

- 1991b. Stinesmindeskibet. Et renæssancevrag. *Hikuin* 18.

Gøthche, M. & F. Rieck 1990. Skibet er ladet med? Et 1600-tals vrag fra Mariager Fjord. *Arbejdsmarken* 1990.

Hägg, I. 1985. *Textilfunde aus dem Hafen von Haithabu.* Berichte über die Ausgrabungen in Haithabu 20. Neumünster.

- 1991. *Textilfunde aus der Siedlung und aus den Gräbern von Haithabu.* Berichte über die Ausgrabungen in Haithabu 29. Neumünster.

Hagberg, U. E. 1967. *The Archaeology of Skedemosse* I-II. Stockholm.

Hammer, C.U., H.B. Clausen & H. Tauber 1986. Ice-core dating of the Pleistocene/Holocene boundary applied to a calibration of the C-14 time scale. *Radiocarbon* 28.

Hansen, B. Als 1985. Middelalderlige Teglovne. *Bygningsarkæologiske Studier* 1985.

Hansen, B. Als & M. Aaman Sørensen 1975. Ishøj kirke. Et kirkerum fra 1100-

årene og op gennem middelalderen. *Arbejdsmarken* 1975.

- 1979. Den usynlige kirke. Butterup kirkes indre i middelalderen. In: R. Egevang (ed.) 1979.

- 1980. Bistrup Teglværk. *Hikuin* 6.

Hansen, H. Jarl 1985. Fragmenter af en bronzebeslået pragtvogn fra Dankirke. *Aarb.* 1984.

- 1990a. Dankirke. Jernalderboplads og rigdomscenter. Oversigt over udgravningerne 1965-70. *Kuml* 1988-89.

- 1990b. Det kulturhistoriske Centralregister. *AUD* 1989.

- 1991. Dankirke. En myte i dansk arkæologi. In: C. Fabech & J. Ringtved (eds) 1991.

- 1992. Content, Use and Perspectices of DKC, the Danish National Record of Sites and Monuments. In: C.U. Larsen (ed.) 1992.

- 1993. European Archaeological Databases: Problems and Prospects. In: Andresen, J., T. Madsen & I. Scollar (eds): *CAA92. Computing the Past. Computer Applications and Quantitative Methods in Archaeology.* Århus.

Hansen, J.M. 1980. Læsøs Postglaciale udvikling i relation til den Fennoskandiske Randzone. *DGF Årsskr.* 1979.

Hansen, K.E. 1944. Kolding Skibet. Foreløbig Meddelelse om Fund af et Middelalderskib. *Handels- og Søfartsmuseet paa Kronborg, Aarbog* 1944.

Hansen, K. Møller & S. Stummann Hansen 1992. Nivå-fjorden - et stenalderlandskab i Nordøstsjælland. *Hørsholm Egns Museum, Årbog* 1992.

Hansen, M. 1980. En enkeltgravshøj fra Kjeldgården, Aars. *Fra Himmerland og Kjær Herred* 1980.

- 1982. Vesthimmerlands Flyveplads. Single-Grave mounds. Recent Excavations and Discoveries no. 17. *JDA* 1.

- 1985. Grave Mounds, Battle Axes and Pottery of the Single-Grave Culture from Southwest Jutland. In: K. Kristiansen (red.) 1985.

- 1986. Enkeltgravskulturens gravmateriale fra Sydvestjylland. In: C. Adamsen & K. Ebbesen (eds) 1986.

Hansen, P.V. & B. Madsen 1983. Flint Axe Manufacture in the Neolithic. An Experimental Investigation of a Flint Axe Manufacture Site at Hastrup Vænget, East Zealand. *JDA* 2.

Hansen, S. 1993. *Jættestuer i Danmark. Konstruktion og restaurering.* København.

Hansen, S. Stummann 1980. Oldtidsagre

296

på Gørding Hede. *Hardsyssels Årbog.*

Hansen, T. Egebjerg 1988. Die eisenzeit-liche Siedlung bei Nørre Snede, Mitteljütland, Vorläufiger Bericht. *Acta* 58, 1987.

Hansen, T. Egebjerg, S. Hvass, D. Kaldal Mikkelsen 1991. Landbebyggelsen i 7. århundrede. In: P. Mortensen & B.M. Rasmussen (eds) 1991.

Hansen, U. Lund 1970: Kvarmløsefundet - en analyse af Sösdalastilen og dens forudsætning. *Aarb.* 1969.

- 1974. Mellem-neolitiske jordgrave fra Vindinge på Sjælland. *Aarb.* 1972.

- 1977: Das Gräberfeld bei Harpelev, See-land. Studien zur jüngeren römischen Kaiserzeit in der seeländischen Insel-gruppe. *Acta* 47, 1976.

- 1978. Himlingøje-gravpladsens høje. Udgravning af den overpløjede høj. *Antikvariske Studier* 2.

- 1979. To nye grave fra Himlingøje. *Arbejdsmarken* 1979.

- 1981. Terra Sigillata - en sjælden import-vare fra Romerriget. *Arbejdsmarken* 1981.

- 1982. Die skandinavischen Terra Sigilla-ta-Funde. Zu ihrer Herkunft, Datie-rung und Relation zu den übrigen römischen Importen der jüngeren Kai-serzeit. *Studien zur Sachsenforschung* 3.

- 1984. Dankirke. Gläser. In: *Reallexikon des Germanischen Altertumskunde* 5. Berlin/New York.

- 1987. *Römischer Import im Norden. Warenaustausch zwischen dem Römischen Reich und dem freien Ger-manien während der Kaiserzeit unter besonderer Berücksichtigung Nord-europas.* NF B, 10.

- 1988a, Handelscentre i Danmark i romersk og ældre germansk jernalder. In: Aa. Andersen *et al.* (eds) 1988.

- 1988b: Hovedproblemer i romersk og germansk jernalders kronologi i Skan-dinavien og på Kontinentet. In: P. Mor-tensen & B.M. Rasmussen (eds) 1988.

- 1991. Himlingøjeundersøgelserne. Om baggrunden for Stevnsområdets rige gravfund i yngre romertid. In: C. Fabech & J. Ringtved (eds) 1991.

- 1992. Die Hortproblematik im Licht der neuen Diskussion zur Chronologie und zur Deutung der Goldschätze in der Völkerwanderungszeit. In: Hauck, K. (ed.): *Der historische Horizont der Götterbild-Amulette aus der Übergangsepoche von der Spätantike zum Frühmittelalter. Bericht über das Colloquium vom 28.11-1.12 1988 in der*

Werner-Reimers-Stiftung, Bad Hom-burg. Göttingen.

- in press. *Himlingøje - Seeland- Europa. Ein Gräberfeld der jüngeren römischen Kaiserzeit auf Seeland, seine Bedeutung und internationalen Beziehungen.* NF B (13).

Hansen, U. Lund & H. Nielsen 1978. En ny Himlingøje-grav. *Arbejdsmarken* 1978.

Hansen, U. Lund, O. Vagn Nielsen & V. Alexandersen 1973. A Mesolithic grave from Melby in Zealand. *Acta* XLIII, 1972.

Hansen, U. Lund & S. Nielsen (eds) 1992. *Sjællands Jernalder. Beretning fra et symposium 24.IV.1990 i København.* Arkæologiske Skrifter 6. København.

Hansen, V. 1964. *Landskab og bebyggelse i Vendsyssel. Studier over landbebyggel-sens udvikling indtil slutningen af 1600-tallet.* Kulturgeografiske skrifter 7. København.

Hansen, V. & H. Nielsen 1979. Oldtidens veje og vadesteder, belyst ved nye undersøgelser på Stevns. *Aarb.* 1977.

Harck, O. 1990. *Archsum auf Sylt. Teil 3. Die Ausgrabungen in den römer-zeitlichen Erdwerken Archsumburg, Tinnumburg und Trælbanken an der Westküste Schleswigs.* Römisch-Germa-nische Forschungen 50. Mainz.

Harder Sørensen → Sørensen, P. Harder

Harrison, R.J. 1980. *The Beaker Folk.* London.

Hartmann, A. 1982. *Prähistorische Gold-funde aus Europa II. Spektralanalytis-che Untersuchungen und deren Auswer-tung.* Studien zu den Anfängen der Metallurgie 5. Berlin.

Hartz, S. 1987. Neue spätpaläolitische Fundplätze bei Ahrenshöft, Kreis Nordfriesland. *Offa* 44.

Haseloff, G. 1981. *Die germanische Tier-ornamentik der Völkerwanderungszeit. Studien zu Salin's Stil I.* Vorgeschicht-liche Forschungen 17, 1. Berlin/New York.

Hassan, F.A. & S.W. Robinson 1987. High-precision radiocarbon chronome-try of ancient Egypt, and comparisons with Nubia, Palestine and Mesopota-mia. *Antiquity* 61.

Hastrup, F. 1964. *Danske landsbytyper. En geografisk analyse.* Århus.

Hatt, G. 1938. Jernalders bopladser i Himmerland. *Aarb.* 1938.

- 1949. *Oldtidsagre.* Arkæol.Kunsthist. Skr.Dan.Vid.Selsk. 2, no. 1.

- 1957. *Nørre Fjand, an Early Iron-Age Village Site in West Jutland.*

Arkæol.Kunsthist.Skr.Dan.Vid.Selsk. 2, no. 2.

Hatz, G. 1966. Zwei münzartige Schmuckstücke des 9. Jahrhunderts aus dem Kreis Lüneburg. *Lüneburger Blätter* 17.

Hauck, K. 1985. *Die Goldbrakteaten der Völkerwanderungszeit.* Münstersche Mittelalter Schriften 24 1,1-2,2.

Hayen, H. 1989. Bau und Funktion der hölzernen Moorwege. In: Jankuhn, H. (ed.): *Untersuchungen zu Handel und Verkehr der vor- und frühgeschichtlichen Zeit in Mittel- und Nordeuropa*, Teil V. Abhandl. Göttingen, Phil.-Hist.Kl., 3. flg. Nr. 180.

Hedeager, L. 1978a. Bebyggelse, social struktur og politisk organisation i Østdanmarks ældre og yngre romertid. *Fortid og Nutid* XXVII:3.

- 1978b. A quantitative analysis of Roman imports in Europe north of the Limes and the question of Roman-Germanic exchange. In: K. Kristiansen & C. Paludan-Müller (eds) 1978.

- 1978c. Processes towards State Forma-tion in Early Iron Age Denmark. In: K. Kristiansen & C. Paludan-Müller (eds) 1978.

- 1982. *Landsbygrundlæggelser på Stevns.* Landsbyer på Stevns - før og nu. Køge.

- 1985. Grave finds from the Roman Iron Age. In: K. Kristiansen (ed.) 1985.

- 1987. Empire, frontier and the barbar-ian hinterland. Rome and Northern Europe from AD 1-400. In: Rowlands, M., M.T. Larsen & K. Kristiansen (eds): *Centre and Periphery in the Ancient World.* New Directions in Archaeology. Cambridge.

- 1988. *Danernes land.* Gyldendal & Poli-tikens Danmarkshistorie 2. København.

- 1990. *Danmarks Jernalder - mellem stamme og stat.* Århus.

- 1991. Gulddepoterne fra ældre germa-nertid - et forsøg på en tolkning. In: C. Fabech & J. Ringtved (eds) 1991.

- 1992. *Iron Age Societies. From Tribe to State in Northern Europe, 500 BC to AD 700.* Oxford.

Hedeager, L. & K. Kristiansen 1982. Bendstrup - en fyrstegrav fra den romerske jernalder, dens sociale og historiske miljø. *Kuml* 1981.

- 1988. Oldtid, o. 4000 f.Kr.-1000 e.Kr. In: C. Bjørn (ed.) 1988.

Hedeager, L. & H. Tvarnø 1991. *Romerne og germanerne. Det europæiske hus* 1 (ed. S. Mørch). København.

Heighway, D.M. et al. (eds) 1972. *The Erosion of History: Archaeology and Planning in Towns*. London.

Helbæk, H. 1954. *Prehistoric food plants and weeds in Denmark. A survey of archaeobotanical research 1923-54*. DGU II, 80.

- 1977. The Fyrkat grain. A geographical and chronological study of rye. In: O. Olsen & H. Schmidt 1977.

Helm, S. & U. Prydsö 1979a. Assement of age-at-death from mandibular molar attrition in Medieval Danes. *Scandinavian Journal of Dental Research* 87.

- 1979b. Prevalence of malocclusion in Medieval and modern Danes contrasted. *Scandinavian Journal of Dental Research* 87.

Henriksen, B. Bille 1976. *Sværdborg I. Excavations 1943-44. A settlement of the Maglemose culture*. Arkæologiske Studier III. København.

- 1980. *Lundby-holmen. Pladser af Maglemose-type i Sydsjælland*. NF B, 6.

Hertz, J. 1985. Lovgrundlag og administration. *AUD* 1984.

- 1991. ICOMOS, ICAHM og Stockholm-charteret. *AUD* 1990.

Hines, J. 1989. Ritual Hoarding in Migration-Period Scandinavia. A Review of Recent Interpretations. *PPS* 55.

Hingst, H. 1971. Ein befestigtes Dorf aus der Jungsteinzeit in Büdelsdorf (Holstein). *Archäologisches Korrespondenzblatt* 1.

Hjelmquist, H. 1975. Getreidearten und andere Nutzpflanzen aus der frühneolithischen Zeit von Langeland. In: J. Skaarup 1975.

Hoff, A. 1990. På sporet af vikingetidens landbrug? *Bol og By. Landbohistorisk Tidsskrift* 1990:2.

Hoff, A. & J. Jeppesen 1992. Thorbjørns Torp. *Skalk* 1992:1.

Holm, J. 1973. Istidsjægere på Ærø. *Fynske Minder* 1972.

- 1993. Settlements of the Hamburgian and Federmesser Cultures at Slotseng, South Jutland. *JDA* 10, 1991.

Holm, J. & F. Rieck 1983. Jels I - the First Danish Site of the Hamburgian Culture. A Preliminary Report. *JDA* 2.

- 1987. Die Hamburger Kultur in Dänemark. *Archäologisches Korrespondenzblatt* 17:2.

- 1992. *Istidsjægere ved Jelssøerne. Hamburgkulturen i Danmark*. Skrifter fra Museumsrådet for Sønderjyllands amt 4. Haderslev.

Holm, L. & L.C. Nielsen 1983. Ottestrup. En ældre middelalder landsby i Vestsjælland. *Museet for Holbæk og Omegn. Årsberetning* 1983.

Horn, Fr. Winkel 1911. *Oversættelse af Saxo Grammaticus: Danmarks Krønike*. Fjortende Bog. Tønder.

Hougaard Rasmussen → Rasmussen, G. Hougaard

Houmark-Nielsen, M. 1989. The last interglacial-glacial cycle in Denmark. *Quaternary International* 3/4.

Huntley, B. & H.J.B. Birks 1983. *An atlas of past and present pollen maps for Europe: 0-13000 years ago*. Cambridge.

Huxtable, J. & V. Mejdahl 1992. Thermoluminescence dating of burnt flint and sediments from Jels. In: J. Holm & F. Rieck. 1992.

Hvass, L. 1986. Keramikken i den jyske enkeltgravskultur. In: C. Adamsen & K. Ebbesen (eds) 1986.

- 1989. Gravkamre i enkeltgravskulturen. In: L. Larsson (ed.) 1989.

Hvass, L. & S. Hvass 1990. Et gravkammer fra enkeltgravskulturen. *Kuml* 1988-89.

Hvass, S. 1978. A House of the Single-Grave Culture Excavated at Vorbasse in Central Jutland. *Acta* 48, 1977.

- 1979. Die völkerwanderungszeitliche Siedlung Vorbasse, Mitteljütland. *Acta* 49, 1978.

- 1981. Vorbasse. The Viking-age Settlement at Vorbasse, Central Jutland. *Acta* 50, 1979.

- 1982. Huse fra romersk og germansk jernalder i Danmark. In: Myhre, B., B. Stoklund & P. Gjærder (eds): *Vestnordisk byggeskikk gjennom to tusen år: tradisjon og forandring fra romertid til det 19. århundre*. AmS-skrifter 7. Stavanger.

- 1983. Vorbasse. The Development of a Settlement through the First Millenium A.D. *JDA* 2.

- 1985a. *Hodde. Et vestjysk landsbysamfund fra ældre jernalder*. Arkæologiske Studier VII. København.

- 1985b. Iron Age settlements. In: K. Kristiansen (ed.) 1985.

- 1986a. En boplads fra enkeltgravskulturen i Vorbasse. In: C. Adamsen & K. Ebbesen (eds) 1986.

- 1986b. Vorbasse - Eine Dorfsiedlung während des 1. Jahrtausends n. Chr. in Mitteljütland, Dänemark. Von der Eisenzeit zum Mittelalter. *Bericht der Römisch-Germanischen Kommission* 67.

- 1987. Et lokalt Danevirke. *Danmarks længste udgravning. Arkæologi på naturgassens vej 1979-86*. København.

- 1988. Jernalderens bebyggelse. In: P. Mortensen & B.M. Rasmussen (eds) 1988.

Hvidt, K., S. Ellehøj & O. Norn (eds) 1975. *Christiansborg Slot 1-2*. København.

Hyldgård, I.M. 1987. Tre træhuse på Hedegård. *META* 1987, 1-2.

Hædersdal, E. 1990. Holme Klosterkirke. In: *Bygningshistoriske Studier*.

Høgsbro Østergaard → Østergaard, K. Høgsbro

Høilund Nielsen → Nielsen, K. Høilund

Højlund, F. 1975. Stridsøksekulturens flintøkser og -mejsler. *Kuml* 1973-74.

Ilkjær, J. 1976. Et bundt våben fra Vimose. *Kuml* 1975.

- 1990. *Illerup Ådal 1. Die Lanzen und Speere*. JAS Skr. XXV:1.

- 1991. Mosefundene i perspektiv. In: C. Fabech & J. Ringtved (eds) 1991.

Ilkjær, J. & J. Lønstrup 1974. Cirkulære dupsko fra yngre romersk jernalder. *Hikuin* 1.

- 1982. Interpretation of the Great Votive Deposits of Iron Age Weapons. *JDA* 1.

- 1983. Der Moorfund im Tal der Illerup-Å bei Skanderborg in Ostjütland (Dänemark). *Germania* 61.

Iversen, J. 1937. *Undersøgelser over Litorinatransgressioner i Danmark. (Foreløbelig Meddelelse)*. Meddelelser fra Dansk Geologisk Forening 9.

- 1941. *Landnam i Danmarks Stenalder*. DGU II. Række, Nr. 66.

- 1967. Naturens udvikling siden sidste istid. In: Nørrevang, A. & T.J. Meyer (eds): *Danmarks Natur 1*. København.

Iversen, M. 1975. Fire slags grave. *MIV* 5, 1975.

Iversen, M., U. Näsman & J. Vellev (eds) 1991. *Mammen: grav, kunst og samfund i vikingetid*. JAS Skr. XXVIII.

Iversen, M. & J. Vellev 1986. Kammergravens alder. *Skalk* 1986:6.

Jacob-Friesen, G. 1967. *Bronzezeitliche Lanzenspitzen Norddeutschlands und Skandinaviens*. Veröffentlichungen der urgeschichtlichen Sammlungen des Landesmuseums zu Hannover 17. Hildesheim.

- 1970. Skjerne und Egemose. Wagenteile südlicher Provenienz in Skandinavischen Funden. *Acta* XL, 1969.

Jacobsen, E. Maagaard 1982. Litorinatransgressioner i Trundholm mose, NV-Sjælland. En foreløbig undersøgelse. *DGF Årsskr.* 1981.

- 1983. Litorinatransgressioner i Trundholm mose, NV-Sjælland. Supplerende undersøgelser. *DGF Årsskr.* 1982.

298

Jacobsen, J.A., C. Madsen & H. Thrane 1985. Nye fynske husfund fra yngre jernalder. *Fynske Minder* 1984.

Jacobsson, B. 1989. En borg i Trelleborg. *Ale* 1989:1.

Jakobsen, B. 1973. Skovens betydning for landbrugets udvikling Danmark indtil år ca. 1300. *Det Forstlige Forsøgsvæsen i Danmark* 33, 1972-73.

Jankowska, D. (ed.) 1990. *Die Trichterbecherkultur. Neue Forschungen und Hypothesen, Teil I.* Poznan 1990.

Jankuhn, H. 1936. Zur Deutung des Moorfundes von Thorsberg. *Forchungen und Fortschritte* 12, Nr.16.

- 1984. Die Befestigungen um Haithabu. In: Jankuhn et al. (eds) 1984.

- 1986. *Haithabu. Ein Handelsplatz der Wikingerzeit.* Neumünster.

Jankuhn, H., K. Schietzel & H. Reichstein (eds) 1984. *Archäologische und naturwissenschaftliche Untersuchungen an Siedlungen im deutschen Küstengebiet vom 5. Jahrhundert n.Chr. bis zum 11. Jahrhundert n.Chr. Band 2 Handelsplätze des frühen und hohen Mittelalters.* Weinheim.

Jansen, H.M. 1986. Report on the Excavation of Plot no. 607a, Møllergade 6, Svendborg 1976-77. In: Jansen, H.M. (ed.): *The Archaeology of Svendborg, Denmark* 4. Svendborg.

- 1988. Svendborg in the Middle Ages - an Interdisciplinary Investigation. (With contributions by Tove Hatting and Ingrid Sørensen.) *JDA* 6, 1987.

Janssen, C.R. 1973. Local and regional pollen deposition. In: Birks, H.E.B. & R. West (eds): *Quaternary Plant Ecology.* Oxford.

Janssen, W. 1987. *Die Importkeramik von Haithabu.* Die Ausgrabungen in Haithabu 9. Neumünster.

Jansson, I. 1991. År 970/71 och vikingatidens kronologi. In: M. Iversen et al. (eds) 1991.

Jantzen, C. 1992. Det første Egholm. Forgængeren til Egholm Slot. *Hikuin* 19.

Jarl Hansen → Hansen, H. Jarl

Jennbert, K. 1984. *Den produktiva gåvan.* Acta Archaeologica Lundensia Ser. in 4, No. 16.

Jensen, B. & J. Vellev 1971. Erobrerfolkets børn. *Skalk* 1971:1.

Jensen, H.A. 1979. *Seeds and other diaspores in Medieval layers from Svendborg.* The Archaeology of Svendborg, Denmark 2 (ed. H.M. Jansen). Svendborg

- 1985. *Catalogue of late- and post-glacial macrofossils of Spermatophyta from Denmark, Schleswig, Scania, Halland, and Blekinge dated 13,000 B.P. to 1536 A.D.* DGU Ser. A, 6.

- 1986. *Seeds and other diaspores in soil samples from Danish town and monastery excavations, dated 700-1536 AD.* Det Kgl. Danske Videnskabernes Selskab. Biologiske Skrifter 26.

- 1991. The Nordic Countries. In: van Zeist, W., K. Wasylikowa & K.-E. Behre (eds): *Progress in Old World Palaeoethnobotany.* Rotterdam.

Jensen, H. Juel 1982. Knivene under mikroskop. In: Brinch Petersen et al. 1982.

- 1988. Functional Analysis of Prehistoric Flint Tools by High-Power Microscopy: A Review of West European Research. *Journal of World Prehistory* 2, 1.

Jensen, H. Juel & E. Brinch Petersen 1985. A Functional Study of Lithics from Vænget Nord, a Mesolithic Site at Vedbæk, N.E. Sjælland. *JDA* 4.

Jensen, J. 1966. Zwei Abfallgruben von Gevninge, Seeland, aus der jüngeren Bronzezeit (Per. IV). *Acta* XXXVII.

- 1967. Voldtofte-fundet. Bopladsproblemer i yngre bronzealder i Danmark. *Aarb.*

- 1971. Rammen. *Skalk* 1971:5.

- 1973. Ein neues Hallstattschwert aus Dänemark. Beiträge zur Problematik der jungbronzezeitlichen Votivfunde. *Acta* 43, 1972.

- 1978. Kultøkser fra bronzealderen. *Arbejdsmarken* 1978.

- 1979a. *Oldtidens samfund. Tiden indtil år 800.* Dansk social historie 1. København.

- 1979b. *Skovlandets folk.* Sesams Danmarkshistorie. Bronzealderen 1. København.

- 1982a. *The Prehistory of Denmark.* London/New York.

- 1982b. Roskilde. Two hollow-cast ankle rings. *JDA* vol. 1.

- 1982c. Neble. New gold finds. *JDA* vol. 1.

- 1983. Et rigdomscenter fra yngre bronzealder på Sjælland. *Aarb.* 1981.

- 1988a. Bronze Age Research in Denmark 1970-1985. *JDA* 6, 1987.

- 1988b. *I begyndelsen. Fra de ældste tider til ca. år 200 f.Kr.* Gyldendal og Politikens Danmarkshistorie 1. København.

- 1988c. Sophus Müller og det moderne gennembrud i dansk arkæologi. In: Aa. Andersen et al. (eds) 1988.

- 1992. *Thomsens museum. Historien om Nationalmuseet.* København.

Jensen, J., J. Nørlem Sørensen, F. Rieck & M. Stief Aistrup 1989. Hjortspringbåden genopstillet. *Arbejdsmarken* 1989.

Jensen, J.Aa. 1973. Bopladsen Myrhøj. 3 hustomter med klokkebægerkeramik. *Kuml* 1972.

Jensen, J. Steen 1977. Kirkegulvsmønter. *Hikuin* 3.

- 1988. Metaldetektorer og møntfund. In: Aa. Andersen et al. (eds) 1988.

- 1992. Næsholms datering - dendrokronologisk eller numismatisk? *Hikuin* 19.

Jensen, J. Steen, K. Bendixen, F. Lindahl, N.-K. Liebgott, K. Grinder-Hansen & G. Posselt 1992. *Danmarks Middelalderlige Skattefund c.1050-c.1550.* NF B, 12.

Jensen, N.M. & J. Sørensen 1990. Nonnebakkeanlægget i Odense. *Kuml* 1988-89.

Jensen, S. 1981. Fredbjergfundet, en bronzebeslået pragtvogn på en himmerlandsk jernalderboplads. *Kuml* 1980.

- 1984. Ribeegnen gennem 10.000 år - et bebyggelseshistorisk projekt. *Mark og Montre* 1984.

- 1987. Gårde fra vikingetiden ved Gl. Hviding og Vilslev. *Mark og Montre* 1986-87.

- 1990. Handel med dagligvarer i vikingetiden. *Hikuin* 16.

- 1991a. Dankirke - Ribe. Fra handelsgård til handelsplads. In: P. Mortensen & B.M. Rasmussen (eds) 1991.

- 1991b. *Ribes Vikinger.* Ribe.

Jensen, S., P.K. Madsen & O. Schiørring 1983. Excavations in Ribe 1979-82. *JDA* 2.

Jensen, V. & J.M. Ulriksen 1989. Sønderø - en anløbsplads fra yngre jernalder og vikingetid. *ROMU* 1988.

Jeppesen, H. 1979. Kollerupkoggen. Et vragfund i en ralgrav. *Handels- og Søfartsmuseet på Kronborg, Årbog* 1979.

Jeppesen, J. & H.J. Madsen 1990. Stormandsgård og kirke i Lisbjerg. *Kuml* 1988-89.

- 1991. Storgård og kirke i Lisbjerg. In: P. Mortensen & B.M. Rasmussen (eds) 1991.

Jeppesen, T. Grøngaard 1981. *Middelalderlandsbyens opståen. Kontinuitet og brud i den fynske agrarbebyggelse mellem yngre jernalder og tidlig middelalder.* Fynske Studier 11. Odense

- 1982. Aastrup II - to sulehuse fra middelalder og renæssance. *Fynske Minder* 1981.

Jespersen, J. Seit 1985. En kvindegrav fra ældre germansk jernalder ved Levka Bugt, Bornholm. *Fra Bornholms Museum* 1984-85. Rønne.

Jessen, N.H. (ed.) 1990. *Vandløb og kulturhistorie. Rapport fra et seminar afholdt på Odense Universitet 16.-17. januar 1990*. Skrifter fra Historisk Institut, Odense Universitet 39. Odense.

Johansen, E. 1977. Alstrup-højen. Enkeltgrave med skeletter. In: S.E. Albrethsen (ed.) 1977.

- 1985. A Burial Mound with Culture Layers from the Early Bronze Age near Torslev, Northern Jutland. *JDA* 4.

Johansen, E., B. Møller Knudsen & J. Kock 1992. *Fra Aalborgs fødsel til Grevens Fejde 1534*. Aalborgs Historie 1. Aalborg.

Johansen, H. 1981. Kirkens huse. *Danmarks Arkitektur* I. København.

Johansen, K. Friis 1917. Jordgrave fra Dyssetid. *Aarb.* 1917.

Johansen, M. 1986. *Middelalderbyen Køge*. Viby.

Johansson, A.D. 1971. Barmose gruppen. Præboreale bopladsfund med skiveøkser i Sydsjælland. *Historisk Samfund for Præstø Amt. Årbog* 1968.

- 1990. *Barmosegruppen. Præboreale bopladsfund i Sydsjælland*. Århus.

Jonassen, H. 1950. Recent pollen sedimentation and Jutland heath diagrams. *Dansk botanisk Arkiv* 13 (7).

Jouttijärvi, A. & H. Lyngstrøm 1990. Fire mænd og deres jernknive - en arkæologisk/metallurgisk undersøgelse. *Aarb.* 1990.

Juel Jensen → Jensen, H. Juel

Junghans, S., E. Sangmeister & M. Schröder 1968. *Kupfer und Bronze in der frühen Metallzeit Europas 3*. Studien zu den Anfängen der Metallurgie 2.3. Berlin.

- 1974. *Kupfer und Bronze in der frühen Metallzeit Europas 4*. Studien zu den Anfängen der Metallurgie 2.4. Berlin.

Jæger, A. & J. Laursen 1983. Lindebjerg and Røjle Mose. Two Early Bronze Age Settlements on Fyn. *JDA* 2.

Jørgensen, A. Nørgård 1991. Kobbeå Grab 1 - ein reich ausgestattetes Grab der jüngeren germanischen Eisenzeit von Bornholm. *Studien zur Sachsenforschung* 7.

- 1992. Weapon sets in Gotlandic grave finds from 530-800 A.D.: A chronological analysis. In: L. Jørgensen (ed.) 1992.

Jørgensen, E. 1975. Tuernes mysterier. *Skalk* 1975:1.

- 1977a. *Hagebrogård - Vroue - Koldkur.*

Neolithische Gräberfelder aus Nordwest-Jütland. Arkæologiske Studier IV. København.

- 1977b. Brændende langdysser. *Skalk* 1977:5.

- 1981. Gravhusenes problem. *Skalk* 1981:3.

- 1985a. Brydningstid. *Skalk* 1985:2.

- 1985b. To gravhøje ved Hjordkær i Sønderjylland. Om særprægede senneolitiske gravanlæg. *Kuml* 1984.

- 1988. Fire storstensgrave i en højtomt ved Lønt. *Arbejdsmarken* 1988.

Jørgensen, G. 1977. Et kornfund fra Sarup. Bidrag til belysning af tragtbægerkulturens agerbrug. *Kuml* 1976.

- 1979. A New Contribution Concerning the Cultivation of Spelt, *Triticum spelta* L., in Prehistoric Denmark. *Archaeo-Physica* 8 (Maria Hopf-Festschrift).

- 1982. Korn fra Sarup. Med nogle bemærkninger om agerbruget i Yngre Stenalder i Danmark. *Kuml* 1981.

- 1986. Medieval Plant Remains from the Settlements in Møllergade 6. In: Jansen, H.M. (ed.): *The Archaeology of Svendborg, Denmark* 4. Svendborg.

Jørgensen, G. & B. Fredskild 1978. Plant remains from the TRB Culture, period MN V. In: K. Davidsen 1978.

Jørgensen, J. Balslev 1954. *The Eskimo Skeleton. Contributions to the physical anthropology of the aboriginal Greenlanders*. Meddelelser om Grønland 146 (2). København.

- 1973. Anthropologie des skandinavischen Neolithikums. In: Schwabedissen, H. (Hrsg.): *Die Anfänge des Neolithikums vom Orient bis Nordeuropa Teil VIIIa (Anthropologie, 1. Teil)*. Fundamenta, Reihe B, 3. Köln.

Jørgensen, L. 1984. Et gravanlæg fra enkeltgravskulturen. *MIV* 12.

- 1988. Family Burial Practices and Inheritance Systems. The Development of an Iron Age Society from 500 BC to AD 1000 on Bornholm, Denmark. *Acta* 58, 1987.

- 1989. En kronologi for yngre romersk og ældre germansk jernalder på Bornholm. In: L. Jørgensen (ed.) 1989.

- (ed.) 1989. *Simblegård-Trelleborg. Danske gravpladser fra førromersk jernalder til vikingetid*. Arkæologiske Skrifter 3. København.

- 1990. *Bækkegård and Glasergård. Two Cemeteries from the Late Iron Age on Bornholm*. Arkæologiske Studier VIII. København.

- 1991a. Schatzfunde und Agrarproduk-

tion - Zentrumsbildung auf Bornholm im 5.-6. Jh. n. Chr. *Studien zur Sachsenforschung* 7.

- 1991b. Våbengrave og krigeraristokrati. Etableringen af en centralmagt på Bornholm i 6.-8. årh. In: P. Mortensen & B.M. Rasmussen (eds) 1991.

- (ed.) 1992. *Chronological Studies of Anglo-Saxon England, Lombard Italy and Vendel Period Sweden*. Arkæologiske Skrifter 5. København.

- 1993. The Find Material from the Settlement of Gudme II - Composition and Interpretation. In: P.O. Nielsen *et al.* (eds) 1993.

Jørgensen, L. Bender 1986. *Forhistoriske Textiler i Skandinavien*. NF B, 9.

- 1991. European Textiles in Later Prehistory and Early History. A Research Project. *JDA* 8, 1989.

- 1992. *North European Textiles until AD 1000*. Århus.

Jørgensen, L. Bender & T. Skov 1981. Trabjerg. A Viking-age Settlement in North-west Jutland. *Acta* 50, 1979.

Jørgensen, M. Schou 1982. To jyske bronzealderveje - og en ny metode til arkæologisk opmåling. *Arbejdsmarken* 1982.

- 1988a. Vej, vejstrøg og vejspærring, Jernalderens landfærdsel. In: P. Mortensen & B.M. Rasmussen (eds) 1988.

- 1988b. Færdsel over stenalderfjorden. Om den ældste vej i Tibirke. *Fortidsminder og kulturhistorie* (Antikvariske studier 9).

- 1990. Vandløbet som forhindring, Vadesteder og broer fra en arkæologisk synsvinkel. In: N.H. Jessen (ed.) 1990.

Jørgensen, M. Schou, U. Lund Hansen, J. Balslev Jørgensen, T. Hatting & H. Nielsen 1978. Himlingøjegravpladsens Høje. *Antikvariske Studier* 2.

Jørgensen, S. 1956. Kongemosen. Endnu en Aamose-boplads fra den ældre stenalder. *Kuml* 1956.

Kaldal Mikkelsen → Mikkelsen, D. Kaldal

Kann Rasmussen → Rasmussen, A. Kann

Kapel, H. 1969. En boplads fra tidligatlantisk tid ved Villingebæk. *Arbejdsmarken* 1969.

Karlsson, L. 1983. *Nordisk form, om djurornamentik*. The Museum of National Antiquities, Stockholm. Studies 3. Stockholm.

Kaufmann, D. 1990. Tagung über "Befestigte neolithische und äneolithische Siedlungen und Plätze in Mitteleuropa" im Jahre 1988. *Jahresschrift für mitteldeutsche Vorgeschichte* 73.

Kaul, F. 1985. Priorsløkke - en befæstet

jernalderlandsby fra ældre romersk jernalder ved Horsens. *Arbejdsmarken* 1985.

- 1987. Sandagergård. A Late Bronze Age Cultic Building with Rock Engravings and Menhirs from Northern Zealand, Denmark. *Acta* 56, 1985.

- 1988a. *Da våbnene tav. Hjortspringfundet og dets beggrund.* København.

- 1988b. Neolitisk gravanlæg ved Onsved Mark, Horns herred, Sjælland. *Aarb.* 1987.

- 1988c. Nogle nye sjællandske helleristningsfund. *Adoranten.*

- 1989a. Klekkendehøj og Jordehøj - 5000-årige ingeniørarbejder. *Arbejdsmarken* 1989.

- 1989b. Priorsløkke: A Fortified Early First Millennium A.D. Village in Eastern Jutland, Denmark. In: K. Randsborg (ed.) 1989.

Kelly, R.L. 1992. Mobility/Sedentism: Concepts, Archaeological Measures, and Effects. *Annual Review of Anthropology* 1992, 21.

Kempfner-Jørgensen, L. 1983. En hellekiste fra yngre stenalder og en vikingetidsgård ved Melsted. *Fra Bornholms Museum* 1983.

Kempfner-Jørgensen, L. & M. Watt 1985. Settlement Sites with Middle Neolithic Houses at Grødby, Bornholm. *JDA* 4.

Kieffer-Olsen, J. 1987. Vorbasse by. *META* 1987, 1-2.

- 1990. Middelalderens gravskik i Danmark. *Hikuin* 17.

Kieffer-Olsen, J. & N. Engberg 1992. Kirkegårdens grøft. Om den ældste indhegning af Danmarks kirkegårde. *Arbejdsmarken* 1992.

Kjer Michaelsen → Michaelsen, K. Kjer

Kjær Kristensen → Kristensen, I. Kjær

Kjærum, P. 1955. Tempelhus fra stenalder. *Kuml* 1955.

- 1967a. Mortuary Houses and Funeral Rites in Denmark. *Antiquity* 41.

- 1967b. Trækisten i stenkisten. *Skalk* 1967:1.

- 1970. Jættestuen Jordhøj. *Kuml* 1969.

- 1977. En langhøjs tilblivelse. In: S.E. Albrethsen (ed.) 1977.

Klindt-Jensen, O. 1957. *Bornholm i Folkevandringstiden.* Nationalmuseets Skrifter, Større Beretninger II. København.

- 1978. *Slusegårdgravpladsen 1-2. Bornholm fra 1. årh. f. til 5. årh. e.v.t.* JAS Skr. XIV,1-2.

Klindt-Jensen, O. & D. Wilson 1965. *Vikingetidens Kunst.* København.

Kling, J. 1992. En medeltida bondgård i Käglinge, Malmö. In: J.-E. Augustsson (ed.) 1992.

Knudsen, B. Møller & O. Schiørring 1992. *Fra grubehus til grillbar. Horsens i 1000 år.* Horsens.

Knudsen, S.Aa. 1982. *Landskab og oldtid. Atlas over Søllerød og Lyngby-Taarbæk kommuner.* De Historisk-topografiske Selskaber for Søllerød og Lyngby-Taarbæk Kommuner. København.

Koch, E. 1990. Aspekte der Feuchtbodenfunde mit Keramik der Trichterbecherkultur aus Seeland. In: D. Jankowska (ed.) 1990.

Koch, H. 1936. *Danmarks Kirker i den begyndende Højmiddelalder I-II.* København.

Kock, J. 1984. Hellum-potter. *Skalk* 1984:3.

Kolstrup, E. 1988. Late Atlantic and Early Subboreal vegetational development at Trundholm, Denmark. *Journal of Archaeological Science* 15.

Kolstrup, E. & K. Havemann 1984. Weichselian *Juniperus* in the Frøslev alluvial fan (Denmark). *Bulletin of the Geological Society of Denmark* 32.

Kossack, G., K.-E. Behre & P. Schmid (eds) 1984. *Archäologische und naturwissenschaftliche Untersuchungen an Siedlungen im deutschen Küstengebiet vom 5. Jahrhundert v.Chr. bis zum 11. Jahrhundert n.Chr. Band 1 Ländliche Siedlungen.* Weinheim.

Kowalewska-Marszalek, H. 1990. Sandomierz - Wzgorze Zawichojskie. Beispiel einer neolithischen befestigten Anlage in Südostpolen. *Jahresschrift für mitteldeutsche Vorgeschichte* 73.

Kristensen, H. Krongaard 1987. *Middelalderbyen Viborg.* Århus.

- 1992. Sandgravvold. *Hikuin* 19.

Kristensen, H. Krongaard & J. Vellev 1982. En ikke ringe ære for byen. *Skalk* 1982:5.

Kristensen, I. Kjær 1991. Storgård IV. An Early Neolithic Long Barrow near Fjelsø, North Jutland. *JDA* 8, 1989.

Kristiansen, K. 1976. En kildekritisk analyse af depotfund fra Danmarks yngre bronzealder. *Aarb.* 1974.

- 1984. Ideology and Material Culture: An Archaeological Perspective. In: M. Spriggs (ed.) 1984.

- 1985. Fortidsmindebevaring i Danmark. Status og fremtidsperspektiver. *Fortidsminder 1985* (Antikvariske Studier 7).

- (ed.) 1985. *Archaeological Formation Processes. The representativity of archaeological remains from Danish Prehistory.* København.

- 1986. Ideologie und Gesellschaft während der Bronzezeit in Südskandinavien. In: D.-W.R. Buck & B. Gramsch (ed.) 1986.

- 1987. Value, Ranking and Consumption in the Bronze Age. In: H.-Å. Nordström & A. Knape (eds) 1987.

- 1990. Ard marks under barrows: a response to Peter Rowley-Conwy. *Antiquity* 64.

- 1991a. Chiefdoms, states, and systems of social evolution. In: Earle, T. (ed.): *Chiefdoms: Power, Economy and Ideology.* Cambridge.

- 1991b. Prehistoric Migrations - the Case of the Single Grave and Corded Ware Cultures. *JDA* 8, 1989.

- 1992. From Romanticism, through Antiquarianism, to an Historical View of Nature: the Case of Denmark. In: Macinnes, L. & C.R. Wickham-Jones (eds): *All natural things: archaeology and the green debate.* Oxford.

Kristiansen, K. & C. Paludan-Müller (eds) 1978. *New Directions in Scandinavian Archaeology. Studies in Scandinavian Prehistory and Early History* 1. København.

Krogh, H. 1973. The early Post-glacial development of the Store Belt as reflected in a former fresh water basin. *DGU Årbog* 1972.

- 1979a. The Quaternary History of the Baltic. Denmark. In: Gudelis, V. & L.-K. Königsson, (eds): *The Quaternary History of the Baltic.* Acta Universitatis Upsaliensis. Symposia Universitatis Upsaliensis. Annum Quingentesimum Celebrantis: 1. Uppsala.

- 1979b. Late Pleistocene and Holocene shorelines in Western Denmark. In: Oele, E., R.T.E. Schüttenhelm, & A.J. Wiggers (eds): *The Quaternary History of the North Sea.* Acta Universitatis Upsaliensis. Symposia Universitatis Upsaliensis. Annum Quingentesimum Celebrantis: 2. Uppsala.

- 1982. Post-glacial submergence of the Great Belt dated by pollenanalysis and radiocarbon. *International Geological Congress, XX Session, Norden* Part IV.

Krogh, K.J. 1960. Stilladser til et kirkebyggeri i 1100-tallet. *Aarb.* 1959.

- 1983. The Royal Viking-age Monuments at Jelling in the Light of Recent Archaeological Excavations. A Preliminary Report. *Acta* 53, 1982.

Krogh, K.J. & O. Voss 1961. Fra hedenskab til kristendom i Hørning. *Arbejdsmarken* 1961.

Kroll, E.M. & T.D. Price (eds) 1991. *The Interpretation of Archaeological Spatial Patterning*. New York/London.

Kromann, A. 1987. Die römische Münzen von Gudme. *Frühmittelalterliche Studien* 21.

Kromann, A., P.O. Nielsen, K. Randsborg, P. Vang Petersen & P.O. Thomsen 1991. Et fynsk rigdomscenter i jernalderen. *Arbejdsmarken* 1991.

Kromann, A. & M. Watt 1984. Skattefundet fra Smørenge. *Arbejdsmarken* 1984.

Krongaard Kristensen → Kristensen, H. Krongaard

Kunow, J. 1983. *Der römische Import in der Germania Libera bis zu den Markomannenkriegen. Studien zu Bronze- und Glasgefäßen*. Göttinger Schriften zur Vor- und Frühgeschichte 21. Neumünster.

Kunwald, G. 1954. De ældste vidnesbyrd om ligbrænding. *Dansk Ligbrændingsforenings beretning*.

- 1962. Broskovvejen. *Arbejdsmarken* 1962.

- 1964. Oldtidsveje. *Danske veje*. Turistforeningens årbog 1964.

- 1970. Der Moorfund im Rappendam auf Seeland. *PZ* 45.

la Cour, V. 1961. *Næsholm*. København.

- 1963. Om studiet af vore danske voldsteder. *Historisk Tidsskrift* 12. rk., 1.

- 1972. *Danske Borganlæg I-II*. København.

la Cour, V. & H. Stiesdal 1957. *Danske Voldsteder I, Thisted Amt*. København.

- 1963. *Danske Voldsteder II, Hjørring Amt*. København.

Langballe, H. 1985. Foulum huset - tempel eller bolig. *MIV* 13, 1985.

Larsen, C.U. 1986. Et spørgsmål om indgange. *Arbejdsmarken* 1986.

- 1989. Gravhøje på Sjælland. *Arbejdsmarken* 1989.

- (ed.) 1992. *Sites & Monuments. National Archaeological Records*. København.

Larsen, E. Benner 1984. Værktøjsspor/På sporet af værktøj. Identifikation og dokumentation af værktøjsspor, belyst ved punselornamenterede genstande fra Sejlflod. *Kuml* 1982-83.

Larsson, L. 1983. Mesolithic Settlement on the Sea Floor in the Strait of Öresund. In: Masters, P.M. & N.C. Flemming (eds): *Quaternary Coastlines and Marine Archaeology*.

- 1984. The Skateholm Project - a Late Mesolithic Settlement and Cemetary Complex at a Southern Swedish Bay. *MLUHM* new series 5.

- 1988. *Ett fångstsamhälle för 7000 år sedan*. Kristianstad.

- (ed.) 1988. *The Skateholm Project I. Man and Environment*. Acta Regiae Societatis Humaniorum Litterarum Lundensis LXXIX. Stockholm.

- (ed.) 1989. *Stridsyxekultur i Sydskandinavien*. University of Lund, Institute of Archaeology, Report Series No. 36.

- 1990a. Dogs in Fraction - Symbols in Action. In: P.M. Vermeersch & P. Van Peer (eds) 1990.

- 1990b. The Mesolithic of Southern Scandinavia. *Journal of World Prehistory* 4, 3.

- (ed.) in press. *Bronsålderns gravhögar*. Lunds Universitets Historiska Museet och Arkeologiska Institutionen. Report Series.

Larsson, L. & M. Larsson 1986. Stenåldersundersökningar i Ystadsområdet. *Ystadiana. Ystad Fornminnesförenings skrift* XXI.

Larsson, T.B. 1986. *The Bronze Age Metalwork in Southern Sweden. Aspects of social and spatial organization 1800-500 BC*. Archaeology and Environment 6. Umeå.

Lauenborg, M. 1980. Kjersing II. En højgruppe fra enkeltgravskulturen. *Mark og Montre* 1980.

- 1982. Hundens grav. *Skalk* 1982:1.

Leroi-Gourhan, A. 1984. Pincevent. Campement magdalénien de chasseurs de rennes. *Guides Archéologique de la France*.

Levin Nielsen → Nielsen, E. Levin

Levy, J. 1982. *Social and Religious Organization in Bronze Age Denmark. An Analysis of Ritual Hoard Finds*. BAR Int. Ser. 124.

Liebgott, N.-K. 1976. Medieval Pottery Kilns at Faurholm in Northern Zealand, Denmark. *Acta* 46, 1975.

- 1979a. *Stakhaven. Arkæologiske undersøgelser i senmiddelalderens Dragør*. Nationalmuseets Skrifter. Arkæologisk-historisk Rk. XIX. København.

- 1979b. Telt, hytte, bod. In: R. Egevang (ed.) 1979.

- 1989. *Dansk middelalderarkæologi*. København.

Lindblom, I. 1984. Former for økologisk tilpasning i Mesolitikum, Østfold. *Universitetets Oldsaksamling Årbok* 1982/1983.

Liversage, D. 1980. *Material and Interpretation. The Archaeology of Sjælland in the Early Roman Iron Age*. Publications of the National Museum. Archaeological-Historical Series I, XX. København.

- 1981. Neolithic Monuments at Lindebjerg, Northwest Zealand. *Acta* 51, 1980.

- 1988. Mortens Sande 2 - A Single Grave Camp Site in Northwest Jutland. *JDA* 6, 1987.

- 1989a. Radiometrisk datering og beaker bosættelse i en nordvestjysk biotop. In: L. Larsson (ed.) 1989.

- 1989b. Early Copper and Bronze in Denmark - a computer-aided examination of the SAM-analyses. In: J. Poulsen (ed.) 1989.

- 1992. *Barkær. Long Barrows and Settlements*. Arkæologiske Studier IX. København.

- in press. Interpreting Composition Patterns in Ancient Bronze: The Carpathian Basin. *Acta* 64, 1993.

Liversage, D. & M. Liversage 1989. A Method for the Study of the Composition of Early Copper and Bronze Artefacts. An example from Denmark. *Helinium* XXIX.

Liversage, D., M. Munro, M.-A. Courty, P. Nørnberg 1987. Studies of a buried Early Iron Age field. *Acta* 56, 1985.

Liversage, D. & D.E. Robinson 1988. Mens havet æder ind i det nordjyske hedelandskab. *Naturens Verden* 1988:7.

Lomborg, E. 1969. Den tidlige bronzealders kronologi. *Aarb.* 1968.

- 1973a. *Die Flintdolche Dänemarks. Studien über Chronologie und Kulturbeziehungen des südskandinavischen Spätneolitikums*. NF B, 1.

- 1973b. En landsby med huse og kultsted fra ældre bronzealder. *Arbejdsmarken* 1973.

- 1976. Vadgård. Ein Dorf mit Häusern und einer Kultstätte aus der älteren nordischen Bronzezeit. In: Mitscha-Märheim, H., H. Friesinger & H. Kerchler (eds): *Festschrift für Richard Pittioni zum siebzigsten Geburtstag* I. Archaeologia Austriaca, Beiheft 13. Wien.

- 1977a. Bronzealderbopladsen på Skamlebæk radiostation. In: S.E. Albrethsen (ed.) 1977.

- 1977b. Klokkebæger- og senere Beakerindflydelser i Danmark. Et bidrag til enkeltgravskulturens datering. *Aarb.* 1975.

Lorenzen, V. 1949. Vore middelalderlige voldsteder. *Fortid og Nutid*.

Lund, C. 1987. Beskyttelse af historiske skibsvrag og fortidsminder på den danske havbund. *Fortidsminder og kulturhistorie* (Antikvariske Studier 8).

Lund, J. 1977. Overbygård - En jernalderlandsby med neddybede huse. *Kuml* 1976.

- 1980. Tre førromerske jordkældre fra Overbygård. *Kuml* 1979.

- 1982. Toftinghuset. Om rekonstruktion af et jernalderhus. *Kuml* 1981.

- 1984. Nedgravede huse og kældre i ældre jernalder. *Hikuin* 10.

- 1988. Jernalderens bebyggelse i Jylland. In: Näsman, U. & J. Lund (eds): *Folkevandringstiden i Norden. En krisetid mellem ældre og yngre jernalder. Rapport fra et bebyggelsesarkæologisk forskersymposium i Degerhamn, Öland, d. 2.-4. oktober 1985*. Århus.

- 1991. Jernproduktionen i Danmark i romersk jernalder. In: C. Fabech & J. Ringtved (eds) 1991.

Lund, J. & J.N. Nielsen 1984. Nordjyske jernalderbygninger med fodremskonstruktion. *Aarb.* 1982.

Lund Hansen → Hansen, U. Lund

Lunt, D.A. 1978. Molar attrition in Medieval Danes. In: Butler, P.M. & K.A. Jowsey (eds): *Development, Function and Evolution of Teeth*. London.

Lysdahl, P., M. Lundbæk, B.A. Gottlieb, J.N. Sørensen & B. Aaby 1992. Lurparret fra Ulvkær i Vendsyssel. *Kuml* 1990.

Løkkegaard Poulsen → Poulsen, K. Løkkegaard

Lønstrup, J. 1988. Mosefund af hærudstyr fra jernalderen. In: P. Mortensen & B.M. Rasmussen (eds.) 1988.

Maagaard Jacobsen → Jacobsen, E. Maagaard

Mackeprang, M.B. 1943. *Kulturbeziehungen im nordischen Raum des 3. bis 5. Jahrhunderts*. Hamburger Schriften zur Vorgeschichte und germanischen Frühgeschichte 3. Leipzig.

- 1944. En Bronzespand med Billedfrise i en Grav fra 3. Aarhundrede. *Arbejdsmarken* 1944.

Madsen, A.P., S. Müller, C. Neergaard, C.G.J. Petersen, E. Rostrup, K.J.V. Steenstrup & H. Winge 1900. *Affaldsdynger fra Stenalderen i Danmark. Undersøgte for Nationalmuseet.* København.

Madsen, B. 1983. New Evidence of Late Palaeolithic Settlement in East Jutland. *JDA* 2.

- 1984. Flint Axe Manufacturing in the Neolithic: an Experiment with Grinding and Polishing of Thin-Butted Axes. *JDA* 3.

- 1986. Nogle taxonomiske og nomenklatoriske bemærkninger til studiet af flintteknologi - eksperimentelt og arkæologisk. *Fjölnir* 5. Uppsala.

- (ed.) 1991. *Eksperimentel Arkæologi.* Studier i teknologi og kultur Nr. 1. Historisk-Arkæologisk Forsøgscenter. Lejre.

- 1992. Hamburgtraditionens flintteknologi ved Jels. In: J. Holm & F. Rieck 1992.

Madsen, B. & R. Fiedel 1988. Pottery Manufacture at a Neolithic Causewayed Enclosure near Hevringholm, East Jutland. *JDA* 6, 1987.

Madsen, B. & A.B. Nielsen 1987. En stenalders højtomt ved Dalbyneder. *Arkæologiske fund. Kulturhistorisk Museum, Randers. Virksomhed og resultater* 1986.

Madsen, C. & H. Thrane 1992. Udgravninger af sydfynske gravhøje fra yngre bronzealder. *Fynske Minder* 1992.

Madsen, H. Brinch 1984. Metal-Casting. Techniques, Production and Workshop. In: M. Bencard (ed.) 1984.

Madsen, H.J. 1971. To dobbeltgrave fra jysk enkeltgravskultur. *Kuml* 1970.

- 1983. Byens ældste rådhus. *Århus Årbog* 1983.

- 1991. Vikingetidens keramik som historisk kilde. In: P. Mortensen & B.M. Rasmussen (eds) 1991.

Madsen, J. Skamby 1984. En regionalundersøgelse af Hads herreds bebyggelse i yngre stenalder. *Fortid og Nutid* 31.

- 1987. Dänisch-wendische Beziehungen am Schluss des 11. Jahrhunderts vom Fund einer Schiffswerft bei Fribrødre Å auf Falster aus beleuchtet. In: Wiberg, B. (ed.): *Bistum Roskilde und Rügen*. Roskilde.

- 1989. Fribrødre Å - en værftsplads fra slutningen af 1000-tallet. *Lolland-Falsters historiske Samfunds Årbog* 1989.

- 1991. Fribrødre Å: A shipyard site from the late 11th century. In: O. Crumlin-Pedersen (ed.) 1991.

Madsen, M.R. & S.H. Thomsen 1972. Nye dobbeltgrave fra yngre stenalder ved Tarp. *Mark og Montre* 1972.

Madsen, O. 1990. Gantrup. En enkeltgravshøj med ringgrøft og grav med dødehus. *Kuml* 1988-89.

- 1992. Midtjysk magt. *Skalk* 1992:2.

Madsen, P.K. 1986. A survey of the research of Danish medieval pottery. *Medieval Pottery, Bulletin of the Medieval Pottery Group* 10.

Madsen, P.K., B.R. Bitsch, S. Gram, D. Mortensen, L. Mortensen, A. Müch, H. Stiesdal & C. Sønderby 1993. *Dendrokronologiske undersøgelser i Hvidding kirkes tagværk*. Den Antikvariske Samling. Ribe.

Madsen, P.K. & J.E. Petersen 1983. Jernkær. *Mark og Montre* 1983.

Madsen, T. 1978a. Toftum ved Horsens, et befæstet anlæg tilhørende Tragtbægerkulturen. *Kuml* 1977.

- 1978b. Bebyggelsesarkæologisk forskningsstrategi: Overvejelser i forbindelse med et projekt over tragtbægerkulturen i Østjylland. In: H. Thrane (ed.) 1978.

- 1979. Earthen Long Barrows and Timber Structures: Aspects of the Early Neolithic Mortuary Practice in Denmark. *PPS* 45.

- 1980. En tidlig-neolitisk langhøj ved Rude i Østjylland. *Kuml* 1979.

- 1982. Settlement Systems of Early Agricultural Societies in East Jutland, Denmark: A Regional Study of Change. *Journal of Anthropological Archaeology* 1.

- 1988. Causewayed enclosures in South Scandinavia. In: C. Burgess *et al.* (eds) 1988.

Madsen, T. & H. Juel Jensen 1982. Settlement and land use in Early Neolithic Denmark. *Analecta Praehistorica Leidensia* 15.

Madsen, T. & J.E. Petersen 1984. Tidligneolitiske anlæg ved Mosegården. Regionale og kronologiske forskelle i tidligneolitikum. *Kuml* 1982-83.

Madyda-Legutko, R. 1986. *Die Gürtelschnallen der römischen Kaiserzeit und frühen Völkerwanderungszeit im mitteleuropäischen Barbaricum.* BAR Int. Ser. 360.

Mahler, D. 1985. Ragnesminde: A Germanic-Early Viking Age House-Site in Eastern Sjælland. *JDA* 4.

- 1986. Jyske enkeltgrave med rav. In: C. Adamsen & K. Ebbesen (eds) 1986.

Mahler, D., C. Paludan-Müller & S. Stummann Hansen 1983. *Om Arkæologi. Forskning, formidling, forvaltning - for hvem?* København.

Malmer, M.P. 1962. *Jungneolithische Studien.* Acta Archaeologica Lundensia, Ser. in 8, no. 2. Lund.

- 1969. *Gropkeramikboplatsen Jonstorp RÄ.* Kungl. Vitterhets Historie och Antikvitets Akademien, Antikvariskt Arkiv 36. Stockholm.

Malmros, C. 1980. Den tidlige enkeltgravskultur og stridsøksekultur. *Aarb.* 1979.

- 1986. A Neolithic Road Built of Wood at Tibirke, Zealand, Denmark. Contributions to the History of the Coppice

Management in the Subboreal Period. In: Königsson, L.K. (ed.): *Nordic Late Quarternary Biology and Ecology*. Striae 24.

Malmros, C. & H. Tauber 1977. Kulstof-14 dateringer af dansk enkeltgravskultur. *Aarb.* 1975.

Marseen, O. 1960. Ferslev-Huset. *Kuml* 1960.

- 1963. Smedegårde og Livø. Grubekeramiske bopladser ved Limfjorden. *Kuml* 1962.

Martens, J. 1990. Borremose Reconsidered. *JDA* 7, 1988.

Mathiassen, T. 1937. Gudenaa-Kulturen. En Mesolitisk Indlandsbebyggelse i Jylland. *Aarb.* 1937.

- 1943. *Stenalderbopladser i Aamosen.* NF III,3.

- 1946. En boplads fra ældre stenalder ved Vedbæk Boldbaner. *Søllerødbogen* 1946.

- 1947. En senglacial boplads ved Bromme. *Aarb.* 1946.

- 1957. Oldtidsminderne og Fredningsloven. *Arbejdsmarken* 1957.

- 1959. *Nordvestsjællands Oldtidsbebyggelse.* Nationalmuseets Skrifter, Arkæologisk-Historisk Række VII. København.

Mathiassen, T., M. Degerbøl & J. Troels-Smith 1942. *Dyrholmen. En Stenalderboplads paa Djursland.* Arkæol. Kunsthist.Skr.Dan.Vid.Selsk. 1,1.

Meiklejohn, C. & M. Zwelebil 1991. Health Status of European Populations at the Agricultural Transition and the Implications for the Adoption of Farming. In: Bush, H. & M. Zwelebil (eds): *Health in Past Societies. Biocultural interpretations of human skeletal remains in archaeological contexts.* BAR Int. Ser. 567.

Mejdahl, U. 1987. Poghøj - et tidligt middelalderligt gårdsanlæg. *META* 1987, 1-2.

Mejdahl, V. 1990. A survey of archaeological and geological samples dated in 1989. *Geoskrifter* 34. Århus.

- 1991. *Aldersbestemmelse ved hjælp af optisk stimuleret luminescens.* Intern rapport. Nordisk Laboratorium for Luminescens Datering. Risø.

Mejdahl, V., W.T. Bell & M. Winter-Nielsen 1980. Datering af keramik fra arkæologiske udgravninger ved hjælp af termoluminescens (TL). *Aarb.* 1979.

Menghin, W. 1983. *Das Schwert des frühen Mittelalter. Chronologisch-Typologische Untersuchungen zu Langschwertern aus germanischen Gräbern des 5.- bis 7. Jahrhunderts n. Chr.* Stuttgart.

Menke, M. 1989. Zu den frühen Kupferfunden des Nordens. *Acta* 59, 1988.

Mertz, E. L. 1924. *Oversigt over de sen- og postglaciale Niveauforandringer i Danmark.* DGU II Rk., 41.

Meulengracht Sørensen → Sørensen, P. Meulengracht

Michaelsen, K. Kjer 1989. En senneolitisk hustomt fra Vendsyssel. *Kuml* 1987.

- 1990. Løkkebjerg. Endnu en romertidsgravplads fra Gudme/Lundeborgområdet. *Årbog for Svendborg & Omegns Museum* 1990.

Midgley, M.S. 1985. *The Origin and Function of the Earthen Long Barrows of the Northern European Plain.* BAR Int. Ser. 259.

Mikkelsen, D. Kaldal 1990. To ryttergrave fra ældre romersk jernalder - den ene med tilhørende bebyggelse. *Kuml* 1988-89.

Mikkelsen, M. 1992. Metode og prioritering i forbindelse med lokalisering og udgravning af bronzealderbosættelser. *AUD* 1991.

Mikkelsen, V. 1986. *Borup. Man and vegetation.* The Royal Danish Academy of Sciences and Letters' Commission for Research on the History af Agricultural Implements and Field Structures 4.

Morgan, R. 1990. Reconstructing a Neolithic Wooden Mortuary Chamber from the Fens in Eastern England through Tree-Ring Study. In: D.E. Robinson (ed.) 1990.

Mortensen, P. & B.M. Rasmussen (eds) 1988. *Fra Stamme til Stat i Danmark 1. Jernalderens stammesamfund.* JAS Skr. XXII.

- (eds) 1991. *Fra Stamme til Stat i Danmark 2. Høvdingesamfund og Kongemagt.* JAS Skr. XXIIn:2.

Müller, S. 1896. Nye Stenalders Former. *Aarb.* 1896.

- 1897. *Vor Oldtid.* København.

- 1898. De jyske Enkeltgrave fra Stenalderen. *Aarb.* 1898.

- 1919. Bopladsfund fra Bronzealderen. *Aarb* 1919.

Müller-Wille, M. 1976. *Das Bootkammergrab von Haithabu.* Berichte über die Ausgrabungen in Haithabu 8. Neumünster.

- 1989. *Heidnische Opferplätze in frühgeschichtlichen Europa nördlich der Alpen: Die archäologiche überlieferung und ihre Deutung.* Joachim Jungius Gesellschaft der Wissenschaften E.V. Hamburg.

- 1991. Wikingerzeitliche Kammergräber. In: M. Iversen *et al.* (eds) 1991.

Munksgaard, E. 1974. *Oldtidsdragter.* København.

- 1987. Spätantikes Silber. *Frühmittelalterliche Studien* 21.

- 1991. Kopien af dragten fra Mammengraven. In: M. Iversen *et al.* (eds) 1991.

Munksgaard, E. & E. Østergaard 1988. Textiles and costume from Lønne Hede. An early Roman Iron Age burial. In: Jørgensen, L. Bender, B. Magnus & E. Munksgaard (eds): *Archaeological Textiles. Report from the 2nd NESAT Symposium 1.-4. V: 1984.* Arkæologiske Skrifter 2. København.

Møhl, U. 1971. Fangstdyrene ved de danske strande. *Kuml* 1970.

- 1980. Elsdyrskeletterne fra Skottemarke og Favrbo. Skik og brug ved borealtidens jagter. *Aarb.* 1978.

Møller, E. 1961. Den middelalderlige kirke som byggeplads. *Fortid og Nutid* XXI.

Møller, E. & H. Græbe 1972. Uggeløse kirke i søgelyset. *Arbejdsmarken* 1972.

Møller, E. & O. Olsen 1961. Danske trækirker. *Arbejdsmarken* 1961.

Møller Hansen → Hansen, K. Møller

Møller, J.T. 1986. Han Herrederne - et gammelt ørige. In: F. Nørgaard *et al.* (eds) 1986.

- 1988. Vadestedet. In: Aa. Andersen *et al.* (red.) 1988.

Møller Knudsen → Knudsen, B. Møller

Møller-Christensen, V. 1953. *Ten Lepers from Næstved in Denmark. A study of skeletons from a Medieval Danish Leper Hospital.* København.

- 1958. *Bogen om Æbelholt Kloster.* København.

- 1961. *Bone Changes in Leprosy.* København.

- 1967. Evidence of leprosy in earlier peoples. In: Brothwell, D.R. & A.T. Sandison (eds): *Diseases in Antiquity.* Springfield.

- 1978. *Leprosy Changes of the Skull.* Odense.

Mårtensson, A.W. (ed.) 1976. *Uppgrävt förflutet för PKbanken i Lund. En investering i arkeologi.* Lund.

Näsman, U. 1988. Analogislutning i nordisk jernalderarkæologi. In: P. Mortensen & B.M. Rasmussen (eds) 1988.

- 1990. Om fjärrhandel i Sydskandinaviens yngre järnålder. Handel med glas under germansk järnålder och vikingetid. *Hikuin* 16.

- 1991a. Det syvende århundrede - et mørkt tidsrum i ny belysning. In: P.

304

Mortensen & B.M. Rasmussen (eds) 1991.
- 1991b: The Germanic Iron Age and Viking Age in Danish Archaeology since 1976. *JDA* 8, 1989.
- 1991c. Grav og økse. Mammen og den danske vikingetids våbengrave. In: M. Iversen *et al.* (eds) 1991.
- 1991d. Nogle bemærkninger om det nordiske symposium "Samfundsorganisation og Regional Variation" på Sandbjerg Slot den 11.-15. april 1989. In: C. Fabech & J. Ringtved (eds) 1989.
Nancke-Krogh, S. 1989. Flere tvillingehænder. *Adoranten.*
Naturfredningsloven 1973. *Naturfredningsloven. Almindelig fremstilling og kommentarer.* København.
Neumann, H. 1982. *Olgerdiget - et bidrag til Danmarks tidligste historie.* Skrifter fra Museumsrådet for Sønderjyllands amt 1. Haderslev.
Newell, R.R., T.S. Constandse-Westermann & C. Meiklejohn 1979. The Skeletal Remains of Mesolithic Man in Western Europe: an Evaluative Catalogue. *Journal of Human Evolution* 8,1.
Nielsen, E. Levin 1966. Det ældste Viborg. Nye synspunkter og tolkninger. *Fra Viborg Amt* 1965.
- 1969. Pederstræde i Viborg. Købstadsarkæologiske undersøgelser 1966/67. *Kuml* 1968.
Nielsen, F.O. 1988. Bornholms bebyggelse i yngre stenalder - et forskningsprojekt. *Fra Bornholms Museum* 1987-88.
Nielsen, F.O. & P.O. Nielsen 1985. Middle and Late Neolithic Houses at Limensgård, Bornholm. *JDA* 4, 1985.
- 1986a. En boplads med hustomter fra mellem- og senneolitikum ved Limensgård, Bornholm. In: C. Adamsen & K. Ebbesen (eds) 1986.
- 1986b. Stenalderhuse ved Limensgård på Bornholm. *Arbejdsmarken* 1986.
- 1990. The Funnel Beaker Culture on Bornholm. In: D. Jankowska (red.) 1990.
- 1991. The Middle Neolithic Settlement at Grødbygård, Bornholm. In: Jennbert, K., L. Larsson, R. Petré & B. Wyszomirska-Werbart (eds): *Regions and Reflections in Honour of Märta Strömberg.* Acta Arcaheologica Lundensia, Series in 8, No. 20. Lund.
- 1992. Early Neolithic Houses at Limensgård, Bornholm. *JDA* 10, 1991.
Nielsen, H.H. 1988. An Early Neolithic Pottery Deposition at Ellerødgård I, Southern Zealand. *JDA* 6, 1987.

Nielsen, I. 1985. *Middelalderbyen Ribe.* Viby.
- (ed.) 1987. *Bevar din arv. Danmarks fortidsminder 1937-1987.* København.
Nielsen, J.L. 1975: Aspekter af det førromerske våbengravsmiljø i Jylland. *Hikuin* 2.
Nielsen, J.N. 1982. Iron Age Settlement and Cemetery at Sejlflod in Himmerland, North Jutland. *JDA* 1.
Nielsen, J.N., L. Bender Jørgensen, E. Fabech & E. Munksgaard. 1985. En rig germanertidsgrav fra Sejlflod, Nordjylland. *Aarb.* 1983.
Nielsen, J.N. & M. Rasmussen 1986. *Sejlflod - en jernalderlandsby ved Limfjorden.* Ålborg.
Nielsen, K. Høilund 1987: Zur Chronologie der jüngeren germanischen Eisenzeit auf Bornholm. Untersuchungen zu Schmuckgarnituren. *Acta* 57, 1986.
- 1991: Centrum og periferi i 6.-8. årh. Territoriale studier af dyrestil og kvindesmykker i yngre germansk jernalder i Syd- og Østskandinavien. In: P. Mortensen & B.M. Rasmussen (eds) 1991.
Nielsen, L.C. 1981a. Omgård. A Settlement from the Late Iron Age and the Viking Period in West Jutland. *Acta* vol. 50, 1979.
- 1981b. Vestjyske gårde og landsbyer fra bronze- og jernalder. *Arbejdsmarken* 1981.
- 1990: Trelleborg. *Aarb.* 1990.
- 1991: Hedenskab og kristendom. Religionsskiftet afspejlet i vikingetidens grave. In: P. Mortensen & B.M. Rasmussen (eds) 1991.
Nielsen, O. Vagn 1970. *The Nubian Skeleton through 400 years.* København.
Nielsen, O. Vagn & V. Alexandersen 1965. Antropologiske og odontologiske undersøgelser af de senneolitiske skeletrester fra Gerdrup. *Aarb.* 1964.
Nielsen, P.O. 1976. De såkaldte "madknive" af flint. *Aarb.* 1974.
- 1979a. Die Flintbeile der frühen Trichterbecherkultur in Dänemark. *Acta* 48, 1977.
- 1979b. De tyknakkede flintøksers kronologi. *Aarb.* 1977.
- 1981a. *Bondestenalderen.* Sesams Danmarkshistorie, Stenalderen 2. København.
- 1981b. Hundredetusind fortidsminder. *Arbejdsmarken* 1981.
- 1984. Flint Axes and Megaliths - the Time and Context of the Early Dolmens in Denmark. In: Burenhult, G. (ed.): *The Archaeology of Carrowmore.* Theses and Papers in North-

European Archaeology 14. Stockholm.
- 1985a. De første bønder. *Aarb.* 1984.
- 1985b. Neolithic Hoards from Denmark. In: K. Kristiansen (ed.) 1985.
- 1989. Neolitiske bopladser. Udgravningsmetodiske eksempler fra nye undersøgelser. *AUD* 1988
- 1991. Neolitikum. *AUD* 1990.
- 1993. Sigersted und Havnelev. Zwei Siedlungen der frühen Trichterbecherkultur aus Seeland. In: Hoika, J. (ed.): *Beiträge zur frühneolithischen Trichterbecherkultur im westlichen Ostseegebiet.* Untersuchungen und Materialien zur Steinzeit in Schleswig-Holstein 1. Neumünster.
Nielsen, P.O., K. Randsborg & H. Thrane (eds) 1993. *The Archaeology of Gudme and Lundeborg. Papers presented at a Conference at Svendborg, October 1991.* Arkæologiske Studier X. København.
Nielsen, S. 1979a. Den grubekeramiske kultur i Norden. *Antikvariske Studier* 3.
- 1979b. En middelalderlig teglbrænderindustri i Pamhule Skov nær Haderslev. *Antikvariske Studier* 3.
- 1982. Den grubekeramiske kultur og stridsøksekulturen. *Aarb.* 1980.
Nielsen, V. 1984. Prehistoric Field Boundaries in Eastern Denmark. *JDA* 3.
- 1987. Ploughing in the Iron Age. Plough marks in Store Vildmose, North Jutland. *JDA* 5, 1986.
Nikkilä, E. 1947. En satakundensisk äsping och dess eurasiska motsvarigheter. *Folk-liv. Acta Ethonologica et Folkloristia Europea* XI. Stockholm.
Nilsson, T. 1989. Senglacial bosættelse i Vendsyssel. *Kuml* 1987.
- 1991. Store Tyrrestrup - en bronzealderhustomt med bronzedepot. *Vendsyssel nu & da* 1989-90.
Noe, P. 1971. Frigivet. En enkeltgravshøjs storhed og forfald. *MIV* 1.
- 1973. Endnu en dobbeltgrav. *MIV* 3.
Noe-Nygaard, N. 1971. Spur dog spines from Prehistoric and Early Historic Denmark. *Meddelelser fra Dansk Geologisk Forening* 21.
- 1974. Mesolithic hunting in Denmark illustrated by bone injuries caused by human weapons. *Journal of Archaeolocical Science* 1.
- 1988a. δ^{13}C-values of dog bones reveal the nature of changes in man's food resources at the Mesolithic-Neolithic transition, Denmark. *Chemical Geology (Isotope Geoscience Section)* 73.
- 1988b. Taphonomy in Archaeology with Special Emphasis on Man as a Biasing

305

Factor. *JDA* 6, 1987.

- 1989. Man-made trace fossils on bones. *Human Evolution* 4, 6.

Nordström, H.-Å. & A. Knape 1987. *Bronze Age Studies*. Transactions of the British-Scandinavian Colloquium in Stockholm, May 10-11, 1985. Stockholm.

Norling-Christensen, H. & K. Bröste 1945. Skeletgraven fra Korsør Nor. *Arbejdsmarken* 1945.

Nyborg, E. 1977. Mikaels-altre. *Hikuin* 3.

- 1985. Om romanske kirketårne i Danmark. In: Blindheim, M. (ed.): *Kongens magt og ære. Skandinaviske herskersymboler gjennom 1000 år*. Oslo.

- 1986. Kirke - sognedannelse - bebyggelse. *Hikuin* 12.

- 1987. Om kirkekunsten, kirkearkitekturen og middelalderens virkelighed. I: *Tradition og historieskrivning*. Acta Jutlandica LXIII:2, Humanistisk serie 61. Århus.

- 1988a. Om kirkekunsten, kirkearkitekturen og middelalderens virkelighed. In: Hastrup, K. & P. Meulengracht Sørensen (eds): *Tradition og historieskrivning*. Århus.

- 1988b. Korbue, krucifiks og bueretabel. In: Larsen, L., E. Levin Nielsen, E. Roesdahl & O. Schiørring (eds): *30 artikler til Olaf Olsen på 60årsdagen 7. juni 1988*. Hikuin 14.

- 1990. Om kirketopografi og middelalderlig bydannelse. *Hikuin* 17.

- 1993. Kirke, sogn og bebyggelse o. 1000-1300. In: Jensen, S. (ed.): *Ribeegnen i 10.000 år*. Århus.

Nyegaard, G. 1985. Faunalevn fra yngre stenalder på øerne syd for Fyn. In: J. Skaarup 1985.

- 1993. Kirkebjerg-bopladsen ved Voldtofte, SV Fyn i zooarkæologisk belysning. In: L. Forsberg & T.B. Larsson (eds) 1993.

Nørgaard, F., E. Roesdahl & R. Skovmand (eds) 1986. *Aggersborg gennem 1000 år*. Herning.

Nørgård Jørgensen → Jørgensen, A. Nørgård

Odgaard, B. 1985. Kulturlandskabets historie i Vestjylland. *Fortidsminder 1985* (Antikvariske Studier 7).

- 1988. Heathland history in western Jutland, Denmark. In: H.H. Birks *et al.* (eds) 1988.

- 1990. Vestdanske lyngheders oprindelse og fortidige udnyttelse. *Bebyggelseshistorisk Tidsskrift* 19.

- 1991a. Cultural Landscape Development through 5500 Years at Lake Skånsø, Northwestern Jutland, as Reflected in a Regional Pollen Diagram. *JDA* 8, 1989.

- 1991b. Pollenanalyser fra Kragsø, 1989. In: Andersen, S.Th., B. Odgaard & P. Rasmussen 1991.

Odgaard, B. og B. Aaby 1988. Vegetationen i det åbne land. *Vækst* 1988:2.

Odgaard, B.V. & H. Rostholm 1988. A Single Grave Barrow at Harreskov, Jutland. Excavation and Pollen Analysis of a Fossil Soil. *JDA* 6, 1987.

Oldeberg, A. 1974. *Die ältere Metallzeit in Schweden I*. Stockholm.

Olesen, L. H. 1988. Begravelsesplads gennem 2000 år i Stendis. *Holstebro Museums Årsskrift* 1987.

Olsen, O. 1958. Kirkegulvet som arkæologisk arbejdsmark. *Arbejdsmarken* 1958.

- 1966. Hørg, hov og kirke. Historiske og arkæologiske vikingetidsstudier. *Aarb.* 1965.

- 1972. Skt. Mikkel i Slagelse. Om en nyfunden 1000-talskirke og dens forhistorie. *Arbejdsmarken* 1972.

- 1973. Die frühen Städte in Dänemark - Forschungsstand. *Frühe Städte im westlichen Ostseeraum. Kiel Papers '72*.

- 1975. Nogle tanker i anledning af Ribes uventet høje alder. *Fra Ribe Amt* 1975.

- 1977. Perspektiver for dansk middelalderforskning. *Hikuin* 3.

- 1979a. Krønike og udgravning. Øm kloster i historisk og arkæologisk belysning. *Convivium*.

- 1979b. Rabies archaeologorum. *Fortid og Nutid* XXVIII.

- 1980. Rabies archaeologorum. *Antiquity* LIV.

- 1982a. The Medieval Town - a Historical-Archaeological Project. *Danish Medieval History. New Currents*. København.

- 1982b. The quantitative approach in urban archaeology. In: *Environmental archaeology in the urban context*. The Council of British Archaeology Research Report 43. London.

- 1989. Royal Power in Viking Age Denmark. In: Bekker-Nielsen, H. & H.F. Nielsen (eds): *Beretning fra syvende tværfaglige Vikingesymposium 1988*. Højbjerg.

- 1992. Dansk arkæologi. In: *Strejflys. Træk af dansk videnskabs historie 1917-92*. København.

Olsen, O. & O. Crumlin-Pedersen 1968. The Skuldelev Ships (II). *Acta* 38, 1967.

Olsen, O. & O. Schiørring 1980. Ti byer. Diskussionsoplæg til møde på Skarrildshus maj 1980. Projekt Middelalderbyen 1980.

Olsen, O. & H. Schmidt 1977. *Fyrkat I. Borgen og bebyggelsen*. NF B, 3.

Olsen, R.A. 1986. *Borge i Danmark*. Århus.

Olsen, R.A. & O. 1972. Nonneliv - især i Jylland. *Skalk* 1972:6.

Olsson, G. 1988. Nutrient use and productivity for different cropping systems in south Sweden during the 18th century. In: H.H. Birks *et al.* (eds) 1988.

Paludan-Müller, C. 1978. High Atlantic Food Gathering in Northwestern Zealand. Ecological Conditions and Spatial Representation. In: K. Kristiansen & C. Paludan-Müller (eds) 1978.

Pauly, B. 1982. EDB og arkæologi. *Fortidsminder og Bygningsbevaring* (Antikvariske Studier 5).

- 1992. Protected Monuments. In: C.U. Larsen (ed.) 1992.

Pearson, G.W. & M. Stuiver 1986. High-Precision Calibration of the Radiocarbon Time Scale 500-2500 BC. *Radiocarbon* 28.

Pearson, G.W., J.R. Pilcher, M.G.L. Baillie, D.M. Corbett & F. Quua 1986. Heigh-Precision 14C Measurement of Irish Oaks to Show the Natural 14C Variations from AD 1840-5210 BC. *Radiocarbon* 28.

Pearson, M. Parker 1984. Economic and ideological change: Cyclical growth in the pre-state society of Jutland. In: Miller, D. & C. Tilley (eds): *Ideology, Power and Prehistory. New Directions in Archaeology*. Cambridge.

Pedersen, J.-Aa. 1986. A New Early Bronze Age House-Site under a Barrow at Hyllerup, Western Zealand. *JDA* 5.

Pedersen, L. 1989. Skolæstøksens kulturhistoriske betydning. In: Pedersen, L. (ed.): *Stammebåd og skolæstøkse. Arkæologiske undersøgelser ved Halsskov forud for etableringen af den faste forbindelse over Storebælt*. København.

- 1992. Ålegård. *Skalk* 1992:6.

Persson O. & E. 1988. Anthropological Report Concerning the Interred Mesolithic Populations from Skateholm, Southern Sweden, Excavation seasons 1983-84. In: L. Larsson (ed.) 1988.

Petersen, B. Fugl 1974. Senpalæolitiske flækkespidser fra Knudshoved Odde, Sydsjælland. *Aarb.* 1973.

- 1993. Rundebakke. En senpalæolitisk boplads på Knudshoved Odde, Sydsjælland. *Aarb.* 1992.

Petersen, E. Brinch 1967. Klosterlund -

306

Sønder Hadsund - Bøllund. Les trois sites principaux du Maglémosien Ancien en Jutland. Essai de typologie et de chronologie. *Acta* XXXVII, 1966.

- 1971. Ølby Lyng. En østsjællandsk kystboplads med Ertebøllekultur. *Aarb.* 1970.

- 1972. Sværdborg II. A Maglemose Hut from Sværdborg Bog, Zealand, Denmark. With contributions from S. Jørgensen and K. Rosenlund. *Acta* XLII, 1971.

- 1973. A Survey of the Late Palaeolithic and the Mesolithic of Denmark. In: Kozlowski, S.K. (ed.): *The Mesolithic in Europe*. Warszawa.

- 1974. Gravene fra Dragsholm: Fra jæger til bønder for 6000 år siden. *Arbejdsmarken* 1974.

- 1977. Udgravning. In: Brinch Petersen *et al.* 1977.

- 1979a. Udgravningerne i sommeren 1978. In: Brinch Petersen *et al.* 1979.

- 1979b. Kvindernes smykker. In: Brinch Petersen *et al.* 1979.

- 1982. Skørbrændte sten og tilspidsede pæle. In: Brinch Petersen *et al.* 1982.

- 1988. Ein mesolithisches Grav mit acht Personen aus Seeland. *Archäologisches Korrespondenzblatt* 18, 2.

- 1989. Vænget Nord: Excavation, Documentation and Interpretation of a Mesolithic Site at Vedbæk, Denmark. In: C. Bonsall (ed.) 1989.

- 1990. Nye grave fra jægerstenalderen. Strøby Egede og Vedbæk. *Arbejdsmarken* 1990.

- 1991. L'Art et les Sépultures Mésolithique en Scandinavie Meridionale. In: *5 Millions D'Annees L'Aventure Humaine*. Bruxelles.

- 1992. Senpalæolitikum og mesolitikum. *AUD* 1991.

Petersen, E. Brinch, V. Alexandersen, P. Vang Petersen & C. Christensen 1979. Vedbækprojektet. Ny og gammel forskning. *Søllerødbogen* 1979.

Petersen, E. Brinch, C. Christensen, P. Vang Petersen & K. Aaris-Sørensen 1976. Vedbækprojektet. *Søllerødbogen* 1976.

Petersen, E. Brinch, H. Juel Jensen, K. Aaris-Sørensen & P. Vang Petersen 1982. Vedbækprojektet. Under mosen og byen. *Søllerødbogen* 1982.

Petersen, E. Brinch, J.H. Jønsson, P. Vang Petersen & K. Aaris-Sørensen 1977. Vedbækprojektet. I marken og museerne. *Søllerødbogen* 1977.

Petersen, E. Brinch, C. Meiklejohn & V. Alexandersen 1993. Vedbæk. Graven midt i byen. *Arbejdsmarken* 1993.

Petersen, J.E. 1988. Farvergade i Næstved. Arkæologiske fund fra germansk jernalder og middelalder. *Aarb.* 1987.

Petersen, K. Strand 1976. Om Limfjordens postglaciale marine udvikling og niveauforhold, belyst ved mollusk-faunaen og C-14 dateringer. *DGU Årbog* 1975.

- 1981. The Holocene marine transgression and its molluscan fauna in the Skagerrak-Limfjord region, Denmark. *Special Publications International Association of Sedimentologists* 5.

- 1985. The late Quaternary History of Denmark. *JDA* 4.

- 1991. Holocene Coastal and Faunal Development of the Skagen Odde, Northern Jutland, Denmark. *Quaternary International* 9.

- 1992. Environmental changes recorded in the Holocene Molluscan Fauna, Djursland, Denmark. *Scripta Geologica*. Leiden.

Petersen, P. Vang 1977. Vedbæk Boldbaner - endnu engang. *Søllerødbogen* 1977.

- 1982. Jægerfolket på Vedbækbopladserne - kulturudviklingen i Kongemose- og Ertebølletid. *Arbejdsmarken* 1982.

- 1984. Chronological and Regional Variation in the Late Mesolithic of Eastern Denmark. *JDA* 3.

- 1987. Zwei Schatzfunde mit römischen Münzen in Gudme - archäologische Untersuchungen. *Frühmittelalterliche Studien* 21.

- 1988. Nydam III - et våbenoffer fra ældre germansk jernalder. *Aarb.* 1987.

- 1990. Eksotiske faunarester i Kongemose- og Ertebølletid - et resultat af udveksling. *Hikuin* 16.

- 1991: Nye fund af metalsager fra yngre germansk jernalder. Detektorfund og danefæ fra perioden 1966-88. In: P. Mortensen & B.M. Rasmussen (eds) 1991.

Petersen, P. Vang & L. Johansen 1993. Sølbjerg I - an Ahrensburgian Site on a Reindeer Migration Route through Eastern Denmark. *JDA* 10, 1991.

Petersen, S. Bødtker & T. Woller 1989. Trelleborggravpladsen til revision. In: L. Jørgensen (ed.) 1989.

Pétrequin, A.-M. & P. 1988. Ethnoarchéologie de l'Habitat en Grotte de Nouvelle-Guinée. *Bulletin du Centre Genevois d'Anthropologie* 1.

Porsmose, E. 1981. *Den regulerede landsby. Studier over bebyggelsesudviklingen* på Fyn i tiden fra ca. 1700 til ca. 1000 e.Kr. fødsel I-II. Odense.

- 1988. Middelalder, o. 1000-1536. In: C. Bjørn (ed.) 1988.

- 1992a. Landsbyen i renæssancearkæologien. *Hikuin* 19.

- 1992b. Bebyggelsesudvikling fra vikingetid til renæssance i Rønninge sogn, Østfyn. In: J.-E. Augustsson (ed.) 1992.

Poulsen, J. (ed.) 1989. *Regionale forhold i Nordisk Bronzealder. 5. nordiske symposium for bronzealderforskning på Sandbjerg Slot 1987*. JAS Skr. XXIV.

Poulsen, K. Løkkegaard 1978. Eisenzeitliche Muschelhaufen in Dänemark. *Offa* 35.

- 1992. Eriksvolde - et uafsluttet fæstningsværk? *Hikuin* 19.

Poulsen, N.J. 1977. Lille Hedinge kirke - en kridtstenskirke i tre stokværk. *Arbejdsmarken* 1977.

Price, T.D. 1985. Affluent Foragers of Mesolithic southern Scandinavia. In: Price, T.D. & J.A. Brown (eds): *Prehistoric Hunter-Gatherers. The Emergence of Cultural Complexity*. London.

Price, T.D. & A.B. Gebauer 1992. The Final Frontier: Foragers to Farmers in Southern Scandinavia. In: Gebauer, A.B. & T.D. Price (eds): *Transitions to Agriculture in Prehistory*. Monographs in World Archaeology 4. Madison.

Price, T. & E. Brinch Petersen 1987. Prehistoric Settlement in Mesolithic Denmark. *Scientific American* 256, 3.

Probst, N. in press. The introduction of flush-planked skin in Northern Europe - and the Elsinore wreck. *Ancient Shipbuilding Traditions. Proceedings of the 6th International Symposium on Boat and Ship Archaeology, Roskilde 1991*. Roskilde.

Raddatz, K. 1970. Religionsgeschichtliche Probleme des Thorsberger Moorfundes. In: Jankuhn, H. (ed.): *Vorgeschichtliche Heiligtümer und Opferplätze in Mittel- und Nordeuropa*. Abhandlungen der Akademie der Wissenschaften in Göttingen, Phil.-Hist. Kl., dritte Folge, Nr. 74. Göttingen.

- 1987a. *Der Thorsberger Moorfund Katalog*. Offa-Bücher 65. Neumünster.

- 1987b. Der Thorsberger Moorfund, Gürtelteile und Körperschmuck, Katalog. *Offa* 44.

Ramskou, T. 1961. To "Naust" ved Harrevig. *Aarb.* 1960.

- 1980. Vikingetidsbroen over Vejle ådal. *Arbejdsmarken* 1980.

- 1981. *Vikingerne som ingeniører*. København.

Randsborg, K. 1974. Social Stratification in Early Bronze Age Denmark: A Study in the Regulation of Cultural Systems. *PZ* 49.

- 1979. Resource Distribution and the Function of Copper in Early Neolithic Denmark. In: Ryan, M. (ed.): *Proceedings of the Fifth Atlantic Colloquium*. Dublin.

- 1980. *The Viking Age in Denmark. The formation of a state*. London.

- (ed.) 1989. *The Birth of Europe. Archaeology and Social Development in the first Millennium A.D.* Analecta Romama Instituti Danici, Supplementum XVI. Roma.

- 1991. *The First Millennium in Europe and the Mediterranean*. Cambridge.

- 1992. Historical Implications. Chronological Studies in European Archaeology. *Acta* 62, 1991.

Rasmussen, A. Kann 1968. En byhøj i Thyland. *Arbejdsmarken* 1968.

Rasmussen, G. Hougaard 1990. Okkergrave fra ældre stenalder på Djursland. *Kuml* 1988-89.

Rasmussen, J. 1972. Æskebjerg - en rensdyrjægerboplads på Knudshoved Odde. *Årbog for Historisk Samfund for Præstø Amt* 1969-70.

Rasmussen, L. Wincentz 1984. Kainsbakke A47: A Settlement Structure from the Pitted Ware Culture. *JDA* 3.

- 1986. Nye C 14 dateringer for grubekeramisk kultur i Danmark. In: C. Adamsen & K. Ebbesen (eds) 1986.

- 1990. Dolkproduktion og -distribution i senneolitikum. *Hikuin* 16.

Rasmussen, L. Wincentz & N.A. Boas 1982. Kainsbakke og Kirial Bro. *Fortidsminder og Bygningsbevaring* (Antikvariske Studier 5).

Rasmussen, L. Wincentz & J. Richter 1991. *Kainsbakke*. Grenå.

Rasmussen, M. 1993. Bopladsstruktur og økonomisk variation i ældre bronzealder - set fra et par nordjyske bopladser. In: L. Forsberg & T.B. Larsson (eds) 1993.

- in press a. Gravhøje og bopladser. En undersøgelse af lokalisering og sammenhænge. In: L. Larsson (ed.) i tryk.

- in press b. *Bopladskeramik i ældre bronzealder*. JAS Skr.

Rasmussen, P. 1990. Leaf Foddering in the Earliest Neolithic Agriculture. Evidence from Switzerland and Denmark. *Acta* 60, 1989.

- 1991. Leaf-Foddering of Livestock in the Neolithic: Archaeobotanical Evi-

dence from Weier, Switzerland. *JDA* 8, 1989.

Rasmussen, U. Fraes 1982. Gård til borg. *Skalk* 1982:2.

- 1992. Karlstrup voldsted. En stormandsgård ved Karlstrup kirke sammenlignet med andre middelalderhuse. *Årbog for Køge Museum* 1991.

Rech, M. 1979. *Studien zu Depotfunden der Trichterbecher- und Einzelgrabkultur des Nordens*. Offa-Bücher 39. Neumünster.

Reinholdt, H. 1985. En middelalderlig pottemagerovn ved Kragelund i Midtjylland. *META* 2,3.

- 1992. *Middelalderbyen Svendborg*. Gylling.

Richter, J. 1991: Rasmussen, L.W. & J. Richter 1991.

Rieck, F. 1972. Bronzer fra Vognserup Enge. *Fra Holbæk Amt* 1971-72.

- 1982. En halv meter høj. *Nordslesvigske Museer* 9.

- 1991. Aspects of coastal defence in Denmark. In: O. Crumlin-Pedersen (ed.) 1991.

- 1992. Krigsbytte. *Skalk* 1992:1.

Rieck, F. & O. Crumlin-Pedersen 1988. *Både fra Danmarks Oldtid*. Roskilde.

Rindel, P.O. 1992. Oldtid i lange baner - arkæologiske undersøgelser på den kommende motorvejsstrækning mellem Vejen og Holsted. *Mark og Montre* 1992.

Ringtved, J. 1988. Jyske gravfund fra yngre romertid og ældre germanertid. Tendenser i samfundsudviklingen. *Kuml* 1986.

- 1991. Fremmede genstande på Sejlflodgravpladsen, Nordjylland. In: C. Fabech & J. Ringtved (eds) 1991.

Robinson, D.E. (ed.) 1990. *Experimentation and Reconstruction in Environmental Archaeology. Symposia of the Association for Environmental Archaeology No. 9. Roskilde, Denmark, 1988*. Oxford.

Robinson, D.E. & I. Boldsen 1991. Et eksperiment til belysning af jernalderens kornbrug. In: B. Madsen (ed.) 1991.

Robinson, D.E. & D. Kempfner 1988. Carbonized Grain from Mortens Sande 2 - a Single Grave Site in Northwest Jutland. *JDA* 6, 1987.

Robinson, D.E., H.K. Kristensen & I. Boldsen 1992. Botanical analyses from Viborg Søndersø: a waterlogged urban site from the Viking Period. *Acta* 62, 1991.

Robinson, D.E. & P. Siemen 1988. A

Roman Iron Age funerary deposit from Præstestien, southwestern Jutland, and the early cultivation of rye in Denmark. *Antiquity* 62.

Roesdahl, E. 1977. *Fyrkat. En jysk vikingeborg. II. Oldsagerne og gravpladsen*. NF B, 4.

- 1980. *Danmarks vikingetid*. København.

- 1983. Fra vikingegrav til Valhal. In: Kisbye, T. & E. Roesdahl (eds): *Beretning fra andet tværfaglige vikingesymposium*. Højbjerg.

- 1986. Vikingernes Aggersborg. In: F. Nørgaard *et al.* (eds) 1986.

- 1987a. *Vikingernes verden*. København.

- 1987b. The Danish geometrical Viking fortresses and their context. In: Brown, R.A. (ed.): *Anglo-Norman Studies* IX. Woodbridge.

- 1988. Vikingetidens befæstninger i Danmark - og hvad der siden skete. In: Madsen, T. (ed.): *Bag Moesgårds Maske*. Århus.

- 1992. Princely Burial in Scandinavia at the time of the Conversion. In: Kendall, C. & P. Wells (eds): *Voyage to the Other World: the Legacy of Sutton Hoo*. Minneapolis.

- (ed.) 1992. *Viking og Hvidekrist. Norden og Europa 800-1200*. København.

Roesdahl, E., J. Graham-Campbell, P. Connor & K. Pearson (eds) 1981. *The Vikings in England and their Danish homeland*. London.

Rosenberg, G. 1937. *Hjortspringfundet*. NF III, I.

Rosenlund, K. 1976. *Catalogue of subfossil Danish Vertebrates - Fishes*. København.

Rostholm, H. 1977. Nye fund fra yngre stenalder fra Skarrild Overby og Lille Hamborg. *Hardsyssels Årbog* 1977.

- 1978. Neolitiske skivehjul fra Kideris og Bjerregårde i Midtjylland. *Kuml* 1977.

- 1982a. *Oldtiden på Herning-egnen. Spor efter mennesker gennem 8000 år*. Herning.

- 1982b. A Grave Complex of the Early Single Grave Culture at Skarrild Overby, Central Jutland. *JDA* 1.

- 1982c. Oldtidsfund fra Vorgod sogn. In: Christensen, V. Nørlund (ed.): *Vorgodbogen. Træk af Vorgod sogns historie*. Videbæk.

- 1986a. Kornaftryk fra Enkeltgravskulturen. In: C. Adamsen & K. Ebbesen (eds) 1986.

- 1986b. Lustrup og andre bopladsfund fra Herning-egnen. In: C. Adamsen & K. Ebbesen (eds) 1986.

- 1987. De første bønder. Landbrug i

308

Danmarks bondestenalder og bronzealder. *FRAM* 1987.

- 1991. En overpløjet gravhøj i Bukkær, Assing sogn. *FRAM* 1991.

Rowley-Conwy, P. 1979. Forkullet korn fra Lindebjerg. En boplads fra ældre bronzealder. *Kuml* 1978.

- 1981. Slash and burn in the temperate European Neolithic. In: Mercer, R. (ed.): *Farming Practice in British Prehistory*. Edinburgh.

- 1982. Forest grazing and clearance in temperate Europe with special reference to Denmark: An archaeological view. In: Limbrey, S. & M. Bell (eds): *Archaeological Aspects of Woodland Ecology*. BAR Int. Ser. 146.

- 1984a. Bronzealderkorn fra Voldtofte. *Kuml* 1982-83.

- 1984b. The Egehøj Cereals. Bread Wheat (*Triticum aestivum* s.l.) in the Danish Early Bronze Age. *JDA* 3.

- 1984c. The Laziness of the Short-Distance Hunter: The Origins of Agriculture in Western Denmark. *Journal of Anthropological Archaeology* 3.

- 1985a. The Single Grave (Corded Ware) Economy at Kalvø. *JDA* 4.

- 1985b. The Origin of Agriculture in Denmark: A Review of some Theories. *JDA* 4.

- 1985c. Mellemneolitisk økonomi i Danmark og Sydengland. *Kuml* 1984.

Ruinkampagnen 1991. *Ruiner - bevaring af forfald. Midtvejsstatus for Ruinkampagnen.*

Rust, A. 1937. *Das altsteinzeitliche Rentierjägerlager Meiendorf*. Neumünster.

- 1943. *Die alt- und mittelsteinzeitlichen Funde von Stellmoor*. Neumünster.

- 1958. *Die jungpaläolitischen Zeltanlagen von Ahrensburg.*Offa-Bücher 15. Neumünster.

- 1972. *Vor 20.000 Jahren. Rentierjäger der Eiszeit*. Neumünster.

Rydbeck, O. 1945. Skelettgraven i Bäckaskog (sittande hukläge) och dess ålder. *MLUHM* 1944-45.

Rønne, P. 1979. Høj over høj. *Skalk* 1979:5.

- 1991. Early Bronze Age Spiral Ornament - the Technical Background. *JDA* 8, 1989.

Sahlins, M. 1972. *Stone Age Economics*. London.

Sarauw, G.F.L. 1903. En stenalders boplads i Maglemose ved Mullerup sammenholdt med beslægtede fund. *Aarb.* 1903.

Sawyer, P. 1988. *Da Danmark blev Danmark. Fra ca. år 700 til ca. 1050*. Gyldendal og Politikens Danmarkshistorie 3. København.

Schiellerup, P.S. 1992. St. Valbyvej - et senneolitisk højkompleks ved Himmelev, nord for Roskilde. *Aarb.* 1991.

Schietzel, K. 1984. Hafenanlagen von Haithabu. In: H. Jankuhn *et al.* (eds) 1984.

Schietzel, K. & O. Crumlin-Pedersen 1980. Havnen i Hedeby. *Skalk* 1980:3.

Schiørring, O. 1983. Århus. Excavation of the Medieval Town Hall and Square. *JDA* 2.

- 1984. Århus 900-1600. *Århus Midtby. Bevaringsplan 1984*. Århus.

- 1988. Das dänische stadtarchäologische Projekt "Mittelalterstadt". Bericht über die Arbeit und die Ergebnisse. *Lübecker Schriften zur Archäologie und Kulturgeschichte* 14.

Schmidt, H. 1985. Om bygningen af et vikingetidshus på Fyrkat. *Arbejdsmarken* 1985.

-1992. Viking Age Buildings. *JDA* 9, 1990.

Schou Jørgensen → Jørgensen, M. Schou

Schovsbo, P.O. 1983. A Late Neolithic Vehicle from Klosterlund, Central Jutland. *JDA* 2.

- 1987. *Oldtidens Vogne i Norden. Arkæologiske undersøgelser af mose- og jordfundne vogndele af træ fra neolitikum til ældre middelalder.* Frederikshavn.

Schuldt, E. 1972. *Die mecklenburgischen Megalithgräber*. Beiträge zur Ur- und Frühgeschichte der Bezirke Rostock, Schwerin und Neubrandenburg 6. Berlin.

Schwabedissen, H. 1979. Der Beginn des Neolithikums in nordwestlichen Deutschland. In: Schirnig, H. (ed.): *Großsteingräber in Niedersachsen*. Hildesheim.

Schwarz-Markensen, G. 1983. Wo liegen die hauptliefergebiete für rohmaterial Donauländischer steinbeile und -äxte im Mitteleuropa? *Archäologisches Korrespondenzblatt* 13.

Seit Jespersen → Jespersen, J. Seit

Sellevold, B. Jansen, U. Lund Hansen & J. Balslev Jørgensen 1984. *Iron Age Man in Denmark. Prehistoric Man in Denmark, vol. III*. NF B, 8.

Shanks, M. & C. Tilley 1987. *Social Theory and Archaeology*. Cambridge.

Shennan, S.J. 1982. Ideology, Change and the European Early Bronze Age. In: Hodder, I. (ed.): *Symbolic and Structural Archaeology*. Cambridge.

Siemen, P. (ed.) 1989. *Bebyggelser og keramik fra 4.-9. århundrede*. Esbjerg.

- 1990. Bebyggelseshistorie øst for Esbjerg - 3000 års landsbyer og enkeltgårde i Novrupområdet. *Mark og Montre* 1990.

- 1991. Middelalder i Tjæreborg og Allerup. *Mark og Montre* 1991.

Simonsen, J. 1979. Dolktidsgrave fra Vejby og Fjallerslev. *MIV* 8, 1978.

- 1981. Bolig eller dødehus. *MIV* 11, 1981.

- 1983. A Late Neolithic House Site at Tastum, Northwestern Jutland. *JDA* 2.

- 1986. Nogle nordvestjyske bopladsfund fra enkeltgravskulturen. In: C. Adamsen & K. Ebbesen (eds) 1986.

- 1987. Settlements from the Single Grave Culture in NW-Jutland. *JDA* 5, 1986.

Skaarup, J. 1973. *Hesselø - Sølager. Jagdstationen der südskandinavischen Trichterbecherkultur*. Arkæologiske Studier I. København.

- 1975. *Stengade. Ein langeländischer Wohnplatz mit Hausresten aus der frühneolithischen Zeit*. Meddelelser fra Langelands Museum. Rudkøbing.

- 1976. *Stengade II. En langelandsk gravplads med grave fra romersk jernalder og vikingetid*. Meddelelser fra Langelands Museum. Rudkøbing.

- 1979. *Flaadet. En tidlig Maglemoseboplads på Langeland*. Meddelelser fra Langelands Museum, Rudkøbing.

- 1980a. Et 1600-tals skibsvrag ved Lundeborg. *Fynske Minder* 1979-80.

- 1980b. Undersøisk stenalder. *Skalk* 1980:1.

- 1981. Lyster. *Skalk* 1981:6

- 1982. Siedlungs- und Wirtschaftsstrukturen der Trichterbecherkultur in Dänemark. *Offa* 39.

- 1983. Submarine stenalderbopladser i Det sydfynske øhav. *Fortidsminder og Bygningsbevaring* (Antikvariske Studier 6).

- 1984. Tiles and Coastal Trade. *JDA* 3.

- 1985. *Yngre Stenalder på øerne syd for Fyn*. Meddelelser fra Langelands Museum. Rudkøbing.

- 1990. Burials, Votive Offerings and Social Structure in the Early Neolithic Farmer Society of Denmark. In: D. Jankowska (ed.) 1990.

Skaarup, J. & O. Grøn 1991. Den våde grav. *Skalk* 1991:1.

Skamby Madsen → Madsen, J. Skamby

Skansjö, S. 1983. *Söderslätt genom 600 år. Bebyggelse och odling under äldre historisk tid*. Lund.

Skov, E. 1979. Almuebænk og herremandsstol. In: R. Egevang (ed.) 1979.

309

Skovgaard-Petersen, I. 1981. The Written Sources. In: M. Bencard (ed.) 1981.

Slomann, W. 1959a. *Sætrangfunnet. Hjemlig tradisjon og fremmed innslag.* Norske Oldfunn IX. Oslo.

- 1959b. Et nytt romertids gravfunn fra Nord-Norge. *Viking* 23.

- 1977. Der Übergang zwischen der späten Kaiserzeit und der frühen Völkerwanderungszeit. In: Kossack, G. & J. Reichstein (eds): *Archäologische Beiträge zur Chronologie der Völkerwanderungszeit.* Antiquitas Reihe 3, 20. Bonn.

Smedstad, I. 1988. *Etableringen av et organisert veihold i Midt-Norge i tidlig historisk tid.* Varia 16. Oslo.

Sobotta, J. 1991. Frühmesolithische Wohnplätze aus Draved Moor, Dänemark. *Archäologisches Korrespondenzblatt* 21.

Solberg, B. 1981. Spearheads in the transition Period between the early and late Iron Age in Norway. *Acta* 51, 1980.

Sonneville-Bordes, D. de 1960. *Le Paléolithique supérieur en Perigord.* Bordeaux.

Speth, J.D. 1991. Nutritional constraints and Late Glacial adaptive transformations: the importance of non-protein energy sources. In: Barton, N., A.J. Roberts & D.A. Roe (eds): *The Late Glacial in North-West Europe: Human Adaptation and Environmental Change at the End of the Pleistocene.* CBA Research Report 77. Oxford.

Spriggs, M. (ed.): *Marxist Perspectives in Archaeology.* Cambridge.

Stapert, D. 1992. *Rings and sectors: Intrasite spatial analysis of Stone Age sites.* Groningen.

Steen Jensen → Jensen, J. Steen

Steensberg, A. 1983. *Borup AD 700-1400. A Deserted Settlement and its Fields in South Zealand, Denmark.* København.

- 1986. *Pebringegården. Folk og dagværk fra oldtid til nutid.* Højbjerg.

Sterum, N. 1976. Hellekister i sen jysk enkeltgravskultur. *Aarb.* 1974.

- 1978. Nogle C-14-frie synspunkter på den Beckerske kontakthypotese. Svar til en "Efterskrift". *Hikuin* 4.

- 1983. Fra klosterets periferi. *Skalk* 1983:3.

Steuer, H. 1974. *Die Südsiedlung von Haithabu. Studien zur frühmittelalterlichen Keramik im Nordseeküstenbereich und in Schleswig-Holstein.* Die Ausgrabungen in Haithabu 6. Neumünster.

- 1984. Dienstedt. In: *Reallexikon der ger-*

manischen Altertumskunde 5. Berlin/New York.

- 1987. Der Handel der Wikingerzeit zwischen Nord- und Westeuropa aufgrund archäologischer Zeugnisse. In: Düwel, K. *et al.* (eds): *Untersuchungen zu Handel und Verkehr der vor- und frühgeschichtlichen Zeit in Mittel- und Nordeuropa 4. Der Handel der Karolinger- und Wikingerzeit.* Abhandlungen der Akademie der Wissenschaften in Göttingen, Phil.-hist. Kl., dritte Folge, 156. Göttingen.

Stidsing, R. 1989. Stendyngegrave ved Ø. Tørslev grusgrav. *Arkæologiske Fund. Kulturhistorisk Museum, Randers. Virksomhed og resultater* 1987-88.

Stiesdal, H. 1968. An Excavation in the Town of Ribe, Denmark. *Rotterdam Papers* I.

- 1974. The medieval palatium in Denmark. Some recent discoveries at Tranekær Castle. *Chateau Gaillard* VII.

- 1981. Types of public and private fortifications in Denmark. *Danish Medieval History. New Currents. V. The History of Castles and Fortifications.* København.

- 1982. Sønder Jernløse-fundet belyst ved andre sjællandske eksempler. *Aarb.* 1980.

- 1983a. Tidlige sjællandske og lolland-falsterske vesttårne. In: Johannsen, H. (ed.): *Kirkens bygning og brug. Studier tilegnet Elna Møller.* København.

- 1983b. Grave i tidlige vesttårne. *Hikuin* 9.

Stilborg, O. 1990. Teknologisk undersøgelse af keramik fra Lundeborg I. *Årbog for Svendborg & Omegns Museum* 1990.

Stjernquist, B. 1974. Das Opfermoor in Hassle-Bösarp. *Acta* 44, 1973.

Storgaard, B. 1990. Årslev-fundet - et fynsk gravfund fra slutningen af yngre romersk jernalder. *Aarb.* 1990.

Stoumann, I. 1981. Sædding. A Viking-age Village near Esbjerg. *Acta* 50, 1979.

Strömberg, M. 1968. *Der Dolmen Trollasten.* Acta Archaeologica Lundensia. Ser. in 8. No. 7. Lund.

- 1971. *Die Megalithgräber von Hagestad.* Acta Archaeologica Lundensia. Ser. in 8. No. 9. Lund.

Stummann Hansen → Hansen, S. Stummann

Stürup, B. 1966. En ny jordgrav fra tidligneolitisk tid. *Kuml* 1965.

Sturdy, D.A. 1975. Some reindeer economies in prehistoric Europe. In: Higgs, E.S. (ed.): *Palaeoeconomy.* Cambridge.

Søgaard, H. 1961. *Det ældste Århus.* Århus.

Sørensen, I. 1980. Datering af elsdyrknoglerne fra Skottemarke og Favrbo. *Aarb.* 1978.

Sørensen, M.-L. S. 1987. Material order and cultural classification: the role of bronze objects in the transition from Bronze Age to Iron Age in Scandinavia. In: Hodder, I. (ed.): *The Archaeology of Contextual Meaning.* Cambridge.

Sørensen, P. Harder 1982. The Use of Photographs in Celtic Field Studies. *JDA* 1.

Sørensen, P. Meulengracht & G. Steinsland 1990. *Før kristendommen. Digtning og livssyn i vikingetiden.* København.

Sørensen, S.A. 1982. En senneolitisk gravplads ved Gundsølille. En foreløbig meddelelse. *ROMU* II, 1981.

- 1988. A Maglemosian Hut at Lavringe Mose, Zealand. *JDA* 6, 1987.

- in prep. *Kongemosekulturen i Sydskandinavien.*

Tauber, H. 1971. Danske kulstof-14 dateringer af arkæologiske prøver III. *Aarb.* 1970.

- 1977. *Investigations of Aerial Pollen Transport in a Forested Area.* Dansk Botanisk Arkiv 32, 1.

- 1980. Kulstof-14 datering af moselig. *Kuml* 1979.

- 1981. 13C evidence for dietary habits of prehistoric man in Denmark. *Nature* 292, 5821.

- 1986a. C-14 dateringer af enkeltgravskultur og grubekeramisk kultur i Danmark. In: C. Adamsen & K. Ebbesen (eds) 1986.

- 1986b. Analysis of stable isotopes in prehistoric populations. In: Herrmann, B. (ed.): *Innovative Trends in Perhistoric Anthropology.* Mitteilungen der Berliner Gesellschaft für Abthropologie, Etnologie und Urgeschichte 7.

- 1988. Danske arkæologiske C-14 dateringer 1987. *AUD* 1987.

- 1989a: Danske arkæologiske C-14 dateringer 1988. *AUD* 1988.

- 1989b. Stabile isotoper sladrer om forhistoriske kostvaner. *Naturens Verden* 7.

- 1990. Danske arkæologiske C-14 dateringer, København 1989. *AUD* 1989.

Taute, W. 1968. *Die Stielspitzen-gruppen im nördlichen Mitteleuropa. Ein Beitrag zur Kenntnis des späten Altsteinzeit.* Fundamenta Reihe A:5. Köln.

- 1975. Ausgrabungen zum

Spätpaläolithikum und Mesolithikum in Süddeutschland. In: Böhner, K. (ed.) *Ausgrabungen in Deutschland*. Teil I. Mainz.

Thomsen, B. 1982. *Historiske vrag i danske farvande*. København.

Thomsen, E. 1983. Bygningsstenen i Grenåegnens kridtstenskirker. *Hikuin* 9.

Thomsen, P.O. 1989. Lundeborg. En foreløbig redegørelse efter 4 udgravningskampagner. *Årbog for Svendborg & Omegns Museum* 1989. Svendborg.

- 1991a. Lundeborg - en handelsplads gennem 600 år. In: C. Fabech & J. Ringtved (eds) 1991.

- 1991b. Lundeborg, A trading centre from the 3rd-7th century AD. In: O. Crumlin-Pedersen (ed.) 1991.

Thomsen, T. 1929. *Egekistefundet fra Egtved, fra den ældre Bronzealder*. NF II, 4.

Thomsen, T. & A. Jessen 1906. Brabrand-Fundet fra den ældre Stenalder, arkæologisk og geologisk behandlet. *Aarb*. 1906.

Thorsen, S. 1977. Krudhøj: Fladhøj, rundhøj og langhøj. In: S.E. Albrethsen (ed.) 1977.

- 1981. "Klokkehøj" ved Bøjden. *Kuml* 1980.

Thorvildsen, E. 1972. Dankirke. *Arbejdsmarken* 1972.

Thorvildsen, K. 1940. Jordgraven fra Volling. In: Norling-Christensen, H. & P.V. Glob (red.): *Fra Danmarks Ungtid. Arkæologiske Studier til Johannes Brøndsted*. København.

- 1941. Dyssetidens Gravfund i Danmark. *Aarb*. 1941.

- 1957. *Ladbyskibet*. NF VI, 1.

- 1978. Registrering og fredning af fortidsminder i Danmark. *Fornvännen* 73.

Thrane, H. 1963. Hjulgraven fra Storehøj ved Tobøl i Ribe amt. *Kuml* 1962.

- 1967a. Stenalders fladmarksgrave under en broncealderhøj ved Gadbjerg. *Aarb*. 1967.

- 1967b. Fornemme fund fra en jernaldergrav i Uggerløse. *Arbejdsmarken* 1967.

- 1973. Det store broncealderfund fra Røjlemose. *Fynske Minder* 1972.

- 1974 Bebyggelsesarkæologi. En arbejdsopgave. *Fortid og Nutid* 25.

- 1975: *Europæiske forbindelser. Bidrag til studiet af fremmede forbindelser i Danmarks yngre broncealder (periode IV-V)*. Nationalmuseets Skrifter, Arkæologisk-Historisk Række XVI.

- (ed.) 1976. *Bebyggelsesarkæologi*. Skrifter fra Institut for Historie og Samfundsvidenskab 17. Odense.

- (ed.) 1977. *Kontinuitet og bebyggelse*. Skrifter fra Institut for Historie og Samfundsvidenskab 22. Odense.

- (ed.) 1979. *Fra jernalder til middelalder*. Skrifter fra Historisk Institut 27. Odense.

- 1980a. Fem lerkar med korn. Om baggrunden for de første udgravninger på Kirkebjerget i Voldtofte. *Aarb*.

- 1980b. Nogle tanker om yngre broncealders bebyggelse på Sydvestfyn. In: H. Thrane (ed.) 1980.

- (ed.) 1980. *Broncealderbebyggelse i Norden. Beretning fra det andet nordiske symposium for broncealderforskning, Odense 9.-11. april 1980*. Skrifter fra Historisk Institut, Odense Universitet 28.

- 1981. Late Bronze Age Graves in Denmark seen as Expressions of Social Ranking. An Initial Report. In: Lorenz, H. (ed.): *Studien zur Bronzezeit. Festschrift für Wilhelm Albert v. Brunn*. Mainz.

- (ed.) 1982. *Om yngre stenalders bebyggelseshistorie*. Skrifter fra Historisk Institut, Odense Universitet 30.

- 1984. *Lusehøj ved Voldtofte - en sydvestfynsk storhøj fra yngre broncealder*. Fynske Studier XIII.

- 1985. Bronze Age Settlements. In: K. Kristiansen (ed.) 1985.

- 1987a. Das Gudme-problem und die Gudme-Untersuchung. *Frühmittelalterliche Studien* 21.

- 1987b. The Ladby ship revisited. *Antiquity* 61.

- 1989. Siedlungsarchäologische Untersuchungen in Dänemark. *PZ* 64.

- (ed.) 1990. *Gudme-rapport*. Skrifter fra Historisk Institut, Odense Universitet 33. Odense.

- 1991a. Danish Plough-Marks from the Neolithic and Bronze Age. *JDA* 8, 1989.

- 1991b. Gudmeundersøgelserne. In: P. Mortensen & B.M. Rasmussen (eds) 1991.

- 1991c. Om Gudmes funktion. In: C. Fabech & J. Ringtved (eds) 1991.

Tixier, J. 1963. *Typologie de l'Epipaléolithique du Magreb*. Mémoire du C.R.A.P.E., Alger, Paris Arts et Métiers graphiques.

Tkocz, I. & N. Brøndum 1985. *Anthropological Analyses. Medieval Skeletons from the Franciscan Cemetery in Svendborg*. The Archaeology of Svendborg, Denmark 3 (ed. H.M. Jansen). Svendborg.

Tornbjerg, S.Å. 1985. Bellingegård, a Late Iron Age Settlement Site at Køge, East Sealand. *JDA* 4.

- 1989. Jernalderbebyggelser ved Køge. *Køge Museum* 1989.

- 1991. Varpelev gennem 2000 år. Rapport fra et arkæologisk recognoscerings- og udgravningsprojekt i Varpelev ejerlaug. *Årbog for Køge Museum* 1990.

Troels-Smith, J. 1942. Geologisk Datering af Dyrholm-Fundet. In: Mathiassen, Th., M. Degerbøl & J. Troels-Smith: *Dyrholmen. En Stenalderboplads paa Djursland*. Arkæol.Kunsthist. Skr.Dan.Vid.Selsk. I:1.

- 1953. Ertebøllekultur - Bondekultur. Resultater af de sidste 10 Aars Undersøgelser i Aamosen, Vestsjælland. *Aarb*. 1953.

- 1967. The Ertebølle Culture and its Background. *Paleohistoria* XII.

- 1982. Vegetationshistoriske vidnesbyrd om skovrydning, planteavl og husdyrhold i Europa, specielt Skandinavien. In: Sjøvold, T. (ed.): *Introduktionen av jordbruk i Norden*. Oslo.

Trolle-Lassen, T. 1984. A preliminary report on the archaeological and zoological evidence of fish exploitation from a submerged site in Mesolithic Denmark. *C.N.R.S. Centre de Recherches Archéologiques. Notes et Monographies techniques* 16.

- 1992. Butchering of Red deer (*Cervus elaphus* L.) - A Case Study from the Late Mesolithic Settlement of Tybrind Vig, Denmark. *JDA* 9, 1990.

Tromnau, G. 1975. *Neue Ausgrabungen im Ahrensburger Tunneltal. Ein Beitrag zur Erforschung des Jungpaläolithikums im nordwesteuropäischen Flachland*. Offa-Bücher 33. Neumünster.

Ulbricht, I. 1978. *Die Geweihverarbeitung in Haithabu*. Die Ausgrabungen in Haithabu 7. Neumünster.

- 1980. Middelalderlig kamproduktion. *Hikuin* 6.

Ulriksen, J.M. 1990. Teorier og virkelighed i forbindelse med lokaliseringen af anløbspladser fra germanertid og vikingetid. *Aarb*. 1990.

Vagn Nielsen → Nielsen, O. Vagn

Vandkilde, H. 1989a. Von der Steinzeit bis zur Bronzezeit in Dänemark. *Zeitschrift für Archäologie* 23.

- 1989b. Det ældste metalmiljø i Danmark. In: J. Poulsen (ed.) 1989.

- 1990a. A Late Neolithic Hoard with Objects of Bronze and Gold from Skeldal, Central Jutland. *JDA* vol. 7.

311

- 1990b. Senneolitikum ved Limfjorden: Fra dominans til anonymitet. In: Ringtved, J. (ed.): *Limfjordsegnens kultur- og naturhistorie. Rapport fra seminar afholdt 4.-5. november 1989 i Nykøbing Mors.* Limfjordsprojektet, rapport 1. Århus.
- 1992a. A Late Neolithic Hoard from Vigerslev, North Zealand. An Archaeological and Metal Analytical Classification. *JDA* 9, 1990.
- 1992b. Metal Analyses of the Skeldal Hoard and Aspects of Early Danish Metal Use. *JDA* 9, 1990.
- 1993. Aspekter af teknologi og samfund i overgangstiden mellem Sten- og Bronzealder i Danmark. In: L. Forsberg & T.B. Larsson (eds) 1993.

Vang Petersen → Petersen, P. Vang

Vebæk, C.L. 1980. Priorsløkke - en befæstet boplads fra ældre romersk jernalder ved Horsens. *Antikvariske Studier* 4.
- 1988. En byhøj i Thy. *Arbejdsmarken* 1988.

Vedsted, J. 1986. *Fortidsminder og kulturlandskab. En kildekritisk analyse af tragtbægerkulturens fundmateriale fra Norddjursland.* Randers.

Vejledning 1993. *Vejledning om naturbeskyttelsesloven.*

Vellev, J. 1971. Oderkistegravpladsen i Skringstrup. *MIV* 1
- 1972. Nye udgravninger på "oderkiste"- gravpladsen i Skringstrup. *MIV* 2.
- 1973. Dobbeltgrav i Skringstrup. *MIV* 3.
- 1975. Skringstrup-pladsen. Nye betragtninger. *Hikuin* 2.
- 1983. Grenåegnens kalkstenskirker. *Hikuin* 9.
- 1985. Et middelalderligt bronzestøberi i Odense. *Fynske Minder* 1984.
- 1990. *Asmild klosterkirke i 900 år.* Højbjerg.

Vermeersch, P.M. & P. Van Peer (eds) 1990. *Contributions to the Mesolithic in Europe. Papers presented at the fourth international symposium "The Mesolithic in Europe".* Leuven.

Vesth, K. Borch 1985. Danske voldsteder. *Fortidsminder 1985* (Antikvariske Studier 7).

Vinner, M. 1986a. Roar fra Roskilde. *Skalk* 1986:3.
- 1986b. Recording the Trial Run. In: O. Crumlin-Pedersen & M. Vinner (eds) 1986.

Vorting, H.C. 1973. Et usædvanligt enkeltgravsanlæg ved Veldbæk. *Mark og Montre* 1973.
- 1977. Gravplads på højtoppen - og andet godt fra en frigivet gravhøj i Vendsyssel. In: S.E. Albrethsen (ed.) 1977.

Voss, O. 1955. The Høstentorp Silver Hoard and its Period. *Acta XXV*, 1954.
- 1967. Dokumentationsproblemer indenfor arkæologien. *Kuml* 1966.
- 1986. Jernudvindingsanlæg i Danmark fra forhistorisk og historisk tid. *AUD* 1985.
- 1991. Jernproduktionen i Danmark i perioden 0-550 e.Kr. In: C. Fabech & J. Ringtved (eds) 1991.

Wagnkilde, H. 1986. Et ringformet gravanlæg fra dolktid og ældre bronzealder. *Fra Bornholms Museum* 1986.

Watt, M. 1978. Hellekiste på Krusegårds Mark i Poulsker. *Bornholmske Samlinger* 2. rk. 12.
- 1983. A Viking Age Settlement at Runegård (Grødby), Bornholm. An Interim Report of the Investigations 1979-82. *JDA* 2.
- 1985. Det antikvariske arbejde. Romertidsgravpladsen ved Grødbygård i Åker. *Fra Bornholms Museum* 1984-1985.
- 1988. Bornholm mellem vikingetid og middelalder. In: A. Aagesen *et al.* (eds) 1988.
- 1991. Sorte Muld. Høvdingesæde og kultplads fra yngre jernalder på Bornholm. In: P. Mortensen & B.M. Rasmussen (eds) 1991.

Wegewitz, W. 1957. Ein Rennfeuerofen aus einer Siedlung der älteren Römerzeit in Scharmbeck (Kreis Harburg). *Nachrichten aus Niedersachsens Urgeschichte* 26.

Weisgerber, G. (ed.) 1980. *5000 Jahre Feuersteinbergbau. Die Suche nach dem Stahl der Steinzeit.* Veröffentlichungen aus dem Deutschen Bergbau-Museum Bochum 22.

Werner, J. 1960. Die frühgeschichtlichen Grabfunde vom Spielberg bei Erlbach, Ldkr. Nördlingen, und von Fürst, Ldkr. Laufen a.d. Salzach. *Bayerische Vorgeschichtsblätter* 25.
- 1988. Danceny und Brangstrup. Untersuchungen zur černjachov-Kultur zwischen Sereth und Dnjestr und zu den "Reichtumszentren" auf Fünen. *Bonner Jahrbücher* 188.

Westerby, E. 1927. *Stenalderbopladser ved Klampenborg.* København.

Wienberg, J. 1986. Gotiske kirkehvælvinger - et økonomisk perspektiv. In: Andrén, A. (ed.): *Medeltiden och arkeologin. Festskrift til Erik Cinthio.* Lund.

Willroth, K.-H. 1985. *Die Hortfunde der älteren Bronzezeit in Südschweden und auf den dänischen Inseln.* Offa-Bücher NF 55. Neumünster.

Wilson, D. & O. Klindt-Jensen 1966. *Viking Art.* London. (Reprint 1980.)

Wincentz Rasmussen → Rasmussen, L. Wincentz

Worsaae, J.J.A. 1865. *Om Slesvigs eller Sønderjyllands Oldtidsminder.* København.
- 1869. Om Mammen-Fundet fra Hedenskabets Slutningstid. *Aarb.* 1869.

Worsøe, E. 1979. *Stævningsskovene.* København.

Wyszomirska, B. 1984. *Figurplastik och gravskick hos Nord- och Nordösteuropas neolitiska fångstkulturer.* Acta Archaeologica Lundensia, Ser. in 4. No. 18. Lund.

Wåhlin-Andersen, V, 1964. Skuldelevskibene i perspektiv. *Skalk* 1964:4.

Zvelebil, M. & P. Rowley-Conwy 1986. Foragers and Farmers in Atlantic Europe. In: Zvelebil, M. (ed.): *Hunters in Transition. Mesolithic Societies of temperate Eurasia and their transition to farming.* New directions in Archaeology. Cambridge.

Ørsnes, M. 1966. *Form og stil i Sydskandinaviens germanske jernalder.* Nationalmuseet. Skrifter. Arkæologisk-Historisk række 11. København.
- 1969-70. Forord til C. Engelhardt: *Sønderjyske og Fynske Mosefund.* (Reprint.) København.
- 1976. Bejsebakken. In: *Reallexikon der Germanischen Altertumskunde* 2. Berlin/New York.
- 1984. *Sejrens pris. Våbenofre i Ejsbøl Mose ved Haderslev.* Haderslev.
- 1988. *Ejsbøl I. Waffenopferfunde des 4.- 5. Jahrh. nach Chr.* NF B, 11.

Ørsnes-Christensen, M. 1956. Kyndby. Ein seeländischer Grabplatz aus den 7.-8. Jahrhunderts n.Chr. *Acta XXVI*, 1955.

Østergaard, K. Høgsbro 1962. Arkæologiske undersøgelser i Brørup kirke 1953-54 og 1962. *Aarb.* 1961.